DISSENT

DISSENT

THE RADICALIZATION OF THE REPUBLICAN PARTY AND ITS CAPTURE OF THE COURT

JACKIE CALMES

TWELVE

NEW YORK BOSTON

Twelve
Hachette Book Group
1290 Avenue of the Americas, New York, NY 10104
twelvebooks.com
twitter.com/twelvebooks

First Edition: June 2021

Twelve is an imprint of Grand Central Publishing. The Twelve name and logo are trademarks of Hachette Book Group, Inc.

The publisher is not responsible for websites (or their content) that are not owned by the publisher.

The Hachette Speakers Bureau provides a wide range of authors for speaking events. To find out more, go to www.hachettespeakersbureau.com or call (866) 376-6591.

Library of Congress Control Number: 2020948685

ISBNs: 978-1-5387-0079-2 (hardcover), 978-1-5387-0081-5 (ebook)

Printed in the United States of America

LSC-C

Printing 1, 2021

To my mother,
Jean Feehan Calmes Morgenstern (1933–2019),

and my youngest sibling,
Connie Calmes Szakovits (1966–2020).

Their memories are our blessing.

CONTENTS

CONTENTS

AUTHOR'S NOTE

As my fortieth anniversary in journalism approached, Donald Trump had just been elected president. While his victory was a surprise, including to himself, he was no political aberration. Trump's rise in the Republican Party was the logical result of the party's ever-rightward, populist, and antigovernment evolution, a shift that coincided with my career in political journalism and was its single biggest story. I'd been witness to that transformation from the midterm election year of 1978, when I arrived in West Texas for my first job at the *Abilene Reporter-News*, to Trump's election, by which time I was a Washington correspondent for the *New York Times*. Parallel to the Republican Party's gradual radicalization was the conservative movement's long game to capture the Supreme Court.

At both the *Times* and, before that, the *Wall Street Journal*, one of the most frequent questions I had gotten from voters since the 1990s was some variation of "What's happened to the Republican Party?" It was typically asked with disdain by Democrats and independents, and pain from current or former Republicans. All sides agreed that the party had moved so far to the right that it was on the wrong side of history on many issues—women's and LGBTQ rights, climate change, race, immigration, and more—and too uncompromising to govern effectively. I began thinking about a book addressing the voters' question. By 2018, I'd taken a job as

White House editor for the *Los Angeles Times*, and as Brett Kavanaugh was poised for confirmation in October, my agent, Gail Ross, and editor, Sean Desmond, came back to me: What about telling the story of the Republican Party's modern transformation as the frame for Kavanaugh's rise to become the justice who gave conservatives their long-sought lock on the highest court?

Their idea made sense, given Kavanaugh's life experiences: coming of age in Reagan's America, inside Washington's Beltway; joining the infant Federalist Society at its founding campus, Yale; prosecuting Bill and Hillary Clinton; representing the Republican side in the partisan legal fights that bookended the 2000 election, first over custody of motherless Cuban refugee Elián González and then in *Bush v. Gore*; advising George W. Bush through the polarizing years after 9/11; being rewarded with a federal judgeship, but only after a prolonged Senate confirmation fight emblematic of the era's partisan court battles.

I agreed to trace his path, through the years and political changes we'd each seen from our respective vantages. It proved to be a challenging period in which to write the story, however. From Antonin Scalia's death in 2016 through the aftermath of Ruth Bader Ginsburg's in 2020, Kavanaugh was just one of three arch-conservatives that Republicans forced onto the Supreme Court. In the process, it was roiled by the hyper-partisanship plaguing the U.S. government more broadly. The dynamic on the court shifted after Kavanaugh's arrival and then again after Amy Coney Barrett's. Chief Justice John G. Roberts Jr. first emerged as the controlling power at the center, and then, by late 2020, at key times found himself alone with the three liberals in dissent against the five right-wing justices. This upheaval created a headache for someone trying to write a book on the court. What was clear was that the court more than ever was showing the political divisions Roberts had been trying to avoid, and was poised to issue rulings outside the American mainstream.

In 1978, a year before Kavanaugh would enter Georgetown Preparatory high school in suburban Washington, I arrived for work in Abilene (home, incidentally, to his future wife, Ashley Estes, then just three years old; I took up jogging on the track at the high school she'd attend). Texas had for more than a century been a near-solid Democratic state, except in presidential elections. That wild midterm year of Jimmy Carter's presidency would mark the beginning of the national Republican Party's post-Watergate reemergence, heralding its ascendance in the Reagan years and the shift of its historic base from the North to the South. I was from two Democratic strongholds in the Midwest—Toledo, Ohio, where I grew up, and Cook County, Illinois, where I finished college. Texas back then was a Democratic bastion of a different sort. Many Democrats I met were more conservative than Republicans I'd known. They often opposed the national party, yet remained "yellow dog Democrats" in state and local elections—so loyal, the saying went, that they'd vote for a yellow dog over a Republican. Texas was a two-party state, my translators joked: conservative Democrats and liberal Democrats, just like elsewhere in the South.

That November, my election-night story included the report of young George W. Bush's defeat for a House seat representing a district west of Abilene, including Midland and Odessa. His loss was expected, yet he did surprisingly well. So did other Republicans across the South, foretelling the wave Reagan would ride two years later. Texans in 1978 elected the first Republican governor since Reconstruction: Bill Clements, a rich and bombastic oilman, a sort of precursor of Trump. Among the Democrats who won, taking congressional seats finally vacated by aged New Deal Democrats, was Phil Gramm. The East Texas professor would become a leader among conservative House Democrats known as "Boll Weevils"— southern pests to Congress's Democratic leaders, but allies to Reagan. Like some other Boll Weevils, Gramm soon would jump to the Republican Party, speeding its rightward, southern-based makeover.

By 1980, when Texas turned on Carter and embraced Reagan, I was in Austin covering politics for a chain of fourteen state newspapers. On election night, I'd barely made it to the state's Republican Party head-quarters to cover the vote watch there before the networks, shortly after polls closed in the East, projected Reagan would be the winner. Not only that, but the Senate would have a Republican majority for the first time since Dwight Eisenhower's first term.

* * *

Two years later, I was covering politics for the *Dallas Morning News* when Texas Democrats had a last hurrah. They swept every statewide office in the 1982 midterm elections as Democrats nationwide exploited Reagan's weaknesses amid a recession and his cuts to Social Security. The Texas party wouldn't come close to achieving that again; by 2020, it was a perennial loser in statewide races and Democrats' hopes of a comeback thanks to their Trump-era gains in the big cities and suburbs proved premature.

I moved to Washington on New Year's Day 1984, the election year of "Morning in America" for Reagan and the Republican Party. Working first for *Congressional Quarterly* magazine, I soon got to know a maverick Republican congressman from suburban Atlanta, Newt Gingrich. Though he was a junior member of the seemingly permanent House Republican minority, Gingrich saw himself as nothing less than the field marshal for a post-Reagan revolution—even as some allies in the so-called Conservative Opportunity Society confided to me that he was more opportunist than conservative. I joined the *Wall Street Journal*'s Washington bureau in 1990, in time to report how Gingrich, by then the second-ranking House Republican leader, nearly sabotaged that year's bipartisan budget deal between President George H. W. Bush and Congress's leaders because it raised taxes to reduce mounting deficits.

Gingrich subsequently predicted to me that Republicans finally could win a House majority in 1994—*if* a Democrat, not Bush, were president. He turned out to be right, of course, and became the House Speaker in 1995. Yet my *Journal* colleague David Rogers and I turned out to be right in predicting to our skeptical New York editors that Gingrich would eventually overreach given his ideological fervor, messianic ambition, and weak grasp of policy details. He and his lieutenants quickly found governing to be harder and less popular than campaigning.

Within a year, voters' disgust with Republicans' hard-line policies and their holiday-season government shutdowns in late 1995 and early 1996 helped revive President Clinton. Republicans' biggest overreach—impeaching Clinton in 1998 for offenses related to an affair with a White House intern—provoked another backlash. The president's party gained House seats in midterm elections for the first time since 1934. Gingrich was forced to resign as Speaker.

In Texas, however, George W. Bush won reelection as governor and was back in my sights. He immediately began building a campaign for president, and I returned to Austin to interview him for the *Journal*. Bush positioned himself as a counter to Gingrich—as a "compassionate conservative"—but also told voters on the right what they wanted to hear: that Jesus Christ was his personal savior, that he'd slash taxes, and that his "humble" foreign policy would eschew interventionist "nation building." (He'd break that last promise big time.)

Bush often mentioned Reagan in his campaign speeches but almost never Reagan's successor, his father, who'd been discredited within their party. Yet privately, Bush sometimes told us reporters on his campaign plane, "History will look kindly on my dad." He said it again as we flew back to Austin on election eve; as he returned to his seat up front, I opted on this final campaign flight to tell him I agreed. I cited some of his father's achievements—passage of clean air and water laws and the Americans with Disabilities Act, cessation of Reagan's covert wars in Central America, brokering the end of the Cold War. Then I ended with the one accomplishment the son could not, politically, credit: that his father, despite his 1988 antitax promise, had signed the landmark 1990 deficit reduction agreement that contributed significantly to the balanced budgets and prosperity the nation enjoyed at that moment. "Interesting," was all Bush said, before walking away. With his subsequent deep tax cuts and spending increases, the annual deficits and mounting debt of the Reagan era returned.

Days after Bush's reelection in 2004, he announced that he would spend his new political capital on partially privatizing Social Security. For the next ten months I covered that doomed effort, which most Republicans in Congress opposed. It finally died when Bush became mired in a separate crisis over his botched response to Hurricane Katrina's devastation of the Gulf Coast in late summer 2005. Together the two failures—on top of rising red ink and bloody Mideast wars—all but wrecked his second term. Once again a Bush presidency spawned a conservative revolt. This one took aim as well against other Republicans, the majority in Congress, who'd built a record of overspending and corruption. The right's revulsion was evident all over the country in 2006 as I reported on midterm campaigns. Democrats won control of both the House and Senate for the first time in twelve years. In 2008 they would also win the presidency. After the near collapse of the financial system that fall, and its bailout by the lame-duck Bush administration, a more militantly conservative movement took root. Soon it would have a name: the Tea Party.

I'd joined the *New York Times* Washington bureau that summer of 2008, and soon was chronicling the U.S. response to the global crisis, and the conservative rebellion. Once Barack Obama became president in 2009, he quickly expanded Bush's bailout program while enacting an economic stimulus plan that ultimately exceeded $1 trillion. The Tea Party grew in opposition and now the Republican establishment joined with it, antagonists united against their common enemy—the new Democratic president, and first African American. In the 2010 midterm elections, the party recaptured the House and gained seats in the Senate.

Republicans now shared responsibility for governing, however, and that required occasional compromise with Obama. Yet compromise was something the Tea Party base would not abide. From 2011 on, especially after Republicans also captured the Senate in 2014, they were the targets of conservatives' ire more often than were Democrats. They'd failed to keep promises to repeal "Obamacare," defund Planned Parenthood, and balance the budget—promises the congressional Republicans knew they couldn't, or wouldn't, keep. Their onetime allies in conservative media also turned on elected Republicans, reflecting the anger of right-wing audiences and stoking it, too, to boost ratings and clicks.

As the crowded Republican presidential field took shape for 2016, Trump quickly became the mouthpiece for this antiestablishment, antigovernment populism, as well as for the racists, xenophobes, and conspiracy nuts that the party had long sought to contain. Trump spoke the language of aggrievement of mostly white, less educated voters, both in rural America and once-proud, now-struggling industrial areas like my Ohio hometown. And he amplified those grievances, with the help not only of Fox News and other conservative media but also of CNN and MSNBC, which were eager for the ratings his unorthodox rantings brought. But many urban and suburban voters, especially women, were repelled. Their numbers would grow.

By Trump's hostile takeover of the Republican Party, he greatly expedited its radicalization. But he didn't cause it. Five years before his election, a moderate Republican author had come out with an exhaustive party history entitled *Rule and Ruin: The Downfall of Moderation and the Destruction of the Republican Party, from Eisenhower to the Tea Party.* "While there are many possible reasons to explain the present American political dysfunction," Geoffrey Kabaservice wrote, "the leading suspect is the transformation of the Republican Party over the past half-century into a monolithically conservative organization." That change, he added, "ought to concern all Americans."[1]

Trump ushered in the fourth revolution in as many decades: The Republican Party became more of a personality cult than a political network, and it jettisoned conservative orthodoxies on trade, immigration, deficits, and foreign relations. With Trump's election, "the GOP will no longer be the home of conservatism," wrote Peter Wehner, a veteran of the three prior Republican administrations. Now the party stood for whatever Trump said, or tweeted.[2]

Yet even Never Trumpers agreed that Trump was good for the courts. In packing them with conservatives, including Neil Gorsuch, Brett Kavanaugh, and Amy Coney Barrett on the Supreme Court, Trump would have an impact decades past his presidency. He'd delegated the job of picking the nominees to others, to leaders of an ascendant conservative legal movement. In doing so, Trump completed the Republican Party's institutionalization of a system that had evolved since the Reagan era with the creation of the Federalist Society in 1982—to identify and promote proven conservatives to be judges. Democrats had no such analog.

In telling Kavanaugh's story alongside his party's, I drew not only on my experiences and past reporting, but also on the works of others, including friendly competitors. I could not have done it, however, without the insights of more than two hundred individuals in both parties, and no party, who generously shared them over more than two years' time. Some were sources going back thirty-five years, but many were new acquaintances. I'm grateful to all of them.

Jackie Calmes
Washington, D.C.

DISSENT

PROLOGUE

On October 8, 2018, President Trump was playing his favorite role: master of ceremonies for his own prime-time show, before a deferential audience in a venue generously accented in gold. The event in the White House East Room, the swearing-in of Brett M. Kavanaugh as an associate justice of the U.S. Supreme Court, wasn't even necessary. Kavanaugh had been sworn in two days earlier in a private ceremony at the court, just after the Senate confirmed him 50–48, the narrowest margin for a justice in 137 years. What *was* real was this: With Kavanaugh's confirmation, Republicans achieved a forty-year dream, taking control of the nation's highest court with an unquestionably conservative majority. Conservatives would "raise the curtain on a new age," commentator Hugh Hewitt exulted.[1] What's more, for now Republicans controlled all three branches of government.

Like much with Trump, this staged ceremony was unusual if not unprecedented.[2] Except for Barack Obama, presidents since Ronald Reagan had hosted ceremonial swearing-ins for new justices at the White House; Obama hosted receptions for his two choices but skipped the oath-taking, in a symbolic nod to the court's independence. Trump, however, revived the swearing-in and did so in prime time. Retired justice John Paul Stevens had written disapprovingly, "I believe that the ceremony should take place at the Supreme Court whenever possible. The three branches of our government are separate and equal. The president and the Senate play critical roles in the nomination and confirmation process. After that process ends, however, the 'separate but equal' regime takes over."[3] Yet Trump had assembled the entire court, leaders of Congress's Republican majority, and senior administration officials, notably White House counsel Donald F. McGahn, the architect along with Senate majority leader Mitch McConnell of what McConnell called "the court project." No Democrats were apparent here, unless one counted the four justices appointed by Presidents Obama and Bill Clinton—Ruth Bader Ginsburg, Stephen Breyer, Sonia Sotomayor, and Elena Kagan—who now comprised the court's minority. Also in attendance: Fox's Laura Ingraham, part of Kavanaugh's social circle of young conservatives in the 1990s, now a star in the firmament of conservative media; Deputy Attorney General Rod J. Rosenstein, who even then was overseeing a criminal investigation of the president; and Republican senators.

While Trump often claimed historic firsts that just weren't so, he in fact had achieved a dubious one with Kavanaugh's and Neil Gorsuch's ascensions to the court (and would do so again with Amy Coney Barrett's confirmation two years later). They were the first justices in history to be chosen by a president who'd failed to win the popular vote, and confirmed by a majority of senators who collectively had been elected with fewer votes—many millions fewer—than the senators who voted "no." In Kavanaugh's case, the fifty senators who backed him together got 24.5 million fewer Americans' votes than the forty-eight who opposed him, according to political scientist Kevin J. McMahon. Gorsuch's fifty-four Senate supporters were elected with nearly 22 million fewer votes than the forty-five senators in opposition. For a court whose chief, John G. Roberts Jr., already worried about public perceptions of its legitimacy, this was an unwelcome milestone to say the least.[4]

Trump strode the red carpet of the White House's first floor Cross Hall into the East Room and to the lectern with the presidential seal, flanked by now-retired justice Anthony M. Kennedy and a nervous-looking Kavanaugh, Kennedy's former law clerk and now his successor. The president began traditionally enough. He said he'd been told that "the most important decision a president can make is the appointment of a Supreme Court justice." Trump had outsourced his decision to conservative activists at the Federalist Society and the Heritage Foundation, thus filling the openings more smoothly than his chaotic administration conducted just about any other business. Trump recognized each of the other eight justices by name, along with the widow of Antonin Scalia, Maureen Scalia. He saluted Kavanaugh's "amazing wife, Ashley," "their two beautiful daughters, Margaret and Liza," and "Justice Kavanaugh's mom and dad, Martha and Ed."

Then Trump said he wanted to begin the proceedings "differently." And so he did. For his next 176 words, he broke with presidential norms, turning a solemn official occasion into a partisan, divisive one. Later Roberts would tell a confidant he'd been promised it wouldn't be political. Trump began: "On behalf of our nation I want to apologize to Brett and the entire Kavanaugh family for the terrible pain and suffering you have been forced to endure." It was an awkward moment even for those in the room who agreed with Trump's sentiment, though most attendees applauded politely. For many watching on television, however, his words were like salt in a wound. The president was purporting to apologize for the country when half of its registered voters opposed Kavanaugh, according to a Fox News poll. Other polls, too, found more Americans against him than for him, making Kavanaugh the most unpopular new justice in polling history. More Americans believed Christine Ford's allegation of sexual assault than believed his denials—that was not true for Anita Hill when she accused Clarence Thomas of sexual harassment twenty-seven years before. Yet here was Trump, calling Ford part of "a campaign of political and personal destruction based on lies and deception."[5]

Trump typically was not a magnanimous winner, one who looked forward with an eye to healing. Nearly three years later he still assailed his vanquished 2016 foe as "Crooked Hillary." His way was to speak exclusively to his conservative base, which embraced the new justice and vilified the accusers, and to always get the last blow. Looking to Kavanaugh, he said—falsely—"I must state that you, sir, under historic scrutiny, were proven innocent."

Next Trump recognized the Senate Republicans in the front rows who made Kavanaugh's confirmation possible, especially McConnell, for whom packing the federal courts with conservatives—not passing laws—was his desired legacy. The enthusiastic applause for McConnell prompted Trump to marvel, "I think that's the biggest hand he's ever received." McConnell was the reason that Kavanaugh was Trump's second justice in as many years—he'd brazenly blocked Obama's final nominee, Merrick Garland, for nearly a year to leave the seat for the new president to fill, with Gorsuch.

Trump went on eloquently—this was Teleprompter Trump, reading words written for him, not Twitter Trump or the Trump of the unpredictable word salads regularly served up to reporters. Finally he extolled Kavanaugh and handed him the mic.

The new justice first gave Trump the flattery and gratitude the president craved. He then paid tribute to Roberts, whose own nomination Kavanaugh had promoted thirteen years before as Bush's adviser. Was his praise a clue? Did it mean Kavanaugh would ally with Roberts, the court's new center now that swing voter Kennedy was gone? Or would he throw in with hard-liners Thomas and Samuel Alito on the right, as Gorsuch had?

Kavanaugh next sought to allay concern about his stunningly partisan and angry testimony at his confirmation hearing, a performance that former justice Stevens had called disqualifying. The Supreme Court, Kavanaugh said, "is not a partisan or political institution. The justices do not sit on opposite sides of an aisle. We do not caucus in separate rooms. The Supreme Court is a team of nine, and I will always be a team player on the team of nine."

He hailed Kennedy as a model of civility and collegiality who "fiercely defended the independence of the judiciary, and zealously guarded the individual liberties secured by the Constitution." Those listening for clues again could wonder: Would Kavanaugh indeed be independent of Trump? And would his own concept of "individual liberties" extend—as they had for Kennedy—to women seeking abortions, or to gay Americans?

Kavanaugh emphasized again, as he had when Trump announced his nomination in this same room three months earlier, that he had long worked "to promote the advancement of women." Now, however, he spoke in the wake of the searing allegations of sexual assault and alcohol-fueled misogyny during his high school and college years. He boasted to applause that all four of his law clerks would be women, "a first in the history of the Supreme Court." Then Kavanaugh closed as Trump had begun, alluding to the toxic confirmation process. But he was conciliatory: "I take this office with gratitude and no bitterness. On the Supreme Court, I will seek to be a force for stability and unity." With Trump looking on, Kennedy performed the mock swearing-in. The president exited with Kavanaugh and his family, followed by Republicans from all three branches of government, to celebrate their power at a reception with toasts and music.

* * *

That morning, as Trump left the White House for the quick trip to Florida, he had spoken to reporters about Kavanaugh. Having dropped any pretense that he took Kavanaugh's accusers seriously, Trump called the new justice "a man that was caught up in a hoax that was set up by the Democrats." He predicted that voters would soon punish Democrats in the midterm elections. He was wrong: A month later, voters put Democrats in control of the House, and Republicans netted just two Senate seats in a year that heavily favored their candidates. Republicans would have to share power in the legislative branch, and Trump faced new doubts about his reelection in 2020.

Yet whatever happened, the party still would claim dominance on the Supreme Court for years to come.

The story of Kavanaugh's rise to become the fifth man, the justice who sealed conservatives' capture of the court, is best told against the backdrop of the Republican Party's transformation—its radicalization—over the four decades from his high school years to his confirmation. In that time, the party underwent successive revolutions: under Ronald Reagan in the eighties, Newt Gingrich in the nineties, the Tea Party in the aughts, and finally Trump. Each pushed the party farther to the right, powered by newly politicized Christian conservatives, the right-wing press, and social media. The "Party of Lincoln," born in the North and dedicated to the abolition of slavery, became fully rooted in the South and rural America, virtually all white and all but openly receptive to racists. The old party of business became as much or more the party of religious conservatives. Republican leaders played to that base, weaponizing judicial politics by promising to put proven conservatives on the federal bench to reverse rulings on abortion, school prayer, gay rights, and more. To that end, the party created a network for nurturing and promoting ideological conservatives, led by the wildly successful Federalist Society.

Kavanaugh, as an ambitious young Republican, knew to join the fledgling society at its birthplace, Yale Law School. The conservative legal network then was just a few years old, yet early members had already landed prestigious jobs in Washington. For all of Kavanaugh's eager-to-please striving, however, there were false notes in his early adulthood, by many classmates' accounts. While he was an athlete and reasonably handsome, he seemed shy around young women and, perhaps because of that, drank excessively. He and his guy friends were known for their drunken antics, usually the kind that involved mocking and demeaning others, male and female. And Kavanaugh, when drunk, was often belligerent.

Rather than go into private practice after law school, for several years he parlayed his Ivy League and conservative legal connections into advantageous clerkships and a Justice Department internship. With them came influential mentors, not least Ken Starr, Justice Kennedy, and ultimately Bush. Kavanaugh joined Starr's wide-ranging probe of Bill and Hillary Clinton and stayed for three years. Soon he was back again when the investigation turned to the president's affair with a White House intern; in returning, he disregarded some Republicans' career advice, gambling that his role in the decade's defining partisan fight would burnish his conservative credentials. He further gilded his résumé by joining Bush's legal team for the 2000 election recount, then easily segued into the White House, and the new president's circle.

As Democratic senator Dick Durbin would say, Kavanaugh was "like the Forrest Gump of Republican politics—you always show up in the picture. Whether it's the Ken Starr investigation, *Bush v. Gore*, the Bush White House, you've been there."[6]

Once upon a time, Republican presidents nominated federal judges mostly from the establishment ranks of corporate lawyers, big-city prosecutors, state magistrates and politicians. Nominees' judicial philosophy generally got little attention. Subsequently, their records as judges—or justices—often disappointed movement conservatives. To remedy that, since the 1980s the right had paved a different career path to the courts.

Kavanaugh followed it.

1

THE EARLY YEARS

"I was lucky."

When Brett Kavanaugh introduced himself to the nation on July 9, 2018, after President Trump announced his nomination in prime time, the first thing he told American viewers was that he was an only child. "When people ask what it's like to be an only child, I say, 'It depends on who your parents are. I was lucky.'" Looking on proudly were Martha Murphy Kavanaugh and Everett Edward Kavanaugh Jr. Their son extolled his mother, as an inner-city schoolteacher turned "trailblazer" lawyer, before praising his dad in far fewer words. That reflected her influence, but also Kavanaugh's desire to blunt opponents' claims of his hostility to women's rights. For the remainder of his remarks, he likewise sought to define himself before his critics did. He described a privileged life but not an elitist one, and one of service to others—from his school days to his current roles as dad, coach, mentor to female law clerks, and server of meals to the homeless.[1]

Contrary to Trump's anti-Washington brand, Kavanaugh was literally a creature of the city, born there on February 12, 1965, the birthdate of the first Republican president, Abraham Lincoln. Nearby in the capital on that Friday, the Democratic First Lady, Lady Bird Johnson, hosted a tea to promote the new Head Start program for underprivileged children, part of her husband's "War on Poverty." That weekend, President

Lyndon B. Johnson met with his advisers about the actual war, in Vietnam; they planned a bombing campaign that would last more than three years, doing more to divide Americans than to force the Asian communists to the negotiating table. In Queens, New York, Trump's hometown, someone threw a firebomb into the home of civil rights activist Malcolm X; he was assassinated a week later. The simmering foreign and domestic struggles were splitting the otherwise prosperous country, sowing seeds that would transform its politics. Democrats controlled the White House and Congress and a progressive majority held sway on the Supreme Court. Yet the year before, after Johnson signed the 1964 Civil Rights Act, he is said to have predicted privately that he'd likely delivered his native South to the Republican Party for years to come.

Those political winds, from the sixties to the Reagan era, were of little moment to the young Kavanaugh, despite his inside-the-Beltway life. "This was just our community," recalled Samantha Semerad Guerry. She also grew up in Washington's Maryland suburbs, attended a private school (befriending classmate Chrissy Blasey), and long dated one of Kavanaugh's friends. Guerry, like many contemporaries, had no memories of political talk among her school friends, even though she was from a pedigreed Republican family. Her father worked in the administrations of presidents Richard Nixon, Gerald Ford, and Ronald Reagan, as well as at the Republican National Committee. Her mother had senior positions in the White House and State Department. As a girl, Guerry met all three presidents, campaigned for Ford, and interned in Reagan's White House. Students in the area's private schools included the sons and daughters of members of Congress, diplomats, and even royalty. In 1975, seniors at Holton-Arms School, which Guerry and Blasey soon would attend, held their prom in the White House East Room, thanks to classmate Susan Ford, the president's daughter.

"Politics was always in the air but it wasn't remarkable to us," she said. "D.C. was a quote-unquote company town so everybody was connected to the government somehow. Your parents would come home and at dinner they would talk about the issues they'd been working on that day and the people they were working with." (Guerry has since left the party, or, as she said, it left her: "The Republican Party that I grew up in is not the Republican Party that exists today.")[2]

The Kavanaughs, like a number of people in the Maryland suburbs, were Irish Catholic. Each Sunday they worshipped at Little Flower Catholic Church in Bethesda, and young Brett would attend the all-boys Catholic elementary school Mater Dei—"Mother of God." Standards for the boys were high. "Fostering competition early on, teachers reported the class academic rankings on a chalkboard. Kavanaugh's name was always at the top," *Vanity Fair* reported.[3] A "profound influence," Kavanaugh would say, was Christopher Abell, who not only taught him English and religion, but also coached football and baseball. Four decades later, Kavanaugh would recall Abell's assignment in seventh grade of Harper Lee's *To Kill a Mockingbird*, telling the 2018 graduating class of Catholic University's law school, "That book forces you to confront the ugly history of racism in this country, and also tells you about one of the key lessons of life: to stand in someone else's shoes, and to try to see things from their perspective. That was the lesson that Atticus Finch taught his daughter, Scout Finch." And, Kavanaugh added, "that was the lesson that Mr. Abell taught us."[4]

Years later Kavanaugh would cite his mother's job teaching in two inner-city schools and the 1980s crack scourge in Washington's Black communities to suggest his familiarity with race issues and with those in less privileged shoes. Yet his suburban enclave was far removed from those afflicted areas. Bethesda, adjacent to the far northwest quadrant of Washington, blended with the capital's wealthiest and mostly white neighborhoods there. Still, Bethesda wasn't as associated with ostentatious wealth as were the smaller nearby suburbs of Potomac and Chevy Chase, Maryland, and McLean, Virginia. It was home to federal employees and public school teachers as well as doctors, lawyers, diplomats, and celebrity journalists. Kavanaugh's parents initially were among the more modest residents, until each advanced in their separate careers when Brett was a teenager. Then came a renovation project so impressive it was featured in a local magazine, and the Kavanaughs' purchase of second homes, first on the Chesapeake Bay and then in the Florida Keys.

Both Martha and Ed Kavanaugh got law degrees in 1978. She had entered the law school at American University in Washington when her son was ten. After graduation she became a state prosecutor in Maryland, serving for a time on a commission addressing spousal abuse. In 1984 she opened a solo practice. Ed Kavanaugh also attended the law school, at night, while working as a lobbyist. His son, in his White House remarks, recalled Ed's "unparalleled work ethic," without saying what work he did. Father and son bonded over sports—watching, playing, and attending, often going to Baltimore to see the Orioles. (Kavanaugh would transfer his loyalties when the Washington Nationals brought baseball back to the capital years later.) The family socialized at area country clubs and spent time at their place on Maryland's Eastern Shore, in the picturesque town of St. Michaels.

It was after Brett was launched on his own career that Martha Kavanaugh was named in 1993 to be a district court judge in Montgomery County, Maryland. Two years later she rose to the county's circuit court of appeals.[5] She presided over a range of cases, from crimes of teen rape and murder for hire to the illegal operation of a trash dump, before she retired in 2001. Ed Kavanaugh, long an executive at the Cosmetic, Toiletry, and Fragrance Association, the lobbying group for about three hundred companies, was promoted in Brett's senior year to its president and CEO. Over the next twenty-two years, until retiring in 2005, he would earn millions, including a reported $13 million retirement package, and lead the industry's fight against regulations from the Food and Drug Administration, arguing that the companies could police themselves given how safe their products were. His son would come to share the father's aversion to federal regulations, a stance that would commend him to Trump.

One prominent fight in the late 1980s was over banning a carcinogenic chemical in hairsprays. It pitted Ed Kavanaugh's group against Representative Ron Wyden, a Democrat from Oregon who would go on to the Senate, and three decades later vote against putting Brett Kavanaugh on the Supreme Court based partly on Kavanaugh's lower court opinions against federal regulations. ("You don't have to look at his genes, just look at his record," Wyden would say.) Ed Kavanaugh also waged a high-profile battle against animal rights activists, who sought a ban on animal testing in the development of cosmetics. In a letter soliciting funds from cosmetics companies for a lobbying and advertising campaign against the ban, he wrote, "We are dealing with zealots who cannot comprehend that a child's life is more important than a dog's, who see nothing wrong with making a child the ultimate guinea pig instead of an animal."[6] Into the 1990s, animal rights protestors would try to disrupt the cosmetics lobby's annual convention at a Florida resort.

In 1990, the year his son graduated from Yale Law School, Ed Kavanaugh was caught in an embarrassing exposé by ABC's *Primetime Live*, which surreptitiously videotaped nine members of Congress cavorting on a Barbados beach with lobbyists. Kavanaugh sponsored one of the parties for the lawmakers, nearly all of whom were members of the House Ways and Means Committee. A Florida columnist for the *St. Petersburg Times* wrote, "I doubt that even Kavanaugh's best products could improve the smell of the Ways and Means fling on Barbados."[7]

A later controversy would involve both Kavanaughs, father and son, and the future chief justice, John G. Roberts Jr., underscoring the small, incestuous world of official Washington. Early in George W. Bush's administration, Ed Kavanaugh hired Roberts as an outside counsel for the cosmetics association, and Roberts successfully lobbied Bush officials against stricter rules for safety labels on sunscreen products. At the time, Brett Kavanaugh was a Bush adviser, including on judicial nominations. After Bush nominated Roberts to be chief justice in 2005, Roberts failed to disclose his prior lobbying for Ed Kavanaugh's group, and, after the negative publicity, corrected his federal ethics forms. The White House told reporters that Brett Kavanaugh had not had anything to do with vetting Roberts's nomination. He had, however, enthusiastically promoted Roberts's name internally.[8]

•   •   •

Most boys at Mater Dei went on to one of two rival all-male Catholic high schools—Gonzaga, in a crowded, run-down area of Washington near Capitol Hill, or Georgetown Prep, a boarding and day school run by Jesuit priests at a lush ninety-three-acre expanse in suburban Rockville, Maryland, complete with a nine-hole golf course. Brett Kavanaugh chose Prep. Tuition was about $4,000 a year for day students; by 2019 it had increased far beyond the inflation rate to $38,330, and $62,090 for boarders.

He entered the school in the fall of 1979, the eve of the Reagan revolution. A broad field of Republicans was competing for the party's nomination to take on the beleaguered Democratic president, Jimmy Carter. Years later, classmates from Prep and Yale could recall little about young Kavanaugh's politics. Yet he would trace his conservatism to this time, and to the influence of his mother's work as a prosecutor, to the long-running saga of Americans held hostage by Iran, and to candidate Reagan's call for a more muscular military. His father was a registered Republican and his mother a Democrat, though she would switch parties years later.[9]

Kavanaugh, who turned sixteen three weeks after Reagan took office in 1981, would lose his one bid for elective office, student body president. What he cared most about, however, was sports of all kinds, and hanging out with his fellow jocks. On the football team he was a cornerback and wide receiver. For a year he also was on the track team. His passion was basketball; over his four years at Prep, Kavanaugh was captain of the freshman, junior varsity, and varsity teams.

No nominee for the Supreme Court, or any other major federal office, would ever have their high school years so closely examined. Georgetown Prep wasn't the most elite of the capital area's private schools. St. Albans and Sidwell Friends were more prestigious. Among those who attended or graduated from St. Albans were Roosevelts, Kennedys, Rockefellers, a Bush, and both the 2000 and 2004 Democratic presidential nominees, Al Gore and John F. Kerry, respectively. Sidwell similarly attracted the children of senators, administration officials, diplomats, and Presidents Theodore Roosevelt, Richard Nixon, Bill Clinton, and Barack Obama.

While academic standards were high at all the private schools, Prep was better known at the time for sports and partying. "The Georgetown Prep guys had a slight chip on their shoulder," said a prominent Washington lawyer who was on the board of a rival school in the 1980s. "They were very good athletically, but when it came to both intellect and social standing, St. Albans and Sidwell were clearly a notch above them." Even so, Prep boasted of the richest history as the first such Catholic school in the country, dating to 1789—the year that George Washington became president, the first Congress met, and the U.S. Constitution took effect. In 1919, Prep moved from Washington to its suburban campus. Its legacy and emphasis on service and fraternity loomed large among alumni. Kavanaugh, describing his Prep years in a 2018 interview on Fox News, said, "I was focused on academics and athletics, going to church every Sunday at Little Flower, working on my service projects, and friendship—friendship with my fellow classmates, and friendship with girls from the local all-girls Catholic schools." At the White House, he noted, "The motto of my Jesuit high school was, 'Men for others.' I have tried to live that creed."[10]

The school also had a darker side, not uncommon at all-boys academies and especially pronounced among athletes. Absent the mixing of the sexes and the Monday-morning accountability of a coeducational school, at Prep a chauvinistic machismo was celebrated. After a weekend of bad behavior, guys wouldn't have to soberly confront the offended girls in the corridors and classes. They'd brag of their exploits at the lockers and cafeteria tables, among the other guys. "There was no answering for their behavior to anyone," said a Kavanaugh acquaintance who attended an all-girls school. To this woman and her friends, Prep guys had a reputation as "over the top" and not "safe." Parents, priests, teachers, and coaches shared a guys-will-be-guys ethos.

Among the top-grossing movies of 1982—the year before Kavanaugh graduated from high school—was number-five hit *Porky's*, "about a group of boys who try to have a lot of sex," in the words of *New York Times* film critic Wesley Morris. Morris used the occasion of Kavanaugh's 2018 nomination for a review of the movies that defined the era for teens, headlined "Boys Had It Made, Girls Were the Joke." Kavanaugh himself would cite the influence of three movies—*Animal House* (1978), *Caddyshack* (1980), and *Fast Times at Ridgemont High* (1982)—to explain to inquiring Democratic senators the crass and sexist content in his senior yearbook. Unlike some contemporary hits, *Porky's* didn't evoke an innocent nostalgia for the years before John F. Kennedy's assassination, Morris wrote. Instead, "All that the boys long for is girls—to talk to, sure, but mostly to peep at, ogle and harass." The plotline includes plans for gang sex with a prostitute. "By 1982, if you were a teen male, your fantasies no longer had to live under a mattress. In a movie theater, you were free, say, to do some vicarious peering into the girls' shower after gym. The drooling voyeurism, the casual racism, the aggressive anti-Semitism, the backhanded homophobia: None of it is quite the reason to bring 'Porky's' up now. The reason to bring up 'Porky's' now is the laughter—the *uproarious* laughter." With that, Morris drew a line to 2018, and the recollections of Kavanaugh accusers Christine Ford and Deborah Ramirez of their alleged tormentors laughing at them.[11]

For Prep guys, the girls in their social circle mostly were from the area's all-female Catholic schools—Immaculata, Visitation, and Prep's so-called sister school, Stone Ridge School of the Sacred Heart—and less from the non-Catholic Holton-Arms, National Cathedral School, or Sidwell. Kavanaugh's close friend and football teammate Mark Judge would provide a revealing window into the guys' attitude toward the non-Catholic girls, writing in his "underground" student newspaper *The Unknown Hoya* that Holton-Arms—Guerry and Blasey's school—"is the home of the most worthless excuses for human females." A Holton girl was an "H.H.," he wrote: Holton Hosebag.

Guerry got to know some boys at Prep after she auditioned for the school's staging of *Oklahoma!* in Kavanaugh's senior year. She was not only chosen for the cast but also tapped to teach the show's choreography to the boys, many of them football players. She ended up dating a friend of Kavanaugh's for more than a year. "That class was really tight; they were a really close group of guys. And I think, by and large, they were a really nice group of guys," she recalled. "They did have sort of a Marines' mentality—a brothers-in-arms kind of thing."

She concluded something else as well: "There's just a profound sense of entitlement there, that sense of birthright—that they were all there because they were above average. They believed they were extraordinary, and they were told on a regular basis that they were the future leaders of the known world. There was no lack of self-confidence among them." Indeed, the future chairman of the Federal Reserve System, Jerome Powell, was a Prep graduate twelve years before Kavanaugh, and future justice Neil Gorsuch, whose mother was Reagan's environmental administrator, entered Prep two years behind him. Christopher Dodd, son of a senator and a future congressman and senator himself, was an alumnus. Kavanaugh's football teammate Michael Bidwill would become president of the National Football League's Arizona Cardinals; his father owned the team. "They worked hard," Guerry said. "And they played hard."

Kavanaugh would be forced to address the "played hard" part years later to the Senate. "Yes, there were parties," he said defensively. "And the drinking age was eighteen, and yes, the seniors were legal and had beer there. And yes, people might have had too many beers on occasion. And people generally in high school—I think all of us have probably done things we look back on in high school and regret or cringe a bit."[12] Kavanaugh would repeat that claim of legal drinking numerous times, yet he never was of legal drinking age in high school. He didn't turn eighteen until February 12, 1983, well into his senior year, and the previous July a new Maryland law had raised the legal age to twenty-one. Kavanaugh was just seventeen during that summer of 1982 when, the former Chrissy Blasey would allege, he drunkenly assaulted her.

Kavanaugh's scrawled notes on monthly calendars from that summer, the ones he would famously produce to the Senate thirty-six years later, suggest the good times he had as a rising senior. Nearly every weekend he was at his parents' house on the Eastern Shore, or staying with classmates at their families' second homes. There was "Beach Week" at the ocean, an annual beach-house bacchanalia for his private-school crowd. During the week, he'd spend one day at the Columbia Country Club and the next at Congressional Country Club. One weekend he visited Connecticut for admission interviews at two Ivy League colleges, Yale and Brown. With his parents, he visited New York for several days.

Humor writer Mike Sacks, who grew up in affluent Potomac, Maryland, four years behind Kavanaugh, milked his memories of Washington's Reagan-era suburbia for his media projects. While his family wasn't rich and he didn't go to a prep school or belong to a country club, Sacks spent time with "this entitled type," as he described Kavanaugh. "Things had a tendency to happen while you were around them. When they got drunk, all bets were off."[13]

As much as Kavanaugh would play down his drinking during his court vetting, his speeches during his years as an appellate court judge are notable for how often he alluded to the alcohol-fueled antics of his high school, college, and law school years. Speaking at the Catholic University law school in 2015, for example, he recognized three alumni who'd been his friends in high school. "Fortunately, we've had a good saying that we've held firm to, to this day," Kavanaugh said. "Which is, what happens at Georgetown Prep stays at Georgetown Prep. That's been a good thing for all of us, I think."[14]

But as the nation would come to know, he and his classmates left a lot of hints in their senior yearbook, the *Cupola*. On Kavanaugh's personal page, he began with standard entries for his athletic achievements and work on the student newspaper, then listed more numerous faux accomplishments— insider jokes suggestive of drunkenness and sex. Among them were the "Keg City Club" ("100 Kegs or Bust"), "Beach Week Ralph Club— Biggest Contributor," "Devil's Triangle," "Judge—Have You Boofed Yet?," "Maureen—Tainted Whack," and the one that would become the most famous, "Renate Alumnius" (*sic*). Kavanaugh's friend Mark Judge, on his page, called himself the founder of "Alcoholics Unanimous" and included a quote, "Certain women should be struck regularly, like gongs."

"Our yearbook was a disaster," Kavanaugh told the Senate Judiciary Committee decades later, to distance himself from the contents. That's when he alluded to the era's teen-oriented movies as the likely inspiration for the student editors, adding, "Many of us went along in the yearbook to the point of absurdity." He and his supporters among his former classmates would deny that terms including "Devil's Triangle" and "boofing" referred to sex acts. Four friends would go to the trouble of writing senators to explain how to play the beer-drinking game they'd named Devil's Triangle, adding, "If the phrase 'Devil's Triangle' had any sexual meaning in the early 1980s, we did not know it."

Another rich source of material on Kavanaugh's high school circle was Judge's prolific later writings about what he described as the debauchery of those years. Judge, who declined to speak to the committee, citing his alcoholism, released a memoir in 1997, fourteen years after high school graduation, entitled *Wasted: Tales of a Gen X Drunk*. He wrote, "If you could breathe and walk at the same time, you could hook up with some-one. This did not mean going all the way for the most part, these girls held to the beliefs of their very conservative families." By 2005, Judge had changed from a liberal to conservative Catholic and wrote *God and Man at Georgetown Prep*—a takeoff on William F. Buckley's famous attack a half century before on liberalism in academia, *God and Man at Yale*—

to fault the Jesuits at Prep for what he considered a too-liberal education. The *New York Times* and the *Washington Post* went so far as to review Judge's oeuvre during Kavanaugh's confirmation. *Times* reviewer Dwight Garner, a Catholic of Kavanaugh and Judge's generation, and someone for whom their teenage drinking excesses rang familiar, wrote, "'Wasted' is the story of a privileged young white man, a cocky princeling among cocky princelings."[15]

On page 59, Judge introduced a thinly veiled "Bart O'Kavanaugh"—"Bart" was Brett Kavanaugh's nickname among his high school pals.

> "Do you know Bart O'Kavanaugh?"
> "Yeah, he's around here somewhere."
> "I heard he puked in someone's car the other night."
> "Yeah. He passed out on his way back from a party."

The actual Brett Kavanaugh would testify repeatedly to the Senate, under oath, that he never passed out from drinking or forgot what happened the night before.

After Trump announced his choice of Kavanaugh, Judge tweeted a photo of eight bare-chested teenage boys on a beach and wrote, "Members of the mighty GP class of 1983." He and Kavanaugh were front and center; the two classmates were all but inseparable, by many accounts. Articles during Kavanaugh's confirmation process generally depicted him as something of a follower of the extroverted and good-looking Judge. Yet Elizabeth Rasor, who would be Judge's girlfriend during and after college, recalled that it was Judge who was more in thrall to Kavanaugh. "Mark worshipped Brett," she said. "I think people have gotten that wrong—that Mark was the really cool one that everyone wanted to hang out with."[16]

One recollection depicting Kavanaugh in Judge's shadow came in a sworn statement that Prep classmate Paul Rendon gave to the Senate Judiciary Committee. "Mark Judge was the class clown. Brett Kavanaugh would always laugh the loudest when it was in response to Mark Judge's jokes and antics," Rendon wrote. Also: "When I heard Dr. Ford describe Brett Kavanaugh and Mark Judge laughing at her, I immediately recalled Brett Kavanaugh and Mark Judge laughing together at someone else's expense."[17]

Without naming anyone, Rendon also said that "Brett Kavanaugh's group of friends," the jocks, routinely "tormented, teased and ridiculed" other students, sometimes shoving them into lockers or closets. He said he never witnessed Kavanaugh joining in the bullying, only standing by and laughing at his friends' actions. Rendon said he did witness, on Mondays during their junior and senior years, Kavanaugh and other athletes bragging about how many kegs of beer they'd killed over the weekend, and about sexual conquests. They often mentioned "a person named Renate, pronounced, REE NATE," Rendon wrote. "I specifically recall one day walking down a hall with Brett Kavanaugh on [the] way to class" as he sang, "REE NATE, REE NATE, if you want a date, can't get one until late, and you wanna get laid, you can make it with REE NATE."

In the 1983 yearbook, Kavanaugh and a dozen other seniors would refer to "Renate" on their personal pages, describing themselves as "Renate Alumni" or "Renate Alumnius." A photo of nine football players, including Kavanaugh and Judge side by side again, is captioned "Renate Alumni." To the Senate, Kavanaugh would insist that the woman—Renate Schroeder, later Renate Dolphin, then a student at one of the nearby girls' schools—was a friend to the Prep guys. The media badly misinterpreted the references, he insisted. She plainly did not see it that way. Dolphin said she'd heard about the slanderous chant back then and asked that the boys stop. But until the *New York Times* contacted her in 2018, she did not know about the material in the Prep yearbook. "I can't begin to comprehend what goes through the minds of 17-year-old boys who write such things," she said, "but the insinuation is horrible, hurtful and simply untrue. I pray their daughters are never treated this way." Through her lawyer, in 2019, she said she had nothing to add.[18]

Early in Kavanaugh's senior year, one of his teammates wrote in Prep's student newspaper, *The Little Hoya*, about the impact on students' parties of Maryland's new law setting the minimum drinking age at twenty-one. Apparently, underage seniors weren't at a loss—some parents agreed to open their large houses to throngs of students, allowing beer and assuming responsibility. "As the 1982 school year progresses, Georgetown Prep has become well known throughout the area for its 'great parties,'" the article began. "Parties in which as many as 600 people at a time come to enjoy themselves and take a breather from the day-to-day school routine, are what is meant by 'great parties.'" The one concern, according to the student author, was that "unruly kids would crash" the parties—that is, guys from rival schools.

Months later, Kavanaugh was featured in a short article. In a photograph, he is wearing his Prep sports jacket. "In addition to his athletic prowess, Brett is an excellent student and a member of the National Honor Society," who'd applied to several Ivy League schools, including Princeton, the University of Pennsylvania, Brown, and Yale, as well as Amherst and Georgetown. "Ideally," the piece closed, "Brett hopes to study English and history at one of the northern colleges." (On the opposite page was a notice that a younger student, Neil Gorsuch, was among three members of Prep's forensics club to qualify for the area finals competition.) For college, Kavanaugh would choose his grandfather's alma mater, Yale.[19]

2

FROM WATERGATE'S RUINS TO REAGAN'S REVOLUTION

"We are different from previous generations of conservatives."

As vice president and beyond, Joe Biden liked to tell his crowds, "Folks, this is not your father's Republican Party." When Brett Kavanaugh became a teenager in 1978, his father's Republican Party was beginning the transformation to which Biden alluded. The years-long battles between the party's ruling moderates and the growing ranks of insurgent conservatives had escalated as Republicans sought to rebuild from the ruins of the Watergate scandal and then the loss of the White House in 1976. From the vantage of decades later, it's clear that the norms-abiding moderates never had a chance. Right-wing activist Paul Weyrich warned, "We are different from previous generations of conservatives. We are no longer working to preserve the status quo. We are radicals, working to overturn the present power structure in the country."[1]

The very survival of the 122-year-old party was at stake. Prominent conservative Clare Boothe Luce wrote in 1975, "There is not the slightest chance, in my view, that the GOP can 'win' in 1976, or for that matter, ever again." By 1977, fewer than one out of five Americans described themselves as Republicans; the rest split between Democrats and independents. President Jimmy Carter, a Georgian, had won all the states of the old Confederacy except Virginia in ousting Gerald R. Ford. Many Republicans feared their race-based dream of capturing the South had been dashed, even as their party was bleeding support in its traditional strongholds of the Northeast and Midwest.[2]

Conservatives seriously debated forming a third party and leaving the shambles of the Grand Old Party to the moderates. Yet by the midterm election year of 1978, Republicans of all stripes were regaining optimism, if only from Democrats' misfortunes. Carter confronted a global energy crisis, high inflation, and a stagnant economy, as well as a liberal rebellion within his party led by Massachusetts senator Edward M. Kennedy. Suddenly, Republicans were battling each other not simply to redefine their party, but also to choose a new leader with a realistic hope of winning the White House. Given the stakes, their warring intensified.

The conservatives' edge, and the first shoots of the Reagan revolution, were evident. Evangelicals, throwing off their longstanding aversion to politics, increasingly were coming into the Republican Party as voters and volunteers. They were even taking over local party organizations, sometimes by ousting Goldwater conservatives for not being conservative enough, especially on social issues. By mid-1978, a property tax revolt in California spurred voters to embrace Proposition 13, writing into the state constitution strict limits on tax increases. Those limits ultimately proved fiscally devastating, but for now conservatives were celebrating. The anti-tax movement was infectious. By year's end, the Democratic-controlled Congress passed a Republican bill to cut federal taxes. Bolder plans were hatching.

In November's midterm elections, conservatives were prominent among the victors as Republicans made gains in the House, Senate, and governorships (though a thirty-two-year-old Democrat, Bill Clinton, was elected governor in Arkansas). George W. Bush lost his House race in West Texas, but first-time Republican winners included Ford's White House chief of staff, Dick Cheney of Wyoming, and history teacher Newt Gingrich in Georgia. Newly elected Democrats from the South were more conservative than the retired Democrats they replaced. Some, like economics professor Phil Gramm in Texas, would become Reagan allies and, with time, Republicans.

Attention shifted to the 1980 presidential race. Reagan had endeared himself to the right four years earlier with his strong challenge to Ford for the 1976 Republican nomination. The former actor had first come to conservatives' attention at the 1964 party convention, when his call to arms for Barry Goldwater nearly stole the show from the nominee. Goldwater's landslide loss to Lyndon B. Johnson put conservatives on the defensive, but Reagan gave hope to many by subsequently winning two terms as California's governor. For the 1968, 1972, and 1976 presidential cycles, Republicans' presidential nominees were establishment candidates, Nixon and Ford. Yet their failures—and then Carter's—paved the way for Reagan. The crises of 1979 and 1980, including the Soviet Union's invasion of Afghanistan and radical Islamists' takeover of Iran and the U.S. embassy there, increased the appeal of his message of economic change and military might.

Reagan vanquished conservatives and moderates, including establishment pillar George H. W. Bush; his last moderate rival for the Republican nomination, Congressman John Anderson of Illinois, quit to run for president as an independent. At the Republican convention, the emboldened pro-Reagan right drafted a platform that broke with the past: Out was a forty-year-old plank endorsing the Equal Rights Amendment for women as well as another for abortion rights. In was a call for both a constitutional amendment banning abortion and an anti-abortion litmus test for federal judges. In a nod to moderates, Reagan chose Bush as his running mate. By then, however, Bush had disavowed his support for abortion rights and endorsed the Reagan tax-cut plan that he'd famously derided as "voodoo economics."

The nominee built a coalition of white southerners and traditional business-oriented Republicans, along with newly politicized evangelical Christians and "Reagan Democrats." The last group were mainly white, working-class voters across the industrial North, where the good jobs with good benefits that residents had taken for granted since midcentury were threatened by globalization and technological change. Many of these insecure workers were open to Reagan's economic ideas, as well as his conservative stands in the culture wars over guns, abortion, gay rights, busing, and affirmative action. Reagan's first appearance after the convention confirmed that he would expand on Goldwater's and Nixon's Southern Strategy playbook, with coded racial appeals to white Democrats. He and

Nancy Reagan went to the Neshoba County Fair, in the Mississippi county best known as the place where civil rights workers James Chaney, Andrew Goodman, and Michael Schwerner were murdered sixteen years before by local racists, including law enforcement officials, who escaped justice. There Reagan resurrected the phrase that had been widely discredited for its association with southern segregationists in the sixties. "I believe in states' rights," he said.[3]

Reagan defeated Carter by 10 points, 51 percent to 41 percent. (Anderson won 7 percent of the vote.)[4] On his coattails, the Republicans unexpectedly won enough Senate seats, a net gain of twelve, to have a majority for the first time in more than a quarter century. With Reagan's election mandate, his Senate support, and an expanded coalition of Republicans and southern Democrats in the Democratic-controlled House, the new president was able to press the most conservative agenda in memory. His inaugural address famously set the tone: "Government is not the solution to our problems. Government is the problem."[5]

Yet by Reagan's second year, that line was no longer broadly popular and neither was he. Many Americans again looked to the government for help amid a severe recession, high interest rates, and Social Security cuts. Rising budget deficits, too, put Reagan and other supply-side conservatives on the defensive as his tax cuts clearly weren't paying for themselves with economic growth as promised. In 1982, Republican senators who were "deficit hawks," an endangered breed in the party, led the way in raising taxes to reduce the fiscal gap. Reluctantly, Reagan signed the tax increases into law. His standing with the right was solid enough that he could get away with such compromises; future party leaders wouldn't find conservatives so forgiving. With an improved economy by 1984, he easily won reelection in a landslide, but without coattails for his party.

While Reagan would be remembered for the massive first-year tax cuts, over time he approved eleven tax increases. Still, annual deficits grew and the federal debt tripled during his presidency. In 1986, he signed other landmark laws overhauling the tax code and the immigration system, giving amnesty to millions of people in the country illegally. He also vetoed a bill imposing sanctions on South Africa's racist government, only to have the Republican-led Senate join with the Democratic House to override his veto. Opposition to that country's apartheid system of racial segregation, and Reagan's tolerance of it, was an issue that roiled campuses nationwide in the 1980s—including the one Kavanaugh now attended, Yale.

By 1987, Reagan's revolution seemed tapped out. Democrats had recaptured the Senate in 1986, giving them full control of Congress for the first time in his presidency. The president, already hobbled by lame-duck status, was weakened further by the Iran-Contra scandal and, a senior Republican senator told me, early signs of dementia.[6]

Yet Reagan's legacy was strong enough to help his vice president win the Republican nomination against conservative challengers, and then the election. Though Bush ran a bare-knuckles campaign, including racial appeals, as president he vowed to be a "kinder, gentler" Republican—an implicit rebuke of Reaganism suggesting a course correction back toward the center. Bush signed landmark legislation strengthening environmental laws, barring discrimination against disabled Americans, and requiring accommodations for them in all places open to the public. He agreed to the bipartisan 1990 budget pact that helped erase projected deficits in that decade, through spending caps and tax increases. On foreign policy, he ended the nation's long involvement in Central America's civil wars, and presided over the end of the Cold War and the integration of formerly communist Eastern Europe after the collapse of the Soviet Union. After he managed the U.S.-led coalition that liberated Kuwait from Iraq in early 1991, his popularity exceeded Reagan's highs.

In that year, however, Bush's fortunes plummeted. The nation was in a recession and conservatives were mutinous that he'd broken his 1988 convention promise to them: "Read my lips: No new taxes." Bush didn't have Reagan's stature with the right to pull off such compromises. And thanks to Reagan's influence, much of the party no longer subscribed to a fiscal conservatism that abhorred deficits more than taxes. Challenged by right-wing pundit Pat Buchanan for the 1992 nomination, Bush emerged weakened for his race against Clinton. Meanwhile, militant conservatives led by Newt Gingrich, the onetime backbench pest, were ascendant in Congress. And they were plotting the Republican Party's next revolution.

•   •   •

Conservatives not only won the long civil war against Republican moderates, they also built a well-funded network of foundations, alliances, and advocacy groups that effectively institutionalized their grip on the party. The Heritage Foundation, financed in the 1970s by brewery magnate Joseph Coors, thrived as the think tank of the Reagan revolution. Its "Mandate for Leadership" was the revolution's manifesto, filling twenty volumes with more than two thousand recommendations covering taxes, trade, regulations, national security, and more, and opposing affirmative action and other civil rights initiatives.[7] The National Rifle Association, which had radicalized in the mid-1970s to focus on politics and gun rights after a century as a nonpartisan promoter of hunting and marksmanship, became a virtual arm of the Republican Party. Southern televangelist Jerry Falwell founded the Moral Majority to galvanize evangelicals for the 1980 election; while the group didn't survive past the Reagan administration, other conservative Christian groups took its place in alliance with Republicans in the culture wars.

Among these new forces on the right, "I would put the Federalist Society front and center," said David Brock, who came to Washington as a right-wing writer during the Reagan years but defected in the Gingrich era. From Reagan to President Trump, Brock said, "the constant was the long game to capture the courts, and the Supreme Court in particular."[8]

•   •   •

In April 1982, just over a year into Reagan's presidency, scores of conservative law students from across the country met in Room 127 of Yale Law School. As they swapped right-leaning legal arguments in that large lecture hall at one of America's most liberal law schools, former Yale professor Ralph K. Winter Jr. excitedly marveled, "I can't believe I'm hearing *these* things in *this* room."[9] Winter was something of a celebrity at this symposium: The conservative scholar had just been nominated by Reagan and confirmed to the New York–based Second Circuit Court of Appeals. Two other attractions were the student organizers' faculty advisers: Robert Bork, a Yale professor who'd recently been confirmed by the Senate for the D.C. Circuit Court of Appeals, and Antonin

Scalia, a University of Chicago professor who'd soon join Bork on the court.

Reagan, by his choices for judges and federal officials, was elevating people and ideas long seen as controversial, even on the fringe, by the legal and political establishments. Three law students who'd been friends as undergraduates at Yale ambitiously decided to organize this symposium, to debate these ideas—among them how to redefine federalism to return more power to state and local governments. By inviting speakers with administration connections, they also could prospect for jobs in Washington. Word spread from Harvard to Stanford. The organizers—Steven G. Calabresi at Yale and Lee Liberman Otis and David McIntosh, now at the University of Chicago's law school—little expected that from their invitation would come a transformational conservative institution, the Federalist Society.

The student-founders gave it that name at the start, and adopted as their logo a silhouette of James Madison, coauthor of the *Federalist Papers*, that also endures. They got a $25,000 grant from a neoconservative foundation.[10] The invitation sent to law schools nationwide became a mission statement: "Law schools and the legal profession are currently strongly dominated by a form of orthodox liberal ideology which advocates a centralized and uniform society. While some members of the legal community have dissented from these views, no comprehensive conservative critique or agenda has been formulated in this field. This Conference will furnish an occasion for such a response to begin to be articulated."

One of the speakers immediately saw the promise of this gathering. Ted Olson, a young assistant attorney general and future solicitor general, told the students, "I sense that we are at one of those points in history where the pendulum may be beginning to swing in another direction. Of course, we do not know now, and no one will really know until many years from now, whether the 1980 elections have wrought a significant and long-lasting change. But I think that there is an opportunity here, and the organization of this society and this symposium is a cause for optimism and a sign that perhaps something is happening."[11]

The forum got national media attention as a sign of the Reagan revolution at work. By summer's end, the founders had money from conservative foundations and sent out an ambitious pitch for more on October 15, 1982:

"Proposal to Form a National Conservative Legal Organization." They called for creating separate divisions for law students, faculty, and lawyers, and correctly predicted that the society would become a conservative placement service—for law clerks, professors at elite law schools, government lawyers, and, ultimately, judges. They drafted a how-to guide for students at other law schools to form chapters. One bit of advice reflected the diversity of views on the right: Chapters "should not use the label 'conservative,'" the founders wrote, to avoid disputes among libertarians, law-and-economics conservatives, "strict constructionists," evangelicals, and others about what the term meant, and to encourage even students who didn't consider themselves conservative to participate.

A year later, the Federalist Society had a Washington office at a conservative think tank, the American Enterprise Institute, and a national director, Eugene Meyer, who would still be at the helm in 2020. Scalia served as a fund-raiser, speaker, and liaison among law schools. Founders Calabresi, McIntosh, and Otis soon all got jobs in the Justice Department after graduation, the vanguard of many young conservatives who'd parlay their Federalist Society connection for career advancement.[12]

In the mid-1980s, the society began holding its annual gatherings at the historic Mayflower Hotel in downtown Washington. The conventions would come to draw thousands of lawyers for a long weekend of legal discussions, career networking, and a gala dinner with a prominent speaker. The organization quickly evolved with its members as they graduated and fanned out: First came scores of campus chapters, then a lawyers' chapter in Reagan's Washington, where the early members got their first jobs, and then lawyers' chapters in cities nationwide. The organization did not endorse or donate to candidates, lobby, or file cases. Its influence flowed from networking among those who did. Rich donors and conservative foundations chipped in through the years, including the John M. Olin, Sarah Scaife, and Lynde and Harry Bradley foundations and billionaires David and Charles Koch.

The Federalist Society soon changed the terms of the debate for conservatives. Nixon-era phrases, including "strict constructionism" and "law and order," were replaced by talk of "originalism" and "textualism"— the beliefs that the Constitution should be interpreted according to the supposed "original intent" of the founders, and laws precisely according to their texts. The society encouraged debate among its libertarian and conservative factions, and liberal lawyers were invited to events as intellectual foils. Some attended simply because they enjoyed the discussions.[13]

Despite the early success, conservatives fretted that the Federalist Society would stall or even dissolve once Reagan left office. Legal scholar Richard Epstein, a faculty adviser to the early chapter at the University of Chicago, said in 1986, "It is still a marginal organization and the key to whether it survives and flourishes will come after 1988."[14] Members took heart when George H. W. Bush's election kept Republicans in control of executive and judicial hiring. Yet the Federalist Society would grow dramatically during Clinton's two terms, reflecting conservatives' hunger to network and debate as a sort of shadow government until the next Republican regime.[15]

•   •   •

It was not surprising that Yale Law School would be the society's birthplace. Since Franklin D. Roosevelt's New Deal, Yale "had decisively embraced liberalism," Steven M. Teles wrote in a history of the conservative legal movement.[16] The school's few conservative students, fired by the Reagan-era ferment, yearned for intellectual exchanges with others of like mind.

Conservative lawyer George T. Conway III, who would become better known as one of President Trump's biggest critics while married to Trump counselor Kellyanne Conway, entered Yale Law School in 1984 and became president of its two-year-old Federalist Society chapter; he remained involved nearly four decades later, on the national society's board of visitors. His reason for joining was simple: "I had conservative views on the law that were basically at odds with the ethos that dominated the law school." Back then, he said, "We'd have weekly meetings in the Yale Law School dining room and usually about a dozen people would show up."[17] The chapter hadn't changed much by the time Kavanaugh entered the law school and joined three years later. Like the broader organization, however, it was growing.

While Reagan provided the spark, the Federalist Society evolved from a conservative legal movement that took root in the 1960s, in opposition to liberal rulings on civil rights and criminal justice from the Supreme Court under Chief Justice Earl Warren. The left would come to see the society's development as nefarious: It was a secretive right-wing cabal, bankrolled by dark money. Yet conservatives' model was liberals' own organizations of the era, including labor unions and public interest groups, and the progressive philanthropies like the Ford Foundation that contributed to them. "Liberals often treat all this conservative mobilization as some kind of conspiracy story. But unless you actually realize how deep liberal entrenchment in professions was, then none of that stuff makes any sense," Teles, the historian, told me. The left also had support in academia, he added. "Conservatives have been more dependent upon organizations of their own."[18]

Nixon promised in his 1968 campaign to deliver conservative courts filled with "law and order" judges. As president he sought young candidates for the lifetime jobs, to ensure a conservative stamp on the judiciary long after he was gone. Later Republican presidents followed his example. Seeking reelection in 1972, Nixon again used the courts as a rallying cry for white southerners, northern suburbanites, business interests, and conservative Christians, including traditionally Democratic Catholics. Each group had its own reasons to be receptive to attacks on the courts' perceived liberalism—opposition to rulings for desegregation and forced busing, abortion, federal regulations, restrictions on religious activities in public schools, expanded rights for criminal defendants, and more. Corporate interests and foundations backed by right-wing donors began bankrolling conservative groups to press the issue.

Despite his aborted presidency, Nixon got an unusually large number of opportunities—four—to reshape the Supreme Court. Ford got another in finishing Nixon's second term. Conservatives hoped that those five justices, a majority, would end the Warren Court's social revolution. Yet the Burger Court, led by Nixon appointee Warren E. Burger, would become known within the conservative movement as "the counter-revolution that wasn't."[19] Of the five justices—Burger, Harry Blackmun, Lewis F. Powell Jr., William Rehnquist, and John Paul Stevens—only Rehnquist satisfied the Republican right.

Conservatives' dismay with the Nixon-Ford justices partly reflected a change in what the right wanted from the federal courts at all levels. Before

Reagan, conservatives mainly sought what Nixon called law-and-order judges. Nominees often were tough-on-crime prosecutors or marquee partners in corporate law firms (and overwhelmingly men). By Reagan's time, however, the right's focus was on the culture war issues—abortion, gun rights, religion, affirmative action, gay rights, and more—as much as on law enforcement and business regulations. Republican presidents increasingly looked to lawyers who'd served in Republican administrations, or to lower court judges, with records that proved their ideological bona fides.[20] George H. W. Bush's choice of David Souter for the Supreme Court was something of an exception, and ultimately one of conservatives' biggest disappointments. Bush picked Souter, an obscure New Hampshire official who'd briefly been on the Boston-based First Circuit Court of Appeals, on the advice of his chief of staff, former New Hampshire governor John Sununu, and the state's senator, Warren Rudman. Yet even the sainted Reagan disappointed the right by two of the four justices he named; while Rehnquist and especially Scalia delighted conservatives, Sandra Day O'Connor and Anthony M. Kennedy did not.

Compared to the Democrats, conservatives had nothing to complain about. Over forty years from 1968 to 2009, just two Democratic-appointed nominees joined the court—Ruth Bader Ginsburg and Stephen Breyer in Clinton's first term. No openings occurred during Carter's one term. After Democrats' loss in *Bush v. Gore* in December 2000, when five conservative justices ended the recount and effectively declared George W. Bush president, some progressive lawyers sought to copy the Federalist Society—to create a network to galvanize the left around the courts as a political issue. Yet the result paled by comparison. Brian Fallon, a founder in 2017 of the progressive group Demand Justice, would tell me just after Kavanaugh's confirmation, "When people say, 'Why does the left not care about the courts and why does the right care so intensely?,' it's two sides of the same coin. The right is the side that has had grievances over the last fifty years against the courts. And by the same token, for all the reasons that the right is upset, the left is complacent." By 2020, however, that was changing.

In 2020, five of the six Republican appointees on the Supreme Court—John G. Roberts Jr., Clarence Thomas, Samuel Alito, Neil Gorsuch, and Kavanaugh—had served in Republican administrations; they were well known to conservatives. And all six, including Amy Coney Barrett, had been members of the Federalist Society; Roberts disputed that, though records showed he had formally participated in society events and in 2007, as chief justice, had sent a video tribute to the society's twenty-fifth anniversary gala.

Affiliation with the Federalist Society, or at least its blessing, had become arguably the most important criterion for vetting judicial candidates by the time of George W. Bush's presidency. After his father's elevation of Souter, suspicious conservatives wanted proof of ideological purity. In 2005, the society for the first time formally supported a nominee, Bush's choice of Roberts to replace Rehnquist as chief justice. But just a few months later, Bush learned the hard way what a force the society had become: Its leaders and other conservative activists forced him to withdraw his nomination of his longtime adviser, friend, and fellow Texan, Harriet Miers, to replace O'Connor. Miers was a virtual stranger to the activists, and her career offered few clues to her jurisprudence. She wasn't one of *them*.

Professor Todd Zywicki at George Mason University Law School, a center of right-leaning legal thought, scathingly wrote that conservatives, led by the Federalist Society, had spent years "building a deep farm team of superbly qualified and talented circuit court judges primed for this moment. The prevailing liberalism of the contemporary legal culture was on the ropes and primed for a knockout—only to have the president let it get off the canvas and survive this round."[21]

The Federalist Society was slow to assume a direct role in putting conservatives on the bench. As early as its first year, 1983, its leaders considered creating a system to rate prospective judges. The idea was dropped as impractical, and risky if the society's imprimatur hurt the right's favorites by suggesting they were biased. Such qualms would seem quaint by the new century. Meyer, the society's leader from the start, would continue to insist that it was a neutral player in court politics. Yet the overt involvement of other leaders—especially Leonard Leo, the executive vice president—undermined Meyer's contention. To maintain appearances, Leo took leaves of absence to work with the White House on nominations.[22]

• • •

By the time Kavanaugh was working with Leo to vet judicial candidates for Bush, the Federalist Society's membership was about thirty thousand, and growing. Yet as influential as it had become, Kavanaugh and other Republicans acted as if affiliation was something to hide. That only fed the left's darkest conspiracy theories.

In March 2001, just weeks into his new job as an assistant White House counsel, Kavanaugh was fed up with what he called the erroneous "whoppers" in the press. He wanted someone to set the reporters straight. Kavanaugh fired off an email to colleagues, objecting in particular to one report that said he had remained a member of the Federalist Society. "This may seem technical," he wrote, "but most of us resigned from the Federalist Society before starting work here and are not now members of the Society." Kavanaugh expressed concern about appearances of a conflict of interest: "The reason I (and others) resigned from Fed society was precisely because I did not want anyone to be able to say that I had an ongoing relationship with any group that has a strong interest in the work of this office." Another lawyer told him to chill. Given how many Bush aides were society members, the lawyer wrote back, "I think it's far better to simply give that 'accusation' a shrug of the shoulders." No way, Kavanaugh replied in turn—they should "aggressively" push back.[23]

Yet in 2018, when Kavanaugh filled out a questionnaire for the Senate Judiciary Committee ahead of its hearings on his nomination to the Supreme Court, he wrote that he had been a member of the Federalist Society since 1988, without any gaps in membership. And in late 2019, when then-justice Kavanaugh was the featured speaker at the society's annual black-tie gala, he emotionally told the nearly three thousand conservatives filling Union Station's grand hall, "I have been coming to these convention dinners for more than twenty-five years. . . . I have always been a proud member of the Federalist Society." The audience broke into spirited applause.[24]

In 2005, as Bush aides promoted Roberts's nomination, they went so far as to demand that newspapers correct reports that Roberts was a member of the Federalist Society. Then the *Washington Post* found a directory that identified him on one of the society's steering committees. Still White House aides pressed their complaints: Roberts, they countered, had not paid a $25 membership fee, so he couldn't be a member.[25] From the Federalist Society's earliest days, membership carried something of a stigma given the left-leaning bias of academia and the American bar. Yet law students and lawyers aspiring to prestigious federal jobs or judgeships knew membership had cachet—a credential of conservatism—when Republicans were doing the hiring. "It was precisely the willingness to bear this stigma that made Society membership a valuable signal of true-believership for conservatives in government," Teles wrote.[26]

Kavanaugh quickly joined after he entered Yale Law School, just five years after the society's founding there. For an ambitious young Republican, it was an important box to check.

3

THE YALE YEARS AND ONWARD

"I got there by busting my tail."

Kavanaugh didn't draw prime real estate on Yale's Old Campus quadrangle when he arrived as a freshman in 1983. He was assigned to Lawrance Hall, a turreted, nearly century-old High Victorian brick dormitory, where many residents had four-bedroom suites with a shared living room. But his was a two-bedroom unit in the basement that was described as "cellar-like," a "dungeon." He didn't improve the place. The shared bathroom typically stank of vomit, suite-mate Kit Winter and others would recall. Kavanaugh's roommate was Jamie Roche, a prep-school all-American swimmer from a nearby town in Connecticut. David White lived in the unit's other room; Winter came later. As often happens with college roommates, Kavanaugh and Roche quickly sensed that they weren't simpatico. They didn't socialize beyond the first days of college.[1]

Decades later, Roche sought to explain why he and Kavanaugh didn't hit it off. "Brett Kavanaugh was very fond of alpha-male athletes," he told me. That didn't describe Roche, though he was a nationally ranked swimmer. "For the football players, there was an alpha-male athlete phenomenon that everybody knows—and it's 'slap each other on the back, get together and watch football, and scream and yell and drink beer'—sort of dramatically." Kavanaugh and his friends, Roche said, "had a way of socializing that was sort of drunken, but not in a nice way, not in a fun way." They'd "egg each other on to doing things that make other people uncomfortable. There was a sort of a threatening air to that group that I just didn't like."[2]

The two guys didn't have a bad relationship. Years later, they both agreed on that. "We talked at night as freshman roommates do and I would see him as he returned from nights out with his friends," Roche wrote in a statement for the Senate Judiciary Committee in 2018. "It is from this experience that I concluded that although Brett was normally reserved, he was a notably heavy drinker, even by the standards of the time, and that he became aggressive and belligerent when he was very drunk." Often, Roche said, Kavanaugh was "incoherently drunk."[3] Kavanaugh denied that. "Like most people in college, I went to parties and had beers," he told the committee's Republican investigators under oath.

The really bad blood was between Roche and White. While Kavanaugh and White were friendly, and partied often, "Jamie and Dave White hated each other," Kavanaugh told the investigators. "They got in fights—fist fights—during the year. One time, Dave White was away for the weekend. When he came back, Jamie had moved all Dave White's furniture, everything, like into some other area of Lawrance Hall in a hallway." Roche stayed away a good deal. Besides swimming and going to classes, he was a cheerleader. A good friend was a woman on the squad, Debbie Ramirez, another freshman from small-town Connecticut.[4]

* * *

Kavanaugh would spend seven years at Yale as an undergraduate and law student, until mid-1990, but those first months in New Haven would be the ones for which he would become best known. He was not yet the ambitious networker he would become, and, as with many students his age, his political views remained unformed. For the first time he was attending school with females. Yet by all accounts, he continued to live in a guy's world, all the way through Yale and long beyond: He hung with the varsity athletes, joined a bad-boys fraternity as well as a males-only secret society with the misogynistic nickname "Tit & Clit," and partied hard. Try as he might, Kavanaugh couldn't make a varsity team himself; he played junior varsity basketball and intramural football, softball, and basketball.

In dozens of interviews with contemporaries, few cited any memory of his intellectual prowess. One classmate, an athlete who knew Kavanaugh all four years as an undergraduate, recalled being stunned on learning at the 1987 commencement ceremonies that Kavanaugh had graduated with honors. Friends and acquaintances had one principal memory: Brett drank a lot. And when he did, he was a sloppy, often belligerent drunk.

•   •   •

Todd Kaplan liked Kavanaugh, except when he drank. "He was a perfectly pleasant guy until about his sixth drink, and then he changed—the kind of guy who would wake up and not recall what had happened at the end of the evening. That was Brett," Kaplan told me. Friends would have to explain to Kavanaugh why they were mad at him the morning after; he had no memory of what he'd said or done to them. Kaplan was not among the former classmates who went public with such reminiscences years later, during Kavanaugh's Senate confirmation process. But Kaplan's memory, a common one among Kavanaugh's contemporaries, was an important one: It contradicted Kavanaugh's insistence under oath that he never forgot what he did while drinking. (For him to say otherwise would suggest that perhaps he could have assaulted a woman when drunk, and simply didn't remember.)

He was "a typical jock-y Irish guy," Kaplan said. "During the week he worked hard. On a 'student scale' of one to ten, he was a nine-and-a-half. He was in the library, he was not screwing around. But when it came time to go get a beer, watch a ball game, play on the intramural basketball team, he was the jock-y guy and he was happy to have too many drinks. When he did, he was no longer the very quiet, shy guy he was when he was sober. But I was the same way." Kaplan also remembered Kavanaugh as the organizer of tailgate parties for home football games: "He would have an Irish flag, and that's how you would find his tailgate."

For Kaplan, growing up in ethnic Irish and Italian neighborhoods near New Haven, gambling on horses and sports was a part of life. At Yale, however, he found that wasn't so for the many upper-class kids. Yet as he continued to place bets on weekend games, other students asked him to take their wagers, mostly small sums. Soon Kaplan had a little side business—an illegal one, his parents reminded him. Some people called him their bookie. Among his occasional clients was Kavanaugh. While Kaplan would come to see that some of his customers had a gambling problem, that didn't describe Kavanaugh. "He was a 'homer,'" Kaplan said, making small bets on teams from back home—the Washington Redskins, the Baltimore Orioles, the University of Maryland. "He just wanted to scream for his team."[5]

Often on weekends, Kavanaugh was screaming in the living room of a suite upstairs from his own in Lawrance Hall, C11. The unit was home to a varsity football player, Paul Lisella, and had a living room with better furniture than most students' digs and, most important, a good TV for watching sports. Kavanaugh was friendly with the suite's other residents—Mark Krasberg, Richard Oh, Daniel Lavan, Steve Kantrowitz, and Scott Ardley—though they didn't socialize outside the dorm. He often came with athletes, like soccer player Kevin Genda and football player Dave White. Kavanaugh was a huge fan of Washington's NFL team, Oh recalled, and especially of John Riggins—Riggo, the team's beer-loving running back, who set a single-season league record for touchdowns that year. (In Kavanaugh's sophomore year, Riggins would make news of a different sort, drunkenly telling Sandra Day O'Connor at a black-tie affair, "Come on, Sandy baby, loosen up. You're too tight.")[6] Even when there wasn't a game on, Kavanaugh and his circle "would congregate regularly in our suite to play drinking games, like Quarters, because we had furniture," Lavan said. Frequently with the guys was a woman, Tracy Harmon, who lived upstairs. On rare occasions her friend, and Roche's—Debbie Ramirez—came with Harmon. Both women, thirty-five years later, would be the subject of allegations that an inebriated Kavanaugh exposed himself to them when they, too, were drunk. Ramirez would say her assault likely occurred there in C11's common room, during a drinking game. Harmon would tell friends she didn't remember, or it didn't happen.[7]

Lavan told me that if he'd heard about the alleged incidents involving Ramirez and Harmon at the time, "I could easily have forgotten it. Because it was absolutely consistent with the kinds of behavior that went on by those guys, even in our suite, with the drinking games and the general misogynistic banter that would go on, and in the way they treated women. It was clear that they would egg each other on to these kinds of humiliations—laughing at women and making them uncomfortable just to have fun together." Echoes of Prep's "Renate Alumni." Still, Lavan saw another side of Kavanaugh as well. As he would write years later to the Senate, in an otherwise critical letter, Kavanaugh "took his studies seriously and was intelligent and at times thoughtful."[8]

By his sophomore year, Kavanaugh sought to join Yale's one fraternity at the time, Delta Kappa Epsilon, well known as a haven for hard-partying jocks. Lynne Brookes, a social friend of Kavanaugh's through their under-graduate years, witnessed the night he was tapped to become a Deke—and gained a nickname. "He was stumbling drunk, in a ridiculous costume, saying really dumb things, and I can almost guarantee that there's no way that he remembers that night," she recalled on CNN in 2018. Kavanaugh was publicly grabbing his crotch, she told me, hopping on one leg, and chanting, "I'm a geek, I'm a geek, I'm a power tool. When I sing this song, I look like a fool." From then on, he was "Brett Tool."[9]

That's the name by which both Jennifer Langa Klaus and Kerry Berchem knew Kavanaugh, when they arrived at Yale the following year. "I just knew him as Brett Tool, like 'He's a tool,'" Klaus told me. "By the time I got to whatever party I was at, he was far gone. He was standing against the wall, swaying, eyes half-mast, spittle around his—I mean, not to be gross, but just sort of out of it." Unlike many other Kavanaugh acquaintances, however, Klaus remembered him at parties as "pleasant, friendly, not mean, not belligerent in any way. I don't recall him being inappropriate with me, but just totally sloshed." Berchem described him to me as a "vanilla" guy, often "drunk in a corner."[10]

"He was a huge drinker all through Yale," Brookes said. "He tried to portray himself as this huge athlete. He was a JV guy. His friends, guys and gals, were varsity. So he was never quite good enough." Kavanaugh drew especially close to the basketball players, and in particular the nearly seven-foot center, Chris Dudley, who would go on to the NBA. Brookes, who by her own description was a hard-drinking athlete as well, said the jocks didn't party every night. "It was Thursday night and Saturday night. Friday was not a big night because most people that were in our crowd had games on Saturday." Brookes, who played varsity hockey and lacrosse, joined a women's group called Sub Rosa, which cohosted drinking parties with the Dekes, including "beer bowling." She recalled driving once in her senior year with Kavanaugh and two other students to a bowling party; they got "so hammered," she said, that they were lucky to get back to campus alive.

DKE's reputation was well established when Kavanaugh became a fraternity brother. The *Yale Daily News*, in a 2018 article on the fraternity's history, described it as "an organization notorious for disrespecting women." It published a photo from the newspaper of January 18, 1985— midway through Kavanaugh's sophomore year—showing two new fraternity pledges (called "buttholes," according to the caption) waving poles to which women's bras and panties were attached, on a march across campus. When a female student objected, one of the guys responded, "But hey, your panties might be here!" A DKE alumnus told the newspaper that women had loaned the lingerie, but a woman, a classmate of Kavanaugh's, said Dekes were known in the dorms for panty raids.[11]

The Dekes wouldn't have an actual fraternity house until 1988, by which time Kavanaugh was in law school. In his time, the brothers typically met in residential colleges. Yet Greek life was reemerging at Yale after a decline in the 1970s. That partly reflected changed societal attitudes in the Reagan era. But it also was a response to a new Connecticut law raising the minimum drinking age to twenty-one from eighteen: Frats offered ready access to alcohol for the underaged. By 1985 three new fraternities and a sorority had opened.[12] Klaus Jensen was part of a group that founded a Sigma Nu chapter, as an alternative to DKE. "It wasn't hard to find thirty people to say, 'Yeah, let's be in a fraternity.' We each paid fifty bucks and we had a few parties. It was really pretty lame insofar as a fraternity goes. Turned out to be mostly soccer players, lacrosse players that didn't really want to have anything to do with the Dekes." The Dekes, he said, "were your classic college-guy buffoons."[13]

Dekes were perhaps best known for sponsoring the annual "Tang" contest, an elaborate speed-drinking competition dating to the early twentieth century, just ahead of final exams. Teams representing Yale's residential colleges squared off in rounds, two at a time, across a ten-foot table; each contestant in turn downed two eight-ounce glasses of warm keg beer. There were penalties for spillage and other infractions. In a photo from one year's event, Kavanaugh intently referees an opposing team. He's wearing a Washington football T-shirt and the goofy leather football helmet for which, like his nickname, he was known.[14]

Kavanaugh joined another all-male group popular with athletes, the secret society Truth & Courage, known as "Tit & Clit," which "fizzled out of existence in the early 2010s."[15] He also was an occasional sports reporter for the *Yale Daily News*, writing two dozen articles over three years.[16] Yet as he would tell the Senate's Republican investigators years later, "Two things I was doing the most at Yale College were studying and going to class . . . and the second thing was basketball."

The future justice's brush with the wrong side of the law—and an example of the beery belligerence so many classmates would remember— came at the start of his junior year. Demery's, a bar popular with both New Haven locals and Yale students for its pizza and cheap beer, was the kind of joint where "town met gown," as classmate Chad Ludington described it to me. Kavanaugh was there late on a September night in 1985 with some varsity basketball players, including Ludington and Dudley, after a concert by the English reggae band UB40. The Yalies kept looking at a guy nearby, wondering if he was the band's lead singer. The man, a local resident, cursed and told them to stop: "I don't like the way you're fucking looking at me."

"Hey, buddy, sorry. We just thought maybe you were the lead singer of UB40," Ludington said, trying to defuse the situation.

"Well, I'm not," the man angrily replied. "Don't look at me that way again."

"That's when Brett said, 'Fuck you,' and threw the contents of his glass at him," Ludington recalled. As the two men "embraced in fighting," Dudley "took his glass and smashed it up against the guy's ear." Ludington sought to pull Dudley away from the ensuing melee.

New Haven police arrived and began questioning people, including Dudley, Kavanaugh, and the victim, Dom Cozzolino, whose ear was bleeding; he was aided by emergency personnel and then taken to a hospital for further treatment. The police put Dudley in handcuffs and took him to their station, though he ultimately wasn't charged. According to the police report, Cozzolino said the fight began when Kavanaugh "threw ice at him for some unknown reason." Dudley denied that he'd attacked Cozzolino, the report said, and "Mr. Kavanaugh didn't want to say if he threw the ice or not." At twenty, the future Supreme Court justice declined to cooperate with police, as was his right.

As an eyewitness, Ludington was in an awkward spot. "I was doing my best to not have to give any details," he said. "Brett had started the fight and Chris had upped the ante by drawing blood, literally. I didn't want to have to rat on my friends, to be frank with you. But I didn't have to, because I wasn't the only guy that saw Brett throw the ice. A lot of people did. In fact, the guy Dom—he pointed and said, 'That guy threw the ice.'"

Ludington returned to campus and sometime after 1 a.m. called the basketball coach: "Chris has been arrested, he's down at the station." In later years, Dudley, who unsuccessfully ran as a Republican to be governor of Oregon, would deny that he'd been arrested. Though the police report doesn't say, Ludington said Dudley "absolutely was arrested. They took him off in handcuffs."[17]

Ludington was already soured on Kavanaugh, because of his penchant for such drunken aggression. After the Demery's episode, they rarely socialized again. Ludington was especially offended by what he saw as Kavanaugh's insensitivity toward the blue-collar "townies" of New Haven. The Yalies were juniors, for God's sake. "By that point, if not earlier," Ludington said, "one should have appreciated the class difference and been more respectful and aware of it—understand that you might be perceived as a jerk or a snob. And if a guy says something snappy, just disregard him. Walk away."

Dudley, however, remained close with Kavanaugh for years. Through-out the 2018 confirmation process, he insisted that Kavanaugh never drank excessively, never behaved badly. He wrote to the Senate Judiciary Committee, "The person sometimes being described in the press is not the Brett Kavanaugh that I have known as a good friend for 35 years. The person they are trying to describe would not be able to function day to day." But Brookes, their college friend, would object when CNN host Chris Cuomo cited Dudley as a reference for Kavanaugh. "I'm not sure he's the best character witness," she said of Dudley. She told, for example, of witnessing both men "very drunk" at a party. Dudley, goaded by Kavanaugh, barged into a room where a male and female student had gone for privacy—just "to embarrass that woman," Brookes said. "They thought it was funny. The girl was mortified. And I was furious."[18]

For Brookes, like Ludington, the bar fight at Demery's defined Kavanaugh. "That incident is Brett," she said to me. "When he's drinking with the boys—Brett was always more popular with the boys than with the girls—he was very much the guy who wanted to make the other guys be like, 'Aw, Kavanaugh, you're such a dude!' He would get drunk enough to loosen his inhibitions, because I think he is a conservative guy, and then he was all about impressing the other guys."[19]

Marc Schindler, a varsity soccer player who knew Kavanaugh throughout their undergraduate years, came away with two memories. One was the common recollection: "Brett was always the guy who would be standing next to the keg at the party, not saying much, just pounding beers, with that red plastic cup in his hand, leaning up against the wall." The second was from their graduation in 1987. Schindler saw that Kavanaugh was graduating with distinction. "And I remember at the time thinking, 'Jesus, Brett Kavanaugh is smart? Who knew?'"[20]

With a bachelor's degree in history, Kavanaugh gave some thought to teaching the subject and coaching high school students, yet his mother's work as a prosecutor intrigued him. As he would tell the Senate, "I got into Yale Law School. That's the number one law school in the country. I had no connections there. I got there by busting my tail in college."

●   ●   ●

One thing that friends and acquaintances don't recall from Kavanaugh's Yale years is much if any indication of his political views. Ronald Reagan was reelected in 1984, in a landslide that included sophomore Kavanaugh's first vote for a president. "I agreed with him on some issues and registered Republican," Kavanaugh would tell senators at a 2006 hearing on his nomination for the D.C. Circuit Court. A booming Wall Street was attracting many students—including some of Kavanaugh's friends—and appalling others by its excesses. There were protests on campus against nuclear arms, against Reagan's "Star Wars" proposal for an antimissile shield in space, and, most of all, against South Africa's apartheid.

Opposition to the brutal white supremacist regime in South Africa—and to Reagan for condoning it—"was a central issue on campus" for several years, said Michael Barr, a Kavanaugh classmate active in the antiapartheid movement, who would become an economic adviser in the Clinton and Obama administrations. Protestors set up a shantytown in Yale's Beinecke Plaza and rallied there in front of the university president's office, calling for the college administration to divest from South Africa.[21]

As for Kavanaugh's views on this and more, Schindler said, "I don't remember his politics at all. But it's not like any of us had a lot of conversations about that, particularly among the athletes."

At Yale Law School, Kavanaugh would publish a law review article on strengthening safeguards against racial discrimination in jury selection. His seven male housemates in his third year of law school, over 1989 and 1990, mostly leaned Democratic. The group shared a brownstone building subdivided into several apartments, conveniently located behind Payne Whitney Gymnasium. Sports more than politics was the topic of choice, and ESPN's *SportsCenter* rather than cable news was the channel of choice. One housemate, James E. Boasberg, would also become a federal judge, nominated by a Democrat, Barack Obama, to the district court in Washington.[22]

"The house was so nasty that all the college frats had turned it down as unsanitary, but the eight of us lived there and bonded and have remained friends," Kavanaugh told Catholic University's law school graduates in 2018. For a quarter century afterward, the former roommates would reconnect in most years for a weekend at various locations—watching baseball's spring training or the World Series, rafting, biking, taking in Las Vegas. "The eight of us have maintained a very tight bond and have carried each other and encouraged each other through the valleys and mountains of life," he said.[23]

Kavanaugh didn't stand out among the best and brightest. "He had a pretty low profile in law school," said a student who attended at the same time. "I would've said he was kind of a corporate-law guy, not a prominent person on campus."[24]

Peter Keisler, a conservative lawyer who also went to Yale College and Law School, five years ahead of Kavanaugh, described the appeal of the law school as being "a small community." At roughly two hundred students in each class of the three-year program, it was about a third of the size of Harvard's law school. "I wouldn't say that everybody knows everybody," Keisler said, "but most people knew a lot of people." Kavanaugh quickly joined the five-year-old founding chapter of the Federalist Society. Keisler, who had been at Yale for the society's birth, said that while its earliest members joined because they "liked getting together and talking" with other conservatives, that didn't mean they felt out of place at the generally liberal law school. "It was not, for me, a place that I felt was hostile or unwelcoming," Keisler said. "Some of my closest friends then and until this day had a wide variety of views. Dinners would be two hours in the dining hall in which you'd be talking about a lot of things and sometimes agreeing and sometimes not. It was a very—for me—warm and exciting place to be at school. That was certainly my experience. And I suspect it was Brett's experience, too."[25]

Yet Kavanaugh described a more isolated experience in a 2017 speech to the American Enterprise Institute about the legacy of William H. Rehnquist, who was the chief justice when Kavanaugh entered law school. "He was my first judicial hero," Kavanaugh told his audience. "In case after case after case during law school, I noticed something. After I read the assigned reading, I would constantly make notes to myself—'Agree with Rehnquist majority opinion.' 'Agree with Rehnquist dissent.' 'Agree with Rehnquist analysis.' 'Rehnquist makes a good point here.' 'Rehnquist destroys the majority's reasoning here.' At that time, in 1987, Rehnquist had been on the Court for fifteen years, almost all of it as an associate justice. And his opinions made a lot of sense to me. In class after class, I stood with Rehnquist. That often meant, in the Yale Law School environment of the time, that I stood alone."[26] When he'd entered law school, Washington was roiled by Reagan's nomination of Robert Bork, the former Yale law professor and mentor to the Federalist Society's founders, for the Supreme Court. To get to classes, law students passed anti-Bork protests, though a few "Confirm Bork" signs competed with those urging "Block Bork."

The Federalist Society that Kavanaugh joined was a fledgling group. He jokingly drew a contrast with what it would become when he spoke at the Yale chapter's annual banquet in 2014. "When I was at Yale, the Federalist Society was basically a lunch table. Annual banquet? Are you kidding? The banquet was a pitcher and a pizza at Sally's"—a no-frills pizza joint in New Haven. "The organization was struggling a bit. Many Yale students back then thought the Federalist Society was crazy. And to be honest, some of the Federalist Society members *were* crazy. Okay, maybe some things haven't changed."[27]

The chapter in his time, like the Federalist Society generally, strove for meetings that allowed conservatives of different viewpoints to debate. One reason, a member said, was simply "to make better events that we would enjoy." Another was to "underscore that we really were about broadening the debate and not about pushing ideas on people." A typical discussion would have a libertarian, who wanted courts to more aggressively strike down federal regulations, facing off against a conservative favoring judicial restraint.[28]

Kavanaugh worked hard at law school, contemporaries said, and tales of his drunken partying are far less numerous than for his undergraduate years. "Yale College is a place where the cool people drink a lot and the people who want to please their peers party hard. Law school is a very different environment," said a Kavanaugh acquaintance who also attended both Yale College and Yale Law School. "If you want to be respected by your peers, you do it by working hard and achieving."[29]

Nonetheless, in that address to Yale's Federalist Society in 2014, Kavanaugh spent more time regaling the students with drinking stories from his own law school days than serving up intellectual food for thought. Yet by then he'd been a judge on the nation's second most prestigious court for eight years. He told the law students how he'd organized a bus trip from New Haven to Boston, for a Red Sox game and bar-hopping, in his final year. He and his buddies chugged from a keg on the ride up. They returned, he said, "falling out of the bus, onto the front steps" of the law school at about 4:45 a.m. Kavanaugh, modifying the old saying of his Georgetown Prep days, added, "Fortunately for all of us, we had a motto: 'What happens on the bus stays on the bus.'" He paraphrased it again for the audience before him: "Tonight you can modify that to 'What happens at the FedSoc after-party stays at the FedSoc after-party.'"

He also told of a class party at the New Haven Lawn Club, a prestigious social and athletic facility near Yale. "It is fair to say that we had a few drinks" before dinner, Kavanaugh said. A friend broke a table in the reception area: "I actually still possess a photo of him sprawled on the floor on top of the table. How did he break it, you might ask? The old-fashioned way. He lost his balance and fell into the table, drink in hand, and the table collapsed. My friend was a big guy. Now you might think that we would have quickly left the Lawn Club after that, with some sense of shame. But you'd be wrong." When a bartender refused to serve the drunken friend, a professor nicknamed "Dukie-stick" intervened, Kavanaugh said. "The moral of the story? Don't ever let it be said that Yale Law professors are not there when you need them most."[30]

During his years as a judge, Kavanaugh gave a number of such speeches in which he went on at length with drinking tales from high school, college, and law school. They had the odd ring of reunion reminiscences among classmates from an all-boys school or brothers from a fraternity—all about guys drinking excessively, going to games, partying, misbehaving. That reflected Kavanaugh's formative world. Yet however endearingly relatable his storytelling might have been to some in his audience, certainly it wasn't the stuff many law students come to hear from such a prominent jurist. (Nor was it the goody-two-shoes version of his early life that he'd tell the Senate and the world in 2018.)

In the Yale remarks, Kavanaugh segued to his memories of a law school mentor, Professor George Priest. He joked that he came into Priest's antitrust class with an advantage, having played on Priest's intramural basketball team, and, sure enough, Priest ultimately got him a "life-changing" clerkship with Judge Alex Kozinski of the Ninth Circuit Court of Appeals, a known feeder of clerks to Justice Anthony M. Kennedy. Priest told the *New York Times*, after Kavanaugh was nominated to the Supreme Court, "You learn a lot about the character of a person by playing basketball with him. He is an incredibly decent person." Like others, Priest said the young Kavanaugh had been "slightly conservative" but not outspoken about it.[31]

* * *

Kavanaugh got an unusual number of the summer jobs so coveted by law students and recent graduates: as an associate at one of Washington's preeminent law firms. After his first year of law school, in 1988, he worked at Pillsbury Winthrop Shaw Pittman. In the summer of 1989 he was an associate at both Miller Cassidy Larocca & Lewin and Covington & Burling. While he was at Covington, Kavanaugh's drunken behavior one evening had the most serious repercussions for him since his bar fight at Demery's.

The law firm hosted the summer associates at a long-popular bar nestled between the Dupont Circle and Georgetown neighborhoods—the since-closed Brickskeller, a beer lover's utopia with more than twelve hundred varieties from around the globe. When one associate arrived a bit late, he saw Kavanaugh, already drunk, cradling a paralegal in his arms and stumbling down the bar's front stairs with her. Kavanaugh fell at the bottom and he and the woman tumbled onto the sidewalk. He was reprimanded for the incident, another associate recalled, and the entire group of about forty law students got a lecture on proper behavior. Such summer stints typically yield job offers at the end; the students, often from Ivy League schools, already have cleared a high bar just by being selected. "It was hard not to get offered a job," the fellow associate said. "You really had to work at it." Yet Kavanaugh did not get one, the associate said, and the Brickskeller embarrassment probably accounted for it.[32]

After graduation in 1990, Kavanaugh worked again as a summer associate, at Williams & Connolly. This time he was offered a job, but he declined it—he'd lined up a clerkship with an appeals court judge. David Kendall, a partner at the firm, said he never worked on a case with Kavanaugh but "had a positive impression—not a deep impression—of an intelligent guy, socially adept." By decade's end, they would be on opposite sides: Kendall as President Bill Clinton's lawyer and Kavanaugh as a junior attorney on Ken Starr's team to investigate and prosecute Clinton and his wife.[33]

Kavanaugh wasn't interested in going into private practice, at least not yet. He first wanted a clerkship for an appeals court judge and, ultimately, for a justice of the Supreme Court. "Different people have different reasons for seeking clerkships," said Gary S. Feinerman, a federal district judge who was a clerk for Kennedy with both Kavanaugh and Neil Gorsuch. "I think for most people it's because it's a really interesting experience—you get to work with a judge for a whole year and see how the courts make decisions."

In 1989, Kavanaugh had interviewed with Walter K. Stapleton, the chief judge on the Philadelphia-based Third Circuit Court of Appeals, and a Reagan appointee. Stapleton took him on for a year over 1990 and 1991. "He had one of the most impressive résumés I have ever seen," Stapleton later told the Senate. "He had received an honors grade in every course he had taken at Yale Law School, save one." Stapleton said Kavanaugh's professors endorsed him and Stapleton's notes from their interview described him as "extremely talented, mature, confident yet modest, good sense of humor." The judge said he later advised Kavanaugh to aspire to become a judge himself, but the young man "in characteristically modest fashion said he doubted that he would get the opportunity to serve."[34]

In the year Kavanaugh did legal research and drafted opinions for Stapleton, the judge wrote the ruling in an important case, *Planned Parenthood v. Casey*, that upheld most of the abortion restrictions of a Pennsylvania law. Years later, when the Senate was considering Kavanaugh's Supreme Court nomination, neither he nor the White House would say what role he played in Stapleton's opinion. Pennsylvania's law was the most significant challenge to abortion rights since *Roe v. Wade*, and a lower court judge held that it was unconstitutional. Stapleton's opinion reversed much of that ruling. In the appellate panel's two-to-one vote for the opinion the dissenter was Samuel Alito, Kavanaugh's future colleague on the Supreme Court. Alito wanted to endorse the entire law, including its requirement that a married woman get her husband's consent for an abortion. Stapleton and the other judge in the majority called that requirement an "undue burden" that left women vulnerable to abuse. Ultimately, the Supreme Court also struck down the mandate for spousal consent while sustaining other abortion restrictions, in a split decision that nonetheless upheld a constitutional right to an abortion.

In 1991, Kavanaugh got a shot at yet another appeals court clerkship, and with it greater opportunity for advancement. The circumstances were odd ones. Alex Azar, who'd been a year behind Kavanaugh at Yale (and would become President Trump's health and human services secretary), was clerking for Kozinski, the well-known conservative on the Ninth Circuit, but he'd left after just six weeks to join another appeals court judge, one who'd help him get a clerkship with Justice Antonin Scalia. Kozinski asked Yale's Priest for recommendations to fill Azar's spot. Priest phoned his hoops-playing protégé, Kavanaugh. Kozinski had a reputation as a hard boss, even a "sadistic" one, according to a 1985 complaint. Yet young lawyers overlooked that rap, given his reputation as a libertarian intellectual force and, even more, because of his record of feeding favored clerks to Kennedy. Kavanaugh got the position for the 1991–92 term.

"When we started as law clerks, he told us we work for the people and we should consider ourselves on the job twenty-four hours a day, seven days a week, 365 days a year," Kavanaugh said at a 2006 hearing on his appeals court nomination. "And I can say from personal experience that Judge Kozinski lived up to that promise."

In 2008, the *Los Angeles Times* would reveal that Kozinski maintained a private but publicly accessible server with sexually explicit content. It included a photo of naked women on all fours painted as cows, a video of a half-naked man with a sexually aroused farm animal, and images of masturbation and contortionist sex. "I think it's odd and interesting," he told the paper.[35] Later the *Times* reported that Kozinski for years had been sending emails with raunchy, misogynist jokes and sexually explicit photos to hundreds of individuals, including former clerks, on what he called his "Easy Rider Gag List." Again he defended the practice.[36] In 2017, however, the sixty-seven-year-old Kozinski suddenly retired after the *Washington Post* reported that at least fifteen women, most of them law clerks or junior aides, alleged sexual misconduct dating to 1986—five years before Kavanaugh would clerk for him. According to the allegations, Kozinski repeatedly showed women pornography in his chambers, kissed and fondled women uninvited, and made lewd comments. By retiring, he short-circuited an investigation.[37]

Kavanaugh maintained a relationship with Kozinski long after his clerkship. As Kozinski wrote in an article the year Kavanaugh worked for him, "Judge and law clerk are tethered by an invisible cord for the rest of their mutual careers." In later years, they would appear on panels together, and vet clerks for Kennedy. Kozinski flew from California to Washington in 2006 to testify for Kavanaugh's appeals court confirmation, calling him "my good friend." Amid Kozinski's disgrace in 2017, Kavanaugh hired Kozinski's son as his clerk. A woman who clerked for another judge on the Ninth Circuit told me, "Everyone who has ever been in Kozinski's presence knew about his behavior."[38] Yet Kavanaugh would insist at his Supreme Court confirmation hearing, under oath, that he never suspected his mentor's misconduct and could not recall Kozinski ever telling or sending him grossly inappropriate jokes.

Some lawyers would publicly suggest in 2018 that it defied credulity that at a minimum Kozinski wouldn't have had Kavanaugh on his Easy Rider Gag List. After all, Kavanaugh was a guy's guy. From high school, with the drunken antics and sexist yearbook entries, through college and his escapades with the jocks and panty-thieving Dekes, to the falling-down-drunk outings in law school and as a law firm associate, Kavanaugh was in on the frat-boy fun. He was, after all, the guy who thought it was funny to barge into a bedroom to humiliate a young woman in a tryst. It's hard to imagine that Kozinski, in Kavanaugh's presence, would have avoided making the nasty, sexist comments for which he was so well known. And given the many former clerks on his email list, men and women, it hardly seems likely that he would have excluded Kavanaugh.

●　　●　　●

After clerking for Stapleton and Kozinski, Kavanaugh made his play for a Supreme Court clerkship—with his hero, Rehnquist. He got an interview, he told people, but was not chosen. Instead, he won a yearlong internship at the Justice Department with President George H. W. Bush's solicitor general, Ken Starr. There he helped prepare legal briefs and Starr's oral arguments for the government's cases before the Supreme Court. Just as with Priest and Kozinski, Kavanaugh fostered a mentor-protégé relationship with Starr that would pay off. But first Kozinski came through: Kavanaugh got a Supreme Court clerkship for the 1993–94 court term, with Kennedy.

He was one of five Kennedy clerks, all white men. Years later, two of them—Miles F. Ehrlich, who became a white-collar trial lawyer in Berkeley, California, and Nathan Forrester, working in the Trump Justice Department—signed a letter with seventy-one other former Kennedy clerks endorsing Kavanaugh's confirmation to succeed their former boss. Feinerman, by now a federal judge, did not sign. Kavanaugh's fellow Georgetown Prep alumnus, Gorsuch, also clerked for Kennedy that year, but part-time because he was hired to assist retired justice Byron White.

Feinerman's path had crossed Kavanaugh's twice before. Both were in Yale's class of 1987, though they didn't know each other well, and together they were summer associates at Williams & Connolly. Only in Kennedy's chambers did Feinerman get a sense of Kavanaugh's political bent. "Certainly at the court you get to know people's jurisprudential views," Feinerman said, and Kavanaugh "was certainly on the right side of the fifty-yard line at the court." By that football metaphor, three of the Kennedy clerks were to the right of the center line (Kavanaugh, Gorsuch, and Forrester), and two (Feinerman and Ehrlich) were to its left.[39]

A clerk for another justice at that time told me that what he remembered of Kavanaugh was his show of temper once, as the court dealt with a case involving Florida's restrictions on antiabortion protesters. The Florida Supreme Court upheld the restrictions, which were intended to protect women entering clinics from aggressive demonstrators seeking to block them. The U.S. Supreme Court agreed in part but struck down some restraints as violations of the protesters' freedom of speech. Several justices, including Kavanaugh's boss, dissented; they would have struck down more restrictions on free-speech grounds. As the opinions and dissents were being drafted and circulated, Kavanaugh angrily confronted some clerks working for justices in the majority. The other clerk couldn't recall the specifics of Kavanaugh's objections, only his over-the-top furor. "He was really pissed off at something that we wrote," the clerk said, "and with an energy and fervor that surprised me."[40]

Once Kavanaugh's clerkship ended, Starr, now back at his law firm, Kirkland & Ellis, recruited the young man to join him there. Yet no sooner had Starr done so than Starr was tapped by a judicial panel to become the independent counsel charged with investigating Bill and Hillary Clinton, for their involvement prior to Clinton's presidency in an Arkansas land investment known as Whitewater. Starr took Kavanaugh with him, for what was supposed to be a short assignment. Instead they worked together for more than four years.

A private law career was not Kavanaugh's chosen path. He would briefly return to Kirkland & Ellis twice more, but between government jobs. In the Office of Independent Counsel with Starr, he would begin the networking that would serve him well once Republicans took back the White House. And his political inclinations, until now clearly Republican but only vaguely partisan, would turn much more so.

4

SUPREME BATTLES:
BORK AND THOMAS

"No one can even agree when the rancor over judicial nominations started."

Kavanaugh was just embarking on his path to a law career when, within four years, the Senate and the nation were roiled by two of the most searing battles in history over Supreme Court nominees, both Republicans. Robert Bork lost in 1987, while Clarence Thomas prevailed in 1991. Three decades later, echoes of each man's saga would resound in Kavanaugh's own confirmation ruckus, and amplify the furor in both parties.

He had just entered Yale Law School in the fall of 1987 when Bork, one of its most famous former professors and a mentor of the Federalist Society founders, was rejected after a divisive debate that nonetheless yielded a bipartisan Senate verdict: He was too far right of the jurisprudential mainstream. Often after such donnybrooks in Congress, the losing party warns that the outcome will have repercussions for years to come. Rarely is that true. Bork's defeat, however, would reverberate. It was the bloody shirt that Republicans would wave for decades in judicial confirmation battles, and again in 2018.

The saga of Bork, a judge on the D.C. Circuit Court, marked the first time that the philosophy of a Supreme Court nominee, rather than his or her integrity and qualifications, was the basis for rejection. And because Bork's candor about his conservative views hurt him, his Senate vetting was the last time that a nominee would be so forthcoming. From then on, nominees from both parties said as little as possible, claiming they didn't want to prejudge issues that might come before the court. In another first, Bork's opposition ran television ads, bringing campaign-style politics to the traditionally staid confirmation process. And because the American Bar Association joined the criticism of Bork, Republicans would come to oppose the venerable group's long-standing but unofficial role as the arbiter of nominees' qualifications.

In the moment, however, what mattered most for Kavanaugh's future was that in Bork's place Ronald Reagan nominated Anthony M. Kennedy of the Ninth Circuit Court, who was confirmed unanimously. Six years later, Kennedy would select Kavanaugh as one of his clerks, forging the tie that would be crucial to Kavanaugh's own nomination years later.

When Thomas won confirmation in 1991, by one of the narrowest margins in history after allegations of sexual harassment, Kavanaugh was a year out of law school and clerking for Alex Kozinski on the Ninth Circuit. Twenty-seven years later (and just a year after Kozinski resigned amid charges of sexual misconduct), Kavanaugh's confirmation process would follow the tawdry trajectory that Thomas's did, showing that the still overwhelmingly male Senate remained an institution incapable of dealing fairly with accusations of sexual misbehavior.

Republican Orrin Hatch of Utah fought in all three confirmation battles from Bork to Kavanaugh, and in others for lower court seats, over his decades on the Senate Judiciary Committee. He wrote in his memoir, "No one can even agree when the rancor over judicial nominations started. Republicans and Democrats point with equal indignation to completely different episodes." He and other Republicans pointed to Bork's rejection as the original sin. That episode and Thomas's each gets its own chapter in Hatch's memoir.[1] Democrats had their own bloody shirts, initially for the sheer number of lower court nominees that Republicans blocked in the Clinton and Obama years. Yet nothing provoked the party like Republicans' unprecedented snub in 2016 of Merrick Garland, President Obama's widely esteemed Supreme Court nominee, allowing President Trump to fill the seat a year later. Then followed Republicans' strong-arming of both Kavanaugh's confirmation in 2018 and Amy Coney Barrett's just days before the election that Trump would decisively lose. Judicial politics had reached a toxicity beyond any known antidote.

•   •   •

That Bork's defeat would become for conservatives like the killing that ignites a gang war, provoking retaliatory hits, showed the superior power of Republicans to craft and sustain a political narrative to fire up their base. Bork did not lose because Democrats were underhanded. He lost because both his record and his candor under senators' questioning showed that he espoused ideologically extreme views that alienated even some Republicans. Sealing his fate, Reagan failed to fight for him. Rather than a harbinger of dysfunction, the episode at bottom was a demonstration of the Senate performing its constitutional role of "advice and consent." Yet the myth took hold. Republicans even turned "Bork" into a verb, recognized by Merriam-Webster: "to attack or defeat (a nominee or candidate for political office) unfairly through an organized campaign of harsh public criticism or vilification."[2] Kavanaugh would apply it to his own confirmation experience.

By 1987, Republican message-meisters were newly abetted by conservative radio talk-show hosts beginning to proliferate nationwide. The Bork debate was right on the heels of the Reagan administration's repeal of the "Fairness Doctrine," which for years mandated that broadcasters airing opinions give free time to opposing views. Now they were free to say what they wanted, unchallenged. Rush Limbaugh, a college dropout and former radio DJ, became nationally syndicated in 1988, his daily shows a megaphone for white male grievances and a caustic no-compromise conservatism that inspired thousands of local imitators. In the next decade, the internet would ease entry for new online sites and give rise to no-holds-barred social media. The ramifications for civil discourse would be devastating.[3]

Bork's rejection was hardly illustrative of Democrats' approach to Republican nominees generally. Of Reagan's five Supreme Court picks, the Senate confirmed three by unanimous votes: Sandra Day O'Connor in 1981, the very conservative Antonin Scalia in 1986, and Kennedy. William

Rehnquist was elevated from associate justice to chief justice in 1986 after a bitter partisan debate, yet by a two-to-one margin, with sixteen Democratic senators supporting him.

Bork was the first of Reagan's nominees to come before the Senate after Democrats won a majority in 1986. And like Kavanaugh thirty-one years later, he was picked to replace the court's swing vote—in Bork's case, Lewis F. Powell Jr. Those two factors argued for nominating some-one less provocatively conservative than Bork. Even Republican leaders said so, notably White House chief of staff Howard Baker, the former Senate majority leader. Yet Reagan had passed over Bork twice before, to conservatives' chagrin. He'd picked O'Connor as the first female justice, to keep a campaign promise to moderate Republicans, and then chose Scalia, who was just as conservative but younger and healthier than the overweight, chain-smoking Bork. Bork "was considered a greater physical risk," as Hatch put it.[4] Now, with Reagan's presidency nearing an end, conservative activists pressed him to name Bork, and for the same reason Democrats would ferociously oppose him: He would decisively shift the court's balance rightward. "We have the opportunity now to roll back 30 years of social and political activism by the Supreme Court," said Dan Popeo, founder of the conservative Washington Legal Foundation.[5]

Democrats also had it in for Bork because he had been Richard Nixon's solicitor general, one of the most famous ever. In what became known as the Saturday Night Massacre, in October 1973, Bork's two superiors at the Justice Department—Attorney General Elliot Richardson and his deputy William Ruckelshaus—resigned rather than obey Nixon's order to fire Watergate special prosecutor Archibald Cox, who'd demanded that the White House produce the tapes of Nixon's Oval Office conversations that ultimately proved his guilt. Bork, next in seniority, carried out the order. In his posthumous 2012 memoir, Bork disclosed that after he fired Cox, to his surprise Nixon promised him the next Supreme Court seat. Bork didn't know whether Nixon actually believed that he still had the political stand-ing to get a nominee confirmed, or whether he simply sought to ensure Bork's loyalty.[6] He and other principals also later revealed that Richardson and Ruckelshaus urged him to carry out Nixon's order—they'd made their point, discrediting the president's directive by their resignations, yet

someone had to stay on to see the Justice Department through the constitutional crisis. When Reagan named Bork to the D.C. Circuit Court in
1981, Senate Democrats did not object, despite their misgivings. Bork was
confirmed by unanimous consent.

The Supreme Court was another matter, however. Within hours of
Bork's nomination on July 1, 1987, Edward M. Kennedy was on the Senate
floor delivering a virulent speech that came to be known as "Robert Bork's
America." It set the tone for Democrats—to the dismay of some—and lent
credence to Republicans' subsequent complaints of character assassination.
"Robert Bork's America," Kennedy said, in his most memorable passage,
"is a land in which women would be forced into back-alley abortions,
Blacks would have to sit at segregated lunch counters, rogue police would
break down citizens' doors in midnight raids, schoolchildren could not be
taught about evolution, writers and artists would be censored at the whim
of government, and the doors of the federal courts would be shut on the
fingers of millions of citizens for whom the judiciary is often the only
protector of the individual rights that are the heart of our democracy."

Kennedy sought to box in Joe Biden, a moderate Democrat and the new
chairman of the Judiciary Committee, yet his divisive hyperbole risked
alienating southern Democrats and moderate Republicans whose votes
were needed to defeat Bork. Bork's record spoke for itself, other Democrats
argued. Back in the early 1960s, he had opposed civil rights laws as federal
overreach and opposed Warren Court precedents on civil liberties. Despite
the Ninth Amendment, which recognizes rights unspecified in the Constitution, Bork opposed "unenumerated" rights; one, a right to privacy,
was the basis of the Supreme Court's precedents on reproductive rights.
Bork's opponents also made much of his support of a 1984 ruling at the
D.C. Circuit Court upholding a chemical company's policy that women of
childbearing age had to be sterilized if they held jobs that exposed them to
toxins unsafe for fetuses. Yet the ruling was unanimous.

In the 1980s, with the arrival of C-SPAN and commercial cable
networks, confirmation hearings and debates were televised for the first
time. In a parallel with Kavanaugh's story decades later, Bork's standing in
national polls would plummet after his hearing in September 1987. He
was not a winning performer, either in demeanor or, perhaps unfairly,

appearance. His Brillo-like hair and beard, furrowed brows, and menacing gaze accentuated his stern delivery of legal arcana. The *Washington Post*'s syndicated TV critic, Tom Shales, said Bork came off as "cold-hearted and condescending," adding, "He looked, and talked, like a man who would throw the book at you—maybe like a man who would throw the book at the whole country."[7]

Also on TV was a precedent-setting sixty-second ad against Bork, paid for by the liberal group People for the American Way and narrated by actor Gregory Peck, conjuring his iconic role as the avuncular lawyer Atticus Finch in *To Kill a Mockingbird*. In the ad, a stereotypically all-American family—mother, father, son, and daughter—gazed toward the Supreme Court edifice as Peck intoned, "Robert Bork wants to be a Supreme Court justice. But the record shows that he has a strange idea of what justice is." Peck suggested that Bork favored poll taxes and literacy tests that had been used to keep Blacks from voting, and opposed privacy rights and First Amendment protections for literature, art, and music. "If Robert Bork wins a seat on the Supreme Court, it'll be for his life—and yours."[8]

By late September, White House officials led by Baker were pushing Bork to withdraw. The proud, strong-willed judge refused. Not only that, he made demands. He came to the White House on a Saturday with his wife and told Reagan advisers that the president should deliver a prime-time address on his behalf. He demanded to see Reagan, alone, then went to the press briefing room to make his case. "A crucial principle is at stake," he said. "That principle is the way we select the men and women who guard the liberties of all the American people, that should not be done through public campaigns of distortion. If I withdraw now, that campaign would be seen as a success, and it would be mounted against future nominees."[9]

The drama dragged on, though the ending was hardly suspenseful. On October 23, Bork became the twenty-seventh Supreme Court nominee in history to be rejected by the Senate, by the widest margin in more than a century, 58–42. Six Republicans joined fifty-two Democrats in voting "no."[10]

"It is difficult to reconcile" Bork's defeat with Scalia's unanimous confirmation vote just a year earlier, Hatch wrote later; the two were "judicial soul mates." Yet Hatch tried: Scalia would be the first Italian American on the court, and Democrats were wary of offending that constituency. Scalia was not replacing a swing-vote justice; he didn't tip the court balance as Bork would. And Scalia's nomination followed the partisan brawl over elevating Rehnquist to chief justice. "No one," Hatch said, "was interested in fighting another battle so soon after the last."[11]

Reagan condemned Bork's opponents as a "lynch mob." While such rhetoric would soon become standard among Republicans, an undecided John Warner, the patrician Republican senator from Virginia, rebuked Reagan for remarks "unbecoming of the office of the president." Biden lobbied Warner hard, going over Bork's record with him; a "no" from the Republican would lend power to the final result, Biden knew. Warner did vote "no." Bork, he said, lacked a "record of compassion, of sensitivity and understanding of the pleas of the people."[12]

Biden, in closing the Senate debate, rebutted Republicans' charge that Bork had been unfairly treated. "This has been a great debate," he said, "a debate about fundamental principle, about how one interprets the Constitution." He called Bork "a fine man, who just had a view of the Constitution that is out of touch with the 1980s and 1990s." As the *New York Times*' Supreme Court reporter, Linda Greenhouse, wrote, "The debate thus ended with Judge Bork's supporters and opponents holding fundamentally irreconcilable views of what had gone wrong for the nominee. His supporters insisted that he had been misunderstood and mischaracterized, while his opponents maintained that he lost precisely because the senators and their constituents did understand his views, and rejected them."[13]

Mark Gitenstein, Biden's chief counsel, wrote several years later in a book on the saga that he remained troubled by both parties' tactics. "There is one thing I have never doubted, however: Americans made a serious, principled decision in rejecting Robert Bork's jurisprudence." He faulted Reagan. "The real tragedy for Robert Bork, his allies, and the philosophy they espoused," Gitenstein wrote, "... is that their greatest champion let them down in the fight, a truth it must be very difficult to face." He said that several Republicans told him that they, too, blamed Reagan, yet the result likely would have been the same if he had engaged.[14]

While Bork didn't get the chance to tip the court the conservatives' way, his defeat spurred conservatives to keep fighting for justices who would. Gitenstein, by then in his seventies, told me in 2019, "I really believe that the most important thing I have ever worked on, maybe that Biden ever worked on, was shaping the court for the next thirty years. I think having Souter and Kennedy on the court made a huge difference." Even so, he said, "The significance of Kavanaugh is that they finally won the Bork fight."

In October 2018, after Kavanaugh's confirmation, Greenhouse similarly wrote that Democrats' fight against Bork was validated in the short term: Anthony Kennedy, while conservative, protected progressives' most cherished precedents. Yet Republicans had been playing "the long game" (a favorite phrase of Senate Republican leader Mitch McConnell, and the title of his memoir), together with the Federalist Society and other groups, building a conservative pipeline from law schools to clerkships to judgeships and ultimately the Supreme Court. It was the pipeline that Kavanaugh had just entered in 1987 at Yale Law and its Federalist Society chapter. "Following Judge Bork's defeat, conservatives didn't waste time licking their wounds," Greenhouse wrote. "They got busy building the infrastructure necessary to accomplish their thwarted goals."[15]

For the Federalist Society, the conviction that Bork was a martyr "translated into a powerful motivation to use the Society to get revenge on the liberal elites who were seen as responsible for Bork's defeat," political scientist Steven M. Teles wrote in his book on the conservative legal movement. The group, long resentful of the ABA's role in rating judicial nominees, was especially bitter that the bar panel had split on giving Bork a "well qualified" rating. It redoubled its efforts to undercut the ABA among Republicans, ultimately succeeding in getting George W. Bush and then Trump to all but ignore the bar. And Bork's loss literally paid off for the Federalist Society: Its budget doubled over the next four years as it appealed to donors to avenge Bork. "We became more political," founding member Steven G. Calabresi said.[16]

Peter Keisler, an early member of the Federalist Society at Yale, had clerked for Bork in 1985 and 1986, then joined Reagan's White House counsel office, where he worked on Bork's nomination. Keisler called the Bork fight "an inflection point." There had long been discussion in both parties, he told me, about "how and to what extent should the Senate take into account a nominee's judicial philosophy"; it was a minority on both sides that said a senator's disagreement with that philosophy was reason enough to vote "no." For Bork to be defeated on philosophical grounds, Keisler said, "was a big jump." Yet as Bork's foes in both parties argued, few nominees ever reflected such a break from the mainstream.

Whether Bork's defeat "is the event from which everything that followed flows, who knows?" Keisler said. It did, however, mark "an escalation. Both sides feel abused." After Bush nominated Keisler for the D.C. Circuit Court in 2006, Keisler recalled, when he met with senators, "I felt like I had parachuted into Northern Ireland. Suddenly you're there, and there are these centuries of encrusted grievances that people have on both sides." He would never get a vote. Keisler and some other Republican nominees became casualties in the Bush-era judicial gang war, with the Democratic minority exacting punishment both for what they considered Republicans' unfair tactics and for their having obstructed so many Clinton nominees. Keisler, while widely respected, also bore a stigma among some Democrats for his associations with the Federalist Society and Bork.

David Brock, a right-wing journalist-provocateur at the time of Bork's defeat, told me three decades later, after he'd defected to the Democratic Party, that Bork's loss was "was defining for the generation of conservatives that Brett [Kavanaugh] is part of and that I was part of." He added, "I can't underline enough how that battle is seared in the minds of conservatives who were—I was twenty-five then—people like me: how the left would stop at nothing, no holds barred, end-justifies-the-means. And there was a reaction to that that carried over far beyond the Bork fight, and beyond nominations—that the struggle with the left was like an apocalyptic kind of struggle. The smashmouth style of conservative politics came out of that, too, because the idea was, 'We're not going to take it anymore.'"

Indeed, an ascendant Representative Newt Gingrich, in a 1988 speech, condemned the left's opposition to Bork in the militant terms that would define the post-Reagan conservative movement Gingrich was building in the House: "This war has to be fought with the scale and duration and savagery that is only true of civil wars. While we are lucky in this country that our civil wars are fought at the ballot box, not on the battlefields, nonetheless it is a civil war."[17]

So it was that in 1991, when George H. W. Bush teed up the next Supreme Court showdown by choosing Thomas, conservatives were ready. "It was like, 'This is *not* going to happen again,'" Brock said. "And, of course, the first thing they said about Anita Hill was that Thomas was being 'borked.'"

•   •   •

Nine months earlier, on October 8, 1990, in the elegant White House East Room, Bush had hosted a celebration celebrating David Souter's confirmation to take the Supreme Court seat long held by liberal William J. Brennan Jr. Prominent conservatives weren't in a party mood, however. Souter, a former New Hampshire attorney general, state judge, and, briefly, federal appeals court judge, was unfamiliar to them, his views on abortion unknown. He'd been sold to Bush mainly by White House chief of staff John Sununu, the former New Hampshire governor whose brand of Yankee Republicanism was disdained by conservatives as old-school—too moderate, and too chilly toward the social issues that moved them. Many already were seething that Bush had broken his "no new taxes" promise in the ongoing budget negotiations with the Democratic-led Congress. Their restiveness was an ill omen as Bush looked to his 1992 election race.

So it was that in the midst of Souter's party, Sununu made a peace offering to conservative activist Thomas Jipping, from right-wing leader Paul Weyrich's Free Congress Foundation: Bush would let the activists choose someone for the next Supreme Court vacancy, and the White House would lead a "knock-down, drag-out, bloody-knuckles grassroots fight" to confirm their choice. Jipping didn't have to wait long to test that promise. Late the following June, Thurgood Marshall, the civil rights icon and first Black justice, announced he was resigning. Sununu called Jipping, who faxed his recommendation that evening: Thomas, a forty-three-year-old African American judge young enough to hold the seat for decades.[18]

Four days later, Bush introduced Thomas from the lawn of his ocean-side estate in Kennebunkport, Maine. "The nomination got off to a rocky start immediately," Hatch recalled, when Bush called Thomas "the most qualified man for the court at this time." That, Hatch said, "was the kind of compliment that begs to be challenged and contradicted no matter who is the nominee." Thomas had never argued before a jury, hadn't practiced law in years, and had been less than two years on the D.C. Circuit Court. Democrats also fumed that Bush seemed to suggest the vacancy was "a Black seat," yet he was nominating a man whose views of the law, civil rights, and affirmative action were opposite Marshall's.[19]

Thomas's race and compelling personal story nonetheless would make him difficult for Democrats to oppose. From poverty in rural Pin Point, Georgia, he had gone to Yale Law School, worked for Missouri attorney general John Danforth, and, after Danforth was elected to the Senate in 1976, joined him in Washington two years later as an adviser. Thomas evolved from a Democrat to a mainstream Republican like Danforth, then shifted farther to the right, with a libertarian, antigovernment streak and disdain for the affirmative action policies that had eased his own path. After Reagan's election, Thomas was nominated and confirmed first to be assistant secretary of education for civil rights in 1981, and then, in 1982, to be chairman of the Equal Employment Opportunity Commission. In 1989, despite Thomas's young age and inexperience, Bush nominated him for the D.C. Circuit to replace Bork, who retired. For months, conservatives and Federalist Society leaders had campaigned for Thomas, eager to promote one of the party's few Black conservatives to a prestigious judgeship.

It proved a short apprenticeship for the highest court, and did little to allay concern about Thomas's inexperience. The ABA gave him a mediocre rating of "qualified"; a minority of the evaluating panel held out for "not qualified." It was the lowest assessment for a Supreme Court nominee in modern times. Yet, as Republicans counted on, Senate Democrats and civil rights groups were torn over the nomination; their opposition to Thomas's record and inexperience was offset by their hesitance to oppose a Black nominee. Conservative and evangelical groups were able to mobilize some Black ministers for him.

Republicans were cautiously confident that Thomas had sufficient Senate support by the time he arrived for his Senate hearing on September 10, escorted by Senator Strom Thurmond, the former segregationist, 1948

Dixiecrat candidate for president, and now the senior Republican on the Judiciary Committee. Thomas was understandably careful to avoid Bork's candor in answering senators' questions about his judicial philosophy, civil rights, affirmative action, and abortion. His responses were widely seen as unimpressive, however, causing some worry among his administration handlers. The hearing ended on September 20, without a word of a drama unfolding behind the scenes. There, a conflicted accuser had information against Thomas, while the senior Democrat privy to her secret—the chairman, Biden—seemed as reluctant to have her testimony as she'd been to give it. The parallels with events a quarter century later in Kavanaugh's case would only become more pronounced.

"I had no plan in my mind to come forward, not one single thought about it," Anita Hill would tell the authors of a book on Thomas's confirmation two years later. Yet Hill, a University of Oklahoma law professor who'd worked for Thomas at the Education Department and EEOC, had told enough friends about Thomas's sexual harassment and graphic talk of sex and pornography that, inevitably, word reached Washington's political bubble. Separately, two Democratic Senate aides contacted her; one was Ricki Seidman, a young aide to Ted Kennedy who years later would advise Kavanaugh's accuser, Christine Ford. Hill, foreshadowing Ford, ultimately decided she had "a duty to report" what she knew, yet initially she would come forward to the Judiciary Committee only on the condition of confidentiality.[20] She didn't realize how that would limit what Biden could do with her allegation. Thomas and the committee's Republicans would have to be told her name. Once she agreed to be named to the senators, Biden asked the White House to send the FBI to interview her and investigate, to avoid any appearance of partisanship by relying on his staff. (Chuck Grassley, the chairman in 2018, would have no such qualms about his Republican gumshoes, insisting that they, not the FBI, would deal with the various allegations against Kavanaugh.)

Hill agreed to speak to the FBI only after she was allowed to fax the bureau a four-page statement of her allegations—about Thomas's repeated pressure to date him, his descriptions of his sexual interests and pornography, and his warning that if she ever told others about his behavior, it could ruin his career. Biden shared her statement with Democrats, but Thurmond did not do the same with all Republicans on the committee. Agents also interviewed Thomas, who unequivocally denied the accusations.

On Friday, September 27, the committee voted on his nomination. Not only was the public unaware of Hill's allegation, but so were some Republicans voting that day. The result surprised reporters expecting a slim majority for confirmation: It was a 7–7 tie, which meant the nomination would go to the Senate without the committee's recommendation. A statement from Biden afterward also piqued journalists' interest: "I believe there are certain things that are not at issue at all.... And that is his character." No one had suggested otherwise, some thought, so why did Biden say that?[21]

By October 5, three days before the Senate was to vote, Hill's explosive charges hit the news wires. Hatch later recalled her anguished vacillation, her naïve idealism, and the impact of her allegations, in words that eerily described Ford's situation three decades later: "Ms. Hill agonized for several months about submitting a statement.... Apparently, she wanted the committee to learn of her accusations without being identified, hoping the nominee would then withdraw rather than have the story become public. Those in Washington knew differently. They understood that her desire to submit her allegations either anonymously or in confidence would significantly diminish the attention they received from the committee. (In other words, they could be ignored.) Now that the accusations had been printed in the media, positions changed. The committee had no choice but to address the charges publicly."[22]

Thomas, like Kavanaugh years later, had looked to be on the verge of confirmation and now he faced an extraordinary crisis for which the Senate had no playbook. Biden scrapped plans for the Senate's vote on the approaching Tuesday, October 8, and instead scheduled a new hearing for Friday the eleventh. Obsessed with seeming fair, he repeatedly acceded to Republicans' demands, including allowing Thomas to speak before and after Hill, though Hill had been told she would testify first. With the change, Thomas could frame the contest. And he did. He dramatically told Democrats at the outset that he would refuse to "provide the rope for my own lynching." With that, he played the race card, though his accuser was of the same race. Democrats were all but paralyzed—not least Kennedy, who already was hamstrung by his involvement in a family scandal in which his nephew had been charged with rape (the young man would be acquitted).[23]

"We were given the understanding that Anita would be the opening witness and we came to the Capitol, we were actually in a little green room, and they came in and said, 'Oh, that's changed, it's now going to be Thomas. He'll go first,'" Janet Napolitano, one of Hill's lawyers, the future Arizona governor and Obama's homeland security secretary, told me. Without what she called "rules of the road" for a hearing of this sort, "I think they were bending over backwards to agree to Thomas's team's requests. And I think the Democrats literally didn't know what to do with this kind of testimony or how to handle it. It's like they'd never heard the term 'sexual harassment' before. And in fact, if any good came out of Hill-Thomas, it's that it raised the public's awareness about sexual harassment in the workplace."[24] The experience did not, however, prod the Senate to devise rules of the road for any future cases, as would become clear twenty-seven years later.

After Thomas finished his statement and departed, Hill was brought in. Alone at a table facing the green baize-covered bench of white males, she read her statement and then for seven hours calmly answered questions. Leading for Republicans was former prosecutor Arlen Specter, a moderate facing a far-right rival for reelection in Pennsylvania and eager to please conservatives there. He chipped away at what he saw as Hill's inconsistencies, and went so far as to accuse her of "flat-out perjury," leaving even some Republicans slack-jawed.

Other Republicans, chiefly Hatch and Alan Simpson of Wyoming, suggested Hill was a scorned woman and she'd fantasized that Thomas had done what she claimed. Watching from the press table, I was taken aback by that turn in the questioning and, during a break, intercepted Thomas's chief Senate advocate, Danforth, as he walked to his office. Were the Republicans actually saying Hill might be mentally unstable? Crazy? "No, Jackie, I wouldn't say 'crazy,'" Danforth said, before elaborating on the possibility that Hill was a fantasist. Hatch publicly suggested that Hill had lifted one of her sensational anecdotes, that Thomas asked her, "Who put this pubic hair on my Coke?," from the movie *The Exorcist*, and another allegation—that Thomas talked of a hardcore porn star, "Long Dong Silver"—from a reference in a court case in the circuit that included Hill's state of Oklahoma.

The Republicans "were so out of line and so out there," Napolitano said, "and no Democrat stepped in to say, 'Professor Hill is not on trial here and that line of questions is inappropriate.' So she had nobody who was kind of her protector on the committee. And Thomas had the whole Republican lineup." Because he was a Black man, Napolitano added, "the civil rights groups that normally would have stepped up and been opposed to Thomas initially were quiet."[25]

Hill was a compelling witness, however, and her testimony dominated the evening news broadcasts. Her poise threw a scare into Republicans, just as Ford would. "Her testimony was mesmerizing," Hatch wrote. Yet when a TV anchor said to him, "It's all over, isn't it?," he replied, "You've only heard one witness. Wait until you've heard from him." McConnell would say much the same, to Trump, after Ford's testimony against Kavanaugh. Hatch rushed to the office where Thomas was waiting to testify again, and told him not to "take any crap from anyone." The senator recalled, "When he returned to the committee that evening, he was a different man. . . . He was ready, and he was angry." Years later, Hatch would give a similar pep talk to Kavanaugh.[26]

Hill's team didn't know that Thomas would get another turn to testify that evening. Only Napolitano was in the hearing room after Hill testified—the rest of the team was at dinner—"and all of a sudden the doors in back of the committee dais open up." The senators and Thomas entered, with White House counsel C. Boyden Gray. "This was before cell phones," she recalled. "I had no way of getting in touch with people to say, 'Get back here!'"[27]

Thomas delivered the scorching counterattack that Kavanaugh would copy, outraging Democrats and many nonpartisans yet rallying Republicans. In his most memorable passage, Thomas slapped down the race card harder than ever: "This is a circus. It is a national disgrace. And from my standpoint, as a Black American, as far as I am concerned, it is a high-tech lynching for uppity Blacks who in any way deign to think for themselves, to do for themselves, to have different ideas. And it is a message that, unless you kowtow to an old order, that is what will happen to you—you will be lynched, destroyed, caricatured by a committee of the United States Senate rather than hung from a tree."

As Hatch left, NPR reporter Nina Totenberg told him, "You just saved his ass." Hatch replied, "No, Nina, he just saved his ass."[28] The hearing that began Friday morning went on through the weekend, until late at night. Republicans openly solicited dirt on Hill. "I am getting stuff over the transom about Professor Hill," Simpson said. "I have got letters hanging out of my pockets. I have got faxes. I have got statements from her former law professors, from people that knew her, statements from Tulsa, Oklahoma, saying, 'Watch out for this woman!'"

Yet Biden agreed, without any Democrats' dissent, to bar testimony about Thomas's private life, including his penchant for pornography. Corroborators for Hill waited to testify, yet Biden decided against calling them: Angela Wright, an EEOC employee who alleged that Thomas had sexually harassed her, too; Rose Jourdain, an EEOC colleague to whom Wright had confided; Sukari Hardnett, another employee who wrote the Senate committee that women working for Thomas "knew full well you were being inspected and auditioned as a female," contrary to his claim under oath that he never commingled his personal and professional lives; Kaye Savage, a friend of Thomas's and Hill's who was shocked to find his apartment papered with nude centerfolds, the floors covered with stacks of *Playboy* magazines; Fred Cooke, an attorney who saw Thomas renting porn videos like those Hill described; the owner of the video rental store; and a number of Thomas's acquaintances from college and law school who contacted the committee to rebut his sworn denials of indulging in porn and graphic sexual talk.

Hill's witnesses would have testified in the middle of the night in any case, because Republicans, with Biden's acquiescence, lined up numerous character witnesses for Thomas and they spoke without limits. Finally, at 2:03 a.m. on Monday, October 14, the hearing ended. Thomas's tirade and Republicans' counterattacks worked. More Americans believed him, polls showed. The next day, the Senate narrowly confirmed Thomas, 52–48. Eleven Democrats, most from the South, joined all but two Republicans in support.[29]

Even more than in Bork's case, the partisan sparring and score-settling continued long afterward. In 1993, Simpson and Thurmond initially blocked a vote to confirm President Bill Clinton's nomination of Napolitano to be a U.S. attorney. A wealthy conservative commissioned David Brock to write a takedown of Hill for the *American Spectator*. In "The Real Anita Hill," published in March 1992, Brock smeared her with the phrase that famously summed up Republican senators' attacks: "a little bit nutty and a little bit slutty." Rush Limbaugh read long excerpts of Brock's hit piece on air; in 1994, Limbaugh would be married in Thomas's home, with the justice officiating. Brock was paid to turn his article into a book, which became a bestseller. In it, he depicted Hill less as a villain, more as a pawn of Democrats assailing a good man.[30] Brock later alleged that the Judiciary Committee's chief Republican counsel, Terry Wooten, illegally gave him a confidential FBI file that he used to discredit Angela Wright, the would-be witness against Thomas. After President George W. Bush in 2001 named Wooten to be a federal judge in South Carolina, Brock—by then a Democrat who disavowed his past work against Hill—gave the Senate committee a sworn affidavit of his allegation. Wooten denied it and was confirmed by a Republican-controlled Senate.[31]

A very different book followed in 1994, *Strange Justice* by Jill Abramson and Jane Mayer, then reporters at the *Wall Street Journal*. It included evidence that undermined Thomas's denials of an interest in pornography, and quoted witnesses who corroborated Hill's complaints about his harassment. The authors concluded that "the truth in this matter favors her much more than was apparent at the time of the hearings."[32]

For years, Thomas mostly kept a low profile, except among conservative groups. He was the featured guest at a 1993 fund-raiser for a Georgia foundation, although the Code of Judicial Conduct—binding on federal judges, but not justices—says judges shouldn't be speakers or honored guests at political fund-raisers. That year he also spoke to another group on the right with cases before the Supreme Court and expressed his "sense of gratitude and a sense of loyalty and friendship."[33] At his hearing, Thomas had portrayed himself as open-minded on abortion rights and insisted he'd never even discussed *Roe v. Wade*. Yet in his first year on the court, he joined Scalia in a dissent calling for *Roe* to be overturned.

With a memoir in 2007, Thomas made clear how bitter he remained.

One chapter was entitled "Invitation to a Lynching." He compared his foes to Klansmen and called Hill "my most traitorous adversary." His wife, conservative activist Ginni Thomas, became more outspoken in right-wing circles, spawning questions about potential conflicts of interest for her husband. In 2009, as the Tea Party took hold, she formed a tax-exempt group and accepted donations as large as $500,000 from unnamed donors, making it impossible to know whether they had business before the court. After I wrote about that for the *New York Times* in 2010, the next morning Ginni Thomas called Hill and left a message: "Good morning, Anita Hill, it's Ginni Thomas. I just wanted to reach across the airwaves and the years and ask you to consider something. I would love you to consider an apology sometime and some full explanation of why you did what you did with my husband." Hill asked the university police to give the recording to the FBI. In a public statement, Thomas said the message was intended as "an olive branch."[34]

Events would continue to periodically revive the memories—and divisiveness—of the Hill-Thomas saga.

Weeks before the 2016 election came the disclosure of the 2005 video in which Trump boasted that, as a celebrity, he "can do anything—grab them by the pussy!" Numerous women were moved to go public with their experiences with sexual misconduct. One, an attorney in Alaska, took to Facebook to lodge a new accusation against Thomas, and one that went to his behavior as a justice. In 1999, she wrote, he'd twice groped her at a dinner party. Weeks later, her charge was reported by the *National Law Journal*. While Thomas denied it, the article included corroboration from the woman's roommates, whom she'd told at the time, and from her former husband. Yet other news that day all but buried the new allegation: FBI director James B. Comey announced that he'd reopened an investigation of Democratic nominee Hillary Clinton and her private emails as secretary of state.

In 2018, Abramson revived the woman's accusation against Thomas in a *New York* magazine article, citing it and the evidence she and Mayer published years before refuting his Senate testimony to argue for Thomas's impeachment. He should be impeached, she wrote, "because of the lies he told, repeatedly and under oath, saying he had never talked to Hill about porn or to other women who worked with him about risqué subject matter. The idea of someone so flagrantly telling untruths to ascend to the highest legal position in the U.S. remains shocking, in addition to its being illegal." The matter got little attention, again, in a media and political world absorbed by Trump's controversies.[35]

The rehashing flared anew with Biden's announcement in the spring of 2019 of his presidential candidacy, though the focus was on his conduct, not Thomas's. The former senator and vice president again was forced to defend his handling of Thomas's confirmation process, but now in the less forgiving light of the #MeToo era. Before he joined the race for the 2020 Democratic nomination, Biden expressed remorse in ways that left many, including Hill, unsatisfied. "My one regret is that I wasn't able to tone down the attacks on her by some of my Republican friends," he said in 2017. "I mean, they really went after her. As much as I tried to intervene, I did not have the power to gavel them out of order."[36] In March 2019 he again made that odd claim of his impotence as committee chairman, saying, "To this day I regret I couldn't come up with a way to get her the kind of hearing she deserved, given the courage she showed by reaching out to us." He added, "I wish I could've done something."[37]

Angela Wright came to Biden's defense, sort of, a couple months later, writing in the *Washington Post*, "By linking questions about his sexual behavior to his race and labeling it a lynching, Thomas put every man on that panel on the defensive. I understand why Biden turned into a prattling, ineffectual lump of nothingness." More deserving of condemnation, she said, were Grassley, Hatch, and Simpson—and Thomas.[38]

Nothing, however, would remind Americans about Thomas's contested confirmation as much as Kavanaugh's nomination fight in 2018. And Republicans, girding for the fight, would reach back more than thirty years to remind the party's base of how the dastardly Democrats had engineered Bork's rejection, only to try to do the same to Thomas four years later.

The echoes between Thomas's and Kavanaugh's confirmations would be extraordinary: Conservative nominees seemingly poised for narrow Senate approval. Potential accusers behind the scenes, torn between a sense of civic duty and a desire for anonymity. Senate Democrats reluctant to prosecute a "she said, he said" case, then forced by media leaks. Republicans damning the Democrats as willful schemers, and the accusers as their misguided pawns. Nationally televised hearings. Riveting, credible women followed by intemperate nominees denying the accusations but focused on condemning the Democrats. Would-be corroborators barred from testifying. The nominees hurriedly confirmed by among the closest votes in history. And finally two justices, disbelieved by many millions of Americans, with lifetime seats on the nation's highest court.

Hill ended her 1997 memoir with an "Open Letter to the 1991 Senate Judiciary Committee." She warned that hers would not be the last allegation of sexual misconduct against a major nominee, and urged the Senate to devise a nonpartisan system to fairly address such matters. "The weight of the Senate and the Executive," she wrote, "should not have been used against an individual citizen called upon to participate in a public process."[39]

Yet it was, and would be again.

5

GINGRICH, STARR, AND A PARTISAN BAPTISM

"Be nasty."

I n the mid-1980s an aide to Republican Newt Gingrich called me. Gingrich, a rebellious House backbencher from Georgia, had read stories I'd done on the ethics scrapes of some Democrats in Congress, and he'd directed this aide to occasionally contact me with dirt on others, usually allegations culled from local newspapers. On this day she had a tip about Representative Mike Lowry from Seattle—or so I thought, until she mentioned San Diego. "Are you talking about Bill Lowery?" I asked. Realizing she'd confused Lowery, a Republican from San Diego, with Lowry, a liberal from Seattle, she ended the call. As comic as the exchange was, the fact that Gingrich would brazenly have a staffer doing such political work was just one sign that he was a new breed of Republican, less interested in passing laws than in ruthless politics. His goal was nothing short of ending Democrats' decades-long House majority, and leading a new Republican revolution beyond Reaganism.

By 1991, Gingrich had decided he could achieve that goal in the 1994 midterm elections, but only if the Republican president, George H. W. Bush, was defeated in 1992. He told me his thinking: Because voters since Franklin D. Roosevelt's time had punished a president's party in every midterm election—to send a message to the man not on the ballot—Republicans in Congress would be at a disadvantage so long as their party remained successful at winning the presidency. (Of the six midterm elections from 1970 to 1990, a Democrat was president during just one, in 1978—the year Republicans did well, though hardly well enough to seize a House majority.) Gingrich boldly predicted that if a Democrat won the White House in 1992, Republicans could try to nationalize the midterm elections against him and his party two years later and win enough seats to break Democrats' forty-year lock on the House majority. He was doing his part to weaken Bush. In 1990, he'd led a conservative revolt against Bush's bipartisan budget deal with Congress's leaders; while unsuccessful, Gingrich continued to criticize the president for breaking his "no new taxes" campaign promise.

Bush indeed lost in 1992, to Bill Clinton, and Gingrich immediately looked toward 1994. Starting in the late 1980s he'd mobilized a nation-wide network of support from among local talk-radio hosts, who regularly echoed his talking points against Clinton and congressional Democrats. On election day 1994, as we spoke in the afternoon at his suburban Atlanta office, Gingrich was unsure whether Republicans would capture the House, but he was confident of big gains—and certain that conservative media had helped. "I think one of the great changes in the last couple of years was the rise of talk radio, which gives you an alternative validating mechanism," he said. In fact, he'd be interviewed the next day by a new local host, a young guy named Sean Hannity.

Republicans triumphed in numbers beyond his dreams, winning major-ities in both the House and Senate for the first time since 1952. Once dismissed as a "gnat" by a House Speaker, Gingrich now was in line for the job. He led a cult of personality in his party, presaging the one for Donald Trump. He solidified Republicans' base in the South and rural America, and kept its voters perpetually angry at Democrats and at govern-ment generally—again, with the help of conservative media. Long after he'd fallen from this height, Gingrich could claim the Republican Party's radicalization as his legacy. It was a straight line from his uncompromising, smashmouth politics to the Tea Party and then to Trump.

•   •   •

"Be nasty." That was Gingrich's advice to local College Republicans in 1978, the year he was elected to Congress on his third try. Also: "You do not want to elect politicians who say 'trust me,' because you can't trust anybody."[1]

The future leader of the post-Reagan Republican revolution came late to conservatism. A Pennsylvania native, Gingrich went south for college and arrived as a relatively liberal Rockefeller Republican; he even worked for New York governor Nelson A. Rockefeller's 1968 presidential campaign. His inner circle for his first two House races in 1974 and 1976 included local Democrats, and in all three campaigns he had support from teachers, labor, and environmental groups. His press aide from that time told me in 1994, "Newt came to me and said, 'We're going to build a new Republican Party. We're going to bring in Blacks and women and be a moderate-conservative voice in American politics.'"

By 1978, however, Gingrich felt the political winds blowing rightward and bent with them. In Congress, he built a following among other young right-wingers elected since Watergate: the so-called Conservative Opportunity Society. Its members saw themselves as Ronald Reagan's revolutionaries, and fought not only Democrats but also Republican leaders, for being too accommodating. Speaker Jim Wright, the powerful Texas Democrat who'd dubbed Gingrich a "gnat," was forced to resign in 1989 amid an ethics investigation sparked by the Republican pest. While many Republicans had decried Gingrich's tactics—conservative columnist George Will drew parallels to red-baiting senator Joseph McCarthy—Gingrich's success as a giant-killer propelled him to election as House Republicans' number two leader. He immediately was a threat to the establishment Republican ahead of him, Minority Leader Robert Michel; the Illinoisan soon retired. Gingrich amped up his divisive, hyperbolic, even messianic rhetoric. "People like me are what stand between us and Auschwitz," he once said.[2]

"It was Mr. Gingrich who helped show candidates how to capitalize on voter cynicism and how to relentlessly attack opponents' weaknesses," a colleague and I wrote in our *Wall Street Journal* story on Republicans' 1994 victory. Long before Trump, Gingrich called Democrats "thugs" and a "corrupt, left-wing machine," even as he built his own multimillion-dollar fund-raising conglomerate, known as Newt, Inc. He'd devised a "Contract with America" to nationalize Republicans' campaign message, promising both tax cuts and a balanced budget, anticrime measures, welfare cuts, and term limits. While the Contract had less impact on the election outcome than often thought, it proved a valuable guide for governing once Republicans found themselves in charge of the House for the first time in the lives of many.[3]

On the new Congress's first day in January 1995, I walked a Capitol corridor where Gingrich's regime had set up "Radio Row"—table after table of visiting talk-show hosts interviewing Republicans for conservative audiences back home. Rush Limbaugh, the king of them all, was declared an honorary House Republican. Collectively, the local celebrities became a power center within the party. Yet they increasingly broadcast an uncompromising, antigovernment populism that would boomerang on party leaders soon enough, and give rise to the reality-TV star who would match their demagogy and ascend to the presidency two decades later.

Significantly, Gingrich's rise coincided with the end of the Cold War. By demonizing Democrats as not simply Republicans' political opponents but as evil enemies, he filled the void for conservatives accustomed to battling an existential threat. "Everything had been organized around the Soviet Union being the enemy, and the Soviet satellites," David Brock, the former right-wing writer, told me. "So Republicans turned inward"—to the culture wars at home. For Gingrich, baby boomers Bill and Hillary Clinton were valuable foils to personify the political and generational shift. He caricatured them as a dual threat: a draft-dodging liberal (Gingrich himself dodged Vietnam with multiple draft deferments) and his feminist wife. "The right," Brock said, "read that as a threat to what was normal."[4]

For any ambitious Republican, taking on the Clintons was a career enhancer. In 1994, Brett Kavanaugh had signed up.

●   ●   ●

That year, twenty-nine-year-old Kavanaugh was entering private practice for the first time. Mentor Ken Starr had recruited him to Kirkland & Ellis, a firm stocked with conservative lawyers. Before Kavanaugh started, however, Starr was named as the independent counsel to take over an investigation of the Clintons and an Arkansas real estate investment called Whitewater. Starr took Kavanaugh with him in September 1994, promising a short gig. It lasted nearly four years. "Starr treated him like a son," said Bruce Udolf, a lawyer on the team. "I assumed he was there just to build a résumé. He was a young, up-and-coming kid."[5]

Kavanaugh's recruitment reflected conservatives' project at work, molding a new generation for power. "Ken saw in Brett what everybody saw in him: an extremely able, ambitious young lawyer who had potential to have a long career," said Paul Rosenzweig, a senior counsel to Starr. "The greatest success of the conservative movement over the last forty years has been building a pipeline of young legal talent. And to a large degree, that's reflective of the fact that the old guard saw it as their obligation and duty. Guys like Ken Starr and [Reagan adviser] Ed Meese built people like Brett."[6]

Young Kavanaugh was by all accounts a Republican without hard edges, neither ideological nor particularly partisan. After several clerkships, his rightward leanings mainly went to matters of jurisprudence. Now he joined other conservative climbers in Starr's orbit—including Alex Azar, who would become Trump's health secretary, and Rod Rosenstein, his deputy attorney general—in working to build a case to unseat a president of the other party. Kavanaugh emerged as a party warrior. For several years he'd collaborate with anti-Clinton conspiracists on the right. While he'd ultimately reject their theories, he grew to share their disgust with both Clintons. Just how partisan Kavanaugh became was stunningly evident two decades later, when he blurted at his Senate hearing that his Democratic opponents were seeking "revenge on behalf of the Clintons."

●   ●   ●

Kavanaugh spent three years and about $2 million on his initial assignment: running down the conspiracists' claims that the Clintons' close friend Vince Foster was murdered, to silence whatever damaging testimony he could make against them. The U.S. Park Police, suburban Virginia police, the FBI, a senior House Republican, and a bipartisan Senate panel had already investigated and concluded that Foster, who suffered from depression, killed himself. His widow, Lisa Foster, had no doubt. Yet Starr revived the case, to the Foster family's anguish, and nothing in the record suggests that Kavanaugh had any qualms about taking the lead. Showing his aggressiveness early on, he proposed in a March 1995 memo that the Starr team consider "whether to issue subpoenas to Foster's mother, Lisa Foster, Foster's children, Foster's siblings, and Foster's friends for documents that might shed light on Foster's state of mind or their perceptions of Foster's state of mind (e.g., letters from Foster, letters to each other before or after Foster's death, notes, personal diaries, etc.)."[7]

Foster, Bill Clinton's friend since childhood and Hillary Clinton's former law partner in Little Rock, had reluctantly followed them to Washington to be the deputy White House counsel. Quickly overwhelmed by the pressure and partisan attacks, he blamed himself for a series of crises that marred the Clintons' first months. He was repeatedly mocked on the *Wall Street Journal's* conservative editorial page. A day after one such column, on the afternoon of July 20, 1993, Foster drove from the White House and across the Potomac River to Fort Marcy Park in Virginia, walked through the trees to a Civil War–era cannon, and shot himself through the mouth with a .38-caliber handgun. A colleague later found a note in the White House—Foster's inventory of complaints against the media, Republicans, and others. It ended, "Here ruining people is considered sport."

Initially Clinton aides barred the Park Police from inspecting Foster's office, which stoked conservatives' suspicions. In January 1994, Attorney General Janet Reno named Robert B. Fiske, a Republican and former U.S. attorney, as a special prosecutor to investigate Whitewater and Foster's death. Six months later, Fiske reported "the overwhelming weight of the evidence" was that Foster shot himself, and "there is no evidence" the Clintons' legal problems had anything to do with it.[8] At about the same time, significantly, Clinton signed a long-promised law reestablishing an office of an independent counsel, to be filled not by the attorney general as Fiske was but by a panel of supposedly impartial judges. Reno and others recommended Fiske, for continuity in the investigation. But the panel of judges, headed by a Reagan appointee close to Republican senators who opposed Fiske, chose the more partisan Starr.[9]

Elated conservatives pressed for yet another Foster probe. Among them were hard-line House Republicans and Christopher Ruddy, a right-wing journalist hired by billionaire Richard Mellon Scaife to investigate Foster's death for Scaife's publications; Ruddy would later become the chief executive of conservative Newsmax Media, and a Trump confidant. Starr was easily persuaded. In late March 1995, Kavanaugh gave him a memorandum justifying a new probe. "We have received allegations that Mr. Foster's death related to President and Mrs. Clinton's involvement" in Whitewater, Kavanaugh wrote—not acknowledging that the sources were the same conspiracists discounted by prior investigators. However Foster died, Kavanaugh added, his death could be related to information he had on the Clintons. Fiske had said otherwise. "It necessarily follows," Kavanaugh ended, "that we must have the authority to fully investigate Foster's death."[10]

The young lawyer threw himself into the work. He reviewed gruesome photos and notes on Foster's body. He visited the site where Foster was found, went with investigators on interviews, and examined Foster's financial records. He ordered analyses of carpet fibers from Foster's home, car, and office for matches of those found on his clothes; conspiracists had suggested that Foster was rolled in a carpet after he was killed, his body taken to the federal park and posed to suggest suicide. Kavanaugh even got a hair sample from Foster's teenage daughter, now long after her dad's death, to compare with strands on his clothes.[11]

A meeting with Starr and the team on June 16, 1995, reflected just how invested Kavanaugh was. "At this point, I am satisfied that Foster was sufficiently discouraged or depressed to commit suicide," he told them, according to his later summary of their discussion. Yet he described six ways in which they should expand the probe. They would search all of Fort Marcy Park and its many trees for the missing bullet; without it, theories would persist that Foster was killed elsewhere and dumped there. To identify a fingerprint on the gun, he proposed searching a family home in Hope, Arkansas, for a print from Foster's deceased father for comparison. The IRS would "perform a full financial analysis of Foster." Investigators would "track down all of Foster's foreign travel," and "investigate an alleged Swiss bank account" in his name (it didn't exist). The sixth step remained under discussion: investigating whether Foster had affairs. "We have asked numerous people about Foster's alleged affair with Mrs. Clinton," Kavanaugh told the team, "but have received no confirmation of it. If we want to pursue this line of investigation further, however, we should ask Mrs. Clinton about the alleged affair at her next interview."[12] The First Lady, according to someone familiar with the case, "was never asked any such question."[13]

In a memo a month later, July 15, Kavanaugh expressed even greater certainty: "To my mind, the evidence clearly establishes that Mr. Foster was sufficiently depressed or discouraged to have committed suicide." Foster had talked to a sister about seeing a psychiatrist. He was found with a list of doctors in his wallet. He'd broken into sobs at dinner with his wife the previous weekend, and had just begun taking antidepressants. He "wrote a note that is a mixture of fury and despair," Kavanaugh wrote, and "was overwhelmed by the sense of failure."[14] (Three days later, FBI agent Chuck Regini similarly wrote to Kavanaugh that "we have established beyond a reasonable doubt" that Foster shot himself.)[15] Kavanaugh also dismissed talk of a White House cover-up, writing in the July memo, "At this point I do not believe there is evidence warranting criminal prosecution of any individual in the Foster documents investigation."

Yet the probe dragged on for over two years more. The same deference to the Republican right wing that led Starr and Kavanaugh to reinvestigate Foster's death now compelled them to drag it out long after their own minds were made up. Where past investigators had dismissed the murder conspiracies, Starr and Kavanaugh were determined to take them seriously and settle the matter, even as that prolonged the Foster family's ordeal. Kavanaugh's files at the National Archives are stuffed with material from and about the conspiracists. Included is a five-page fund-raising letter from conservative televangelist Jerry Falwell, hawking a $38 video "exposé" entitled *The Death of Vince Foster: What Really Happened?* and seeking additional money "to help us with this vital truth campaign."[16]

Exchanges between the Starr, Clinton, and Foster legal teams became increasingly tense with time, and offer early evidence of the petulance Kavanaugh would one day show the nation. In late 1995, two and a half years after Foster died, the Starr team pressed for more material and interviews even as Lisa Foster was preparing to remarry at the new year. When she said through her lawyer, James Hamilton, that only Starr could review Vince Foster's diary, Kavanaugh took umbrage. It was "an implicit attack on my integrity and credibility," he wrote in an October memo intended "for posterity" in the office files, echoing complaints to his colleagues.[17] In December, Kavanaugh drafted a three-page response to Hamilton after he balked at some demands from the Starr office. Starr's deputy, John D. Bates, cut the draft letter in half by deleting or editing Kavanaugh's most truculent parts. Bates moved up high a note of empathy for the family's pain. Gone was Kavanaugh's bloodless line, "It is an unfortunate fact that the desires of family members and the needs of law enforcement may diverge, and they appear to have done so here." Also struck was Kavanaugh's swipe at Hamilton: "We are fully prepared to deal with any criticism by you or others that may be directed at our Office for the time and effort spent . . . so any veiled threats in that vein do not affect us."[18]

The Clintons' lawyer, David E. Kendall, reached out to Kavanaugh early on, to see what he might need, and to renew their acquaintance from Kavanaugh's summer as an associate at Williams & Connolly. Kendall initially was baffled that Starr had opened the probe on the heels of Fiske's report, but by the investigation's second year he'd become "enraged," he told me. "They seemed to be chasing every possible conspiracy theory. When you start doing that, it's endless. And it's partisan. Starr would every now and then give a speech saying, 'There are many unanswered questions.' Well, the unanswered questions were from conspiracy crazies." Yet, Kendall added, "All you can do is smile sweetly, and say, 'We're cooperating fully. We hope this will come to an end.'"[19]

On October 10, 1997, Starr finally announced the finding: Foster had committed suicide. In a statement for the family, sister Sheila Foster Anthony assailed Starr for having indulged the conspiracists and giving credence to "any thought that the president of the United States somehow had complicity in Vince's death." The conspiracy-mongers were enraged as well, proving just how wrong Starr and Kavanaugh were to think that the far right could be persuaded to accept any finding other than murder. Ruddy wrote a book alleging a Clinton cover-up, abetted by Starr's team. Two decades later, Ruddy's friend Trump, running for president, still insisted Foster's death was "very fishy." He told the *Washington Post*, "I will say there are people who continue to bring it up because they think it was absolutely a murder."[20]

Starr, in a memoir published twenty-one years later as the Senate considered Kavanaugh's Supreme Court nomination, hailed the Foster report as "the definitive word on the cause of death." He did acknowledge, "Obviously, we couldn't lay entirely to rest far-fetched theories."[21] Kavanaugh himself praised the Foster investigation in 1999. "What's important in these investigations," he said on CNN, "... is that the American people, at the end of the day, have confidence that the person was dogged at getting at the truth."

A quarter century after Foster's death, Bill Clinton attested to the bitterness that lingered. He told an audience in May 2019 that Kavanaugh's ordeal during his confirmation process the year before was a sort of karmic payback for what Foster's family and friends endured. "He didn't have any problem making us put up with three years of Vince Foster nonsense," the former president said.[22]

With the Foster report in, Kavanaugh belatedly joined Kirkland & Ellis. But the case still wasn't closed: Starr summoned Kavanaugh back months later to handle a lawsuit against Hamilton, seeking his notes of a conversation with Foster nine days before the suicide. Starr initially sought reams of Hamilton's material, for evidence implicating Hillary Clinton in particular, but a federal court ruled against him. On appeal, Starr limited his quest to Hamilton's notes from his and Foster's final talk. Hamilton argued that attorney-client privilege shielded the notes, and associations of lawyers and even hospices backed him, fearful of the chilling precedent that an adverse ruling would set.

Arguing before the D.C. appeals court he would one day join, Kavanaugh countered that Foster would have been "a critical witness" in the Whitewater investigation, and the attorney-client privilege lapsed with his death. The court panel agreed, holding two to one that posthumous disclosure was permissible for a criminal investigation. Hamilton appealed to the Supreme Court, which expedited the important case. On June 8, 1998, Kavanaugh made his only appearance at the high court before he'd arrive as a justice. Some observers were puzzled that the proud Starr didn't take the lead. Associates told me Starr liked to delegate to favorites and, besides, Kavanaugh had asked for the role when he agreed to return to the office.

Facing the justices, Starr sitting beside him, Kavanaugh said of the attorney-client privilege, "death ends it" in a criminal inquiry. Most of the justices expressed concerns. Kavanaugh's hero, Chief Justice William Rehnquist, told him a client must "feel free to tell a lawyer the truth, and the whole truth." When Kavanaugh speculated that deceased clients, if they could speak to the issue, might see disclosure in criminal cases as their posthumous civic duty, David Souter countered that the opposite could just as well be true. Anthony M. Kennedy seemed receptive to his former clerk's arguments, only to turn protective of the privilege.[23]

Kennedy indeed was in the majority later that month when the court ruled 6–3 against Starr, and Kavanaugh. A celebratory Hamilton told reporters he received "a very gracious phone call" from Kavanaugh, and added, "Brett is a lawyer of great competence. He will be a force in this town for some time to come." Two decades later, Hamilton said, "I thought Starr was overreaching, perhaps to find negative information on Hillary. But to be up-front about it, Brett won in the court of appeals. And while I won in the Supreme Court, he got three votes. So it was not a slam dunk. He did okay with what I thought was a very bad case that would have made bad law had Starr's argument prevailed."[24]

Even then Kavanaugh's work with Starr wasn't finished. A new controversy had emerged, over the president's apparent affair with a White House intern.

•   •   •

By late 1997, more than three years into his Whitewater investigation, Starr had little to show for the time and taxpayers' money—certainly nothing that might lead to Clinton's impeachment. Then he got wind of the salacious story of the president's relationship with Monica Lewinsky.

While Kavanaugh didn't officially rejoin Starr's office until April 1998, he'd remained involved as the Lewinsky story broke, records and interviews indicate. Kendall recalled a colleague returning from Starr's office one day with news: "Brett Kavanaugh is back." Kendall considered that significant: The young lawyer had spent years on the dead-end Foster probe and had finally entered private practice. "You had to ask, 'Why is he doing this?'" Kendall said. The allegation that Clinton had an affair and lied about it "was like a lifeline" for Starr's team, as Kendall saw it. "This long, fruitless investigation, which had ground on so long, and come up with nothing, finally has a chance to embarrass the president. It was a deeply partisan investigation, and Brett is returning at a time when it looks like all of a sudden, for the first time in years, the investigators have the upper hand."[25]

Starr's new lead had roots in Clinton's first term, and an earlier sex scandal. Paula Jones, a former Arkansas state employee, had filed a civil lawsuit against Clinton in 1994 alleging sexual harassment. She said he'd exposed himself to her in a Little Rock hotel in 1991, when he was governor and just months away from announcing his presidential bid. The legal wrangling dragged on for several years—long enough to merge with the Lewinsky affair.

Over the winter of 1995–96, as Gingrich led congressional Republicans in forcing a series of government shutdowns, unsuccessfully trying to get Clinton to accept deep cuts in social programs, twenty-one-year-old Lewinsky came to the White House as a volunteer to replace furloughed federal workers. She answered phones and delivered documents, including to the Oval Office. There, she met Clinton. They began an episodic affair that lasted for the next year and a half.[26]

In late 1997, Jones's lawyers learned about Lewinsky from a small clique of conservative attorneys and were eager to question her, to establish a pattern of misconduct by Clinton that would buttress Jones's case. Lewinsky's secret had gotten out after she'd disclosed it to an older, seemingly sympathetic coworker, Linda Tripp. That fall, Tripp was surreptitiously recording their phone calls at the suggestion of a conservative literary agent, Lucianne Goldberg, and maternally coaxing the lovesick Lewinsky to talk about Clinton. Goldberg, in turn, told the anti-Clinton lawyers— "the Elves." Among them was George T. Conway III, the future Never Trumper. Far-right pundit Ann Coulter assisted, too, as did Robert Bork and conservative lawyer Ted Olson, a Federalist Society stalwart and a future solicitor general under George W. Bush.

Lewinsky, unaware of the conniving, on January 7, 1998, gave Jones's lawyers a sworn statement denying any sexual relationship with the president. She urged Tripp to lie as well. The next day, the Elves got word of Lewinsky's deception to the Starr team through Rosenzweig, the senior counsel; he'd gone to law school with a couple of them. One told him there was a witness with damning evidence: Tripp. The connection was made and soon she turned over copies of her recordings.

Events moved rapidly. The following week, Starr got authorization from Reno and the three-judge panel overseeing his investigation to expand it into Clinton's relationship with Lewinsky, based on evidence that the president had encouraged her to lie under oath. Starr's action was controversial within his office (Kavanaugh wasn't back yet). Several lawyers said that probing the president's sexual behavior would trivialize their work. Among them was Bruce Udolf, a former assistant U.S. attorney. Years later, Udolf dropped his reserve about discussing the prosecutors' deliberations, after a Starr colleague publicly said the #MeToo movement vindicated Starr's probe of Clinton's affair with Lewinsky. Udolf, incensed, told me it did no such thing. As if addressing the former colleague, he said, "Do you mean to tell me you put a young girl in the grand jury, and through all that, when you knew there was no way in the world that you'd ever be able to prove a case against her—just to humiliate the president of the United States? And you're proud of that?"

Just as Starr had gotten a green light to expand his investigation, a group including the Elves, Starr investigators, and Tripp's lawyer met at a Howard Johnson's restaurant across from the Watergate apartment building where Lewinsky stayed with her mother—Starr's folks were staking it out. An elaborate relay game ensued: The Starr team, to avoid being the leaker, returned the copies of Tripp's recordings to her lawyer, who gave them to the Elves, who got them to *Newsweek* reporter Michael Isikoff and his editors.[27]

Separately, over the river in Virginia, several Starr lawyers and FBI agents had intercepted Lewinsky at a mall. She'd gone there to meet Tripp, who'd set her up. The investigators, threatening Lewinsky with decades in jail, persuaded her to go with them to the nearby Ritz-Carlton Hotel for what became twelve hours of intermittent, often emotional interrogation— "Prom Night," the team would dub its operation. Lewinsky tried at one point to surreptitiously call Clinton's secretary, Betty Currie; Clinton was being deposed the next day by Jones's lawyers and Lewinsky wanted to get word to him that they knew about the affair. She was unsuccessful. Clinton denied under oath that he'd had sexual relations with Lewinsky, opening the door to the perjury charge for which he'd be impeached.

The story of their relationship broke on that Sunday, January 17. Matt Drudge, the blogger-provocateur, posted online that *Newsweek* was blocking Isikoff's report. Four days later, the *Washington Post* splashed its story across its front page, opening a thirteen-month constitutional drama that split the nation.

•　•　•

Kavanaugh also had doubts about the investigation's new direction as he returned that spring. He'd expressed them in February on a panel discussing the independent counsel law at Georgetown University Law Center. "Congress has to take responsibility for overseeing the conduct of the president," he said, adding, "That's the role I believe the Framers envisioned and that's the role that makes sense if you just look at the last twenty years. It makes no sense at all to have an independent counsel looking at the conduct of the president." When the moderator asked which panelists believed a sitting president cannot be indicted, Kavanaugh raised his hand along with more than half the group. The Constitution empowered Congress to take action through impeachment, he argued. Later that month he expressed the same view to the *Washington Post*, calling it "absurd" that the Republican-led Congress "is doing nothing."[28]

Offsetting Kavanaugh's doubts about independent counsels, however, was his loyalty to Starr, which was why he'd rejoined the office. "By that time, Brett and I were very close. I think he responded to a friend in need," Starr said.[29] For Kavanaugh, who by now aspired to be a judge like his mother, this man who still liked to be called "Judge" Starr— for his time on the D.C. Circuit, before he was solicitor general—was a most valuable mentor. Soon enough Starr would emerge from his Clinton prosecution widely disparaged even among some Republicans. At this point, however, he remained an influential figure within conservative legal circles, as Kavanaugh knew. At a "Kenneth Starr Appreciation Dinner" in November 1999, Kavanaugh suggested in his tribute that Starr might become an ambassador, or even "Mr. Justice Starr."[30] He later would defend Starr repeatedly in speeches and writings as "a hero" who exposed "a massive effort by the president to lie under oath and obstruct justice." In doing so, of course, Kavanaugh also was defending, and extolling, his own role.

* * *

He returned as a long-simmering controversy was coming to a boil over the Clinton side's complaints about leaks from Starr's office, allegedly including confidential grand jury information. Kavanaugh was well known to be accessible to reporters in his first years on the team, but he wasn't publicly implicated in illegal disclosure of nonpublic information. In late 1997 and early 1998, however, before he was back on Starr's payroll, two prosecutors separately told at least one reporter, Dan Moldea, that their office shared nonpublic information with reporters of whom Starr approved, and Kavanaugh was "the main guy" to see, according to a sworn statement from Moldea to the Senate in 2018. The journalist said Kavanaugh subsequently called him and they met for an off-the-record lunch a block from the White House on January 19—just as the Lewinsky story was breaking.[31]

In a speech four months later, Moldea discussed the leaks controversy and his own experience, without naming Kavanaugh. He decried the Starr office's partisanship and "well-timed leaks which have turned gossip into gasoline." The judge overseeing the grand jury for the Clinton investigation named a semiretired judge to look into the matter. His report, which remained secret until a government watchdog group forced its release during Kavanaugh's 2018 confirmation process, said Starr's office made "clumsy, unwise" decisions in providing information to reporters but did not violate grand jury secrecy rules. It did not name Kavanaugh. However, as the watchdog group complained, the judge only investigated the Starr office's actions after the Lewinsky story broke, not in the prior three years when Kavanaugh was there.[32]

Through the years-long Clinton probe, the Starr lawyers did little socializing given the workload. A few played poker occasionally, but one recalled Kavanaugh joining just once. As a single man who was twenty-nine years old when he took the job, Kavanaugh hung out with other young conservatives-on-the-make. It was "a close circle of cold, cynical and ambitious hard-right operatives being groomed by GOP elders for much bigger roles in politics, government and media," Brock wrote in 2018, describing a group that included him, Coulter, Drudge, Azar, future Fox firebrands Laura Ingraham and Tucker Carlson, Mark Paoletta, the future chief counsel to Vice President Mike Pence—and Kavanaugh. "Each of them partied at my Georgetown townhouse amid much booze and a thick air of cigar smoke."[33]

In late 1998, Kavanaugh and Ingraham, who hosted a show on MSNBC, made the *Washington Post*'s gossip column when they attended Senator John McCain's holiday party together, prompting speculation of a romance. The headline conveyed Ingraham's answer: "The TV Host & the Ex-Starr Deputy: Just Friends."[34] The previous January, just after the Lewinsky news broke, Kavanaugh attended a party at Ingraham's townhouse. She'd invited young conservatives to watch a humiliated Clinton deliver the State of the Union address to Congress, amid speculation that he might soon be forced to resign. When Hillary Clinton appeared onscreen, Kavanaugh mouthed the word "bitch," according to Brock. "I can still see it now," he told me in 2019.[35]

Such visceral loathing of both Clintons was common among conservatives. Kavanaugh, immersed for years in the world of anti-Clinton conspiracists, showed his contempt not just by that utterance at a TV but also in his work for Starr. On August 15, 1998, he gave Starr a blistering memo suggesting ten questions for the prosecutors to ask when they grilled Clinton for the grand jury. Seven were shockingly graphic. "Slack for the President?," Kavanaugh wrote in the memo's subject line, and immediately answered: No. "After reflecting this evening," he wrote, "I am strongly opposed to giving the President any 'break' in the questioning regarding the details of the Lewinsky relationship—unless before his questioning on Monday, he either (i) resigns or (ii) confesses perjury and issues a public apology to you. I have tried hard to bend over backwards and to be fair to him and to think of all reasonable defenses to his pattern of behavior. In the end, I am convinced that there really are none. The idea of going easy on him at the questioning is thus abhorrent to me." He went on, "It is our job to make his pattern of revolting behavior clear—piece by painful piece."

Kavanaugh's proposed questions included: "If Monica Lewinsky says that you inserted a cigar into her vagina while you were in the Oval Office area, would she be lying?" "If Monica Lewinsky says that on several occasions in the Oval Office area, you used your fingers to stimulate her vagina and bring her to orgasm, would she be lying?" "If Monica Lewinsky says that you ejaculated into her mouth on two occasions in the Oval Office area, would she be lying?" When the *Washington Post* published the document in 2018 (a month before allegations of nonconsensual sexual misconduct by Kavanaugh surfaced), former Starr deputy Robert Bittman said Kavanaugh had "immediately regretted the tone of the memo." Still, both Bittman and Starr defended it.[36]

"Brett was not alone in thinking that the president's game-playing forced us to ask him direct, impolite questions," Rosenzweig told me. The lawyers had held mock interrogations in which a folksy southerner among them, Hickman Ewing, played Clinton. Thanks to Ewing's performance, Rosenzweig said, "We pretty much proved to ourselves that if we asked vague questions the president would rope-a-dope us to death and make us look like idiots. I frankly shared Brett's view."

Even so, the sex-related questions they asked Clinton over four hours at the White House, a session that was broadcast to the grand jury over closed-circuit television, were not as explicit as Kavanaugh's versions. Clinton surprised the lawyers by conceding at the outset, for the first time, that he had "inappropriate, intimate contact" with Lewinsky. Anticipating their suggestion that he lied in his January 1998 deposition to Jones's attorneys, Clinton justified his denials of sexual relations with Lewinsky because they did not have intercourse. When the Starr lawyers asked about other sexual acts, Clinton fell back on his initial statement acknowledging "wrong" conduct. They returned to the office downcast, believing he'd bested them. Yet Kavanaugh, who was too junior to be among the president's interrogators, patted prosecutor Sol Wisenberg and congratulated him for the "sex questions," adding, "You got what you needed to get."[37]

Kavanaugh was busy as one of two principal authors—"the chief word-smith," Starr would say—for what would famously become the "Starr Report," the voluminous case to impeach a president for only the second time in as many centuries. The team was riven by disagreement over how to handle the most prurient details. Kavanaugh, despite his X-rated questions for Clinton, opposed being explicit in a document for history. If the racy anecdotes were to be included, bury them in an appendix, he suggested.[38] But Starr sided with those, including Rosenzweig, who argued otherwise—that only graphic detail would show how brazenly Clinton lied in denying he had sexual relations with Lewinsky. Starr wouldn't say "hell" or "damn" in conversation, yet he sanctioned a report describing the president performing and receiving oral sex, inserting a cigar into a woman's vagina, and ejaculating into a sink off the Oval Office. The production was stressful and exhausting; for weeks, Kavanaugh pulled all-nighters. Late one night, he was so tired as he drove home that he stopped, parked, and hailed a cab.[39]

On September 9, two vans with armed guards delivered thirty-six boxes containing the 445-page report and supporting materials to the Capitol. Starr attached a cover letter warning that the findings "contain information of a personal nature that I respectfully urge the House to treat as confidential." It soon became clear that the House Republicans would ignore the caution and release everything, with little protest from Democrats. "This is really bad, and we're going to get blamed," Kavanaugh told Starr. The boss directed him to draft another, more pointed warning. When other aides objected, however, Starr backed down.[40] In later years, he and his lieutenants, including Kavanaugh, would insist they had no idea that the House Republican leaders would quickly release the entire report, without even reading it. "This possibility had never occurred to us," Starr wrote.[41] If so, they'd naïvely misread Gingrich's House, led by a man who'd built a movement on the mantra "Be nasty."

A year later, Kavanaugh would tell CNN—he occasionally appeared on cable news programs in his post-Starr years—"Our goal was to be thorough. It was also to be fair. And we think we accomplished both of those goals."[42] Testifying several years later for his nomination to the D.C. appeals court, however, Kavanaugh told senators that the House's quick release of the report "caused unnecessary harm, combined with the way the report was structured." He often distanced himself from the report's steamy narrative of Clinton's affair, saying he wrote the other part, the legal grounds against the president. Even so, he defended the sexual details as "relevant to the facts in the case."

Lewinsky was in a New York hotel room when the report became public, and called it up on her laptop. "I remember waiting as the pages would slowly appear. The more I read, the more mortified I was. I couldn't believe the level of detail that was in there," she said in a 2018 documentary. "Reading something that was so mortifying and knowing that everyone else in the world who is connected was reading it at the same time, knowing how my family was going to be affected—my dad, my stepmom, my mom, my stepdad—I had taken on what I imagined they felt, too, how humiliated they were. I felt terrible for Mrs. Clinton. I felt awful for Chelsea."

Blame Bill Clinton, not us—that was the attitude of Starr, Kavanaugh, and the rest of the team. As for Lewinsky, "She brought this on herself. She should have cooperated," Starr told his communications adviser, Judi Nardella Hershman.[43] Kavanaugh summed up his service under Starr in his 1999 tribute: "Doing the right thing, doing the hard thing, doing it very well, enduring the attacks. He taught us . . . what it means to be the man in the arena."[44] Much of the country, however, saw something else: Starr, the moralistic, self-righteous son of a small-town Texas preacher, had become the nation's partisan high priest, leading his apostles on a four-year, $45 million crusade to expunge a sinner from the White House temple. Typical of the media coverage was ABC News host Ted Koppel's summary: The Starr Report mentioned "sex" or variations of the word 548 times and "Whitewater"—the investigation's original objective—just twice. It back-fired on Starr and the House Republicans, creating widespread sympathy for the Clintons. With the approaching midterm elections becoming something of a referendum on impeachment, the First Lady—standing by her man—was Democrats' favorite campaigner.

National polls consistently showed that at a time of prosperity and peace, about two-thirds of Americans approved of Clinton's job performance and opposed his impeachment. Thus reassured, Democrats backed the president even as they deplored his personal conduct. For many House Republicans, however, sentiment in their solidly conservative, gerrymandered districts favored Clinton's removal, spurring them on despite the danger to colleagues in the relatively few swing districts. They pressed on even after Democrats gained House seats in November, breaking the midterm elections jinx against the president's party that dated to FDR's time.

Three days after the elections, facing a mutiny, Gingrich announced he would resign as Speaker and, after twenty eventful years, from Congress. The Republicans' midterm losses were the final straw for his former followers. They had grown tired of Gingrich's inability to switch from revolution to governance, and of his chronic unpopularity and ethics scrapes. Where they divided was on whether Gingrich's sin was that he'd grown too pragmatic, cutting occasional deals with the hated Clinton, or that he was too right-wing. Exiting, Gingrich bitterly complained of the cannibals in his party—ironically echoing Jim Wright's barb in his farewell address a decade earlier, condemning the "mindless cannibalism" Gingrich represented.[45]

What some Republicans knew—and everyone else would soon learn—was that even as Gingrich pursued the impeachment of a president based on a consensual sexual relationship, the married speaker had been having an affair for five years with a young House aide. She would become his third wife after his divorce a year later.

Against this backdrop of election losses and recriminations, some House Republicans pressed for the lesser step of censuring Clinton. Their cause gained strength when Senate majority leader Trent Lott, a Mississippi Republican, made clear that the Senate could not muster the two-thirds vote needed to convict the president. But militant House conservatives vetoed the censure idea. "National polls are meaningless to these people," Scott Reed, a leading party strategist, told me at the time. "They'd rather fight and go down with principles than cave and go with this censure thing."[46]

With impeachment hearings beginning two weeks after the elections, Kavanaugh's final task was to help prepare Starr to testify. Starr brought on Merrie Spaeth, a Dallas-based communications consultant who'd long worked with Republicans, and Hershman, a family friend and Republican operative. In the first practice days before Starr was to appear at the House

Judiciary Committee, Hershman fired questions at him as if she were the panel's Democrats. "Isn't it true," she said at one point, "that this is a personal vendetta against the president of the United States, and this is about your own personal beliefs of how people should lead their lives—like you're the sex police?" Spaeth, her boss, recorded Starr and they assessed how well— or not—he projected composure and control. Kavanaugh didn't like it. He told Starr after more such sessions, "You're too programmed."[47]

One day, after a staff meeting, Hershman remained in the conference room to clear the table of papers left behind. She heard the door open, but before she looked up, Kavanaugh was at her side, badgering her angrily. Frightened, she circled the table a full rotation to evade him, but he followed.

"You are going to tell me exactly who you are and why you are here."

"I am here at the invitation of Judge Starr," she stammered, "and he shared with the group who I am and why I'm here."

"No, I'm telling you—" Kavanaugh said, pointing a finger at her face, so near she felt his breath. She cut him off: "And I'm telling you to go talk to Judge Starr."

Kavanaugh, suddenly deflated, left. Hershman, troubled by his intimidating show of temper to her, one of the few women in the office, complained to Starr. "He said he had never seen something like this from Brett before," she recalled. Starr suggested that Kavanaugh was just stressed, and protective of him with an unfamiliar person in the mix. He added, "Brett is very smart. He is going places—possibly the Supreme Court." She retorted, "Not if he treats women like that, he won't."[48]

Twenty years later, Hershman told me she saw that same "almost feral belligerence" in Kavanaugh's face as he testified before the Senate committee about the allegations of sexual assault. She decided then to share her account with senators undecided about him, and with the media. Starr told the news site *Slate* he did not recall her telling him about the episode.[49]

• • •

On November 19, 1998, Starr took his seat at the witness table for the House impeachment hearing. Kavanaugh sat just behind him in the first row. A senior Democrat, the quick-witted Barney Frank of Massachusetts, challenged Starr. Why had he given Congress such a damaging report on Clinton's affair *before* the election, but only afterward sent material exonerating the president in all the matters Starr had been investigating for years: Whitewater, Foster's death, the White House travel office firings and alleged misuse of FBI files?

"We felt we didn't have proof beyond a reasonable doubt," Starr replied. Yet he'd known that long before the election. In any case, that strict legal standard applied to criminal prosecutions, not impeachment referrals.

"In other words," Frank snapped, "don't have anything to say unless you have something bad to say."

A week later, ABC's Diane Sawyer interviewed Starr and several aides for the news program *20/20*. Sitting with Kavanaugh and three other lawyers in one segment, she asked them to recall the moment they first learned of Clinton's affair with Lewinsky. "Are you saying that there was no one in this office who said, 'This is not of sufficient gravity to investigate and report?'" Kavanaugh jumped to answer: "No one. No one." He added emphatically, "It wasn't our choice. The question and the debate was, what should we do about it?" Sawyer alluded to the widespread criticism of the Starr investigation, and asked, "What happens when you meet people, and they say, 'Where do you work?'" Kavanaugh replied again: "It depends who the person is."[50]

On December 19, the House voted mostly along party lines to impeach Clinton for perjury and obstruction of justice. But before it did, there was more drama. The Republican in line to succeed Gingrich as Speaker, Robert Livingston of Louisiana, called for Clinton to resign during his remarks on the House floor. As angry Democrats shouted, "*You* resign!," Livingston announced he would do just that. He was one of a half dozen Republicans caught in the crossfire after the porn publisher Larry Flynt offered rewards for proof of Republicans' own philandering. The story of Gingrich's adultery came out, too, making him the ultimate symbol of hypocrisy.

The Republican-led Senate reluctantly held a trial, with Rehnquist presiding, that stretched for twenty-one days into mid-February. Neither count against Clinton got a majority, let alone the necessary two-thirds vote, and the president was acquitted.[51]

"For some of my colleagues, lying about marital infidelity was not behavior sufficient to be disqualified for holding public office," Orrin Hatch explained in his memoir. Then he focused not on the political price Republicans paid for so avidly prosecuting Clinton, but on what Clinton had cost Democrats, and himself. Indeed, the president had squandered both time and the political capital that came with an economic boom and historic budget surpluses. He would not leave the legacy he'd envisioned—resolving Social Security's long-term solvency, climate change, and immigration reforms. And as Hatch saw it, Democrats lost the White House in 2000—and with it the power to name federal judges—because Clinton, "the best national campaigner in the Democratic Party," was sidelined. "If Bill Clinton had simply told the truth," Hatch wrote during George W. Bush's first term in 2002, "in all probability Al Gore would be President today."[52]

•   •   •

For all the fervor that Kavanaugh brought to prosecuting Clinton, his takeaway that future presidents should be immune to such actions while in office would enrage Democrats. It was a cynical conversion, they said, benefiting Republican presidents—and his patrons—Bush and Trump. Kavanaugh's views would be an issue at all three of his confirmation hearings, in 2004, 2006, and 2018. In fairness, however, he'd first expressed them while Clinton was president, at the 1998 Georgetown University forum and in a law review article the same year.

The extent of Kavanaugh's change of heart was apparent at the 2006 hearing. Kavanaugh—who'd advocated for yet another Foster investigation, and written the cut-no-slack questions for Clinton—now testified that it had been a mistake to expand Starr's mandate beyond the Whitewater land deal. "It created the impression," he said, "that Judge Starr was somehow the permanent special investigator of the administration." Another counsel could have probed the other issues, he said. In 2009, having served in Bush's White House, Kavanaugh wrote an article for the *Minnesota Law Review* reflecting his firsthand familiarity with a president's burdens. The country, he said, "would have been better off if President Clinton could have focused on Osama bin Laden without being distracted by the Paula

Jones sexual harassment case and its criminal investigation offshoots."

"I think he comes by the change of heart honestly," Rosenzweig told me. "I think many of us saw the disruption that the Clinton investigation wrought on our society and are not 100 percent sure that it was the right course." Rosenzweig noted that Robert Ray, Starr's successor who concluded the investigation, was set to indict Clinton when the president left office, but agreed to let him admit fault, pay a fine, and forfeit his law license. Had Clinton been indicted, Rosenzweig said, his trial— assuming the usual course of white-collar trials—might have started around September 11, 2001. "To some degree," he said, "the Clinton investigation was a product of a time when the country didn't have that much to worry about."

For Starr, his widely panned role in the prolonged drama dashed what-ever last hope he had for his dream job: "Some have been kind enough to suggest I would have been on the Supreme Court had I not taken on the Whitewater investigation," he wrote in his memoir. With explicit bitterness, he noted that he'd been passed over once, when he was solicitor general to George H. W. Bush, for Souter—"an unknown judge from New Hampshire." Bush thereby made "a costly and unforced presidential error," Starr wrote, given Souter's record as a "reliably liberal vote."[53]

In contrast, Kavanaugh's role on the Clinton investigation contributed to his realizing Starr's dream, and his own. It was a solid credential in Republican circles. "If you were a Republican coming out of that, that was a good mark," Rosenzweig said. In his 2018 confirmation hearing, Kavanaugh would even turn his years on the Starr team to advantage— to defend against allegations of sexual misconduct. "I and other leading members of Ken Starr's office were opposition-researched from head to toe, from birth through the present day," he said. "Recall the people who were exposed that year of 1998 as having engaged in some sexual wrongdoing or indiscretions in their pasts."

Yet, he added, "Nothing about me."

6

BECOMING A "BUSHIE"

"Love the guy."

By the time the Senate acquitted Bill Clinton on February 12, 1999—Kavanaugh's thirty-fourth birthday—Kavanaugh was back at Kirkland & Ellis. It seemed pretty apparent, however, that this third time might not last much longer than his prior two stints. But even in private practice, the ambitious young lawyer was burnishing his credentials among Republican Party leaders and conservative groups. In under two years, he scored something of a trifecta, three times popping up Zelig-like in Republicans' most significant culture wars and political battles of the time.

First, as Florida governor Jeb Bush sought to create a statewide voucher program to subsidize parents' costs of sending their children to private religious schools—a priority of conservatives—Kavanaugh helped him defend his initiative against legal challenges that it violated the separation of church and state. In 2006, long after Kavanaugh's involvement, the Florida Supreme Court indeed struck down the program as unconstitutional. But he'd been on the "right" side.[1] Another opportunity for Kavanaugh to take sides arose after a five-year-old Cuban boy, Elián González, was found floating at sea in an inner tube three miles off Florida's coast on Thanksgiving Day 1999. A small boat full of Cuban refugees had capsized and most, including his mother, drowned. What ensued was a partisan custody fight that gripped the nation. Anti-Castro Republicans, including Governor

Bush and his brother, Texas governor and Republican presidential candidate George W. Bush, sided with the boy's Miami relatives, who sought to keep him. Many Democrats sided with the father in Cuba who demanded his son back (the parents were divorced). In the months-long legal wrangling, Kavanaugh worked pro bono on the Florida relatives' team. A federal court ruled for the father and the case ended in the Supreme Court, which declined to hear the relatives' appeal. Elián returned to Cuba, but anger lingered among Cuban Americans, enough to be a factor in George W. Bush's disputed Florida victory that sealed his win over Al Gore.

Then came Kavanaugh's third and perhaps most politically advantageous move: He joined Bush's legal team in the weeks-long Florida recount fight that ended with the Supreme Court's conservative majority deciding for Bush, 5–4. Several years later, Kavanaugh would minimize his role when Democrats quizzed him about it during the 2004 Senate hearing on his nomination to be an appeals court judge. He said he was just "part of a group of Republican lawyers" that monitored the "relatively quick and uncontroversial" recount in Florida's Democratic-leaning Volusia County, one of four counties that were the focus of the parties' fight for the presidency.[2] But his contribution, together with the reputation he'd built since the Starr years, was enough that his reward was a job in the new administration—a prized one that put him in the White House, as an associate counsel. By 2003, he was promoted to be the senior associate counsel and then staff secretary, controlling the paper flow to Bush from a desk just outside the Oval Office. Kavanaugh's new mentor, the president, quickly determined to promote him further—to a top federal judgeship.

•   •   •

Bush's ascendance in 2000 to the pinnacle of the Republican Party and then the White House was hardly predictable. His father had been ousted after one term just eight years before, weakened by his own party's conservative insurgents. But by the time Newt Gingrich, Republicans' standard-bearer for much of the 1990s, resigned in disgrace after 1998, disillusioned conservatives and party leaders alike looked to George H. W. Bush's namesake son for a "new" face and message. George W. Bush twice had been elected governor of the most populous red state. And the ambitious Texan, as much as he loved his dad, essentially promised the right that he'd be what his father was not: a *true* conservative.

In Bush's campaign, his father was he-who-must-not-be-named. The candidate would praise Ronald Reagan and condemn Clinton, but almost never mention the president who served between them. When conservatives called on him to account for his dad's broken tax promise and appointment of David Souter to the Supreme Court, Bush would tell audiences, "My father can defend himself." The son promised not only "no new taxes" but "tax cuts, so help me God." He said his models for the Supreme Court were his dad's other nominee, Clarence Thomas, and the most conservative justice, Antonin Scalia.[3]

Still, Bush emphasized that he'd be a "compassionate conservative," implicitly breaking from the Gingrich breed. He also did not subscribe to the forces growing within the conservative base—"isms" that Donald Trump later would harness and make his own. "Among social conservatives and some economic conservatives, a more nationalistic, protectionist and even nativist populism runs deep, calling into question the party's traditional fealty to free trade and internationalism," I wrote at the time with a colleague at the *Wall Street Journal*.[4] Bush sought to blur conservatives' hard lines, and bridge their differences with mainstream Republicans. It worked for a while, just long enough to get him elected and reelected.

Eight months into Bush's presidency, the terrorist attacks of September 11, 2001, erased many Americans' lingering questions about his legitimacy, and a suddenly united nation gave him extraordinary political capital. Bush and his strategist he dubbed "The Architect," Karl Rove, quickly pressed that edge to partisan ends. While invading Afghanistan after 9/11 to rout terrorists there had bipartisan support, Bush went beyond that—with an eye to painting Democrats as weak on national security going into the 2002 midterm election season. He pushed into law the so-called Patriot Act, with provisions expanding government surveillance and curbing civil liberties, a number of which later would be found unconstitutional. More controversially, Bush and Vice President Dick Cheney immediately began making the case for invading Iraq, and won a split Congress's authorization of military force just weeks before the November elections. The strategy worked: For only the second time since 1934, the president's party gained seats in Congress at his midterm, giving Republicans full control. Their net gain of two Senate seats was enough to end the bare 51–49 majority Democrats unexpectedly won in early 2001 when Senator Jim Jeffords of Vermont left the Republican Party to protest its rightward turn.[5]

Bush and Rove envisioned nothing less than a realignment of the parties much like Franklin D. Roosevelt had achieved to Democrats' decades-long advantage. With early victories enacting tax cuts, a bipartisan education law, and a Medicare prescription drug benefit, Bush sought to make inroads among suburban and older voters, especially women, and independents alienated by Gingrich-era Republicans. He planned to overhaul immigration law and give millions of undocumented, longtime residents a path to citizenship, to counter Democrats' edge among the growing ranks of Latino voters as well as Asian Americans and other immigrant groups. Yet the increasing nativism and xenophobia in his party foiled those plans, and twice he was unable to get bipartisan legislation through Congress. By the 2006 midterms, the conservative grass roots had grown disgusted with the entire party establishment. Six years of control in Washington had produced corruption among House Republicans, a swing from budget surpluses to mounting deficits, seemingly endless wars, a bungled response to Hurricane Katrina, and Bush's attempted Social Security makeover.[6] Democrats would capture the House and Senate in the 2006 elections.

In one way, however, Bush consistently pleased the right: by his zeal for putting young, proven conservatives on the federal bench after eight years of a Democratic president. Early on, Jeffords's defection had complicated prospects for Bush's judicial nominees by giving Democrats control of the Senate, and thus the confirmation process. Bush was fortunate, at least, that the new chairman of the Senate Judiciary Committee was Patrick Leahy of Vermont, an institutionalist whose respect for rules and traditions checked his partisanship. To many Democrats' chagrin, Leahy rushed through most of Bush's early nominees. Only a relative few considered too ideologically extreme were held back. Yet the intensity of the fights over those nominations added to the bad blood that had built between the parties since Robert Bork's defeat. In the White House, Kavanaugh played a significant behind-the-scenes role—bigger than known, until years later.

* * *

Kavanaugh's hiring into the new Bush administration was a slam dunk. By 2001, the thirty-five-year-old lawyer was well known to the partisans doing the hiring, and well vetted given his past, politically charged work. White House counsel Alberto Gonzales chose Kavanaugh as an associate counsel, tasked along with other young conservatives in the office with identifying and vetting prospective judges. A *New York Times* article described the group as "a cadre of young lawyers who have a strong ideological commitment to conservative jurisprudence," credentials as former Supreme Court clerks and Federalist Society members, and, in some cases, "impeccable anti-Clinton credentials." Its example: Brett Kavanaugh.[7]

"Kavanaugh is well-liked by ideological friends and foes," the *Washington Post* reported, and "known for his work ethic—staying at the office until three or four in the morning."[8] By the following year, a *Post* profile on the Zelig-like striver began, "Where there is controversy, there is Brett Kavanaugh." It contrasted his past and current roles: As Starr's deputy, "he was devoted to restricting the powers of the president. Now, as a lawyer in the Bush White House, he is devoted to expanding the chief executive's powers." Allies said the shift simply reflected that Kavanaugh was dealing with potential criminal matters in President Clinton's case, but civil proceedings in Bush's. Yet a former Starr team colleague, Mark Tuohey, told the *Post*, "It's a stretch" to say that Kavanaugh's work had been ideologically consistent.[9]

Just how involved Kavanaugh was in some of Bush's most controversial judicial nominations would be a matter of contention in his own confirmation hearings, leaving Democratic senators convinced he'd lied to them about his role. Certainly Bush relied on his advice. He would say that Kavanaugh helped persuade him to nominate John G. Roberts Jr. to be chief justice in 2005.[10] The White House lawyers, Kavanaugh in particular, enlisted the Federalist Society as a full partner, "an ideological gatekeeper in vetting judicial nominees," according to a scholar of the conservative legal movement, in her 2015 book.[11]

Caroline Fredrickson, chief of staff in 2001 to Democratic senator Maria Cantwell of Washington, recalled meeting Kavanaugh when he and

Gonzales came to see Cantwell early on about judicial nominees from her state. "Who's that guy? He looks so familiar," Fredrickson asked a colleague. "You've seen him all over TV because he wrote the Starr report," the woman replied. "Ah, it's Brett Kavanaugh," Fredrickson said. According to Fredrickson, who later would head progressives' belated answer to the Federalist Society, the American Constitution Society, Kavanaugh and Gonzales had come to tell Cantwell that Bush wanted a change in her state's bipartisan commission that recommended individuals for judgeships. Because Cantwell had just beaten a Republican incumbent, Washington had two Democratic senators. Bush wanted to keep the panel balanced by adding a loyal Republican congresswoman from Washington. Cantwell, as a new senator with a lot on her plate, didn't object. It is hard to see a Republican being so amenable with federal judgeships at stake.[12]

Kavanaugh was a natural fit for Bush's inner circle, sharing a Yale pedigree, sports fanaticism, and political chops. He developed an enduring bond with the president; some described him as being like the son Bush didn't have. Long after his White House years, Kavanaugh often cited Bush and his homespun aphorisms in speeches. "Live on the sunrise side of the mountain, not the sunset side of the mountain. Be optimistic. See the day that is coming, not the day that is gone," he told the graduates of Catholic University's Columbus School of Law in 2018. "This was a favorite saying of President George W. Bush's. I worked for him for five and a half years. Love the guy."[13] During Bush's frequent getaways to his ranch in Crawford, on the scrublands of central Texas, Kavanaugh often came along in the years that he was White House secretary. He was part of an elite fraternity—and it was mostly men—but it wasn't glamorous duty. He lived in a double-wide, five-bedroom trailer alongside those for Secret Service agents, pilots, and aides who monitored secure communications to keep the president in touch with the world. Much like firefighters, the men would go as a posse for groceries, cook their own meals, grill outside, or grab a meal at Crawford's sole restaurant, the Coffee Station, and watch videos at "home." When Bush cleared brush, Kavanaugh sometimes helped.[14]

Still single, in Washington Kavanaugh socialized with other conservative lawyers on the rise, again mostly guys, including Noel Francisco, another associate White House counsel who'd been on the *Bush v. Gore* team (and would become President Trump's solicitor general); Viet Dinh, an assistant attorney general who'd investigated Whitewater as a Senate aide; John Yoo, the Justice Department official who would write the so-called torture memos to legally justify what the administration euphemistically called "enhanced interrogation techniques" for terrorist suspects; Eugene Scalia, son of the justice; and Paul Clement, who would become Bush's solicitor general. There was an all-male dinner group—the Eureka Club, named apparently for Reagan's alma mater—that would meet monthly for a boozy steakhouse dinner.[15]

In the late summer of 2001, Kavanaugh spent a weekend with a group of guys on a rented boat off Maryland's coast. "Su Ching is booked," the organizer had written in the subject line of an email before the trip. "Although you may be hoping that I've lined up a hostess for a rub-n-tug massage session, 'Su Ching' actually is the sailboat (a Tayana 55) we've got for Friday, Sept. 7 to Sunday, Sept. 9 out of Annapolis." The ethnic slur and sexist humor in the email, which was among those released during Kavanaugh's 2018 confirmation process, was further evidence of the frat-like air that suffused his professional and social lives. Afterward, he wrote to his buddies on Monday, September 10, 2001: "Excellent time. Apologies to all for missing Friday (good excuse), arriving late Saturday (weak excuse), and growing aggressive after blowing still another game of dice (don't recall)." He added, oddly: "Reminders to everyone to be very, very vigilant w/r/t confidentiality on all issues and all fronts, including with spouses."[16]

In 2018, Democratic senator Sheldon Whitehouse of Rhode Island asked Kavanaugh, in written questions, what "issues" he was so eager to keep secret. Kavanaugh replied that he was referring to his approaching first date with Bush's personal secretary, Ashley Estes. "I had discussed Ashley at some length" on the trip, he wrote. "I was asking my friends not to share my interest in and upcoming date with Ashley with their spouses." Some senators and their aides didn't buy it; they suspected something—they didn't know what—more embarrassing. His response struck them as another example of Kavanaugh not being honest about some seemingly small matter, thus raising questions about his truthfulness about more damning allegations.[17] Whatever the case, Kavanaugh's caution to his boating pals was in keeping with a running theme of his boys-only outings since his teens, variations on the motto "What happens at Georgetown Prep stays at Georgetown Prep."

The boating adventure was the end of such frivolity for some time. A day after his return, September 10, Kavanaugh indeed had a first date with Estes. And the morning after that, as he'd tell the nation when he was picked for the Supreme Court, "I was a few steps behind her when the Secret Service shouted at all of us to sprint out the front steps of the White House because there was an inbound plane." After the September 11 attacks, Kavanaugh and everyone else in the White House was working impossibly long hours—he immediately pulled an all-nighter to research Bush's emergency powers. The couple's relationship got off to a slower start than it otherwise might have.

Estes was from Abilene, a small, conservative city of churches on the West Texas plains, more than two hours' drive from either Dallas–Fort Worth to the east or Odessa and Midland, Bush's former home, to the west. She was nearly a decade younger than Kavanaugh. She'd graduated from the University of Texas at Austin in 1997—her future husband was then three years into his work on the Starr team—and got a job in then-governor Bush's office. When Bush was elected president, he brought her along.[18]

As Estes and Kavanaugh continued dating from one year to the next, Bush good-naturedly prodded them to marry. They did so in 2004, and with the president and First Lady in attendance, the marriage at the Catholic Christ Church in Washington's Georgetown neighborhood drew society-column coverage. The *Washingtonian* magazine quoted the wedding planner: "It was the only wedding in the hundreds I have planned where all of the guests were in their seats 15 minutes early. There's no lollygagging when Secret Service are holding machine guns outside of the church."[19]

*　　*　　*

A year before, on July 25, 2003, Bush had nominated his staff secretary to a seat on the D.C. Circuit Court of Appeals, the nation's second most prestigious bench and the launchpad to the Supreme Court for Justices Scalia, Thomas, Ruth Bader Ginsburg, and, soon, Roberts. Another young White House lawyer, D. Kyle Sampson, early in the administration had suggested to Gonzales that Kavanaugh would make a good judge. Yet a first potential appointment quietly fizzled. In 2002, when Democrats had a Senate majority, Gonzales discussed with Kavanaugh a seat on the Richmond-based Fourth Circuit Court, whose jurisdiction includes Kavanaugh's home state of Maryland. But Maryland's senators, both Democrats, opposed nominating him, ostensibly because he never practiced law there, Kavanaugh disclosed on a Senate questionnaire when he was subsequently picked for the D.C. Circuit.

Democrats' threat to filibuster Kavanaugh's nomination, because of his perceived partisanship, would block a vote until 2006. Democrats also were peeved that Bush was trying to fill two openings on the D.C. court, the venue for cases involving the federal government and in particular its regulation of air, water, labor, civil rights, energy efficiency standards, consumer protections, and other matters central to daily life. Republicans had blocked Clinton's nominees for the court by claiming it didn't have enough work. One of the failed nominees was future justice Elena Kagan, who instead became dean of Harvard Law School (where she'd hire Kavanaugh to teach).

His nomination stalled, Kavanaugh bided his time in the West Wing as staff secretary. For more than half of his time in the White House—nearly three years—he was a judge-in-waiting. He described his job to senators in 2018, emphasizing his proximity to power: "As staff secretary I was by President Bush's side for three years and was entrusted with the nation's most sensitive secrets. I traveled on Air Force One all over the country and the world with President Bush. I went everywhere with him, from Texas to Pakistan, from Alaska to Australia, from Buckingham Palace to the Vatican." He vetted virtually all proposed statements, speeches, executive orders, and interagency communications before they went to the president, often negotiating among administration officials on the content. "I was selected for that job to be the honest broker for the president in making sure he got competing views," Kavanaugh testified at his confirmation hearing in 2004.

Simultaneously, he did what he could to promote his nomination, including trying to paper over hard feelings about the Starr investigation. Having worked on judicial nominations for Bush's first couple years,

Kavanaugh knew that Clinton lawyer David Kendall had vouched for Ken Starr's deputy, John D. Bates, after Bates was nominated in 2001 to be a federal district judge. Bates had called Kendall to see whether he'd oppose Bates's nomination, potentially influencing Democratic senators. Kendall told Bates he would not, and even offered to write a recommendation. Now Kavanaugh likewise called Kendall. "David, what would your position be?" he asked. "Brett, personally I think highly of you," Kendall said. "But I do have two serious questions I don't know the answer to. Maybe you can help me. First of all, were you responsible for the pornographic excess of the Starr report? And second, were you involved in the leaks?" As Kendall recounted the exchange to me in 2019, "His response was, 'David, good to talk to you. Thank you very much.' Click. He didn't engage, didn't admit or deny. I tried not to make it a hostile thing, but I had the same two questions then that I have now."[20]

Democrats protested that, his Starr role aside, the thirty-eight-year-old Kavanaugh was too young and inexperienced for such an important court. "He'd barely handled any cases in court," said Lisa Graves, then Leahy's chief counsel for nominations. His legal work primarily had been in the service of Republican causes: the Clinton impeachment, Jeb Bush's Florida school vouchers, Elián González, *Bush v. Gore*, and, lately, President Bush. What's more, Kavanaugh was nominated at a particularly contentious time. The White House and congressional Democrats were bitterly jousting over a group of especially conservative judicial nominees and post-9/11 policies involving U.S. citizens' privacy, racial profiling, and the alleged torture of combatants in Iraq and Afghanistan. They suspected Kavanaugh had been involved in all those matters. "It's the summer of 2003: All hell had broken loose," Graves recalled. For months, international organizations and media had been reporting on the alleged torture, sexual abuse, and even murder of suspected terrorists in American hands. In April 2004, CBS's *60 Minutes* and the *New Yorker* magazine revealed photos, taken by U.S. service members at Iraq's Abu Ghraib prison, offering proof of the gruesome and dehumanizing treatment of detainees.

"The really big issue at the time was the Bush legal framework around torture and interrogation," said Jeremy Paris, a Democratic counsel when Kavanaugh was a D.C. Circuit nominee. "We suspected then, just based on his position in the White House, that he would have known."[21] Democrats were able to block Bush's nominee for the Fourth Circuit, William J. Haynes II, who as Pentagon general counsel had helped draft interrogation policies for the naval base at Guantánamo Bay, Cuba. They had help from Republican senator Lindsey Graham. As a former reserve judge advocate in the military, Graham reflected the opposition to Haynes from the Judge Advocate General's Corps, which felt unduly pressured to accept the harsh interrogation policies. Democrats failed, however, to block Ninth Circuit nominee Jay Bybee, the Justice Department official who had signed off on the Yoo torture memos.

Democrats believed Kavanaugh had a hand in both the Haynes and Bybee nominations, as well as others that split the Senate. Then another issue arose. Four months after he was nominated, an unusual scandal broke in the Senate that seemed to implicate him: "Memogate." At issue were thousands of emails of Democratic senators and their aides secretly accessed by a senior Republican aide in the thick of judicial politics, Manuel Miranda. Democrats were sure that Kavanaugh had to be a recipient, perhaps *the* primary one, of the stolen goods.

•   •   •

Miranda was a fiercely partisan Cuban American whose activism among conservative Christian groups led in 2001 to a job with Senator Orrin Hatch on the Judiciary Committee, to work on judicial nominations. He was promoted to the office of Senate majority leader Bill Frist, a Tennessee Republican. As the parties battled over nominees from 2001 through 2003, the man widely known as "Manny" distinguished himself among Republicans in the Senate and the White House for his real-time intelligence about what Democrats were up to.[22]

On joining the committee in December 2001, Miranda learned from a clerk that they could access Democratic aides' emails, thanks to a shared server. However, the clerk told Miranda, his supervisors had admonished him to quit copying Democrats' messages and to delete any that he possessed—one supervisor even shredded printouts the clerk had given her. Miranda gave him other instructions. As the clerk later told investigators,

Miranda said, "Senator Hatch wanted the staff to use any means necessary to support President Bush's nominees." When Miranda moved to Frist's office in 2003, he had the clerk keep sending him copies of Democrats' communications.[23]

Over time, Miranda acquired an estimated 4,670 emails—Democrats' memos, speech drafts, research, and political talking points about Bush nominees—and shared his purloined intel with Republican aides in the Senate and Bush administration. As would become apparent only years later, prominent among the recipients was Kavanaugh. During the Senate's consideration of one particularly conservative appeals court nominee, Priscilla Owen, the clerk gave Miranda Democrats' emails almost daily. Miranda later would insist that he never told anyone his source. Yet the frequency and rich details of his information—including a four-thousand-word memo for Leahy from the senator's counsel, Graves—should have left anyone suspicious, and certainly anyone like Kavanaugh smart enough to be working in the White House.

Graves, recalling that period nearly two decades later, said Democrats were mystified at Republicans' unusual savvy in Judiciary meetings. "There were times in 2002 or 2003 when something would happen at a hearing, and we'd go, 'Wow, that's weird. How do they know that?,' or 'Why are they making that point?' And in hindsight, you go, 'Oh, because they had this memo that we didn't know they had.'" At one point she emailed two colleagues, "Do we have some sort of leak? What's happening?" She added, "Because I was the chief counsel on nominations, I had in my file our memo on every single judicial nominee—'Here's why you should vote against this nominee' or 'Here are the questions we recommend be asked about this nominee.' Other staffers' emails had my memos and whatever they would provide for their bosses."[24]

Then, on November 12, 2003, Miranda organized a rare overnight protest by Senate Republicans to counter Democrats' filibusters of several nominees. He emailed all fifty-one Republicans' offices, urging them to come to the Senate at 6:02 p.m. because Fox News would broadcast their demonstration at the start of its evening news show. When his email was leaked to Democrats, the ploy backfired. Democrat Frank Lautenberg of New Jersey read it from the Senate floor, with an enlargement of the email beside him. "It is good to see a bunch of penguins walking down here fifty-one deep," he said.[25] Democrats' mockery enraged Miranda. But his retaliation would lead to his exposure, and then an unprecedented two-year investigation that would leave Democrats stewing for years—not least because his suspected accomplice, Kavanaugh, was destined for the Supreme Court.

To embarrass Democrats in return, Miranda leaked emails suggesting that they colluded with liberal advocacy groups to oppose Bush nominees (as if Republicans didn't do the same with conservative groups against Democratic candidates), giving them to conservatives at the *Wall Street Journal*, the *Washington Times*, and the Coalition for a Fair Judiciary. Two days later, a biting *Journal* editorial against Senate Democrats cited their "staff strategy memos" and quoted from three senators' correspondence. The *Washington Times* ran a story the next day with similar information. And the Coalition for a Fair Judiciary, a conservative group, posted twenty-eight pages of Democrats' material on its website.

Seeing the *Journal* piece, Edward Kennedy's chief counsel contacted the Senate sergeant-at-arms about a potential computer breach. The Capitol Police seized materials from the Judiciary Committee's network and sealed its computer room. Democrats demanded an investigation and Hatch, the chairman, authorized one. Senate Sergeant-at-Arms William Pickle probed for more than three months, with help from a computer forensics firm and Secret Service agents. The clerk, Miranda's source, quickly admitted his culpability and fingered Miranda. On March 4, 2004, Hatch released Pickle's sixty-five-page report, which detailed the "circumstantial evidence" implicating Miranda and said other Republican aides might have been involved. But Pickle could not compel them to testify, and journalists who'd received and published Democrats' documents predictably declined to reveal their sources. Conservative activists who were implicated, including C. Boyden Gray, the former White House counsel to George H. W. Bush, refused to be interviewed. "Without their cooperation," the report said, "the investigation faced a significant impediment to identifying the source of the disclosure."

The lack of cooperation extended to the White House, which did not allow Senate investigators to speak to administration officials who had communicated with Miranda. Kavanaugh, by then a nominee to the second-highest court, didn't volunteer anything about his many exchanges with Miranda. While Miranda gave some information, the report said, he wouldn't identify his White House contacts. Hatch and Leahy had jointly asked Pickle to determine whether a crime had been committed. The sergeant-at-arms suggested grounds for possible charges: making false statements to Congress, receiving stolen property, and computer fraud. Pickle noted that prosecution under the 1984 Computer Fraud and Abuse Act could extend to "government employees who 'obtain information' by merely reading it." White House officials like Kavanaugh, for example.

In response to Pickle's report, Leahy decried "this unprecedented case of partisan spying in the Senate," and lamented that the sergeant-at-arms couldn't compel testimony or prosecute, given the apparent criminal behavior. "There are still outstanding questions that demand answers," he said. "We do not know who at the Department of Justice or the White House benefited from this wrongdoing and worked with staff of these Republican offices or their intermediaries." Leahy said Democrats had written to the White House and Justice Department, adding, "We do not have responsive answers."[26] He wrote separately to Gonzales, asking if the White House counsel's office had received any of the Democrats' emails. Gonzales's reply was far from a flat denial, more a statement of willful ignorance: "I am not aware of any credible allegation of White House involvement in this matter. Consequently, there has been no White House investigation or effort to determine whether anyone at the White House was aware of or involved in these activities." Yet emails released in 2018, during Kavanaugh's Supreme Court confirmation process, would show that both Gonzales's office, which then included Kavanaugh, and the Justice Department received Democrats' material or information derived from it. In Miranda's emails forwarding the material to the Bush officials, Kavanaugh was frequently listed among the recipients; for some messages, he was the only one.

Hatch told reporters, "I am mortified that this improper, unethical, and simply unacceptable breach of confidential files occurred." Chuck Schumer of New York, a senior Democrat on the Judiciary Committee, futilely called for an independent counsel with subpoena power to investigate further.[27] A bipartisan group of senators referred Pickle's report to the Justice Department for possible prosecution, and Justice assigned a U.S. attorney for the Southern District of New York to investigate whether Republican aides had violated the computer fraud act. That referral, in April 2004, came on the eve of Kavanaugh's initial hearing on his nomination to the D.C. appellate court. No action was taken.[28] A year later, Beryl A. Howell, a former Leahy counsel who would become a federal judge, outlined in the *Yale Journal of Law and Technology* the legal arguments that Miranda had violated both criminal and civil statutes.[29]

So it was that Kavanaugh, a nominee for a lifetime seat on the country's second highest court, escaped being identified and publicly implicated in what were, at a minimum, unethical acts, if not criminal ones. As the Pickle Report noted, the American Bar Association's Model Rules of Professional Conduct state that it is professional misconduct for a lawyer to "engage in conduct involving dishonesty, fraud, deceit, or misrepresentation." Kavanaugh would profess ignorance and innocence at his hearings, under oath, even after emails came to light in 2018.

Paris, the former Leahy counsel, said Kavanaugh should have confronted Miranda early on: "Hold on, where are you getting this? Why do we know this?" Graves, whose emails were among Miranda's most frequent targets, told me after Kavanaugh's ascent to the Supreme Court, "He knew he was getting our most sensitive memos, letters, and strategies—he's not stupid."[30]

*   *   *

The Miranda story would be a recurring issue for Kavanaugh at his confirmation hearings, given Democrats' doubts about his veracity. As for Miranda, a postscript on his fate is useful as a window into the right's zealotry in Republicans' long war for the courts.

Miranda not only escaped prosecution, he was hailed as a hero among movement conservatives. "You have no ethical duty to your opposition," he would say.[31] After losing his Senate job, he formed first one group and then another to fight for conservative justices. He was often quoted in the media—promoting successful Bush nominees Roberts and

Samuel A. Alito Jr., warning against any Supreme Court appointment for Gonzales, and opposing Bush's failed nomination of another confidant from Texas, White House aide Harriet Miers. Edwin Meese, Reagan's longtime adviser and attorney general, got Miranda a job at the Heritage Foundation for a time. And in 2006, at the Conservative Political Action Conference—the once-fringe, now-mainstream gathering known as CPAC—Miranda received the Ronald Reagan Award for his role in Miers's demise and Alito's subsequent confirmation.

In presenting the award, David Keene, the president of the American Conservative Union, alluded to the Memogate scandal but suggested that Miranda hadn't stolen Democrats' information, he'd "merely come upon it." Senate Republicans, Keene groused, were "more interested in getting along with fellow members of the Senate club than truth, justice or even partisan advantage"—and thus they allowed Miranda "to be sacrificed, fired and publicly humiliated." Miranda, in continuing to battle for conservative justices, "served notice on a Republican president that we conservatives haven't worked as hard and as long as we have so that he can put his friends and cronies on the court regardless of their qualifications," Keene said. Alito wouldn't have been chosen "but for Manny Miranda."[32]

•   •   •

Kavanaugh finally got a hearing before the Judiciary Committee, on April 27, 2004; it would be the first of two, reflecting the controversy of his nomination, and the second wouldn't be held until 2006. Memogate loomed large: The hearing was the first chance for Democrats who were Miranda's targets to try to hold the White House to account. As they saw it, Kavanaugh's likely complicity was more proof that he was too partisan, and too dishonest, to be a judge. That he denied any inkling of Miranda's wrongdoing, and under oath, was the last straw.[33] But it was Hatch who first raised the subject, and quickly, to give Kavanaugh a friendly serve: "Now, this is an important question. Did Mr. Miranda ever share, reference, or provide you with any documents that appeared to you to have been drafted or prepared by Democratic staff members of the Senate Judiciary Committee?"

Kavanaugh: "No. I was not aware of that matter ever, until I learned of it in the media late last year."

Hatch asked variations on the question. Kavanaugh gave the same answer.

Schumer was next: "Did you ever come across memos from internal files of any Democratic members given to you or provided to you in any way?"

"No."

Democrat Dick Durbin of Illinois identified himself as Miranda's biggest victim, with more than two thousand emails stolen. To his questions, Kavanaugh conceded that he knew the conservative activists who'd posted Democrats' emails on their group's website—he'd worked with them to mobilize support for Bush nominees. Durbin noted the irony of that answer: Conservative editorialists had expressed shock—shock!—that Democrats' emails proved they met and communicated with liberal groups about nominees, and now Kavanaugh was conceding that such coordination "turns out to be a sin committed by the administration as well?"

"I think it is quite proper, and certainly we did it, and appropriate, for anyone to speak to members of the public who are interested in public issues," Kavanaugh replied.

Durbin emphasized just how much insider intelligence Miranda passed on, such as Leahy's schedules and the senator's questions for Bush nominees. "Did it ever raise a question in your mind that perhaps he knew just a little bit too much for a staffer on Capitol Hill?"

"I have thought about this," Kavanaugh acknowledged, but "there was nothing out of the ordinary." Democrats were incredulous. In subsequent written questions, which senators routinely give nominees after a hearing, Leahy had twenty-six queries about Miranda, and Kennedy had several more. Kavanaugh's replies were unresponsive, yet he took seven months to submit them, further infuriating the Democrats. In 2006, he again denied under oath knowing or suspecting Miranda's wrongdoing. Democrats still had no evidence to refute him. In 2018, they would.

*   *   *

Other controversies stymied Kavanaugh's promotion to the D.C. Circuit. When the Senate didn't vote on it before adjourning in 2004, Bush renominated him in the new Congress in 2005, and again in 2006. The president abandoned some nominees in the face of Democrats' opposition, but not his protégé sitting just outside the Oval Office.

Schumer had summed up Democrats' view of Kavanaugh at the first hearing, calling his nomination "among the most political in history." He went on, "Some might call Mr. Kavanaugh the Zelig of young Republican lawyers, as he has managed to find himself at the center of so many high-profile, controversial issues in his short career, from the notorious Starr Report to the Florida recount, to this president's secrecy and privilege claims, to post-9/11 legislative battles...to controversial judicial nominations. If there has been a partisan political fight that needed a good lawyer in the last decade, Brett Kavanaugh was probably there." Similarly, Durbin told Kavanaugh he was "the Zelig or Forrest Gump of Republican politics—you show up at every scene of the crime." He added, "Would you not understand that an attorney coming before the D.C. Circuit Court, looking at your résumé, has to assume—just assume—where you are going to end up? There are so few exceptions, if any, in your legal career that point to objectivity."

Kavanaugh countered, "My background has not been in party politics."

Schumer and Durbin voiced many Democrats' feelings: A president of their party wouldn't be so brazen as to nominate someone who'd not only been part of so many partisan brawls, but also worked to impeach a president of the other party. Bush had promised to be "a uniter, not a divider," Schumer said, yet picking Kavanaugh was "not just a drop of salt in the partisan wounds, it is the whole shaker!" The Democrats noted that they'd backed two other Bush nominees involved in Clinton's impeachment and Senate trial, because both men had long records of nonpartisan, professional experience. Kavanaugh did not. Republicans, in response, played down Kavanaugh's role with Starr, though it accounted for nearly a third of his legal career at that point. Arlen Specter of Pennsylvania, the committee chairman at the 2006 hearing, said Kavanaugh "was not counsel, he was not deputy counsel. He was one of a tier below."

Kavanaugh's evaluation from the American Bar Association emerged as another flashpoint. In a rare move, in 2006 the group downgraded his rating from those in 2003 and 2005, reflecting concerns that judges and lawyers familiar with his career had raised confidentially. The ABA's action exacerbated its already strained relations with Republicans, who'd complained since the Bork and Thomas fights that the group was biased against conservatives. In fact, Republican nominees typically got its highest rating: "well qualified."

Since Dwight Eisenhower's time, an ABA committee had vetted judicial candidates "strictly on professional qualifications: integrity, professional competence and judicial temperament," and not "philosophy, political affiliation or ideology." It privately canvassed hundreds of lawyers, judges, and other associates *before* an individual's nomination; that allowed those consulted to be candid, the thinking went, and presidents could quietly nix someone who didn't rate highly, as Clinton had (and Obama would). But Bush broke with tradition, to conservatives' delight, naming judges without first getting evaluations. He couldn't cut out the ABA altogether, however: The Judiciary Committee still insisted on a report before its hearing.[34]

When Kavanaugh was first nominated, conservatives were prominent on the ABA's judiciary panel. The chair was Carol E. Dinkins, a deputy attorney general in the Reagan administration who'd been appointed to several positions in Texas by then-governor Bush. Kavanaugh was rated "well qualified," a fact that Republicans trumpeted at his 2004 hearing. Yet when his evaluation was updated before his second hearing on May 9, 2006, conservatives complained that the bar group's chief investigator was biased. One prominent writer—the same Kavanaugh friend who years later would publish a false theory of mistaken identity to exonerate him of sexual assault allegations—dismissed the lawyer as "a fervent gender activist" and alleged without evidence that she was in cahoots with Senate Democrats.[35] Yet three-quarters of the members who'd previously rated Kavanaugh "well qualified" now switched to the middling rating: "qualified." "A substantial majority" of the fifteen-member panel voted for the lesser rating, the ABA reported.

Stephen L. Tober, a New Hampshire lawyer who chaired the committee, wrote in a nine-page explanation that the change reflected interviews with thirty-six individuals—nineteen judges and seventeen lawyers—beyond the fifty-five professionals consulted in 2003. Also, "new and different developments" had troubled members. (At the subsequent hearing, Durbin would tell Kavanaugh that among ABA members' new concerns was how "dismissive" he'd been of Miranda's heist of Democrats' documents; Kavanaugh acknowledged that the ABA had asked him about it.) Tober wrote that those interviewed also shared concerns that others had raised earlier: "that he had never tried a case to verdict or judgment; that his litigating experience over the years was always in the company of senior counsel; and that he had very little experience with criminal cases." Tober gave damning examples of the critiques: A judge said Kavanaugh's performance in court was "less than adequate," "sanctimonious," and showed "experience on the level of an associate"—a junior lawyer in a firm. A lawyer in a separate case said Kavanaugh "did not handle the case well as an advocate and dissembled." Another called him "immovable and very stubborn and frustrating to deal with on some issues." Tober wrote that some lawyers raised "a new concern": Kavanaugh's temperament.

Kavanaugh was given a chance for rebuttal; Tober did not say whether he took it. At his hearing, Kavanaugh declined Republicans' invitations to criticize the ABA and said he was pleased by its report. Tober emphasized that the distinction between "well qualified" and "qualified" was, "at its most basic, the difference between the 'highest standard' and a 'very high standard.'" Republicans seized on his reassurance—"not a tinker's bit of difference," Specter said. Even so, they didn't have Tober testify, as was customary, thus minimizing attention to the ABA report's unflattering reviews of Kavanaugh from judges and lawyers who'd dealt with him. But Democrats read them in committee, and in the Senate.[36]

Democrats also interrogated Kavanaugh, without much effect, on his work in the White House counsel's office promoting Bush's most controversial appeals court choices. It had been Kavanaugh's job to recommend candidates for judgeships and to vet and interview them, coordinating with conservative activists—notably Leonard Leo of the Federalist Society. Once Bush made his picks, Kavanaugh would track nominees' prospects in the Senate, with Miranda among other aides there, and figure out how best to pressure or persuade balky senators. He prepared talking points for administration officials, nominees, and senators. He'd speak to reporters privately, to influence coverage. And he'd review documents on a nominee's record to help decide which to release or withhold. Lawyers in the White House counsel's office divided the workload of nominations, though the lines often blurred. Kavanaugh denied to Democrats that he played any part on the appeals court nominations they most opposed: of Charles W. Pickering Sr.; William H. Pryor Jr., who called *Roe v. Wade* an "abomination" and said rights for same-sex couples would "logically extend" to "necrophilia, bestiality, and pedophilia"; and William J. Haynes II, a former Pentagon counsel who drafted its interrogation policies. As with Miranda's scandal, Democrats had no evidence to contradict Kavanaugh's denials, yet.

They also sought without success to plumb his role in developing Bush's hotly contested wartime policies for warrantless wiretapping, and for detaining and interrogating combatants picked up in Iraq and Afghanistan. Again, Kavanaugh denied involvement or even much knowledge. Information seeming to contradict him would come out only after he'd been confirmed to the appellate court, and more after he'd become a justice, the result mainly of outside groups' Freedom of Information Act requests and lawsuits. Starting in late 2018, the National Archives released thousands of Kavanaugh's White House emails, including hundreds on surveillance programs, after a lawsuit by the Electronic Privacy Information Center, known as EPIC. Releases in October 2018 included eleven emails from Kavanaugh to his friend Yoo, author of the "torture memo" and the legal justifications for the surveillance policies, in the months after the September 11, 2001, attacks. Several hundred more emails were about other programs for U.S. surveillance, such as airline passenger profiling.

Material released in January 2019 included an email from Yoo to Kavanaugh six days after 9/11, with Yoo's analysis of constitutional issues regarding "random electronic surveillance for counter-terrorism purposes." Kavanaugh wrote the same day, "Any results yet on the 4A [Fourth Amendment] implications of random/constant surveillance of phone and e-mail conversations of non-citizens who are in the United States when the purpose of the surveillance is to prevent terrorist/criminal violence?" Kavanaugh was the staff secretary, and thus Bush's communications filter, when Attorney General John Ashcroft in 2004 confronted White House officials about the legality of the surveillance program. Under Bush's secret order, the National Security Agency was eavesdropping on calls and emails of U.S. citizens—without the warrants required by law—to track any contacts with Al Qaeda suspects. In 2006, Kavanaugh testified, "I learned of that program when there was a *New York Times* story" in December 2005. In 2019, EPIC reported that a new batch of Kavanaugh emails from the National Archives suggested otherwise. There were 573 messages he sent or received *before* the story's publication with the names of the two reporters working on it.[37]

Whether Kavanaugh had been in the loop on the NSA's program at the start, he quickly joined it. Five days after the *Times* story ran, he emailed senior White House aides, including Karl Rove and Chief of Staff Andrew Card, "It is not good if Americans or members of Congress think we did something that is a good thing but stretched the law in doing it, so we need to fight back hard on that legal part in the court of public opinion and the court of Congress."[38]

Democrats also quizzed Kavanaugh about Bush-era detention policies that violated the Geneva Conventions. "I was not involved and am not involved in the questions about the rules governing detention of combatants," he told them in 2006. Yet those questions—including whether detainees should have legal counsel, and what constituted torture—were matters of running debate among the White House counsel's office, Cheney and his aides, the Justice and State departments, the Pentagon, and the CIA. And in 2007, after Kavanaugh joined the appeals court, National Public Radio and the *Washington Post* reported that he'd been part of a heated exchange in 2002 over whether terrorist suspects who were U.S. citizens had a right to legal counsel; Cheney was opposed. With the issue likely headed to the Supreme Court, Kavanaugh and another White House lawyer who'd clerked for Anthony M. Kennedy argued that Kennedy, the court's swing vote, would likely recognize a right to counsel for detained citizens. Consequently, they said, the policy should reflect that. But Cheney prevailed. (The court later did indeed rule, 8–1, that citizen detainees had a right to counsel.)[39]

After the *Post* and NPR reports on Kavanaugh's role in the debate, Leahy—again chairing the Judiciary Committee—wrote to Gonzales, now

Bush's attorney general, seeking a criminal investigation "and prosecutorial action" into whether Kavanaugh lied to Congress. Through a spokesperson at the D.C. Circuit Court, Kavanaugh said he was truthful. The Justice Department declined comment, and again did not act.[40]

•   •   •

Democrats' three-year logjam to Kavanaugh's confirmation in 2006 had begun to break a year earlier, in May 2005, when a bipartisan "Gang of 14"—seven Republican senators, led by John McCain of Arizona, and seven centrist Democrats—forced a detente in the court wars. They'd allied to block Frist, the majority leader, from acting on his threat to have Republicans disallow filibusters of judicial nominees, by changing a long-time Senate rule. Under the rule, sixty votes were needed to overcome a filibuster; Democrats, by routinely obstructing the Senate's consideration of Bush's most conservative nominees, in effect had erected a supermajority hurdle to their confirmation. It would take a simple majority of fifty-one senators to change that rule, and there were fifty-five Republicans. Yet doing so was called the "nuclear option" for a reason: Filibustering was a Senate tradition, to protect the minority party's rights and encourage compromise. The bipartisan gang wanted to preserve it.

After weeks of negotiating in McCain's office, in May 2005 the members announced a deal. Republicans would not back Frist if he tried to end the filibuster for judicial candidates, leaving him short of the votes he'd need. And the Democrats would no longer support filibusters against three of the ten nominees their party was blocking, including Priscilla Owen and William H. Pryor Jr., in effect clearing them to be confirmed by a simple majority. Two other nominees were explicitly marked for defeat; several more, their fate left hanging, soon withdrew. As for other current and future Bush nominees, the gang's Democrats would support a filibuster only in "extraordinary circumstances."

Amid the two sides' bargaining, the Democrats separately had huddled with Minority Leader Harry Reid of Nevada, or his chief counsel, Ronald Weich. While Kavanaugh was not among the ten nominees known to be under discussion, he was prominent in the Democrats' private talks. Reid intensely opposed him, reflecting Democrats' conviction that Kavanaugh was a partisan hack. "And remember," Weich told me, "Hillary Clinton was in the Senate at that time. People felt it was especially insulting to her to have one of the Clintons' persecutors elevated to this judicial post." Weich, later dean of the University of Baltimore law school, tried to persuade Democrats in the gang to add Kavanaugh's name to those singled out for defeat. "We'll see how it goes," they'd say. Nothing was ever decided. "He was neither blocked nor guaranteed confirmation," Weich said. "It was left open to further deliberations."[41]

Kavanaugh was in limbo, and would remain there for a third year. For the remainder of 2005 and into 2006, the Senate was preoccupied with Bush's first Supreme Court nominations—confirming Roberts as chief justice and Alito as an associate justice and, in between, considering the aborted Miers nomination. By the spring of 2006, Bush and his Senate allies pushed again to confirm Kavanaugh. The gang's Democrats split over whether "extraordinary circumstances" justified a filibuster. They extracted a concession: Specter agreed the Judiciary Committee would call Kavanaugh for another hearing, as Leahy and others had long sought after he replied so tardily and feebly to their written questions following the 2004 hearing. At the new hearing, Leahy asked him: Why had he taken seven months to reply?

Kavanaugh: "Senator, I take responsibility for that, and I'm happy to answer any additional questions."

Leahy, trying again: "Why did you take seven months?"

"Senator, again, I take responsibility for that and—"

"Of course you take responsibility for it. Obviously, they are your answers. But why seven months?"

"Senator, if there was—I take responsibility for that. I think I had a misunderstanding, which is my responsibility. I'm happy to answer additional questions today that you may have, or other members of the committee may have. Again, I take—"

"What was the misunderstanding?"

"Senator, I take responsibility for that."

The audience broke into laughter. Not Leahy. "Mr. Kavanaugh, we are not playing games. I am just asking you a question."[42]

While Kavanaugh was cagey throughout the session, to Democrats' vexation, the fix was in without the threat of a filibuster. Two days later, on May 11, the committee approved his nomination by a party-line 10–8 vote. In late May, the Senate debated over two days, each side rehashing its arguments. Hatch lauded Kavanaugh at length, and his lobbyist father, too: "The apple did not fall far from the tree." Kavanaugh "was not a political partisan," Hatch insisted, dismissing the liberal groups opposed to him as so extreme that they even favored same-sex marriage. (Nine years later, the Supreme Court would recognize such unions as a constitutional right, in an opinion by Kavanaugh's mentor, Kennedy.) Schumer countered that the young and relatively green Kavanaugh should be in line for a district court seat, at best. But Republicans, he said, "value ideology and political service above judicial experience and depth."[43] Leahy complained that Kavanaugh repeatedly said he wanted to make Bush proud on the court. "This is an independent branch of government. He's not supposed to make any president, Republican or Democratic, proud!" The vote for confirmation was 57–36, with all Republicans and four Democrats in favor.[44]

Leahy, given his emphasis on judicial independence, couldn't have approved of Kavanaugh's swearing-in ceremony on June 1, 2006. The president hosted it in the Rose Garden, an all but unprecedented event for an appeals court judge but one reflecting Bush's affection for Brett and Ashley Kavanaugh. Also there were Cheney, Gonzales, Starr, Alex Kozinski, Walter K. Stapleton, and dozens of administration officials. In the years since Kavanaugh's nomination, he had married and had a daughter; nine-month-old Margaret was in the audience with her grandparents. Bush joked that Ashley's marriage "was the first lifetime appointment I arranged for Brett."[45] Months later, a national magazine reported that Bush already had Kavanaugh in mind for the Supreme Court, should an opening occur in his last two years. It did not.[46] Yet as Bush had written in a fatherly handwritten note to Kavanaugh on the eve of the Rose Garden ceremony, "Who knows? Some future President may be wise enough to name you to the Supreme Court."[47]

7

THE JUDGE AVOIDS A TEA PARTY

"A partisan shock trooper
in a black robe."

The new judge left the political arena for the relative cloister of the court just in time. Republicans were in trouble. It was already clear, a year and a half before George W. Bush left office, that he was shaping up as a failed president. While his early tax cuts and response to the 9/11 attacks had been hugely popular among conservatives, many of those same conservatives came to see much of his legacy as a betrayal: An education law giving the federal government too big a role in local schools. A costly new federal entitlement, the Medicare prescription drug benefit. Trillions of dollars more in federal debt. An immigration reform proposal that, as the right saw it, gave amnesty to millions of "illegal aliens." A tragically inept response to Hurricane Katrina. And unending wars, along with the very "nation building" candidate Bush condemned.

By 2006, many conservatives were fed up with both the president and the Republicans who'd run Congress for his first six years. The midterm elections that year became a referendum on all-Republican government, and Democrats won control of Congress for the first time since the Gingrich revolution of 1994. Their freshman class in the House was Democrats' largest since that of the "Watergate babies" elected after Richard M. Nixon's resignation in 1974. The Republican casualties, meanwhile, included some of the best known of the revolutionaries elected in

1994. After a dozen years in power—forget the Contract with America's promised three-term limits—they personified the broken promises, dysfunction, and scandals that had come to define Republican governance. Typical was Representative J. D. Hayworth Jr., a bombastic former sportscaster from suburban Phoenix who was among those called to account for contributions and favors from prison-bound Republican lobbyist Jack Abramoff. To try to mollify his constituents, Hayworth secured pork-barrel projects for his district; collectively, House Republicans' use of congressional appropriations as an incumbent protection racket resulted in nearly ten thousand spending items totaling $29 billion in fiscal year 2006 alone. Republicans created a database to track members' requests, and instructed new lawmakers on how to get their share. "You're told you have to do that to be reelected," then-representative Jeff Flake told me that year.[1]

Party leaders also dangled pork to buy members' votes on controversial bills—most dramatically during a middle-of-the-night vote for Bush's Medicare drug bill in 2003. With the bill seemingly defeated at the end of the fifteen-minute vote, doomed by conservatives' opposition to new spending, the leaders extended the voting period by nearly three hours, to 6 a.m., and openly bartered with holdouts on the House floor until they had enough support. It was "one of the most breathtaking breaches of the legislative process in the modern history of the House," political scientists Thomas Mann and Norman Ornstein wrote.[2] Republicans had turned for leadership after Gingrich's ouster to more pragmatic players, Speaker Dennis Hastert of Illinois and Majority Leader Tom DeLay of Texas. DeLay, the real power of the two, was best known for the "K Street Project," named for the location of many lobbyists' firms; he openly enlisted them as legislative partners, if they hired only Republicans. Facing indictment for corruption in 2005, DeLay nearly succeeded in changing the rules so he could remain as majority leader. In 2006, he resigned from Congress. Three other Republicans left in scandal, one to prison for selling spending earmarks for defense projects. Joe Scarborough, a '94 class Republican who'd left Congress for MSNBC, quoted Lord Acton when he and I discussed his party's self-inflicted plight: "Power corrupts, and absolute power corrupts absolutely."[3]

The Republicans' losses in the Bush years depleted the ranks of party moderates, which helped solidify Congress's partisan polarization. Compromise became a four-letter word. Those Republicans still inclined to make deals with Democrats often drew right-wing challengers, and risked defeat in their states' party primaries or nominating conventions where hard-line conservatives increasingly dominated. Even incumbents once seen as right-wingers themselves now were scorned as "establishment" Republicans, or worse, RINOs—Republicans in Name Only. They lamented that even the sainted Ronald Reagan wouldn't win a party primary—he was for free trade, signed an immigration law giving amnesty to millions of undocumented residents, and compromised often, including on deficit reduction bills that raised taxes. Yes, Reagan had said, "Government is not the solution to our problem; government *is* the problem," but he wasn't speaking in absolute terms—he'd begun by saying, "In this present crisis," referring to the economy. He also famously said that anyone who agreed with him 80 percent of the time was a friend. Now conservatives demanded 100 percent.

When Orrin Hatch was first elected to the Senate in 1976, he was, as he later put it, "the darling of the so-called ultra-conservatives" (he still was when I began covering him in 1984). He was shocked, then, in 2000 to be greeted at the Utah Republican convention with "lusty, full-throated, enthusiastic boos." He recognized some critics, including a woman who objected that he'd worked on legislation with Democrats, and a man irate that he was opposed to allowing guns in churches, schools, and mental institutions.[4] Despite the unexpected opposition, Hatch prevailed over three more conservative rivals to win nomination for a fifth term. His foes were more noisy than numerous. That would change, however. They were in the vanguard of what would become, in a decade, the nationwide Tea Party revolution.

In 2010, Utah Republicans ousted Hatch's respected Senate colleague, Robert Bennett, for a Tea Party challenger. Bennett's mortal sin? Compromising with Democrats, in particular on a health care bill. His loss stunned Republican incumbents across the country, but it was only the first of such mutinies—further discouraging incumbents from making the compromises essential to legislating. Bennett would again draw national attention six years later, for a story after his death in May 2016 that captured how radical his party was becoming. His son revealed that Bennett, in his last months, tried to counter the anti-Muslim talk of then-candidate Donald Trump, even offering kind words to veiled women in airports. "I want to go to every Muslim and say thanks for being in our country, and I want to apologize on behalf of the Republican Party for Donald Trump," he'd say, according to his son. Even in his final days, ill with cancer, he'd ask, "Are there any Muslims in the hospital?" Republicans like Bennett were literally dying off.[5]

In charting the increasingly nationalist, antigovernment, and uncompromising right-wing populism of grassroots Republicans in the years from Gingrich to Trump, the role of an expanding conservative media in the internet age—not just local radio-show hosts but websites like Breitbart News as well—cannot be overestimated. Fox News, born in 1996, was hugely influential, but the broader megaphone of conservative media was more overtly right-wing. These websites and broadcast celebrities both animated the party's base and reflected it, provocatively playing to their audiences' prejudices in the interests of gaining eyes and ears.[6] Of the four Republican revolutions in as many decades, three were led by men—Reagan, Gingrich, and, later, Trump—who each gave voice to a conservative movement farther right than its predecessor. But the third of the four upheavals, that of the Tea Party, was a bottom-up phenomenon, a headless movement of radicalized antigovernment and xenophobic conservatives taking their voice from talk-radio hosts, and vice versa. While conservative media had been allies with Gingrich-era Republicans, a decade later it had come—like its audience—to distrust the party as insufficiently militant, and attacked Republicans as much or more than it did Democrats.

None felt conservatives' sting more than Bush. His response to the economic crises late in his presidency—federal bailouts for banks, insurers, and automakers—only confirmed his perfidy for many on the right. They came to view his tenure as a lamentable bridge between two revolutions: beginning as a response to Gingrich's failures and, with Bush's own, giving the impetus for the Tea Party's rise. The Tea Party network would not take shape by that name until 2009 and 2010, when it arose nationally to oppose President Obama's economic stimulus and health care measures.

Yet the movement took root in Bush's final years. He'd inherited a nation that was prosperous, enjoying rare budget surpluses, and at peace, and left to Obama the worst recession since the Depression, a trillion-dollar budget deficit, and two Middle East wars. Bush had entered office amid high hopes in the party establishment that he and strategist Karl Rove would position mainstream Republicans for preeminence in the new century: Bush's "compassionate conservatism" and appeal to many Latinos would check the right-wing forces threatening to reduce the Grand Old Party to a reactive white man's club. Instead, once he'd retired to Texas, establishment Republicans sought to get right—literally—with their grass roots. They allied against a common enemy: Obama.

In Congress, Republicans would obstruct and oppose the new Democratic president from the start, as their leaders decided over steaks and red wine while Obama danced at his inaugural balls.[7] Almost eight hundred thousand Americans lost their jobs in January 2009, yet there would be no coming together. Given Republicans' defiance—and his need to act fast to save the finance, auto, and housing industries—Obama relied on the Democratic majorities in the House and Senate. Then he lost them in the 2010 midterm elections. Voters' dismay at the slow recovery, deficits, and his unpopular health care law allowed Republicans to ride the Tea Party wave. They recaptured not only the House but also numerous state legislatures. In 2014 they would seize the Senate as well.

To achieve their comeback in those years, Republican leaders played to the far-right base. They cynically made the promises—repeal "Obamacare," "defund" Planned Parenthood, balance the budget—they knew they couldn't keep. When they did regain power, congressional Republicans' failure to keep those promises revived the old intraparty tensions. So did the compromises they had to make with Obama now that they shared responsibility for governing. Trying to placate conservatives with a show of combativeness, Republican leaders repeatedly engaged in brinkmanship with Obama by opposing essential bills to fund the government and raise the nation's debt limit. But repeatedly they had to retreat and cut deals, lest they be blamed for shutting down the government or, worse, provoking a global debt crisis. Such risks meant little to the Tea Partiers and conservative media celebrities, however, and they slammed Republicans for backing down.

"They don't give a damn about governing," former representative Tom Latham told me over breakfast in Des Moines in 2015. The Iowa Republican, first elected in the Gingrich revolution, had just left Congress in frustration after twenty years. Republicans' race for the party's 2016 presidential nomination was under way. Neither conservative activists nor media stars had a favorite among the contenders. They only knew who they didn't want: Bush's brother Jeb, the former Florida governor, or any other establishment types. In the end, no one played the antiestablishment part better than a real estate developer turned reality-TV star, Donald Trump.[8]

* * *

Kavanaugh was far removed from the turmoil in his party, one of a panel of presumably impartial judges on the U.S. Circuit Court of Appeals for the District of Columbia, and raising a family in tony Chevy Chase, Maryland. Soon the Kavanaughs would have a second daughter, Liza. The charming, century-old homes in their community are large, but spaced closely enough that the blocks have a neighborly feel. Ashley Kavanaugh became the town manager for their village. Nearby, just over the state line in Washington, is the Shrine of the Most Blessed Sacrament, where the family attended Mass and the girls would go to school. Parishioners have included politicians, members of Congress, and national journalists, among them Edward M. Kennedy, Kavanaugh's Democratic antagonist on the Judiciary Committee; Kennedy's sister and brother-in-law Eunice and Sargent Shriver; conservatives William Bennett and Pat Buchanan; journalists Chris Matthews, Mark Shields, Cokie Roberts, Gerald Seib, and myself.

On the court, Kavanaugh continued to be "the consummate networker," as a longtime acquaintance described him, including at events for Democrats and journalists. Nan Aron, founder of the Alliance for Justice, a liberal group on the front lines against conservative judicial nominees, recalled Kavanaugh as among the first to arrive and the last to leave at ceremonial investitures for new judges named by Democratic presidents. He'd attend the twice-a-year parties of NPR's Supreme Court reporter, Nina Totenberg, and book-signing parties for authors of court-related works.[9]

When Kavanaugh first arrived at the federal courthouse near the Capitol, the balance on the appeals court favored Republican appointees. After Obama's first term, however, Democratic appointees were a majority; Kavanaugh more often found himself dissenting. He took predictably conservative positions, became known for his clear writing, and built an enviable record of having his opinions endorsed by the Supreme Court. Conservative and liberal justices often hired his former clerks, a signal of confidence in his judgment.[10]

Yet Kavanaugh's hiring practices would become a matter of some controversy. Women who'd been recent law students at Yale told several publications after his Supreme Court nomination that they were advised before their clerkship interviews that they should dress attractively, that Kavanaugh liked "a certain look," as one put it. The Yale advisers were well-known professors Jed Rubenfeld and Amy Chua, a married couple and friends of Kavanaugh's with a reputation for getting law students placed with federal judges. Chua was the author of a provocative best-seller, *The Battle Hymn of the Tiger Mother*. Rubenfeld in 2018 came under investigation for sexual misconduct at Yale Law School and in mid-2020 was suspended from the faculty for two years.[11]

One lawyer who interviewed with Kavanaugh and other judges in 2013 told me that Rubenfeld warned her about Alex Kozinski, saying he was well known for sexually harassing his clerks (further raising questions about Kavanaugh's claims in 2018, under oath, that he was unaware of any bad behavior by Kozinski, his mentor and friend). The woman added, "Then he said, 'Kavanaugh only hires women with a certain look.' He didn't say anything else." Chua, she said, told her to dress for her interview with Kavanaugh in a way suggesting she was "outgoing" and added, "Dress up, but do *not* wear a suit"—even though Kavanaugh's female clerks were known for wearing suits at his chambers. Friends told her that Chua told them to show off their legs, the lawyer recalled. "We all noticed that his female clerks were all very good-looking, conventionally attractive."[12]

She said her interview with Kavanaugh was "totally unremarkable." He fondly shared stories about George W. Bush. "I'm thought of as a conservative judge," he said at one point, to gauge how she felt about that. She told him she leaned Democratic but wasn't political. "He didn't seem too concerned," she said. Kavanaugh was known as the only prominent conservative judge who didn't show favor to students in the Federalist Society. The woman was hired by another appellate judge; Kavanaugh chose a friend of hers, another left-leaning woman.

The reports in 2018 of Chua's advice to female students, including in the *Yale Daily News*, prompted the law school to open an inquiry. "This is the first we have heard claims that Professor Chua coached students to look 'like models,'" an official said. "We will look into these claims promptly." Nothing came of it. Chua said that in the decade she'd known Kavanaugh, his "first and only litmus test in hiring has been excellence."[13]

Kavanaugh gained a well-deserved reputation for favoring Yale law students as his clerks, and students with family and professional connections. That is hardly uncommon among judges; certainly he benefited from such favoritism as a young man. "But he was kind of infamous for that," said a recent Yale graduate. "It was something that we would joke about a lot."[14] Among Kavanaugh's clerks on the appeals court were the children of Kozinski; Samuel Alito; J. Harvie Wilkinson III, a judge on the Fourth Circuit Court; and Michael Chertoff, a Bush administration colleague who became an appeals court judge and then secretary of homeland security. Just after Kavanaugh's Supreme Court nomination, Chua wrote a column in the *Wall Street Journal* headlined "Kavanaugh Is a Mentor to Women," and subtitled "I can't think of a better judge for my own daughter's clerkship." Indeed, he had just hired Sophia Chua-Rubenfeld, and ended up bringing her along with him to the Supreme Court.[15]

Kavanaugh set out to be known as a promoter of women. Yet lawyers and clerks at the court also saw his hiring practices as part of the ambitious judge's "long game," as one said, to build support for a future Supreme Court nomination. He certainly wanted to be noticed. "I wrote pieces over the years about the lack of female clerks and he would always email back and say, 'What about me?,'" said journalist Dahlia Lithwick, a former Ninth Circuit clerk. "He wasn't mean or defensive about it, just very much, 'Have you seen what I've been doing? I've been working really hard to fix this.'"[16] At his 2018 hearing, Kavanaugh recalled that after joining the D.C. bench in 2006, he read a *New York Times* story about the dearth of female clerks at the high court.[17] "I took action," he testified. Just over half of his clerks on the appeals court—twenty-five of forty-eight—were women. Most went on to be Supreme Court clerks. A quarter of his hires were minority students.

* * *

Lawyers who practiced at the D.C. court generally praised Kavanaugh as a good judge, who predictably favored corporations, police, and executive power. "He would be well prepared. He would be gracious at the arguments to attorneys on both sides, including the side he was going to rule against. He was never a bully," said Peter Keisler, who often argued before him. "You can disagree with particular outcomes or reasoning, but it was a very constant record he built." Of the criticisms when he was nominated—that he was partisan and inexperienced—the latter would be moot by the time he was named to the Supreme Court. Over twelve years as a judge, he wrote about three hundred opinions, lectured at law schools, and taught at Harvard for a decade, including a course on the Roberts Court he was destined to join.

Given the unique docket of the D.C. court, heavy on cases related to the federal government, Kavanaugh's record provided little evidence of his stance on women's and civil rights, the rights of LGBTQ people, or the death penalty. On the frequent cases involving regulatory agencies, he was a reliable vote for businesses, for employers over workers, and against environmental protections. When Trump nominated Kavanaugh for the high court, the White House released an unusual memo citing scores of times that he'd sided against regulators in cases dealing with clean air and water measures, consumer protections, and net neutrality.

Having worked for a president, Kavanaugh took an expansive view of executive power, especially in matters of national security. He was a proponent of the controversial military commissions created to try noncitizen terrorist suspects. Perhaps unsurprisingly for a former counsel to a president accused of condoning violations of international law, Kavanaugh proved hostile to claims that it could constrain U.S. government action.

On domestic issues, two of his stands—against gun control and the Affordable Care Act—would draw much attention during his Supreme Court confirmation process. Kavanaugh dissented in 2011 when the D.C. court upheld Obama's signature health insurance law,[18] and again in 2015 when it dismissed another challenge to the act. He called it "a law that is unprecedented on the federal level in American history." The mandate that individuals get insurance or pay a tax penalty, he said, "could usher in a significant expansion of congressional authority with no obvious principled limit." Yet in the 1990s, when President Clinton had unsuccessfully sought to require that employers insure their workers, it was Republicans who called instead for a mandate on individuals to have coverage. Republicans said their proposal, from the conservative Heritage Foundation, would promote personal responsibility. When Obama adopted the concept, conservatives abandoned it.[19]

Kavanaugh again was the dissenter on a three-judge panel in 2011, in *Heller v. District of Columbia*, when two Republican-appointed colleagues upheld a gun control law that Washington's city council had enacted to replace one the Supreme Court struck down. He argued for holding such laws to a legal standard that his colleagues explicitly rejected. In his dissent, he said semiautomatic rifles should not be banned because they now were in "common use." He also echoed the gun lobby in taking umbrage at the term "assault weapon."[20]

Among his most noted actions taking aim at government regulation was Kavanaugh's majority opinion in 2013 for a split three-judge panel, against the Environmental Protection Agency's landmark rule holding states responsible for air pollution generated within their boundaries that harms other states downwind. The Supreme Court decisively overturned his ruling by a 6–2 vote in 2014, with a rebuke that must have stung. While Kavanaugh, like many conservatives, called himself a textualist—that is, a judge who sticks narrowly to the precise text of a law in question— the high court chided him for suggesting "unwritten" requirements in the Clean Air Act. A court's job, it said, "is to apply the text [of the statute], not to improve upon it."[21] That slap cheered Kavanaugh's critics to the left. They often called him a judicial activist, usurping the phrase that conservatives for years had leveled against liberal judges. The EPA's rule had been two decades in the making, negotiated among states, scientists, industries, and environmentalists. The proponents said it would prevent up to thirty-four thousand premature deaths, and save up to $280 billion in health costs—many times more than the estimated $2.4 billion cost to industries. Kavanaugh's opinion throwing out the rule provoked a *Washington Post* columnist, Steven Pearlstein, to write a scathing column. Kavanaugh, he said, was "a partisan shock trooper in a black robe waging an ideological battle against government regulation," one of a new breed of conservative judges who "genuflect before the tabernacle of judicial restraint even as they throw themselves lustily into [the] pit of judicial activism."[22]

A further sampling of his antiregulation, pro-business record: In 2008, Kavanaugh dissented when the court upheld the constitutionality of the Public Company Accounting Oversight Board, a financial regulator Congress created in 2002 after costly scandals at Enron and other corporations. In 2012, he dissented from the full court's decision backing the EPA's authority to regulate greenhouse gases, saying the agency hadn't adequately weighed the costs to industry. In 2014, he dissented when the court supported the EPA's regulation of mercury and other pollutants from power plants; again he cited the expense to industry. In 2016, his target was the Consumer Financial Protection Bureau, established after the Great Recession to guard against the sorts of banking abuses that led to widespread home foreclosures. He ruled it unconstitutional, but the full appeals court reversed him.

In late 2013, a celebrated case pitted SeaWorld of Florida against Obama's secretary of labor, Thomas Perez. The government had fined the theme park company after the Occupational Safety and Health Administration found that SeaWorld was willfully negligent in the death of an animal trainer, who was attacked and drowned by a killer whale during a performance. A court panel upheld the penalty. Kavanaugh dissented. The majority backed the Labor Department based on what was known as "*Chevron* deference." The doctrine dated to a 1984 Supreme Court ruling for the oil company and against environmental groups. There, the justices had upheld an industry-friendly rule from Reagan's EPA—its chief was Anne Gorsuch, mother of the future justice—holding that when laws are ambiguous, judges should defer to the agencies Congress charged with enforcing those laws. Despite the Reagan-era origin of the *Chevron* deference, overturning it had become a priority for judicial conservatives, including Anne Gorsuch's son, who weren't inclined to be deferential to regulators in Democratic administrations. The hostility that Neil Gorsuch and Kavanaugh showed as appeals court judges to the precedent, and to regulatory agencies generally, made them especially attractive Supreme Court candidates to the like-minded Donald F. McGahn, soon to be Trump's counsel and judicial headhunter. (In another fluke of history, SeaWorld's lead lawyer against the Labor Department was Eugene Scalia, the justice's son and Kavanaugh's friend, who would become the department's chief under Trump.)

Kavanaugh, in dissent, assailed his colleagues' decision. He listed numerous unregulated activities, including rodeo riding and stock car racing, to suggest the broad ramifications of holding companies liable for harm to employees who accept the risk of their work—as SeaWorld argued its animal trainer had. This was the nanny state at its worst, Kavanaugh suggested: "When should we as a society paternalistically decide that the participants in these sports and entertainment activities must be protected from themselves?"[23]

Despite the rarity of women's issues before the court, two cases stood out as Kavanaugh increasingly was seen as a high court candidate for some future Republican president. In each, he pleased neither conservatives nor liberals. Yet by staking a middle ground, he arguably protected his prospects for being confirmed. After all, Kavanaugh was no naïf to Republicans' judicial politics: He'd had a lead role in putting judges on the bench for Bush, from vetting to seating.

In a case in 2015, *Priests for Life v. HHS*, Kavanaugh objected when the D.C. court in effect approved the Obama administration's concession to employers who, for religious reasons, opposed covering contraceptives in employees' insurance plans, as the Affordable Care Act required. The administration proposed that employers could avoid the coverage mandate by filing a form stating their objections with either their insurer or the government. Conservative groups, including Catholic organizations, weren't assuaged. But a three-judge panel decided the proposed form was not a burden, considering the government's interest in promoting access to contraceptives to reduce unwanted births. The full appeals court declined to review that ruling. Kavanaugh dissented. Requiring the form of employers infringed on their religious freedom, he said. Yet his stand didn't satisfy some conservatives because, even as he echoed their view of religious freedom, he acknowledged the Supreme Court precedent that the government has a "compelling interest" in contraceptives' use.[24]

The second case involved abortion rights. Kavanaugh had provided a clue to his views in September 2017, in a speech at the conservative American Enterprise Institute about the legacy of Chief Justice William Rehnquist. In it, he seemed to lament Rehnquist's inability to muster a majority against *Roe v. Wade* in 1973 and in subsequent challenges to it.[25] To that point, more than eleven years into Kavanaugh's tenure, no significant abortion case had come to the appeals court. A month later, one did.

Garza v. Hargan was a case bound to get attention in the Trump administration. It combined not only the question of abortion rights, but also the president's priority issue: immigration. In early September 2017, a seventeen-year-old immigrant illegally entered Texas from Mexico, escaping "severe child abuse," according to court records. Taken into custody, she was held at a shelter, where she was found to be eight weeks pregnant. She wanted an abortion. Because Texas law requires either parental consent or a judge's order bypassing that prerequisite, she went to a local court with help from the American Civil Liberties Union. On September 25, a judge decided that she was mature enough to act in her best interest, granted a bypass, and named a guardian, Rochelle Garza. Yet government officials refused to let her leave the shelter for the procedure, citing an administration policy against doing anything that "facilitates" abortion. Garza sued. On October 18, a district court judge ordered that the young woman—now more than fourteen weeks pregnant—be allowed to leave for an abortion. The government appealed and filed an emergency motion to stay the judge's order.

That's when Kavanaugh entered the story. On October 20, he was on the three-judge panel that heard arguments in the case. That evening he wrote the opinion for a split panel, reversing the lower court's green light for an abortion. Kavanaugh gave the government eleven days to find a sponsor for the young woman, by which time she'd be nearly four months pregnant;

if it failed, she could resume her lawsuit. His decision, and the prospect of more delays, plainly infuriated his dissenting colleague, Patricia Millett, an Obama appointee. She condemned the constraints on the young woman, called "Jane Doe," as unconstitutional—"a full-on, unqualified denial of and flat prohibition on J.D.'s right to make her own reproductive choice." The government didn't have to facilitate anything, she wrote—the teen had a judge's approval and a guardian ready to transport her and pay for the procedure.

Two days later, Jane Doe's lawyers appealed to the full ten-judge court, which quickly reversed Kavanaugh's order. Only he and two other Republican appointees dissented. Kavanaugh wrote their opinion, objecting that the majority's ruling was "ultimately based on a constitutional principle as novel as it is wrong: a new right for unlawful immigrant minors in U.S. Government detention to obtain immediate abortion on demand." He called it "a radical extension" of abortion rights. Seeking to convey compassion, even as he'd sought to delay if not deny the young woman's wishes, he described her as a girl "alone and without family or friends" in a foreign land. The government, he wrote, is "merely seeking to place the minor in a better place when deciding whether to have an abortion." He didn't mention her guardian, or the fact that she'd made her decision nearly seven weeks earlier, long before she'd reached the second trimester of pregnancy.

Millett, now writing for the majority, likewise evoked "a child who is alone in a foreign land," abused and pregnant: "She did everything that Texas law requires," and had a constitutional right to have an abortion despite being an undocumented immigrant. Yet the government would not allow her to exercise that right unless, "like some kind of legal Houdini," she could escape from detention. Her choice was to leave the United States and return to the life she'd fled, or stay and seek the unnecessary sponsor Kavanaugh proposed, even as her pregnancy advanced. That, Millett said, was the sort of "undue burden" that the Supreme Court held unconstitutional, and Jane Doe was now fifteen weeks pregnant—just five weeks short of Texas's twenty-week limit for abortions. Millett acidly dismissed Kavanaugh's claim that the court was permitting "abortion on demand" for undocumented minors: "Abortion on demand? Hardly." And she derided Kavanaugh for making an argument the government hadn't even raised—that the teen would be in "a better place" with a sponsor. More judicial activism.

With the appeals court's go-ahead, the district court judge in Texas ordered that the teen be allowed an abortion "promptly and without delay." She had the procedure the next day.[26]

Abortion-rights advocates were predictably outraged by Kavanaugh's actions, but so were some antiabortion conservatives. He pleased them by writing that the government "has permissible interests in favoring fetal life, protecting the best interests of a minor, and refraining from facilitating abortion." Yet he did not endorse a separate dissent by the more conservative Karen LeCraft Henderson, holding that a minor in the country illegally does *not* have a right to an abortion. The antiabortion group Americans United for Life came to Kavanaugh's defense. "Why Judge Kavanaugh didn't join Judge Henderson's dissent is a matter of speculation," conservative lawyer Steven H. Aden wrote. But Kavanaugh's dissent, Aden added, "states a pro-life view and supports the government's arguments, in a way that appears both pragmatic and wise under the circumstances."[27]

Kavanaugh threaded a needle, just as he had in the contraceptives case. He was on the "right" side in *Garza*—blocking an abortion, if temporarily, and using the antiabortion forces' language about "abortion on demand." Yet he hadn't gone so far as to reject the teen's right to an abortion—that might alienate the few moderate Republicans in the Senate, and hurt his chances for confirmation were he picked for the high court. His balancing act defined his dozen years on the appeals court. Throughout, he sided with business against federal agencies' regulations, building a record of apparent enmity toward *Chevron* deference that would recommend him to any Republican president. He checked other boxes for conservative activists: against gun control, the Affordable Care Act, and then, late in the game, abortion. All the while, he promoted the careers of women lawyers, including some left-leaning ones who stood ready to return the favor.

8

NUCLEAR WAR
AND A SUPREME STEAL

"You will regret this, and you may regret it a lot sooner than you think."

Barack Obama had been in office for six weeks by early March 2009, and it was no honeymoon. No president other than Franklin D. Roosevelt had inherited an economic crisis more calamitous: The financial, housing, and auto sectors faced ruin, and the entire economy by extension. Yet in Congress, nearly every Republican dug in against Obama's emergency stimulus plans. And now, all forty-one of those in the Senate—just enough to sustain a filibuster—chose this perilous time to send him a letter on March 2 that they'd also oppose his judicial nominees unless he first got their approval for any candidates from their states. As it turned out, Republicans also would oppose him when he did get their blessing.[1]

Even before the Republicans' warning, Obama had consulted closely with one of the Senate's most admired senior Republicans, Richard Lugar of Indiana, as he weighed his first nomination for a judgeship. The president wanted to elevate David Hamilton, a moderate district judge from Lugar's state, to the Chicago-based Seventh Circuit Court of Appeals. During Obama's few years in the Senate, he and the decades-older Lugar had built a rapport despite their differences in age and politics; they'd traveled overseas together and sponsored an arms control program. (Such bipartisanship didn't endear Lugar to the Tea Party; three years later, the six-term senator was trounced in Indiana's Republican primary.) On

March 17, with Lugar's support, Obama announced Hamilton's nomination. All other Republicans, however, aligned behind their leader, Mitch McConnell, in opposition. Those on the Judiciary Committee boycotted Hamilton's hearing, forcing a later one. Republicans filibustered on the Senate floor, even knowing that they couldn't prevail without Lugar's vote. It was seven months before Hamilton was confirmed. Among Republicans, only Lugar voted yes.

"That set the tone for the next seven years," said Chris Kang, an Obama adviser.[2] Democrat Patrick Leahy, the Judiciary Committee's chair, told his counsel, "They are not going to give Obama anyone without a fight." He was floored that Republicans were so eager to stymie the Democratic president that they'd snub the venerable Lugar. "David Hamilton went to Lugar's church," Kristine Lucius, Leahy's counsel, recalled. "His father was the pastor there, and his mom was in the church choir with Lugar's wife. Lugar was personally vouching for him!"[3]

Obama's bid for bipartisanship stood in contrast to his predecessor's first act on judges. At a televised White House event in May 2001, George W. Bush announced eleven appeals court nominees at once, a group that on balance thrilled the conservative activists in his audience. His choices had been vetted by Bush's team of right-leaning headhunters, including Brett Kavanaugh, with little consultation of Democrats. Eight years later, progressive activists unsuccessfully pressed for Obama to hold a similar event and introduce a lineup of liberals. Many would complain to the end of his presidency that Obama never tried to fill the courts with progressives like Republicans battled for conservatives—just as they groused that Democratic senators didn't fight hard enough against the right-wing nominees of Republican presidents. Senate Democrats generally saved their battles for the most ideological conservatives, though that label came to define most Republican nominees. In contrast, Senate Republicans opposed nearly every Democratic pick, even moderates—as Judge Hamilton's experience showed, and Merrick Garland's would.

After a quarter century of escalating battles, the nation's process for picking supposedly nonpartisan judges had become a full-fledged partisan war. From its start to the present, however, Republicans had an edge. They had a system to put proven conservatives on the courts—no more

Blackmuns, Stevenses, and Souters—and were single-minded in pressing it. They were backed by the institutional strength of the Federalist Society and other advocacy groups well financed by right-wing donors, and by millions of motivated voters. As for tactics, Republicans not only fought harder, but increasingly they played dirty. The rules-respecting Democrats never had a chance. "One of us is fighting with a rolling pin," Lucius said, "and the other is fighting with a gun."

• • •

Like Obama, Bill Clinton had also vexed many Democrats: After twelve years in which Ronald Reagan and George H. W. Bush filled the courts with conservatives, Clinton was picking mostly centrist Democrats and even moderate Republicans. "He didn't put his political capital in the courts at all," a party strategist said, echoing others. He also gave in too easily to Republicans, the critics said—chiefly Orrin Hatch, the chair of the Senate Judiciary Committee for six of Clinton's eight years in office. Before McConnell took power, for years Hatch was the Republican senator most tenacious about packing the courts.[4]

Clinton had been president just five months when Byron White announced he was resigning, giving Democrats their first opportunity to seat a justice in twenty-six years, since Thurgood Marshall. Clinton wanted to pick Bruce Babbitt, his interior secretary, a two-term Arizona governor and one-time presidential candidate. Then he called Hatch. The senator warned that he and other western Republicans would oppose Babbitt because of his record at the Interior Department of favoring the environment over ranching, mining, and other industries. "I explained to the President that although he might prevail in the end, he should consider whether he wanted a tough, political battle over his first appointment to the Court," Hatch wrote in his memoir.[5]

Having blackballed Clinton's candidate, Hatch suggested alternatives— and later took some credit for the only two justices Clinton would name: appeals court judges Stephen Breyer of the Boston-based First Circuit and Ruth Bader Ginsburg of the D.C. Circuit. "I knew them both and believed that, while liberal, they were highly honest and capable jurists,"

Hatch said.[6] (Years later, he'd say much the same about Merrick Garland to Obama, only to join McConnell in blocking Garland's nomination to the Supreme Court.) Clinton took three months and weighed forty-two prospects before picking Ginsburg. Contrary to Ginsburg's later status as a liberal icon, and an early legal career as a pioneering feminist, Clinton introduced her to the nation as a moderate consensus-builder based on her thirteen years on the D.C. court. There, she overlapped with Robert Bork and began a lifelong friendship with Antonin Scalia. A Clinton adviser confided at the White House announcement, "Our friends in the liberal community are not very excited."[7] She was confirmed 96–3 on August 5, 1993. Within a year, Clinton just as easily put Breyer on the court after Harry Blackmun retired. Again, Republicans weren't opposed, and Democrats weren't excited. While Breyer had been chief counsel to Edward M. Kennedy when Kennedy chaired the Judiciary Committee, Democrats there considered him "milquetoast." The Senate voted overwhelmingly to confirm him, 87–9, on July 29, 1994.

Clinton's ease in filling the high court vacancies was remarkable considering that he struggled from the start against Republicans' resistance to his lower court choices, as well as their opposition to his policies and their various investigations of him. The Republican-controlled Senate all but ceased confirming judges in 1996, in the hope that Clinton would not be reelected. Democrats seethed. Four years earlier, they'd had a Senate majority, but then-chairman Joe Biden shepherded numerous nominees of George H. W. Bush to confirmation even as Bush headed to defeat.

In Clinton's second term, two female nominees drew especially strong opposition. Sonia Sotomayor was a Manhattan district court judge, one of Bush's successful election-year nominees in 1992. Yet when Clinton sought to promote her to the New York–based Second Circuit Court, Republicans tried to block her. Rush Limbaugh warned that the liberal Sotomayor was on a "rocketship" to the Supreme Court, so eager were Democrats to seat the first Latina justice. It took more than a year, but she was confirmed 67–29.[8] Elena Kagan wasn't so fortunate. Clinton chose her for the D.C. Circuit in 1999, but with his presidency winding down, Republicans refused to give her even a hearing. She wasn't alone. Republicans' roadblocks left about a hundred judicial vacancies for the next president. That might have been Democrat Al Gore, Clinton's vice president and would-be successor. But by a 5–4 vote, the Supreme Court's conservative majority decided the disputed 2000 election for George W. Bush.

•   •   •

Kavanaugh and his colleagues in the new Bush White House worked at a furious clip in early 2001 to vet potential judges for all those vacancies, even meeting prospects in the evenings. By March, they'd interviewed more than fifty candidates to compile an initial list for Bush to announce in May.[9] Senate Democrats, meanwhile, retreated to a resort in rural Pennsylvania; they needed a strategy for dealing with nominees in an era when Republicans had come to value conservative ideology and youth over practical legal experience. In a 50–50 Senate where Vice President Dick Cheney was the tiebreaker, Democrats were the minority—and then Jim Jeffords defected. Suddenly in control, a senior Democrat, the Brooklyn battler Chuck Schumer, served notice: "We will not have nominations of rightwing after rightwing after rightwing judges. Judges will have to be moderate. The president will get some he wants, we will get some we want."[10]

Early on, many Democrats saw Bush as an illegitimate president. Now he was asking them to confirm hard-core conservatives, who'd mostly made a name in Republican administrations and politics, and to seats Clinton had been blocked from filling. Yet Leahy, like Biden before him, moved most of the nominees through the Judiciary Committee and the Senate. He shelved a relative few to whom Democrats most objected, including John G. Roberts Jr. for the D.C. Circuit. Several years later, when Republicans again were in the majority and attacking Democrats for their obstructions of Bush's nominees, Leahy had a ready retort: In his seventeen months as chairman, the Democratic-led Senate had confirmed one hundred of them—more than Republicans had in the two years since they retook control.[11]

Indeed, Leahy's pace angered some Democrats, including party leaders. "We were like, 'Slow down, you're killing us,'" recalled a leadership aide. "Leahy *so* did not want to be criticized for being unfair." A committee aide had a T-shirt made that said, "I confirmed 98.2% of George W. Bush's judges, and all I got was this lousy t-shirt." But Republicans focused on the few Democrats blocked, and none more than Miguel Estrada, the victim of the first successful filibuster of an appeals court nominee in history. Estrada's long ordeal so incensed Republicans that his name joined Bork's and Thomas's on the bloody shirts that conservatives waved in subsequent battles against Democratic nominees. Even some Democrats came to regret blocking Estrada, who was less conservative than some Republican nominees later confirmed to the D.C. court.

Estrada, a Honduran immigrant who arrived in the United States with limited English skills at seventeen and became a Harvard-educated lawyer, was among Bush's first choices for judgeships in May 2001. But Democrats didn't hold a hearing on him until the fall of 2002, too close to Congress's adjournment for Estrada to get a Senate vote. While he'd received the American Bar Association's highest rating, Democrats said the forty-one-year-old lawyer lacked the experience that should be required for the second most prestigious court. They also objected that the administration withheld records from Estrada's time in the solicitor general's office during Bush's father's administration; an unnamed supervisor had told the committee that Estrada showed an intemperate conservative bias in some memos he wrote there. An unspoken factor also loomed large against Estrada, one that recalled Republicans' own resistance to Sotomayor. "He was clearly going to be headed to the Supreme Court, and I think there was a real concern about that," said a Democratic counsel from that time. Bush, who was elected governor and president with more support from Latinos than Republicans usually got, was eager to make history, and score political points, by naming the first Hispanic justice. Democrats, protective of their edge among the growing population of Hispanic voters, were just as eager to prevent him. If Estrada were confirmed, the D.C. Circuit would be his springboard to the Supreme Court, as it had been for other justices.[12]

Republicans moved quickly to confirm Estrada after taking over the Senate after the 2002 midterm elections, but Democrats filibustered. They demanded Estrada's memos, though former solicitors general of both parties said such legal advice should remain private.[13] Seven times through 2003, the Republican majority leader, Bill Frist, held cloture votes to end debate but failed to get the sixty votes needed. Exasperated, he warned that he would resort to the so-called nuclear option, forcing a change in Senate rules to ban filibusters. But on September 4, Estrada gave up.

The fallout was immediate and enduring. Frist adviser Manuel Miranda was so enraged that soon he leaked to conservative media some of the Democratic emails he'd been poaching—triggering the events that would expose his theft and raise questions about Kavanaugh's complicity that would follow him onto the Supreme Court. Among the emails Miranda leaked was one confirming that liberal groups had urged Democrats to block Estrada to keep him out of line for the high court. Seven years later, still-resentful Republicans would question Kagan about Estrada at her Supreme Court confirmation hearing; the two had been friends since Harvard Law School. Did she believe he had been qualified for the D.C. court? Lindsey Graham asked. Yes, Kagan said, and the Supreme Court, too. The irony was rich: Kagan was being held to account for Democrats' blocking Estrada when Republicans had kept her off the same court.

The issue of court appointments became central to Bush's pitch for re-election in 2004. He needed conservatives to vote in large numbers. To that end, he loudly opposed efforts in some states to legalize same-sex marriage and vowed to keep picking judges who'd oppose the unions. "This difficult debate was forced upon our country by a few activist judges...who have taken it on themselves to change the meaning of marriage," he complained on July 10, in his weekly radio address. Afterward he and Laura Bush went to nearby Georgetown, for a wedding of the traditional sort—uniting Brett and Ashley Kavanaugh.[14]

*   *   *

No vacancy at the Supreme Court occurred in Bush's first term, and then he got two in the first year after his reelection. In filling those seats— he would get no others—the Democrats weren't the president's problem. Conservatives were.

His first appointment went relatively smoothly, despite a late twist. On July 1, 2005, Sandra Day O'Connor, the first female justice, announced she was retiring. Eighteen days later, Bush nominated Roberts, who'd been on the D.C. appeals court for two years, to replace her. As Roberts awaited confirmation, however, on September 3, Chief Justice William Rehnquist died. Bush nominated Roberts instead to be chief justice, and urged the Senate to confirm him before the first Monday in October, the start of the court's term. Within two weeks, Roberts was approved by the Judiciary Committee and then by the Senate, 78–22, with support from all Republicans, half of the Democrats, and Jeffords.

Then things got messy. As Roberts joined the high court on October 3, Bush announced his new choice for O'Connor's seat: Harriet Miers, his White House counsel. Conservatives were gobsmacked. She was not one of them, specifically not of their legal fraternity, the Federalist Society. They barely knew her, except as one of Bush's Texas cronies. Among the most outspoken critics, ironically, was the man still embittered by attacks against his own nomination years before: Robert Bork. Interviewed by conservative Tucker Carlson, then the host of a show on MSNBC, Bork called Miers's nomination "a disaster on every level." He went on, "So far as anyone can tell, she has no experience with constitutional law whatever. But the other level is more worrisome, in a way—it's kind of a slap in the face to the conservatives who've been building up a conservative legal movement for the last twenty years. There's all kinds of people now on the federal bench and some in the law schools who have worked out consistent philosophies of sticking with the original principles of the Constitution. And all of those people have been overlooked."[15]

Bork, a founding father of the Federalist Society, had identified why Miers was doomed: The conservative legal movement was too formidable by 2005 to be ignored by a Republican president. Leonard Leo, the society's vice president and a judge-whisperer in the Bush White House, had acquiesced in the choice of Miers. Now he was on the defensive. So were the Senate's Republican leaders. They'd bowed to Bush and said Miers could be confirmed by Thanksgiving, but rage on the right stopped them cold. She withdrew four days before Halloween. All the while, Democrats mostly stood back, enjoying the Republicans' infighting. "We worked really hard to get Democrats *not* to tank her," said Lucius, the former Leahy counsel. "We thought it would be *way* better if they did it."[16]

Bush immediately made amends to the right. He nominated Samuel

Alito, a Federalist Society member who'd been elevated to the Third Circuit by Bush's father in 1990. This was someone conservatives knew, given Alito's hard-right record, and they were appeased. (A prominent nonconservative also backed him: Maryanne Trump Barry, Donald Trump's older sister and Alito's court colleague, testified for him in the Senate; Barry, a Reagan appointee to a district court, was named to the Third Circuit by Clinton in 1999, as a compromise after Republicans opposed his first pick.) Democrats, including then-senator Obama, filibustered Alito but failed. On January 31, 2006, he was confirmed 58–42. All but four Democrats opposed him, along with one Republican and Jeffords.

•　　•　　•

With Obama's arrival in the White House, Senate Republicans made clear by filibustering Hamilton that the detente forced by the Gang of 14 was over. They put up more obstructions to his lower court nominees than they had to Clinton's. Yet, like Clinton, Obama filled the two seats on the Supreme Court relatively easily within his first two years, when Democrats ran the Senate. David Souter, out of sync with his party and comfortable with Obama choosing a successor, gave the White House a heads-up in April that he was retiring. On May 26, 2009, Obama selected Sotomayor to be the first Hispanic justice. For Obama, like Clinton as well as Jimmy Carter, diversity on the courts was more important than ideology, the Republicans' litmus test.

Conservatives and some Republican senators slammed Sotomayor as a liberal extremist. They made much of her statement in past speeches, "I would hope that a wise Latina woman with the richness of her experiences would more often than not reach a better conclusion than a white male who hasn't lived that life." Limbaugh and others on the right called her a racist. Separately, Republicans' allies at the National Rifle Association for the first time weighed in against a Supreme Court nomination, telling senators that a vote for Sotomayor would be held against them at election time. Her sin was joining a Second Circuit opinion that affirmed some government power to regulate gun ownership. (As she awaited a vote, well-known conservative judges on another appeals court ruled the same way in a separate case.)[17] On August 6, Sotomayor was confirmed 68–31; nine Republicans voted with all Democrats and two independents in her favor.

John Paul Stevens, another Republican appointee now seen as a liberal by a party moved so far to the right, announced his retirement the following spring. Obama picked Kagan, a second woman whom Republicans had once opposed for an appeals court, but successfully. Now Obama's solicitor general, the first woman in that job, Kagan had been among his finalists for the seat that went to Sotomayor. Scalia had confided to Obama adviser David Axelrod at the time, "I hope he sends us Elena Kagan."[18] Scalia's private endorsement reflected his regard both for Kagan's work before the Supreme Court as solicitor general and for her reputation as a pragmatic consensus-builder—in contrast with his own ideological fervor.[19] As the first female dean of Harvard Law School, she'd been known for welcoming more conservatives there; she hired then-judge Kavanaugh as a lecturer for what would be a decade-long stint. On August 5, 2010, she was confirmed 63–37, getting four fewer votes from Republicans than Sotomayor.[20]

High among Obama's finalists for both vacancies was Kavanaugh's colleague on the D.C. court, Merrick Garland, a highly respected moderate who had Hatch's endorsement. As the *New York Times* put it, "Mr. Obama ultimately opted to save Judge Garland for when he faces a more hostile Senate and needs a nominee with more Republican support."[21]

That time indeed was coming. Democrats lost their House majority in the 2010 midterm elections, and their Senate majority shrank by six seats; they'd lose it, too, in 2014. Republicans could make more trouble for his nominees, and did. They began filibustering nominees for the district courts as well as appeals courts, a first. Other nominees simply died in the Judiciary Committee without a vote when Republicans wouldn't return their "blue slips"—the forms, on blue paper, that the two senators from a nominee's state would give to the committee to signal approval. By a tradition dating to 1917, if a home-state senator withheld a slip, which was rare, the committee buried the nomination. A chairman could make exceptions. But Leahy was a stickler for tradition, even as he complained that Republicans were abusing it. In effect, a single senator could veto Obama's nominees.

In his first term, Obama couldn't fill any of four vacancies on the pivotal D.C. Circuit, where Republican appointees were a majority. Republican senators finally allowed Sri Srinivasan to be confirmed early in Obama's second term but blocked four other nominees—three women and an African American man. They argued that the court's caseload was light, that it didn't need more judges. Republicans had used the same argument to block Clinton nominees, but dropped it in the Bush years to put Kavanaugh and other conservatives on the D.C. bench. Ahead of a vote in the Judiciary Committee for one Bush nominee, Democratic counsel Jennifer Duck sardonically reminded a Republican counterpart of his boss's Clinton-era claims about the court having enough judges. He laughed. "Jennifer, we don't care what he said back then."[22]

After nearly five years of such obstructions against Obama nominees, the Senate majority leader, Reid, had had enough. On November 21, 2013, he resorted to the nuclear option—the extreme step that he'd so opposed when Frist threatened it in 2005. Most Senate Democrats predictably voted for their leader's motion, effectively banning filibusters of presidential nominees other than those for the Supreme Court. No longer would those chosen for lower courts and executive branch posts need sixty votes to be confirmed; a simple majority would do. Three Democrats joined Republicans in opposition, and some who voted yes did so reluctantly: While Democrats were the majority for now, they knew they would be powerless to stop right-wing nominees in such times—not so far off— when Republicans controlled both the White House and the Senate. The dissident Democrats included Schumer, who soon would succeed Reid.

McConnell delivered a warning to Democrats—a self-fulfilling prophecy, really: "You will regret this, and you may regret it a lot sooner than you think." Just over three years later, when he'd become the majority leader and Trump the president, McConnell led Republicans in ending filibusters of Supreme Court nominees as well, to confirm Neil Gorsuch. Some Democrats would blame themselves for inviting McConnell's action. But many believed that he would have gone nuclear in any case, given his ruthless quest to pack the courts.

For just over a year, through 2014, Obama and Democrats made important gains, thanks to the change: Three nominees finally were confirmed for the D.C. Circuit and more than a hundred others became judges. To many Democrats' chagrin, however, Leahy hewed to the blue slip tradition, allowing Republicans to block some nominees. Texans Ted Cruz and John Cornyn withheld their slips for two nominees for the Fifth Circuit, which handles cases from Texas, Louisiana, and Mississippi; Trump would fill the seats, giving conservatives control. After 2014, when Republicans won a majority, the Senate confirmed just two appellate judges in Obama's final two years—the fewest during a Congress since the nineteenth century.

McConnell, as majority leader, even blocked consensus candidates. A prime example involved a seat on the Seventh Circuit for a nominee from Wisconsin. It had been vacant since 2010, largely because the Tea Party senator elected that year in Wisconsin, Ron Johnson, opposed Obama's pick. When the president named a compromise nominee, Johnson finally returned his blue slip—in 2016. The Judiciary Committee approved the nomination, yet McConnell would not hold a Senate vote. Trump got to fill that seat, too: In 2018, the Senate narrowly confirmed his nominee— Michael Brennan, cofounder of Milwaukee's Federalist Society chapter— though Wisconsin's other senator, Democrat Tammy Baldwin, withheld her blue slip. Baldwin objected not only because McConnell had blocked Obama's nominee, but also because Trump, in picking Brennan, snubbed Wisconsin's bipartisan judicial selection commission—the sort of panel that some states use to reduce the politics in picking judges. Grassley, unlike Leahy, had the Judiciary Committee vote for Brennan despite Baldwin's opposition. "The blue slip courtesy is just that—a courtesy," Grassley said— ignoring his own prior fealty to the tradition. To Democrats, Brennan's subsequent Senate confirmation was especially revolting: He had vocally defended Johnson's right to use his blue slip to block Obama nominees. Now he was a judge only because his state's Democratic senator had been denied that right.[23] Numerous Trump nominees similarly would be confirmed despite objections from home-state Democratic senators.

Republicans' hardball tactics prevented Obama from filling another Seventh Circuit seat, which would have huge ramifications for the Supreme Court. In 2016, he chose Myra Selby, who'd been the first woman and African American on Indiana's Supreme Court. Dan Coats, then a Republican senator from Indiana, withheld his blue slip and Grassley declined to give Selby a hearing. The next year, Trump picked Notre Dame law professor Amy Coney Barrett, a former Scalia clerk well known for opposing *Roe v. Wade*. She was confirmed, and Trump added her name to his short list of Supreme Court prospects.

For all of Republicans' obstructions, Obama's overall tally of confirmed judges wasn't bad, helped as he was by Reid's nuclear strike and Democrats' control of the Senate for six of his eight years as president. When he took office, Republican-named judges were majorities on ten appeals courts, and Democratic appointees on just one—the California-based Ninth. Two courts were split. When Obama retired, nine courts had majorities of Democratic appointees and four had Republican majorities. Neither Clinton nor Bush had achieved a similar shift in eight years. Clinton inherited Republican-appointed majorities on every appeals court and flipped the balance on just three. Bush restored the conservative edge on one of those and increased conservative majorities on the others.[24] Kang, the Obama adviser, noted that in a federal judiciary with a combined 852 seats on the appeals and district courts, Obama and Bush each won confirmation of 324 judges. By rights, however, Obama should have filled more seats.

Obama, Bush, and Clinton all faced a Senate controlled by the other party in their last two-year Congress, but their respective records for confirmed judges show just how obstructive the Republicans, under McConnell, had become in Obama's time. Clinton and Bush had strikingly similar outcomes in their final two years: Clinton saw seventy judges confirmed, fifty-seven for district courts and thirteen for appeals courts; Bush got sixty-eight approved, fifty-eight on district courts and ten on appeals courts. Obama's tally? Just twenty judges, eighteen for district courts and two for appeals courts—the lowest total since Harry Truman.[25]

Kang's regret was that in the first six years of Obama's presidency, when Democrats controlled the Senate, they didn't focus more on trying to shape the judiciary philosophically, as Republicans did. That sentiment moved him to become a founder and general counsel for Demand Justice, a liberal group formed after Trump's election to counter those on the right, like the Federalist Society. Its mission: to spur Senate Democrats to fight harder against Republican nominees, and to persuade left-of-center voters to cast their ballots for presidents and senators with the courts top of mind—in short, for Democrats to be as single-minded and cutthroat as McConnell.

•   •   •

The midwinter Presidents' Day weekend is a popular time for many in Washington to get away to warmer places. In 2016, with the Senate in recess, McConnell and his wife, Elaine Chao, escaped to the Virgin Islands. They'd just arrived on sunny St. Thomas on Saturday, February 13, when an aide interrupted with news: Scalia, the Supreme Court's longest-serving justice and a conservative icon, had been found dead that morning in his bed at a luxury ranch in remote West Texas, where he'd gone to hunt. A Scalia family member told the Federalist Society's Leo, who quickly called McConnell's adviser for judicial nominations. McConnell and Scalia were friends going back to the 1970s, when McConnell was a junior staffer at the Justice Department and Scalia headed its Office of Legal Counsel. Even so, no sentimentalist, McConnell instinctively turned to politics—to considering what a fight for control of the nation's highest court would mean for mobilizing conservative voters in that election year. Obama's pick, if confirmed, could give the left a majority on the court for years to come. So what if he still had a year to serve? McConnell resolved that Obama would not fill Scalia's seat.[26]

The chain of communications within hours of the discovery of the body—from Scalia's family to Leo to McConnell—captured just how invested each of those parties was in the long game to lock up the courts for conservatives. Scalia had mentored the creators of the Federalist Society thirty-four years before. Leo was the group's liaison to Republican presidents and senators. And McConnell was committed to making the realization of "the judges project" his legacy. Ultimately, this one senator's brazen and unprecedented decision would shake all three branches of government, and succeed even beyond his hopes.

McConnell mainly wanted to rally conservatives to reelect Republicans' Senate majority. Neither he nor most other Republican leaders really expected their party to win the White House, especially if the clownish Trump were its nominee. Yet Trump did win, and Senate Republicans, too. Now, thanks to McConnell, the party could take the third branch of government as well. The nation paid a price, however: The events would not only poison the Senate's confirmation politics far beyond their already noxious state, but also persuade many Americans that the judicial branch was no less partisan than the other two. Against that backdrop, the Senate just over two years later would take up Kavanaugh's nomination to the Supreme Court.

McConnell would later say of his decision that day on a Caribbean island, "The first thing that came into my mind was that I knew, if the shoe was on the other foot, [Democrats] wouldn't fill this vacancy. I knew it for sure."[27] Democrats angrily rejected his contention—a Democratic-controlled Senate confirmed Anthony M. Kennedy in early 1988, a presidential election year. "The circumstances were as close as they could be, and we went forward with Kennedy as Democrats," Senator Dick Durbin told me. Speaking of McConnell, he added, "What he has done, sadly, is really damaging to the Senate as an institution, more damaging than anything else in the twenty-plus years I've been here. To deny to a president the opportunity to fill a vacant seat in the Supreme Court is as serious a constitutional decision as any Republican leader can make. And the way they did it was so low-rent—wouldn't even entertain meeting with Garland."[28]

·   ·   ·

McConnell moved fast on that Saturday—he was anxious to put down his marker before the Republican presidential candidates met that night for a debate in Greenville, South Carolina. He feared that Cruz, his grandstanding Senate nemesis, would issue his own call to block any Obama nominee, and then other Republican senators might balk at seeming to follow the unpopular Texan's lead. Just after 6 p.m., pre-debate, McConnell released his bombshell statement: "The American people should have a voice in the selection of their next Supreme Court justice. Therefore, this vacancy should not be filled until we have a new president."

He emailed it to Republican senators, noting falsely, "It has been 80 years since a new justice was confirmed in an election year." Few Republicans seemed troubled then or in subsequent weeks by the precedent being set. But three years later, Jeff Flake of Arizona, by then retired from the Senate, lamented McConnell's move against Garland's nomination to me: "It was pretty much, 'This is what's going to happen, whether the Judiciary Committee wants to do this or not.' The leader would not bring it to the floor, so it was pretty much a done deal. But it wasn't right, in my view."[29] Flake and Hatch at one point each suggested that the Senate might act in a post-election lame-duck session—in other words, if Hillary Clinton won, Republicans might allow a vote.

Obama and his advisers weren't shocked by McConnell's statement, having dealt with him for seven years. The question was whether he could sustain his ploy on something so constitutionally momentous as a Supreme Court seat. "It was stunning but not surprising because it was consistent with the pattern he'd established from the very first day President Obama was elected," senior adviser Valerie Jarrett told me. Yet it was "inconsistent with our Constitution, which gives the president a four-year term and the power to appoint people to the Supreme Court—with the expectation that the Senate would do its job and provide a hearing and then a vote." She was among those in Obama's circle who believed McConnell could pull it off, however: "I can't think of times when his party bucked him." Even so, the president and his team mobilized to fill the seat. "The chances of being successful were not very great," Jarrett said. "But we owed it to our country to try."[30]

Ron Klain had been at the center of confirmation battles for decades, as an aide to Senate Democrats, including Biden on the Judiciary Committee, and then in the Clinton and Obama administrations. He pressed for the president to quickly nominate Garland, now the D.C. Circuit's chief judge. After all, Obama had held Garland in reserve for just such a time, when only a consensus candidate could get confirmed. The sooner the president acted, the longer the blockade that McConnell would have to defend. Yet Obama and other advisers decided to vet several other candidates as well. Advocacy groups on the left lobbied for a more liberal choice, someone who'd excite the party's liberal base.[31]

Obama met with congressional leaders in the Oval Office on March 1 and asked the Republicans for recommendations. McConnell was blunt:

Don't waste your time. Leahy tartly reminded McConnell that every Senate Democrat had voted for Justice Kennedy in 1988. The Republican leader was unmoved. Months later, McConnell would tell a crowd back home in Kentucky, "One of my proudest moments was when I looked at Barack Obama in the eye and I said, 'Mr. President, you will not fill this Supreme Court vacancy.'" Obama pressed ahead. Just over a month after Scalia's death, on a mid-March day pleasant enough to assemble in the Rose Garden, Obama introduced Garland as his choice. But he did something more, which perhaps no president before him had felt compelled to do: He pleaded for the Senate to give his nominee a vote. "If you don't," Obama said, "then it will not only be an abdication of the Senate's constitutional duty. It will indicate a process for nominating and confirming judges that is beyond repair" and "provoke an endless cycle of more tit-for-tat."[32]

Republicans, somewhat defensively, recycled old quotes from Democrats to suggest that McConnell's move really wasn't so outrageous. For example, Reid had once said "advice and consent" didn't mean "vote." (Never mentioned was that Frist, Reid's Republican predecessor, had said in 2006, "As majority leader, I have fought to uphold a simple principle on judicial nominations: Qualified judicial nominees deserve a fair up-or-down vote in the Senate. It's our constitutional duty.")[33] Republicans got the most mileage, however, out of something Biden had said in 1992, a presidential election year. Should an opening occur on the Supreme Court, Biden said, George H. W. Bush should not fill it. Biden spoke in late June, however, not early February, and described a vacancy owing to a justice's retirement, not sudden death. He also made an exception if Bush were to pick a consensus candidate. Yet his quote rang true enough to the current circumstances to give Republicans a political talking point.

Most Republican senators wouldn't even allow Garland the traditional courtesy call, let alone agree to a hearing and a vote. Still, some Republicans, especially those up for reelection, were forced to defend McConnell's blockade back home. One blinked, and his experience showed just how effectively the nexus of conservative media and activists kept Republican politicians in line. Jerry Moran told constituents in Kansas that the Senate should allow Garland a hearing and a vote, saying, "I would rather have you complaining to me that I voted wrong…than saying I'm not doing my job." Conservative websites attacked him, talk-radio hosts howled, and Tea Party activists threatened to find a challenger to run against him. Moran hastily retreated, with a craven statement calling Garland "unacceptable to serve on the Supreme Court."[34] McConnell was even more biting. Ignoring Garland's centrist record, and Hatch's former endorsement, the majority leader absurdly sniped, "From a conservative point of view, I don't think you could have a worse nominee than Merrick Garland."

Not that it mattered to Republicans, but the American Bar Association gave Garland its highest rating, unanimously, and more. Its evaluation was likely unprecedented in its praise of a nominee. "Most remarkably," it said, "in interviews with hundreds of individuals in the legal profession and community who knew Judge Garland, whether for a few years or decades, not one person uttered a negative word about him." Sample remarks included, "Judge Garland has no weaknesses," and "He may be the perfect human being."[35]

While some in the White House hoped that McConnell couldn't sustain his roadblock against such a nominee, Democrats couldn't mount a counteroffensive to pressure enough Republicans to break ranks. Their failure demonstrated the gulf between the parties when it came to making political hay over the courts. Obama aides and party strategists said Democratic voters just didn't care the way Republicans' voters did, but it was equally true that Democratic leaders did little to try to rile their supporters about the high stakes as their Republicans counterparts did. Even Obama promoted Garland little after the first weeks, leaving politics generally to the party's standard-bearer in that election year. Yet Clinton was all but silent, stoking talk that she might nominate someone more liberal once— not if—she became president. With neither Democratic leader putting up a fight, the media and voters weren't going to remain interested. At bottom, the reason for Democrats' passivity was simple: They did not imagine that Trump could win. Clinton would fill the seat.

Garland wasn't even mentioned from the stage at the Democrats' convention that summer. In her speech accepting the presidential nomination, Clinton referred to the Supreme Court only in a generic promise to name justices who would back campaign spending limits and voting rights. Democrats forfeited the opportunity—a multi-night, prime-time national audience—to rouse voters against Republicans' unparalleled power play. "The convention is a political event and it's not an appropriate place to be talking about a Supreme Court nomination," Jarrett told me much later. "The American people wanted to hear about why [Clinton] is best positioned to be the president of the United States. Every minute you're talking about something else, you're not promoting her agenda."[36]

Trump was talking plenty about the Supreme Court nomination, however. He told an Iowa crowd that week, "If you really like Donald Trump, that's great. But if you don't, you have to vote for me anyway. You know why? Supreme Court judges."[37] For conservatives—particularly evangelicals wary of a thrice-married former casino owner who'd once favored abortion rights—it was a crude but winning argument.

Progressive groups active in judicial politics were livid that Democrats had squandered the moment. Not long after the convention, Jarrett called some of their leaders to the White House for a strategy meeting, and began with a question: "What are you all doing to get Merrick Garland confirmed?" Nan Aron, president of the Alliance for Justice, fumed until it was her turn. "With all due respect," she said then, "I sat through four days of a perfect convention but I don't think I heard the words 'Supreme Court' once. And the convention would have been a perfect opportunity for the president, who has the bully pulpit, to talk about the courts." Aron went on, "If this was a Republican president who was denied the opportunity to name a Supreme Court justice, that's all that person would have talked about."[38] Jarrett told me she did not recall the exchange. Speaking of Garland, she added, "There is absolutely nothing we could have done to get him through, no matter what effort we went through, because McConnell had made the political calculus that he was willing to take whatever heat came his way in order to preserve that seat for a potential Republican president."[39]

In September and October, as both parties anticipated Clinton's victory, Flake privately marshaled support from other Republican senators for a letter advocating a post-election vote on Garland. He'd planned to send it, he told me, "after a Hillary Clinton victory that just didn't come."[40] As McConnell and many Republicans saw it, the open seat—and Trump's promise of a nominee bearing the Federalist Society's imprimatur—got

Trump elected. On that, if nothing else, Kang agreed with McConnell: "That fight ended up getting Donald Trump the presidency."[41] Of those voters who said in exit polls that the Supreme Court was "the most important factor" in their vote for president, nearly six in ten voted for Trump. More than a quarter of Trump voters said they chose him over Clinton with the Supreme Court in mind.[42]

McConnell reveled in just how well his gamble had paid off. Fired-up conservative voters not only returned Republican majorities to Congress, but also elected a Republican president in an upset. Trump now would partner with McConnell to put much of the government's third branch—starting with the Supreme Court—under the sway of Republicans, too. In victory, McConnell belatedly conceded Garland's qualifications. Having cynically claimed conservatives couldn't imagine "a worse nominee," two years later McConnell called Garland "obviously a well-qualified nominee" in remarks to the 2018 Federalist Society convention. But, McConnell added, his blockade wasn't about the man, it was about politics: "It was about who would make the nomination." He told his grateful audience that his philosophy for confirming judges dated to his time as a Senate Republican aide in the Nixon era: "Advice and consent means whatever the majority at any given moment thinks it means."

9

THE LURE OF A LIST

"Game on!"

Just hours after Antonin Scalia was found dead in Texas, he literally loomed over the six Republican presidential candidates assembled on-stage in Greenville, South Carolina, for a nationally televised debate. His enlarged likeness was projected above them. Moderator John Dickerson of CBS asked for a moment of silence to remember "the court's leading conservative," and five of the Republicans bowed their heads, eyes closed. Donald Trump looked straight ahead. Predictably, the first question was about the vacancy on the Supreme Court, and Mitch McConnell's just-announced stand that President Obama should not fill the seat. Dickerson put it to Trump: "If you were president, and had a chance with eleven months left to go in your term, wouldn't it be an abdication, to conservatives in particular, not to name a conservative justice with the rest of your term?"

"If I were president now, I would certainly want to try and nominate a justice," Trump readily acknowledged. But, he added, "I think it's up to Mitch McConnell, and everybody else, to stop it. It's called delay, delay, delay." Then, to impress conservatives, Trump name-dropped: He mentioned two appellate judges familiar to activists on the right—Diane S. Sykes and William H. Pryor Jr.—as possible nominees if he were president. He'd just learned their names that afternoon, from campaign counsel Donald F. McGahn. Trump and McGahn had quickly talked by phone after the Scalia news broke; Trump had to be prepped for the night's debate. McGahn suggested a third name—Brett Kavanaugh—but they decided that the George W. Bush protégé might not go over well among conservatives soured on the whole Bush family.

Ted Cruz, the Texas senator, also came prepared to use Scalia's death to advantage—and to undercut Trump, the rival shaping up as his biggest threat. Cruz name-dropped, too, saying he'd known Scalia for twenty years and familiarly offering condolences to "his wife, Maureen, whom he adored, his nine children, his thirty-six grandkids." Then he attacked: "The next president is going to appoint one, two, three, four Supreme Court justices. If Donald Trump is president, he will appoint liberals." Trump angrily interrupted repeatedly, twice calling Cruz "the single biggest liar." Cruz, an award-winning college debater, parried. He pointed to Trump's history of contributions to Democrats: "You know how I know that Donald's Supreme Court Justices will be liberals? Because his entire life he's supported liberals.... Nobody who cares about judges would contribute to John Kerry, Hillary Clinton, Chuck Schumer, and Harry Reid."[1] Trump soon would vanquish Cruz for their party's nomination. Yet the vulnerability Cruz had sought to exploit—Trump's weakness among conservatives who obsessed over the federal courts and the social issues they decided— was not so easily overcome. He'd need their energy and votes to win in November. Trump and McGahn had work to do.

•   •   •

Through the winter and into the spring, Cruz continued to fan the doubts about Trump. He'd remind conservative audiences, for example, that Trump had named his sister, Third Circuit judge Maryanne Trump Barry, as a potential justice; Cruz called her "a radical pro-abortion extremist."[2] As the candidates battled in the states' nominating contests, McGahn campaigned in Washington to win over Trump skeptics influential with social conservatives. Prominent among them was Leonard Leo, the Federalist Society's judge-maker, and an ally with other conservative Catholics in the antiabortion wars. McGahn asked Leo to draft a list of potential Supreme Court candidates for Trump. Then he hosted a get-acquainted meeting at his downtown law office between Trump and a small group that included Leo, Newt Gingrich, a few members of Congress, and Jim DeMint, the former South Carolina senator now heading the conservative Heritage Foundation. Afterward, Trump, McGahn, and Leo met separately. As McGahn had arranged, Leo gave the candidate a short list of prospects.[3]

McGahn intended it as a sort of private cheat sheet for Trump, so he could drop names at rallies or in conversations to impress dubious conservatives. Trump had a bolder idea: Make the list public. "Game on!" McGahn thought. Recalling the moment in late 2018, before a black-tie Federalist Society audience that included four Supreme Court justices, McGahn said, "I'd love to take credit, but it was his political instinct."[4] It was the instinct of a reality-TV showman, looking to boost his ratings. After the meeting in McGahn's law office, Trump teased reporters at a previously scheduled news conference to stay tuned for the "biggest breaking news:" Within days, he'd release a list of Supreme Court candidates. He had "already shown it to a lot of people," Trump said, which of course wasn't true—he'd only just seen it himself.

Speaking slightly over a week after Scalia's death, Trump then underscored the stakes of the 2016 election: "You might have five Supreme Court justices to be picked over the next four years, because we already have one and you'll probably have four more. So you could change the balance of the court very quickly, very easily." Trump noted that "some of the people that are against me say, 'We don't know if he's going to pick the right judge. Supposing he picks a liberal judge, or supposing he picks a pro-choice judge?'" Given that, he said, he would do what no presidential candidate had ever done: tell voters who he would consider nominating, and stick to that list as president. "That's a good idea, right?"[5]

It took more than a few days—eight weeks, actually—for the campaign to produce the list. In that time a few names were added and all of them had to be vetted. Though the Heritage Foundation was involved, Leo took the lead. A father of six, always nattily dressed, Leo was the face of the Federalist Society, more widely known than either its more reticent president, Eugene B. Meyer, or its still-active founders. His high profile rankled some members, who privately complained that he was a self-promoter and too absorbed with antiabortion politics; many Federalist

Society members were of a libertarian bent, more interested in questions of restraining government power than in social issues. "He only has power because he speaks for a network that's much larger than he is," a network that over nearly four decades had become part of "the infrastructure" of the Republican Party, Steven M. Teles, a scholar of the conservative legal movement, told me. Leo typically took a leave from the Federalist Society when he worked on Supreme Court nominations, to maintain appearances: The society insisted that it is nonpartisan and does not lobby. He was so identified with the group, however, that few people separated the two. That vexed Meyer. In July 2019, the *Washington Post* published his objection to its coverage: "The Federalist Society has never participated in the judicial selection and confirmation process. Individuals associated with the society have, but never representing themselves as speaking or acting for the organization."[6]

Trump's list became known as the society's work, not least because he said himself that his high court prospects were "all picked by the Federalist Society."[7] Meyer aside, "The Federalist Society was perfectly happy not to disabuse the press and public of the association," said a longtime member and officer, "because, frankly, we like the judges." Meanwhile, conservative leaders scoffed at Democrats' criticism that Trump's candidates—like George W. Bush's judicial appointees—were nearly all members of the Federalist Society. With membership at more than seventy thousand lawyers, "It's a little like saying, 'Wow, everyone who was nominated was a Republican!'" said longtime member Peter Keisler.[8]

Trump's release of the list on May 18 would prove to be one of his most impactful acts for his candidacy, and ultimately his presidency. It named eleven conservatives—six appeals court judges named by George W. Bush and five state supreme court justices appointed by Republican governors. All the candidates were white, eight of the eleven were men, and most were young, in their forties or early fifties. Included were the two appellate judges Trump had named in the South Carolina debate—Sykes and Pryor. Democrats years before had tried to block Pryor from the Atlanta-based Eleventh Circuit Court, but the Gang of 14 deal cleared the way for his approval. As Alabama's Republican attorney general, Pryor had denounced *Roe v. Wade* as creating "a constitutional right to murder an unborn child," and he argued that a right to "homosexual sodomy" would "logically extend" to necrophilia, bestiality, incest, and pedophilia.[9]

Longtime court watchers puzzled over a couple names that were missing, one in particular. Trump's list "omits two of the biggest stars of the conservative legal world," the Associated Press reported—former solicitor general Paul Clement, and Kavanaugh.[10] John Malcolm, the director of the Heritage Foundation's Edwin Meese III Center for Legal and Judicial Studies, had recommended eight people and only Kavanaugh and Clement didn't make Trump's cut.[11] CNN analyst Joan Biskupic, a biographer of several justices, later wrote, "For years it was practically a Washington parlor game: Who would be first to the Supreme Court, Kavanaugh, a veteran of a prominent U.S. appeals court, or Clement, a high-profile appellate lawyer?" Kavanaugh, she said, was "a Republican golden boy with insider connections."[12] Yet it was just those connections that—for now at least—apparently worked against each man. Both were Washington insiders with Ivy League pedigrees, and candidate Trump was running against inside-the-Beltway elites. His court prospects were nearly all from places between the coasts, and graduates of law schools there. Like many Republicans on the rise, most of the judges on the list had served in George W. Bush's administration, so clearly Trump hadn't let that association work against them. Yet none were nearly as close to the former president as Kavanaugh. He was a Bushie. Still, McGahn knew the list would grow. He kept Kavanaugh's name in reserve—along with that of another conservative, Neil Gorsuch of the Tenth Circuit Court in Denver—partly to discourage early scrutiny of either.[13]

Just a month later, Trump confirmed that he'd expand his list. On June 21, he appeared before nearly a thousand conservative evangelical leaders at a hotel in Times Square. All of his picks would be "great intellects, talented men at what they do—and women—but also be pro-life," he told his audience.[14] Marjorie Dannenfelser, president of the antiabortion group Susan B. Anthony List, was sold: "When he said several times today 'pro-life Supreme Court justice,' that's the first time I've ever heard a candidate use those words together in one sentence."[15]

One after another, influential conservatives who'd publicly opposed Trump now supported him solely to prevent a President Hillary Clinton from picking Supreme Court justices. "It's the Supreme Court, Stupid," was the headline on a column endorsing Trump, by influential talk-radio host Hugh Hewitt.[16] Trump made it a staple of his speeches to raise the specter of Clinton filling Scalia's seat and three or four more. Stoking the issue days before the rivals' first debate in late September, Trump added ten names to his Supreme Court list. Again he opted for conservatives far from the Washington–Boston corridor of the eastern elites. His new group included justices on state supreme courts in Iowa, Georgia, Florida, and Michigan; two district court judges, among them McConnell favorite Amul Thapar in Kentucky; a Utah senator, Mike Lee (his brother, Utah Supreme Court justice Thomas Rex Lee, was on Trump's initial list; their father, Rex Lee, had been Ronald Reagan's solicitor general); and three appeals court judges, including Gorsuch.

Steve Bannon, the former chief of right-wing Breitbart News, who was now running Trump's campaign, had pressed Trump to include Lee as an olive branch both to the senator and to his good friend, Cruz. Each remained bitter about Trump's campaign attacks, in particular his unfounded charge that Cruz's father was complicit in the assassination of John F. Kennedy. The list "does not change Sen. Lee's mind about Trump in any way whatsoever," said a statement from his office. Like most Republican officials, however, Lee ultimately would fall in line behind Trump. And so would Cruz.

●　　●　　●

When a president wins in an upset as Trump did, many factors can be said to have made the difference. Virtually all analysts agreed, however, that a big one was Trump's unprecedented play using the court as catnip for conservatives. The exit polls of voters bore that out.[17]

And now Trump would be the rare president since George Washington to take office with a Supreme Court vacancy to fill—one of a chief executive's most enduring acts. He'd delegated his selection process to McGahn, the Federalist Society, and the Heritage Foundation, and the players went to work immediately so that Trump could name his choice within days of his swearing-in. Trump wasn't totally removed, however, especially since

McGahn and Leo sometimes disagreed. Early on, Leo flew to New York to see the president-elect at Trump Tower. The former Trump skeptic came away persuaded both that he'd have ready access to the president and that Trump would keep his promise to pick from the list of twenty-one proven conservatives. Leo was so thrilled, said a conservative with direct knowledge of the meeting, that he "could have flapped his arms and flown home without taking the shuttle."[18]

The man notably missing from the expanded list—Kavanaugh—was weighing another option in the wake of Trump's election. After a decade on the appeals court, he was restless; despite its prestige, its government-focused caseload could be especially dry. Kavanaugh privately made soundings about the opening for Trump's solicitor general, according to someone who spoke with him during the presidential transition. He apparently decided against putting his name in play, however. After all, he was on the court that had become the main feeder for Supreme Court justices. And he was still young, not quite fifty-two years old.

●　　●　　●

With so much advance work done, the process for naming a successor to Scalia moved quickly, and more smoothly than much else about the Trump team's amateurish operation. On January 5, 2017, two weeks before the inauguration, McGahn interviewed Gorsuch—his own favorite, and the top contender among six—at his Washington law office. On January 14, McGahn accompanied Gorsuch to meet with the president-elect at Trump Tower; separately, Trump met briefly with three other finalists as well. On January 31, eleven days after Trump took office, he called Gorsuch in Colorado to offer him the seat. The next evening, they appeared together in the White House for the televised announcement.[19]

Gorsuch had been confirmed as an appeals court judge without opposition in 2006, but the Supreme Court was another matter. Democrats were the minority in the Senate but they weren't going to make it easy for Republicans to fill a seat that rightfully belonged to Garland, as they saw it. Also, Trump had shown just days into his presidency how brazenly he would test legal and constitutional limits, underscoring the need for an independent judiciary to act as a check. He had banned travel to the United States from Muslim-majority nations, provoking chaos at airports and immediate lawsuits, and then fired the acting attorney general for refusing to defend his order. He'd mused about reauthorizing the waterboarding of detainees, in violation of federal law, and falsely alleged that up to five million noncitizens voted, costing him a majority of the popular vote.[20] Senate minority leader Chuck Schumer served notice that Democrats would filibuster the nomination.

The president told reporters that he advised McConnell, "Go nuclear." McConnell hardly needed Trump's spur. He had been ready for this moment for more than three years, since he told his predecessor, Reid, that he and the Senate Democrats would regret their votes ending filibusters of all presidential nominations except for those to the Supreme Court. Now McConnell and his Republican majority would remove the exception: No longer would nominees to the high court need a sixty-vote supermajority to be confirmed. They voted to do so as soon as Democrats started their filibuster. The next day, April 7, the Senate voted mostly along party lines, 54–45, to confirm Gorsuch.

In other ways, McConnell moved to prevent Democrats from slowing his race to pack the courts. He served notice in the fall of 2017 that for nominations to the thirteen appellate courts, the Judiciary Committee would not honor the blue slip tradition. Democrats could no longer block nominees from their states by withholding their slips. Republicans now argued that because each appeals court had jurisdiction over multiple states, senators from one state shouldn't have a veto. In going along with McConnell, committee chairman Chuck Grassley broke a published pledge. Two years before, in his state's largest newspaper, the *Des Moines Register*, he had extolled the century-old practice as important to consensus between the White House and the Senate on judges who served for life. He'd lauded Patrick Leahy, his Democratic predecessor as Judiciary Committee chairman, for upholding the tradition despite objections in his party, then added, "I... also intend to honor it."[21]

With McConnell, Grassley, and McGahn clearing the way, Trump was all but unstoppable in filling the scores of seats left open by Republicans' obstruction of Obama's nominees. Further infuriating Democrats, Trump repeatedly suggested at his political rallies that it was Obama's ineptitude or laziness that accounted for the vacancies. As he told a crowd in Richfield, Ohio, "When I got in, we had over 100 federal judges that weren't appointed. Now, I don't know why Obama left that. It was like a big beautiful present to all of us. Why the hell did he leave that? Maybe he got complacent."[22] In his first year, Trump won confirmation of more circuit court judges, twelve, than any president since 1945.[23]

McConnell gloated to thousands at the Federalist Society's 2018 Washington convention about his and McGahn's achievement: "I said, 'Don, you get them up here, and I'll make them a top priority.'" And with no risk of Democrats' filibusters, a narrow Republican majority could confirm even the most far-right nominees. "No Republican president could get the kind of nominee we'd want with sixty votes," McConnell said. At the prior year's Federalist Society convention, McGahn had delighted the audience by confiding that he'd come to the White House with two lists for judgeships—one of "mainstream folks," another of prospects "too hot for prime time"—and Trump told him to throw out the first.

Month after month, the White House announced Trump's latest judicial nominees in statements that numbered each new "wave." It was apt metaphor for the regularity with which conservatives were washing into the Senate for confirmation, and then onto the federal bench.

•   •   •

McGahn, meanwhile, sought to hasten the next Supreme Court opening— by making octogenarian Anthony M. Kennedy comfortable with the idea of retiring. Starting with Gorsuch, the justice's protégés were purposely prominent among Trump's judicial nominees; the aim was to reassure Kennedy that the otherwise capricious and impulsive president would choose well in naming a successor. Both Gorsuch and another finalist for the Scalia seat, Raymond Kethledge of the Sixth Circuit Court, were former Kennedy clerks, as were a number of Trump's lower court nominees.

Trump himself flattered the justice. When Trump delivered his initial address to a joint session of Congress and other dignitaries on February 28, 2017, he paused on his way out to greet Kennedy. "Say hello to your boy.

Special guy," the president told him. Kennedy's son Justin, as an executive at Deutsche Bank, had helped secure loans for Trump's company when other big banks declined to do so, given Trump's record of bankruptcies and stiffing creditors. When Kennedy came to the Rose Garden in April to administer Gorsuch's oath for the Supreme Court, Trump called the justice "a great man of outstanding accomplishment." In truth, conservative activists so reviled Kennedy—for his support of abortion rights, limits on the death penalty, and expanded gay rights—that some had called for his impeachment.[24] After Gorsuch's swearing-in, Kennedy privately met with Trump and recommended another of his former clerks for the high court: Kavanaugh.[25]

Seven months later, Trump took the first step toward fulfilling Kennedy's wish. In time for McGahn's special address to the Federalist Society convention in November 2017, the White House released another update of Trump's Supreme Court list, adding five candidates to the twenty left after Gorsuch's confirmation. There were two state supreme court justices, from Georgia and Oklahoma, two appeals court judges from heartland circuits, including Amy Coney Barrett, and Kavanaugh. "The minute the third list was put out with Kavanaugh's name," said Nan Aron of the liberal Alliance for Justice, "we knew what was coming."[26]

Many on the left were convinced that Kavanaugh's dissent a month earlier in *Garza v. Hargan*, the rare abortion-rights case to come before the D.C. Circuit Court, had tipped him into contention. A Democrat on the Senate Judiciary Committee, Richard Blumenthal of Connecticut, would say as much to Kavanaugh at his confirmation hearing. Kavanaugh candidly responded that the reason he finally was added to Trump's list was much simpler: "A lot of judges and lawyers made clear to various people" that he should be on it. That wasn't an accident—it reflected a behind-the-scenes promotional campaign that Kavanaugh was part of, conservative sources would later say.

Yet Kavanaugh had long been on McGahn's list. The White House counsel had to bide his time, however, to sell Trump on a "Bushie," and one who literally was born and raised inside the Beltway. "Trump came in promising to drain the swamp and to take on the establishment, and this is a guy who represents the Republican Bush establishment," said one Republican familiar with the backstory of Kavanaugh's nomination.

Kavanaugh appealed to McGahn especially for his opinions against federal regulations, for broad presidential power, and, now, as he'd written in his *Garza* dissent, against "abortion on demand." The two men, just three years apart and by now longtime players in Washington's politics, were social friends as well. In 2008, when Bush named McGahn to be on the Federal Election Commission, Kavanaugh swore him in to office. After the small ceremony, McGahn told his then-fiancée, "That guy's going to be on the Supreme Court someday." He could hardly have imagined that his prediction would become a self-fulfilling prophecy. By the meeting on January 5, 2017, when McGahn and other Trump insiders interviewed Gorsuch for the court opening, McGahn not only had decided that Gorsuch would get the nomination, but also that he and Bannon had their man for the next vacancy. "It was Gorsuch and Kavanaugh, back-to-back. The play was called," said an official who was present.[27]

It turned out, however, that Kennedy wasn't ready to retire. Often justices announce their retirements when the court's annual term ends in June. But as the 2016–17 term closed, no announcement came. Another year passed, and in the spring of 2018 another court term was winding down. Grassley, for one, was impatient. He wanted to steer another nominee onto the high court before the 2018 midterm elections, he told Hewitt, the conservative pundit, in an interview on May 19. "So," Grassley said, "my message to any one of the nine Supreme Court justices? If you're thinking about quitting this year, do it yesterday."

Seven weeks later, the justices met for the last time that term on June 27, a Wednesday. Trump called McConnell: Would Kennedy retire? McConnell was doubtful. McGahn knew better, but, to prevent Trump from leaking the news, he hadn't let the president in on the secret. Kennedy had secretly dispatched a former clerk, now a Trump appointee at the Justice Department, to give McGahn a heads-up that he was giving up his seat. Kennedy told his colleagues at their final luncheon that day, then went downstairs to meet McGahn, who was waiting in a government car to take him—and his resignation letter addressed "My dear Mr. President"—to see Trump in the White House. After a short visit between the president and the justice in the residential quarters, McGahn saw Kennedy off. His first call was to Kavanaugh. "We need to talk on Friday," McGahn said.[28]

Just before 2 p.m., both the court and the White House announced Kennedy's news.[29] Though long rumored, it still came as a surprise. The court's term had ended that morning without any retirement announcement, and reporters filed stories to that effect. Democratic lawyers on the Senate Judiciary Committee were relieved. Without a nomination to process, one exulted, "We'll be able to take summer vacations!" At the Alliance for Justice, Aron said, "We thought we were home free for about three hours." At about 2 p.m., she got a call from her office: "Nan, Kennedy's retiring!'" "Oh, God!" she exclaimed. Aron expected Kavanaugh to be Trump's nominee, but Democrats and Republicans in the Senate were skeptical, for good reason. McConnell had openly discouraged talk of Kavanaugh. The majority leader feared that Kavanaugh's long paper trail—from the Starr investigation, through the Bush administration and in hundreds of court decisions—would not only give Democrats an excuse to drag out the confirmation process but potentially provide them with ammunition against him, including proof that he'd been untruthful in his past confirmation hearings.

Speculation also centered on Raymond Kethledge and Amy Coney Barrett. Two days after Kennedy's announcement, a Friday, Kavanaugh met with McGahn late in the afternoon for the initial "SDR" interview— for "sex, drugs, and rock and roll," a joking take on the all-too-serious question of whether the candidate had anything embarrassing or even disqualifying in his or her past. They talked in Kavanaugh's court office for about four hours, "going through the usual kinds of questions you would go through when you're embarking on a process like this," Kavanaugh recalled later.[30] Over Monday and Tuesday, July 2 and 3, Trump met briefly with Kavanaugh and several other candidates, including Barrett, Kethledge, and Amul Thapar, McConnell's preferred pick.

As McGahn knew, Kavanaugh would have a broad network of support should he be nominated. Bush-era colleagues could be influential with Republican senators; one, Ohio's Rob Portman, was a senator himself, and friendly with swing-vote moderates Susan Collins of Maine and Lisa Murkowski of Alaska. Ready to help publicly and covertly were fellow members of the Federalist Society, former clerks, Yale alumni, judges whose nominations Kavanaugh had helped grease in the Bush years, and conservative media figures he'd courted since the Clinton years.

Yet Kavanaugh had his detractors on the right, for not being conservative enough. On Tuesday, the right-wing website *Daily Caller* carried a column headlined "Movement Conservatives Fume at Trump Scotus Favorite." One name on Trump's short list "has some influential conservatives cringing behind the scenes. That name is Judge Brett M. Kavanaugh," the columnist began. He quoted outraged leaders of several prominent groups, and said their criticisms "are beginning to reach Trump." One unnamed source went so far as to say, "Kavanaugh is crashing and burning today." According to the writer, activists complained that McGahn—one of Kavanaugh's "cocktail circuit buddies"—hadn't been honest with Trump about Kavanaugh's "weaknesses," including his Bush ties and his squishy rulings on Obamacare and abortion.[31] Another article said that "sources familiar with Trump's thinking say he is likely to be turned off by the judge's former work with Bush and his marriage to Bush's former secretary."[32]

As similar reports appeared elsewhere in conservative media, Kavanaugh's allies, including former clerks, pushed back in his defense on other websites. They worked out of the judge's chambers, alongside Kavanaugh; after all, few had more experience than he did at Republicans' judicial politics game. Kavanaugh also faced trouble from the party's moderate side. When McGahn brought Collins and Murkowski to the White House to speak with Trump following Kennedy's announcement, Collins encouraged the president to set aside his list and "to look instead for a candidate who had previously been confirmed with bipartisan support." That hardly described Kavanaugh. Collins recommended Joan Larsen, a Trump appointee to the Sixth Circuit Court who'd been confirmed with the support of the two Democratic senators from Larsen's home state, Michigan.[33] Even Ashley Kavanaugh was not pulling for her husband. "Perhaps because that earlier confirmation battle had been so brutal, Ashley prayed that God would deliver them from another," conservative activists Mollie Hemingway and Carrie Severino wrote in their account of the nomination. "She was proud he was a front-runner for the Supreme Court, but she hoped he would not be nominated."[34]

Trump, in his usual reality-show fashion, put out the word that he would reveal his choice in prime time on Monday, July 9. On Saturday, he tweeted from his Bedminster, New Jersey, golf club, "Big decision will soon be made on our next Justice of the Supreme Court!" Yet he remained undecided. McConnell, in phone calls with Trump and McGahn, pressed for either Kethledge or Thomas Hardiman, another appeals court judge; Thapar was out of the running. McConnell warned Trump that Kavanaugh's paper trail at a minimum would delay confirmation and at worst could sink him.[35] Simply rehashing the Bush-era controversies on presidential war powers, government surveillance, and detainees' torture could alienate Kentucky's other senator, libertarian Rand Paul. Conservative media was predicting that Paul would oppose Kavanaugh.

"That entire weekend, it was really up in the air. Trump had truly not made up his mind," said a conservative privy to the insiders' deliberations. Leo also was having second thoughts about Kavanaugh. Trump adviser Kellyanne Conway favored Barrett, who shared her staunch anti-abortion views.[36] From Bedminster, Trump canvassed friends by phone. On Sunday he called Leo, who suggested that the president meet with Kavanaugh again.

Kavanaugh was on his way to the 5:30 p.m. Mass at Blessed Sacrament when he got a call to come to the White House at 7:00. After the Mass, he changed into a suit that his wife had brought to him, while his security guard drove downtown. In the White House residence, he met for more than an hour with the president and Melania Trump. Trump's qualms apparently were allayed: He ended the visit by telling Kavanaugh the Supreme Court nomination was his.

10

THE MODEL NOMINEE

"What rings true?
What rings false?"

Just twelve days after Anthony M. Kennedy informed President Trump that he would retire, the president was ready to announce his choice for a successor. In prime time, he strutted alone the length of the White House Cross Hall to a lectern just inside the East Room, and then stood there, taking in the standing ovation from the mostly Republican assemblage. He began much as he had in nominating Neil Gorsuch, by noting that "other than matters of war and peace, this is the most important decision a president will make." Trump paid tribute to the absent Kennedy, who was in Europe, for his thirty years on the court—a reminder that for presidents, naming justices is one of their most long-lived legacies. Like his modern Republican predecessors, Trump chose from among candidates young enough to match Kennedy's longevity; Gorsuch was not yet fifty when he was confirmed. And now the president introduced his latest pick: fifty-three-year-old Brett Michael Kavanaugh.

As Trump announced the name, the nearby door to the Green Room opened and out came the nominee, his wife, Ashley, and daughters, Margaret and Liza. Kavanaugh looked nervous as the standing ovation lasted more than a minute, longer than Trump's. The president, obsessed with TV ratings and crowd sizes, quipped, "I know the people in this room very well. They do not stand and give applause like that very often, so they have some respect." He called for Kavanaugh's "swift confirmation" and then motioned his nominee to the mic. Kavanaugh audibly expelled a breath as he opened a binder of prepared remarks. He began by thanking Trump. Then he added a bit of hyperbole that struck many people—those looking for signs of his judicial independence—as troublingly obsequious: "No president has ever consulted more widely, or talked with more people, from more backgrounds, to seek input about a Supreme Court nomination." While Trump had indeed consulted with aides and allies—including Fox host Sean Hannity, while they'd played golf that weekend—any well-informed American knew that the president had picked, again, from a list compiled by officials of the Federalist Society and the Heritage Foundation.

Kavanaugh paid additional tributes: to Kennedy, his family, and even a priest he'd attended as an altar boy and with whom he now served meals to the homeless. He especially extolled his mother, for her work as a teacher, prosecutor, and county judge, and cited what he called her standard line on passing judgment: "Use your common sense. What rings true? What rings false?" He couldn't know how fully those questions would come to loom over his confirmation.

He recalled the motto of his Jesuit high school—"Men for others"—and said his career had been one of public service. He defined his judicial philosophy, echoing conservatives' mantra: A judge "must interpret the law, not make the law." He noted his eleven years teaching hundreds of law students, mostly at Harvard, and thanked the former dean who hired him there, Elena Kagan; if that suggested a tacit endorsement, so be it. Besides Kagan and his mother, Kavanaugh emphasized his relationships with other females. He boasted that a majority of his dozens of clerks had been women. He praised his daughters for their sports acumen, turning to slap hands with the precocious Liza, and drawing laughter by noting his nickname from Margaret's teammates—"Coach K," a nod to Duke University's legendary men's basketball coach, Mike Krzyzewski. And he told of his first date with his wife—on September 10, 2001—and of their years in the Bush White House in the aftermath of the next day's terrorist attacks.

"If confirmed by the Senate," he closed, "I will keep an open mind in every case. And I will always strive to preserve the Constitution of the United States and the American rule of law."[1]

* * *

After just fifteen minutes, the ceremony was over, and the president escorted the Kavanaughs to a reception. As the Republican VIPs celebrated, however, the scene across town at the Supreme Court foretold the fight ahead. Hundreds of protestors with signs reading "Stop Kavanaugh" and endorsing reproductive rights faced off on the pleasant summer night with antiabortion, pro-Kavanaugh demonstrators, each side vying to be in the camera shot behind reporters broadcasting live. Several senators—including two who would soon be rivals for the 2020 Democratic presidential nomination, Kirsten Gillibrand of New York and Bernie Sanders of Vermont—addressed the anti-Kavanaugh crowd, promising resistance.

Yet even as the left was warning that Kavanaugh would be the court's deciding vote against abortion rights, some conservatives remained worried that he was a squish on the issue. Tony Perkins, head of the influential Family Research Council, said he and other Christian conservatives would "trust but verify," adapting Ronald Reagan's famous phrase for dealing with the former Soviet Union. But the Judicial Crisis Network, the tip of conservatives' spear in court fights since 2005, said it was "ready on day one with a $12 million war chest" to promote Kavanaugh. It quickly launched a website, ConfirmKavanaugh.com, and a $1.4 million ad campaign in Alabama, Indiana, North Dakota, and West Virginia—all red states with Democratic senators, three of whom faced tough reelection contests in November. Republican activists, already going door-to-door mobilizing voters for the midterm elections, added support for Kavanaugh to their talking points.[2]

Republicans were poised for a bigger fight than Democrats had given them over Gorsuch. While Gorsuch was more conservative than Kavanaugh, he was seen as an even trade for Scalia. Kavanaugh would replace Kennedy, the court's swing vote, who'd protected abortion and gay rights and other precedents paramount to the left. In the Eisenhower Executive Office Building next to the White House, the administration set up a war room larger than its operation for Gorsuch. It included eleven lawyers—former Kavanaugh clerks and political appointees from the Justice Department—and communications specialists to deal with the media, marshal surrogates to speak for Kavanaugh on television, and generate op-ed pieces in his favor. The White House quickly distributed talking points praising the scores of times that Kavanaugh, on the appeals court, had overruled federal agencies' "job-killing regulations." In time, however, some tension would develop among Republicans as those in the Senate groused that the administration operatives, especially White House counsel Donald F. McGahn, weren't holding up their end of the confirmation effort. "They didn't really have a political or press operation," a Republican Senate aide complained to me. "They had an operation to find nominees, not really sell them."[3]

Most Democrats were predictably opposed to Kavanaugh. Only three had voted to confirm Gorsuch—Joe Manchin of West Virginia, Joe Donnelly Sr. of Indiana, and Heidi Heitkamp of North Dakota—and all three now were under greater political pressure, with elections in their pro-Trump states just months away. Republicans assailed Democrats, including Minority Leader Chuck Schumer, for announcing their opposition to Kavanaugh before he'd even had a hearing—an especially hypocritical attack from senators who just two years before had refused to give Merrick Garland even a meeting. Also, Kavanaugh was not a blank slate to Democrats. Schumer and others, notably Patrick Leahy and Dick Durbin, still harbored hard feelings from the past decade's confirmation battle, convinced that Kavanaugh had misled the Senate about his involvement in Bush-era controversies and the Memogate scandal.

Schumer was especially primed to oppose Kavanaugh, even as he was realistic that without the filibuster and its sixty-vote hurdle, Democrats likely had little chance of stopping the nominee. They had to put up a fight, more than they had against Gorsuch, given that both the stakes for the court and the expectations of Democratic voters were higher. After Trump announced Kavanaugh's nomination, Schumer met with aides to draft a response. "You should go look at what you said last time," one told him. They didn't have to search the *Congressional Record* for Schumer's 2006 speech in the Senate against Kavanaugh. Instantly another aide used his phone to call up a video of it. With Schumer at the center, the group huddled around the small screen, replaying his complaints that Kavanaugh was too young and inexperienced, that his career had been "almost exclusively political," and that his nomination to the appeals court smacked of "repayment for services rendered to the political operation of the White House and the Republican Party."[4]

Kavanaugh had since spent a dozen years as a respected jurist on the D.C. court, making the inexperience argument moot and criticism of his credibility and partisanship more difficult. Still, Democrats were confident that there had to be evidence of what they could only allege in 2004 and 2006—that he'd lied to them under oath. Just as Mitch McConnell feared, Democrats would press for full disclosure of Kavanaugh's records, including emails from his five and a half years in the White House, that were unavailable before his prior confirmation. Durbin and Leahy recalled now that Kavanaugh never responded to them in 2007—after he'd become a judge—when evidence surfaced in the media that seemed to confirm he'd lied about his knowledge of Bush's warrantless surveillance order. "Still waiting for a response to my 2007 letter," Durbin quipped after Kavanaugh's nomination to the Supreme Court.[5]

Schumer quickly took the lead in trying to corral Democrats and the Senate's two independents behind a strategy of opposition that would keep them all united—including Manchin, Donnelly, and Heitkamp—and pick off a couple of the moderate Republicans. Given Republicans' slim 51–49 majority, Democrats' hopes hinged on defections by Lisa Murkowski of Alaska, retiring Arizonan Jeff Flake, and perhaps Susan Collins, an abortion-rights advocate up for reelection in 2020. Schumer would call the Democrats on the Judiciary Committee together in his office, or hold conference calls. An incessant phone caller, he also reached them individually. While Schumer's zeal reflected the political animal that he was, his hands-on role also was a matter of necessity: The committee's senior Democrat, eighty-five-year-old Dianne Feinstein, wasn't up to the job, given the toll of age and the distraction of her reelection race in California. Yet her colleagues on the panel weren't willing to challenge her to take charge.

The strategy called for Democrats to argue that Kavanaugh, in replacing swing vote Kennedy, would be a threat to both reproductive rights and the

Affordable Care Act. Eight years after President Obama signed that landmark law, its popularity had grown despite Republicans' constant attacks. Fears about the act's future weren't hypothetical. Republican officials in twenty red states, led by Texas, had filed a lawsuit seeking to have it struck down as unconstitutional; inevitably the case would make its way to the Supreme Court on appeal. "We set out from the very beginning to be really disciplined about how we're going to make the case," a Senate leadership aide said. Democrats would emphasize another issue as well: that Kavanaugh, with his expansive view of presidential power and immunity, was the wrong man for the high court in the era of Trump. Some Democrats argued that Trump had picked Kavanaugh for just those views, given the multiple investigations and legal cases in which the president was implicated.

Lacking the resources of Republicans who controlled the White House and the Senate, Democrats recruited outside help to comb through Kavanaugh's records and to mobilize opposition among women's, labor, and civil rights groups. A former Senate aide, Laurie Rubiner, returned to oversee about fifteen lawyers, who worked alongside staff lawyers to the committee's ten Democratic senators. Rubiner had begun work in the Senate years before on the Republican side, for John Chafee of Rhode Island, one of a vanishing breed of liberal northern Republicans in Congress. Later she switched sides, and worked first for Hillary Clinton and then for Richard Blumenthal of Connecticut.

Outside groups chipped in. We The Action was a new one, a nonprofit clearinghouse for progressive lawyers willing to volunteer assistance. It had formed only the year before, at a time when the new president's policies were leaving refugees, immigrants, and others in need of legal help. After Kennedy announced his retirement, groups on the left that were mainstays of judicial fights—including the Alliance for Justice and the Lawyers' Committee for Civil Rights—posted notices on the We The Action website seeking help in vetting Kavanaugh. "It was more of an information-gathering than a 'let's find the smoking gun' exercise," said Sarah Baker, president of We The Action, who'd worked on judicial nominations in the Obama White House. "A lot of lawyers volunteered."

•   •   •

At Kavanaugh's White House introduction, his emphasis on his relationships with women—his mother, wife, daughters, their teammates, his clerks and law students, Kagan—was impossible to miss, as his Republican handlers intended. Democrats and nonpartisan observers alike initially assumed that Republicans simply were trying to preemptively blunt opponents' image of Kavanaugh as a threat to women's rights, and to appeal in particular to Collins and Murkowski. Second-guessing about other motives would come later.

Collins had her private courtesy call from Kavanaugh—perhaps his most important—on August 21, two weeks before his confirmation hearing was to begin. Their meeting lasted more than two hours, and afterward she released a statement expressing confidence that he would respect court precedents, particularly on abortion. "I specifically asked Judge Kavanaugh if he had made any commitments or pledges to the Federalist Society, or the White House, about how he would decide any legal issues," she said. "He unequivocally assured me that he had not made any such commitments and he expressed his deep respect for the independence of the judiciary. I was also pleased to learn that Judge Kavanaugh believes, as I do, that Article III of the Constitution was intended to include the concept of precedent." Also, she wrote, Kavanaugh agreed with the statement of Chief Justice John G. Roberts Jr. at his confirmation hearing "that *Roe* is settled precedent and entitled to respect under principles of *stare decisis*."[6]

In remarks to reporters staked outside her office, Collins also emphasized that Kavanaugh told her *Roe* is "settled law," as if that were a guarantee he would not vote to overturn it. Critics derided her as either credulous or willfully misleading, noting that while Supreme Court precedents bind lower courts, the high court can—and sometimes does—reverse its prior rulings. As Schumer countered, "Everything the Supreme Court decides is settled law until it unsettles it." He also met with Kavanaugh that day, for more than an hour, and asked whether he believed *Roe* had been correctly decided in 1973. Kavanaugh's answer to that question would have been more telling as to whether he'd vote to overrule the precedent. But he predictably demurred, following the practice of nominees since Bork to avoid saying anything suggesting how they would decide an issue. Similarly, Kavanaugh dodged Schumer's inquiries about whether the

Affordable Care Act was unconstitutional, or whether a president can be subpoenaed.[7]

Collins remained publicly noncommittal. "You never know what questions are going to come up at a Judiciary Committee hearing where twenty-one individuals will be questioning him," she told reporters. Yet she had never opposed a Supreme Court nominee, Democrats knew, and her positive take on her meeting with Kavanaugh only seemed to confirm their hunch that she'd been favorable toward him all along. The White House had made sure of that before Trump nominated the judge.

•   •   •

Republicans settled on a novel way to deal with the Kavanaugh paper trail that so worried McConnell and so intrigued Democrats—they simply put much of it off-limits. For the two summer months between Kavanaugh's nomination and the post–Labor Day start of his hearing, the two parties sparred over what documents from his White House years would be made public. Republican leaders, working with McGahn, devised an unprecedented system for deciding. For decades, the National Archives had been responsible for reviewing and releasing nominees' records, in consultation with the White House; documents were withheld or redacted only if release of the information would violate certain grounds, including national security, personal privacy, and executive privilege. For Kavanaugh's nomination, however, the Archives would work with the George W. Bush Presidential Library to produce papers each had, but the decision on what to release would be made by William Burck, a former senior aide to Bush who'd been Kavanaugh's deputy in the White House, and remained his friend. The Republicans justified this apparent conflict of interest by arguing that Burck, as Bush's personal representative, would have to approve of the release of documents from the Bush Library in any case. By law, both the former and the current president had a voice in which presidential papers became public.

Even vetting the documents that Burck permitted would be a challenge given the deadline Republicans set: They wanted Kavanaugh confirmed and on the court before the October 1 start of its new term. Democrats erupted, objecting that he was being rushed through without a full vetting. Relations between the parties on the Judiciary Committee, already among the worst of Senate committees, deteriorated further. They became toxic between Democratic aides and the scrappy Republican lawyer who loomed large over the process: Mike Davis, the chief counsel for nominations to Chairman Chuck Grassley of Iowa.

The forty-year-old Davis had grown up in Iowa and was drawn to Washington—like many young people in a state where politics is a preoccupation, given its outsized role in picking presidents. He was a mail-opening intern in Grassley's Senate office for a short time, volunteered in Bush's first presidential campaign, and, in his early twenties, got a low-level job in the Bush administration. In the White House Office of Political Affairs, Davis helped to check the political suitability of prospects for federal jobs and appointments. He returned to Iowa to get a law degree, then clerked for Gorsuch on the Tenth Circuit Court in Denver. A decade later, in private practice there, Davis was a volunteer lawyer for the Trump campaign in Colorado; he'd brashly take credit for working his contacts to get Gorsuch's name onto Trump's second court list in September 2016. After Gorsuch was nominated months later, Davis returned to Washington to help him get confirmed and then briefly served as his law clerk at the Supreme Court. He reconnected with Grassley and soon joined his staff on the Judiciary Committee. There, he quickly became known in both parties as a political pit bull who'd do anything to win. As he'd proudly acknowledge to anyone, he was "crazy."[8]

While Davis would become a tenacious fighter for Kavanaugh, prior to the nomination he was as disdainful of Kavanaugh as he was loyal to Gorsuch. Like other Republican committee aides, he favored other conservatives on Trump's list. "To Davis and some other Republicans in D.C., Kavanaugh was a loser whose only constituency was blond wives who spent their summers at country club pools in Bethesda, Maryland," two reporters for *Politico* wrote in a book. "He took to calling Kavanaugh 'Bushy, swampy, chiefy,' meaning he was seen as a Bush acolyte who had spent his life in the 'swamp' of Washington and was too similar to John Roberts, the chief justice who disappointed conservatives by voting to uphold the Affordable Care Act. Kavanaugh, Davis was known to say, would be conservative '95 percent' of the time but would abandon conservatives on the 5 percent of cases that mattered. Davis and other Judiciary aides were also concerned that Kavanaugh would be outed as a partier—a frat boy of sorts."[9]

A Republican Senate aide conceded Davis's combustible, take-no-prisoners style, but added, "When you're in the middle of a war, and I mean *this* was a political war, you need someone—or multiple people—like that, who are leading the charge on a day-by-day basis."[10]

In the Kavanaugh war, Davis was on the front line of the documents battle. Democrats, as the outgunned minority, never had a chance. Lawyers who'd once worked on the Judiciary Committee staff in senior posts and came back to help were shocked by what they saw as Republicans' shameless break with committee practice. Jeremy Paris, Leahy's counsel for nominations from roughly 2006 to 2013, said he'd worked well with his Republican counterparts despite the confirmation fights of those years, under two presidents. "We would try to work in good faith," Paris said. "Sure, we had fights over documents before. But the sheer audacity of their process with Kavanaugh eroded all norms—in service of a partisan power play to put him on the bench, come hell or high water."[11]

Grassley, as chairman, was responsible for requesting records from the National Archives. Yet he didn't ask for anything from Kavanaugh's three years as White House staff secretary, on the specious argument that his job mostly entailed shuffling other advisers' papers to Bush, and the president's to them. The Archives said it couldn't finish even that limited assignment until sometime in October—too late for Republicans. On July 18, nine days after Kavanaugh's nomination, the committee's Republican staff lawyers summoned their Democratic counterparts to a meeting. The Democrats arrived to find Burck and attorneys from his firm there as well. The Republicans explained that they simply wanted to hasten the Kavanaugh records review by including the Bush team at the front end. Democrats objected. "You can't have a partisan, interested actor decide what documents the committee gets to see," the Democrats argued, according to Paris. As he told me, "The Archives—the non-partisan professional archivists—should do it. Then, if President Bush's lawyers come in and want to assert claims that a limited set of documents should be withheld, on such grounds as personal privacy, national security, or executive privilege, they should make the claims. And the archivists and committee can work it out. But the presumption should be, it must be, that the records belong to the American people, and the committee and the people deserve to see them."

The Republicans stood their ground. They also outlined a process further limiting access to documents. Some of those released, they said, would be labeled "committee confidential," a category used sparingly in the past for papers so sensitive that only senators on the committee could see them, and even then they could not publicly describe them. If Democrats wanted to refer to such papers during Kavanaugh's hearing, they would have to ask Grassley, who in turn could—*could*—seek their release from Burck. "I explained this whole process very methodically," Davis told me later.

Across the table, he recalled, Rubiner and another Democratic lawyer, Heather Sawyer, "were so angry." They challenged him: How is this legal? Rubiner suggested that Davis imagine himself in a parallel situation. Suppose a Democratic president picked a former Obama adviser for the Supreme Court, then designated the nominee's former White House colleague to decide which of the nominee's documents the Republicans would get to see. "So," Rubiner said, "If we nominated John Podesta to be a Supreme Court justice, you would be fine if we had David Axelrod go through the documents?"[12] They continued to press for Kavanaugh's records as Bush's staff secretary—after all, he'd once said in a speech that those three years "were the most interesting and informative" in shaping his judicial mindset.[13] Davis countered that the Democrats' demand was impractical given that Kavanaugh had arguably touched every paper that went into and out of the Oval Office; it would mean releasing up to seven million documents. He told the Democrats to suggest digital search terms, to narrow the documents to be retrieved. The argument went on. "You guys are completely unreasonable," he snapped, and walked out.

Schumer got involved. He called the archivist of the United States, David Ferriero, to challenge the Archives' stance that it could only respond to a request for documents from the committee chairman—not from Feinstein, or Schumer. Schumer's counsel called Archives officials as well. The Archives' position wasn't unreasonable, a Democratic leadership aide conceded: "From their perspective, if they were always going to be having to respond to two different document requests, it's going to become an unmanageable thing for them." But, the aide went on, "What we were trying to say is, 'You guys are enabling a process that is a really bad policy for you. Your job as the archivist is to protect history. And you're allowing this partisan process to cause a result which is, basically, ignoring or self-editing or covering up history.'"[14]

Other Democratic senators took action. In the month before Kavanaugh's hearing, Democrats on the Judiciary Committee filed Freedom of Information Act requests for documents from Kavanaugh's White House years—to the National Archives, the Justice Department, the Department of Homeland Security, and the CIA. Even months after Kavanaugh's confirmation, they had little to show for it. Throughout August, Democrats held news conferences, trying to interest reporters—and by extension the public—about what they called a Republican cover-up of Kavanaugh's past untruths under oath. But reporters took little interest, dismissing the controversy as a boring "process fight." Other matters grabbed attention and cable TV airtime—in particular the mid-August release of a tell-all book by one of the few African Americans in Trump's White House, Omarosa Manigault Newman, in which she called the president a racist. The Kavanaugh "process fight" couldn't compete. "We said he was perjuring himself," Rubiner said. "But every morning I would get up and I would turn on the television and it would be about Omarosa. I remember saying, 'What the—?'"[15]

Burck finally informed the Judiciary Committee of the results of his records review on August 31, the Friday of Labor Day weekend—a virtual black hole for news—with Kavanaugh's hearing due to start on Tuesday. Of more than 600,000 pages of documents from Kavanaugh's two and a half years as a White House counsel—the number was actually over 900,000, but Burck said about a third were duplicative—the committee would get 415,084. To justify withholding 204,778 pages, Burck mainly cited "constitutional privilege"—a vague, novel claim distinct from the familiar "executive privilege," which Trump had not invoked. Of the pages to be released to the committee, Burck labeled more than a third as "committee confidential"; senators could not publicly discuss them or ask Kavanaugh about them unless Grassley said so, after consulting Burck.

Kavanaugh "dealt with some of the most sensitive communications of any White House official," Burck wrote, by way of justification. Most papers withheld related to Kavanaugh's role advising Bush on judicial nominations—"the confidentiality of which is critical to any president's ability to carry out this core constitutional executive function." The Archives agreed with the "vast majority" of his decisions, he added.[16] Burck's letter only whetted Democrats' desire to know just which of his decisions the archivists hadn't supported. They noted that Presidents Obama and Clinton had not invoked any privilege to bar documents related to Kagan, the previous court nominee who'd also been a White House aide. Schumer dubbed Burck's action a "Friday night document massacre" and asked, not for the last time, "What are they trying so desperately to hide?"

Throughout Kavanaugh's hearing the following week, the argument—as consequential as it was—devolved into a glass half-full/half-empty partisan spat. Never before, Democrats charged, had so many documents been withheld from the Senate as it considered a Supreme Court nominee. Never before, Republicans countered, had so many documents been released. Both were right. What records were selectively released, however, held enough troubling material to vindicate Democrats' demands to see more. "The small number of documents we did see," Paris said, "suggested Kavanaugh had lied in his previous hearing, and they undermined his testimony at this hearing. If it wasn't clear before then, it was abundantly clear there were relevant documents the committee needed to see and be able to ask him about before going any further." It didn't get the chance.

•   •   •

The paper chase, and the sheer volume of Kavanaugh's record, preoccupied his Democratic opposition. "It ended up distracting us, and taking our time," said Helaine Greenfeld, a committee counsel with long experience.[17] That's just what Republicans had hoped. One party strategist said the documents proved "a double-edged knife" for Democrats: "If Democrats were fighting about documents, they were fighting against the void. You could barely get reporters to care."[18]

Separately, Democrats were getting reports, mostly vague gossip, about

Kavanaugh's behavior in his years from Yale and onto the appellate court. "Early on, I heard a lot about 'He's a partier,' and then of course there were the rumors about him and the judge, Kozinski, and how much he knew about Kozinski's sexual harassment," said a Democratic lawyer whose social circle overlapped with Kavanaugh's. Liberal groups contacted sources nationwide to run down rumors. Senators on the Judiciary Committee heard from constituents. About a half dozen people offered damaging information; none would agree to go public. "It was a while before we started hearing specific rumors and specific stories," said a committee lawyer. "We were hearing a lot of chatter from folks about Yale, that he had a reputation at Yale of being a hard drinker and a party boy."

Davis had said as much before Kavanaugh's nomination, and Republicans were anticipating that line of attack, and more. "I thought there would be a '#MeToo' problem because I knew that we were hearing rumblings," Davis told me later. But, he believed, Democrats would try to link any male whom Trump picked to the movement against sexual misconduct that lately had taken down titans of Hollywood, the media, and corporate America. Yet during Gorsuch's confirmation process the year before, Democrats hadn't heard any talk of misconduct on his part, or suggested any.

With Kavanaugh, Davis said, "I thought their angle would be that 'You're close to Kozinski. Kozinski is this monster. How did you not know?'" In anticipation, Republican investigators sought to determine whether Kavanaugh was among those on Kozinski's email list for sexist, often misogynist jokes and didn't find evidence that he was. However, Kozinski had listed many recipients by code names.[19]

*   *   *

Kavanaugh's nomination had electrified Yale's class of '87; even left-leaning alumni expressed pride in their newly famous classmate. Former acquaintances got on social media to revive friendships and swap memories about a prospective Supreme Court justice. Who would have thought that of the frequently drunk guy they'd known as "Brett Tool," for the stupid song he'd once had to sing in public, trashed and clutching his crotch, for a fraternity pledging rite. Klaus Jensen, who'd been a year behind Kavanaugh at Yale, texted a soccer teammate, David Todd, who was closer to Kavanaugh. "What is your take?" he asked Todd.

"Great guy, good friend, don't agree with some of his politics," Todd replied.

"Levelheaded or an ideologue?" Jensen asked. "I can't quite place him in my foggy memory but vaguely recall him being on the party circuit right alongside us. Not sure if that is good or bad."

"Very levelheaded. Likes a few cold ones."

"Hopefully he's got the moral compass and 'nads to stand up to Don the Con if and when it comes to it."

Jensen also contacted Jennifer Langa Klaus, another friend who'd been part of Kavanaugh's circle. "I cannot believe that you don't remember Brett," she said. "He was this fall-down-drunk guy always holding up the walls, wearing a stupid leather helmet to parties."[20]

Meanwhile, Kavanaugh and his allies privately were reaching out to Yalies as well, partly to protect against their sharing just such recollections, or worse, with the media. In early July, old friends of Kavanaugh began seeking a copy of a photo from 1997 in which he had posed with six other Yale alumni at a wedding rehearsal dinner a decade after their graduations. In the middle were the bride and groom, Karen Yarasavage and Kevin Genda, flanked by two bridesmaids and three groomsmen, all in casual dress, smiling cheerily. There was Kerry Berchem and David White. And on opposite sides of the photo, as far apart as they could be in a group shot, were Kavanaugh and Debbie Ramirez. On July 16, a week after Kavanaugh's nomination, Yarasavage texted Berchem that she'd sent a copy of the photo to "Whitey," who'd sought it for the *Washington Post*. Berchem was confused by the text; she hadn't known White except for that 1997 wedding, as Yarasavage knew, and she had no idea why they'd want the *Post* to get that old photo. But she didn't press. When Yarasavage didn't object, Berchem posted the photo on her Facebook page for kicks, now that Kavanaugh was a man in the news.

That post, in turn, got a few classmates exchanging messages—vague recollections about some drunken incident involving Kavanaugh and Ramirez in their freshman year. Berchem, in the dark because she'd been a year behind the others at Yale, became increasingly suspicious: *Why* did Kavanaugh's pals want that photo? She and Yarasavage traded texts. Berchem wondered, could Kavanaugh and his friends—the ones helping him get through the Senate confirmation process—consider the photo as potential evidence, should it be needed, that nothing untoward had happened between him and Ramirez? After all, they could say, "Just look how cheery they were together more than a decade later." Eventually Berchem would conclude that Yarasavage had meant to send that text message about "Whitey" and the *Post* not to her but to someone else—someone close to Kavanaugh, someone helping him and his Washington handlers to defuse potential land mines to his confirmation. Before long, she would regret posting the photo on Facebook. As events played out, she and Yarasavage—friends since middle school in Milford, Connecticut, teammates on high school volleyball, basketball, and softball teams, friends at Yale—would no longer be talking.[21]

· · ·

As the buzz among Yale alumni percolated to Washington, separate rumors had made their way east from California, about some woman in Palo Alto who'd supposedly had a bad experience with Kavanaugh when they were young. Given the connections among progressive activists in California and people in Washington, it didn't take long for the gossip to jump across the country.

Brian Fallon, a former adviser to Schumer and Hillary Clinton, had become director of Demand Justice, a liberal group formed after Trump's election to counter the right's formidable lobby on judicial nominations. Soon after Kavanaugh's was announced, he got a call from Fatima Goss Graves, president of the National Women's Law Center in Washington. Graves also headed a new legal defense fund for the #MeToo movement, based in Los Angeles, to help women alleging sexual assault. She told Fallon she'd heard that the *Post* had spoken with a woman—a Stanford professor perhaps—with a tale about Kavanaugh. She didn't know much more. Fallon fished for information from reporters he knew, but came up empty.

Graves and other feminists mostly had been trying to find women who would confirm on the record that Kavanaugh, contrary to his denials, had witnessed Kozinski's bad behavior. Then she started hearing the Palo Alto rumors. Allies in California told her the woman apparently did not want to go public. Months later, Graves would describe to me the tension of that time among those opposing Kavanaugh: "People were frustrated because they knew this information" yet the alleged victim "had decided not to come forward." Meanwhile, "you have Kavanaugh's nomination moving forward and we weren't getting the documents. Republicans were going to ram it through." Even so, she was adamant that no one should force an assault survivor to come forward. From July on, she'd tell reporters who kept calling, seeking whatever information she had, "I believe survivors get to tell their own stories."[22]

Yet the *Post* already knew the California woman's story in July. Before long, so did *New Yorker* writer Ronan Farrow, who had just shared a Pulitzer Prize for exposing movie mogul Harvey Weinstein as a sexual predator. The rumor "became the talk of Palo Alto," his coauthor, Jane Mayer, later told an interviewer. "It was so far from the conspiracy view that someone leaked her name."[23] At the same time, Mayer was checking out the chatter among alumni at Yale, her alma mater, about some incident involving Kavanaugh and Ramirez.

Kavanaugh, meanwhile, was busy filling out the piles of paperwork required of a nominee going through the invasive Senate confirmation process. To one of the many standard questions, he answered that no, he had never "committed any verbal or physical harassment or assault of a sexual nature."

11

ONE WOMAN'S CIVIC DUTY

"Oh, my God, they picked him."

Since college, Christine Ford had made a good life in coastal California, a continent away from where she'd grown up in Washington's affluent Maryland suburbs, as Chrissy Blasey. She'd earned master's and doctorate degrees and now, fifty-two years old in 2018, had settled into a routine of science and teaching, sun and surf, marriage and motherhood, with two teenage sons. By her only half-joking description, she'd all but fled the East, though her youth was far from an unhappy one. She went back to Maryland each summer with her husband, Russell Ford, and the boys to see her parents and grandmother and to enjoy the other ocean just as she'd done as a child, at Rehoboth Beach in Delaware. Wherever Ford was, however, she never fully escaped what she, as a research psychologist, called sequelae—the lingering aftereffects of a disease, injury, or trauma, in her case an assault by two teenage boys when she was fifteen.

Over the years, she'd told various people about that incident and about her subsequent anxieties—of flying, and of rooms without clear escapes. She saw an individual therapist. She'd attended couples counseling with Russell. She confided in a few friends, including neighbors in Palo Alto and colleagues at Stanford and Palo Alto universities, where she taught and did research. On very rare occasions, her memories of that 1982 evening were triggered by some news: Her main attacker, a boy she'd known in high school, was making a name for himself back east; a White House adviser to George W. Bush, he'd been picked for a prominent federal judgeship in Washington. She once Googled his name—Brett Kavanaugh—and read an article about Bush attending his wedding. She thought then that he might one day be in line for the Supreme Court, and briefly considered contacting someone in Washington—but who?—to tell of her experience. She decided not to risk her family's privacy. Now, more than a decade later, she saw in the news that he was indeed the top prospect among President Trump's candidates for the nation's highest court. Ford began expressing her concerns to a few friends. A judgeship on the U.S. Court of Appeals for the District of Columbia, as important as it is, was one thing; a lifetime seat on the Supreme Court was quite another. She had to make a decision.[1]

* * *

Chrissy Blasey was one of three children of Paula and Ralph Blasey Jr., their only daughter and the younger sister to Tom and Ralph III. Ralph Blasey had been a business executive and a Republican in affluent Montgomery County, Maryland, just outside Washington. Life revolved around private schools, sports, and country clubs. The Blaseys belonged to the Columbia Country Club in Chevy Chase, one of several local clubs that formed the social hub of Washington elites. Barack Obama joined Columbia in his first year as a former president. In summer, Chrissy spent nearly every day there, swimming and diving; her brothers mostly played golf.

In the late 1970s, in seventh grade, Chrissy entered Holton-Arms School, a private institution in Bethesda, Maryland, for girls from grades 3 through 12. While many private academies nearby were single-gender Catholic schools, Holton-Arms was nondenominational and its students included Protestants, Jews, Catholics, a few Muslims, and Mormon members of the Marriott hotel family. Tuition was more than many parents pay to put their kids through college—for the 2019–20 academic year, it was $44,610—though financial aid was available. The price covered a wide range of classes and sports, as well as resources that public school administrators could only dream of. Two women, Jessie Moon Holton and Carolyn Hough Arms, had founded Holton-Arms as a boarding and finishing school in a

Washington mansion in 1901. The students' motto: "I will find a way or make one." In 1963, the school moved to the suburban campus, which allowed for expanded facilities, sports fields, and larger enrollment.[2]

Classes remained small, however, and the class of 1984 that Blasey joined was about seventy girls. She was a good student and athletic, picked for the soccer, softball, and cheerleading teams. While educational standards were high, much of the girls' drive was self-imposed. "Everyone put a lot of pressure on themselves to do well academically, and if you look at the profile of women in our class and the classes all around us, many of them went on to Ivy League colleges and became exceptional professionals in their fields," her friend Samantha Semerad Guerry recalled. "It was sort of the *Prairie Home Companion* thing: Everybody was attractive, everybody was above average, everybody had a certain means."

Years later, Blasey would profess to being an introverted and insecure teen, but that wasn't how friends saw her. In a photo in the 1982 yearbook, from the end of her sophomore year, she is pretty and, like so many girls of the time, has long blond hair blown back at the sides in the style of actress Farrah Fawcett on the TV show *Charlie's Angels*. That summer, however, Blasey took to wearing her hair straight, held back with a headband. She was in the Community Service Club, whose members visited nursing homes, collected litter, and did other good works, as well as the "Teen-age Republicans," identified by their elephant pins. In 1981, members campaigned for the Republican candidate for governor in next-door Virginia, who lost to Democrat Chuck Robb, son-in-law of former president Lyndon B. Johnson. According to the 1982 yearbook, the *Scribe*, "the club rolls from election to election, always giving a loud cheer for the Grand Old Party."

Must reading for Holton-Arms girls was *The Preppy Handbook*, a bestseller full of advice on how girls should dress, talk, and act around boys. "We were all Pappagallo and Espadrilles, and turtlenecks and monogrammed sweaters and horribly bright pinks and greens with little whales and ducks and things," Guerry said. For social activities, each of the all-girls high schools came to be paired with an all-boys school, based on proximity and whether the schools were religious or nondenominational. The matchups of "brother" and "sister" schools defined the teens' social web in almost tribal ways. For Holton-Arms girls, the brother school was nearby Landon; for Blasey, that was literally true—her two brothers attended Landon. She was a cheerleader for the school. (Years later, alumnae of Stone Ridge School of the Sacred Heart would cheer on an alumnus of their brother academy, Georgetown Preparatory School, writing letters and giving interviews in support of Kavanaugh after the sexual assault allegations broke.)[3]

Especially during summer breaks, however, kids from all of the private schools intermingled, at the country clubs or at parties in large houses when the parents were away. By the summer of 1982, between her sophomore and junior years, Blasey had met some of the jocks from Georgetown Prep, including Kavanaugh, who were a year ahead of her in school. She went out for a short time with one of his friends, Chris Garrett—"Squi"— whose family also belonged to Columbia Country Club. Her friend Leland Ingham, a vivacious athlete, had a crush on another Kavanaugh pal, the cute and funny Mark Judge.

By Ford's later account, one evening those connections brought together a small group—including Chrissy and Leland, Brett, Mark, and their classmate "P. J." Smyth—to a house in Bethesda where the parents were absent. Leland, having turned sixteen, drove the two girls there. The gathering was low-key, a sort of early evening pre-party; there wasn't even music. Blasey wasn't going anywhere afterward. She was just fifteen and mindful of her strict dad (though not so mindful that she wouldn't accept a beer). Brett and Mark arrived drunk, drank more beer, and planned to head to an actual party later. She would always remember P.J. because he was "a strikingly nice person," and not as drunk as the other boys. At some point, she went upstairs to the bathroom. When she came downstairs, she was upset and quickly left—with Leland, she presumed years later, when she tried to recall the evening. Yet she apparently didn't tell Leland what had happened upstairs. Ford was scared and embarrassed, but a single factor dictated silence: "Not getting in trouble with my parents was the number one thing," she told me.

Guerry also knew nothing about Ford's experience until years later; she recalled "a period of time where she got quiet in high school. But it wasn't a big, dramatic thing." Ford would later say, including under oath, that the four years after the attack were the worst. She finished high school and had "a fairly disastrous first two years of undergraduate studies at the University of North Carolina, where I was finally able to pull myself together." She graduated in 1988 with a degree in experimental psychology, then went west to California. In Los Angeles, she felt reborn. She enrolled at Pepperdine University, a Christian school near Malibu, for graduate school and thrived there, getting straight A's and, in 1991, a master's degree in clinical psychology. She became a surfing fanatic, indulging that passion in Hawaii while doing a psychology internship. In 1996 she got a doctorate from the University of Southern California; her dissertation suggested a distinctly personal interest: "Psychometric Development of a Measure of Children's Coping Strategies."

While she wasn't much interested in politics, science was important enough to her that, years later, she participated in a local march that was part of the nationwide protests by scientists opposed to Trump's early policies and personnel choices. A report in the *San Jose Mercury News* included a photo of her group's "brain hats"—knitted caps intended to resemble the gray cerebral cortex, inspired by the pink "pussy hats" at the women's marches after Trump's inauguration. It also quoted her: "'It's a science party!' said biostatistician Christine Blasey of Palo Alto. . . . 'Getting introverted people to the march—that's huge.'"

By then Blasey was her professional name; in June 2002, she had married Russell Ford, a medical devices engineer, in a ceremony amid the redwoods at Half Moon Bay. Before they wed, she confided without details that she'd been sexually assaulted as a teen. She filled in the details a decade later, when tensions over a home renovation project led them to see a marriage counselor. Russell was doing most of the construction, and taking years to finish. Christine wanted a second front door, for easy exit from the master bedroom, though she conceded it would look out of place. She tried to explain why to her husband and their counselor. As Russell Ford related sixteen years later, in a sworn statement to the Senate, "She said that in high school she had been trapped in a room and physically restrained by one boy who was molesting her while another boy watched. She said she was eventually able to escape before she was raped, but that the experience was very traumatic because she felt like she had no control and was physically dominated. I remember her saying that the attacker's name was Brett Kavanaugh, that he was a successful lawyer who had grown up in Christine's home town, and that he was well-known in the Washington, D.C. community."

The notes of the couples therapist refer to Christine Ford's account of being attacked at fifteen by teens from an elite all-boys school in north Bethesda. She also saw an individual therapist; in 2013 they discussed whether Ford would have been helped had Kavanaugh and Judge apologized. While an apology years later could help, the therapist said, it could just as well be counterproductive by reviving bad memories.[4] She continued to talk to Russell about the incident. "We spoke a number of times about how the assault affected her," he said in his Senate statement. "Before the President had announced that Judge Neil Gorsuch was the nominee, I remember Christine saying she was afraid the President might nominate Mr. Kavanaugh."[5]

Ford also confided in several friends. In June 2013, she was "freaking out," she recalled, after talking about the incident with her therapist. She contacted a friend who'd experienced a similar trauma, Adela Gildo-Mazzon, and asked to meet. The women, whose children attended elementary school together, chose a midpoint, at the Pizzeria Venti in nearby Mountain View. As Gildo-Mazzon recalled in 2018, in a sworn declaration, "Christine said she had been having a hard day because she was thinking about an assault she experienced when she was much younger. She said that she had been almost raped by someone who was now a federal judge. She told me she had been trapped in a room with two drunken guys, and that she then escaped, ran away, and hid. Christine said it was a scary situation and that it has impacted her life ever since."

Three years later, in June 2016, a local sex crime had upset Ford, bringing back bad memories, and this time her confidant was Keith Koegler, a lawyer and family friend. Koegler's two sons played soccer, tennis, and basketball with the Ford boys; Koegler had coached soccer for his older son and the Fords' younger one. The families vacationed together in Hawaii. "I can tell you firsthand what it's like when she has to fly," Koegler told me. "She's very nervous and has to take medication." On that summer day, he and Ford were at a local park for one of the kids' sports events. Under a big cedar tree, they got to talking about the topic roiling Palo Alto: the paltry six-month jail sentence that county judge Aaron Persky had given to former Stanford University swimmer Brock Turner after his conviction for sexually assaulting a drunk and unconscious young woman. People were so infuriated that an effort to recall Persky was under way. Ford told Koegler that she "was particularly bothered by it because she was assaulted in high school by a man who was now a federal judge in Washington, D.C.," he said in a sworn statement to the Senate. "I didn't push," Koegler told me. "I looked at her to try to see if she wanted to say more." She did not, not yet.[6]

The next year, 2017, neighbor Rebecca White was walking her dog and passing the Fords' house when Christine approached. Their children went to the same school and played basketball together. It was the beginning of the #MeToo movement, and women nationwide were sharing their long-ago experiences on social media. Ford told White that she'd read White's recent post, and offered both comfort and commiseration: She'd been attacked, too, as a young teenager, she said, and her teenage attacker was now a federal judge. White—like Russell Ford, Gildo-Mazzon, and Koegler—recalled her exchange with Ford in a sworn statement, under penalty of perjury, to the Senate Judiciary Committee in September 2018. All four expected to be contacted by the committee or the FBI. They were not.

•   •   •

When Justice Anthony M. Kennedy announced on June 27, 2018, that he was retiring, Ford's fears that Kavanaugh would be nominated were instantly revived. The media reported he was high on Trump's short list. As Russell recalled, "Christine was very conflicted about whether she should speak publicly about what Mr. Kavanaugh had done to her, as she knew it would be emotionally trying for her to relive this traumatic experience in her life and hard on our family to deal with the inevitable public reaction."

Kennedy's news came just as Ford was looking forward to beach season. Annually after the academic year ended, she'd retreat to a house the Fords owned about forty-five miles away in Santa Cruz; they rented it to students during the school months. She often spent the day at the ocean with her "beach friends," Kirsten Leimroth and Jim Gensheimer. They would set up shade tents where they could change into and out of wetsuits—"my summer office," Ford called her tent—and gab away while their kids were nearby in a program called Junior Lifeguards. Ford had told her friends about the four-week program, which was a fraction of the cost of most area summer camps. Leimroth had four teenage daughters, including triplets, and Gensheimer a son. Both knew from past chats that Ford had had a bad experience when she was young, which accounted for a rocky start to college and lingering anxieties. But they didn't know the details.

On June 27, neither Leimroth nor Gensheimer had arrived at the ocean by the time the Kennedy news broke that morning. Gensheimer got there soon after. As usual for their first day of beach season, he and Ford caught up on each other's lives. He told her about his latest freelance photography work, and about a biopsy he was getting to check for cancer. Then Christine began: "Well, I've got something I want to talk about, but you can't tell anybody." She referred to the speculation about Kennedy's successor, and added, "The guy that attacked me in high school—he's in the news as one of Trump's candidates." Gensheimer later told me that he couldn't recall whether Ford named Kavanaugh that day. She was worried, she told him, because she couldn't remember some things about the incident. "I've been trying to forget about this all my life," she said, "and now if I come forward with this, they're going to want to know every little detail."

Ford compared herself to a person with a sexual harassment complaint against a coworker: "I should go talk to people who do the hiring, and let them know about it, right? And this can be a confidential thing, and they can figure out what they want to do with it. Maybe they can pick someone else." In her idealistic view, she'd somehow get word to White House officials about what Kavanaugh had done to her, and they'd look deeper into his past. She and Gensheimer talked about whom she should tell. She wanted to go "the civic route," as she put it, by telling her representative in Congress, Anna Eshoo. But should she call, write, or just show up at Eshoo's local office? They discussed the fact that Kavanaugh was just seventeen at the time of the alleged incident. "What if that was the only bad thing he'd ever done?" she said. Still, what he'd done to her was really bad, and she'd spoken to therapists and a few friends about it, she told Gensheimer. That was corroboration, she figured.

Yet she kept returning to how she'd be denigrated if she went public, or dismissed: "It's going to be 'he said, she said.'" So many Americans hadn't cared when multiple women alleged that Trump sexually assaulted them, she noted. Gensheimer, having been a staff photographer at the local newspaper, became her crisis communications consultant. The media storm would be intense, he said, "and the conservative press is going to want to just assassinate your character." She would need a lawyer. That advice shocked her. They agreed she faced a "lose-lose" situation: Most likely, her information wouldn't make a difference to Kavanaugh's confirmation, and she'd have upended her life and her family's. And if Trump did name someone else, it would be someone at least as conservative. She understood all that, she told him. "She just felt motivated by civic duty," he said later, "and feeling like somebody needed to know about this."

They shared some gallows humor. She recalled how badly Anita Hill was treated, and at one point asked Gensheimer, "Do you think anybody will try to shoot me or kill me?" No, he told her, "but you'll get tweeted."

•   •   •

Two days later, Ford called her boss, Bruce Arnow, to confide how troubled she was. She also emailed Koegler: "So the favorite for SCOTUS is the jerk who assaulted me in high school. He's my age so he'll be on the court [the] rest of my life."

"Holy fuck," Koegler replied. "I remember you telling me about him, but I don't remember his name. Do you mind telling me so I can read about him?"

"Brett Kavanaugh."

Koegler recognized the name. As a lawyer, he had become interested in the politics surrounding the federal courts, and the influence of the Federalist Society, in the two years since Mitch McConnell blocked President Obama's nomination of Merrick Garland. Now Koegler indeed began reading up on Kavanaugh. From that point on, he became Ford's all-around confidant, legal aide, and character witness. On Monday morning, July 2, he emailed her a link to a *Washington Post* story that Trump had interviewed four candidates and Kavanaugh was described as the favorite.

She replied that she'd found how-to information for sending tips to the *Post* and the *New York Times*, and added, "Considering." He cautioned her, "I wouldn't do anything if it's going to force you to relive the whole thing." The next day she emailed him a link to a *Wall Street Journal* op-ed, "The Case for Brett Kavanaugh," and wrote, "Sounds likely he will be" the nominee. Koegler countered just after midnight with a *Post* article that Kavanaugh was taking flak from wary conservatives. Later Wednesday morning, the Fourth of July, she replied, "Regretting not having acted sooner—will call my govt representative tomorrow."

Ford, at the beach, frequently texted with Koegler, his wife, Elizabeth, and another friend, Deepa Lalla, a health industry executive. Through that holiday week, her self-imposed pressure built as media reports had Trump close to a decision. On the Fourth, she told her older son her story. He was fifteen, the same age she was when she was attacked, and she knew he suspected something was wrong; he'd noted she wasn't surfing as much, and that she, Leimroth, and Gensheimer were more often giving the kids money for treats—to buy the adults time alone to talk. Ford told him that Trump might pick a man for the Supreme Court who'd done something bad to her when they were teenagers. "Is he going to get the job?" her son asked. "It doesn't really matter," she said. "What matters is that I do my duty to tell the president what I know." The boy replied, "That's really nice of you." Days later, in the inscrutable way of teenagers, he told her that he thought he knew what happened, then said he didn't want to talk about it.

On Friday, July 6, Ford resolved to act. Before dawn, Lalla had emailed her a *Post* link for confidential tips, adding, "Whatever decision you make will be OK." From the beach that morning, sitting in her car in the parking lot, she first called Eshoo's office. She spoke only to a receptionist, who said that Eshoo's chief of staff, Karen Chapman, would call Ford on Monday. Impatient, Ford decided to contact the *Post* as well. At 10:26 a.m., she sent a WhatsApp message to its encrypted tip line: "Potential Supreme Court nominee with assistance from his friend assaulted me in mid 1980s in Maryland. Have therapy records talking about it. Feel like I shouldn't be quiet but not willing to put family in DC and CA through a lot of stress." An hour later, she provided names: "Brett Kavanaugh with Mark Judge and a bystander named PJ."

Ford said she thought she was doing so anonymously, but she later fretted to Gensheimer that the *Post* would "figure out who I am." Indeed, her phone number identified her, but she wouldn't know that until September. She believed, naïvely, that she could provide her information to both politicians and the media as an anonymous whistleblower, and that word would reach the White House and persuade the president to pick someone else. Some friends assured her as much; Gensheimer told her that the *Post* could use her tip as the basis for seeking any other such allegations against Kavanaugh. She was eager to act before Trump made his choice. As she'd later tell senators, "On July 6, I had a sense of urgency to relay the information to the Senate and the president as soon as possible, before a nominee was selected. I did not know, specifically, how to do this."

Events were moving faster than she was, however. Early on Monday, July 9, the White House scheduled a prime-time event for Trump's announcement, and that night he confirmed the speculation that Kavanaugh was his pick. Ford had to reconsider her decision to tell her story: Should she proceed now that he was the nominee? She contacted a few friends. Lalla had just gotten off a plane when she read Ford's text. She favored Ford going public, and had sought advice from local #MeToo activists about her unnamed friend—widening a gossip circle that eventually would ripple to Washington. Yet she declined to tell Ford what to do. "Everyone knew at that point what the pros and the cons were," Lalla said. "And Christine was very sensitive to the fact that this had the potential to have a very negative impact on her family, especially her children."

Eshoo insisted to me that her chief of staff, Chapman, called Ford early on Monday, before Kavanaugh's nomination, but Ford disputed that. Chapman didn't call her until Tuesday morning, she said, after Trump's announcement. Ford told Chapman that the nominee had assaulted her in high school, but said that she'd wanted to tell the congresswoman about Kavanaugh *before* the president acted, in hopes that word would get to the White House and Trump would pick another candidate—without anyone else knowing about her accusation. With Ford's sense of urgency now diminished, and Eshoo in Washington, Chapman scheduled a meeting for the following week, on Friday, July 20. Eshoo made sure that Ford was her last appointment that day, "so I would have as much time with her as I wished or that we needed."[7]

Ford said Chapman advised her not to tell anyone else about her allegation. That morning, however, she'd contacted the *Post* tip line again. Having not heard from the paper since her initial post, at 8:03 a.m. she sent a message sure to get attention: "Been advised to contact senators or NYT. Haven't heard back from WaPo." A reply came at 9:21: "I will get you in touch with [a] reporter."

Then she texted Gensheimer: "Oh, my God, they picked him."

Gensheimer said he'd meet her at Rio del Mar Beach. After he arrived, she texted from her car in the parking lot that she'd been delayed—a *Post* reporter, Emma Brown, had just called. By then Ford had spoken with Chapman, and she told Brown that she no longer wanted to talk. The reporter said she'd be available if Ford changed her mind; Brown gingerly followed up in subsequent weeks. Ford finally joined Gensheimer on the beach, and spent the day second-guessing herself. Maybe she shouldn't have contacted the *Post*. Would the paper out her? Gensheimer, the former newspaper employee, assured her that if the *Post* had agreed to respect her confidentiality, it would do so. At the same time, he said, "They want to make sure you're not some loose cannon making something up." Reporters might be asking around, and her identity could slip.

The next day, Leimroth met them at Capitola Beach for their children's day-camp program. The three parents watched the kids from a beachside restaurant, Zelda's, while discussing whether Ford should take an action that could roil the nation. They talked about her upcoming meeting with Eshoo and her decisions not to speak to the press or get lawyers—perhaps it was enough to just tell someone in Washington "and be done with it," Ford said. For the first time, she provided details of how she'd been assaulted thirty-six years before, by the teen who'd become a nominee for the highest court.

She spoke in a hushed tone, Gensheimer said, making her hard to hear over the ocean winds, but he reconstructed her account: She and a girlfriend went to someone's house after a day at the pool, for a spur-of-the-moment gathering. Two boys, Kavanaugh and a friend, were drunk when they arrived; she and her friend had a beer. She went upstairs to the bathroom and the two guys "jumped me and wrestled me" into a bedroom. She screamed and struggled, finally getting away and into the bathroom, locking the door. Once she thought she safely could, she rushed downstairs and out of the house.

Ford told them that if her attacker were Barack Obama's nominee, she would still try to get the word out. "Her whole profession is based on being accurate and telling the truth. It would just ruin her career if she was found to be not telling the truth," Gensheimer said. He sensed that for all her evident angst, Ford felt some release in telling them her secret. She had considered speaking out years before, she told them, when the Senate considered Kavanaugh to be an appeals court judge. Now the stakes were so much higher.

Even so, Leimroth said, "Christine kept rehashing, 'Do I do it? Do I not do it?' 'Is it worth it?'" As the trio sat side by side in their shade tents, "I was more of a sounding board," Leimroth said. "It's not my place to tell somebody what to do." Ford was flummoxed that they, like other friends, said she should get a lawyer. They joked that she should get "that guy" who represented porn star Stormy Daniels in her claims of a sexual encounter with Trump—Michael Avenatti. They brainstormed about all sorts of options: contacting Mark Judge on social media, phoning Kavanaugh, calling or writing the White House. Ford kept returning to her conviction that those in power wouldn't care.

On that Tuesday after Kavanaugh's nomination, Ford took another significant step. She sent a text to the high school girlfriend who'd gone with her to the alleged gathering—Leland Ingham, now Leland Keyser, the athletic golden girl who became a professional golfer and college coach before succumbing to injuries and, consequently, to drug problems. Years before, Ford had attended Leland's wedding to former Democratic strategist Bob Beckel—former vice president Walter Mondale was there, too—but that marriage and then another ended in divorce amid Leland's travails. Ford was all but certain that Keyser wouldn't remember anything, but she had to find out. She wrote to Keyser that Kavanaugh had assaulted her back then, in high school. Keyser, who was in a rehabilitation program, replied days later: "Yikes." That was all. Ford thought then, "I'm on my own." They wouldn't communicate again until September 18, two days after Ford's story became public. Then Keyser texted Ford, to tell her how proud she and her daughter were of Ford. For weeks, the two women texted. The messages show Keyser repeatedly saying that she wished she could be more helpful and that she was in awe of Ford, and Ford telling Keyser to focus on getting better, and not worry that she couldn't recall that long-ago evening.

Ford's agonizing continued in talks with the Koeglers and Lalla at a club where their kids swam and played tennis. "I was walking my dog one day and we had this very intense conversation," Lalla recalled. "I think she was strongly inclined toward not going forward. She was really concerned about being smeared, and about the impact this would have on her family."

* * *

Yet the first ripples of the story already were moving out from Ford's inner circle. A few friends, like Lalla, had reached out to people in the press and politics for advice—keeping Ford's identity confidential, they later claimed, but with enough detail perhaps to allow for educated guesses or easy digging. The Palo Alto community was fertile ground for such rumors, home to many Democratic donors and politically connected women— "the Democratic Party's ATM," some called it. Area residents included Facebook executive Sheryl Sandberg; her sister Michelle Sandberg, a pediatrician and a founder of Moms Demand Action for Gun Sense in America, a group formed after the 2014 Newtown, Connecticut, massacre of twenty first-graders and six adults; Michelle's husband, Marc Bodnick, a Silicon Valley venture capitalist; and Mary Hughes, wife of the county supervisor and founder of a political action committee devoted to electing progressive women to California's legislature. A group spawned during Hillary Clinton's 2008 presidential campaign, Electing Women Bay Area, still met monthly, often inviting candidates for various offices.

The Bay Area already was in the throes of a #MeToo moment. Santa Clara County voters had just ousted Judge Persky for the light sentence he'd given Brock Turner, after a two-year recall campaign organized by Stanford law professor Michele Dauber, a well-known advocate for campus policies against sexual misconduct. Ford and others recalled that early summer of

2018 as a time when women in the Stanford community swapped talk about their own long-suppressed experiences. Many in the Palo Alto area now were eager to know more about this possible Kavanaugh accuser, and to spur her to go public. Koegler said "the immediate group that Christine told"—him and his wife, Lalla, Gensheimer, and Leimroth—"would not have disclosed her name." Lalla, however, wondered whether she'd inadvertently helped Ford's identity slip. "I know I talked to friends," she said, to get advice on Ford's behalf. "I never used her name, I never used background." Lalla reviewed her texts to confirm that. Even so, Ford conceded long after that she and her confidants could well bear some responsibility for the leak of her identity.

The ripples spread. Michael Bromwich, a Washington lawyer, had been a prosecutor in the Reagan-era Iran-Contra scandal and the Justice Department's inspector general in the late 1990s. In July he was approached by a lawyer friend, who asked if Bromwich would represent a "completely credible" woman with an accusation against the court nominee. Maybe, Bromwich said. But he heard nothing more. John Clune, an attorney in Boulder, Colorado, nationally known for representing victims of sexual assault—including cases against professional basketball player Kobe Bryant, and Florida State and Baylor universities—got a call in July from Dauber; the two had worked together to address sexual misconduct on college campuses. Dauber said she knew of a woman in Palo Alto—she didn't name her—who'd been sexually assaulted. Would Clune speak with a friend of the woman? He said he would, but the friend never called. He later asked Dauber what happened to the case, and she told him she didn't know. Clune forgot about the matter until Ford's allegation became public in mid-September; he correctly assumed that Ford was the woman Dauber had in mind. By then Clune was about to take on the case of another, still-secret Kavanaugh accuser, Debbie Ramirez.[8]

Some people, including in Ford's circle, initially figured that Dauber—fresh off her Persky recall victory—played a part in circulating the word about Ford. Dauber adamantly denied that to me, saying she'd never used Ford's name, and for a time didn't even know it. In August, Eleanor Smeal, the longtime women's rights leader who now headed the Feminist Majority Foundation, called Jennifer Duck, chief counsel to California senator

Dianne Feinstein, seeking information about the rumored allegation of sexual assault involving Kavanaugh. She cited Dauber as her source, yet Smeal had no details, no name. Duck volunteered nothing. Dauber later told me she never talked to Smeal, though she had spoken to another woman at the Feminist Majority Foundation, to get recommendations for a lawyer to represent an accuser.

When Ford retained lawyer Debra Katz in early August, Katz quickly heard from a number of people that Dauber was their source. She called the professor on September 5. "You can't keep doing this," Katz said—assault survivors should decide if they go public. Dauber denied to Katz that she'd ever identified Ford or spread her story to anyone. "Debbie told me that she represented the victim and that the victim did not wish to come forward," Dauber said to me much later. "I told Debbie that I had heard about the situation from a friend in Palo Alto and that there appeared to be much discussion of the allegations circulating in the local community. I also told Debbie that, should the matter be brought up to me in the future by anyone, I would be happy to share Debbie's request not to discuss the situation further because the victim did not want to come forward. That is precisely what I did."[9]

Given Dauber's local fame on sexual abuse issues, she was an obvious touchstone for others checking out rumors. Through July and August, they did. But Clune vouched for Dauber's discretion: "She cared a lot about Brett Kavanaugh's nomination, but she would never think that it was her role to out somebody." The only thing that was clear was that many people, including Dauber, were talking, and many of them with little information; in this game of Telephone, inevitably word would reach reporters. But the later focus on identifying a leaker was wasted time. If anything, there were many leakers, including Ford and her friends.

* * *

On Wednesday, July 18, Ford drove from Santa Cruz to Palo Alto to meet with Chapman at Eshoo's office. Two days later, she returned to speak with Eshoo. The congresswoman also would come to be suspected for leaking Ford's name. She, too, flatly denied that to me.[10]

Eshoo, sensing Ford's nervousness, sought to make her comfortable. "The first thing I told her was that she was in a safe place," Eshoo said, and that their conversation would be "totally private." Ford spoke haltingly. "It was difficult for her," Eshoo recounted later, in her Washington office. "I asked her questions along the way. She was always forthcoming. I could tell she was an intelligent woman. She didn't have a political bone in her body—she had no idea how anything works here." Ford told Eshoo that she'd followed Kavanaugh's career and added, "I just always had the thought that he could be nominated for the Supreme Court." Eshoo was impressed by what details Ford recalled after thirty-six years. After they'd talked for nearly two hours, she said, "I want you to know, Dr. Ford, that I believe you." Ford said she believed that it was her civic duty to let "people in the government" know her story—without being identified.

Eshoo, who later said she was wary of being seen as using Ford and her allegation for political advantage, asked her, "What is it you'd like me to do?"

"Well, what can you do?"

For Eshoo, Ford's question was "a showstopper." She paused for about ten seconds. "I've met with many victims of abuse over the years," Eshoo told me, but in that moment she felt "the enormity" of being entrusted with such combustible information against a Supreme Court nominee. She suggested that Ford contact Feinstein, because Feinstein was both Ford's senator and the senior Democrat on the Senate Judiciary Committee.

According to Eshoo, Ford asked her to tell Feinstein. But Ford told me that she didn't recall Eshoo even mentioning Feinstein, only that Eshoo said she'd talk to someone "at the next level" about how to proceed. Eshoo told Ford to go ahead with her plans to visit her dying grandmother, but to stay in touch through Chapman. And, like Chapman, she cautioned, "You cannot tell anyone else."

Eshoo said she called Feinstein the next day. The two women had known each other for about forty years; in the 1980s, Eshoo was on the San Mateo County Board of Supervisors while Feinstein was mayor of San Francisco. The congresswoman said she described to Feinstein what Ford had divulged, and added, "I want you to know, Dianne, that I believe her." According to Eshoo, Feinstein said the accuser should write a letter to her

and the Judiciary Committee chairman, Republican Chuck Grassley, out-
lining the allegation. Eshoo said she had Chapman tell Ford of Feinstein's
request for a letter.

Yet Feinstein does not recall such a conversation with Eshoo; the first
she knew of Ford and her allegation was when she got Ford's letter,
hand-delivered from Eshoo's office on July 30. Feinstein's counsel, Duck,
said she was present when the senator read the letter and Feinstein seemed
genuinely stunned—not like someone who already knew the information.
Eshoo stood by her account of the call with Feinstein. In any case, Ford
wrote the letter while visiting her parents—secluding herself on their porch
with her laptop computer—and emailed it to Chapman on July 30. She'd
addressed it only to Feinstein. Ford feared that Grassley would not keep
her identity confidential. Feinstein and Eshoo, her elected representatives,
had promised to do so.

Chapman emailed the letter to Eshoo's Washington office, where a copy
was put in an envelope stamped "Member's Personal Attention." An aide
walked it across Capitol Hill to the Senate Judiciary Committee, and, as
directed, would only give the letter to Duck. She took it to Feinstein's
office, and to the senator's personal assistant. Once Feinstein had the
envelope, she summoned Duck back. Then, with her counsel present,
Feinstein opened it and read aloud:

> Dear Senator Feinstein: I am writing with information relevant in
> evaluating the current nominee to the Supreme Court. As a constitu-
> ent, I expect that you will maintain this as confidential until we have
> further opportunity to speak.
>
> Brett Kavanaugh physically and sexually assaulted me during High
> School in the early 1980's. He conducted these acts with the assistance
> of his close friend, Mark G. Judge. Both were 1-2 years older than
> me and students at a local private school. The assault occurred in a
> suburban Maryland area home at a gathering that included me and
> 4 others. Kavanaugh physically pushed me into a bedroom as I was
> headed for a bathroom up a short stairwell from the living room. They
> locked the door and played loud music, precluding any successful
> attempts to yell for help. Kavanaugh was on top of me while laughing

with Judge, who periodically jumped onto Kavanaugh. They both laughed as Kavanaugh tried to disrobe me in their highly inebriated state. With Kavanaugh's hand over my mouth, I feared he may inadvertently kill me. From across the room, a very drunken Judge said mixed words to Kavanaugh ranging from "go for it" to "stop." At one point when Judge jumped onto the bed, the weight on me was substantial. The pile toppled, and the two scrapped with each other. After a few attempts to get away, I was able to take this opportune moment to get up and run across to a hallway bathroom. I locked the bathroom door behind me. Both loudly stumbled down the stairwell, at which point other persons at the house were talking with them. I exited the bathroom, ran outside of the house and went home.

I have not knowingly seen Kavanaugh since the assault. I did see Mark Judge once at the Potomac Village Safeway, where he was extremely uncomfortable seeing me.

I have received medical treatment regarding the assault. On July 6, I notified my local government representative to ask them how to proceed with sharing this information. It is upsetting to discuss sexual assault and its repercussions, yet I felt guilty and compelled as a citizen about the idea of not saying anything.

I am available to speak further should you wish to discuss. I am currently vacationing in the mid-Atlantic until August 7th and will be in California after August 10th.

In Confidence,
Christine Blasey
Palo Alto, California

•　　•　　•

Feinstein told Duck to find a lawyer who could be hired for an independent investigation. Then she tried to call Ford. They didn't connect until the next day, and Ford's voice gave her nervousness away. Feinstein asked several questions. Did Ford tell anyone about the assault at the time? No. Did Ford have any medical documentation or corroborators? Yes.

Would she talk with investigators? Maybe. Feinstein assured Ford that she'd stay in touch, through Duck. Eshoo said that she bowed out, believing she had done all she should do—Feinstein would take over. Meanwhile, she said, word was spreading locally: "There was some buzz in the Palo Alto community of people that knew. People have friends that they trust, they chat with them." In fact, Eshoo was among those people—she'd already told her friend Nancy Pelosi, the House Democratic leader, and by September, frustrated that Feinstein seemed to be doing nothing with the letter she had, Eshoo was contacting others as well.

In August, Ford expressed frustration to Chapman that nothing was happening. After weeks of resisting, she decided to get a lawyer. She'd returned east early in the month to vacation with her family. "I was interviewing lawyers during that period of time," she later testified to the Senate, "sitting in the car—in the driveway and in the Walgreens parking lot in Rehoboth, Delaware—and I'm trying to figure out how the whole system works of interviewing lawyers, and how to pick one."

She ultimately settled on Katz and Lisa Banks, whose Washington firm was prominent in the legal niche representing clients with sexual abuse and harassment claims. She also would get advice from Larry Robbins, a Washington lawyer she knew, and Barry Coburn of New York. Republicans later would claim that Duck connected Ford with the feminist duo of Katz and Banks, as if to suggest Senate Democrats were controlling Ford. In fact, Ford said Coburn was the first to recommend Katz and Banks to her. Ford called Katz, and they arranged to meet the night of August 6 at a hotel near Baltimore-Washington International Airport. Ford was at the Hilton hotel there ahead of flying to a funeral for her grandmother; Katz was returning to Washington by way of BWI. Ford quickly discerned that Katz and Banks were near opposites—Deb the hard-charging crusader, Lisa more relaxed and funny. The lawyers quickly learned from Ford that she'd already talked to enough people—Eshoo and Feinstein, a *Post* reporter, friends in and around Palo Alto—that she was not likely to remain anonymous. They disabused her of the idea that any reputable media outlet would run her story without identifying her, and giving Kavanaugh a chance to respond. And by the meeting's end, they also were convinced of her credibility.[11]

"There was no question in our minds that she was really credible, and for all sorts of reasons," Katz said. "She was careful to describe exactly what she could recall, and she was honest about what she didn't recall. But, most notably, people who make up stories don't put a third person in the room." That person could deny her account, or at least fail to corroborate it—as indeed Mark Judge would. Nonetheless, the lawyers asked Ford to take a polygraph test. "We knew," Banks said, "that if she came forward, people would likely say, 'You're a liar.' So it's always helpful to say, 'They took and passed a polygraph.'" The next day, Banks met Ford at the Hilton, where polygraph examiner Jeremiah Hanafin awaited. At his instruction, Ford drafted a statement of what she alleged. She wrote in a childlike scrawl—that reflected her nervousness, she said—and scratched out words as she edited herself. She gave the paper to Hanafin and, with him and Banks as witnesses, swore to its accuracy and signed her name. It read:

"One high school summer in [the] 80s, I went to a small party in the Montgomery County area. There were 4 boys"—she'd crossed out "people" to write "boys"—"and a couple of girls. At one point, I went up a small stairwell to use the restroom. At that time, I was pushed into a bedroom and was locked in the room and pushed onto a bed. The boys were in the room. Brett laid on top of me and tried to remove my clothes while groping me. He held me down and put his hand on my mouth to stop me from screaming for help. His friend Mark was also in the room and both were laughing. Mark jumped on top of us 2 or 3 times. I tried to get out from under unsuccessfully. Then Mark jumped again and we toppled over. I managed to run out of the room across to the bathroom and lock the door. Once I heard them go downstairs, I ran out of the house and went home."

Banks left the room while Hanafin interviewed Ford to devise questions for the test. She added details: No parents were present at the house. The teens were drinking beer. Brett and Mark were "extremely intoxicated." She'd met Kavanaugh at other parties and she'd briefly dated a friend of his. She recalled another male at the gathering, "P.J.," as "a very nice person." She didn't know whether Brett or Mark pushed her into the bedroom.

In his report, Hanafin wrote, using Ford's professional name, "She stated she expected Kavanaugh was going to rape her. Blasey tried to yell for help and Kavanaugh put his hand over her mouth. Blasey thought if PJ heard her yelling he may come and help her. Blasey stated that when Kavanaugh put his hand over her mouth that this act was the most terrifying for her. She also stated that this act caused the most consequences for her later in life. Blasey stated that Kavanaugh and Mark were laughing a lot during this assault and seemed to be having a good time. Kavanaugh was having a hard time trying to remove Blasey's clothes because she was wearing a bathing suit underneath them. She stated Mark was laughing and coaxing Kavanaugh on. Blasey recalls making eye contact with Mark and thinking he may help her. Mark continued to encourage Kavanaugh. On a couple of occasions, Mark would come over and jump on the bed. The last time he did this, all three became separated and Blasey was able to get free and run to the bathroom. She stated she locked herself in the bathroom until she heard Kavanaugh and Mark go downstairs."

Hanafin connected Ford to the device that would gauge her physiological responses as she answered, and conducted his exam.

"Is any part of your statement false?"

"No."

"Did you make up any part of your statement?"

"No."

In his report three days later, Hanafin wrote that he applied various professionally accepted tests to the results, and concluded that she was not lying.[12]

Despite Katz and Banks's certainty that Ford's story was too widely known to remain secret, Ford had all but decided she would not go public. By mid-August, the media consensus seemed to be that Republicans would ram Kavanaugh to confirmation as soon as possible in September so he could be on the court when its term began in October. Why upend her life, Ford thought, if the die was cast? Still, she remained conflicted. How could she allow the Senate to act without knowing what he'd done to her?

Her lawyers wanted to be prepared should Ford step forward, voluntarily or otherwise. In Washington, that meant enlisting advisers on crisis communications and strategy. Ricki Seidman was all in one. A former Democratic strategist now in a boutique communications consulting firm, Seidman provided a link back to Anita Hill: As a young investigator for

Edward M. Kennedy in 1991, Seidman had brought Hill and her troubling allegations about Clarence Thomas to the Senate's attention. Before that, she had worked for the Judiciary Committee when it was riven by Robert Bork's nomination. Over the next three decades, Seidman was involved in some way with the confirmation process for every subsequent Supreme Court nominee except Gorsuch; she'd helped prepare the four nominees of Democratic presidents—Ruth Bader Ginsburg, Stephen Breyer, Sonia Sotomayor, and Elena Kagan—for their Senate hearings, and assisted in Democratic senators' strategies for opposing Republican nominees John G. Roberts Jr. and Samuel Alito. Seidman was effective, tenacious, and seemingly did nothing but work.

On August 16 she joined Katz and Banks on Ford's case. "Our go-to on everything," Katz called her. Seidman flew to California and quickly established a rapport with Ford. She was candid: She told Ford that her coming forward would not prevent Kavanaugh from being confirmed and that—no question—she would be hurt in the process. It was pointless, she said, to make an allegation anonymously—neither the media nor the Senate would do anything with that.[13]

•   •   •

Now that Feinstein and Duck harbored Ford's allegation, they endured their own anxiety that August. Democrats on the Judiciary Committee, unaware of the accusation, were preoccupied with their losing battle for Kavanaugh's records. Duck began seeking an investigative lawyer, as Feinstein instructed. But she confronted hurdles. Under Senate rules, Feinstein would need approval to hire a lawyer from both Grassley and the chair of the Rules Committee, Republican Roy Blunt. They would have to be told the reason for the request, which would violate Feinstein's pledge of confidentiality to Ford. Then Duck learned that Ford was retaining lawyers; one, Katz, was on Duck's list, too. So Duck stood down, figuring that Ford's new lawyers would do their own investigation and soon send a letter to the committee, to Grassley and Feinstein, formally notifying them of Ford's complaint. Then the two senators, who had an amicable relationship on the otherwise polarized panel, would decide how to proceed.

Yet Duck worried that word would get out before then. She also had been surprised to learn how many people Ford had told, including a *Post* reporter. While Feinstein and Duck had promised Ford they would honor her confidentiality, both women were mindful of history here, and how Joe Biden, as chairman of the Judiciary Committee in 1991, mishandled Thomas's nomination by seeming to sit on Hill's allegation and stifle potential corroborators. The backlash then from women voters had helped elect Feinstein in 1992. If Ford's charge surfaced in September, with Kavanaugh's hearing under way or even concluded, the timing would inevitably look political—like Democrats were trying to sabotage him on the brink of confirmation. In late August, Duck told Ford's lawyers that Feinstein needed a letter before the hearing opened on September 4, either authorizing Feinstein to share the allegation with Grassley or clearly stating that Ford did not intend to press it.

No letter came; Ford continued to vacillate. After all the steps she'd taken—lawyers, polygraph, conversations with a *Post* reporter—she despaired at her inability to influence Washington without going public. "I am stopped," she told friends. Yet coming forward remained scary, given what exposure could mean for her family on both coasts. She was concerned as well for her ailing friend Leland Keyser. Then she would change her mind and resolve to go public, spurred by outrage that Kavanaugh would become a justice for life. At such times, she'd be vexed that her lawyers were opposed, warning that she'd end up as Washington roadkill. "You can't just jump in front of a train, and we can't let you," they'd say.

Feinstein, without a letter from Ford, decided she would take the initiative. She had to have a record documenting that Ford did not want to go public. She sent Ford a letter to that effect dated August 31. Yet even as Feinstein did so, Ford's intentions shifted again.

•   •   •

Early in that last week of August, Ford's lawyers told their frustrated client that, despite Seidman's doubts, she could send an anonymous "Jane Doe" letter to Feinstein and Grassley. But Seidman asked her: Had she told her parents yet about the assault? Ford never had. Seidman urged her to do so, given the likelihood that her name would get out.

The next day, Ford called her eighty-four-year-old father from a Stanford campus parking lot. For any parent, such news would be a bombshell; for Ford's father, it was nuclear. Ralph and Paula Blasey's comfortable world in suburban Maryland had long intersected with that of Kavanaugh's parents. Ralph Blasey and Ed Kavanaugh both belonged to the exclusive, men-only Burning Tree Country Club in Bethesda. Now the Blaseys' daughter was telling them that the Kavanaughs' son had sexually attacked her, and that the allegation could soon be national news, potentially dooming his nomination to the highest court in the land. Perhaps as consequential to Ralph Blasey was how that news might be received at the club that was central to his life. He'd been president from 2004 to 2006 and in retirement spent nearly every day there. He was, a member said, "a very quiet and nice man."[14] Until Sandra Day O'Connor became the first woman on the Supreme Court in 1981, Burning Tree had given membership privileges to all justices, as well as to presidents and other political leaders, including former House Speakers Thomas P. "Tip" O'Neill, a Democrat, and John Boehner, a Republican. Few elected officials were members now, given the political stigma of the club's policy barring women.

Ford's father was shaken by the news, but said "Okay" to her plans. His daughter tried to reassure him that the story would be perhaps a one-week news event, and then—who knows?—Trump would do or say something controversial and the media's attention would shift elsewhere.

On Tuesday, September 4, Kavanaugh's hearing opened and proceeded through four long days without a hint of the drama unfolding. Yet rumors were contagious among reporters on Capitol Hill. When the hearing ended on Friday afternoon—with Kavanaugh headed to a Senate vote the following week—the rumors suddenly spiked. Reporters besieged senators and committee aides with calls, emails, and text messages seeking confirmation of some alleged sexual misconduct.

Nearly three thousand miles away in placid Palo Alto, at least two reporters—from the *New Yorker* and BuzzFeed—were way ahead of the others. They knew Ford's name and about the letter she'd written to Feinstein in July. A woman from BuzzFeed showed up at the Fords' home.

One of their sons let her in; Ford demanded that she leave. On the following Monday, the start of a new school year, the woman showed up in Ford's graduate class in clinical psychology. The young reporter blended in with the students, whom Ford didn't yet know, and then she followed Ford to her car, asking questions that Ford angrily refused to answer. "I know about the letter," she told Ford. Once in her car, Ford drove around aimlessly, fearful of being tailed.

On another day, a neighbor called to say that a young man in a navy blazer and white slacks, looking snazzily out of place in hypercasual Palo Alto, was walking about the Fords' house. Ford furtively looked out the window and spied him. He sought to leave a note, and the Fords' dog barked madly. Weeks later Ford would tell the Judiciary Committee how she'd seen a reporter "trying to talk to my dog through the window to calm the dog down." Ford quickly called Katz and described the man. "I think it's Ronan," Katz replied—she knew *New Yorker* writer Ronan Farrow; she'd been a contact of his for stories on sexual misconduct. Katz told Ford she'd take care of it, and immediately called Farrow. Before long Ford saw the dapper man drive away. Farrow, who'd been calling around to Ford's coworkers, later was able to contact Ford, but she did not speak with him.

Following those incidents, Ford knew that her story—and her name— would get out. She decided she would be the one to tell it. Katz recommended that Ford talk to a reporter at the *New York Times* who, like Farrow, had written the exposés about Harvey Weinstein that ignited the #MeToo movement. Ford said no, she would talk to the *Post* reporter she'd first spoken with in July, who'd respected her privacy since. She called Emma Brown, who flew to California after Labor Day. The two women secluded themselves at Half Moon Bay for a couple days. Brown returned to Washington to write her report, to be published when—*if*— Ford agreed. Ford was still vacillating.

12

QUESTIONS OF CREDIBILITY

"I start these hearings with questions about your credibility..."

On Labor Day, the eve of Kavanaugh's hearing, Senate minority leader Chuck Schumer had a conference call—an intervention, really—with the divided Democrats on the Judiciary Committee. They had little hope of defeating Kavanaugh, and what hope they did have required excavating his paper trail for proof of his past dishonesty. Yet Republicans were blocking much of the record, and preventing Democrats from publicizing many documents that were available. And now they were convening his hearing before all the material was in—they'd dump an installment of forty-two thousand pages later that evening. But what could Democrats do about it? A few wanted to boycott the hearing, as some progressive groups urged. At the least, most wanted to disrupt the proceedings in protest. Yet the committee's senior Democrat, the institutionalist Dianne Feinstein, opposed even that. She didn't make the decision, however; Schumer did: Democrats would attend the hearing and immediately interrupt with objections. "We had to expose the bum's rush Chairman Grassley was running," a leadership aide said.[1]

They also sought a strategy for questioning Kavanaugh, hard as it was to get senators to agree to any sort of script. It was understood that senior senators would focus on certain pet subjects—Feinstein on abortion rights, for example, Patrick Leahy on Kavanaugh's involvement in Manuel

Miranda's Memogate, Dick Durbin on Kavanaugh's knowledge of the illegal surveillance and torture policies of the Bush years, and both Leahy and Durbin on his role in the contentious judicial nominees of that time. The objective was to show, if possible, that Kavanaugh had lied to them, under oath, at his prior confirmation hearings. That was likely the only way they'd persuade a couple of Republicans to oppose him. What wasn't part of the strategy: Ford or any other #MeToo accuser. Feinstein and Jennifer Duck were sure that Ford wasn't going public; other senators were mostly in the dark.[2]

Republicans just wanted to get the hearing over with. Kavanaugh, having handled judicial appointments for George W. Bush, was as seasoned a nominee as they could have. He could no longer be assailed for inexperience—he'd spent a dozen years on the federal bench and teaching constitutional law in the Ivy League. The nominee rehearsed at length with former clerks and administration advisers to anticipate Democrats' questions and polish his answers—or his non-answers as more often would be the case. In the years since Robert Bork paid a price for candor, high court nominees became practiced at dodging queries.[3]

●   ●   ●

The next morning, red-cloaked women evoking the victims of the totalitarian patriarchy in *The Handmaid's Tale* lined the halls outside hearing room 216 in the Hart Senate Office Building. Other demonstrators were inside the building and out; scores would be arrested by day's end. At 9:33, Chairman Chuck Grassley entered from the Republicans' side of the dais, followed by ten-year-old Liza Kavanaugh, who pulled her father by the hand, thirteen-year-old Margaret, and then Ashley Kavanaugh. They squeezed past senators and aides to the witness table and the chairs just behind it. Grassley held out the hot seat at the table for Kavanaugh as photographers shot away. The whirrs and clicks of their cameras resounded for nearly a minute and a half while the nominee unsuccessfully tried to look relaxed.[4]

Supporters occupied the first two rows. Donald F. McGahn and Ed Kavanaugh were there, but females filled most of the chairs—the nominee's mother, wife, daughters, friends, former coworkers, law clerks—in a less-than-subtle tableau suggesting this man couldn't be so bad for women. Finally Grassley tapped his gavel for order and began. "Good morning, I welcome everyone to this confirmation hearing on the nomination of Judge—"

"Mr. Chairman?" interrupted Kamala Harris, Feinstein's younger and more fiery fellow senator from California.

"—Brett Kavanaugh," Grassley continued, as if he'd heard nothing.

Three times more Harris interrupted, "Mr. Chairman!" As she complained of the document dump the night before, Republicans shouted, "Regular order!" to silence her. Grassley proceeded, unfazed. "I extend a very warm welcome . . ." But Harris kept talking, now joined by Democrats Amy Klobuchar and Richard Blumenthal. Blumenthal moved to adjourn, calling the hearing "a charade and a mockery of norms." Protestors heckled, "This is a travesty of justice!" and "Please vote no!" Their sporadic outbursts would punctuate the hearing for hours. When police removed demonstrators, new ones took their seats, awaiting their turns to disrupt. Cory Booker appealed to Grassley's "sense of decency and integrity" to delay a hearing until all of Kavanaugh's records were produced. "What is the rush?" Booker asked. "What are you trying to hide?"

"You're taking advantage of my decency and integrity," Grassley replied. Leahy and Sheldon Whitehouse took up the "What's the rush?" refrain. Durbin reminded Republicans that they'd kept a Supreme Court seat open for more than a year rather than confirm Merrick Garland. Unmoved, Grassley boasted that his staff had reviewed all forty-two thousand new pages overnight. Whitehouse marveled facetiously, "Seven thousand pages an hour! That's superhuman!" Leahy mockingly interjected, "They're amazing!" After Whitehouse, a former prosecutor, said any court would delay a proceeding after such a document dump, Republican John Cornyn countered that if the committee were a court, Democrats would be in contempt.

Finally Feinstein spoke, only to confirm her weakness as the Democrats' ostensible leader. Grassley, now deferential, invited her to deliver her opening statement. She seemed befuddled, but agreed—effectively silencing her fellow Democrats and quashing their motion to adjourn. She read her prepared statement, summarizing Democrats' grievances and contrasting Republicans' rush to confirm Kavanaugh with their treatment of Garland. Grassley objected; he wasn't doing anything that Leahy hadn't done, he said. Leahy wasn't having it, and the fight resumed. When he was chairman, Leahy said, 99 percent of Elena Kagan's record from her years as a White House aide was made public, and nearly two weeks before her hearing began, compared to 7 percent for Kavanaugh at the hearing's start. "What is being done here," he said, "is unprecedented."

Durbin complained that a former Bush aide and Kavanaugh friend was deciding which documents the senators would see. "Who is Bill Burck?" he asked sarcastically. "He's not in Article II"—the Constitution's section that sets out the Senate's advice-and-consent role. When Democrats groused that Grassley had refused to seek any records from Kavanaugh's three years as Bush's staff secretary, the chairman dismissed that stint as "the least useful to understanding his views"—never mind Kavanaugh's public claim that it had shaped his judicial outlook.

The sparring continued for more than an hour before the hearing assumed its routine: Republicans praising Kavanaugh and Democrats lodging criticisms. Typical were the back-to-back turns of Feinstein and Orrin Hatch. Feinstein sternly told Kavanaugh that his handling of the Texas abortion case had shown "You are willing to disregard precedent," and that his views against limits on gun ownership were "far outside the mainstream of legal thought." Then came Hatch: "You are a great nominee. I don't think there's any question about it."

Leahy recalled that Trump had promised to name justices who would strike down *Roe v. Wade* and the Affordable Care Act, implying that Kavanaugh fit that bill. But, he told Kavanaugh, what really must have recommended him to Trump—a president under investigation, and one who routinely tested norms—was "your expansive view of executive power and executive immunity." Then Leahy turned to the issue of Kavanaugh's credibility, with an ominous note: "From the bits and pieces of your record we've received, it appears you've provided misleading testimony about your involvement in controversial issues of the Bush White House during your previous confirmation hearings." Recalling that he'd raised the matter when he and Kavanaugh met privately, Leahy said, "I'll do so again when you're under oath."

Durbin piled on: "I wanted to trust you the last time you testified before this committee in 2006, but after you were confirmed to the D.C. Circuit, reports surfaced that contradicted your sworn testimony before this committee. You said to me unambiguously, under oath, the following: 'I was not involved and am not involved in the questions about the rules governing detention of combatants.'" But, the senator added, "Just a week or so ago you acknowledged in my office that you *were* involved. For twelve years you could have apologized and corrected this record but you never did." He closed, "After my personal experience, I start these hearings with questions about your credibility as a witness."

Republican Mike Lee jumped to Kavanaugh's defense. Lee wasn't even a senator at the time of the 2004 and 2006 hearings, but he told Kavanaugh, "The suggestion that you misled this committee at any point in your previous hearings is absurd."

The senators' opening statements took up much of the first day, and then Kavanaugh was "introduced" by a trio of supporters, each picked for symbolic value. Two were women—Condoleezza Rice, Bush's secretary of state, and Lisa Blatt, a liberal appellate lawyer who favored abortion rights. The other was a Republican senator, Rob Portman, who'd served with Kavanaugh in the Bush administration and was popular with his swing-vote Senate colleagues. Blatt, a former clerk to Ruth Bader Ginsburg, said she'd "received many angry calls from friends and even strangers for supporting Judge Kavanaugh." The two had met nearly a decade before, she said, after he'd written to compliment an article she wrote about arguing before the Supreme Court. He became a mentor for her and other women lawyers. "Judge Kavanaugh," Blatt said, "is the best choice that liberals could reasonably hope for in these circumstances."

●   ●   ●

Over the next two days, Republicans served up softball questions. "What makes a judge a good one?" Grassley asked Kavanaugh. Three colleagues would ask the same thing. Many of their queries were intended to allow Kavanaugh to endorse judicial independence, and to cite cases in which he'd ruled against the Bush administration, thereby trying to allay concerns that he'd be "a Trump justice." Democrats quizzed Kavanaugh on the same issues that had vexed them more than a decade before. Only now—as Leahy hinted—even the limited record available included emails showing that Kavanaugh had misled senators back then.[5]

Feinstein cited one email exchange, between Kavanaugh and a Republican lawyer on the Judiciary Committee in March 2003, to underscore the flimsiness of his assurances to Collins that he believed *Roe* is settled law. The lawyer had asked Kavanaugh to review a draft op-ed in support of controversial judicial nominee Priscilla Owen, a Texas Supreme Court justice; it was to be published under the names of pro-choice Republican women, to counter Democrats' claims that Owen would be a threat to abortion rights if confirmed to the Fifth Circuit Court. The draft said that "legal scholars across the board" accept "that *Roe v. Wade* and its progeny are the settled law of the land." Kavanaugh objected to that line, emailing back, "I am not sure that all legal scholars refer to *Roe* as the settled law of the land at the Supreme Court level since [the] Court can always overrule its precedent, and three current Justices on the Court would do so." He suggested writing simply that Owen, if confirmed for the appeals court, could not overrule a Supreme Court precedent. But Kavanaugh, if confirmed to the Supreme Court, *could* do so, just as his email established.[6] Yet in response to Feinstein, he said of his email, "I'm not sure what it's referring to." He called *Roe* an "important precedent...that's been reaffirmed many times."

Leahy focused on emails that undercut Kavanaugh's past denials of any knowledge of, let alone collusion in, the Senate's Memogate scandal of 2001 through 2003—"a digital Watergate," Leahy called the theft of nearly five thousand Democratic emails about Bush's judicial nominees. To more than a hundred questions on the subject in 2004 and 2006, verbal and written, Kavanaugh swore he'd never seen anything from Miranda that caused him to be suspicious about how the Republican Senate aide obtained such insider information. "I was not aware of that matter in any way whatsoever until I learned it in the media," he said in 2004. Back then, he gave Schumer a flat "no" when the senator asked whether "memos from internal files of any Democratic members [were] given to you or provided to you in any way?" In 2006, Kavanaugh had again pleaded ignorance:

"I'm not aware of the memos. I never saw such memos that I think you're referring to."[7]

Now, twelve years later, Kavanaugh conceded that he'd gotten such intelligence from Miranda. He could hardly do otherwise: While Miranda was never forced to identify his Bush contacts to investigators for the Senate and Justice Department, the newly available emails showed that the first recipient named on many—often the only person—was Kavanaugh. Now, in 2018, he went from pleading ignorance about Miranda's inside dope to testifying repeatedly—and disingenuously, to anyone familiar with Congress—that it was typical of the information-sharing between Republican and Democratic aides on Capitol Hill. Among the emails was one Kavanaugh wrote to Miranda on July 16, 2003, with news that he'd become Bush's staff secretary and would no longer work on "the judges docket." He added, "I'm still here though and of course always happy to talk. I very much enjoyed and appreciated all of our joint work together on this important issue and look forward to continuing to support the effort, albeit in a different capacity. I'll see or talk to you soon."

"Will miss you in the trenches," Miranda wrote back. "But not goodbye."

In Leahy's first questions, he asked, "Did Mr. Miranda ever provide you with highly specific information regarding what I or other Democratic senators were planning in the future to ask certain judicial nominees?" Rather than his quick "no" of the past, Kavanaugh said it was his job to know what Democrats were up to: "During those meetings, of course it would be discussed—'Well, I think here's what Senator Leahy will be interested in.'" Ever the prosecutor, Leahy turned to some emails to show that Kavanaugh apparently knew much more than he should have about what Leahy, among others, was interested in. One, from Miranda to Kavanaugh just before a 2002 committee hearing on Owen's nomination, described precisely what questions Leahy would ask her—hardly the kind of thing Democratic aides shared with Republicans. Another from Miranda—marked "highly confidentail" (sic)—warned that then-senator Joe Biden wouldn't attend a committee meeting that day, so Democrats likely would rely on the more aggressive Leahy. In a third email from 2003, Miranda sent Kavanaugh a letter that Democrats were drafting to their Senate leader, Tom Daschle, about strategy on nominations. And in another, Miranda asked Kavanaugh and Justice Department lawyer Don Willett (now a Trump appointee on the Fifth Circuit) to meet him secretly away from Capitol Hill, so he could "provide useful info" about Feinstein and Biden.

Kavanaugh answered Leahy evasively, often stammering. Repeatedly he said he didn't recall, or that it was routine for Republicans and Democrats to share information.

"But here you're getting obviously very private Democratic emails," Leahy countered. "You weren't concerned how Mr. Miranda got them?"

"Well, I guess I'm not sure about your premise," Kavanaugh said, unconvincingly.

Initially Leahy was stymied in showing how suspect Miranda's information was because the Republicans had designated many emails "committee confidential"; he could only vaguely describe them, not copy or quote from them. He told Kavanaugh, "There is evidence that Mr. Miranda provided you with materials that were stolen from me, and that would contradict your prior testimony." Several emails clearly showed "that you had reason to believe materials were obtained inappropriately at the time." Finally Grassley acquiesced in lifting the lid on some emails. Leahy made them public the following day when he next questioned Kavanaugh.

In one dated March 18, 2003, Miranda sent Kavanaugh an eight-page memo that Leahy's counsel Lisa Graves had written to him, including legal research and responses to Republicans' arguments for a nominee. Miranda wrote on the subject line, "For use and not distribution." Leahy asked Kavanaugh, "Why would you ever be asked to keep secret Democratic talking points if they were legitimately obtained?" Again Kavanaugh ducked the question. Leahy read more emails; in one, Miranda wrote "spying" in the subject line. Yet Kavanaugh said no emails ever raised "red flags" about Miranda's source. Leahy, exasperated, told him, "Judge, I was born at night, but not last night."

An email from July 2002 was particularly sensitive—and incriminating. Miranda began by telling Kavanaugh and three Bush appointees at the Justice Department that his message "must be confidential to the recipients of this email and up your chains of authority only." He told them that

Democrats had received a letter against Owen's nomination from a Texas lawyer who'd represented pregnant minors in abortion cases. The lawyer gave examples of what she called Owen's "appalling insensitivity" on the Texas Supreme Court. She had written to the Democrats "in the strictest confidence," Miranda told the four Republicans, "because she is up for partner, and believes she will be fired if it is publicized." He added, "Leahy's staff is only sharing with Democratic counsels."

With that email alone, Miranda put the lie to Kavanaugh's claim that the information was the sort of stuff that Democratic aides commonly shared with Republicans. And twenty-five minutes after Miranda sent it, Kavanaugh emailed him a rebuttal to the Texas lawyer's criticisms of Owen— ammunition for Republican senators to use against Democrats.[8]

Graves was watching Leahy's exchange with Kavanaugh from her home in Wisconsin, and fuming. As she saw it, Kavanaugh had lied under oath a decade before when he denied that he'd seen the Democrats' emails, and now—confronted with proof to the contrary—he was dishonestly describing Republicans' possession of them as standard operating procedure. Immediately she began writing an op-ed, and by week's end it appeared on the website *Slate*. The Senate should not only reject Kavanaugh for the Supreme Court, Graves argued, but he should be impeached and removed from the appeals court for lying under oath at all three of his confirmation hearings.

"Even if Kavanaugh could claim that he didn't have any hint *at the time he received the emails* that these documents were of suspect provenance— which I personally find implausible—there is no reasonable way for him to assert honestly that he had no idea what they were *after* the revelation of the theft" in late 2003, Graves wrote. Yet "he did nothing," she added, providing no help to Senate or Justice Department investigators in a potential criminal case, and then claiming ignorance under oath in 2004 and 2006. In the late '90s, she wrote, Kavanaugh worked to impeach and remove a president, Bill Clinton, for lying under oath in a civil case about a consensual sexual relationship. "By his own standard," Graves wrote, "he clearly should be impeached."[9] Also that day, the last of the hearing, the *Washington Post* reported that Miranda said in an interview, "I never told him that I got this from the Democrats."[10]

Graves, sure that the email evidence against Kavanaugh would be big news, flew to Washington that weekend to be on hand for questions people might have. But reporters had begun chasing another story: a rumored sexual assault. Instantly, the obscure Miranda scandal and Kavanaugh's alleged lies were all but forgotten. Later, however, the *Post*'s popular "Fact Checker" column would give Kavanaugh three "Pinocchios" for falsehoods related to his Miranda testimony—one short of its worst rating. It wrote, "An elite Republican lawyer who was immersed at the time in Washington's inside baseball, Kavanaugh strains credulity by claiming this extraordinary window he had into Democrats' thinking seemed aboveboard."[11]

●　　●　　●

The Miranda emails, along with others from the records at the Bush Library, contradicted or undermined not only Kavanaugh's claims of ignorance about them and their sourcing, but also his denials of any role in picking or vetting Bush's most controversial appeals court nominees. Those included William H. Pryor Jr., who won confirmation to the Eleventh Circuit and now was on Trump's list of Supreme Court candidates, and two nominees who failed to get confirmed—Charles W. Pickering Sr. and William Haynes.

In 2004, Ted Kennedy had asked Kavanaugh a series of questions about the vetting of Pryor, who as Alabama attorney general called *Roe* "the worst abomination of constitutional law in our history" and defended a state law against "homosexual sodomy." Kavanaugh testified that Pryor's nomination "was not one that I worked on personally." Yet fourteen years later, emails showed that Kavanaugh had recommended Pryor's nomination, interviewed him, participated in the Bush administration's "Pryor Working Group," and discussed the nominee with a reporter. With Kennedy long dead, Leahy asked Kavanaugh to reconcile his prior sworn testimony with the new information. Again he didn't answer directly, but stood by his prior answer.

Pickering, a federal district judge in Mississippi, had drawn Democrats' opposition for several reasons. He'd espoused a constitutional amendment to ban abortion, had significantly reduced the sentence of a man convicted for a cross-burning at an interracial couple's house, and sought support for his nomination from lawyers who practiced before his court.[12] In 2006, Kavanaugh had testified that Pickering also "was not one of the judicial nominees that I was primarily handling," and he didn't list Pickering when Democrats, in written questions, asked, "Which nominees did you work on, *in any capacity*?" Again, newly available emails suggested he was significantly involved, even if he wasn't primarily responsible for shepherding the nomination: Kavanaugh had helped stage a pro-Pickering event, reviewed and distributed material supporting Pickering, arranged meetings, drafted remarks for administration officials, and advised White House counsel Alberto Gonzales on strategy. Schumer said the new information raised "serious questions about whether Kavanaugh misled the Senate."[13]

Haynes's nomination had fallen to bipartisan opposition given his role in drafting Pentagon interrogation policies, including forced nudity and use of dogs. Kavanaugh told senators in 2006, "I know Jim Haynes, but it was not one of the nominations that I handled." Twelve years later, he insisted he'd testified accurately in denying any role in Haynes's nomination, yet newly disclosed emails showed he had taken several actions. He'd evaluated whether Haynes was an "across the board judicial conservative"; played golf with Haynes at Gonzales's invitation, as they sized him up; apprised other Bush officials before Haynes's nomination; and consulted with an administration colleague on "q[uestion]s about Haynes."

Kavanaugh also said he didn't know of Haynes's work on the objectionable Pentagon policies, and then he went further, volunteering of his own role, "I was not involved and am not involved in the questions about the rules governing detention of combatants." Yet the media reports in 2007, after he was confirmed for the D.C. court, seemed to contradict him, disclosing that he'd been part of the White House debate about whether terrorist suspects who were U.S. citizens had due process rights, including a right to a lawyer.

Durbin, who'd written to Kavanaugh back then to complain that the judge had misled the Senate, and never received a reply, now had Kavanaugh again before him under oath. "I still don't understand," Durbin said, "...how you could state as clearly and unequivocally 'I was not and am not involved' in the questions about the rules governing the treatment of detained combatants." He noted that Kavanaugh not only was part of administration deliberations over detainees' rights, but was also involved in legal cases involving citizen-detainees Yaser Hamdi and José Padilla. Kavanaugh had worked on Bush's official statement after signing the 2005 torture ban into law that a president could decide to bypass the ban. Given all that, Durbin asked, "Did you really disclose accurately your role?" Yes, Kavanaugh said.

There was also the issue of Kavanaugh's involvement in the development of the secret warrantless surveillance program. Leahy played a video clip from 2006, of Kavanaugh testifying that he knew "nothing at all" about it until he'd read the *New York Times* exposé just months before, in December 2005. Yet among the emails was one that Kavanaugh wrote to Justice Department official John Yoo six days after the attacks on September 11, 2001, asking Yoo about the constitutional implications of random phone and email surveillance.[14] A Yoo memo that day was the administration's initial legal justification for what became the warrantless wiretap program. Kavanaugh's September 17, 2001, email seemed clear evidence that he was involved in its early development. Yet he defended his testimony on the pinched rationale that he'd never been "read into" the actual program once it was in place.

Republicans dismissed the compelling new evidence that Kavanaugh had, at best, misled the committee and, at worst, lied under oath on a range of subjects—Miranda, judicial nominations, surveillance, and detainee policies. Hatch, in a friendly exchange, invited Kavanaugh to offer a blanket refutation.

"Did you mislead this committee in 2006?" he asked.

"I told the truth and the whole truth in my prior testimony."

•   •   •

Democrats repeatedly tried to get Kavanaugh to answer questions gauging his expansive view of presidential power. Feinstein at one point used the topic of torture to do so. "Today we have a president who said he could authorize worse than waterboarding," she said. "How would you feel about that?"

"Senator, I'm not going to comment on—and I don't think I can," he said.

By his response, Kavanaugh demonstrated not only his trepidation at saying anything critical of Trump but also the lengths to which nominees of both parties would go in ducking questions post-Bork—even when the question was about something clearly illegal, like waterboarding. Over days of testifying, Kavanaugh repeatedly cited Ginsburg's demurrals at her 1993 hearing—"no forecasts, no hints, no previews"—to avoid all sorts of questions. Like nominees before him, he said he didn't want to be seen as prejudging issues that might come before the court. Democrats tried to get him to say whether he believed Congress could block a president from firing a special counsel without cause. They were mindful of Trump's threats against Robert S. Mueller III, leader of the ongoing Justice Department investigation into whether Trump tried to obstruct its probe of Russia's meddling in the 2016 election. The usually restrained Chris Coons of Delaware, peeved by Kavanaugh's dodges (and Republican spin), snapped, "You are clearly a capable and good man and a good neighbor and a good coach, and we've heard a lot about that. What I want to hear more about is an honest answer about your view of presidential power."

Feinstein at one point summarized Kavanaugh's views on presidential immunity, based on her take from his past writings or statements: that presidents can't be investigated, indicted, or prosecuted while in office, and can fire special counsels at will. But he declined to engage, insisting he had an open mind. Several Democrats asked Kavanaugh to promise to recuse himself from any case involving Trump's civil or criminal liability. He would not. But the oddest exchange about the edge that "Justice" Kavanaugh might give Trump on the court was between him and Kamala Harris. It lapped over two days and produced no winner, to say the least.

The back-and-forth began with Harris's first, loaded question: "Judge, have you ever discussed special counsel Mueller or his investigation with anyone?" Kavanaugh, looking either guilty or flummoxed, sputtered and sought more information from her. Specifically, Harris asked, had he talked with anyone at the New York law firm representing Trump, Kasowitz Benson Torres? Kavanaugh continued to stammer—"Is there a person you're talking about?"—rather than simply say yes or no. Harris left the question hanging and went on. The next day several Republicans tried to come to his defense, though against what still wasn't clear. Kavanaugh said he'd had no "inappropriate conversations" with anyone. Harris, resuming her interrogation, claimed she had "reliable information" that he'd talked about Mueller or his probe with someone at the firm. The atmosphere was tense as the senator and the nominee awkwardly circled each other again. Finally Kavanaugh said, "The answer is no." Harris never clarified what exactly she was alleging.

Still, the question of how Kavanaugh would come down on issues of presidential power and prerogatives was a compelling one—so much so that Richard M. Nixon's former White House counsel, John Dean, testified against him. Dean said that Kavanaugh's apparent views reflected a fundamental change in the Republican Party from a time, just decades before, when conservatives opposed strong executive power. "If Judge Kavanaugh joins the court," he testified, "it will be the most presidential-powers friendly court in the modern era."

Reproductive rights, as usual, was a focal issue for Democrats. On the third and final day of Kavanaugh's grilling, Mazie Hirono of Hawaii contrasted his disparate stands in two cases at the D.C. Circuit. What they had in common, she said, was that "you reached your desired outcome, which is against women's reproductive rights." In *Priests for Life*, involving the Affordable Care Act's mandate that employers' insurance benefits include coverage for workers' contraceptives, Kavanaugh had argued that a rule requiring religious groups to fill out a two-page form to get an exemption from the mandate was itself a burdensome infringement on their First Amendment right to freely exercise their religion. Yet in *Garza v. Hargan*, involving the young immigrant seeking an abortion, Kavanaugh held that it was not an undue burden to ask the teenager, who'd complied with Texas's strict requirements, to meet additional conditions and remain in custody until she did.

"In each case, Senator, I was doing my best to apply the precedent on point," Kavanaugh said.

"See, that's the thing about following precedent," Hirono countered. "...Oftentimes your own perspective, a judge's ideological viewpoints, et cetera, come into play."

To that point, Kavanaugh's embrace of a precedent that William Rehnquist defined in a 1997 court opinion, the so-called *Glucksberg* test, was especially concerning to Democrats. In *Washington v. Glucksberg*, the court unanimously had ruled that there is no constitutional right to physician-assisted suicide. The test for such unenumerated rights—those not explicit in the Constitution—is that they must be "deeply rooted in this Nation's history and tradition," Rehnquist wrote.[15] For many conservatives, *Glucksberg* offered new hope of reversing rights to abortion, contraceptives, gay marriage, and more; none had deep roots in history and all would have been unimaginable to the founders.

Twenty years after Rehnquist's opinion, in September 2017, Kavanaugh celebrated it and the late chief justice in an address to the conservative-leaning American Enterprise Institute. He hailed Rehnquist for "turning the Supreme Court away from its 1960s Warren Court approach, where the court in some cases had seemed to be simply enshrining its policy views into the Constitution, or so the critics charged." That last phrase served to distance Kavanaugh from "the critics" of the Warren Court's landmark liberal decisions, even as he made plain he was one of them. Also, Kavanaugh all but telegraphed his opposition to *Roe*: He seemed to lament that Rehnquist was in the minority on that ruling, noted the justice's criticism of the *Roe* majority for creating an "unenumerated right," and endorsed his subsequent *Glucksberg* test for such rights. "Even a first-year law student," he said, "could tell you that the *Glucksberg* approach to unenumerated rights was not consistent with the approach of the abortion cases," including both *Roe* and the 1992 decision reaffirming it, *Planned Parenthood v. Casey*."[16]

Several Democrats, Coons especially, zeroed in on the issue. Kavanaugh replied that he'd said nothing in support of *Glucksberg* that Kagan hadn't also said. But Coons noted that Kagan, as a justice, hadn't applied the test in abortion and gay rights cases, and neither had Anthony M. Kennedy. The senator displayed placards with blowups of two Kavanaugh quotes. One was from his 2017 speech, lauding Rehnquist for "stemming the general tide of freewheeling judicial creation of unenumerated rights that were not rooted in the nation's history and traditions." The second was from Kavanaugh's testimony the previous day, when he'd said "all roads" lead to the *Glucksberg* test in gauging the constitutionality of any right not specified in the Constitution.

That view "gives me pause and concern," Coons said. "If applied rigidly, it would blow up precedent in contraception, abortion, protection from sterilization, marriage, a whole range of areas." He pointed to the Fourteenth Amendment as the basis for many unenumerated rights: The Reconstruction-era authors, Coons said, intended "to right historical wrongs" by its guarantee of "due process of law" and "the equal protection of the laws" for all persons. Kavanaugh did not have to respond. Instead, Grassley helpfully called on a Republican senator for questions.

•   •   •

The question of whether Kavanaugh knew of the alleged sexual misconduct of Alex Kozinski, the mentor for whom he'd clerked on the Ninth Circuit Court, proved much less of an issue than Republicans had feared. Women who could have undermined Kavanaugh's sworn denials were unwilling to go public; most were lawyers whose careers could suffer. No evidence had surfaced that Kavanaugh was on Kozinski's "Easy Rider Gag List" for smutty emails; the disgraced judge had used codes for many recipients' names. Yet even some conservatives doubted Kavanaugh. Early opponents of his nomination, who'd hoped Trump would pick someone further to the right, circulated a six-page document against him entitled "#MeToo and the Kavanaugh-Kozinski Collaboration." It said the two men had long been so close that for Kavanaugh, "ignorance of 'open secrets' about [Kozinski's] sexual abuse is highly unlikely."[17]

The White House referred reporters to a few former Kozinski clerks, including women, who similarly claimed ignorance of his misconduct. At the hearing, Hatch raised the subject to give Kavanaugh an early opening to restate his denials. "I don't remember anything like that," Kavanaugh said of Kozinski's emails. He also knew "nothing" of the sexual harassment allegations. When he heard the news, he said, "it was a gut punch for me." He was "shocked and disappointed, angry, a swirl of emotions."

In the hearing room and beyond, people familiar with one or both judges were disbelieving. A counsel to a Democratic senator, sitting not far from Kavanaugh, silently recalled the warnings she'd gotten about Kozinski when she applied for clerkships in 2005. "Those sorts of rumors had been flying for a long time," she told me. Heidi Bond, one of the Kozinski accusers, wrote in *Slate* that Kavanaugh's claim "leaves me wondering whether Kavanaugh and I clerked for the same man. Kozinski's sexual comments—to both men and women—were legendary."[18] A prominent conservative lawyer told me, referring to Kozinski's emails, "*I* saw these things sitting in my office on Sixth Avenue in New York. *Repeatedly* I saw these things, and got them from more than one source. It was a topic of conversation—what a lunatic the guy was. They were crude jokes you just would not send around. Maybe you'd tell them late at night smoking cigars. It's really not something a federal judge should send around. They were misogynistic."[19]

According to an anecdote shared privately among some female lawyers, Kavanaugh, as an appeals court judge, once was visiting Kozinski in his California chambers when Kozinski humiliated a female clerk. Yet neither the woman nor a friend in whom she confided were willing to speak on the record then, or later, given the professional risks. A third lawyer, who heard the story from the abused woman's confidant, told me, "It would have been really wonderful for him—and I think he still could have been confirmed as a justice—to say, 'You know what? I did see this kind of stuff and it's unacceptable. And I didn't say anything because there are strong norms against doing so, and because he was my mentor, and because he still exerted a lot of power over my own career. And that was wrong.'" She added, "A lot of people would have respected that, and it would have been very healing for victims of harassment and sexual abuse."

Kavanaugh testified publicly for more than thirty hours over three days. By the end, Democrats were of two minds about whether they'd succeeded in stoking doubts about his truthfulness—in showing him to be "a dishonest political hack," as one put it to me. His professed ignorance of Kozinski's widely distributed dirty jokes, let alone the open secret of the judge's sexual harassment, was all but impossible to believe, especially for a protégé as close to the man as Kavanaugh was. Yet no evidence or testimony was offered to refute him. By itself, Kavanaugh's suspected dissembling about Kozinski could be dismissed. But there was more.

The emails from his Bush years had provided damning evidence that this nominee to sit on the nation's highest court had perhaps lied under oath on multiple matters. Kavanaugh's denials of complicity in, or even suspicion of, Miranda's computer theft were as hard to believe as his Kozinski statements. He'd changed his testimony from one decade to the next, from claiming to know nothing about Miranda's ill-gotten intelligence on Democrats to acknowledging the information came from Democrats but contending it reflected routine bipartisan sharing. He had received a private eight-page memo of Leahy's, the questions Leahy would ask a Republican nominee, Democrats' draft letter to their Senate leader, and a private lawyer's letter explicitly intended only for the Democrats. Yet none of it made him suspicious, he testified. And just as Kavanaugh in college had declined to answer questions from police about his belligerence at Demery's bar, he never offered investigators any help in the months after the Miranda scandal broke in November 2003.

The White House emails seriously undercut Kavanaugh's testimony since 2004 that "I was not involved" in handling Bush's most divisive judicial nominees, or in helping on policies involving warrantless surveillance and the detention and torture of overseas combatants. Such work was not disqualifying, just controversial. Why state under oath that he'd had nothing to do with those subjects? He could have said from the start that his role was minimal, instead of waiting to do so when faced with evidence of it. Together with the obfuscations or worse about Kozinski and Miranda, Kavanaugh's statements suggested a troubling pattern of clouding the truth.

Even so, was it enough to persuade a couple of Republican senators to oppose him? Most Democrats, and Republicans, were doubtful. Democrats took some heart in polls showing that Kavanaugh was among the least popular Supreme Court nominees in the history of polling. Yet Republicans in Congress were moved not by national polls, but by whatever Trump and his loyal party base wanted.

When Kavanaugh's public testimony ended on Thursday, June 7, the committee met that evening for a private session with him—a routine chance to raise sensitive topics with a nominee. As Republican Ben Sasse said later, "Senators could ask questions that are awkward or uncomfortable about potential alcoholism, potential gambling addiction, credit card debt, if your buddies floated you money to buy baseball tickets"—all questions and rumors about Kavanaugh that had bounced around social media. The senators did not ask him about any sexual allegation.[20]

Yet by Friday afternoon, after witnesses for and against Kavanaugh had testified, and Grassley gaveled the hearing to a close, a burst of calls and messages came to Feinstein's aides: "We've heard you've got this letter."

13

A LEAK, AND A LEAP

"I'm not ever telling anyone this."

Through August, Ford's lawyers had hoped that other women would come forward with complaints against Kavanaugh, or that reporters mining his life would find others. They could not believe Ford was the only one with a story to tell. If she were, how seriously would people take her and her thirty-six-year-old allegation? The lawyers, as well as some Democrats and reporters in New York and Washington, were separately hearing rumors about Kavanaugh—of sexual misconduct, excessive drinking, alcohol-fueled belligerence, gambling, or firsthand knowledge of Alex Kozinski's sexual harassment—from people who knew him at Yale, or as a young summer associate at Washington's elite law firms, on Ken Starr's Clinton investigation, and even as a federal judge. Yet for all the reasons, personal and professional, that held Ford back, people didn't want to put their name to anything that would instantly make national news. Lawyers who argued before the D.C. Circuit Court or the Supreme Court, or whose partners did, could not take the risk. Nor could other professionals whose careers would suffer if they entered Washington's partisan fray.[1]

By early September, however, having been ambushed in Palo Alto by two East Coast reporters, Ford was no longer waiting for someone else to emerge. "I'm getting pulled off this cliff whether I want to or not," she told friends. Meanwhile, as Kavanaugh's hearing wound down, capital reporters had begun pumping Democratic senators and aides about a rumor of Kavanaugh's sexual misconduct years before. No one seemed to have many details or even a name. But the word was that Dianne Feinstein did, in a letter from the alleged victim. Her fellow Democrats on the Judiciary Committee were irked that she might be secreting information about the nominee—none more than California's junior senator, Kamala Harris.

Harris complained to Dick Durbin, a committee ally and the second-ranking Senate Democrat, and to Minority Leader Chuck Schumer. She "believed that committee members had the right to know about the allegations in a closed or open setting, and that the letter should be sent to the FBI," Harris's spokeswoman, Lily Adams, told me. "She did not believe members should be asked to take a vote on a lifetime appointment to the Supreme Court without full information about the nominee."[2] That forced a private meeting of committee Democrats on the evening of Wednesday, September 12, to hear from Feinstein. Some senators were surprised by the sudden scheduling, uncertain of the purpose. The Senate was about to recess before a hurricane slammed the Carolinas; East Coast members were eager to go home. As the Democrats assembled near the Senate chamber in the President's Room, a salon of gilt and Constantino Brumidi frescoes historically intended for visiting presidents, the first news hit online: It confirmed the existence of the rumored letter. Yet its headline—"Dianne Feinstein Withholding Brett Kavanaugh Document from Fellow Judiciary Committee Democrats"—was about to become moot.

The story, on the left-leaning news website *The Intercept*, had few details. "The specific content of the document, which is a letter from a California constituent, is unclear," reporter Ryan Grim wrote. He incorrectly suggested that the letter-writer wasn't Kavanaugh's accuser but someone from Stanford University who was told of the allegation. Grim reported that his sources' accounts varied, "but the one consistent theme was that it describes an incident involving Kavanaugh and a woman while they were in high school."[3]

Senators were seeing the news on their cell phones even as they entered the President's Room. Once the door was closed, Feinstein told them she'd been withholding the seven-week-old letter at the accuser's request. Now, with Ford's knowledge, she read it aloud. She did not name Ford, or provide copies. Feinstein passed the letter around, with most names redacted, and then Jennifer Duck—the only staff member allowed in the room—reclaimed it. Frustrated by this secrecy, Cory Booker of New Jersey told the Democrats that Ronan Farrow of the *New Yorker* knew the accuser's name and her allegation and likely would report it soon. (A former Booker aide worked with Farrow.) He and the other Democrats agreed: Feinstein must turn the letter over to the FBI.

She did so that night, with no redactions. The next day, September 13, she issued a statement confirming what had been buzzed about for days: "I have received information from an individual concerning the nomination of Brett Kavanaugh to the Supreme Court. That individual strongly requested confidentiality, declined to come forward or press the matter further, and I have honored that decision. I have, however, referred the matter to federal investigative authorities." The *New York Times*, going a step beyond *The Intercept*, reported, "Two officials familiar with the matter say the incident involved possible sexual misconduct."

The FBI, in a statement, confirmed receipt of Ford's letter but indicated it would literally file it away, nothing more: "We included it as part of Judge Kavanaugh's background file, as per the standard process." That file was available to the Judiciary Committee members. The FBI did not open an investigation; it took its orders from the White House. There, spokeswoman Kerri Kupec dismissed the development as a partisan attack on Kavanaugh, an "eleventh-hour attempt to delay his confirmation." Senate Republicans said they could do nothing with an anonymous accusation—"unverifiable," Orrin Hatch said. Yet they could read Ford's unredacted letter in the bureau file.

For months afterward, Republicans from President Trump on down would assail Feinstein or her staff for leaking Ford's accusation, though they had no evidence and the facts showed otherwise. And while Republicans ever after dismissed Ford's allegation as part of a last-minute Democratic smear campaign, in fact many Democrats did not welcome a replay of Hill versus Thomas. "When we found out about the allegation, I just had this very strong feeling—and I said it in a staff meeting—that the institution is not equipped to deal with this right now. This is not going to go well," said Erica Songer, a committee counsel to Chris Coons.

Feinstein, facing an election challenge in California from a more liberal candidate, was thrashed by some Democrats and media pundits for bottling up Ford's accusation. But most Democrats on the Judiciary Committee came to sympathize with Feinstein and Duck's dilemma. "I don't know what they could have done differently," said Helaine Greenfeld, a counsel to Mazie Hirono. "They had someone who said, 'Here's a thing I want to tell you, but you can't tell anyone else.' You have to respect that. And they couldn't trust the Republicans."[4] Laurie Rubiner, the former Senate aide who'd returned to help on the Kavanaugh hearing, lamented that the institution remained incapable of fairly handling sexual misconduct allegations more than a quarter century after botching Anita Hill's. "There is no good process in place for the Senate writ large, for what to do when you get something like this," she said. "So it puts somebody like Feinstein, and then Jennifer by extension, in an untenable position. If somebody asks you to keep a sexual assault allegation confidential, what are you supposed to do?"[5]

The committee had long been politically divided, more than most, and nothing brought out members' partisan passions like a Supreme Court opening. Three Democrats—Harris, Booker, and Amy Klobuchar—were planning to seek their party's 2020 presidential nomination and thus were eager to stand out and to please progressive groups. And now a mysterious sexual assault allegation was thrown into the mix, like a match onto kindling, and in the midst of the nation's #MeToo moment. The tension was evident when the committee met publicly on that Thursday, September 13, to move toward a vote on Kavanaugh's nomination. Republicans, with their 11–10 majority, easily defeated Democrats' six motions to first subpoena witnesses and documents from Kavanaugh's time as staff secretary, as well as papers reflecting his views on presidential power.

At one point, Feinstein and Grassley retreated into a private anteroom off the hearing room; she wanted to discuss Ford's allegation with him. A few people, senators and aides, were in the room, and they soon watched in shock as Grassley, seeking privacy, pulled Feinstein into a small bathroom along with their respective counsels, Kolan Davis and Duck. As Feinstein spoke, Davis seemed perplexed by her account; it wasn't the allegation he seemed to expect. "The White House knows there is an issue," Davis told her and Duck, "but it's because he didn't *report* something, not because he *did* something." The two women were confused by Davis's remark. He had in mind other rumors, about Kavanaugh's partying at Yale. In any case, Davis implicitly confirmed that the Republicans had anticipated a #MeToo–related issue.[6]

On Friday, September 14, Farrow and coauthor Jane Mayer reported more details in the *New Yorker* about the allegation. As Booker had indicated, they knew who the accuser was. Yet as their piece said—reflecting Farrow's brief exchange with Ford after visiting her home—she asked not to be named and declined to be interviewed. The article made public for the first time the gist of Ford's letter: that a drunken Kavanaugh forced himself on her at a high school party as his friend watched, that he tried to muffle her cries with loud music and then his hand over her mouth, that she finally broke free, and that she had long suffered from the trauma. The magazine also included Kavanaugh's blanket denial: "I categorically and unequivocally deny this allegation. I did not do this back in high school or at any time."[7] The *New York Times* next reported much the same details, similarly sourced to "three people familiar with the contents of the letter." The paper included the same denial from Kavanaugh. It was the first to identify Mark Judge, and reported that he said he did not recall any such incident.[8]

The Republican counteroffensive began. Grassley quickly released a letter, sent to him and Feinstein, from sixty-five women who said they knew Kavanaugh in high school and attested to "his friendship, character and integrity." They wrote, "In particular, he has always treated women with decency and respect." (One was Renate Schroeder Dolphin, who would soon change her mind.) Susan Collins, whose vote could decide Kavanaugh's fate, had a previously scheduled phone call with him and they spoke for an hour. Most of those involved with the nomination, in both parties, knew they were likely feeling only the initial tremors of an earthquake.

Across the country, Ford was in final discussions with the *Post*.

•   •   •

On Saturday evening, Ford was at the Koeglers' home, on a back patio with an outdoor fireplace and sofas. In that laid-back setting, she had a tense final talk with Keith Koegler and Deepa Lalla about giving the *Post* a green light and then participated in a conference call with *Post* editors. At about 7:30—10:30 in the East—she gave the go-ahead. Ford later went home. She slept in her own bed, fitfully, for what would be the last time in months, until Christmas.

At midmorning Sunday, Lalla texted that the newspaper had posted its story. There, finally, was her name in the first sentence: Christine Blasey Ford. "Since Wednesday," it began, "she has watched as that bare-bones version of her story became public without her name or her consent.... Now, Ford has decided that if her story is going to be told, she wants to be the one to tell it." The account confirmed details in prior reports—the small gathering, Kavanaugh and Judge "stumbling drunk," his assaulting her on a bed while Judge egged him on, his stifling her cries, loud music, her escape, and her lingering anxieties. Kavanaugh's denial was the same statement the White House had provided to the *New Yorker*, the *Times*, and others. What was new was Ford's voice.

"I thought he might inadvertently kill me," she said, by covering her mouth and nose. She described the boys laughing "maniacally," then Judge inadvertently freeing her when he jumped on top of her and Kavanaugh and sent them all tumbling. "My biggest fear was, do I look like someone just attacked me?"—because, she said, she'd resolved instantly, "I'm not ever telling anyone this. This is nothing. It didn't happen, and he didn't rape me." Turning to the present, the story told of her message to the *Post*'s tip line more than two months before, her contacts with Eshoo and Feinstein and requests to them and the *Post* for secrecy, her resort to lawyers, and her polygraph test.[9]

Within minutes, the Koeglers watched as the *Post* story was reported on the Sunday talk shows. Koegler couldn't reach Ford; her phone was blowing up. But after noon, she came to his house for refuge. Koegler's wife, Elizabeth, took their sons and one of the Fords' to their tennis club for lunch and swimming. Ford and Koegler watched the news, each with a sense of an out-of-body experience, then joined the others. After a neighbor reached Ford to tell her that TV trucks and reporters had swarmed her house, she had a friend go there to get clothes and the dog and bring them to the club. The friend told reporters, "They're not coming back, so you can go."

With that, the Fords began their months-long odyssey of living in hotels and a friend's house. They first went to a secure resort hotel in nearby Menlo Park. A few friends would keep Ford company there. Within days, she had a security detail; several guards stayed in an adjacent suite, working in round-the-clock shifts to electronically monitor who came and went. The threats had been immediate—ominous voicemails, texts, emails, and messages on Facebook and LinkedIn. Ford took down her Facebook page and changed her phone number. She and Russell began consulting with security experts about how to modify their home before they moved back. Backers quickly set up GoFundMe accounts to defray such costs.

On the weekend after the *Post* story, Ford went to the FBI's San Francisco office to tell agents about threats she'd received and to get advice on how to separate the serious ones from the harmless. She had asked for an FBI interview and investigation of her allegation. The White House was opposed.

•   •   •

In suburban Maryland, Ford's old friend from Holton-Arms School, Samantha Semerad Guerry, was having Sunday brunch with girlfriends. The women discussed the rumors about Kavanaugh; Guerry said she'd known him in high school. "Three hours later," she recalled, "when Chrissy's name came through, I just about hit the floor." As a communications professional, Guerry immediately worried: "She's about to get run over by a train—I just knew how this was all going to go down. I also was sure that she was telling the truth, because I knew that she would never take this risk without it being true."

Guerry sent an email to the roughly seventy members of the Holton-Arms class of 1984. An exchange ensued among the alumnae asking what they should do, could do, to help "Chrissy." They sent a letter of support to members of the Judiciary Committee, and on Monday night they released it publicly. Now it was Guerry who underestimated the reaction. She was so overwhelmed by media calls on Tuesday that she never changed out of her nightgown. "I did not realize, really, the extent of the firestorm we were getting into. I thought I was just stepping in to be supportive of Chrissy, as a character witness," she said. She became the de facto class spokeswoman, one of the few people besides the lawyers vouching for Ford.

Initially Guerry said no to TV bookers. But when an assistant to CNN host Chris Cuomo failed to persuade her, he called to urge her to come on his evening show. Cuomo argued that a friend needed to speak for Ford, to humanize her, or the other side would be free to define her—as not credible. She made Cuomo talk to her husband and grown son; if she were going to jump into an incendiary national news story, it must be a family decision. Days of interviews and TV appearances followed, and then the backlash. Rush Limbaugh mocked Guerry, slowly spelling out her last name so his listeners could troll her. She would not go on Fox News, though anchor Martha MacCallum was a sorority sister at St. Lawrence University in New York. "There was nothing that I was going to say that was going to change their opinion of Chrissy," she said of Fox viewers.

Not all of their classmates signed on to the letter supporting Ford. The reasons reflected Washington's unique vibe—like that of a small town dominated by one industry, in its case, the federal government. "Quite a few members of the class are still in D.C., and work for the government, or their husbands work for the government," Guerry said. "Or they work for organizations that get funding from the government." The risk was running afoul of powerful people or even of the law limiting government employees' political activity. Also, some moved in the same social circles as the Kavanaughs. Those women's ambivalence didn't surprise Guerry. What did was the number of classmates who wrote back, in essence, #MeToo, disclosing their own experiences with sexual abuse over the years.[10]

•   •   •

For Republicans, the *Post*'s news came as a shock, even though the prior days' rumors had provided warning. Insiders had expected since July that any #MeToo problem that Kavanaugh might face would be related to Kozinski or to some incident at Yale. From the White House to the

Capitol, Republicans went into crisis mode. Grassley immediately told aides to investigate Ford's allegations, and they contacted Katz to schedule an interview with her client. Ford's lawyers resisted; she wanted an independent FBI investigation first.[11] One anecdote served to underscore the potential political ramifications: Collins had planned to announce the next day, Monday, that she would support Kavanaugh. Now she would make no such statement.

Negotiations between the committee's and Ford's lawyers were fraught from the beginning. Ford's life had been upended, yet Republicans wanted immediate answers: How and when would she be available for questioning? Would she provide a biography and a prepared statement by Friday? After Katz told CNN that Ford was willing to testify, Grassley scheduled a hearing for the coming Monday, September 24. Katz continued to demand an FBI interview first; Grassley insisted his staff would do any investigating. Katz and Lisa Banks, who'd built a practice representing women alleging sexual abuse or discrimination, now met their match in Mike Davis, Grassley's combative counsel for nominations (and no relation to Kolan Davis).

Before Kavanaugh's nomination, Davis had badmouthed the judge and promoted another, more conservative choice. But once Trump picked Kavanaugh, Davis was all in. Relations between him and the committee's Democratic lawyers had long been toxic; they would only communicate with him by email, several said, so they would have a record. Ford's team quickly came to mistrust him as well, and he returned the sentiment. Katz and Banks objected when they realized that Davis was not including the Democratic aides on conference calls. They objected again when Davis said a sex crimes prosecutor—not the Republican senators—would question Ford and Kavanaugh at the hearing. He wouldn't identify the prosecutor, citing security reasons.

On Wednesday night, just three days in, Davis caused an uproar that went beyond the committee. Shedding any veneer of impartiality, he tweeted, "Unfazed and determined. We will confirm Judge Kavanaugh. #ConfirmKavanaugh." After midnight, he added, "I personally questioned Judge Kavanaugh under penalty of felony and 5 years imprisonment, if he lies. I'm waiting to hear back from the accuser's attorneys, who can't find time between TV appearances to get back to me." Even Republicans conceded Davis's impropriety in signaling publicly that they had prejudged Ford and were hell-bent on confirming Kavanaugh. Davis deleted the tweets and temporarily locked his Twitter account. On Thursday, he tweeted a third time, "to clear up any confusion," though his post did no such thing: "I was referring to Democrats' partisan political attacks and their refusal to take part in the committee's thorough and fair investigation. I deleted the tweet to avoid any further misinterpretation by left wing media as so often happens on Twitter."

The distrust of Davis was such that Ford's lawyers and advisers wouldn't accept Grassley's offer to send committee lawyers to California to meet with her, rather than have her come to them. "Mike Davis? He'd tweeted 'Confirm Kavanaugh'!" Koegler said. Ford was willing to fly to Washington, her lawyers said on cable TV and in a letter to Grassley, but not as soon as Monday. Ford was receiving death threats, had been forced from her home, her email was hacked, and her identity stolen online, Katz and Banks told Grassley. Yet "you and your staff scheduled a public hearing for her to testify at the same table as Judge Kavanaugh in front of two dozen U.S. Senators on national television...six short days from today," to be interrogated "by Senators who appear to have made up their minds that she is 'mistaken' and 'mixed up.'" They asked him to delay a hearing by three days, to Thursday, September 27. The lawyers also requested that the hearing be held in one of the committee's smaller rooms, that Grassley limit the questioning and the number of cameras, and that Kavanaugh not be present when Ford testified.

On Thursday the twentieth, Ford adviser Ricki Seidman texted Michael Bromwich, the former Justice Department inspector general who was approached in July about representing an unnamed Kavanaugh accuser, but then heard nothing more. He was needed now, Seidman said. The Ford team had contacted other lawyers, but their firms were wary of controversy and fearful of alienating Kavanaugh; even if he weren't confirmed for the Supreme Court, he would remain on the appellate court that heard their clients' cases. Bromwich had extensive experience testifying before Congress, and he had assistants who were public relations professionals. He was in Chicago when Seidman texted, working with the city on police reform measures. Bromwich flew back to Washington on Friday afternoon and, after a brief stop at home, went to Katz and Banks's office downtown. The group worked through the weekend to prepare for the hearing six days away—still unsure whether Ford would be there.

Bromwich had his first conversation with Mike Davis early Saturday while at a gym; he ducked into an empty spin-cycling room to take the call. Davis still insisted on a hearing Monday. Bromwich refused. There were more calls and emails, talk of various options—a private interview of Ford, an open hearing or a closed one—and debate over whether Ford could have her lawyers with her at the witness table. Most witnesses sit alone, as Anita Hill did.[12]

Yet Hill's much-criticized treatment, including her hours alone at a table facing a dais of male senators, was not something that either side wanted to repeat. That's why Republicans were hiring a female prosecutor to question Ford, so they wouldn't be at risk of any backlash. Amid the wrangling, Hill had weighed in with her hard-won perspective: "How to Get the Kavanaugh Hearings Right" was the headline on her op-ed in the New York Times. In 1991, she wrote, the Judiciary Committee failed to show that it took sexual harassment claims seriously, or that it recognized "the need for public confidence in the character of a nominee to the Supreme Court." She counseled, "Select a neutral investigative body with experience in sexual misconduct cases that will investigate the incident in question and present its findings to the committee." And, presciently: "Do not rush these hearings. Doing so would not only signal that sexual assault accusations are not important—hastily appraising this situation would very likely lead to facts being overlooked that are necessary for the Senate and the public to evaluate." None of her advice described the process Republicans had set in motion.[13]

Majority Leader Mitch McConnell made plain just how far from neutral and unrushed the Republican-controlled investigation would be. "Don't get rattled by all of this," he told about two thousand Christian conservatives at their annual "Values Voters Summit" on Friday, September 21. "We're gonna plow right through it and do our job"—confirming Kavanaugh. The exultant reaction of the religious-right crowd, representing the central pillar of his party's base, underscored just how perilous it would be for a Republican to oppose Trump's nominee. One attendee told a Post reporter that Ford's allegation was the work of "a bunch of ungodly women who don't like the values of conservative women." A talk-radio host said the allegation undercut survivors of "real" abuse, because Ford described typical teenage behavior. The radio host, like some other attendees, falsely said that Ford worked for liberal billionaire George Soros, a villain to conspiracy theorists on the right. "I heard it from a good source," she said.[14] (Reflecting the resonance on the right of anti-Soros sentiment,[15] Trump would tweet that Soros funded the protests against Kavanaugh,[16] and a later summary from Senate Republicans on Kavanaugh's confirmation would oddly report that an unidentified source said a client had a photo of Ford with Soros, though they knew that had been debunked. And what if it did exist?)

Later that Friday, having reassured conservative activists, McConnell also assured Trump that he'd get Kavanaugh through the Senate. The senator, who'd argued against Kavanaugh's nomination, now said he was "stronger than mule piss" for the nominee.[17]

At the end of that hellish first week, Ford wrote a personal letter to Grassley to try to cut through the rancor. "There has been a lot of back and forth between your staff and my counsel, and I appreciate the chance to communicate with you directly," she began. She'd learned early that summer that Kavanaugh was on a short list "of what seemed to me as similarly-qualified candidates," she wrote, and contacted her congresswoman "in an attempt to provide information that could be useful to you and the President when making the selection." She wanted "to be a helpful citizen—in a confidential way that would minimize collateral damage to all families and friends involved." She was willing to testify under oath and to meet directly with him and other senators; her lawyers would continue talking with his staff to arrange something. "I am relying on them and you to ensure that the Committee will agree to conditions that will allow me to testify in a fair setting that won't disrupt families and become a media TV show." She described the threats, invasions of privacy, and upheaval she and her family were enduring, and said she'd declined numerous requests to go on TV. "While I am frightened, please know, my fear will not hold me back from testifying and you will be provided with answers to all of your questions. I ask for fair and respectful treatment."

*   •   •

Privately, Ford also was corresponding with her old friend Leland Keyser, who was still battling drug addiction. She hadn't named Keyser in the *Post* article, or P. J. Smyth, the "nice" Kavanaugh friend she'd remembered being at the gathering that long-ago summer. The two women's exchanges began the day after the news in the *Post*. Keyser texted, "You're my hero." At Keyser's request, the women spoke by phone. Keyser texted again, "Everyone wants to talk to me. What am I going to say?" Ford replied, "Say whatever you know. And if you don't know anything, then say you don't know anything. Don't worry about it. Don't stress out about it."

"My head hurts when I try to remember."

"Don't try to remember anything. If you don't remember, you don't remember," Ford reassured her. "You're OK, alright?"

Days later, on September 22, Keyser gave a statement to the Judiciary Committee, through a lawyer, in lieu of the interview Republicans requested. She did not corroborate Ford, though Ford never expected her to. It said, "Simply put, Ms. Keyser does not know Mr. Kavanaugh and she has no recollection of ever being at a party or gathering where he was present, with, or without, Dr. Ford."

In a text that day to Ford, Keyser wrote, "I love you and I'm really proud of you." She said she wished "that my statement was more helpful. I'm really ill and need medical attention. So I had my lawyer do it. I'm sorry if I let you down." Ford replied with a heart emoji and wrote, "I so totally understand. You need to take care of your health first and foremost. Wish he could be different but I will forge on. It was an unremarkable, random evening for you and a very remarkable one for me. Please take care of YOU."[18]

Keyser continued to write to Ford in the weeks ahead. In one text, she wrote that her daughter also was proud of Ford for coming forward. In early October, however, a right-leaning British tabloid, the *Daily Mail*, would cite an anonymous Keyser family member saying Keyser was blindsided by Ford, who "just threw her under the bus," and that "as far as I know they haven't really spoken for several years and they're certainly not close anymore."[19] The text messages suggested otherwise.

That weekend, even Ford's friends couldn't say for certain that she'd go to Washington for the fast-approaching hearing. To allay her fear of flying and protect her privacy, a small plane was made available by its co-owners—local billionaires and Democratic donors Reid Hoffman, cofounder of the LinkedIn networking site, and Mark Pincus, a gaming company entrepreneur—whose identities were unknown to Ford at the time. On Sunday she and Koegler made a list of passengers. Russell Ford would stay home with their sons. Going along would be Koegler; family friends Jay Backstrand and Chris Conroy; beach buddy Kirsten Leimroth; and two colleagues from Stanford, psychiatry professors Bruce Arnow and Allison Thompson. Thompson also was a Holton-Arms graduate. That day Koegler also signed his sworn statement that Ford described her alleged attack to him twice, in 2016 and just before Kavanaugh's nomination.

Ford told friends she was realistic. By herself, she did not expect to stop Kavanaugh's ascent to the highest court—not with a "he said, she said" controversy dating to their high school years. It would likely take more than one allegation to make a difference, she and her lawyers knew. But perhaps other women were waiting, they thought, and her example would bring them out.

14

A CLASSMATE'S SECRET, REVEALED

"Those memories never left me..."

Ford's emergence was one of those rare stories that convulsed Washington and the nation equally. It was easy to understand; there were no complicated policy details. Americans predictably divided along ideological lines, and each side could believe what it wanted—Ford's allegation or Kavanaugh's denial—because the truth likely could never be known. He said, she said. As the capital became the new front in the era's culture war—the #MeToo reckoning—the 24/7 coverage on cable news networks reflected the nation's split. A week in, talk of Ford's accusation and anticipation of her Senate testimony dominated the Sunday talk shows. On Fox News, Lindsey Graham was defiant: "Unless there's something more, no, I'm not going to ruin Judge Kavanaugh's life over this."

By day's end, there would be something more—from a woman whom some on Kavanaugh's team apparently had been bracing for, and preparing for, all along.

* * *

Debbie Ramirez, Yale class of '87, was by now far removed from New Haven in time and distance, having built a quiet, fulfilling life in Boulder, Colorado. Unlike Ford, she was giving no thought to upending that life by revealing her own charge against Kavanaugh. She hadn't even been aware of his prominence back east until the news that Anthony M. Kennedy would retire. As Ramirez and her husband, Vikram Shah, drove to Taos, New Mexico, for a getaway, she heard Kavanaugh's name on the car radio, mentioned as a possible successor. She told Shah that she knew Kavanaugh in college, that he drank a lot, and that "the things he did at Yale were going to come back to haunt him." But she didn't think much more about him. She would remain unaware until September that the news had set some Yale contemporaries abuzz, vaguely recalling some story involving her and Kavanaugh freshman year. Just as gossiping in California about Ford eventually reached media and political figures in New York and Washington, a parallel game of Telephone among Yalies would likewise out Ramirez.[1]

Like Ford, Ramirez had grown up in the east and ultimately moved west, for a change. She was the oldest of three children raised in working-class Shelton, Connecticut; her father was a cable splicer and manager for the phone company, her mother a medical technician. After her parents divorced, Ramirez's mother went back to school and earned a nursing degree at fifty, becoming a registered nurse and then a nursing home manager, setting an example of drive and self-sufficiency for her daughters. Ramirez, whose father is Puerto Rican, was among the few students of color in the Catholic schools she attended. She was co-valedictorian of her eighth-grade class, excelled at St. Joseph High School, and was accepted by Yale—"quite an accomplishment," boasted her mother, Mary Ann LeBlanc. Debbie's younger sister Denise would follow her there. As proud as LeBlanc was, she feared that Debbie—"still a child"—would feel like an outsider among the many affluent and cosmopolitan Ivy Leaguers. "My biggest concern was we were barely middle class and here she was with all those very wealthy people from all over the world," LeBlanc said. "I was scared stiff. She was just totally out of her class."

"She knew this was going to be really hard for me," Ramirez told me. "I can look back and say, 'If I had only listened to my mom, this probably would've never happened.'" But, "I went through it, and there were bad consequences, and we make the choices the best we can at that time and just cope with it." She was drawn to Yale's brand and the opportunity it would open up. Yet Ramirez underestimated her vulnerability as an unworldly biracial woman, she came to believe. She worked in the dining hall at Yale, serving those of greater means. In freshman year, trying to fit in, she became a cheerleader—only to learn that for many at Yale in the 1980s, cheerleading was no longer cool.

Ramirez stood out to friends there for her innocence. "She was the kind of person you wanted to protect," said Kerry Berchem, who was a year behind her at Yale but close to Denise Ramirez. "She was guileless. There were people who were supremely confident in their right to be at Yale, but then there were the rest of us who felt like we were imposters—we were going to fake it until we made it. She didn't even try to fake it. She just was this projection of innocence." Another friend, Lynne Brookes, also said she felt protective of Ramirez. "Debbie was like the classic person that's likely to be victimized," she said. "Kind of insecure, unsure of herself, and I don't think she drank that much in high school. So she was very easily inebriated, especially freshman year."

Yet her mother's worries eased as Ramirez related the fun she was having with her new friends, especially Tracy Harmon, roommate Liz Swisher, and Jamie Roche, a big brother type on the cheerleading squad. "And then one day, she calls me to a restaurant," LeBlanc recalled. "I don't remember the restaurant, I just remember it was very dark—maybe it was dark because that's what I was seeing. She was crying hysterically, and I didn't know what to do. I just sat there and I listened, and then she said something horrible happened to her. I don't remember the exact words, because I think my brain was shut off and she was saying something to me, that something happened to her that was horrible. I thought she was raped. My brain registered rape. So, I said to her, 'Do you want me to go to the school?' And she said no. Back then, reputation meant everything, and all I kept thinking was about her reputation. She couldn't even tell me what happened, she was that embarrassed at that time." She added, "I don't remember us ever talking about it again," but "I never forgot that day."

LeBlanc, fast-forwarding through her memories to 2018, angrily recalled President Trump asking why Kavanaugh's accusers didn't call the police. "I never even thought of the police back then" for "women that got hurt," LeBlanc said. She wanted Debbie to report the incident—whatever it was—to Yale officials, but her daughter refused even that. "What was I going to do—report who I thought were my friends?" Ramirez said to me. Also, "my parents were trying to put me through Yale. Never mind paying for lawyers."

After graduating in 1987, Ramirez worked for five years selling insurance and for a decade as a medical sales representative. For a time she lived north of Boston with other women, including college friend Jennifer Klaus. They'd meet sometimes with other Yalies, in Boston or at the beach. In 2001, she moved to Boulder. In a place so different from what she'd known, Ramirez began what she would call her "journey," coming to appreciate her Latina identity and the significance of gender, race, class, and sexual orientation in society. She joined a running group, became an active skier and rock climber, and volunteered at a community organization for victims of domestic violence. "She was really figuring out her identity and working through things, lots of really hard things," said Dana James, a friend from the running group.[2]

She lost touch with Yale friends. After 2004, Ramirez even became distant from one of her best friends, Karen Yarasavage, now married to classmate Kevin Genda. That year, she was the godmother to their third child. While she was back east for the baptism, Genda snidely remarked on the book Ramirez was reading, *This Bridge Called My Back: Writings by Radical Women of Color*.[3] She let the comment pass, but it lingered in memory, part of the wedge coming between her and Yarasavage. Later Ramirez married Shah, an Indian immigrant she met in Boulder.

＊　　＊　　＊

On Sunday, September 16, 2018, much of the nation learned the news of Ford's allegation. But Ramirez wouldn't hear about it until the next day, when she got a call from Ronan Farrow. Suddenly she was reminded of the memories she'd long suppressed: of Kavanaugh and some other drunks sexually humiliating her and laughing boisterously. She told Farrow she couldn't say for sure that Kavanaugh was the one to expose himself. Within days, however, she remembered it was him; the recollection of his laughter as he zipped up his pants convinced her. Republicans and other skeptics would seize on Ramirez's initial hesitance to name Kavanaugh, yet it also raised the question: If she were lying, why wouldn't she have identified him from the outset? Months later, at home in Boulder, she emotionally recalled the episode for me.

One night in freshman year, she and a roommate heard about a party in Lawrance Hall, in the Gothic quadrangle known as Old Campus, and walked over. There, in the living room of a suite, the two women and a small group of guys, including Kavanaugh, Genda, and David Todd, were playing a drinking game around a table. When each guy won a round, he chose Ramirez to take a drink. "Why are they all picking on me?" she blearily wondered. Her roommate does not remember the evening. "I have no recollections of her being in the room when this happened," Ramirez said, "so it would make sense that she doesn't remember."

Earlier, one of the guys—she was not sure which—had waved a plastic penis at her. Ramirez suddenly saw a penis again, in front of her face. Drunk, thinking it was the fake penis, she pushed it away. Genda and Todd laughed as she recoiled upon realizing the penis she'd touched was real. Genda, a short, scrappy soccer player, teased her, "Do you want to kiss it?" Then he chanted, "Kiss it. Kiss it," and spurred on the guy exposing himself—Kavanaugh.

"Those memories never left me," Ramirez said. "The laughing, the penis. The laughing, David and Kevin laughing. I was closer to them, they were my friends, laughing at me. I'm not sure how well I knew Brett at that time. And pushing it away and touching it and being mortified. Those never left. Vivid thirty-five years later." She had another memory, and rose from her couch to demonstrate. Mimicking Kavanaugh, she stood and wobbled drunkenly, her hips thrust back and then forward as if to pull up a zipper. "And his face—'Ha-ha-ha-ha-ha.'" Another guy, David White, kept yelling down the hall, "Brett Kavanaugh just put his penis in Debbie's face!"

Ramirez began to cry, recalling her mortification decades ago. "First of all, my identity up until Yale was I didn't drink, I didn't really date. I may have gone out on a few dates but I didn't have a serious boyfriend. I had very limited exposure to boys—definitely not touching penises. In my mind, I'm probably still thinking maybe I'll wait until I get married. So just the mortification that that's how I touched the penis. That and the blame. I was drinking; my parents probably didn't even know I drank at that point. So there was all this. I didn't want anybody to know anything. A lot of it was around self-blame and self-judgment. And I don't think I really felt I had to tell anybody because I thought, 'They're all talking about it.'"

She inevitably saw Kavanaugh over the next several years. He hadn't been among her close male friends, like Todd, but they moved in the same circle. "So if I wanted to stay away from him, then I'd have to stay away from all my friends," Ramirez said. "My most prominent memories of Brett are him being drunk," she added. When Ford went public, Ramirez was shocked by his response—not that he denied Ford's accusation, but that he vehemently denied the drunkenness she described. "To lie about the drinking—the one thing we all remember about Brett? He's got lots of witnesses for the drinking. If you're going to lie about that, that's a basic thing that everybody saw him do. So how can any of the rest of it be credible?"

•   •   •

Ramirez and her husband had just returned from visiting his family in India when Ford's story broke. Her mom was in Boulder to care for their pets and stayed for a time after the couple got back. LeBlanc vaguely knew that Trump's nominee had been in Debbie's class at Yale. One day she was watching the news with Shah in the living room; Ramirez was in the second-floor kitchen that overlooked the room, thanks to a two-story cathedral ceiling. At one point, the TV screen was filled by Kavanaugh's face, and Ramirez, looking down, exclaimed, "Oh, my God, he drank *a lot.*" Instantly, LeBlanc was reminded of the traumatic talk with her daughter years before. "I just knew that was the boy that had hurt her," she said. Yet mother and daughter kept their thoughts to themselves. LeBlanc soon returned to Connecticut.

When Ramirez got the call from Farrow about a week later, she thought he was a local reporter; it was part of her job to talk to the Boulder media. "I was taken off guard at work when I realized what he wanted to talk about," she said. Farrow told her he was investigating stories about Kavanaugh at Yale, and one involved "sexual misconduct" toward Ramirez. "Huh?" she said. "What I remember is he was drunk all the time. I don't—sexual misconduct? I can't really think of anything."

"A penis?" Farrow said, as a hint.

"Oh, that! Like, literally, *that* I never forgot."

Ramirez told him that she couldn't speak further at work. They talked that evening, when she was at home. Farrow and colleague Jane Mayer had been calling Ramirez's classmates for weeks. When she recounted to him what had happened, Farrow said she'd described the episode "exactly" as he'd heard it from a source, whom he never identified. "I still don't know who's telling the story," she told me the following year. "There's only a few people I'd reached out to."

Her mother still wasn't one of them, but Ramirez called the next day, Tuesday, to warn that she might be in the news soon—Farrow had interviewed her and other reporters were trying to reach her. "What should I do?"

"Debbie, you have to do what you want," LeBlanc said. She finally confided that she'd come to suspect that Kavanaugh was the perpetrator in Ramirez's freshman-year nightmare. "You were hysterically sobbing," LeBlanc said. "You wouldn't tell me what happened." Until then, Ramirez had forgotten that restaurant meeting. Her mother offered some advice: Ramirez was "perfectly matched" to the moment, LeBlanc said, given her social work with women. And "Christine needs help"—together, two women's stories would have more credibility. "It was terrible for me to say that to her," LeBlanc said later. But, "I felt as though if she stayed quiet she was going to regret it for the rest of her life. Because I thought she would make a difference."

That day, Ramirez retained a lawyer she knew of from her work on domestic violence cases, Stan Garnett, the former district attorney for Boulder County. She also contacted her old Yale friends—Swisher, Harmon, and Roche—hoping she'd told them at the time, and that they could corroborate her story. The people she recalled being in the dorm room were her antagonists—Genda, White, Todd, and, of course, Kavanaugh—so they wouldn't be any help. Farrow said he'd talked to two classmates—he didn't name them—who recalled hearing about the incident soon after. In later articles he identified them: Kenneth Appold and Richard Oh.

Ramirez didn't need the others to tell her what had happened, or to coordinate their stories, as Republicans would later allege—she said she wanted to fill in gaps and get corroboration, as Farrow encouraged her to do. "It was a very emotionally challenging week for her," said her friend Dana James, who kept Ramirez company. The two women were so close that James and her husband named Ramirez and Shah, who had no children, as guardians for their three children should the parents die or be unable to care for them.

While Ramirez previously had told James that she'd had a bad experience at Yale, now she told her friend details. "I absolutely, 100 percent, believe her," James said. "She wasn't super thrilled to have people know she had been drunk, and didn't have really clear memories." But "she was so inspired by Ford," and wanted to provide support to the other woman.[4] Still, Ramirez wrestled with whether to go public. Two factors exerted a push and pull. "Number one, another survivor, Dr. Ford, was out there and we had the same perpetrator," she said. She could either "join her publicly in the scrutiny" or not, and "I chose what I could live with." Yet there was that second consideration: Her former best friend, Yarasavage, was married to Genda, the man Ramirez recalled egging on Kavanaugh, laughing at her, telling her to "kiss it." She asked herself, "How could I tell this without bringing harm on Karen and her three girls?" While Genda, White, and Todd were Kavanaugh's accomplices, "this was about what Brett did to me." She decided to allow Farrow to tell her story, but only if he didn't identify Kavanaugh's friends.

As she saw her decision, "I was standing up for my young self. It wasn't just Dr. Ford. By that time I was standing up for me, just to say, 'This happened to me, and it shouldn't have happened to me.'" The decision "transformed this dark part of my life into something completely different that brings hope."

*   *   *

For the time being, Ramirez's personal drama played out backstage, as Kavanaugh's nomination was roiled by Ford's accusation—by Republicans' investigation and Democrats' demand for an FBI probe; by lawyers' battling over what was shaping up as a replay of the Hill-Thomas show-down; and by nonstop debate on cable news networks and social media. Ramirez and Kavanaugh's Yale classmates continued to swap memories and rumors, and were either dodging reporters or reaching out to them. Significantly, some heard from Kavanaugh, who took an unusually hands-on role in his own confirmation campaign. Would-be justices typically remained sheltered, boning up on the jurisprudential questions that senators would ask at the hearing and leaving strategy to the political operatives—the role Kavanaugh played for Bush nominees. Now he was the nominee *and* a strategist, contacting former acquaintances, fishing for weak links among them, and urging friends to speak to the media or sign endorsements.

In time the evidence would strongly indicate that Kavanaugh anticipated the Ramirez allegation—which implicitly suggested there was something to it—and took steps to be prepared to discredit her charge.

● ● ●

In August, several women backing Kavanaugh circulated a letter of support to women in his Yale class to get their signatures. It extolled him as a student, basketball player, and a friend who treated women as "equals in all respects." Taking the lead was Porter Wilkinson, who did not go to Yale but was a former law clerk to Kavanaugh and the daughter of prominent conservative appellate judge J. Harvie Wilkinson III. Among those she emailed was Lynne Brookes, the college friend of Ramirez and a varsity athlete who'd known Kavanaugh and partied with him often. Wilkinson identified herself as his former clerk and asked Brookes to call her "about an effort we're organizing to support the Judge."

"I went to school with Brett. I know him well," Brookes wrote. "No need."

Thirteen minutes later, Wilkinson emailed again, to ask specifically if Brookes would sign the endorsement. Brookes replied immediately: "No."

A second woman, a classmate, called to press her to sign. Brookes again said no. While a lifelong Republican, Brookes said she didn't support Kavanaugh and was certain he would undo *Roe v. Wade*. The other woman insisted that the letter had nothing to do with politics; it spoke to his character. Brookes was unmoved. She learned later that Kavanaugh himself then called a mutual friend to ask why Brookes wouldn't sign.

In retrospect, Brookes was certain that Kavanaugh, fearing Ramirez's accusation, saw the letter as a way to identify validators as well as anyone among their classmates who might pose a danger. "I think he was trying to figure out what we knew," Brookes said. Ultimately just ten alumnae signed the letter, which was sent to Chuck Grassley and Dianne Feinstein.[5]

About a month later, on Thursday, September 20, two other class-mates were speaking by phone about a business matter. Kathy Charlton mentioned to David Todd that the *New York Times* had called her about Kavanaugh. Todd said he'd had a call from the *New Yorker*'s Farrow. Charlton got straight to the point. "I know about the dick-in-the-face story," she said, having heard from others that Farrow was asking about it. Todd said he'd told the reporter he had no memory of that. Then, according to Charlton, he confided that Kavanaugh also had called, appar-ently to ensure that Todd wouldn't tell reporters anything incriminating. "Hey, Dave," Kavanaugh had said. "No bad. No bad, Dave." To Charlton, that seemed inappropriate behavior for a Supreme Court nominee. She changed the subject.

The next morning, Todd texted her, believing she'd told a journalist what he'd said, and misinterpreted it: "Don't Fucking TELL PEOPLE BRETT GOT IN TOUCH WITH ME!!! I TOLD YOU AT THE TIME THAT WAS IN CONFIDENCE!!!"[6]

• • •

Farrow reached out to other Yale classmates, and doubled back to some. He'd spoken weeks earlier to Roche, Kavanaugh's freshman roommate and Ramirez's friend, but Roche would not talk on the record. Now Farrow tried again. Roche, a software executive in the San Francisco Bay Area, provided some information on background, but still didn't want to be named, for personal and business reasons. He asked Farrow to tell Ramirez he'd be happy to talk with her.

She called him on Wednesday, September 19. She'd been wary to do so for fear it would seem as if she were coordinating accounts among classmates. "I don't want you to say anything that you don't 100 percent remember," she said. At Yale, the two had talked almost daily. Ramirez said she'd gone to him after Kavanaugh's assault, upset, and Roche had tried to make her laugh it off. He soon bought her a penis-shaped water pistol and said, "Why don't you just get him back?" Roche told me he only vaguely recalled the exchange she described, but the anecdote rang true—the gag gift was the kind of thing he'd have done as a freshman.[7]

Farrow also contacted Kerry Berchem, Yarasavage's friend since childhood, who was a year behind her and Ramirez at Yale. Berchem, now an attorney at a prestigious New York law firm, also didn't want to get involved. She and Yarasavage had resumed the conversation-by-text that they began in July about Kavanaugh's nomination, but their exchanges had gone from lighthearted to fraught, especially on Yarasavage's part. Early Friday, September 21, Yarasavage wrote, "The whole Brett thing is so hard. Reporters calling here. Kevin['s] name sullied. Think they are trying to get college dirt on him."

"I am sure it has been hard," Berchem replied. She said she'd had a call from a *Washington Post* reporter, who saw that Berchem was in a sorority and wanted to ask about Kavanaugh and the Dekes. She didn't return the call. But, she told Yarasavage, she'd spoken to a classmate who had talked to Farrow the day before. Berchem wouldn't name the person or tell Yarasavage anything more, given the sensitivity of the information she'd received. The classmate—Genda's former soccer teammate, Klaus Jensen—had phoned to tell Berchem he'd given her name to Farrow. Berchem had never heard about "the dick-in-the-face story"—she was a high school senior that year—or that Genda was involved. Jensen told her that Farrow was investigating the story.

That afternoon, Yarasavage texted Berchem again. She'd had a call from Robin Pogrebin of the *New York Times*, who was in Yale's '87 class and now was reporting on Kavanaugh's college years. "She got no help from me," Yarasavage wrote. She pressed Berchem to tell her which classmate talked with Farrow, but Berchem still would not.

Berchem got to the point: "I think I now know about the alleged incident."

"You weren't even on campus, lucky you." With that, Yarasavage implied that indeed something bad did occur between Kavanaugh and Ramirez, then added, "I never heard a word of this ever happening."

"But if he did this he just needs to come clean," Berchem wrote. "Or step down. And stay an appellate judge."

Neither woman spelled out what "this" was. Months later, Berchem told me they spoke in riddles because at the time she didn't know what exactly had happened to Ramirez, and Yarasavage was protecting her husband.

"I'm being asked to be involved," Yarasavage wrote the next day, Saturday, September 22. She was signaling what soon became clear: At Kavanaugh's request, she had vouched for him to the *New Yorker*, to counter Ramirez's allegation. "I'm a wreck thinking what I say will possibly affect 2 people's lives." She mentioned to Berchem the photo of her wedding party, the one showing Ramirez and Kavanaugh smiling, that she'd allowed to be sent to the *Washington Post* in July. "I had to send it to Brett's team too," she wrote.

Early Sunday, they picked up the conversation for a third day. "My phone hasn't rung since I spoke to *The New Yorker* so I hope that is a good sign," Yarasavage said. "Selfishly, I hope that this story dies as it pains me to be involved."

"Hoping you have a good/boring day," Berchem said.

Soon Yarasavage replied: "As of 2 min ago, not looking that way . . ."

"What happened? Another call?"

"From Brett's guy."

Just after 4 p.m. Berchem texted that she had gotten a call from the *Times*' Pogrebin, who said the *New Yorker* was about to break a story on Kavanaugh, and the *Times* was trying to compete. Yarasavage told Berchem that was the story she'd hinted at: "Brett asked me to go on record." Berchem warned her against it—the allegation could be true, she said, which could explain Ramirez's vulnerability in college. She was too late. Yarasavage wrote, "My story is that we"—she and Ramirez—"were such close friends who shared many intimate details with each other and I never heard a word of this." She said Ramirez's accusation could be a case of mistaken identity (just as Kavanaugh's supporters would suggest), and named another classmate who'd "pulled his unit out once." Berchem dismissed that idea of a doppelganger; she was puzzled about why Yarasavage would name a student who'd been a year behind Kavanaugh and Ramirez at Yale, and thus would not have been on campus at the time. She ended, "Not trying to be melodramatic but he has something to lose. What does she have to gain? I dunno Karen. Just be careful. There would be no going back."

Their exchange had gone on for two hours, past 6 p.m. Three hours later, the *New Yorker* posted its article. As Ramirez had asked, it did not name Genda, White, or Todd, but only described three unnamed men who egged on Kavanaugh. When Berchem read the piece, she was infuriated to see in print an anonymous quote skeptical of Ramirez that she knew was from Yarasavage. Sleepless, at 2:33 a.m. she texted her, "I am at a complete loss for words."[8]

* * *

For a second straight Sunday, the week began with a #MeToo bombshell for Kavanaugh's nomination. The *New Yorker* account said Ramirez's most haunting memory was of the guys' "laughter at her expense." She confessed to having become so inebriated that she was "on the floor, foggy and slurring her words" as two male students—Genda and Todd—stood by laughing as Kavanaugh exposed himself. Farrow and Mayer reported that they'd contacted several dozen classmates but couldn't confirm Kavanaugh's presence at the party Ramirez described. Some couldn't recall the party but many didn't respond or declined to comment. The unnamed Genda, Todd, and White said they had no memory of it.

Four people—two classmates, and Ramirez's mother and sister—offered some corroboration. Former classmate Kenneth Appold, a theology professor who did not agree to be identified by name until the magazine's follow-up piece, said a witness told him what happened, either that night or in the next couple days. Appold, who did not know Ramirez, said he was "100 percent sure" the witness named Kavanaugh as the person who exposed himself; Appold described other details that echoed her account, including the exact place and the fact that another guy encouraged Kavanaugh. "It's been on my mind all these years when his name came up. It was a big deal," he said, because the alleged act was beyond the bounds of campus party behavior. Like others, Appold recalled Kavanaugh as "relatively shy" when sober, but "aggressive and even belligerent" when drunk.

Richard Oh, a classmate who did not know Ramirez well, recounted overhearing a female student tearfully tell someone how a male student had exposed himself to a woman, after another student taunted her with a fake penis. Oh—a resident of C11, the suite in Lawrance Hall where Kavanaugh often watched sports, and where the incident allegedly occurred—told me that after Kavanaugh's nomination, he and some Yale friends had been trading "shady stories" about him. When Oh recalled the tearful woman's tale, his friends prodded him to contact the *New Yorker*, knowing it was making inquiries. When he called, he learned that its reporters already were investigating a story like the one he'd heard.[9]

The article quoted a statement from a half dozen classmates undermining Ramirez and implying she had political motives; it was provided by Kavanaugh's attorneys. Only one signator, Dan Murphy, was named. The others were Todd and White (oddly, Genda did not sign but his wife, Yarasavage, did), Louisa Garry, and Dino Ewing. "We were the people closest to Brett Kavanaugh during his first year at Yale," their statement said. "He was a roommate to some of us, and we spent a great deal of time with him, including in the dorm where this incident allegedly took place. Some of us were also friends with Debbie Ramirez during and after her time at Yale. We can say with confidence that if the incident Debbie alleges ever occurred, we would have seen or heard about it—and we did not. The behavior she describes would be completely out of character for Brett. In addition, some of us knew Debbie long after Yale, and she never described this incident until Brett's Supreme Court nomination was pending."

The statement almost immediately became suspect. The *New Yorker* reported that Garry and Ewing asked after publication that their names be deleted. One signer told me, not for attribution, that the statement came from "the Brett camp" and complained that it was released without the signer seeing the final language, which "seemed to slander Debbie."

The magazine separately quoted Yarasavage—anonymously—saying of Ramirez (just as she'd described to Berchem), "This is a woman I was best friends with. We shared intimate details of our lives. And I was never told this story by her, or by anyone else." Several Yale alumni did vouch for Ramirez in the article, including Roche. He described Ramirez as "exceptionally honest and gentle" and Kavanaugh as "frequently, incoherently drunk." Ramirez told the magazine she'd blamed herself for years but now held all four men as culpable, but especially Kavanaugh. "What does it mean that this person has a role in defining women's rights in our future?" She agreed to go public, the magazine said, for much the same reason Ford had. Realizing that the media was on to her story, she wanted to tell it in her own way: "I didn't want any of this, but now I have to speak."

Would this second allegation sink Kavanaugh? To stoke skepticism, Republicans quickly cited the magazine's acknowledgment that Ramirez at first did not name him as her main antagonist: "In her initial conversations with *The New Yorker*, she was reluctant to characterize Kavanaugh's role in the alleged incident with certainty. After six days of carefully assessing her memories and consulting with her attorney, Ramirez said that she felt confident enough of her recollections to say that she remembers Kavanaugh had exposed himself at a drunken dormitory party, thrust his penis in her face, and caused her to touch it without her consent as she pushed him away." Ramirez would later say that passage was misinterpreted—she was sure from the start of what happened, she said, yet she didn't want to attest to blurry details when first contacted, unexpectedly, by a reporter.

Kavanaugh, in a statement, called her allegation "a smear, plain and simple." He said, "This alleged event from 35 years ago did not happen. The people who knew me then know that this did not happen." White House spokeswoman Kerri Kupec similarly blamed Democrats for "a coordinated smear campaign" and noted that Ramirez's account was "denied by all who were said to be present." What she didn't say was that all those present, in Ramirez's telling, were complicit in her humiliation. Kupec's statement included the words Kavanaugh most needed to hear: "The White House stands firmly behind Judge Kavanaugh."

The White House and Senate Republicans also would make much of a line in a subsequent *New York Times* report that it, too, was unable "to find witnesses acknowledging the episode." Republicans ever after would erroneously say the *Times* had concluded that Ramirez's allegation did not meet its standards for news.

•   •   •

Just ahead of the *New Yorker* article's posting, hints of a third allegation surfaced on Twitter from Michael Avenatti, the showboating lawyer for porn star and Trump accuser Stormy Daniels. Avenatti tweeted that he was representing a woman with "credible information" he'd soon release, "of multiple house parties in the Washington, D.C. area during the 1980s during which Brett Kavanaugh, Mark Judge and others would participate in the targeting of women with alcohol/drugs in order to allow a 'train' of men to subsequently gang rape them." Grassley counsel Mike Davis quickly emailed Avenatti asking for his evidence.[10]

•   •   •

Ramirez was stunned when she read the *New Yorker* by what she came to call "the betrayal." There was the anonymous quote casting doubt on her account that she knew was from Yarasavage, once her best friend. And both Yarasavage and Todd, another old friend, had signed the anonymous statement challenging her credibility. She'd tried to protect them, refusing to let the magazine identify Genda, Todd, or White. "I did not see that coming," she told me. "I never imagined. I could understand if they just said, 'I don't remember. I couldn't remember that.' But to take it a step further and sign a statement in support of Brett? I never imagined."

Berchem, also outraged, waited all day on that post-publication Monday for Yarasavage to respond to her predawn text of disappointment. That evening she wrote again: "The silence speaks volumes." Again she sided with Ramirez: "If she has anything to gain, it's closure, not fame. I believe her. I do love you Karen. And I am sorry and I am mad. At him." Berchem recalled that at Yarasavage and Genda's wedding, Ramirez seemed to avoid Kavanaugh. "It was odd to me then," she wrote, but now "it all seems to make sense." Finally Yarasavage replied. "The silence is because this whole situation is awful. Many people have been affected by this, not just her and him." She added sardonically, "CNN was very polite when they knocked on our front door this morning at 8:20am."

CNN had tried to reach her, too, Berchem said. The women commiserated about the media attention. Then Berchem came back to Kavanaugh: "I wanted to go on record that this process is victimizing so many. That he is moving forward—in my view—is just selfish."

"I understand that thinking," Yarasavage wrote. "I respect it. I also understand the other side. Ha, see, that is why I'm an independent."

"You just made me laugh. Did not think that was possible today."

*　　*　　*

In the days before the *New Yorker*'s publication, Ramirez had connected with Stan Garnett, the well-known Colorado lawyer, thanks to the chief of staff to the state's Democratic senator, Michael Bennet. Garnett, the former Boulder County D.A. who'd run unsuccessfully for Colorado attorney general in 2010, was now at the politically connected law firm of Brownstein Hyatt Farber in Denver. One morning he was in a board meeting for Colorado's Legal Aid Foundation when he kept seeing phone messages from Bennet's Washington office. Another call came just as he was leaving. It was Bennet's aide, Jonathan Davidson. "We're getting reports of a woman who lives in Boulder who had an encounter with Brett Kavanaugh and we want somebody to size up what this is," Davidson said. "Would you do that?"

Garnett, familiar with Ramirez from their work against domestic violence, met her that evening at a law firm in Boulder. He was unsettled to learn that the *New Yorker* was about to publish her story, and that the *Washington Post* was on the scent—from the start, he knew to prepare for the fallout of a bombshell.

"I've dealt with lots of witnesses through the years. She remembered what you would expect her to remember," Garnett said months later in his office above downtown Denver, decorated with framed front pages of newspapers chronicling cases he'd won. "She clearly wasn't getting any pleasure out of talking about what happened and she clearly wanted no part of somebody else's drama. Debbie is a very thoughtful and philosophical person. She cares about politics in a big sense, but she doesn't want to be part of other people's political food fights." He quickly decided she was credible: "You didn't have the slightest sense she was making things up, or she was guessing, or that she was trying to make herself look good."[11]

Garnett knew he'd need help from lawyers more familiar with representing assault victims and navigating Washington. He called John Clune, a Boulder friend nationally known for handling cases of sexual assault and discrimination. In 2003, Clune had represented a nineteen-year-old hotel worker in the mountain town of Edwards, Colorado, who alleged that basketball star Kobe Bryant raped her. Ten years later he represented a Florida State University student who said she'd been raped by quarterback and future Heisman Trophy winner Jameis Winston, and more recently he had sued Baylor University for a former student who alleged she was gang-raped by two football players. He won settlements in each case. For a savvy Washington hand, Garnett reached out on Davidson's advice to Ricki Seidman, but she was part of Ford's team. Seidman arranged for a security consultant to meet with him and Ramirez to secure her house against threats, and for a public relations professional to help with the media. Garnett also called Boulder's police chief and sheriff for a heads-up on the incendiary story about to explode.

Clune agreed to help, given Garnett's assurance of Ramirez's credibility. On Sunday night, just as the *New Yorker* was about to post its story, the lawyers had a conference call with her. Initially Clune would be juggling cases—he had to fly to Montana in the morning for a child sexual assault case. Before dawn on Monday, he met with Ramirez before his flight, passing a CNN reporter outside his house at 5 a.m. From Montana, Clune appeared on TV to speak for Ramirez. A lawyer in Washington, William Pittard, emailed Garnett to offer his expertise in dealing with Congress. Pittard had been a nonpartisan counsel for the House of Representatives for more than five years. Garnett called later Monday. As with Ford's team, none of the lawyers were paid.

They never learned how national reporters came to hear Ramirez's tale. "Apparently, Debbie's story was one of the worst-kept secrets on Capitol Hill before Ronan called her," Clune told me. "So either somebody on Capitol Hill or somebody politically tied decided to try to get the story out, or it could have been that a lot of the classmates were talking with one another about the old days and Kavanaugh's general behavior." Farrow was an obvious choice for tipsters; he'd become famous for his coverage of sexual abuse. Clune said, "All these people that were in her class back at Yale started saying, 'Oh my God, are they going to find out what happened with Brett and Debbie Ramirez?' But nobody called Debbie about that, because they were no longer that close."[12]

After the article was posted, Grassley's nominations counsel contacted Garnett, opening days of jousting by email. Mike Davis was eager to have Republican investigators interview Ramirez. Clune said he wanted to talk with Davis first. But Davis repeatedly refused to consider a call with the Ramirez lawyers until she provided "her evidence," as he put it, to Grassley's staff. Her lawyers said they had no idea what he was talking about—their client was simply a citizen with pertinent information about a nominee for the Supreme Court. Exasperated, they told Davis they wanted the FBI to investigate, though she would agree to be interviewed by the committee lawyers "on appropriate terms." Heather Sawyer, a senior Democratic counsel on the Judiciary Committee, emailed Clune on Tuesday, September 25, that Democratic aides were available to discuss how to proceed even if Republicans weren't. "The Committee does not usually refuse to talk with counsel (or whistleblowers), and also does not usually place preconditions on getting on the phone to discuss next steps," she wrote, "so I'm not sure why that is happening here." Sawyer also offered to provide an FBI contact.[13]

In Boulder, Ramirez had a friend affix a sign to a garbage can near her curb: "Please demand an FBI investigation for Dr. Christine Blasey Ford and Debbie Ramirez's claims."

Pittard, for all his past experience as a congressional lawyer, was stumped by Davis's demands and by Grassley's public claims that Ramirez and her lawyers were not cooperating. On Wednesday, he ended the increasingly tense email traffic with Davis, and went directly to Grassley and Feinstein. In a letter emailed and hand-delivered to them, Pittard said the committee's refusal to seek an FBI investigation was "illogical." It would, he wrote, "allow a credible, efficient, and professional development of the facts—free from partisanship." Ramirez wanted to cooperate, he reiterated, yet Republican aides refused to talk with her lawyers until they produced evidence. "Ms. Ramirez has not conducted an investigation to gather materials that she now somehow can present, gift-wrapped, to the Committee," he wrote, then closed, "Ms. Ramirez has no agenda. She did not volunteer for this. But nor has she, or will she, shy away from truthfully recounting the facts." Her lawyers got no response from Grassley or Davis.[14]

Ramirez's Boulder friend, Dana James, tried to help. Ben Sasse, a young Republican senator on the committee, was a childhood friend. They had grown up together in Fremont, Nebraska, a town of roughly twenty-five thousand people outside Omaha, and were classmates, played sports, and attended the American Legion's annual Boys' State/Girls' State event—Sasse was "governor." She called his office several times, and twice explained to aides her connections to him, and that she wanted to attest to Ramirez's character and ask for an FBI investigation. Sasse never called, but on September 28, James was interviewed by a Grassley aide.

Ramirez's mother, in Connecticut, recoiled at the media coverage. "They started broadcasting Debbie like this down-and-out drunk," LeBlanc said. She secluded herself at home in Shelton, "because the whole town knows Debbie." She got a call from an old friend, a woman to whom LeBlanc had confided long before, after Ramirez wept over her unspecified shame at Yale. "I remember when you told me that!" the friend said. As a devout woman who'd sent her children to Catholic schools, LeBlanc was angry that Kavanaugh, who also had a Catholic education, could have done what her daughter and Ford were alleging.

Clune, with his experience in sexual assault cases, also was bothered by the coverage and the reaction—in particular, the peculiarly Washington way that Ramirez and Ford were immediately examined for their political leanings. Both were registered Democrats, but not particularly political, they said, and friends agreed. But, Clune said, the question should be, "Did this nominee commit these acts?" He also criticized those who dismissed the allegations because they dated to Kavanaugh's high school and college years—a variation on the "boys will be boys" trope. That stance, Clune said, suggested that the critics believed Kavanaugh might have done what was alleged *and* accepted that he had perhaps lied, under oath, in denying it. "That seems to me to be something that nobody in the country would be comfortable with for a potential Supreme Court justice."

●   ●   ●

Republicans rapidly decided that their best defense of Kavanaugh was a good offense, not directly against the accusers—that could backfire—but against Democrats, for their supposed smear campaign. Never mind that such a claim rejected the women's allegations and diminished them as independent actors, making them into political pawns. Senate Republicans had committed to granting Ford a public hearing, but they would all but ignore Ramirez, giving her story as little oxygen as possible to avoid suggesting a pattern of behavior by Kavanaugh.

As usual, Majority Leader Mitch McConnell set the tone, with a twelve-minute diatribe from the Senate floor on Monday, September 24. The man who had vowed within hours of Antonin Scalia's death that he would oppose any Obama replacement now lambasted Democrats for rushing to oppose Kavanaugh. "Before they reviewed a lick of evidence, before they'd heard a minute of testimony, Democrats had already made up their mind and chosen their tactics—delay, obstruct, and resist," he said, adding, "Even by the far left's standards, this shameful, shameful smear campaign has hit a new low."

McConnell recapped events with his own spin, first about Ford. She had given Democrats her letter eight weeks earlier and "requested the matter be handled discreetly and confidentially. The responsible next step would have been alerting the full committee so a confidential bipartisan investigation could begin." At best, that misrepresented Ford's wishes. She wanted to be anonymous, dealing only with her home-state senator and refusing to involve Grassley until her identity had leaked. The only investigation she wanted was by the FBI. McConnell charged that Democrats leaked the letter, citing a statement from Chris Coons of Delaware as proof. Yet Coons repeatedly denied that he'd suggested any such thing. The Republican leader said "all four supposed witnesses either flatly contradict or are unable to back up" Ford, and gave statements under oath—"under penalty of perjury," he repeated for emphasis. But none contradicted her; they said they didn't recall the party. Of the four, only Kavanaugh had given a sworn statement.

Turning to Ramirez's allegation, McConnell falsely said, "This claim is so dubious that the *New York Times* passed on the story entirely after looking into it" and getting "multiple on-the-record denials." In fact, while the newspaper hadn't found a witness to corroborate Ramirez, it did not refute the allegation and published no on-the-record denials. The *Times* ran its own in-depth piece on Ramirez's account, the work of ten reporters, the day after the *New Yorker* article. Finally, McConnell vowed, "This fine nominee to the Supreme Court will receive a vote, in this Senate, in the near future."[15]

Behind the scenes, however, some confidants were telling Trump to replace Kavanaugh with one of the other conservatives on his list. Among them, it was widely reported, was his daughter Ivanka.[16] As Trump said a year later of the naysayers, "Mitch knows this—there were plenty of other people that were saying, 'Let's go to maybe another choice.' And they didn't say it so nicely."[17] By Republicans' accounts, McConnell kept Trump in check behind Kavanaugh.

Typically, nominees remain closeted until confirmation except for courtesy calls to senators. In an unprecedented move reflecting Kavanaugh's peril, his White House handlers on Monday put Brett and Ashley Kavanaugh on Fox News in prime time. The idea, said a Republican strategist, was that "it could be beneficial if Kavanaugh's face was out there, and that way it wasn't just people defining him without him having the ability to define himself."[18] Trump promoted the show in advance to his millions of Twitter followers, tweeting, "This is an outstanding family who must be treated fairly."[19]

For twenty minutes, Fox host Martha MacCallum was gentle but tough in her questions. She didn't shy from embarrassing details, and fairly characterized Ford's memory gaps as typical of trauma victims, who often recall details of an assault but not tangential matters like date and place. Kavanaugh again denied the allegations. But his performance was by turns so rote and mawkish that Trump—his essential audience—roundly panned it privately, aides said. An emotional Kavanaugh, resolutely on message, repeated some variation of "I want a fair process and to be heard" no less than thirteen times, often to evade questions. MacCallum was visibly exasperated. Even Republicans privately mocked him. "'I just want a fair process, I just want a fair process'—Yeah, thanks, we got that," one senior Senate aide said. Six times he said, "I've never sexually assaulted anyone," four times he insisted, "I've always treated women with dignity and respect," and three times he oddly disclosed that he didn't have sex in high school or "for many years" afterward. "I was focused on trying to be number one in my class and being captain of the varsity basketball team and doing my service projects, going to church. The vast majority of the time I spent in high school was studying or focused on sports and being a good friend to the boys and the girls that I was friends with," Kavanaugh said. "I'm a good person. I've led a good life. I've tried to do a lot of good for a lot of people."

When MacCallum asked Ashley Kavanaugh whether the FBI should investigate—"If there's nothing to worry about and nothing to hide, why not have that process, Ashley?"—Kavanaugh interrupted before she could answer. "I want to be heard," he repeated, "...in whatever forum the Senate deems appropriate." His wife told MacCallum, "This process is incredibly difficult, harder than we imagined, and we imagined it might be hard. But at the end of the day, our faith is strong and we know that we're on the right path." Both said he would not quit. Asked if Trump would stand by him, Kavanaugh replied, "I know he's going to stand by me. He called me this afternoon and said he'd stand by me."[20]

Trump's post-show tweet seemed to confirm that, however displeased he was privately by Kavanaugh's TV presence. "The Democrats are working hard to destroy a wonderful man and a man who has the potential to be one of our greatest Supreme Court Justices ever," he wrote, "with an array of False Accusations the likes of which have never been seen before!" The next morning, he tweeted, "Rush Limbaugh to Republicans: 'You can kiss the MID-TERMS goodbye if you don't get highly qualified Kavanaugh approved.'"

Even as Kavanaugh took to the air, Ford's team got unsolicited advice from the camera-loving Avenatti to have her do the same. "You gotta get her on TV! I've had great experience with that," he told Debra Katz and Michael Bromwich in a phone call. "We don't think it's right for her," Bromwich replied. (He told me later, "And we're thinking to ourselves, 'You represent a goddamn porn star, okay? We represent a very private person.'") Avenatti told them to circulate a new photo to replace the ubiquitous one showing Ford oceanside in sports garb and sunglasses. "That picture of her makes me want to vomit every time I see that on TV," he said. Katz and Bromwich ignored him. They asked, when would Avenatti produce the third accuser he'd been teasing about on social media and TV? He wasn't saying.[21]

•   •   •

The next morning, Tuesday the twenty-fifth, Berchem texted Yarasavage from her train to work in Manhattan. Yarasavage wanted to talk by phone instead. As Berchem mostly listened, given the commuters around her, Yarasavage said that her husband denied Ramirez's allegation. Berchem, unswayed, replied by text, "I believe Deb. Brett is a selfish prick and hurting people all over again. There is no reason to pile on and assist him on that."

Berchem said she'd learned from the *Times'* Pogrebin that the newspaper was going to use the wedding-party photo in a story about Ramirez. Yarasavage objected. Berchem was confused—back in July, Yarasavage herself had arranged for the *Washington Post* to have the photo, and, more recently, she'd been willing to give it to both the *New Yorker* and the *Times*. Privately she surmised that because the *New Yorker* did not name Genda and Yarasavage, to their relief, they didn't want the photo in circulation now, to publicly tie them to the alleged assault. Soon Yarasavage texted Berchem: She'd found a media lawyer, who'd told the *Times* it wasn't authorized to use the photo. That also puzzled Berchem—both she and Yarasavage had posted the picture on Facebook; it was hardly private. And how had Yarasavage found a media lawyer so quickly—Brett's team? Before long the *Times* posted its Ramirez story, headlined "In a Culture of Privilege and Alcohol at Yale, Her World Converged with Kavanaugh's"—without the photo.[22]

The next day Berchem sent Yarasavage what would be the final text in their months-long chain. No response. More than two years later, the two women had not spoken, a friendship of four decades shattered on the crucible of Kavanaugh's confirmation. Severed, too, were Yarasavage's ties to Ramirez.[23]

Kavanaugh's nomination divided Yale alumni more broadly as well, though sentiment favored Ramirez. In the week after she went public, about forty-five hundred alumni and students signed two letters of support for her and Ford, one from women, the other from men. "Yale in the 1980s had not been co-educational very long; the drinking age in Connecticut jumped from 18 to 21, helping fuel the rise of fraternities and sororities," the men wrote. "Many of our female friends and classmates struggled to forge new paths in centuries-old male-only traditions; some of our male friends and classmates did not make this process easy. The harrowing accounts we've recently heard—of harassment, misconduct and assault— are sadly consistent with the campus culture at the time. We can't change what happened then, but we can speak out today."[24] Current students, in black, protested at Yale and outside the Supreme Court.

•   •   •

On Wednesday, September 26—as Ford prepared to testify the next day, and Ramirez's lawyers were trying to get a hearing for her, too—Avenatti finally revealed the accuser he'd promised. He released a sworn declaration from a Washington-area web developer, Julie Swetnick, making the most salacious charges yet.

Swetnick grew up in Gaithersburg, Maryland, about fifteen miles from Washington and less affluent than the suburbs familiar to Kavanaugh and Ford. She had graduated from the public high school there. She was several years older than Kavanaugh, yet she said she'd attended "well over ten" large house parties from 1981 to 1983 where she saw him and Judge excessively drunk, molesting girls, spiking punch "with drugs and/or grain alcohol," and waiting in a "train" of guys for their turn to rape girls. Swetnick said she ultimately became a victim herself, after being incapacitated by drugs in her drinks. Kavanaugh and Judge were present, she said, but she did not know if they were among the guys that raped her. Swetnick told "at least two" people shortly afterward, she said, and other witnesses could attest to her statements. To buttress Swetnick's credibility, her declaration noted that she had held security clearances for government technology contracts, including from U.S. embassies and the departments of State, Defense, Treasury, and Homeland Security. Yet even some women's advocates were skeptical that someone would repeatedly attend parties where gang rapes occurred; many assumed Avenatti had exaggerated her claims. Kavanaugh said her allegation was "from the Twilight Zone." Yet Susan Collins, still publicly undecided, told reporters minutes after the statement's release, "Obviously I take it seriously and believe that it should be investigated by the committee."[25]

Republicans quickly found legal records to paint Swetnick as litigious and a serial tax dodger. By the morning, they'd all but persuaded Collins of her lack of credibility. Mostly, however, Republicans focused on Swetnick's controversial celebrity lawyer, to further discredit her by extension. And as they succeeded in undermining Swetnick, increasingly when they referred to her allegation they'd lump in Ford's and Ramirez's as well, conflating the three to suggest they were equally suspect, when they were not. Within days, Republicans were able to persuade many Americans that the trio of accusers didn't suggest a pattern of behavior that would be fatal to Kavanaugh's nomination, but instead reflected a suspicious piling on, a concerted smear. Separately, reporters were skeptical of Swetnick's account given its inconsistencies and her failure to produce the promised witnesses.

Her disclosure, so soon after Ramirez's, played right into Republicans' effort to ignore the more credible Ramirez. It was "a disaster for this process," Clune said later. "Debbie Ramirez's story was starting to gain some of the attention that it deserved and then suddenly we had Avenatti, who'd been dripping out little hints here and there that something big was coming. And then he had this bombshell disclosure with affidavits. It was too much to process at once. Avenatti didn't have credibility because of some of the political fights that he had been in with the president. Suddenly we had a situation where people are willing to throw their hands up and say, 'Okay, now this is just getting ridiculous.'"

On that, both parties agreed. "I think the whole thing could have had a different outcome without the Swetnick allegations and with more investigation around the Ford and Ramirez allegations," said a Democratic Senate counsel. Once Avenatti surfaced, "The feeling changed here overnight." Davis echoed that, but from the opposite vantage: "I think Michael Avenatti did a tremendous disservice to the entire process, and especially to the Democrats' ability to block Brett Kavanaugh. He was manna from heaven."[26]

•   •   •

In the ten days between Ford's allegation and Swetnick's, Trump dropped the uncharacteristic restraint he had initially showed in reacting to the controversy—the influence, aides speculated, of Ivanka Trump and senior adviser Kellyanne Conway. He reverted to form, the champion of any man accused of sexual misbehavior, thumbing his nose at the #MeToo movement. Just after Ford surfaced, Trump issued a measured call for "a complete process" to examine her allegation, adding, "I'd like everybody to be very happy." Conway told reporters, "This woman should not be insulted and she should not be ignored." The next evening, Trump attacked Democrats in a tweet, not the accuser: "The Supreme Court is one of the main reasons I got elected President. I hope Republican voters, and others, are watching, and studying, the Democrats Playbook."[27]

Five days in, however, Trump loosed a tweetstorm against both Democrats and Ford. "I have no doubt that, if the attack on Dr. Ford was as bad as she says, charges would have been immediately filed with Local Law Enforcement Authorities by either her or her loving parents," he wrote mockingly. "I ask that she bring those filings forward so that we can learn date, time, and place!"[28] Fifteen minutes later came another, assailing her legal team as well: "The radical left lawyers want the FBI to get involved NOW. Why didn't somebody call the FBI 36 years ago?"[29] When Ramirez's allegation broke two days later, Trump was hostile from the start—even breaching diplomatic protocol in the process. At the United Nations on September 25 for an annual gathering of world leaders, he flayed her before reporters and cameras as he met with Colombia's president: "The second accuser has nothing. She said she was totally inebriated and she was all messed up, and she doesn't know it was him, but it might've been him." The next morning, addressing the new Swetnick allegation, Trump focused on her attorney, his nemesis, tweeting, "Avenatti is a third rate lawyer who is good at making false accusations, like he did on me and like he is doing now on Judge Brett Kavanaugh. He is just looking for attention and doesn't want people to look at his past record and relationships—a total low-life."

Later at the U.N., Trump held a news conference that was extraordinary even for him. He suggested that Kavanaugh's accusers were "evil people," and sympathized with men who, like himself, faced "false allegations." He wouldn't ask the FBI to act, he said, because "there was nothing to investigate." Democrats "know it's a big, fat con job," he said. "And they go into a room, and I guarantee you, they laugh like hell at what they pulled off on you and on the public." Asked if he believed the women were liars, Trump said "these are all false to me." Why did he always side with accused men—Alabama Senate candidate Roy Moore, an alleged pedophile; former White House aide Rob Porter, accused of abusing two wives; Fox News' Roger Ailes and Bill O'Reilly, both accused of sexual assault? Easy, Trump replied. "I never saw them do anything wrong." Was he influenced by his experience facing allegations of misconduct? "It does impact my opinion. You know why? Because I've had a lot of false charges made against me....I know friends that have had false charges. People want fame, they want money, they want whatever. So when I see it, I view it differently than somebody sitting home watching television where they say, 'Oh, Judge Kavanaugh, this or that.'"

Did he have a message for "the young people of America" in "this cultural moment"? Yes, he said: "Honestly, it's a very dangerous period in our country and it is being perpetrated by some very evil people....When you are guilty until proven innocent, it is just not supposed to be that way." He mentioned the next day's hearing featuring Ford and Kavanaugh: "I think it is going to be a very, very important day in the history of our country."[30]

•   •   •

After days of focus on Ramirez, and then Swetnick, attention returned to Ford on the eve of her coming out at the Judiciary Committee. On Tuesday, she and her small party had left California. "We didn't know until we heard she'd gotten on the plane that she definitely was going to come," Bromwich said. Ford took medication to allay her fear of flying; she seemed nervous on the small plane but joined in her friends' conviviality. They landed at Dulles International Airport outside Washington in late afternoon, earlier than expected, and had to wait for the security detail hired because of the death threats against Ford. The cost, about $60,000 for several days' protection, was covered by the new GoFundMe accounts. Finally, two large black vehicles arrived, each with a driver and another guard, and the Californians were taken to the Watergate Hotel.

Ford met with her lawyers while the others went sightseeing. "She was completely wiped out," said Bromwich, who was meeting her for the first time. The group mostly chatted, saving substantive preparations for the next day. By the time her friends returned, Ford had agreed to do the public hearing rather than ask for private sessions with senators. "Ultimately this was her decision," Katz said, "but we knew—she knew—that if she did not testify publicly, it would be buried"—as Republicans would effectively bury Ramirez's story without a hearing. "If the nation had not seen the power of her testimony, so what?"

Ford and her lawyers huddled all day Wednesday. She bristled at their talk of the partisan maneuvering. "Why is it so political?" she asked. Once, as they criticized Republicans, Ford admonished, "I don't want to hear the word 'Republican' or 'Democrat' again." That morning, they had given her a draft of her opening statement to the senators. By noon she returned it, edited. "It was a sea of red ink," Bromwich said. They revised the draft and gave it to her. "She did it again, another sea of red ink," Bromwich said. "She made it her own."[31]

* * *

Across town that night, Ashley Schapitl, a spokeswoman for committee Democrats, was in bed when she got a text from an editor at National Public Radio at 10:35: "Can you talk quickly?" She called the man, who told her that Grassley's office had just put out a press release suggesting that Ford's allegation against Kavanaugh might be a case of mistaken identity. Did Democrats have a response? The editor sent Schapitl the release: Two unnamed men had separately volunteered to Republican aides that they might be the person Ford described, but the sexual encounters were consensual. Democrats had been told of no such "witnesses."[32]

Republicans later justified publicizing such anonymous and unverified claims—and others that undercut and even slandered Ford, without seeking her response—by saying they did so in the interest of transparency. Such tactics also served to buttress Republicans' strategy of having it both ways: saying they believed Ford, but that Kavanaugh was not her assailant. Republicans soon would offer theories of mistaken identity in Ramirez's case as well.

15

SHE SAID...

"Indelible in the hippocampus
is the laughter..."

Ford and her California contingent, strangers in a strange land, awoke in the Watergate on the overcast morning of Thursday, September 27, and immediately began following the game plan Ricki Seidman had given them. Separate cars with security waited to take them to Capitol Hill, one for Ford, the other for her friends. She was driven into a protected cargo bay at the Dirksen Senate Office Building, where the Judiciary Committee was located; the others were dropped at a side entrance, where a young woman took them through the security checkpoint and another to the committee suite, down corridors with police and television cameras at the ready.[1]

They assembled in a small, two-room staff office. Republican aides had designated a room for Kavanaugh directly across the hallway, but Ford's team nixed that, fearful of an encounter. He now had a waiting room far down the corridor. Ford was surprised to be greeted by friends from Holton-Arms School, some of whom she hadn't seen since graduation, and a few current students. Samantha Semerad Guerry had been working since before dawn, putting her P.R. skills to work for Ford. With Seidman's logistical help, Guerry had been picked up in the darkness at her house in suburban Maryland and driven to a TV studio near the Capitol where the networks took turns interviewing her for their morning shows.

The former classmates' greetings were short—Ford quickly retreated to the rear room with Debra Katz, Lisa Banks, Michael Bromwich, and Barry Coburn. She reread her statement, the pages now in plastic sleeves, then removed each one to edit yet again. As the hearing time neared, Chairman Grassley entered to welcome Ford, as unwelcome a witness as she was to him and other Republicans. "I'm going to do this and be as fair as I can," Grassley told her. When he left, Ford's friends were taken to be seated at the front of the hearing room.

The dark-paneled Dirksen 226, one of the Senate's smallest hearing rooms, held about a hundred people. It was packed. Thanks to an array of TV cameras at the rear, millions more would watch in homes, offices, campuses, and bars—more than twenty million, according to Nielsen, would tune in to six networks that preempted regular programming, and countless others would stream the hearing on phones and computers.[2] This was a drama that mixed politics and sex, with the Supreme Court's balance at stake. Kavanaugh had the most to lose, but he also was the more practiced at Washington politics and public speaking. Ford, like Anita Hill decades before, was the very private mystery woman. Regulars on Capitol Hill—the members of Congress, staff, press, lobbyists—were used to dealing with people accustomed to public attention, who sought it out. After eleven days of nonstop coverage, Ford's ambivalence was well known. She was awaited with anticipation but also with apprehension on her behalf, from all sides—did she really know what was about to hit her?

A scrum of photographers waited in the well between the senators' raised dais and the witness table, eager to capture the accuser the nation had been hearing so much about but only knew from a snapshot behind dark glasses. Finally, as senators were still taking their seats, a door from a back room opened on the Democrats' side and out came a bespectacled blond-haired woman in a conservative navy blue dress and jacket, led by the hand by her new friend "Jay," a gentle giant of a security guard and a fellow basketball fan who would stay with her through her return to California. Her lawyers followed. Ford shyly kept her gaze down as she passed the senators, who stood by their chairs and didn't try to greet her. She'd later compare her experience to being the nervous bride coming down the aisle, the center of all attention, but flanked by lawyers instead of bridesmaids. "And you're like, 'Okay, here we go.'" At the table, Jay pulled the chair out. A large card at her place read "Dr. Christine Blasey Ford." She was plainly unsettled by all the cameras clicking at her. As agreed, Katz and Bromwich flanked her at the table. Ford would not be alone as Anita Hill was.

Another change from the usual format was a small table to her left. There sat Rachel Mitchell, looking more like a middle-aged aunt at the kids' Thanksgiving table than a Republican prosecutor from Phoenix, hired to question Ford so that the eleven male Republican senators wouldn't have to. They had caucused after Ford's story broke and decided that by delegating Ford's interrogation to an experienced female lawyer, they could avoid the shellacking senators got in 1991 for their treatment of Hill. "People didn't know necessarily how to question victims," a Republican aide explained. Republicans had considered thirty women for the job; many said no.[3]

"They had to go and rent a person to come and to be the stand-in female to do the questioning," scoffed former senator Carol Moseley Braun, an Illinois Democrat elected in 1992's "Year of the Woman" blowback after Clarence Thomas's confirmation.[4] Grassley, perhaps to offset Mitchell's Republican pedigree, introduced her by noting that Janet Napolitano, Arizona's former Democratic governor and President Obama's homeland security secretary, had named Mitchell "the outstanding Arizona sexual assault prosecutor of the year." Napolitano told me she had no memory of Mitchell. "When you're a governor, you recognize a lot of people for a lot of things. I don't think I ever actually met her," she said. Napolitano laughed: "That surprised me—being used as a validator."[5]

Katz handed Ford a binder with her statement, which she immediately began rereading. Bromwich patted her forearm; she shot him a wan smile. At one point, she nervously turned to the friends behind her, smiled, and waved slightly. Turning back, she faced the senators, visibly breathed deep, and swallowed hard. The tension was palpable—hers, and everyone else's.

"Remember, none of us had ever met her or had any idea how she was going to be as a witness," Chris Coons told me months later. "I remember having this lump in my throat as she came walking in." He'd heard from several Delaware constituents who knew the Blasey family, and he'd received mixed views about Ford—her appearance would be either "a disaster" or "riveting." Then, Coons said, "As she starts talking, and it's clear this is a measured, professional person who really doesn't want to be here, and really doesn't want to be talking about this, but is credible, my phones start just blowing up. And I heard over those next few hours from complete strangers, from classmates, from high school friends, from family, from extended community members, from people I've known for decades and people I've never met, with their own stories of sexual assault. That hasn't stopped yet." He was speaking a year later.[6]

Grassley thanked Ford as well as the absent Kavanaugh for "accepting our committee's invitation to testify," his graciousness belying his aide's hardball tactics in prior days, and his own public grousing about Ford and her team. "Both Dr. Ford and Judge Kavanaugh have been through a terrible couple weeks. They and their families have received vile threats. What they have endured ought to be considered by all of us as unaccept-able and a poor reflection on the state of civility in our democracy." Ford, ramrod straight, seemingly frozen, nodded assent. "So I want to apologize to you both for the way you've been treated," Grassley continued. "And I intend, hopefully, for today's hearing to be safe, comfortable, and dignified for both of our witnesses. I hope my colleagues will join me in this effort of a show of civility."

He segued immediately, however, to a partisan swipe at the Democrat to his left, Feinstein. He complained that she'd received Ford's letter nearly two months earlier and "took no action," did not share it with him, his staff, or other senators until a week after Kavanaugh's regular hearing ended. "These allegations could have been investigated in a way that maintained the confidentiality that Dr. Ford requested," he said—a claim that Ford, her lawyers, and Feinstein did not accept, given their mistrust of Grassley's staff and of Republicans generally. Feinstein sat without expression as Grassley continued his indictment: She hadn't raised the allegation when she'd met privately with Kavanaugh in August or during his confirmation hearing, and she hadn't even attended a closed session for senators to ask him any sensitive questions. (Feinstein aides had said then that she was ill.) "Throughout this period, we did not know about the ranking member's secret evidence," Grassley said. Finally Feinstein shot him a nasty look and shook her head disapprovingly.

"Only at an eleventh hour, on the eve of Judge Kavanaugh's confirmation vote, did the ranking member refer the allegations to the FBI. And then, sadly, the allegations were leaked to the press. And that's where Dr. Ford was mistreated."

Feinstein, in turn, countered that, yes, she'd received a letter from Ford and kept it secret at Ford's request. She segued to welcome Ford, adding archly that "the chairman chose not to do this." Grassley, ever quick to take umbrage when his fairness and midwestern manners were challenged, snapped that he'd planned to introduce Ford before she testified. Ignoring him, Feinstein segued to the broader issue. "Sexual violence," she said, is experienced by one in three women and one in six men, yet most goes unreported "due to the trauma they suffered and fearing their stories will not be believed. I think it's important to remember these realities as we hear from Dr. Ford about her experience." She recalled in 1991 "walking through an airport when I saw a large group of people gathered around a TV to listen to Anita Hill tell her story. What I saw was an attractive woman in a blue suit before an all-male Judiciary Committee"—an obvious parallel with Ford, in her blue ensemble facing the Republican men—"speaking of her experience of sexual harassment. She was treated badly, accused of lying, attacked, and her credibility put to the test throughout the process."

Feinstein noted that within thirty-six hours of Ford reluctantly coming forward, Republicans had ignored her request for the kind of FBI review Hill's allegations had received and instead quickly scheduled a hearing; only a public outcry forced them to give Ford more time. While the committee heard twenty-two witnesses in 1991, now it was hearing only from Ford and Kavanaugh and refusing Democrats' request to at least subpoena the alleged witness and accomplice, Mark Judge. "What I find most inexcusable is this rush to judgment," she said. As for Debbie Ramirez and Julie Swetnick, Republicans were refusing them even a hearing, let alone an FBI probe. Yet Kavanaugh's credibility was at issue, she said, as "more and more people have come forward" to rebut his claims of "never" drinking to such excess that he'd forget what he'd done. She quoted three of the most damning classmates.

"This is not a trial of Dr. Ford, it's a job interview for Judge Kavanaugh,"

Feinstein closed. "Is Brett Kavanaugh who we want on the most prestigious court in our country? Is he the best we can do?"

Grassley objected to Feinstein invoking what he called the "unsubstantiated allegations" of Ramirez and Swetnick. "We'll consider other issues other times," he snapped, though they never did. He then asked Ford to stand to be sworn in.

Solicitously, Grassley told Ford that whenever she wanted a break or needed something, "just ask us." Jet-lagged and stressed, she jumped at his offer: "I anticipate needing some caffeine, if that is available." With that, Americans finally heard the voice of the woman whose accusation had derailed a Supreme Court nomination. She then began to read her statement, her voice girlish and quaking. An unruly lock of long hair repeatedly obscured her face, and dark-rimmed glasses framed frightened eyes.

•　　•　　•

Ford rotely introduced herself: research psychologist, wife, mother of two boys. Then, her voice breaking, she got to her point: "I am here today not because I want to be. I am terrified. I am here because I believe it is my civic duty to tell you what happened to me while Brett Kavanaugh and I were in high school."

She told of her all-girls school and socializing with boys from the all-male schools in the Washington area. "This," she added matter-of-factly, "is how I met Brett Kavanaugh, the boy who sexually assaulted me." Under oath, she testified to the now-familiar story, which in her telling was newly gripping.

During her freshman and sophomore years, she'd become close to a friend of Kavanaugh's and went to "a number of parties" where he was present. "We did not know each other well, but I knew him and he knew me." One summer evening in 1982, after a day of diving at the Columbia Country Club, she joined "a small gathering" at a house in Bethesda. "There were four boys I remember specifically," she said—Kavanaugh, Judge, "P.J.," and one whose name she couldn't recall—and her girlfriend Leland Ingham, now Leland Keyser. "Like many that summer, it was almost surely a spur-of-the-moment gathering," Ford said—an implied counter to the fact that Kavanaugh had produced his 1982 calendar, on which he'd purportedly registered his every move, as evidence that he went to no such party. She admitted up front to her memory lapses: "I truly wish I could be more helpful with more detailed answers to all of the questions that have and will be asked about how I got to the party and where it took place and so forth. I don't have all the answers, and I don't remember as much as I would like to. But the details about that night that bring me here today are the ones I will never forget." Again her voice quavered. "They have been seared into my memory, and have haunted me episodically as an adult."

The teens were drinking beer in a living room. She had one beer. "Brett and Mark were visibly drunk." Early on, she ascended narrow stairs to a bathroom. "I was pushed from behind into a bedroom. . . . Brett and Mark came into the bedroom and locked the door behind them." She described music playing and one of the boys raising the volume, then audibly drew breath and exhaled before going on.

"I was pushed onto the bed and Brett got on top of me. He began running his hands over my body and grinding into me. I yelled, hoping that someone downstairs might hear me, and I tried to get away from him, but his weight was heavy. Brett groped me and tried to take off my clothes. He had a hard time, because he was very inebriated, and because I was wearing a one-piece bathing suit underneath my clothing. I believed he was going to rape me. I tried to yell for help. When I did, Brett put his hand over my mouth to stop me from yelling. This is what terrified me the most, and has had the most lasting impact on my life. It was hard for me to breathe and I thought that Brett was accidentally going to kill me. Both Brett and Mark were drunkenly laughing during the attack. They seemed to be having a very good time."

She sobbed slightly, and went on. "Mark seemed ambivalent, at times urging Brett on and at times telling him to stop. A couple of times, I made eye contact with Mark and thought he might try to help me, but he did not. During this assault, Mark came over and jumped on the bed twice while Brett was on top of me. And the last time that he did this, we toppled over and Brett was no longer on top of me. I was able to get up and run out of the room." She fled into the bathroom and locked the door. She heard the boys go downstairs, laughing and "pinballing off the walls," and waited to make sure they wouldn't return. Then she descended the stairs and went outside. "I remember being on the street and feeling this enormous sense of relief that I had escaped that house and that Brett and Mark were not coming outside after me."

Ford was a portrait of fragility unfamiliar to those who knew her as their confident, accomplished, and athletic friend and neighbor, without glasses. "That doesn't look like her," beach friend Jim Gensheimer thought as he watched at his Saratoga, California, home. Yet the image of a buttoned-up woman in dark-framed glasses became so iconic that *Time*, when it later chose Ford for its annual "Time 100" feature on influential Americans, pressed her to wear the glasses for her photo shoot. Kirsten Leimroth, Ford's other beach buddy, sat behind her and thought, "She did really well." Only later, when she watched video clips, did Leimroth see how nervous Ford had been. Keith Koegler said, "I knew when I was sitting there, 'She's fucking kicking ass!'" Some Senate aides—Democratic women—fought tears. Senators of both parties listened raptly.

"For a very long time, I was too afraid and ashamed to tell anyone these details. I did not want to tell my parents that I, at age fifteen, was in a house without any parents present, drinking beer with boys. I convinced myself that because Brett did not rape me, I should just move on and just pretend that it didn't happen." She told "very, very few friends" over the years. Before she married Russell Ford, she confided that she'd endured a sexual assault, but she provided details only a decade later, during couples counseling to allay tension over a home renovation project. "In explaining why I wanted a second front door, I began to describe the assault in detail. I recall saying that the boy who assaulted me could someday be on the U.S. Supreme Court, and spoke a bit about his background at an elitist all-boys school in Bethesda, Maryland. My husband recalls that I named my attacker as Brett Kavanaugh."

Beyond that, she only brought up the incident in occasional individual therapy sessions—"talking about it caused more reliving of the trauma so I tried not to think about it or discuss it." Then Kavanaugh's name showed up in media accounts of President Trump's Supreme Court candidates. She contacted her congresswoman and the *Washington Post* in hopes that her information—but not her identity—could somehow get to the president and persuade him to name one of the other conservatives on his list. "This was an extremely hard thing for me to do," she said, near tears, "but I felt that I couldn't not do it." Once Kavanaugh was the nominee, she was "very conflicted as to whether to speak out." She met with her congresswoman, Anna Eshoo, and at her direction wrote the now-famous letter to Feinstein. "My hope was that providing the information confidentially would be sufficient to allow the Senate to consider Mr. Kavanaugh's serious misconduct without having to make myself, my family, or anyone's family vulnerable to the personal attacks and invasions of privacy that we have faced since my name became public."

Ford defended Feinstein, who'd been flayed for two weeks by Trump, other Republicans, and conservative media, both for bottling up the letter and for leaking it. She said the senator promised in writing not to share her letter "without my explicit consent. And I appreciated this commitment." Feinstein, who'd had her head down to follow Ford's remarks from a copy of the statement, looked up at Ford and smiled. Ford continued: "Sexual assault victims should be able to decide for themselves when and whether their private experience is made public."

She described her months of vacillating over the "terrible choice" between civic duty and her family's privacy. When the media reported that Kavanaugh was likely to be confirmed, "I believed that if I came forward, my single voice would be drowned out by a chorus of powerful supporters." She resolved to remain quiet—until reporters showed up at her home and classroom, "making it clear that my name would inevitably be released." After the *Post* story, the attacks "rocked me to my core"— threats of death and violence, hacked emails, her life "picked apart" in the media by people "who have never met me or spoken with me."

She denied "partisan political motives"—"I am no one's pawn." Closing, she invited the senators' questions and asked for "some caffeine." She seemed spent. Handed a cup of coffee, Ford jauntily held it aloft, smiled, and declined the chairman's offer of a break.

•   •   •

Ford had nailed it, and Republicans knew it. But now came question time. Grassley began an unusual, awkward process: Republican senators would remain mute from their perch on the dais while Mitchell took their five-minute turns to interrogate Ford. She would have to stop, even in midsentence, whenever a red light at her table signaled time's up, that it was a Democrat's turn. The prosecutor began empathetically. She introduced herself to Ford—"Nice to meet you," Ford replied—and went on: "The first thing that struck me from your statement this morning was that you are terrified. And I just wanted to let you know I'm very sorry. That's not right."

Ford, in her answers to both Mitchell and Democratic senators, repeatedly showed a scientist's technical precision that was by turns disconcerting, comedic, and oddly effective. When Mitchell asked about Ford's initial text to the *Post*, Ford first corrected her wording of that July message: "I've misused the word 'bystander' as an adjective. 'Bystander' means someone that is looking at an assault, and the person named P.J. was not technically a bystander," because he was downstairs. When Feinstein invited Ford to explain why she'd kept her story to herself for years, Ford noted that she'd told a therapist—"where I felt like it was an appropriate place to cope with the sequelae of the event." She went on, "I think that the sequelae of sexual assault varies by person. So, for me personally, anxiety, phobia, and PTSD-like symptoms are the types of things that I've been coping with. So, more specifically, claustrophobia, panic, and that type of thing."

When Feinstein asked Ford, "How are you so sure that it was he?"—to counter Republicans' suggestion that she'd mistaken Kavanaugh for someone else—Ford didn't pause: "The same way that I'm sure that I'm talking to you right now. It's just basic memory functions. And also just the level of norepinephrine and epinephrine in the brain that sort of, as you know, encodes. That neurotransmitter encodes memories into the hippocampus. And so the trauma-related experience, then, is kind of locked there, whereas other details kind of drift."

Feinstein translated: "So what you are telling us is this could not be a case of mistaken identity?"

"Absolutely not."

Democrat Patrick Leahy would draw from Ford the most enduring line of her three-hour testimony, the one that would be most remembered, and cited, for its unique combination of science, emotion, and memory of a teenage girl's humiliation. Leahy asked her, "What is the strongest memory you have—the strongest memory of the incident, something that you cannot forget?"

Ford replied instantly: "Indelible in the hippocampus is the laughter—the uproarious laughter between the two—and their having fun at my expense." Previously composed, she teared up and hung her head. The room was silent. A Democratic staffer cried. Even Ford's lawyers weren't expecting that line. "I'm thinking to myself, 'Hippocampus? What the hell?,'" Bromwich said. "I frankly never dreamed it would be as incredibly effective and powerful as it was. That was just her speaking in the language that she's most comfortable with about how she had that level of certainty."

Her recollection of the boys' laughter resonated with one TV viewer. In Boulder, Ramirez was watching the hearing at home. When Ford recalled the laughter "at my expense," Ramirez exclaimed to her husband, "Oh my God! She's using the same words that I do!"[7]

*   *   *

Mitchell also asked Ford about her memories, to emphasize her gaps, including about where the gathering was and how she got home. The prosecutor suggested she was skeptical about Ford's claimed anxieties, such as fear of flying. She got Ford to acknowledge that Kavanaugh's name did not appear in the therapist notes Ford offered as corroboration. Yet minutes later, prompted by Democrat Amy Klobuchar of Minnesota, another former prosecutor, Ford clarified that she had talked about Kavanaugh many times with her individual therapist, "but therapists don't typically write down content as much as they write down process. They usually are tracking your symptoms, and not your story and the facts." She noted that her husband, in his sworn statement, affirmed that she had named Kavanaugh in their counseling.

Klobuchar, to offset Mitchell's focus on what Ford couldn't remember, asked her, "Can you tell us what you don't forget about that night?"

"The stairwell, the living room, the bedroom, the bed on the right side of the room as you walk into the room. There was a bed to the right. The bathroom in close proximity. The laughter, the uproarious laughter"—Ford's voice broke again—"and the multiple attempts to escape and the final ability to do so."

Mazie Hirono, a senator from Hawaii, expressed Democrats' disgust that Republicans had hired a prosecutor rather than question Ford themselves. She objected to what she saw as Mitchell's—Republicans'—strategy of emphasizing Ford's memory lapses to diminish her account of the actual assault. "The prosecutor should know that sexual assault survivors often do not remember peripheral information such as what happened before or after the traumatic event," Hirono said. "And yet she will persist in asking these questions, all to undermine the memory and basically the credibility of Dr. Ford."

Leahy singled out for opprobrium another Republican, Ed Whelan, a friend and former colleague of Kavanaugh's, a conservative lawyer long active in judicial nomination politics. The week before, on Thursday night, September 21, Whelan had posted a Twitter thread offering an elaborate theory for mistaken identity. His tweets were complete with floor plans of a suburban Maryland house and senior photos from the Georgetown Prep yearbook, all suggesting Ford confused Kavanaugh for his classmate Christopher Garrett—"Squi." Whelan's defamatory theory was quickly discredited. The next day, he apologized on Twitter for his "appalling and inexcusable mistake of judgement."[8] But the question remained: What did Kavanaugh know of his friend's plan to make a case for an alternative attacker? Days before Whelan tweeted, a Republican aide to Orrin Hatch had urged his Twitter followers to watch Whelan's account. Clearly, others in Kavanaugh's camp were in on the scheme.

Ford forcefully rebutted Whelan's doppelganger theory. In answering Leahy, she would not say Garrett's name, in deference to his privacy and in protest of Whelan's action. She said she knew him well from the club their families belonged to, and that she had gone out with him that summer; he had introduced her to Kavanaugh. She would not have confused the two.

Dick Durbin gave Ford another chance to rebut the suggestion that she'd mistaken Kavanaugh's identity—this one from Kavanaugh himself. The senator read from an advance copy of the remarks the nominee would soon deliver: "I never had any sexual or physical encounter of any kind with Dr. Ford. I am not questioning that Dr. Ford may have been sexually assaulted by some person in some place at some time." Durbin also noted that Grassley's staff had told reporters only the night before that two men separately contacted the committee to say they might be the person Ford described, but that she was a willing partner. Durbin asked, "Dr. Ford, with what degree of certainty do you believe Brett Kavanaugh assaulted you?"

"One hundred percent."

•   •   •

Mitchell, ignoring Democrats' evident disdain, shifted from the alleged events of a summer night in 1982 to the present, probing for evidence that Ford was indeed their pawn to bring down Kavanaugh. She quizzed Ford about who was paying for her expenses, including for the polygraph test, until Katz finally interjected, "Let me put an end to this mystery. Her lawyers have paid for her polygraph." "As is routine," Bromwich added. Mitchell asked Ford whether she expected to repay the costs. She said she didn't know, that she hadn't had time to consider such matters.

"Do you know how that letter became public?" Mitchell asked. No, Ford replied. Who helped her choose her lawyers? Family members and friends, she said. Prompted by Mitchell, she acknowledged that Feinstein's office had offered suggestions. Was it Ford's idea to demand an FBI investigation? Who else was covering her expenses? Bromwich interrupted again: "Both her counsels are doing this pro bono. We are not being paid and we have no expectation of being paid." Tired after nearly three hours, Ford whispered to him, "How many more?" Not many, he reassured her. She squeezed his hand.

Mitchell returned to the alleged assault. Was Ford aware that the three people besides Kavanaugh whom she'd identified as being at the gathering—Judge, P. J. Smyth, and her friend Leland Keyser—all said they had no memory of it? Ford was unfazed. Leland "has significant health challenges," she said, "and I'm happy that she's focusing on herself and getting the health treatment that she needs." She said she wouldn't expect

Keyser or Smyth to remember "because nothing remarkable happened to them that evening." However, she said, "Mr. Judge is a different story. I would expect that he would remember that this happened." Left unspoken: Kavanaugh should, too.

Finally it was over. Grassley thanked Ford "for your bravery coming out, and trying to answer our questions as best you could remember." He was the good cop. Within weeks, his bad-cop staff would produce a voluminous memorandum on its "investigation," slandering her in parts and leaving her depressed for weeks. Someone in the audience yelled, "Thank you, Dr. Ford." Mitchell, who would soon give Republicans a five-page memo to debunk Ford's allegation, walked to the witness table and, after chilly handshakes with Katz and Bromwich, leaned in close to Ford and said she'd pray for her. Ford wondered: Why did she need prayers? Her lawyers called the gesture creepy.

* * *

As Ford left, through the back room again, she was greeted by senators there—Feinstein, whom she'd never met, Hirono, and Arizona's Jeff Flake, the one Republican considered a swing vote on the committee. Flake was months from retirement—he'd opted not to seek reelection given the party backlash to his criticisms of Trump—and that effectively freed him to vote as he wanted.[9] "I was so relieved afterward I didn't even hear what people were saying," Ford said. Security guards guided her and Koegler to the Dirksen Building's basement, where they got into a car behind two other guards. Ford called her husband, who'd watched on television, and asked how the boys were doing. Fine, Russell Ford said, and he told her he was proud of her. She was remarkably calm as they headed back to the Watergate, Koegler thought, or perhaps in shock.

Katz and Bromwich stayed for Kavanaugh's testimony, taking seats in the audience where they could be seen on camera behind him. And just behind them was actress Alyssa Milano, a sexual assault survivor whose 2017 tweet in the Harvey Weinstein scandal—"#MeToo"—sparked the movement; her wide-eyed look of wonder as Kavanaugh testified would be so noticeable in the TV coverage that it would be parodied days later on *Saturday Night Live*. Ford's friends returned to the Watergate with Guerry, in the chauffeured van she'd been using since her morning TV hits. There, the small group assembled in a suite stocked with beverages and watched Kavanaugh off and on until Ford arrived. When she walked in, Guerry thought she looked overwhelmed. But amid much praise for her performance, she relaxed.

Before long her parents entered, along with the wife of one of her brothers. The trio hugged and kissed Ford. "I'm so proud of you," her mother said. "They were so supportive," said Leimroth, who'd met Ford's parents on their visits to California. Their drive from their summer home in Delaware to the Watergate offered evidence, if only privately, to counter Washington chatter that the public silence of Ford's parents, registered Republicans, must mean they weren't behind her. The *Washington Post* that morning had quoted Ralph Blasey telling a reporter, in a brief phone exchange, "I would think all of the Blasey family would support her. I think her record stands for itself—her schooling, her jobs and so on." He hung up, but then answered a second call and added, "I think any father would have love for his daughter."[10] Ford had told friends that she didn't want her parents to join her in the harsh spotlight. "If I asked them to do it, they would. But I don't need them to do it," she said. Referring specifically to the Senate hearing, she told me, "I would have preferred that no one was there, so it never crossed my mind that my parents should be sitting behind me for the cameras."

She was protective of them. Her mother was a stroke survivor, and the Blaseys' longtime social network overlapped with the Kavanaughs'. Nowhere was the awkwardness greater than at the all-male Burning Tree Country Club, where Ralph Blasey and Ed Kavanaugh were members, and Blasey the former president. One club member saw the two fathers together once when a third man walked up and told Kavanaugh that he believed "your son"; Blasey seemed unbothered. Republicans privately claimed that Blasey told friends at the club that even he didn't believe his daughter. When Ford asked her father about such rumors, he denied them; he told her he'd once approached Ed Kavanaugh, shook hands, and said he was sorry that the controversy had been so hard on both families. According to Ford, he also told her that some men confided they believed her.[11]

The next morning, Ford left early to return to California with her friends. Home was still an undisclosed hotel, where security awaited; at dinner in its restaurant that night with Koegler, she wore a hat and disguise while a watchful guard ate at a separate table. She was certain that nothing she had said would upend Kavanaugh's confirmation, yet she was glad that she'd said it. For months after, however, she second-guessed how she'd handled her coming out. "I should have done a better job," she told me, should have said some things differently, been more clear. But just what, she didn't say. Still, she did not regret coming forward: "I truly believe anyone would have shared this information, and not withheld it. Whether through a letter or phone call, they would have shared it. On the other hand, I'm starting to realize that not everyone is in a place in their life where they could afford to take that risk."[12]

•   •   •

Back at the Dirksen Building, and far beyond, Ford's appearance had elicited the first bipartisan agreement of the divisive saga: She had been "a compelling witness" and "very credible." Those were Trump's words. Immediately after she'd ended, the fretful president called Majority Leader Mitch McConnell for a reality check. "We are only at halftime," the wily senator told him.[13]

Yet Democrats and liberal activists were—most of them for the first time—entertaining the notion that Kavanaugh might actually be beatable, or that the White House would withdraw his nomination. "She was just so, so credible and so riveting, there was a moment of 'How on earth does anyone let this guy go forward, in light of this?'" a Democratic committee counsel said. Another recalled, "We all thought, in the intermission, that he was going to withdraw when he came out, or he would withdraw and not come out at all." Many on Kavanaugh's side despondently shared that view. In Republicans' committee offices, "All of us were in a pretty dismal state," said one aide. They wanted Kavanaugh to come out and "make a moment," as the aide put it.[14] A woman who attended the hearing as Kavanaugh's guest told a reporter for a conservative magazine that after Ford's testimony, "Unless something changes, I think we're toast."

The reporter would write, "It appeared that Ford's gut-wrenching and emotionally gripping testimony would convict Kavanaugh in the court of public opinion, or at least in the opinion of enough of the senators who would decide his fate."[15]

But Donald F. McGahn, the White House counsel and impresario of Kavanaugh's nomination, was having none of that. He'd watched Ford testify from the office of Thom Tillis, a North Carolina Republican on the committee, just a floor below. Now McGahn was receiving texts and emails from hand-wringers. "Disaster," one Republican wrote to him. McGahn went upstairs to the holding room for Kavanaugh, who'd just arrived with his wife and hadn't watched Ford. A few supporters and former Kavanaugh clerks also were there. When one suggested that Kavanaugh show some humility in his statement, and sympathy toward Ford, McGahn ordered everyone but the Kavanaughs out.

McGahn had taken to sending Kavanaugh video clips from a movie both men loved: *Miracle*, the Disney tribute to the legendary U.S. men's hockey team that upset the Soviets at the 1980 Winter Olympics. He quoted Coach Herb Brooks's locker-room pep talk: "This is your time. Now go out there and take it!"[16] After Kavanaugh's whiny Fox News interview, McGahn and other Republicans had urged the nominee to be more forceful, even adversarial, in his own defense. Now, in the wake of Ford's impressive presentation, McGahn doubled down. He told Kavanaugh, "You need to reboot the room."[17]

16

...HE SAID

"What goes around comes around."

It was showtime. The nominee and his wife walked up the room's center aisle hand in hand. She didn't release her grip until he took his chair at the witness table. In a funereal touch, Brett and Ashley Kavanaugh, his parents, and nearly all the women who filled the front row of supporters were dressed in black. Kavanaugh nervously rearranged the nameplate, papers, and water bottles before him. Chairman Grassley gaveled to resume the hearing and began by charging again that Democrats had "sat on Dr. Ford's letter for weeks"—though Ford had just testified that Dianne Feinstein did so at her request. At Grassley's direction, Kavanaugh stood, raised his right hand, and swore to tell the truth. Sitting, he began his statement, making immediately plain that he'd kicked his docile Fox News persona to the curb. Angrily defiant, his face contorted and his voice at a near shout, he emphasized that no handler had written his words: "This is *my* statement!"[1]

Kavanaugh again denied Ford's accusation "immediately, categorically, and unequivocally." Stabbing the table with his fingers, he complained that he'd waited "ten long days" for this hearing, "and as I predicted, my family and my name have been totally and permanently destroyed by vicious and false additional accusations." His wife, just behind him, teared up for the first of many times, her chin quivering.

The committee, and the nation, were seeing something they hadn't in more than a quarter century, since Clarence Thomas's confirmation hearing. A nominee was auditioning for a job on the highest court, one for which core criteria are judicial temperance and nonpartisanship, and displaying the opposite traits.

"This confirmation process has become a national disgrace," Kavanaugh shouted. "The Constitution gives the Senate an important role in the confirmation process, but you have replaced advice and consent with search and destroy." He complained of "a frenzy on the left to come up with something, anything, to block my confirmation." Glaring at the Democrats, he charged, "You sowed the wind for decades to come. I fear that the whole country will reap the whirlwind.

"The behavior of several of the Democratic members of this committee at my hearing a few weeks ago was an embarrassment. But at least it was just a good old-fashioned attempt at Borking. Those efforts didn't work. When I did at least okay enough at the hearings that it looked like I might actually get confirmed, a new tactic was needed. Some of you were lying in wait and had it ready."

More caustically than Grassley had, Kavanaugh accused Democrats of a premeditated smear. That was, he had to know, vastly at odds with the truth: Ford, and Debbie Ramirez, were forced into the open by haphazard and all-too-human dramas that took shape far from Washington, from the West Coast whispering about Ford to the gossiping of Yale alumni about Ramirez.

"The first allegation was held in secret for weeks by a Democratic member of this committee and by staff," he charged. Feinstein stared at him, inscrutable. "It would be needed only if you couldn't take me out on the merits. When it was needed, this allegation was unleashed and publicly deployed over Dr. Ford's wishes. And then, and then, as no doubt was expected if not planned, came a long series of false last-minute smears designed to scare me and drive me out of the process before any hearing occurred."

Kavanaugh next delivered his most controversial broadside of all: "This whole two-week effort has been a calculated and orchestrated political hit, fueled with apparent pent-up anger about President Trump and the

2016 election, fear that has been unfairly stoked about my judicial record, revenge on behalf of the Clintons, and millions of dollars in money from outside left-wing opposition groups. This is a circus. The consequences will extend long past my nomination. The consequences will be with us for decades. This grotesque and coordinated character assassination will dissuade competent and good people of all political persuasions from serving our country. And as we all know, in the United States political system of the early 2000s, *what goes around comes around*."

Democrat Sheldon Whitehouse of Rhode Island was not alone in thinking that Kavanaugh was building toward withdrawing. "Having gone so far over the line of what is acceptable conduct, there was just no way to believe that this was part of his strategy to continue to pursue a seat on the Supreme Court," Whitehouse later recalled.[2] Conservative David Frum, the anti-Trump writer and former speechwriter for George W. Bush, tweeted, "Kavanaugh's message—'the Left'; 'Borking'; 'revenge on behalf of the Clintons'; 'goes around comes around'—is that of a man who has already lost his Court seat, preparing for his next career." Yet no sooner had Frum posted his tweet than Kavanaugh proved such conventional thinkers on both sides wrong.

"I will not be intimidated into withdrawing from this process," he said. "You've tried hard. You've given it your all," he went on, glowering at Democrats Kamala Harris and Cory Booker. "You may defeat me in the final vote, but you'll never get me to quit. Never!" He insisted that "there is no corroboration" for Ford's allegation, "and indeed it is refuted by the people allegedly there"—a mischaracterization he would repeat several times. Ford had offered corroboration: the sworn statements from her husband and several friends that she had told them about the alleged attack long before Kavanaugh's nomination. Mark Judge, P. J. Smyth, and Leland Keyser had not "refuted" Ford's account; rather, they had said they had no memory of such an event, and Keyser had said she nonetheless believed Ford. Any lawyer, certainly one in line for the Supreme Court, knew that corroboration isn't limited to eyewitness accounts, and that not remembering something isn't the same as refuting it. Yet Kavanaugh and Republican senators would continue to misuse the terms.

Kavanaugh segued for a powerful personal note, invoking his wife and younger daughter. "The other night, Ashley and my daughter Liza said their prayers. And little Liza, all of ten years old, said to Ashley, 'We should pray for the woman.' It's a lot of wisdom from a ten-year-old." Near crying, he paused to compose himself. Then came the mistaken-identity defense: "I am not questioning that Dr. Ford may have been sexually assaulted by some person in some place at some time." He repeated the line for effect. He named the five area high schools for Catholic girls—the girls with whom he and other guys from Georgetown Preparatory School socialized—and noted that Ford attended a secular school. "She and I did not travel in the same social circles," he said—just after Ford had testified to dating one of his friends and attending parties where he was present. "It is possible that we met at some point at some events," he conceded, "although I do not recall that."

He became emotional again as he introduced what he considered his proof of innocence: pages from his 1982 calendar, the days of the summer months marked with his scrawls about weightlifting and work-outs, parties and gatherings for brew-skis, country club visits, football and basketball camps, beach trips, a golf tournament, ball games. "Why did I keep calendars? My dad started keeping detailed calendars of his life in 1978," Kavanaugh said. Overcome, he stopped a full eleven seconds before resuming, then stopped for fifteen seconds more. He was overcome a third time as he recalled working out "with other guys at Tobin's house—he was the great quarterback on our football team." By now Kavanaugh was repeatedly pausing, each time sniffling, rolling his tongue inside his cheeks, gulping water, and audibly expelling breath. It was a bizarre, cringey performance that unsettled even supporters. That weekend, when NBC's *Saturday Night Live* lampooned him in a skit that went viral, actor Matt Damon's impersonation was hardly more over the top than the real thing.[3] Republicans, however, defended his behavior as simply that of a man rattled at being wrongly accused.

Kavanaugh testified that he drank legally—the drinking age was eighteen. He was wrong, and should have known it. Maryland raised the age to twenty-one that summer; in any case Kavanaugh didn't turn eighteen until well into his senior year, in 1983. He went on, "I drank beer with my friends. Almost everyone did. Sometimes I had too many beers. Sometimes others did. I liked beer. I still like beer. But I did not drink beer to the point of blacking out, and I never sexually assaulted anyone."

He boasted of his good relationships with women since high school, but first addressed some contrary evidence. The *New York Times* had reported how he and his football teammates, in numerous entries in their senior yearbook, had called themselves "Renate Alumni," suggesting they'd each had sex with a student at a local girls' school. At least that's how it was widely read, including all these years later by the woman, Renate Schroeder Dolphin. She told the paper in a statement, "I can't begin to comprehend what goes through the minds of 17-year-old boys who write such things, but the insinuation is horrible, hurtful and simply untrue. I pray their daughters are never treated this way." For Kavanaugh, father to two daughters, it was an especially stinging rebuke.

Now he swore under oath that it was all a media-fanned misunderstanding. Those entries were "clumsily intended to show affection, and that she was one of us," he insisted, implausibly. "But in this circus, the media's interpreted the term as related to sex." He nonetheless apologized. As he had on Fox News, Kavanaugh addressed his early sex life—"not a topic I ever imagined would come up at a judicial confirmation hearing"—saying again that he never had sex in high school, "or for many years after that." He cited endorsements from women, including the letter signed by sixty-five women he knew in high school. Yet one was Dolphin, who'd signed before she learned of the yearbook entries.

He bragged of his record of hiring female clerks, adding, "If confirmed, I'll be the first justice in the history of the Supreme Court to have a group of all women law clerks." Kavanaugh read testimonials from women who were former law students, then looked toward the Democrats and snapped, "But thanks to what some of you on this side of the committee have unleashed, I may never be able to teach again." He angrily turned the page in his binder and read the next bit of praise, for his work coaching girls' teams. Again he laced into the Democrats: "But thanks to what some of you on this side of the committee have unleashed, I may never be able to coach again." For him and his wife, he said, "explaining this to our daughters has been about the worst experience of our lives."

Kavanaugh closed, "I swear today, under oath, before the Senate and the nation, before my family and my God, I am innocent of this charge." He slapped his binder shut, pushed it aside, and blew his nose, awaiting Rachel Mitchell's questioning.

●　●　●

The disjointed process resumed: five minutes of Mitchell speaking for a Republican senator, followed by five minutes of a Democrat's questions, back and forth. The prosecutor, in Grassley's turn, asked Kavanaugh about his relationships with those Ford said were at the gathering. Judge had been a friend since ninth grade, he said. "Funny guy, great writer, popular, developed a serious addiction problem that lasted decades. Near death a couple times from his addiction. Suffered tremendously from"— Kavanaugh stopped, emotional again.

Feinstein, citing all three accusers, challenged him, "If you're very confident of your position, and you appear to be, why aren't you also asking the FBI to investigate these claims?" Not answering, Kavanaugh angrily complained again of his wait for a hearing, the "nonsense" accusations, and his family "destroyed." When Feinstein tried to talk, he cut her off, almost shouting. When Mitchell next asked him about his high school drinking, he petulantly repeated variations on what was becoming a widely mocked mantra: "We drank beer. I liked beer. Still like beer. We drank beer." Again he acknowledged sometimes drinking too much, but denied ever blacking out or not remembering what he had done. Mitchell asked, one detail at a time, whether he'd done what Ford claimed. Push her into a bedroom? Grind his genitals into her? Cover her mouth? Try to strip off her clothes? To each he said no, emphatically.

Patrick Leahy, like Feinstein and each Democrat who followed, was met with the same antagonism. Kavanaugh's disrespect was that of a man who figured he had nothing to lose—these Democrats already opposed him. Yet the repeated intemperance from a federal judge was jarring. Leahy asked whether Judge was referring to Kavanaugh when he wrote in his memoir, *Wasted: Tales of a Gen X Drunk*, about a passed-out, vomiting "Bart O'Kavanaugh." Rather than answer, Kavanaugh attacked Leahy for trying to "make fun of some guy who has an addiction."

"Judge Kavanaugh, I'm trying to get a straight answer from you under oath," Leahy replied. "Are you Bart O'Kavanaugh that he's referring to, yes or no?"

"You'd have to ask him," Kavanaugh said snarkily.

"Well, I agree with you there," Leahy said. "And that's why I wish that the chairman had him here under oath."

When Leahy began to ask about the yearbook references to drinking and sexual exploits, Kavanaugh cut him off. "Senator, let me take a step back and explain high school. I was number one in the class..." He interrupted Leahy's attempts to return to the question until Leahy, peeved and defeated, gave up.

Mitchell next was poised to question Kavanaugh in place of Lindsey Graham, but the Republican senator wouldn't yield. He'd had enough. The back-and-forth was not helping Kavanaugh, as Republicans saw it, and he was at risk of going too far with the partisan bellicosity; he could end up alienating the few swing-vote senators in both parties. Graham wanted to remind his side that this was political war, for the highest stakes, and *they* had to do the battling. He was about to show them how. Graham started by lobbing friendly questions to Kavanaugh, premised on criticisms of Feinstein and Senate Democratic leader Chuck Schumer. Then he swung toward the Democrats across the room. With his face convulsed with rage and his finger piercing the air, he attacked with a fury that rallied Republicans but also underscored how far they would go to confirm Kavanaugh. Was it real or feigned? Probably both, knowing the savvy, shape-shifting Graham.

"If you wanted an FBI investigation, you could have come to us! What you want to do is destroy this guy's life, hold this seat open, and hope you win in 2020." He went on, "Boy, y'all want power. God, I hope you never get it. I hope the American people can see through this sham—that you knew about it and you held it. You had no intention of protecting Dr. Ford. None."

He turned back to Kavanaugh: "Would you say you've been through hell?"

"I've been through hell and then some."

Closing his four-and-a-half-minute philippic, Graham threw down a gauntlet for the few undecided Republicans: "If you vote no, you're legitimizing the most despicable thing I have seen in my time in politics."

Ford's three hours of testimony, and her compelling certainty that it was Kavanaugh who had attacked her, suddenly seemed a distant memory. Graham had reinforced the Republicans' wobbly line. From Trump on down, they would blame Feinstein and Democrats generally for betraying Ford, trying to seem sympathetic to her even as they rejected her accusation and depicted her as Democrats' dupe.

It fell to Whitehouse to follow Graham. "Should we let things settle a little bit after that?" he asked Grassley. Months later, Whitehouse remained reluctantly impressed by Graham's performance. It was, he told me, "probably the single most effective piece of political theater I have ever seen in my life." Kavanaugh's nomination was saved. "That plane was going down. And single-handedly—by changing the emotional tone, by reverting to tribalism, by being even more histrionic than Kavanaugh, giving him cover—it was the pivot point that put Kavanaugh back on the path to confirmation. Part of me was horrified and part of me was awestruck with technical admiration for that performance."[4]

Whitehouse quizzed Kavanaugh about his yearbook, not so much to mock the sophomoric activities he'd boasted of back then but to raise doubts about his truthfulness in describing them now. "Have at it, if you want to go through my yearbook," Kavanaugh sniped, twice. Whitehouse did, inquiring about specific entries.

"'Beach Week Ralph Club—Biggest Contributor'?"

"I'm known to have a weak stomach."

"Did it relate to alcohol?"

"I like beer. I like beer. I don't know if you do. Do you like beer, Senator, or not? What do you like to drink?"

Whitehouse ignored him. Kavanaugh persisted: "Senator, what do you like to drink?"

The senator asked about references to "boofed," a term widely associated with anal sex (for example, a Frank Zappa song released in the summer of 1982, "Valley Girl," called a teacher "Mr. Bu-Fu.")

"That refers to flatulence. We were sixteen."

The fourteen derisive references to "Renate"?

Kavanaugh objected, without irony, to having "her name dragged through this hearing."

When Republicans' turns came, every one now followed Graham's example, ignoring Mitchell and championing Kavanaugh. John Cornyn of Texas, the second-ranking Senate Republican, told him, "Judge, I can't think of a more embarrassing scandal for the United States Senate since the McCarthy hearings."

"I'm never going to get my reputation back," Kavanaugh replied. "My life is totally and permanently altered."

"Well, Judge, don't give up."

"I'm not giving up."

It was Amy Klobuchar's turn. No one would have predicted that it would yield perhaps the day's most dramatic moment—and for Kavanaugh, the most threatening. The Minnesota senator had been one of the least confrontational Democrats throughout the hearings, reflecting her "Minnesota nice" persona and moderate record. Like many Democrats, she began by asking Kavanaugh to seek an FBI probe. But she was so genial that Kavanaugh, even in dodging her request, said, "I have a lot of respect for you." She segued to his drinking in high school and college, prefacing her queries by poignantly recalling the struggles of her alcoholic dad. Now Kavanaugh became defensive, peevishly interrupting her as he had the others. Then came the exchange that would have Republicans fearing his defeat.

"Drinking is one thing," Klobuchar said, "but the concern is about truthfulness. And in your written testimony, you said sometimes you had too many drinks. Was there ever a time when you drank so much that you couldn't remember what happened, or part of what happened the night before?"

"No. I—no. I remember what happened. And I think you've probably had beers, Senator, and so I—"

"So you're saying there's never been a case where you drank so much that you didn't remember what happened the night before, or part of what happened?"

"You're asking about, you know, blackout. I don't know. Have you?"

Klobuchar, taken aback at his insolence, was mute for three long seconds. Behind her, one of the usually poker-faced staff lawyers looked aghast. The senator stammered, "Could you answer the question, Judge? I just—so you—that's not happened? Is that your answer?"

"Yeah, and I'm curious if you have."

"I have no drinking problem, Judge."

"Yeah," he snapped. "Nor do I."

"Okay. Thank you."

Klobuchar turned off her mic and all but collapsed back into her chair, looking slightly upset. She turned to the aides seated behind her and asked no one in particular, "Did that just happen?" Durbin immediately thought, "That is going to be a problem for Kavanaugh."[5]

The Republicans thought so, too. While Kavanaugh just moments before had had a similar smart-alecky exchange with Whitehouse, most Republicans saw his disrespect toward Democrats as strategically deft, solidifying the support of combative conservatives—and Trump. Now he'd crossed a line. He had been rudely belligerent toward a female senator—and one who'd just told of her family's suffering with alcoholism—even as he faced allegations of assaulting women.

White House counsel Donald F. McGahn, sitting behind Kavanaugh, slipped him a note on yellow legal paper. Kavanaugh unfolded it, read for eight seconds, covered it with his legal pad, and looked down. Republican aides huddled on the dais. As Grassley sought to proceed, and called on Orrin Hatch for questions, his aide Mike Davis whispered into his ear—audibly, given an open mic—"Take a break." The elderly Hatch, seemingly oblivious to the maneuvering of fellow Republicans around him, objected. He wanted to speak. But Grassley announced a fifteen-minute break. When it ended, a momentarily humbled Kavanaugh asked to speak. Glancing at Klobuchar, he said, "Sorry I did that. This is a tough process. I'm sorry about that."

Hatch, finally getting his turn, gave a boys-will-be-boys defense of the nominee: "He was an immature high schooler. So were we all. That he wrote or said stupid things sometimes does not make him a sexual predator."

President Trump walks down the White House's first-floor Cross Hall with newly retired Supreme Court Justice Anthony M. Kennedy and his successor, Brett M. Kavanaugh, to Republicans' celebration of Kavanaugh's confirmation in the East Room, October 8, 2018. *Photo credit: Doug Mills/The New York Times/Redux*

Senate Majority Leader Mitch McConnell (left) shakes hands with conservative lawyer Edward Whelan at the White House announcement of Kavanaugh's nomination, July 9, 2018. Whelan, a close friend of Kavanaugh, would later concoct an elaborate theory implicating another man for the sexual assault that Christine Ford alleged; amid an outcry, he apologized for his "appalling" action. *Photo credit: Saul Loeb/AFP via Getty Images*

Trump, Kavanaugh, and Kennedy enter the East Room for the celebration and ceremonial reenactment of Kavanaugh's swearing-in for the Supreme Court, October 8, 2018. *Photo credit: Official White House Photo by Amy Rossetti*

Chief Justice John G. Roberts Jr. swears in Kavanaugh as a justice while wife Ashley Kavanaugh holds the Bible and daughters Margaret (left) and Liza (right) look on, in a private ceremony at the Supreme Court just after Kavanaugh's Senate confirmation, October 6, 2018. *Photo credit: Fred Schilling/Supreme Court of the United States/Wikimedia*

Kavanaugh joins his new colleagues on the Supreme Court for their official group photo, November 30, 2018. *Photo credit: Jabin Botsford/The Washington Post via Getty Images*

Kavanaugh's senior-year photo from the 1983
Georgetown Preparatory School yearbook,
at left, and, at right, as No. 12 and the captain
of Prep's varsity basketball team. *Photo credit:*
WhiteHouse.gov

Brett Michael Kavanaugh
Bethesda, Maryland 20816

sity Football 3, 4; J.V. Football 2; Freshman Football 1; Varsity
ketball 3, 4 (Captain); Frosh Basketball (Captain); J.V. Basket-
(Captain); Varsity Spring Track 3; *Little Hoya* 3, 4*** Landon
ks and Bowling Alley Assault — What a Night; Georgetown vs.
isville — Who Won That Game Anyway?; Extinguisher; Sum-
of '82 — Total Spins (Rehobeth 10, 9 . . .); Orioles vs. Red Sox
Who Won, Anyway?; Keg City Club (Treasurer) — 100 Kegs or
st; ████████ — I Survived the FFFFFFourth of July;
ate Alumnius; Malibu Fan Club; Ow, Neatness 2, 3; Devil's
angle; Down Geezer, Easy, Spike, How ya' doin', Errr Ah; Reho-
h Police Fan Club (with Shorty); St. Michael's . . . This is a
ack; ████ ███ Fan Club; Judge — Have You Boofed
?; Beach Week Ralph Club — Biggest Contributor; ████ —
nted Whack; ████ ████ Beach Week 3-107th Street;
ose Prep Guys are the Biggest . . .; GONZAGA YOU'RE LUCKY.

Christine Blasey Ford, pictured in the
yearbook for her senior year in high
school at the Holton-Arms School in
Bethesda, Maryland. *Photo credit:*
Holton-Arms Scribe, 1984

Photos of Debbie Ramirez and Kavanaugh, Class of 1987, in Yale's yearbook. A week after Ford's allegation against Kavanaugh, Ramirez came forward to say that he had exposed himself to her during a drinking game in their freshman year. Republicans did not give her a hearing. *Photo credit: Yale Banner*

Kavanaugh, wearing a Washington Redskins T-shirt and the antique leather football helmet for which he was known on campus, helps to referee an annual beer-chugging contest—"Tang," sponsored by his fraternity—during his senior year, 1986–87. *Photo credit: Courtesy of Jordan D. Warshaw*

Kavanaugh with his parents, Edward Kavanaugh Jr. and Martha Murphy Kavanaugh, at his Yale College graduation in 1987. *Photo credit: WhiteHouse.gov*

After his nomination, Kavanaugh and his backers got this photo from Yale classmates Karen Yarasavage and Kevin Genda (couple at center), taken before their
wedding in 1997. The couple is flanked by members of their wedding party who
also attended Yale, including Kavanaugh (second from right) and, on the far left,
Debbie Ramirez and Kerry Berchem. Berchem believed that Kavanaugh sought
the photo in anticipation of Ramirez's allegation, to suggest a lingering friendli-
ness between them that would belie her account of an assault years before. *Photo
credit: Courtesy of Kerry Berchem*

Kavanaugh, an associate counsel to Independent Counsel Ken Starr for the years-
long investigation of President Bill Clinton and First Lady Hillary Clinton,
watches intently as Starr testifies before the House Judiciary Committee on possible grounds for the president's impeachment, November 19, 1998. *Photo credit:
David Hume Kennerly/Getty Images*

Karl Rove, chief strategist for President George W. Bush, embraces Kavanaugh, then the White House staff secretary, after a flight during Bush's 2004 reelection campaign, in a photo that captures Kavanaugh's place in the president's inner circle. *Photo credit: Paul J. Richards/ AFP via Getty Images*

Bush reviews documents with Kavanaugh at the president's ranch in Crawford, Texas. The trailers were home to Bush's aides and security detail when they were with him in Texas. *Photo credit: WhiteHouse.gov*

Kavanaugh is at Bush's right at a table in the first family's private dining room of the White House. Between them, seated in the background, is Bush's personal secretary and Kavanaugh's future wife, Ashley Estes Kavanaugh. *Photo credit: WhiteHouse.gov*

MAY 31, 2006

THE WHITE HOUSE
WASHINGTON

Dear Brett,

I have mixed emotions as I write this letter. One, I'm thrilled that you were confirmed to the court. You will be an excellent judge in all respects. Who knows? Some future President may be wise enough to name you to the Supreme Court. Secondly, I will miss your advice, your leadership, and your presence. You have been a valuable member of the team and have been a close friend. I care for you and Ashley a lot. I thank you for your service. I wish you all the best.

Bush wrote this personal note after Kavanaugh's prolonged fight for Senate confirmation to the Circuit Court of Appeals for the District of Columbia, a court second in prestige only to the Supreme Court. "Who knows?" Bush wrote to his protege. "Some future President may be wise enough to name you to the Supreme Court." *Photo credit: WhiteHouse.gov*

Former president Bill Clinton greeted Kavanaugh, who in the previous decade had spent years investigating Clinton and seeking grounds for his impeachment or prosecution, aboard Air Force One in early 2006. Clinton was accompanying President Bush for the funeral of Coretta Scott King in Atlanta. *Photo credit: WhiteHouse.gov*

Kavanaugh takes the oath to join the D.C. Circuit Court, administered by his mentor, Supreme Court Justice Anthony Kennedy, on June 1, 2006, as Chief Justice John G. Roberts Jr. looks on. The partisan standoff in the Senate over his nomination had lasted three years. *Photo credit: WhiteHouse.gov*

Kavanaugh awaits the start of the hearing before the Senate Judiciary Committee on his Supreme Court nomination, September 4, 2018. His wife, daughters, and parents are in the first row over his right shoulder; on his left are Republican supporters, including White House Counsel Don McGahn (second from the aisle, in blue tie). *Photo credit: Chip Somodevilla/Getty Images*

Dr. Christine Blasey Ford, at the Senate Judiciary Committee on September 27, 2018, testifies about her allegation that a drunken Kavanaugh sexually assaulted her in high school. Afterward, President Trump called her a "credible" and "compelling" witness, but soon, before political audiences, he took to characterizing her as a liar. *Photo credit: Michael Reynolds-Pool/Getty Images*

Debbie Ramirez, shown in October 2020 in Boulder, Colorado, was refused a hearing by Senate Republicans. They also worked with the White House to block the FBI from questioning people she suggested could help corroborate her account. *Photo credit: Vikram Shah/Courtesy of Debbie Ramirez*

Kavanaugh, who followed Ford in testifying to the Senate committee, vehemently denied her allegation and blamed Democrats for seeking "revenge on behalf of the Clintons," as his wife looked on. His performance was widely criticized, yet it rallied Republicans to his side. *Photo credit: Jim Bourg-Pool/Getty Images*

Democrats so far had done little to try to undermine Kavanaugh's denials by reviving questions about his honesty on other subjects from his past confirmation hearings. Finally Democrat Chris Coons did so. "It's against that backdrop that I'm seeking to assess your credibility today," he told Kavanaugh.

Even more than Klobuchar, Coons was an unlikely antagonist. A soft-spoken consensus-builder from Delaware, he was the son and grand-son of Republicans of the old-school, eastern establishment variety—pro-business, hawkish, fiscally conservative, and socially moderate. Coons had been a teenage volunteer for Ronald Reagan in 1980 and a founder of College Republicans at Amherst College. But in 1984, as Reagan sought reelection, Coons switched parties and joined the Progressive Students Alliance; he even debated his College Republicans cofounder at a standing-room-only forum. A semester in Africa had left Coons dis-illusioned about Reagan's policies, especially his support of South Africa's racist government. He went to Yale for postgraduate studies and got a divinity degree—in 2018, he was still preaching—and a law degree, two years after Kavanaugh.[6]

Coons posed a new idea: "Why not agree to a one-week pause to allow the FBI to investigate all these allegations?" Kavanaugh was as unreceptive as he'd been to other Democrats. But one Republican—Jeff Flake, the swing vote—was intrigued, as would soon be clear.

Mazie Hirono of Hawaii, one of the last Democratic interrogators, zeroed in on the new issue that had arisen just that day, by Kavanaugh's own conduct and words. "Is temperament also an important trait for us to consider?" she asked.

Kavanaugh readily replied: "For twelve years, everyone who has appeared before me on the D.C. Circuit has praised my judicial temperament."

Republicans continued to pummel Feinstein. To Democrats' frustration, their senior member remained mostly mute. While she was headed to an easy reelection, many in her party wished the eighty-five-year-old had retired in favor of a younger, more dynamic Democrat. Only when a last attack came from Ted Cruz of Texas, an unpopular figure in both parties, did Feinstein demand time to respond. "Let me be clear," she said, "I did not hide Dr. Ford's allegations. I did not leak her story.... I was given some information by a woman who was very much afraid, who asked that it be confidential. And I held it confidential until she decided that she would come forward." Cornyn was unsatisfied. Did her aides leak it? Feinstein's response was embarrassingly confused. First she said her aides wouldn't leak—she hadn't even asked them if they had. Then, visible to the audience, her two counsels behind her, Jennifer Duck and Heather Sawyer, whispered to Feinstein that in fact she had asked them, and that they'd denied leaking. Looking puzzled, she turned back to her mic and corrected herself. For days afterward, Trump mocked her shaky response and mimicked her at political rallies.

The Democrats' final interrogator, Kamala Harris, returned to his vituperative opening salvo alleging a Democratic conspiracy. She noted that Neil Gorsuch had been confirmed just the year before, without much drama. Harris, a former San Francisco prosecutor, reviewed the parallels between Gorsuch and Kavanaugh: graduates of Georgetown Prep and elite law schools, clerks to Anthony M. Kennedy, appeals court judges, Supreme Court nominees. "The only difference is that you have been accused of sexual assault," she said. "How do you reconcile your statement about a conspiracy against you with the treatment of someone who was before this body not very long ago?"

Kavanaugh was unresponsive. A final friendly Republican, John Neely Kennedy of Louisiana, closed with suitable theatricality. "Do you believe in God?" he asked in his folksy, high-pitched drawl. "I do," Kavanaugh replied. Kennedy gave him "a last opportunity, right here, right in front of God and country," to deny each of the three women's allegations. Kavanaugh did. "You swear to God?" Kennedy mock-challenged him.

"I swear to God."

•   •   •

Grassley ended the nearly nine-hour hearing and immediately a security guard was up and near Kavanaugh. The room was quiet as he and his wife were escorted out the rear door. Then America loudly debated how he'd done, illustrating just how opposite are the prisms through which the left and right had come to view things. To his critics, Kavanaugh was unpersuasive and his behavior disqualifying for the court. To supporters, he was justifiably angry and compellingly convincing. Yet both sides generally agreed he'd likely be confirmed. By his partisan defiance, Kavanaugh had solidified the Republican base behind him and, by extension, probably the Senate's Republican majority.

Nearby in the Capitol, in Vice President Mike Pence's Senate office, aides cheered, gave high fives, and pumped fists.[7] That night, Graham was on Sean Hannity's Fox show to collect the host's accolades for his act that day—and to gratuitously shame Kavanaugh's main accuser: "Miss Ford has a problem, and destroying Judge Kavanaugh's life won't fix her problem."[8]

Among Kavanaugh's opponents, the optimism they'd flirted with after Ford testified all but vanished. Keith Koegler, watching replays and commentary that night in his hotel room, decided Kavanaugh—with Graham's help—had likely prevailed. "I don't think we ever had any real confidence" that Ford's testimony would matter, he told me much later. "It's just the way Washington is these days."[9] One of Ramirez's lawyers, William Pittard, had watched the hearing with colleagues at his law firm blocks from the White House. After Ford's testimony, he said, "I thought it was over" for Kavanaugh. And as Kavanaugh began, "I thought he was killing himself with the anger." But, Pittard said, his anecdote of his daughter praying for Ford "was a powerful, powerful story. And they're humans up there—it's not hard for them to see themselves as Brett Kavanaugh."[10]

That ambivalence described Flake, the only undecided Republican on the committee and one of just three in the Senate. He left the hearing less inclined toward the nominee than before, reflecting the risk of Kavanaugh's angry-man strategy. "I didn't like the way he lashed out, obviously, and it did suggest intemperance, and somebody who may not be suited for the court," Flake told me months later, after he'd retired from the Senate. The contemptuous responses to Klobuchar especially bothered him. Yet he asked himself, "How would I act if I felt that I had been unjustly accused?" He canvassed Kavanaugh associates, including judicial colleagues and clerks. "There was not one example we could find in the twelve years he'd been on the circuit court that he was anything but a model of decorum and decency," Flake said. "So that was so out of character, what he had exhibited, that you say, 'Well, you have to weigh that.' And that's what I did."

Yet something more bothered Flake: Republican leaders' actions. Hours after the hearing, Mitch McConnell met with some Republicans in the Capitol. Susan Collins—considered Kavanaugh's make-or-break vote—said she wanted a sworn statement from Mark Judge rebutting Ford. For days, other senators, including Flake and undecided Democrat Joe Manchin of West Virginia, had complained that all the Senate had was a statement from Judge's lawyer, not testimony or an affidavit from the alleged accomplice himself. "I'd been troubled the whole week before by the reasons we'd been given by McConnell and others why we couldn't have one—'Mark Judge wouldn't talk,' 'He'd lawyered up,' 'We can't find him,'" Flake said. But once Collins made her demand, "all of a sudden—BOOM!—they found him in a half an hour and he signed it. So, I thought, 'Hey, this whole thing that he can't be found and can't be talked to, that's a canard.'" With the committee set to vote the next day, Friday, Flake said he had "one of the longest nights I've ever had before, trying to decide what I do."[11]

Senators in both parties wondered why Kavanaugh hadn't borrowed a page from his former boss, Bush. In his 2000 campaign, Bush dismissed all inquiries about his misbehavior as a hard-drinking young man with the same self-deprecating line: "When I was young and irresponsible, I was young and irresponsible." One senator, who declined to be identified, told me, "I thought of that so often. If Kavanaugh would have said, 'I drank a lot of beer, sometimes I drank too much beer, and I don't remember everything that happened. I never thought I hurt anybody. I'm sorry if I did, I don't remember this at all'—that's kind of like a George Bush. Or, 'I was a kid and I did stupid things that kids do, and I don't remember this young lady or what happened, and that's the best I can give you.' I mean, that—to me—might have been the end of the story." Instead, Kavanaugh "doggedly" stuck to his blanket denials, even to heavy drinking.

For those who had lived through the Clarence Thomas–Anita Hill showdown twenty-seven years earlier, the parallels were eerie. "It was like déjà vu all over again," said Janet Napolitano, the veteran of Hill's legal team. Again, she said, Americans saw a "poised and credible" accuser and an "over-the-top response" from the accused. Yet Kavanaugh's response "made Thomas look tame. And then Lindsey Graham followed up."[12]

Ominously, in the fallout of the day's drama the American Bar Association that evening sent a letter urging the committee to halt action until the FBI investigated the allegations. "The basic principles that underscore the Senate's constitutional duty of advice and consent on federal judicial nominees require nothing less than a careful examination of the accusations and facts by the FBI," ABA president Robert Carlson wrote. Without that, he said, the Senate would harm its reputation and "the great trust necessary for the American people to have in the Supreme Court." Heather Gerken, dean of Kavanaugh's alma mater, Yale Law School, endorsed the ABA's message.[13]

More threatening perhaps, Kavanaugh's testimony had stoked doubts about his integrity far beyond Washington. Formerly reticent college and high school classmates suddenly were willing to speak to the media about what they saw as his needless lying—under oath!—about his drinking and silly yearbook entries. Lynne Brookes, Kavanaugh's college friend who wouldn't sign a letter of support, also wouldn't speak out against him. But that night she agreed to go on CNN. "There were a lot of emails and a lot of texts flying around about how he was lying to the Senate Judiciary Committee today," she told host Chris Cuomo. Brookes, a registered Republican, said Kavanaugh was often "stumbling drunk" in college, "and there had to be a number of nights where he does not remember."[14]

Seth Hagan, a Prep classmate, posted on Facebook after the hearing, "So angry. So disgusted. So sad. Integrity? Character? Honesty?"[15] Leland Keyser released a new statement, through her lawyer, responding to Kavanaugh's repeated claims that she had "refuted" Ford's story. She "does not refute Dr. Ford's account," the statement said, "and she has already told the press that she believes Dr. Ford's account." (Keyser would reverse herself nearly a year later.)

Yale classmate Chad Ludington released a statement that he'd "cringed" at Kavanaugh's claims of innocence and harmless drinking in both his Fox News interview and his Senate testimony. Ludington, a professor at North Carolina State University, recalled drinking often with Kavanaugh and seeing him "staggering from alcohol consumption, not all of which was beer," "often belligerent and aggressive." He wrote of the Demery's incident, of Kavanaugh throwing his drink in a man's face at the campus bar, starting a fight that landed a friend in jail. "I do not believe that the heavy drinking or even loutish behavior of an 18- or even 21-year-old should condemn a person for the rest of his life," Ludington wrote. "I would be a hypocrite to think so." Yet, "I do believe that Brett's actions as a 53-year-old federal judge matter. If he lied about his past actions on national television, and more especially while speaking under oath in front of the United States Senate, I believe those lies should have consequences."[16]

Ramirez's friends were startled that Kavanaugh testified he had first heard of her allegation when the *New Yorker* reported it on September 23. They believed—and Kerry Berchem had texts to perhaps prove— that Kavanaugh and his backers had anticipated such an accusation since July. After he was nominated, they had contacted classmates about their memories and sought the 1997 photo that included Ramirez and Kav- anaugh. Berchem previously had resisted prodding from Yale friends to speak out. But after his testimony, she resolved to act. Berchem contacted the Hartford, Connecticut, office of her senator, Richard Blumenthal, a member of the Judiciary Committee. She sent fifty-one screenshots of her texts with Karen Yarasavage, along with a note explaining them and a timeline suggesting that Kavanaugh had expected Ramirez's allegation and sought to line up former classmates to rebut it. Blumenthal's chief counsel, Sam Simon, reached Berchem that night, and gave her information to Grassley the next day. Berchem also contacted the offices of Republican fence-sitters Flake, Collins, and Lisa Murkowski of Alaska, asking them to demand an FBI investigation.

•   •   •

Ramirez watched the hearing at home with her husband. By the time Ford was finishing, Shah had developed a stomachache so painful that he was buckled over. The couple left for the hospital before Kavanaugh began. No sooner had they gotten to the emergency room, however, than Shah told his wife, "I don't feel the pain anymore." They concluded it must have been stress-related. Much later Ramirez watched some of the Kavanaugh testimony that she'd missed—"the part where he lies and said that what happened with me was not true." She despaired of getting a hearing of her own, or an FBI investigation. The committee was set to vote on Kavanaugh the next day.[17]

•   •   •

Thursday had been among Washington's most momentous days in memory, yet Republican leaders awoke Friday resolved to proceed as if nothing much had happened, as if no clouds hung over the nominee for the nation's highest court. Grassley was intent on holding a committee vote that morning. Democrats were just as intent on delaying it until there was an independent investigation of Ford's allegation—with Judge questioned under oath—and a hearing for Ramirez.

"There was someone in the room, according to Dr. Ford's account, when she was assaulted. And the idea that we would never call Mark Judge before the committee—and he just got away with sending a letter saying, 'I don't know anything'—is crazy," said Coons's counsel, Erica Songer. As for Ramirez, "We saw this with Dr. Ford: There's something about having someone say in their own words what happened, before the entire committee."[18]

Yet the power of Ford's testimony had not moved Republicans from their course. The Republicans' nominations counsel, Mike Davis, gave me a simple reason for not giving Ramirez a hearing: "The senators didn't want to hear from her." The Republican senators, that is. Why not? "I don't think they found her allegations credible," Davis said. That went without saying for Julie Swetnick, represented as she was by Michael Avenatti.[19]

•   •   •

Early Friday, Flake validated Republican leaders' rush to a vote by issuing a statement that he would support Kavanaugh. As Flake walked to the committee room, he was accosted at an elevator by two women who identified themselves as survivors of sexual assault. One blocked the elevator doors, trapping him inside while reporters and cameras recorded the encounter.

Ana Maria Archila, executive director of the liberal Center for Popular Democracy, pointed a finger and cried, "What you are doing is allowing someone who actually violated a woman to sit in the Supreme Court! This is not tolerable! You have children in your family—think of them!" Flake, looking pained, repeatedly muttered, "I need to go to the hearing." The second woman, Maria Gallagher, jumped in: "You're telling all women that they don't matter, they should just stay quiet because if they tell you what happened to them, you're going to ignore them." Flake looked down. "Look at me when I'm talking to you!" she chided. "You're telling me that my assault doesn't matter, and that you're going to let people who do these things into power!"

Now Archila challenged him: Did he believe Kavanaugh told the truth? Flake said only "thank you" as he looked for an escape. "Saying 'thank you' is not an answer," she admonished. A reporter asked if he'd care to respond. Flake said no. Finally the doors closed. The nearly five-minute clash made for dramatic television and was replayed all day. As CNN aired the moment live, analyst David Gergen, who'd advised presidents of both parties, declared it "just the beginning." He added, "We are on the brink of what is likely to be the most divisive vote in our lifetime." Ford spoke for millions of women, Gergen said, "and if you have a group of eleven white males sitting there on the Republican side, you have to ask, do they get it?"[20]

●   ●   ●

Coons had a bad moment of his own walking to the committee room, thanks to his friend Flake. He'd stopped in a corridor to chat with reporters when one of them noticed a news alert on her phone and showed it to him: Flake would vote for Kavanaugh. "Oh, fuck," the usually unflappable Coons uttered, tearing up. He went on, "We each make choices for our own reason. I'm struggling. Sorry."

Like others, Coons was exhausted by the furor. He had worked since dawn on the remarks he would make before the committee voted—editing them in the hope of winning over Flake. "I was overcome with emotion partly because I was genuinely surprised," Coons explained much later.

He and Flake had one of the rare bipartisan friendships in Congress, and Coons had hoped that he could persuade Flake to support a delay, to slow the train until the FBI could investigate. Now that seemed moot.[21]

As soon as Grassley opened the meeting, Democrats—Blumenthal—sought again to subpoena Judge. Suddenly the chairman brandished a letter from Judge, signed and sworn—the letter that Republican leaders had secured the night before, only after Collins demanded it. Grassley read it aloud. Judge asked—"as a recovering alcoholic and cancer survivor"—that the committee accept his letter denying any memory of the party Ford alleged, in lieu of his personally testifying. The committee predictably voted along party lines against a subpoena, and Grassley set the vote on Kavanaugh for 1:30. That left several hours for all twenty-one senators to make final statements. Ignoring Democrats' protests, Grassley signaled for a vote on his motion. Leahy objected that Grassley was violating committee rules. Hirono erupted, "What a railroad job! My answer is no, no, *no!*" Booker and Harris refused to vote. The Republican majority of course prevailed.[22]

Grassley led off the senators' final statements. As other Republicans would, he again falsely stated that all three people Ford named at the long-ago gathering refuted her "version of the facts." He concluded, "There is simply no basis to deny Judge Kavanaugh a seat on the Supreme Court on the basis of evidence presented to us." Feinstein followed, admonishing Republicans—and Kavanaugh—with an intensity she hadn't previously shown: "Candidly, in the twenty-five years on this committee, I have never seen a nominee for any position behave in that manner. Unbelievable!" She noted that Republicans had lambasted her for not giving Ford's letter to the FBI, yet they'd refused to direct the bureau to investigate in the two weeks since she'd turned it over. As for Ramirez and Swetnick, Republican strategy "is no longer attack the victim, it is ignore the victim."

Hatch followed, and all but proved Feinstein's point. It was time to "end this circus," he snapped. "We've had enough time on this to choke a horse!"

Leahy, like Feinstein, condemned Kavanaugh for his partisanship. By his "conspiratorial madness" and vehemence, Kavanaugh outdid Thomas, Leahy said. "In my time in the Senate, I have never seen such volatility, partisanship, and lack of judicial temperament from any nominee, for any court, in any administration." Then it was a Republican's turn, and Graham expressed the opposite view: "I've never heard a more compelling defense of one's honor and integrity than I did from Brett Kavanaugh. He looked us in the eye, everybody in the eye, and he was mad, and he should have been." Then Graham, who would become chairman in 2019 if Republicans kept their majority, issued a vague threat to Democrats. "I'm going to remember this," he said. A former prosecutor, he ended with an appeal to Flake: "I cannot tell you, Jeff, what happened thirty-five years ago. I *can* tell you this—that through any legal system, this thing would not get out of the batter's box."

Two former Democratic prosecutors—Whitehouse and Klobuchar—disputed him. "I don't want to hear about 'respecting Dr. Ford' when we are not giving her the respect of having an investigation of the case that she made to us yesterday," Klobuchar said, a tear in her eye. "She did this before the nominee was even picked.... So don't argue that she is part of some massive political strategy. Those aren't the facts!"

For all the passion exhibited, and some of it was even real, the statements were predictable from Democrats and Republicans. And the outcome seemed certain. That was all the more reason that attention from the audience, and reporters, normally should have waned by the time more junior lawmakers got their turns to speak. On this morning, however, Coons would prove an exception. His advisers had worked until after 1 a.m. on a draft statement. He read it at 6:30 and wasn't at all satisfied. He still believed he could get Flake to back a delay, he told his counsel, Songer, "and this is exactly the wrong speech if I'm trying to persuade him." They softened criticism of Republicans and amplified Coons's rebuttal to their claims that Democrats had sandbagged Kavanaugh by springing the allegation late in the process. When it was finally his turn to speak, he began by saying that he had only learned of the allegation, but not Ford's name, at the Democrats' September 12 caucus where Feinstein was forced to disclose it. He did not know how it leaked. "I cannot rule out that the person who leaked this information had a partisan agenda," he said, "but I am certain that ranking member Feinstein and her staff did *not* disclose Dr. Ford's account before that date." That was Coons's remonstrance to

McConnell, who'd claimed in his Senate speech that Coons had implicated Feinstein.[23]

"To suggest," he went on, "that Senate staff interviews or letters from lawyers are an adequate substitute for a robust FBI fact-gathering process, that we might then weigh, is not credible and reflects, sadly, a willful blindness to the dysfunction of our institution." He appealed to Republicans' sense of his fairness—"*You know me*," he said. "If I were convinced this were nothing more than a partisan hit job to take down a good man and hold a position vacant past the election, I would not stand for it." Abandoning his prepared remarks, he held his cell phone aloft. Now emotional, Coons said that while Ford testified he'd gotten messages from five friends—"Five!"—revealing that they'd been sexually assaulted. "That suggests that there is an ocean of pain in this nation not fully heard, not yet fully addressed, not yet appropriately resolved. And I for one will not countenance the refrain said by too many in response to these allegations by Dr. Ford, that 'It happened too long ago' and that 'Boys will be boys.'"

Coons, a former prosecutor, reminded his colleagues that Ford had provided corroborating evidence that she'd told people of her assault in 2002, 2012, 2013, 2016, 2017, and 2018. He criticized Kavanaugh for saying that the individuals Ford named had refuted her account: "That's not the case, and Judge Kavanaugh knows it." He referred to the allegations from other women: "Their claims have varying credibility but deserve to be heard."

Opposite Coons, on the Republicans' side, Flake was riveted. When Coons finished, Flake walked over and tapped his shoulder. They exited into an anteroom.

Later accounts would ascribe Flake's subsequent call for an FBI investigation to the unsettling elevator encounter. That was just one factor, he told me. He was upset at the nation's division, he said, and troubled by Republican leaders' initial, false claims that Judge couldn't be found to provide a sworn statement or testify. "When I got to the committee, I wasn't sure I was going to ask for the delay. I didn't know." Then Coons spoke, making the case "why we shouldn't rush this. And it made sense to me."[24]

It was a measure of how polarized Congress had become since the 1990s that Flake and Coons's friendship was so rare. Parties aside, they had much in common. Flake was fifty-six, Coons fifty-five. Both had spent time in Africa when they were young—Flake as a Mormon missionary, Coons as a college student and volunteer relief worker—and returned together as senators. They were in a Bible study group, and their wives were friends. In Congress, Flake said, "you can go years without any meaningful interaction with those on the other side." Once they were alone in the back room, Flake began, "This is tearing the country apart." They tried unsuccessfully to reach FBI director Christopher Wray, but Rod Rosenstein, the deputy attorney general, called them back. He assured them that an investigation could be done in a week. Flake reached Collins and Lisa Murkowski, who said they would back him—the Republican trio would leverage their votes to demand a one-week FBI probe.

By now, Republicans in the hearing room had become unnerved by Flake's and Coons's absence. No less than George W. Bush tried to reach Flake. He'd called the previous week, too, just to assure him that Kavanaugh "was a good guy." This time Flake didn't answer. "My guess is that somebody had said, 'Hey, now would be a good time to talk to Jeff again. He's going wobbly.' " Senators and aides began filling the L-shaped back room, crowding the small space for what became a mix of partisan showdown and bipartisan negotiation. Flake and Coons squeezed into an old-fashioned wooden phone booth for privacy.[25] In the hearing room, Grassley had little choice but to call a break. He and a few other senators sat idly by, waiting.

When Flake left the booth, he was besieged by Republicans pressing him to relent, Graham and Cornyn most forcefully. Backed into a corner, literally, he looked distraught. The Republicans told him an FBI probe wouldn't accomplish anything. "Of course the FBI can do something— it's the FBI!" Coons interjected. "There are leads to follow and they could be followed in a short period of time." The Republicans countered that Flake would be rewarding the Democrats for their scheming, "and you'll gain nothing." Long after, Flake said of the squeeze, "It was the same kind of pressure that all Republicans are now under—'You stick with the team, stick with your tribe.' "[26]

A separate clash pitted Whitehouse and Republican Ben Sasse of Nebraska. Sasse confronted the Democrat about an undisclosed allegation that Whitehouse had recently passed on to Grassley and Feinstein. A Rhode Island constituent claimed that in August 1985, two men named Brett and Mark sexually assaulted a woman on a boat in Newport Harbor, and that he and another person accosted them hours later, physically injuring both. Republican aides privately questioned Kavanaugh under oath; he denied the claim. Inexplicably, they also read to him unrelated anti-Trump tweets by the accuser, thereby effectively identifying the man and making his partisan views part of the interview transcript released to the public. Consequently, the man was assailed on social media; he recanted the allegation and apologized for his "mistake."

Sasse charged that Whitehouse had leaked a false allegation to smear Kavanaugh. When their exchange grew so heated that it drew the others' attention, the two senators retreated to the hearing room and the near-empty dais to continue talking, now in low voices. On camera, but not overheard, Sasse and Whitehouse went back and forth until both were smiling. "Ben gave me the courtesy of the time to explain what had really gone on," Whitehouse said later. He explained to Sasse that he'd told Grassley and Feinstein of the allegation so the committee staff could investigate, privately, but it became public because of the Republican aides' irrelevant questions to Kavanaugh about the accuser's past tweets.[27]

More than an hour after Flake and Coons had gone to the back room, Grassley moved to resume the meeting. Flake privately asked him for a minute to address the committee. Grassley agreed, and Flake publicly described his understanding of what had been hashed out: He would vote for Kavanaugh now, sending his nomination to the Senate with the panel's party-line endorsement. But the Senate would delay its vote—no more than a week—while the FBI investigated "the current allegations that are there."

"We ought to do what we can," Flake said, "to make sure that we do all due diligence with a nomination this important."

Grassley immediately ordered a vote, but Leahy objected. Feinstein asked, "What are we voting on?"—was it the nomination, or the agreement Flake had outlined? It was the nomination, which was approved 11–10 along the usual party lines. Only then, with Flake's vote in hand, did Graham warn about the so-called agreement, saying, "We're not the majority leader."

That is, McConnell called the shots in the Senate, and neither he nor the White House were parties to this "deal." Grassley similarly said that he could only promise Flake that he'd advocate for it with McConnell and Trump. But Flake implicitly reminded them that his vote in the Senate was at stake, and Klobuchar correctly added that Murkowski's and Collins's votes might be as well.

Suddenly Grassley adjourned the meeting after nearly four and a half hours. Again Leahy and Feinstein protested. They wanted clarity: What exactly had been agreed to? It's done, Grassley dismissively said. "Well, *is* it done?" Feinstein demanded.

"This is all a gentlemen's and -women's agreement," Grassley told her.

17

THE "INVESTIGATION" THAT WASN'T

"Don't worry, we're going to do it by the book."

Democrats' doubts about the FBI's investigation were soon validated. With no votes to spare, McConnell persuaded Trump to direct the bureau to act, to placate Flake, Murkowski, and Collins. Flake told reporters the probe would cover "the current allegations," but that turned out to be those of Ford and Ramirez—ostensibly—but not Julie Swetnick's. Perhaps most egregiously, it also would not cover a still-secret allegation, from a reputable figure in Washington, that Kavanaugh had exposed himself to a second woman at Yale.

Only the trio of swing-vote Republicans had the clout to ensure a credible probe. Yet Flake, when asked by reporters about the bureau's mandate, said, "We'll leave that to the FBI." The FBI, however, left it to the White House. And White House counsel Donald F. McGahn, along with McConnell, saw to it that the bureau was tightly constrained. After the committee adjourned on Friday, McConnell met with its Republican members, and Murkowski and Collins, to decide how to limit the investigation. Flake, recalling the meeting later, said, "Obviously [they] had to talk to Mark Judge," and to the others Ford placed at the gathering: Leland Keyser and P. J. Smyth. "You stopped at hearsay. We would talk to anybody with firsthand knowledge of what might have occurred. If something specific came out of those interviews that the FBI would need to follow up on, they would follow up."[1]

That wasn't what happened. People allegedly with firsthand information, or close to it, were not contacted, and there was no FBI follow-up. The FBI initially was told to interview just four people: Judge, Keyser, Smyth, and Ramirez. Not on its list were Ford, Kavanaugh, and the three men Ramirez identified as witnesses and accomplices of Kavanaugh—Kevin Genda, David White, and David Todd. The bureau would also ignore the dozens of people that both women's lawyers recommended as having useful information. Democrats only knew who was on the FBI's list by reading news accounts; when they asked for copies of the White House's directives to the bureau, McGahn and FBI director Christopher Wray did not respond.[2]

That Friday night, Graham took Flake to dinner at Café Berlin on Capitol Hill. Flake brought along his twenty-five-year-old son Austin, a Senate employee, and Collins and Murkowski eventually joined them. "It was just a casual dinner," Flake said. "I know people find that hard to believe, that it wasn't a strategy kind of session at all." At a minimum, however, the wily Graham was trying to keep his colleagues in the party fold.[3]

In Boulder, Ramirez was elated, unaware of the limits on the FBI. "I finally slept that night, and Saturday night," she said, believing the FBI "would actually want to investigate, and find out more information after I shared what I shared." Her lawyer William Pittard had watched Friday's TV coverage at his Washington law office—from the protestors' ambush of Flake at a Senate elevator through the committee drama that ended with the proposed one-week investigation. Pittard, like other attorneys for the accusers, was confused about what the probe would mean, but he quickly flew to Colorado to help prepare Ramirez to meet with FBI agents.[4]

Debra Katz and Michael Bromwich expected to dash to California to advise Ford, but got no indication that the FBI wanted to speak with her. "I'd never heard of an investigation where you don't talk to the complainant," said Bromwich, once the Justice Department inspector general. Republicans justified snubbing Ford by noting that she'd gotten a Senate hearing. Bromwich scoffed, telling me, "No self-respecting FBI agent in a trillion years would rely on a Senate hearing as everything they need for a real investigation. They would insist on doing it their way, and having the ability to ask follow-up questions in a way that just doesn't happen in Senate hearings." He tried repeatedly that night to reach Wray, to learn who would supervise the investigation and to arrange for agents to question Ford and others helpful to her case. Finally, FBI general counsel Dana Boente called and gave Bromwich email addresses for two lower-level agents.

Unsatisfied, on Saturday Bromwich emailed Boente seeking a supervisory agent's contact information and asking him to forward a letter to Wray. The letter said Ford was eager to cooperate, and included five pages with names and phone numbers of potential witnesses and corroborators, as well as possible evidence to either buttress her account or challenge Kavanaugh's credibility. Boente passed the buck, replying, "Michael, I have forwarded your letter to the Security Division." That "was a bad sign," Bromwich knew—the division was an FBI backwater. He persisted on Sunday: "Dana, we still haven't heard anything. Who is running the investigation?" No response. He and Katz wrote again to Boente and Wray. Still Boente wasn't helpful; he emailed cryptically hours later, "The Security Division is coordinating investigative steps with various field offices." Bromwich gave up trying to reach higher-ups. He asked Boente to relay his and Katz's letter to the Security Division and field offices.[5]

In short, the lawyers for Ford—Kavanaugh's prime accuser—could not even learn who was leading an investigation into her allegation. And no one told them that she wasn't even on the White House–approved list for FBI interviews. They learned that from reporters.

By Saturday, attorneys for Ramirez, Judge, Keyser, and Smyth confirmed to reporters that their clients were cooperating with the FBI. Agents interviewed Keyser that day. Her lawyer, in a statement, said she told them she did not recall the gathering Ford described. But the lawyer reiterated, "Notably, Ms. Keyser does not refute Dr. Ford's account, and she has already told the press that she believes Dr. Ford's account."[6] Ramirez was to meet agents Sunday, in Boulder. As she prepared with her lawyers on Saturday, they were fielding calls with other tips against Kavanaugh. The lawyers had no way to vet them all, and they feared that some could be bogus—from conservative activists trying to "sting" them. They passed some tips on to the FBI.[7]

Swetnick's lawyer, Michael Avenatti, tweeted that the FBI had not tried to contact her; he called the probe a sham. Democrats, while keeping distant from him, also complained. As questions mounted about the FBI's mandate, White House spokesman Raj Shah pointed reporters toward the Capitol, saying in a statement, "The scope and duration has been set by the Senate." Senate Republicans pointed back at the White House. Trump, meanwhile, told reporters as he left for a political rally in West Virginia that the FBI is "all over talking to everybody." Agents "have free rein," he said. "They can do whatever they have to do, whatever it is that they do." Late Saturday, after NBC News and the *New York Times* reported that the White House had restricted the FBI to interviewing four people, Trump tweeted that it was fake news. Agents should "interview whoever they deem appropriate," he wrote. Such words from any past president would be an order. Not in the cynical world of Trump's presidency. The only order for the FBI was the one from McGahn and Republican senators, and it was the opposite of what Trump said. They felt free to ignore him, certain he didn't mean what he'd written.

To his rapturous rally-goers, Trump predicted that the investigation "will be a blessing in disguise." That was a self-fulfilling prophecy, of course: By design, the limited probe would turn up nothing to incriminate Kavanaugh. Yet just the fact of it would blunt criticism that Republicans were ignoring the allegations. As usual, the president accused Democrats of a hoax: "They don't care who they hurt, who they have to run over in order to get power and control."[8]

On Sunday, the one Democrat with any standing among Republicans—Coons—reached out to McGahn to protest the restrictions. McGahn reassured him, "Don't worry, we're going to do it by the book."

"Well, where is this book?" Coons countered. "I want to know what you're going to do and what procedures you're going to follow."

When Coons didn't get satisfactory answers, he sent a letter to McGahn to memorialize McGahn's assurances to him "that the White House will not micromanage the investigation or limit FBI resources dedicated to this task in order to achieve a predetermined outcome." He again asked McGahn to spell out what procedures the FBI was following, and said those should include interviewing any individuals identified by other witnesses or FBI agents. McGahn did not respond. As Coons came to see it, Republicans did the minimum necessary to satisfy Flake and Collins.[9]

*   *   *

On Sunday, three agents traveled from Denver to Boulder to meet Ramirez at the office of her attorney John Clune. Among them was supervisory agent Todd E. Stanstedt (his identity still a mystery to Ford's team). Stanstedt and Garnett knew each other from Garnett's years as Boulder County D.A.; they'd both worked on a serial murder case against an FBI informant. "Great guy," Garnett said of Stanstedt. "He bleeds FBI. Thoroughly trained." They spoke in a separate room, while agents Kevin Hoyland and Amy Howard interviewed Ramirez in a conference room, visible through glass walls.

For two hours the agents sat across the table from her, taking extensive notes but not recording. Her lawyers mostly listened. Ramirez was grateful that one agent was a woman, and that both were sensitive in asking hard questions. She took a break once when she became emotional. They asked some questions to plumb whether she was in cahoots with Democrats or politically motivated, as Republicans alleged. She denied it. Was she in contact with Ford? No. Did she know how reporters got her name? No. One question surprised her: Did she remember any distinctive marks on Kavanaugh's penis? No, she said. "I just wanted it out of my face and I pushed it away."

Her lawyers said they would provide names of other people to interview. The agents made clear as they left, however, that they weren't free to speak to anyone else. When one lawyer asked whether the agents or someone else would follow up on Ramirez's information, the agents said they didn't know. "Should I give people a heads-up that you'll be calling?" she asked. No, they replied. Hoyland said something else as they left, to the lawyers: "You won't see it in the report, but she's very credible."

Two hours later, Ramirez's lawyers emailed Stanstedt the names and contact information for twenty-five people to interview, mostly Yale classmates, including two of the three men Ramirez had named as Kavanaugh's wingmen. "I know he was not able to do so, and I know that was frustrating to him," Garnett said later.[10]

The next day was First Monday, for 101 years the statutory October opening of a new Supreme Court term. Republicans had failed to get the ninth justice seated in time, but they were determined to confirm Kavanaugh by the weekend. The FBI probe was two days old, its findings unknown, yet McConnell pronounced, "We'll be voting this week." Republican leaders did give a bit of ground on the FBI limits, only because Flake and Collins asked that others be questioned. About a half dozen names were added to the bureau's list. While they were not disclosed, almost none were from the accusers' recommendations. Trump continued to confuse the matter, having it both ways. He told reporters that the FBI had no limits, and agents could interview all three known accusers and Kavanaugh as well. Then in the next breath, he deferred to the Senate, saying he wanted "a very comprehensive investigation, whatever that means according to the senators and the Republicans." He added, "I want to make the Senate happy."[11]

Smyth was interviewed on Monday. He told the FBI "he has no knowledge" of the gathering or the alleged "improper conduct" by Kavanaugh, his lawyer said in a statement. Agents spoke with Judge more than once. They also interviewed Christopher Garrett—Kavanaugh's friend who'd dated Ford briefly, and the man Ed Whelan had implicated as Ford's possible attacker in his discredited Twitter thread. Garrett's lawyer said he had no information to provide. The FBI contacted eleven people and interviewed ten. Among them was Kavanaugh's high school classmate Timothy Gaudette. Kavanaugh had written Gaudette's name, along with those of Garrett, Judge, and Smyth, on his calendar for July 1, 1982, for a gathering at Gaudette's house to drink beer—possibly the get-together Ford described, some speculated. Agents questioned two of the three men Ramirez named as egging on Kavanaugh—David Todd and Kevin Genda—and Genda's wife, Karen Yarasavage. The third man, lawyer David White, declined to be interviewed.[12]

Swetnick was ignored. The FBI, White House, and Senate weren't alone in being dismissive. Many, including some reporters and women's group advocates, were dubious of Swetnick's account of frequent gang rapes at suburban Washington house parties in the early '80s—not least because of the disrepute of her lawyer, Avenatti. Even so, Swetnick's claims seemed to get some support in an affidavit to the committee from Elizabeth Rasor, Judge's girlfriend in college and after. Rasor said Judge had confided to her in about 1988 that a few years before, he and some high school friends had taken turns having sex with a drunk woman. "I do not have any information to suggest, one way or another, that Brett was one of them," she attested. Judge, she said, considered the sex consensual, not gang rape. (Judge denied her account through his lawyer; unlike Rasor, he was not under oath.)[13]

The doubts about Swetnick's allegation built as reporters and Republicans spoke to acquaintances and found legal records suggesting a troubled personal, financial, and professional history. Avenatti never produced the witnesses he had promised to back her account. He did release a sworn statement from an unidentified corroborator, but the woman disavowed much of it in late October, after Kavanaugh's confirmation. "I do not like that he twisted my words," she told NBC News.

Swetnick appeared for the first time publicly on Tuesday night, October 2, in a prerecorded interview on MSNBC. Reporter Kate Snow began by telling the audience that the network had not been able to independently verify her claims of Kavanaugh's complicity at parties where guys spiked drinks and took turns raping intoxicated women. Also, Snow said, Swetnick's responses in the interview differed from her sworn statement. On air, Swetnick disputed the claim in her statement that she saw Kavanaugh "spike" punch containers, telling Snow, "I saw him by them." Her statement said she saw him and Judge in lines outside rooms "waiting for their turn with a girl inside," but she told Snow they weren't in lines "but definitely huddled by doors." Swetnick did explain some puzzling parts of her statement. Snow asked why she, an older, community college student, attended parties with high school guys. Swetnick said large parties commonly drew people ranging from their teens to their midtwenties. Why would she go to so many parties where gang rapes occurred? Swetnick said she didn't realize what went on in the rooms until she was drugged and taken into one herself, at a party where Kavanaugh and Judge were present. Had she known, she said, she would have called the police.

The day after she was assaulted, Swetnick said, she did contact the police—she named a Montgomery County, Maryland, officer, whose service NBC confirmed—and also confided in her mother. Both were now dead, Snow reported, and county police said it could take a month to search for a record of Swetnick's filing. Snow asked Swetnick about Kavanaugh's response that her accusation was "a joke" and "a farce." "He's a liar," she said. To questions about lawsuits that she had been involved in, either suing past employers or being sued by them, Swetnick denied any wrongdoing and said the lawsuits were dismissed or settled. Snow said she'd asked Swetnick and Avenatti for names of any corroborators, and Swetnick identified four people. One didn't remember her, another had died, and two didn't respond to NBC's contacts, Snow said.[14]

County officials never did search for any Swetnick police filing. The 1982 records had not been digitized, and the county records custodian told me in September 2019 that no one, including Avenatti, would pay the $1,260 charge for looking through three boxes of hundreds of microfiche files for the year. I paid the county to do so, but rescinded the work order when Swetnick, in a brief interview before the search began, retracted her claim that she was assaulted in 1982. She'd specified that year in both her sworn statement and her NBC appearance, but a year later told me it could have been 1980 or 1981.[15]

Snow's NBC report confirmed for Democrats as well as Republicans that Swetnick's allegation could work to Kavanaugh's benefit, given her credibility problems as well as Avenatti's. Trump and the Republicans happily focused on it, ever after conflating the other accusers with Swetnick to paint all the women as liars.

Trump also was on TV that Tuesday night, holding a political rally in Southaven, Mississippi, and he unloaded his harshest attack to date on Ford. Leaving the White House, he'd underscored to reporters his view about who the real #MeToo victims were: men. "It's a very scary time for young men in America, when you can be guilty of something that you may not be guilty of." At the rally, he stunned even some aides by mimicking the voices of Ford and a faux interrogator to mock her: " 'I had one beer!' 'Well, do you think it was—?' 'Nope, it was one beer.' 'Oh, good—how did you get home?' 'I don't remember.' 'How'd you get there?' 'I don't remember.' 'Where is the place?' 'I don't remember.' 'How many years ago was it?' 'I don't know. I don't know. I don't know. I don't know.' 'What neighborhood was it in?' 'I don't know.' 'Where's the house?' 'I don't know.' 'Upstairs? Downstairs? Where was it?' 'I don't know. But I had one beer! That's the only thing I remember.'" Amid his supporters' laughter and cheers, Trump returned to character: "And a man's life is in tatters. A man's life is shattered." A fan held up one of the Trump campaign's manufactured signs: "Women for Trump."[16]

In Washington, meanwhile, lawyers, senators, and reporters were learning that the FBI had already completed its investigation, in three days short of a week.

• • •

The probe's brevity only proved its limits. "Given that the FBI is a very PR-conscious organization, I found it stunning that the word was coming out that they were done as of Tuesday evening," Bromwich said, speaking from his Justice Department experience. "There clearly was no interest in talking to people who might be able to undermine Kavanaugh's claims of the way he lived his life in high school and in college. If you're looking to determine somebody's fitness for the Supreme Court, you might want to know whether he has told the truth under oath in his confirmation hearing."[17]

Republicans continued their circular game with reporters—the FBI deferred to the White House, which punted to senators, who sent the journalists back to the White House or FBI. The bureau justified the limits on agents as standard operating procedure for background investigations of nominees—so-called BIs. Those are less rigorous than criminal investigations, they said. Yet lawyers from past administrations disputed that Kavanaugh's investigation was "by the book," as McGahn had said. Robert Bauer, President Obama's White House counsel, called the process "contaminated at the core."[18]

Sarah Baker, who worked on nominations for Obama, told me, "The thing the FBI got most frustrated with us about, which I'm sure is true for every administration, is that we'd say, 'And can you do it by tomorrow?' 'No, we can't.' And we'd say, 'Okay, how about two days?' We would negotiate how long it would take. But we would *never* say, 'You've got to do these four people in this amount of time, and if somebody comes forward with relevant information, you can't talk to them.' That is unbelievable."[19]

On Wednesday, the FBI delivered its finished product to the White House and Senate. While its work was commonly called a report, it actually was just a compilation of so-called 302s, the designation for agents' summaries of each interview. The FBI drew no conclusions. Yet some Republicans would say the FBI exonerated Kavanaugh. No one could contradict them because the bureau's work was never released, and senators who read it were supposed to stay mum. Nearly a year later, the FBI rejected House Speaker Nancy Pelosi's request under the Freedom of Information Act for its 527-page file.[20]

For weeks, especially after the FBI reopened the investigation, citizens nationwide had called, written, or visited FBI offices to volunteer information. None were heeded. Lawyers for Ford and Ramirez together had recommended more than fifty individuals with information. Most of the ten people the FBI interviewed were on the lawyers' lists, but that left more than forty others who were ignored—because they didn't have first-hand knowledge of the known allegations, Republicans said. That wasn't entirely true. Five Yale classmates of Kavanaugh and Ramirez were on both lists, and none were contacted although two—Elizabeth Swisher and Tracy Harmon Joyce—were said to have possibly been in the dormitory suite on the night Ramirez described. Then there was the classmate whose eyewitness account (more below) suggested that the assault Ramirez alleged was not Kavanaugh's only such offense at Yale.

Especially odd was that the FBI never questioned Kavanaugh or two of the three accusers, Ford and Swetnick. That, along with the bureau's shunning of so many people trying to perform a civic duty, presented a damning picture of an investigation that wasn't—with a lifetime seat on the Supreme Court at stake.

The sheer number of classmates who came forward to rebut Kavanaugh's sworn testimony—many of them former friends—by itself suggested a stunning indictment of a sitting federal judge. Kavanaugh had urged Fox

News' Martha MacCallum to talk to people who knew him at the time of the alleged incidents: "The women I knew in college and the men I knew in college said that it's inconceivable that I could've done such a thing." Yes, some said that. But others said the opposite: After the Fox broadcast and then Kavanaugh's Senate testimony, at least twenty men and women he knew at Yale made clear to the FBI and the Senate that they were willing to swear, under oath, that he was indeed capable of "such a thing." As Daniel Lavan had told me, when he recalled the frequent visits to his freshman-year suite by Kavanaugh and his friends, what Ramirez described "was absolutely consistent with the kinds of behavior that went on by those guys." He had written to the Senate saying as much.

•   •   •

To illustrate the flagrant shortcomings of the FBI "investigation," first consider Ford's allegation. Among the individuals who were not contacted, though they had offered to provide information or contest Kavanaugh's testimony, were these:[21]

- Russell Ford, Keith Koegler, Adela Gildo-Mazzon, Rebecca Olson. Ford's husband and three California friends corroborated her account with sworn statements to the committee. Each said she told them of the alleged assault long before Kavanaugh was nominated and that she either named him or described the culprit as a federal judge in Washington.
- Kirsten Leimroth and Jim Gensheimer. Ford's beach friends both spoke with her throughout the weeks before and after Kavanaugh's nomination, as she wavered over going public. Once she did, each spoke to the media.[22]
- Elizabeth Rasor. Judge's former girlfriend cast doubt on his and Kavanaugh's denials of misconduct with women and of excessive drinking. She did so in comments to the media and in her affidavit alleging that Judge had confided to her about gang sex in high school. Rasor contacted the New Yorker, and later the Judiciary Committee and the FBI, after reading Judge's denials in the press. "I was very angry when

I saw that he had lied," she told me. Also, knowing Judge, she found credible Ford's description of how he'd both goaded Kavanaugh and then seemed as if he might stop him, and of how he jumped on the bed, drunk and laughing: "That was exactly how Mark behaved when he drank—annoying and hyper one moment, abusive the next." She also thought his tale of gang sex might corroborate Swetnick. "Mark said 'a drunk older woman,'" Rasor said—to boys of seventeen, that might describe a woman just a few years older, like Swetnick. Rasor, a special education teacher, tried to contact the FBI through Roberta Kaplan, the lawyer who successfully argued the same-sex marriage case at the Supreme Court and cofounded the TIME'S UP Legal Defense Fund. An FBI official told Rasor to call its tip line. Like others who did so, she got no response.[23]

- Monica McLean. Ford's high school friend wanted to rebut a letter to the Senate from a former boyfriend of Ford, who cast doubt on her polygraph results. The California man, contacted by Senate Republican aides, wrote that Ford helped McLean prepare for a polygraph test in the 1990s. Both women denied that, but Republicans seized on the man's claim to suggest that Ford was so practiced at lie detector tests that the results of her own examination in August 2018 were suspect. While neither the aides nor the FBI contacted McLean, the Republicans on the Judiciary Committee gave her name to the Justice Department for possible investigation of witness tampering—for her talks with her longtime friend, Keyser, while Kavanaugh's nomination was pending.

- Jeremiah Hanafin. The polygraph examiner, a former FBI agent, could describe Ford's test results and independent reviews he sought, and allow the FBI to inspect his data, Ford's lawyers told the bureau. Hanafin also could have addressed criticisms from Republicans and prosecutor Rachel Mitchell that he had tested Ford too soon after her grandmother's death for the results to be reliable.

- Renate Schroeder Dolphin. She made plain to the *New York Times* and the *New Yorker* that she did not believe Kavanaugh when he testified that the references to her in his senior yearbook were meant affectionately, not as sexual mockery. She removed her name from the list of sixty-five female supporters that Kavanaugh and Republicans repeatedly cited as proof of his good relations with women. "There is nothing affectionate or respectful in bragging about making sexual conquests that never happened," she said in a statement.

- Angela Walker. Dolphin's high school classmate also did not believe Kavanaugh, telling the *New Yorker* that the yearbook entries were "a terrible betrayal." She sent the FBI a sworn statement taking issue with Kavanaugh's claim that he and his friends didn't behave badly with females. She recalled a large party hosted by Georgetown Prep boys, where one of them "warned me not to go upstairs, where the bedrooms were, cautioning me that it could be dangerous."

- Seth Hagan. The Prep classmate said he saw Kavanaugh and his friends mocking Dolphin. "They were very disrespectful, at least verbally," he told the *New York Times*. "I can't express how disgusted I am with them, then and now."

- Paul Rendon. Another Prep classmate, Rendon gave the San Francisco FBI office and the Senate committee a sworn declaration that Kavanaugh had lied under oath. Rendon said he had witnessed Kavanaugh and other athletes joking about their drinking and "sexual conquests," in particular "a girl named Renate." Rendon said he had heard Kavanaugh sing a rhyme that he recalled as "REE NATE, REE NATE, if you want a date, can't get one until late, and you wanna get laid, you can make it with REE NATE." He wrote, "I thought that this was sickening at the time I heard it, and it left an indelible mark in my memory." He took his statement—dated October 1, the third full day of the FBI's probe—to the local bureau office. He was told to file a report online or by phone. He did, to no avail.

- Joseph A. Hennessey. An athlete at a rival all-boys Catholic school when Kavanaugh was at Prep, Hennessey gave the committee a sworn statement that began, "From my personal knowledge, Judge Kavanaugh did not tell the whole truth about his drinking in high school or about the possibility that his heavy drinking contributed to memory loss." Hennessey described in detail his first, bad impression of Kavanaugh in late 1980 or early 1981: Invited by a Prep friend to a party, he saw Kavanaugh "lying on the couch, seemingly unconscious." Kavanaugh then "bolted up," plainly "'stupid' drunk, i.e. stumbling/swaying, glassy-eyed, and slurring his words," and demanded to know who Hennessey was. "He became pugnacious and confrontational" when he learned that Hennessey was from the rival school and "angrily and loudly demanded that I leave. He had to be held back by others." Hennessey subsequently attended other Prep parties, he said, and Kavanaugh "was regularly stupid drunk, aggressive, and confrontational towards me because l did not attend Prep." Their mutual friends assured Hennessey that Kavanaugh was a good guy, and "that he probably and genuinely had no memory of meeting me because he had been so intoxicated." That, of course, contradicted Kavanaugh's claims under oath that he never was so drunk he'd forget something. Yet Hennessey, like the others, never heard from an investigator.

•   •   •

Now, consider Ramirez's allegation. A number of people tried and failed to speak to the FBI about her account and about Kavanaugh's behavior at Yale. They included:

- Vikram Shah, Mary Ann LeBlanc, and Denise Ramirez. Ramirez's husband, mother, and sister each learned from her something about the alleged incident years before Kavanaugh's nomination, making each a potential corroborator. LeBlanc's and Denise Ramirez's recollections might have been especially valuable: They said Debbie confided in them soon after the alleged episode, though without providing many details, and both recalled her emotional trauma then.[24]
- Jamie Roche. One would think the FBI would talk to the one person who both shared a bedroom with Kavanaugh in the year of the alleged assault and was a close friend of Ramirez. On October 3, as the bureau ended its investigation without contacting Roche, he criticized all seven federal background checks of Kavanaugh since the 1990s. "The FBI didn't find Debbie's story because they were not looking for it," he wrote on *Slate*. "I still haven't been called, even though they are supposedly looking into Debbie's case. How will they learn what

happened if once again they are not allowed to truly and thoroughly investigate?"

He added, "I do not know if Brett attacked Christine Blasey Ford in high school or if he sexually humiliated Debbie in front of a group of people she thought were her friends. But I can say that he lied under oath. He claimed that he occasionally drank too much but never enough to forget details of the night before, never enough to 'black out.' He did, regularly. He said that 'boofing' was farting and the 'Devil's Triangle' was a drinking game. 'Boofing' and 'Devil's Triangle' are sexual references. I know this because I heard Brett and his friends using these terms on multiple occasions. I can't imagine that anyone in the Senate wants to confirm an individual to a lifetime appointment on the United States Supreme Court who has demonstrated a willingness to be untruthful under oath about easily verified information."[25]

Kavanaugh dismissed Roche's recollections by deflecting: He noted that Roche had a contentious relationship with a third suitemate, perhaps to imply Roche didn't get along with anyone. Roche acknowledged his tiff with the other roommate, but told me it had no bearing on what he knew of Kavanaugh.[26]

- Lynne Brookes and Elizabeth Swisher. The names of both women, Yale athletes who roomed with Ramirez and often partied with Kavanaugh, were given to the FBI by both Ford's and Ramirez's lawyers. Each publicly accused him of lying to Fox News and the Senate committee about his college drinking and behavior.

Brookes, a pharmaceutical executive and registered Republican, was the former Kavanaugh friend who'd appeared on CNN within hours of his testimony, telling of the text messages that day among classmates astonished by what they considered his lies about his behavior at Yale. She recalled the night he joined his fraternity—sloshed, hopping while holding his crotch and singing the ditty that gave him the nickname "Brett Tool." She added, "I can almost guarantee that he doesn't remember that night." On ABC News, Brookes said, "I drank in excess many nights with Brett Kavanaugh," and, "Knowing Brett the way that I did, I just find it hard to believe—it is not plausible to me—that he remembers everything that he did when he was drinking."[27]

Swisher, a physician, a professor of gynecological oncology, and a Democrat, described Ramirez as an innocent and Kavanaugh as often "very drunk." She told CNN, "I would have stayed on the sidelines if he had said, 'I drank to excess in high school, I drank to excess in college, I did some stupid things. But I never sexually assaulted anybody.'" Instead, Swisher said, he lied under oath. "In the highest position in the judiciary in our land, to not know the difference between truth and lies—that's just terrible."[28]

- Kenneth Appold. A professor at Princeton Theological Seminary, Appold was a suitemate of Kavanaugh's at the time of the alleged incident. He didn't know Ramirez. Just after Kavanaugh's nomination—more than two months before Ramirez's allegations became public—he tried repeatedly to give the FBI information that matched her account. He then spoke with the *New Yorker*. He was "100 percent certain," he told the magazine, that he'd heard a story identical to Ramirez's from an eyewitness, on the night of the event or soon after, and that his source implicated Kavanaugh. "I believe her because it matches the same story I heard 35 years ago, although the two of us have never talked," Appold said. He recalled Kavanaugh as a mix of the reserved scholar his allies described and the nasty drunk that detractors remembered. Appold said he was reminded of the young, obnoxious Kavanaugh while watching him testify, and added, "What he said about drinking was not accurate."[29]

His account in the *New Yorker* was weakened, however, by the magazine's report that his source didn't recall the incident Appold described. Yet Appold hadn't identified an eyewitness to the reporters; he remained unsure which of several classmates it was. Jane Mayer, cowriter of the piece, acknowledged that. "The edited version of the story unfairly undercut Appold, who had always said he was hazy about who told him about the Ramirez incident," she told me. "But he was completely sure that he learned of it almost immediately after it happened. Further, Appold's account was corroborated by a Yale roommate in whom he confided a few years later, and whom we interviewed."[30]

That roommate in graduate school at Yale, Michael Wetstone, and another, Daniel Lavan, who'd known Kavanaugh since the freshman-year partying in Lavan's suite, each recalled that Appold told them in late 1988 or early 1989 about the alleged incident. Ramirez's lawyers gave their names to the FBI.

Just after Trump nominated Kavanaugh in early July, Appold contacted an FBI official in Washington but was told to call a field office. There, he got a recording. After several attempts, he reached a human who gave him an 800 number for tips. He called that number and left his message and contact information. He also spoke with Ramirez's attorneys. One of them, Clune, wrote to the supervisory FBI agent, Stanstedt, that Appold recalled "more than has been reported" by the *New Yorker* and "is eager to share what he knows with you." Clune provided Appold's phone number and email address. No one contacted him.

Even so, Appold told me in an email exchange the following year, "Unlike many, I'm not particularly critical of the FBI in this instance. They surely could have done more, and I wish they had." But "the real problem," he wrote, was the agents' restricted mandate: "That wasn't their fault—it was the fault of Congress and the President, who authorized the investigation. This was a political investigation, whose goal was expediency, not fact-finding."[31]

- Richard Oh. When Oh, an emergency room physician in San Francisco, learned that his Yale classmate had been nominated for the Supreme Court, he was "impressed and happy," he told me, even though he disagreed with Kavanaugh's politics. Yet Oh also remembered an offensive story that he'd heard freshman year—involving Kavanaugh, a plastic penis, a drunk woman, and a guy who'd exposed himself to her. What he didn't know, yet, was that Kavanaugh allegedly was the guy who had thrust his penis at the woman. He now learned details from old friends, when they reconnected to reminisce about their now-famous classmate; the friends said Kavanaugh was the subject of some "shady" stories in college.

"I don't know of anything like that," Oh told them, "except this particular story I recall about a plastic penis"—one that likely occurred in the living room of their own dormitory suite, Lawrance Hall C11. As Oh told me later, "When someone says, 'Somebody stuck a plastic dildo in my face, and I tried to push it away and it was real,' that stuck with me." Encouraged by his former suitemates, he contacted the *New Yorker* and spoke with Mayer, who was already investigating the Ramirez story. After the FBI reopened its investigation on September 28, Oh tried to reach someone there. When no one replied, he got a lawyer and swore a statement summarizing his recollection.

Like Appold, Oh didn't know Ramirez, which should have made his corroboration of interest. "My memory was completely independent of anybody else talking about it," he told me. The FBI did "a complete whitewash. They just did not take the time to look at all sides and try to investigate, or talk to people who are very credible and had things to say."[32]

- Mark Krasberg. An assistant professor of neurosurgery at the University of New Mexico, Krasberg was one of the friends who pressed Oh to contact the *New Yorker*. He had already talked to its reporters. He also called an FBI field office in Colorado, Ramirez's home state, and told a woman there that he could identify the location of the incident Ramirez described—his freshman-year suite—as well as potential witnesses and corroborators. She told him she'd relay his information, but couldn't guarantee he'd hear from anyone. The bureau also got Krasberg's name from Ramirez's attorneys and Senate Democrats; he'd reached out to the office of his home-state senator, Democrat Martin Heinrich. Krasberg later made a timeline of his many unsuccessful efforts to engage the FBI. He was driven, he told me, by two things: disbelief of "Brett's blanket denial that he had never sexually assaulted anyone," and a desire to support Ramirez against the sort of partisan attacks Anita Hill endured. Also, for more than two months, he and his friends had been discussing vague recollections of another alleged incident involving Kavanaugh and a different woman—apparently the same assault an eyewitness was trying to report.[33]

- Daniel Lavan. A Washington-based adviser for international development programs, Lavan had roomed with Oh and Krasberg at Yale. Lavan was quoted in the *New York Times* disputing Kavanaugh's testimony that he didn't drink excessively and was always able to remember things afterward. Lavan tried to reach the FBI, unsuccessfully. Separately,

Ramirez's attorneys told agents that Lavan could identify other alumni "familiar with the matters described by Ms. Ramirez."

Much later Lavan told me he had "zero doubt" of Appold's account, from an eyewitness, that Kavanaugh exposed himself to Ramirez. Yet by itself, Lavan said, that act by a drunk nineteen-year-old shouldn't disqualify him from the Supreme Court decades later. What *should* disqualify Kavanaugh "was his really pathetic lying about it and other things that he did," under oath. "I certainly saw him very drunk on multiple occasions, to the point where it's absurd to say that he would have remembered everything that he did, or that he always was in complete control of what he was doing." Lavan also objected to the charge from Republicans that Ramirez's story was part of "an orchestrated smear" by Democrats. "If you actually know these people who are describing what they heard and saw at the time, that's just laughable."[34]

- Stephen Kantrowitz. Another resident of C11, Kantrowitz also reached out to the FBI. He later texted the *New Yorker*, "No one who lived in Lawrance Hall (so far as I know) has been contacted by the FBI[.] What a charade."[35]

- Charles Ludington. "Chad" Ludington, one of the Yale basketball players Kavanaugh hung out with, at first declined reporters' interview requests after Kavanaugh's nomination. He still held back after the news of Ramirez's allegation broke because he had no firsthand knowledge, though he did remember hearing something about the alleged incident at the time. Like other classmates, however, Ludington only decided to act—he called the FBI—after watching Kavanaugh on Fox News and at the Senate committee. Kavanaugh, he believed, lied under oath about his behavior at Yale. (Kavanaugh agreed to make the Fox News transcript part of the official Senate record, meaning that he swore to the truth of everything he'd said in the TV interview.) "Why not 'Yes, I was a drunk, but, no, I didn't do anything I'm being accused of'?" Ludington said to me. "Instead he lied, certainly about the drinking. Which makes me think he was probably lying about the other things, too."

A professor at North Carolina State University, Ludington had written a statement for the *New York Times* on September 30 attesting, "I can unequivocally say that in denying the possibility that he ever blacked out from drinking, and in downplaying the degree and frequency of his drinking, Brett has not told the truth."[36] Next Ludington drove toward the FBI office in Raleigh to make a report. En route, he got a call from the office—don't come, file a report online instead. He did so. He never heard back.[37]

- James Polsky. Kavanaugh's roommate for two years, Polsky withdrew his endorsement of the nomination and publicly said he could refute Kavanaugh's denials of drunken, crude behavior in college. He declined to be interviewed by reporters after Kavanaugh's confirmation.

- Jennifer Langa Klaus. Ramirez's former roommate was quoted in the *New Yorker* story vouching for her honesty. The FBI never contacted Klaus. On Thursday, October 4—as senators reviewed the bureau's documents in a secure Capitol room—Klaus unexpectedly got a call from a Republican aide on the Judiciary Committee. After he'd questioned her for ten to twenty minutes, she told me, she concluded he was fishing for information to undermine Ramirez. "I don't understand why you're calling me," she told him—she thought it was the chairman, Grassley, but his aides denied that. She was puzzled because she'd read that the investigation was over. The man asked whether Ramirez drank excessively. "We all did at times," Klaus said. He asked about other male students exposing themselves—as if to imply, she said, that someone other than Kavanaugh could have done what Ramirez alleged. When Klaus said such antics weren't unheard of, the man inferred that the behavior was common. "I just kept on saying, 'No, no, no. That's not what I said.' 'No, I don't agree with that.' I said I believed Debbie— she has nothing to gain in this if she was lying. But if Brett was willing to lie about how much he drank, then I'm concerned that he would lie about anything."[38]

- Kit Winter. Clune included Winter, a freshman-year suitemate of Kavanaugh's, in his list to the FBI. Winter "may have information about Judge Kavanaugh's heavy use of alcohol while at Yale," Clune wrote. In an online interview, Winter had described Kavanaugh and his crowd as "loud, obnoxious frat boy-like drunks" and said Kavanaugh's bathroom reeked of vomit.[39]

- Marc Schindler. Schindler was among the alumni trading stories after Kavanaugh's nomination about his behavior at Yale. He had connections to two of the guys Ramirez identified as egging on Kavanaugh and laughing at her—Todd, who was Schindler's roommate for three years, and Genda, a soccer teammate.[40]
- Kathy Charlton. Charlton, another Yale classmate, had reconnected with Todd in recent years and was consulting with him about a business project after Kavanaugh's nomination. She went to the FBI, and to the media, after exchanges with Todd suggested to her that Kavanaugh was trying to influence what he might say if contacted by reporters.[41]
- A post-college friend of Ramirez, who did not want to be identified. After the news of Ramirez's allegation broke, a woman she had befriended after college contacted Ramirez's lawyers and then the FBI to offer corroboration. According to a sworn affidavit she gave the bureau, in 1991 or 1992 she and Ramirez were together at the woman's apartment—two twentysomethings talking "about men, generally, and relationships." "At this time," the woman said, "Ms. Ramirez specifically mentioned that a male classmate exposed his penis to her without her consent." The woman did not speak with Ramirez before coming forward; they had lost touch. She told the FBI she was willing to be questioned, but did not want to be named publicly. Ramirez's lawyer, Pittard, separately gave the woman's name and affidavit to the FBI because, as he wrote to Director Wray, "this witness, through her lawyer, made multiple attempts to engage the FBI, only to be rebuffed."[42]

● ● ●

A closer look at two other individuals' futile efforts to engage the FBI illustrates just how bogus the investigation was.

Kerry Berchem, a year behind Kavanaugh and Ramirez at Yale, didn't expect or want to get drawn into their controversy. A mother of three and a lawyer at a marquee firm in Manhattan, she was drowning in work on corporate mergers and acquisitions in the summer of 2018, and paying little attention to the news. Nonetheless, with a Yale acquaintance picked for the Supreme Court, she texted with old college pals, especially her friend since middle school, Karen Yarasavage. It was the two women's exchanges, from Kavanaugh's nomination nearly to his confirmation, that Berchem gave to the Senate and FBI.[43]

Yarasavage had sided with Kavanaugh. Ramirez was her best college friend, a bridesmaid at her wedding, and the godmother to her youngest daughter. But Genda, implicated in the alleged assault, was her husband. Yarasavage joined several others, including Todd and White, in giving the statement to the *New Yorker* that undermined Ramirez. Berchem, on the other hand, believed Ramirez, though the two weren't close and hadn't seen each other since they were Yarasavage's bridesmaids twenty-one years before. With time, Berchem decided that Yarasavage's texts to her provided evidence that Kavanaugh had anticipated Ramirez's accusation, which to her gave the allegation credibility. He and his circle had contacted classmates to shape their public comments. They'd suggested that someone else might have done what Ramirez alleged. And they'd acquired Yarasavage's wedding party photo showing Ramirez and Kavanaugh seemingly happy and untroubled by any past event.

(Kavanaugh was plainly aware of the inappropriateness of contacting people to influence their accounts: In one interview under oath with Republican committee aides, he angrily alluded to the *New Yorker's* reporting that Ramirez had called former classmates to see what, if anything, they recalled. "What is going on here?" he snapped. "When someone is calling around to try to refresh other people—is that what's going on? What's going on with that? That doesn't sound—that doesn't sound good to me. It doesn't sound fair. It doesn't sound proper. It sounds like an orchestrated hit to take me out.")

When Ford and Kavanaugh separately testified, Berchem stayed home to watch. Several things that he said moved her to act, but most of all his claim that he knew nothing about what Ramirez might allege until the *New Yorker* broke the news. She reviewed her texts. "I had reason to believe he may have been lying, and perjury is illegal," she later told me. "Given that he was interviewing for one of nine positions on the highest court in the country, I thought the texts, and what they might mean, should be looked into."

That day, Thursday, September 27, she contacted the Hartford,

Connecticut, office of her senator, Blumenthal, and provided screenshots of her texts with Yarasavage, which were shared with Grassley's office. The next morning, she also sent material to the offices of Republicans Flake, Murkowski, Collins, and Bob Corker of Tennessee and asked them to support an FBI probe—only hours before Republican leaders reluctantly agreed to just that. Berchem expected investigators to call. When they had not by Sunday, September 30, she wrote a nine-page summary of her texts and emailed it to agent J. C. McDonough, whose name she got from a reporter. She told him she had no direct knowledge of what Ramirez alleged, but "I am writing to you because of my belief and concern that, based upon information obtained in a series of texts dating from July 4, 2018, through September 25, 2018, between myself and Karen Yarasavage, that Brett and/or his friends or representatives may have initiated an anticipatory narrative in an effort as early as July to conceal or discredit the Ramirez Allegations."

At nearly 8 p.m., McDonough replied. He told Berchem to post her material on the FBI's website for tips. She said she'd already done so. She wrote him again on Monday and submitted more information to the tip line. The same day, NBC News reported on her texts and the wedding photo. Berchem didn't know who provided them to the reporter, she told me, and she was pained by the disclosure because it publicly identified Yarasavage—"I did not want Karen or her family to suffer." Berchem began sending emails daily to Mike Davis, copying Senate aides of both parties. Each time, Davis simply replied "Received" or "passed along to committee investigators." A spokesperson for Grassley told NBC, inexplicably, that Berchem's texts "do not appear relevant."

McDonough replied a second, final time, again telling Berchem to post her information online or call the nearest FBI office. On Tuesday, she called the one in Bridgeport, Connecticut. She was passed among three people over thirteen minutes, repeatedly put on hold, and ultimately told, "We'll get back to you."

On Wednesday, as the media reported the FBI had finished, Berchem put more of her records on its online portal. Acquaintances also copied her posts onto their Facebook pages. That afternoon, she heard for the first time from the Senate committee, a brief call from a Republican lawyer.

The woman seemed unfamiliar with her material, Berchem said, and asked few questions. (Republicans' official summary of their investigation, a month later, would describe the call as an interview of Berchem and deride her complaint that the committee ignored her.) That night, Berchem wrote her eighth and final email to McDonough, a lengthy complaint summarizing her unsuccessful efforts to engage the bureau. "The FBI is so busy that it cannot spare one agent to call me back?" All she wanted "was to perform my civic duty, to have a private discussion with the FBI, and to possibly assist in the investigation ordered by President Trump." Again she got no reply.

She did hear from an adviser to Murkowski, Nathan Bergerbrest, one of the few aides who was responsive to her. He said he appreciated her efforts. But, she told me, "he was sort of suggesting I stop beating my head against the wall."

●   ●   ●

A second individual was nearly as persistent as Berchem in trying to talk to the FBI and senators about Kavanaugh, confidentially. He was just as unsuccessful, though he had much more serious information: This was the classmate who said he'd witnessed a drunken Kavanaugh lewdly assault another female classmate, who was severely intoxicated.

Rumors of a separate incident like Ramirez described had circulated since Kavanaugh's nomination, mostly within a limited circle of Yale alumni. When the FBI reopened its investigation, on page 4 of the letter from Ford's attorneys listing people the agents should contact was the name "Tracy Harmon Joyce," and this: "We have been advised that while at Yale, Mr. Kavanaugh exposed himself to Ms. Harmon Joyce and forced her to touch his penis. Witnesses were present and we have been advised that they will be contacting the FBI with their first-hand accounts."[44]

The eyewitness—Max Stier, the founder of a nonprofit well known and respected in Washington, the Partnership for Public Service—even then was privately trying to interest the bureau in his account. He went so far as to enlist a senator, Chris Coons, to reach Wray; Coons and Wray both graduated from Yale Law School in 1992, a couple years after

Kavanaugh. Stier hoped to keep his information out of the press—he wanted to share it only with the bureau, and with senators before they voted on confirming Kavanaugh. On Sunday, September 30, two days into the FBI's work, Coons gave Stier's name and contact information to Wray. Nothing happened. On Tuesday, Coons wrote to the FBI director. Still no one contacted Stier. Separately, another Democratic senator passed along information about him to Ramirez's lawyers, after getting it from a Yale graduate.

Stier would not agree to speak on the record, before or after Kavanaugh's confirmation. Yet individuals familiar with his account said he would have told the FBI and senators this: One night on campus, Harmon Joyce was debilitatingly drunk when she was dragged by two guys to Kavanaugh, who was standing with his erect penis exposed. They made her touch it. Harmon Joyce told friends she had no memory of such an incident and declined to talk to the media. Yet several friends told me they believe it happened, and she likely was too drunk to remember.[45]

The story remained secret. Kavanaugh was confirmed on October 6. Yet word of the allegation spread. I first heard of it on October 25, just after beginning work on this book. Through FBI spokespersons, Wray declined requests for an interview. Nearly a year later, in September 2019, two reporters for the *New York Times* first publicly disclosed the episode in a book about Kavanaugh. But they made the mistake, in a *Times* article promoting their book, of initially failing to note that the alleged victim disputed the account. That allowed Republicans and other Kavanaugh supporters to dismiss the allegation, and to attack the *Times'* credibility. Stier remained unwilling to go public to describe what he saw.

Even so, just as he'd feared, Kavanaugh's defenders—including the president—immediately assailed Stier as a Democratic hack with a partisan motive. In the late 1990s, Stier was a junior lawyer at Williams & Connolly, which represented President Bill Clinton; he was assigned to the team defending Clinton in the impeachment stemming from the Starr investigation. If that made Stier a party hack, then so was Kavanaugh, as Ken Starr's protégé. And so was Trump's former White House counsel Emmet Flood, who also was on Clinton's legal team. But Stier was no partisan. He'd previously worked for a Republican congressman and clerked for

Justice David Souter. After Clinton's Senate acquittal, he left Williams & Connolly and in 2001 founded the Partnership for Public Service, to promote service in government and best practices at federal agencies.

•   •   •

Little noticed amid the FBI's probe, the Republicans' prosecutor released a five-page "Analysis of Dr. Christine Blasey Ford's Allegations." In it, Mitchell made misleading or false statements and omitted facts to conclude that no "reasonable prosecutor" would pursue a case based on Ford's account. She wrote, "A 'he said, she said' case is incredibly difficult to prove. But this case is even weaker than that." While saying she was "not a political or partisan person," Mitchell addressed the memo only to "All Republican Senators."[46] She noted that no legal standard of proof applied to Senate testimony—the confirmation process is not a trial. Yet she went on to assess Ford's account in just that context, saying that's "the world in which I work." It was not, however, the world of politics in which Ford's allegation was being weighed. No preliminary investigation was done, as would be routine prior to trial. Ford could not call witnesses or cross-examine Kavanaugh's. Mitchell's memo was "preposterous," a Republican prosecutor told the *Washington Post*. A Republican attorney who had worked for Mitchell, and praised her hiring, said her analysis "demonstrates she's abandoned what she knows to be true in favor of being a political operative."[47]

Feinstein issued a five-page rebuttal. She noted Mitchell's inaccuracies and countered her claim that no prosecutor could build a case based on Ford's account. "The question before the Senate," Feinstein said, "is to determine whether Brett Kavanaugh has the suitability and trustworthiness of an individual nominated to serve for a lifetime appointment on the Supreme Court."

•   •   •

Even before the FBI finished, the Judiciary Committee's Republican majority took to Twitter to claim that the bureau's six previous background investigations of Kavanaugh through three decades had found no "whiff of ANY issue—at all—related in any way to inappropriate sexual behavior or alcohol abuse." Eight Democratic senators wrote to Grassley to object that the claim was false and violated the confidentiality of such FBI reports: "If the Committee Majority is going to violate that confidentiality and characterize this background investigation publicly, you must at least be honest about it." They demanded the tweet be corrected. It was not.[48]

The White House received Kavanaugh's seventh background check on Wednesday and Trump was briefed Thursday morning. Press secretary Sarah Huckabee Sanders said the FBI had done everything the Senate asked—a laughable assertion given that the Senate asked for so little. Anyone who complained Ford "wasn't given ample opportunity to make her case and state her case has been living in a cave," Sanders added, ignoring the fact that Ford never got to speak to the FBI. She was silent about Ramirez, in keeping with Republicans' strategy of pretending the second credible accuser didn't exist.

A former FBI agent, who left the bureau after Kavanaugh's confirmation, deplored what he described as the politicization of the bureau in the matter. "A lot of the coverage" in the media, the former agent told me, reflected "what was being portrayed by the White House and Republican senators—that the bureau had done a complete investigation as if it was a criminal matter." Instead, agents could only follow White House instructions, and did not treat the case as a criminal investigation. "Most presidents would probably want everything" investigators could find, the former agent said, but Trump did not. "I get defensive for the bureau because it's not like the agents didn't want to go out and keep going."[49]

Senators closeted themselves in the secure room in the Capitol complex, taking turns reading the only copy of the agents' interview summaries. Murkowski spent hours there, took a break to meet with sexual assault survivors in her office, and was back at 10:30 p.m. A Senate aide who saw her there said she looked distressed. Oddly, she clutched a rock. "It's my comfort rock," she told Coons.[50]

Despite all evidence to the contrary, Collins told reporters, "It appears to be a very thorough investigation." Flake, to Coons's chagrin, called the FBI's work "reassuring." Their responses signaled the success of

Republicans' ploy: As flawed as the so-called investigation was, it provided political cover for the fence-sitters. "The career agents of the FBI have done their work independent of political or partisan considerations," Grassley said, falsely. Maybe the agents had done so, but their bosses at the White House and Senate had not. McConnell told reporters, "What we know for sure is the FBI report did not corroborate any of the allegations against Judge Kavanaugh"—a most cynical statement, given that McConnell and the White House had made sure the FBI *couldn't* corroborate Ford's or especially Ramirez's accounts. Asked about criticisms that agents didn't talk to potential corroborators, he scoffed, "There's no way anything we did would satisfy the Democrats."[51]

About twenty Democrats went to the hideaway to share reading duties, divvying the papers among themselves. "At the end of it, we put them down and talked to one another, and said, 'Can you believe this?'" Dick Durbin recalled. "Witnesses mentioned names that were never followed up. This was the most cursory, unprofessional thing I've seen come out of the FBI." He didn't suggest that the interviews contained any smoking gun, but, he told me, "There was plenty of evidence to pursue the investigation. And they didn't."[52]

Democrats pressed the issue with Wray long after the Kavanaugh vote. In late October, Kamala Harris quizzed the FBI director at a hearing of the Senate Homeland Security Committee. Wray conceded the obvious—that the White House had limited the bureau's scope—but said little more. Nine months later, at a Judiciary Committee hearing in July 2019, he repeated that to Sheldon Whitehouse but said the bureau had followed "long-standing policies, practices and procedures for background investigations." Whitehouse wasn't buying it: "It looked to me like every time somebody went to try to get an FBI agent to take information, they got fended off, and that the tip line actually became a tip dump, into which information was dumped and never, ever reviewed."[53] Days later, Whitehouse and Coons wrote to Wray, asking him to answer eighteen questions about the Kavanaugh investigation by August 30, 2019. The senators challenged Wray's explanation that a background check typically is less rigorous than a criminal probe: "This was no longer a typical background check; the FBI was tasked with investigating specific and serious allegations of sexual misconduct by a nominee to a lifetime appointment on the highest court in the nation." Nearly two years later, Wray still hadn't replied; Whitehouse appealed to the new attorney general—Merrick Garland.[54]

The accusers' lawyers condemned the FBI's work. "The 'investigation' conducted over the past five days is a stain on the process, on the FBI and on our American ideal of justice," Ford's attorneys wrote to Wray. Ramirez's lawyer Pittard wrote, "We can only conclude that the FBI—or those controlling its investigation—did not want to learn the truth behind Ms. Ramirez's allegations." Garnett, the former D.A., was incredulous. "I get politics," he told me, but "I don't understand Washington, D.C., politics particularly well, and especially these confirmation battles." He didn't fault the FBI: "When the FBI gets assigned something to investigate, they want to be able to go investigate it. You don't curtail their ability to investigate for political reasons."[55]

Even holding the FBI's "investigation" to the lower standard of a background check as opposed to a criminal probe, as Wray would have it, this was a sham. Limited to a week, itself a farcical deadline, the bureau took just half that time to interview the few people Republicans allowed. Trump repeatedly lied about the FBI's scope. Neither Ford nor Kavanaugh was questioned. Ramirez was—only so Republicans could avoid another nationally televised Senate hearing—but the three witnesses/accomplices she named initially were not to be questioned, until the swing-vote senators objected. Agents didn't follow up with potential corroborators. Appold and Oh, just to name two, didn't even know Ramirez at Yale, yet four decades later they independently supported her account even before she came forward—only to be ignored. The "investigation" of Ramirez's claim, then, amounted to talking only to Ramirez. Knowing Stier was intent on remaining anonymous, Republicans felt confident that they could bury his eyewitness account of a separate assault. And in the end, they would falsely claim that the FBI had cleared Kavanaugh of all allegations. With the FBI's work a secret, superficial as it was, who could dispute them?

Beyond the allegations of sexual assault were the many accusations that Kavanaugh had lied under oath about his drinking and other conduct in high school and college. The FBI could argue, and did, that such accusations weren't part of its mandate. The senators could not. If so many of Kavanaugh's former friends and associates recognized that dishonesty under oath should disqualify a Supreme Court nominee, why couldn't U.S. senators?

Ramirez, so ecstatic when the investigation reopened, was equally crushed by its outcome. "I never imagined they would never contact the people that support my story," she told me. The Senate's refusal to give her a hearing was also a surprise: "I wanted to get them information, and I was never given that option."[56] As senators voted on Kavanaugh, she issued a 214-word statement. It began, "Thirty-five years ago, the other students in the room chose to laugh and look the other way as sexual violence was perpetrated on me by Brett Kavanaugh. As I watch many of the Senators speak and vote on the floor of the Senate I feel like I'm right back at Yale, where half the room is laughing and looking the other way. Only this time, instead of drunk college kids, it is US Senators who are deliberately ignoring his behavior."[57]

18

CONFIRMATION

"I will vote to confirm Judge Kavanaugh."

Lisa Murkowski walked into the Senate on Friday morning, October 5, still unsure how she'd vote on a pending motion that would signal where senators likely stood on confirming Kavanaugh. All her hours reviewing the FBI's notes hadn't resolved it for her. And the assault allegations weren't the only hurdle to deciding whether to support Kavanaugh. He'd erected another—by his over-the-top behavior at the Judiciary Committee. When the Senate clerk called Murkowski's name for the preliminary vote, she chose "no." Reporters mobbed her as she left the chamber: Did this mean she'd also be a "no" on the next day's confirmation vote? "I don't have a statement right now," she said, "because I did not come to a decision on this until walking onto the floor this morning." She would speak that evening, Murkowski said. Then she offered a preview: "It just may be that, in my view, he's not the right man for the court at this time."[1]

•   •   •

Republicans had said that Kavanaugh's partisan bellicosity at his hearing saved his nomination. But he wasn't confirmed yet, and they were nervous—fearful he'd gone too far. War rooms were fully mobilized, with outposts next to the White House in the Eisenhower Executive

Office Building, in McConnell's Capitol suite, and in Grassley's committee offices. The war council under General McConnell didn't want or need Trump's "help" to sway fence-sitters or to keep wobbly senators in line— one characteristically toxic comment from the president could push them the other way.[2] "In terms of the people that we needed to, in the end, win over, it's sometimes the less said is better," said John Thune of South Dakota, a member of the Republican leadership.[3]

In the weeks after the sexual allegations erupted, "There were really only two senators who, the entire time, were solid on Kavanaugh and never wavered," a senior Republican aide claimed. "It was McConnell and Grassley. I can tell you that for sure. All the rest of them, even on the Judiciary Committee, were wavering and running for the hills."[4] At the center of the tempest were Grassley's aides, led by the eager brawler, Mike Davis. "Those guys were doing a lot of the hand-to-hand combat on a day-by-day basis, rebutting things or providing facts," said a Republican Senate aide. But the direct liaison to the swing-vote Republicans was Rob Portman, a senator from Ohio who was as mild-mannered as Davis was pugnacious. He'd served in the Bush administration with Kavanaugh and now vouched for him, or, coordinating with Kavanaugh behind the scenes, put senators in touch with others—including Bush—who did the same.[5]

That inside game—securing at least fifty votes for Kavanaugh's confirmation, with Vice President Pence as tiebreaker—was the priority; Republican Senate leaders and their top aides handled that. Nearly as important, however, was the outside game: managing public opinion. It could affect the other. Early on, the White House sent press assistant Raj Shah to head a media operation. Oddly, the team included Bill Shine, the White House communications chief who'd lost his job as a Fox News executive for covering up years of sexual harassment by CEO Roger Ailes. Only in Trump World would a man with Shine's history be considered a good choice to help defend a nominee accused of sexual misconduct, and amid the very #MeToo reckoning that brought down Ailes. A Republican strategist, with extraordinary understatement, told me, "Frankly, they needed a woman to respond to all of the allegations." The job as front woman went to Kerri Kupec, a Justice Department spokeswoman. Also key to the White House effort was Megan Lacy, a former Grassley aide who was a liaison to Senate Republicans (later Kavanaugh would make her one of his first clerks at the court).[6]

Furor over Kavanaugh's conduct at his hearing tested the communications team. Within a week, more than twenty-four hundred law professors across the philosophical spectrum signed a letter urging senators to reject him. Kavanaugh, they wrote, had "displayed a lack of judicial temperament that would be disqualifying for any court, and certainly for elevation to the highest court of this land."[7] Perhaps the more astonishing rebuke came from a single legal scholar: former justice John Paul Stevens. The ninety-eight-year-old Stevens told retirees at an event in Boca Raton, Florida, on Thursday, October 4, that while he initially supported Kavanaugh, "his performance during the hearings caused me to change my mind." Stevens associated himself with other Kavanaugh critics: "They suggest that he has demonstrated a potential bias involving enough potential litigants before the court that he would not be able to perform his full responsibilities. And I think there is merit in that criticism and that the senators should really pay attention to it."[8]

There was more. The next day, the American Bar Association said it was reviewing its "well qualified" rating, given concerns about Kavanaugh's judicial temperament. A week earlier, when the ABA president urged the Senate not to vote until the FBI investigated the allegations against Kavanaugh, Republicans dismissed his letter as one man's opinion. This subsequent letter, however, was from the ABA's entire Standing Committee on the Federal Judiciary, the broad group that the Senate had relied on for a half century to evaluate nominees.[9]

Kavanaugh had to respond. The *Wall Street Journal* on that Friday included his op-ed—it had been posted online Thursday evening—mixing self-defense with a faint admission of error for "a few things I should not have said." He didn't specify which "things," however, and his column was not an apology. The headline summed it up: "I Am an Independent, Impartial Judge." It continued, "Yes, I was emotional last Thursday. I hope everyone can understand I was there as a son, husband and dad."[10] Kavanaugh was delivering just enough penitence to assuage would-be supporters, but not so much as to anger a president who viewed apologies and admissions of error as signs of weakness. He closed with a promise: "You can count on me to be the same kind of judge and person I have been for my entire 28-year legal career: hardworking, even-keeled, open-minded, independent and dedicated to the Constitution and the public good."

In prior eras, it would have been unimaginable that the Senate would confirm a Supreme Court nominee after the partisan intemperance Kavanaugh had shown. He'd gone beyond Clarence Thomas, whose fiery testimony in 1991 was the only parallel. Thomas, unlike Kavanaugh, had public polls on his side. Even so, his margin of victory was one of the slimmest ever for a justice up to that time, and narrower than his Republican handlers expected. As the vote on Kavanaugh neared, Republicans had no margin for error.

•   •   •

Among the mostly female protestors who thronged Capitol Hill ahead of the Kavanaugh vote, and especially the offices of Murkowski, Susan Collins, and Jeff Flake, was Judi Hershman. The longtime Republican— Ken Starr's communications adviser at the end of his Clinton investigation, before and during the impeachment—said she was inspired by Ford to act: Hershman wanted to tell senators of the time that an inexplicably angry Kavanaugh had so frightened her, following her around a table at the Starr office as she tried to evade him, demanding, "You are going to tell me exactly who you are and why you are here!" On Tuesday she'd sent a written account to the offices of Flake, Murkowski, Chris Coons, and Mazie Hirono; aides to all four confirmed the senators saw it, she said. On Friday she joined protestors at the Senate office buildings and left additional copies of her statement. A Hirono aide asked if Hershman wanted the FBI to get it. She declined. "My story is hardly earth-shattering," she told me. "There was no physical contact, let alone criminal behavior. I was rattled but not traumatized." Still, she said, "It does suggest that Kavanaugh's alleged belligerence extended beyond high school and college and was not confined to the drinking hours."[11]

As she told the senators, when she'd watched on TV as Kavanaugh testified, "I saw the face of the person that tried to bully me that day in 1999."

• • •

With Murkowski's "no" vote, the Senate tally on Friday's motion to consider Kavanaugh's nomination was 51–49. As expected, that foretold Saturday's final result. Jeff Flake said he would vote to confirm Kavanaugh "unless something big changes." Collins and Joe Manchin said they'd reveal their decisions later Friday, but neither one's vote was much in doubt. McConnell had lunch with Collins and later claimed that he didn't ask for her decision, nor did she volunteer it. But from her easy demeanor, he said, "I intuited that she was going to vote for Kavanaugh."[12]

Collins took the Senate floor at 3 p.m. for her announcement. Nearly two dozen Republicans were on hand, some smiling and easily chatting—another clue that she wasn't going to disappoint. She'd told party leaders her decision in the Senate dining room; Grassley cried. No senator had come under greater pressure. George W. Bush had called Collins twice, and she'd visited his father at the family's Kennebunkport compound; George H. W. Bush died the following month. Protestors against Kavanaugh shadowed her in Maine and Washington, including at her home. A GoFundMe campaign was raising money for whatever Democrat would challenge her in 2020.

Sitting behind Collins, forming a backdrop for the cameras, were several other Republican women. Protestors in the gallery shouted, "Vote no! Show up for Maine women!" As Capitol police led hecklers away, Collins kept her eyes down. She would speak for about forty-five minutes, but her decision was evident from her first sentences. She excoriated Democrats and progressive groups for "over-the-top rhetoric." Point by point, she explained why she disagreed with foes who said a Justice Kavanaugh would be a threat to the Affordable Care Act, to same-sex marriage, to abortion rights, and that he would side with President Trump should a case against him come to the court. Kavanaugh, Collins insisted, was "more of a centrist than some of his critics maintain."

She said nothing about Kavanaugh's behavior at his hearing. She noted that the ABA "gave him its highest possible rating," without mentioning that it was reconsidering. Then Collins got to the question of whether Kavanaugh "committed sexual assault and lied about it to the Judiciary

Committee." She started with the most incendiary, and least credited, allegation—Julie Swetnick's—dismissing it as "outlandish." Collins said nothing about the more credible accuser, Debbie Ramirez—in keeping with Republicans' virtual erasure of her. As for Ford, Collins similarly echoed other Republicans: She believed Ford had been sexually assaulted, but not by Kavanaugh. Soon came her anticlimactic close: "I will vote to confirm Judge Kavanaugh."[13]

McConnell led a standing ovation of Republican senators, who took turns shaking Collins's hands. "I've not heard a better speech in my time here," McConnell said. Grassley, tearful again, hugged her.[14] Soon after, Manchin also confirmed his support for Kavanaugh—despite reservations, he said—and removed any doubt about the next day's outcome.[15]

By contrast, Murkowski spoke that evening in a near-empty Senate. She'd been abandoned by her party before: Eight years earlier, after a far-right candidate wrested the nomination from her in a party primary, national Republican leaders supported the man despite widespread doubts about him. Murkowski mounted an audacious write-in campaign and won. She returned to the Senate, owing her party nothing. The Kavanaugh controversy also had personal resonance, as it did for many women. A reporter for Alaska Public Media had asked Murkowski if she'd ever experienced any "MeToo moments." The senator replied emphatically, "Yes." The reporter wrote, "That's about all she wanted to say about that."[16]

Murkowski began by agreeing with Collins: She did not believe Kavanaugh would vote to overturn *Roe v. Wade* or Obamacare, or Alaskan Natives' rights. Unlike Collins, she raised the issue of Kavanaugh's temperament: For her, his conduct at his hearing was disqualifying. She took on Republicans who said his words and behavior were justifiable from a man under such attack—the bar for the court is higher than that, she said. She read from the Code of Judicial Conduct, that judges must "act at all times in a manner that promotes public confidence in the independence, integrity, and impartiality of the judiciary and shall avoid impropriety and the appearance of impropriety." In Kavanaugh's hearing, she said, "it became clear to me...that that appearance of impropriety has become unavoidable."[17]

She and Collins, two friends, had each cited the high bar for confirmation to the Supreme Court. Only Collins decided that Kavanaugh cleared it.

• • •

Following Murkowski, Democratic senators spoke through the night and into Saturday, pushing the confirmation vote into the afternoon. Then each senator stood at his or her desk to vote, a formality reserved for the most solemn, historic roll calls. Donald F. McGahn watched from the gallery. Murkowski voted "present" rather than "no," because she'd agreed to a so-called pair with Republican Steve Daines of Montana, a Kavanaugh supporter who was at his daughter's wedding. The arrangement, under a Senate rule intended as a courtesy, did not change the result, only the tally. Instead of 51–49, the vote was 50–48. The margin was the closest for a justice since 1881. "This is a stain on American history!" a woman yelled from the gallery when Pence, as president of the Senate, announced the vote.[18] He quickly left for his motorcade; waiting on the Capitol drive, hundreds of protestors chanted "Shame!" and "Vote them out!"[19]

Republicans scattered to celebrate. McGahn, other White House aides, McConnell, and Grassley gathered in the vice president's ceremonial office near the Senate floor for a toast.[20] At the White House, Trump called Kavanaugh to congratulate him, then flew to a political rally in Kansas. He told the *Washington Post* that Alaskans "will never forgive" Murkowski. (Sarah Palin, the former Alaska governor, vice presidential nominee, and Tea Party favorite, had tweeted threateningly, "Hey @LisaMurkowski— I can see 2022 from my house.")[21] Speaking to reporters after arriving in Topeka, Trump singled out the FBI—usually his piñata—for praise: "I thought the FBI was incredible. They worked hard and they worked really fast. I heard the report was really detailed—thorough, professional report." He'd initially opposed an investigation, but now Trump called it "a terrific thing for the process."[22]

For hours, demonstrators protested at the Supreme Court building. Police and security guards struggled to keep them off the marble steps but by early evening, the guards gave way. The mostly young and female protestors pressed to the massive doors, at times touching the guards who stood shoulder-to-shoulder, backs against the wall. Several demonstrators banged on the doors. One woman successfully clambered onto the lap of Lady Justice, the massive statue near the entrance, yelling and pumping a fist. Some demonstrators wore T-shirts reading "November Is Coming." Signs read "Kava-Nope," "Lied Under Oath," and "I Believe Dr. Blasey-Ford." They chanted, "We believe survivors!," trying to be heard inside.[23]

There, in a small private ceremony that evening in the justices' conference room, Kavanaugh was sworn in by Chief Justice John G. Roberts Jr. as an associate justice. Soon the chief would have to deal with more than a dozen complaints against Kavanaugh for judicial misconduct, based on his behavior in his confirmation hearings.

●　　●　　●

No one explanation accounts for how Republicans prevailed in confirming Kavanaugh. High among the factors is the nature of Washington in polarized, politically tribal times. After the #MeToo movement began in 2017, seemingly invincible men in media, entertainment, and business had been brought low, from Harvey Weinstein to Roger Ailes. Yet Washington seemed somehow exempt. Trump, a serial philanderer, had been elected weeks after the release of a video in which he crudely boasted of routinely sexually assaulting women. Now the Supreme Court had a second justice confirmed after allegations of misconduct. In tribal politics, as Bill Clinton first showed, roughly half the nation didn't care when the accused was one of their own.

Second, Republicans had successfully limited attention to Ford, all but ignoring Ramirez's account against Kavanaugh and fully ignoring Max Stier's allegation of a similar assault at Yale by the nominee. The Republicans purposely conflated Ford and Ramirez with the less credible Swetnick and her politically toxic lawyer, Michael Avenatti, further blunting any narrative suggesting a pattern of bad behavior by Kavanaugh. And while even Trump called Ford credible and compelling, the fact remained that hers was a vague thirty-six-year-old account from high school, without real-time corroborators. Laurie Rubiner, an adviser to the Judiciary Committee Democrats, said that when the Ford story broke, "I had somebody who is one of us—a woman—say to me, 'It was in high school!' I thought, 'Yeah, we're not going to win this.'"[24]

Third, Republicans from Trump on down repeatedly and effectively noted that the FBI had checked Kavanaugh's background six times in his quarter century in government jobs and never came up with the sorts of allegations that surfaced in 2018. Yet anyone familiar with such FBI checks knew the point was specious. "That, to me, was always like a red herring," said Sarah Baker, who vetted nominees in the Obama administration. Both Baker and a former FBI agent told me that rarely, if ever, does the FBI contact people who knew a nominee in high school or college. "They typically don't go back that far," Baker said, "unless there is some lead—for example, a legal filing or something that comes up in the course of the FBI's interviews for the investigation."[25]

A fourth factor: Long after the Hill-Thomas debacle, the Senate still lacked a system for handling such explosive complaints against a nominee in a nonpartisan way. That worked to Kavanaugh's advantage, given Republicans' control of both the White House and the Senate. Ramirez attorney Stan Garnett was a deputy district attorney in Denver during the Hill-Thomas episode, and said he thought then, "This is a horrible way to find the truth about anything, to just have somebody testify and then get questioned by eight or nine folks on the committee who each have their agenda. And she doesn't have subpoena power. You can't call corroborating evidence." Yet twenty-seven years later, Garnett said, Ford's hearing likewise "felt like a kangaroo court." That made him and Ramirez's other lawyers disinclined to fight for her to have a hearing. "The American justice system has its problems," he said, "but it does a really good job of getting to the truth of contested facts. And it does it methodically, publicly, and carefully. A Senate committee just procedurally simply cannot do that."

Then there was the related factor: the combined power and resolve of Republican leaders McConnell, Grassley, and McGahn.

Together, the men ensured that the FBI did an investigation unworthy of the name. With McConnell's control of the Senate floor, Grassley's of the Judiciary Committee, and McGahn's of the White House strategy, the trio was able to rush Kavanaugh through to confirmation just days after their original October 1 deadline, despite the serious allegations that had unexpectedly arisen. Their success in keeping a lid on Kavanaugh's records from his Bush years handicapped opponents in building a case for Kavanaugh's past dishonesty, which could have undermined his subsequent denials of Ford's and Ramirez's claims. And they denied a platform not only to Ramirez, but to dozens of citizens who sought to corroborate Kavanaugh's accusers or attest that he'd lied under oath.

Ultimately, however, Kavanaugh owed a fourth Republican: Trump. Another president might well have withdrawn support, especially in the intensity of the #MeToo moment. Not Trump, despite—or because of— his own misconduct. He wobbled only when he thought Kavanaugh seemed weak in his self-defense. And Trump was shameless in shaming the alleged victims, playing yet again to the sense of aggrievement among his many male supporters and women, too, who resented perceived elites— including the feminists leading the #MeToo charge.

*　　*　　*

Driving Republicans' timetable were the approaching midterm elections. Seating another justice would be a bragging point to spur conservative voters; failing to do so could enrage them and depress turnout. Though Republicans had far fewer Senate seats to defend in 2018 than did Democrats, the political winds generally favored Democrats. Republicans needed all the voters they could mobilize, especially because their majority in the House was endangered. From Trump down, party leaders predicted a backlash against Democrats for opposing Kavanaugh.

"There is nothing that unifies all stripes of Republicans more than a court fight," McConnell told the *New York Times*. "They stupidly handed us the best issue they possibly could going into the fall election. And it totally underscores the importance of keeping a Republican Senate." An exultant Grassley told Iowa Republicans at a party dinner the day after Kavanaugh's confirmation, "I hope the battle cry of Republicans for the next 30 days will be 'Remember Kavanaugh.'"[26]

At Trump's rally in Topeka hours after the Senate vote, he got thunderous applause at the mention of Kavanaugh's name. The president reminded the crowd of the importance of electing Republicans, given the prospect of future court openings as aged justices retired. "It could be three, it could even be four, it could be a lot!" he said. Trump kept up the pro-Kavanaugh, anti-Democrats drumbeat over the next month at more than a dozen rallies. After little-noticed news that a Kavanaugh accuser had recanted— a woman who'd gotten no publicity or serious attention from either party after contacting the Senate—Trump promoted the report, implying that the faker was Ford. "A vicious accuser of Justice Kavanaugh has just admitted that she was lying, her story was totally made up, or FAKE!" he tweeted. "Where are the Dems on this?"[27] In Bozeman, Montana, he told about five thousand fans, "She made up the lie!"—never identifying "she." On election eve in Cape Girardeau, Missouri, home of Rush Limbaugh, Trump again said that "the accuser of Brett Kavanaugh" had recanted, as if there were only one: Ford. "It was a scam, it was fake, it was all fake."

The Republicans' triumphalism over Kavanaugh's confirmation stoked a backlash the opposite of what they intended—among Democrats, especially women. In one measure of the moment, a video of Lady Gaga's emotional remarks on CBS's *Late Show with Stephen Colbert* went viral. Gaga, a sexual assault survivor, called the Kavanaugh-Ford hearing "one of the most upsetting things I have ever witnessed." The audience burst into applause. She condemned Trump for mocking Ford for her memory gaps at his Mississippi rally. "If someone is assaulted or experiences trauma," Gaga said, "there is science and scientific proof—it's biology—that people change, the brain changes. And literally what it does is it takes the trauma and it puts it in a box and it files it away and shuts it so that we can survive the pain." Ford, Gaga went on, opened that box when she realized Kavanaugh might sit on the nation's highest court: "She was brave enough to share it with the world to protect this country." The audience clapped, whistled, and cheered.[28]

Ana Navarro, a longtime Republican strategist and Trump critic, excoriated her party's leaders for their handling of the allegations and their subsequent celebrating. "This spiking of the football that has been going on since that confirmation—by the president, and by his allies in the Senate and outside of government—has totally discounted the pain and trauma out there," she said on a popular podcast. She slammed Kavanaugh, too: "I initially thought, 'Okay, this guy seems like a decent guy. He certainly seems to have the intellect, and he seemed at first blush to have the moral fitness and the judicial temperament and judicial independence.'" Then she watched his hearing. The saga had "opened up the floodgates" for women, she said. "I think it's going to change the country."[29]

A Gallup poll ahead of the vote had captured Americans' partisan divide, with Republicans overwhelmingly supportive of Kavanaugh, Democrats equally opposed, and independents split down the middle. "No prior nominee has been as politically polarizing as Kavanaugh," the pollster said, "and that pattern was well-established long before sexual assault allegations against him surfaced." Overall, a majority opposed him—a sharp break from past nominations for the Supreme Court. In the previous seven confirmations of a justice, public support exceeded opposition by an average of 24 percentage points, according to Gallup.[30]

Kavanaugh's unpopularity nationwide was of little help to Democratic senators fighting for reelection in red states. For Heidi Heitkamp, challenged by a Republican House member in pro-Trump North Dakota, there was no good vote on Kavanaugh: Vote "no" and she'd further energize conservatives against her; vote "yes" and demoralized Democrats might stay home. She reluctantly decided to back Kavanaugh, just as she had voted for Neil Gorsuch. Then she watched Kavanaugh's testimony—twice, the second time without sound—and changed her mind. "Of course, he was going to be angry. But I think there's a way to express that anger in ways that maybe can communicate anger but maintain judicial decorum," she said on CNN. As for Ford, "I believed her."[31]

Campaigning at a Scandinavian festival in tiny Rutland, North Dakota, Heitkamp performed in a guitar-and-fiddle duet of "Me and Bobby McGee." She belted out the refrain: "Freedom's just another word for nothing left to lose..."[32] She did lose on November 6, along with three other Democrats from pro-Trump states who'd voted against Kavanaugh— Joe Donnelly in Indiana, Claire McCaskill in Missouri, and Bill Nelson in Florida. Yet all but Nelson had been widely expected to lose before the Kavanaugh vote. Five other Democrats who opposed Kavanaugh won their races in competitive states: Jon Tester in Montana, Bob Casey in Pennsylvania, Sherrod Brown in Ohio, Tammy Baldwin in Wisconsin, and Deborah Stabenow in Michigan. Manchin, the only Democrat to vote for

Kavanaugh, also won in West Virginia. But Dean Heller of Nevada, the only Republican seeking reelection in a state that Hillary Clinton carried in 2016, voted for Kavanaugh and lost. Republicans ended with a gain of just two seats, despite their lopsided advantage in the seats up for grabs.

Democrats swept the House races, taking a net forty seats and winning the majority for the first time in a decade. Trump ignored that walloping and focused on Republicans' small Senate gain to boast, falsely, that voters had "clearly rebuked the Senate Democrats for their handling of the Kavanaugh hearings." Among those who didn't buy it were fellow Republicans in Arizona. Senate nominee Martha McSally had lost to Democrat Kyrsten Sinema in the race to fill Flake's seat, and a party postmortem partly blamed McSally's endorsement of Kavanaugh. Republican women, it said, "proved very difficult to bring home to a Republican candidate that supported President Trump and the confirmation of Justice Kavanaugh."[33]

•   •   •

Little noticed on the Friday before the elections, November 2, Grassley's staff released an unusual 414-page memorandum summarizing its Kavanaugh investigation and including hundreds of pages of statements and exhibits. This was not an official congressional committee report—that would require bipartisan agreement, and Democrats weren't even aware this summary was in the works. This memorandum was an official Senate document nonetheless, the committee's last word on Kavanaugh, justifying his confirmation for the historical record—and smearing the accusers to do so. For that reason, it deserves attention here.[34]

When asked about the memorandum months later, some Republican senators said they knew nothing about it. One person who did immediately read it was Ford; she was depressed for days afterward. She had no idea it was coming and was given no opportunity to rebut the contents. Most disturbing was the memorandum's vague sexual innuendo, including several unsupported references to her "very robust and active social life" at the University of North Carolina—"slut-shaming stuff," said her friend Keith Koegler. Also, Grassley aides had contacted a former boyfriend and they included his signed statement "casting doubt on Dr. Ford's credibility," as the memorandum put it. He stated—falsely, Ford told me—that she fraudulently used his credit card after they'd broken up. He said that in six years she didn't mention a fear of flying, one of the anxieties she'd ascribed to the high school assault; she told me he knew better—she'd grip his arm in dread when they flew together. A woman who said she attended UNC when Ford did, and whose name was redacted, claimed Ford bought drugs there. Untrue, Ford said, though of course her denial wasn't included.[35]

Ramirez, too, was upset, especially since she had not even gotten a Senate hearing. Both women said Republicans had victimized them all over again. Ford faulted Democrats, too, for not publishing a rebuttal. Democrats told lawyers for Ford and Ramirez that if they responded, it would only draw attention to a document few people read. "Well, I read it," Ford said. "And it's there, it's on your committee website. And trust me, there are people online quoting it all the time."[36]

The Republicans included information from people supporting Kavanaugh without question, while expressing skepticism or worse about information from his critics, and the accusers. For example, they gratuitously wrote that despite Ford's alleged fear of flying, "Dr. Ford acknowledged that she flew to the hearing and traveled by plane for work and leisure"—as if that put the lie to her claimed fear, when countless people fly daily despite their phobia. In contrast, they included without comment Mark Judge's assertion, in a statement from his attorney, that he had never gone to any gathering like Ford outlined and "never saw Brett act in the manner Dr. Ford describes."[37] Nowhere in the memorandum did the Republicans mention Judge's books about the partying of his high school crowd—including the antics of "Bart O'Kavanaugh"—that undermined his statement.[38]

Those who maligned Ford went mostly unnamed. The Republicans wrote, "A large portion of individuals providing testimony in support of Justice Kavanaugh asked that their names be redacted out of fear" of personal or professional harm.[39] Yet the opposite was also true, that people withheld negative information about Kavanaugh for the same reason—as Republican aides surely knew, or would have known if they had coordinated with Democrats on the committee staff. A senior Republican aide told me that the memorandum's authors included anonymous and unsubstantiated information against the accusers in the interest of transparency. "All the evidence that we got, we put it in the report so people can see the good and the bad," he said.[40] In fact, much that was unfavorable to Kavanaugh was left out.

The memorandum opened with the Republicans' blanket conclusion: "Committee investigators found no witness who could provide any verifiable evidence to support any of the allegations brought against Justice Kavanaugh."[41] They didn't say how they chose the individuals they interviewed. In Ford's case, the Republicans listed fourteen interviewees who took a side; the names of all but three were redacted. Seven were Kavanaugh supporters and seven offered unsubstantiated negative aspersions against Ford. In other words, all were helpful to Kavanaugh.[42]

The Republicans described two unnamed men as possible doppelgangers for Kavanaugh, to buttress their theory of mistaken identity—the men first mentioned in the press release from Grassley on the eve of the Kavanaugh-Ford hearing. Each man had supposedly volunteered to the committee's staff that *he* might have been the person Ford described, but that she was a willing partner. What evidence did the Republican aides have that the men were credible? They didn't say. According to the memorandum, one man claimed that in 1982, after graduating from high school in Hampton, Virginia, he traveled to Washington and "attended a house party where he kissed and made out with a woman he met who he believes could have been Dr. Ford." The other man said that he visited Washington as a nineteen-year-old college student and "kissed a girl he believes was Dr. Ford" in a bedroom of a house. He reportedly recalled that she "was wearing a swimsuit under her clothing, and that the kissing ended when a friend jumped on them as a joke." According to the Republicans, the man said that "the woman initiated the kissing and that he did not force himself on her." In short, the Republicans suggested not only that Kavanaugh was a victim of mistaken identity, but that fifteen-year-old Ford was a sexual aggressor.[43]

The memorandum also cited the letter endorsing Kavanaugh signed by sixty-five women who knew him in high school, to note that he had "a reputation for treating women with decency and respect."[44] It didn't note that a couple of women had removed their names, notably Renate

Schroeder Dolphin, after the news of the sexual innuendo in Kavanaugh's yearbook. It accepted Kavanaugh's innocent explanations of that yearbook entry and others by pointing to supportive letters from his friends.[45] Yet it was silent about other Kavanaugh contemporaries who contradicted him in media interviews. Arguably the most outrageous knock against Ford was this bit of hearsay in Republicans' summaries of their interviews: An unidentified woman, who said her family knew the Blasey family from the country club, "told the Committee she was in contact with several individuals who knew Dr. Ford from high school and who have information regarding her drinking and partying, but none are willing to come forward and identify themselves." The Republicans quoted her: "I wish I could say all of the things I know, but I don't want to put myself out there."[46]

Inexplicably, they included a puzzling contribution from yet another unnamed person, described as an investment firm employee with a client who "has a photograph of Dr. Ford with George Soros"—the billionaire philanthropist loathed by conspiracy theorists on the right. The memorandum's authors conceded, "Reports of the existence of this photo surfaced in the media and have been proven not to be accurate."[47] So why include the claim? The Republicans didn't say. Nor did they explain what would have been wrong if Ford *were* photographed with Soros.

The memorandum briefly acknowledged the sworn statements from people seeking to corroborate Ford, including them in the voluminous appendix. Those were from her husband and three friends, who swore under oath that Ford had told them of Kavanaugh's alleged assault long before he was nominated, and that she had identified him by name or as a federal judge in Washington.[48] The Republicans also included material unfavorable to Kavanaugh from several individuals, without comment. There was the sworn affidavit from Mark Judge's college girlfriend, Elizabeth Rasor, in which she told of going to drinking parties with "Brett and Mark," and of Judge confiding that he and some Georgetown Prep classmates once "took turns having sex with a woman who was drunk."[49] Also included were sworn statements from two men who knew Kavanaugh in high school— Paul Rendon, the Prep classmate who recalled Kavanaugh's complicity in his friends' bullying and his mockery of Renate Schroeder Dolphin,[50] and Joseph A. Hennessey, who recalled how Kavanaugh's friends excused his belligerence toward Hennessey by saying he was too drunk to know or remember what he was doing.[51] The Republicans didn't note that Hennessey's recollection contradicted Kavanaugh's contention—central to his denial of Ford's and Ramirez's allegations—that he never was so drunk that he forgot his actions.

The two-sentence conclusion on Ford's allegation said investigators "found no verifiable evidence" and added, "The witnesses that Dr. Ford identified as individuals who could corroborate her allegations failed to do so, and in fact, contradicted her." The memorandum thus memorialized the falsehood that Kavanaugh and Republicans repeated throughout his hearing—that the people Ford named had "refuted" her when they simply said they had no memory of what she described, and one, Leland Keyser, said at the time that she believed Ford. The memorandum did not include that fact.

*   *   *

The memorandum's treatment of Ramirez was similar in several respects to that of Ford. The section on her allegation also began with skepticism about her credibility. The first paragraph noted that the *New York Times* reported it wasn't able to corroborate Ramirez's account, and that she had contacted Yale classmates "to refresh her recollection." She later would say that she was certain it was Kavanaugh who was zipping up his pants after a penis was thrust in her face, but, because she had been drunk, she sought corroborators before she went public.[52] The memorandum likewise criticized Ramirez and her attorneys for not cooperating with the Republican investigators, without explaining that both women wanted an FBI investigation first. It suggested weaknesses in Ramirez's account, and her supporters', but not in statements from individuals favorable to Kavanaugh. And again the Republicans offered a doppelganger for Kavanaugh. Here, too, their theory was a ludicrous one, based on a tip from a Republican lawyer who, like Kavanaugh, had worked on the *Bush v. Gore* recount in 2000.

The lawyer, whose name was redacted, was Joseph Smith of Denver, who was a year behind Kavanaugh and Ramirez at Yale.[53] According to the memorandum, Smith told the Republican investigators that another student in Kavanaugh's fraternity "had a reputation for exposing himself publicly." As evidence, Smith provided a photo from the Yale yearbook of 1988—the year after Kavanaugh graduated. It showed the young man Smith named exposing himself as he stood among more than fifty fraternity brothers outside their frat house, all of them in ties and sport coats over boxer shorts.[54] What the memorandum didn't say was that the student, like Smith, was a year behind Kavanaugh and Ramirez—he wouldn't have been at Yale during their freshman year, at the time of the alleged assault.

The Republicans included unsworn statements from two of Kavanaugh's friends at Yale who, like some of his Prep classmates, denied they ever saw him blackout drunk. "Not one time," said Chris Dudley, the former Yale basketball player who later was in the NBA.[55] They were contradicted by a number of other Yale alumni who wrote on-the-record accounts for the media and the committee, some under oath, attesting to Kavanaugh's frequent, excessive drunkenness and to Ramirez's trustworthiness. But few were mentioned in the memorandum. Within the thick appendices, it did include Kerry Berchem's screenshots of her text messages with Karen Yarasavage, with redactions.[56]

The Republicans omitted Berchem's contention that the texts showed that Kavanaugh had anticipated Ramirez's allegation and tried to marshal evidence to rebut it. The memorandum only acknowledged briefly that the messages suggested "Kavanaugh and his team may have contacted classmates about Ramirez's claims." It didn't say whether committee investigators asked Yarasavage about Kavanaugh's contacts when they questioned her through her attorney, yet it emphasized her hearsay that Ramirez had reached out to classmates to "refresh her recollection." The memorandum conceded that Yarasavage "could not remember whether she heard that from mutual friends or from news reports and was unsure who Ramirez contacted"—raising the question of why the Republicans included her statement at all.

Missing altogether was a statement that another Yale classmate, Kathy Charlton, gave to Grassley's and Feinstein's offices, and the FBI. In it, she said that David Todd, one of the three men Ramirez had implicated, told her that Kavanaugh had advised him against talking to the media. Like

Berchem, Charlton believed those communications implied that Kavanaugh directed his own confirmation campaign behind the scenes, contacting classmates and seeking to influence their remarks to the press.[57]

*   *   *

As for Swetnick, the Republicans devoted nearly twice as much space to undermining her and her lurid allegation as they gave to Ramirez's more credible account. They filled those pages with anonymous innuendo about her sex life and mental health, including negative statements from two ex-boyfriends as well as eight unnamed individuals who weren't under oath. An example: "[Redacted], a friend of [Redacted], called Swetnick 'a gold digger who hangs out with older guys.' He stated that he believes Swetnick is not trustworthy." Other individuals said Swetnick's mother complained that she was "always a problem," was "bleeding them dry financially," had substance abuse problems, and was guilty of "elder abuse"; that Swetnick was "beyond crazy" and a "serial manipulator," and that "they heard" from others "who witnessed Swetnick at bars after work where she would get drunk and rub up against men at the bar."[58]

Grassley referred the cases of several individuals, including Swetnick and Avenatti, to the Justice Department, seeking further investigations. The referrals for Swetnick and Avenatti cited possible violations of federal laws on conspiracy, false claims, and obstructing a congressional investigation. A year later, in October 2019, Swetnick told me she had not heard from the FBI or Justice. (Avenatti had separate legal problems: By early 2020, he'd been convicted and incarcerated for unrelated charges including fraud, extortion, and tax evasion.) Grassley referred to the Justice Department another woman, Judy Munro-Leighton, who he said had claimed authorship of an anonymous "Jane Doe" letter sent to Kamala Harris's office alleging that Kavanaugh and a friend raped her in a car; contacted by Senate investigators, she'd recanted. A fourth referral named the man from Rhode Island who'd told Sheldon Whitehouse's aides that two men named "Brett and Mark" assaulted a woman on a boat in Newport Harbor in 1985.[59]

*   *   *

On Monday morning, November 5, Fatima Goss Graves discovered the Grassley staff's memorandum on the Judiciary Committee website. Graves, the president of the Washington-based National Women's Law Center and a cofounder of the TIME'S UP Legal Defense Fund for sexual abuse cases, coincidentally met with me later that day, a month after Kavanaugh's confirmation. She quickly brought up the one-sided memorandum: "I thought I was fine, but no, I'm not fine. I was so enraged by this."

Referring to Ford, Graves said Republicans "were trying to discredit her, to make her seem confused or crazy from the beginning. They went back to that playbook"—the Anita Hill playbook. Graves saw Kavanaugh's confirmation as a setback for a movement that had been making strides in increasing understanding of sexual assault and its victims. "The president and members of the Senate basically are bringing back tropes that we were starting to shed," she said. "Our institutions need to catch up with our culture. And the Senate"—older, whiter, and more male than many organizations—"is always going to be a hard institution to move."[60]

When Berchem saw the memorandum, she emailed Mike Davis: "The Ramirez section is an interesting piece of fiction."[61] In Colorado, attorney Garnett said right-wing radio stations used the memorandum to suggest that Garnett had "manufactured" Ramirez's allegation. "It was slanderous of Debbie," he said, and ignored individuals he'd recommended to corroborate her.[62]

Democratic lawyers on the Judiciary Committee tried without success to get their Republican counterparts to identify the people who had anonymously provided information against the accusers. Feinstein issued a statement assailing Republicans for "attacking victims of sexual assault," for falsely claiming that Ford and Ramirez had no corroborating evidence, and for ignoring supportive testimony in the FBI's secret summary of interviews. The "smear campaign," Feinstein said, "sends a terrible message to women who face sexual assault and harassment."[63] Despite Ford's and Ramirez's desire for a more in-depth response countering the Republicans' work, Democrats decided not to draw attention to the memo by rebutting it further.

"We've been of many minds about it," Democratic counsel Helaine Greenfeld said months later. Ford, she went on, "came to us with such pure motives, that made me cry. First she thought, 'If I just write this letter, and the White House knows about this, they would never nominate him. I just want them to know it.' And then she thought, 'Well, if someone can just tell the senators, that would stop this.'" Given that, Greenfeld said, "I worry, just on a personal level: Why would you want to put her through bringing it up again?"[64]

19

JUSTICE KAVANAUGH

"I hope you are proud of what we've done."

A month after Kavanaugh's private swearing-in at the Supreme Court, and President Trump's reality-show reenactment at the White House, a last ceremony remained: Kavanaugh's formal investiture on November 8. Breaking with tradition, the chief and the newest justice did not take the traditional walk for the cameras down its front steps—"out of an abundance of caution, due to security concerns," the court spokeswoman said. With Republicans and a few Democrats assembled in the courtroom, at 10:01 a.m. Kavanaugh entered wearing black robes. Following custom, he sat below the bench in a mahogany chair that had belonged to John Marshall, the longest-serving chief justice, from 1801 to 1835. At 10:04 the audience stood as Donald and Melania Trump arrived. Then, as the marshal called "Oyez, oyez," seven other justices took their seats; the ninth, eighty-five-year-old Ruth Bader Ginsburg, had been hospitalized the previous day after a fall, alarming progressives nationwide who feared losing yet another seat.

Among the attendees were the men who made this moment possible: Mitch McConnell and Lindsey Graham, Donald F. McGahn and Leonard Leo. Also present was Merrick Garland, who would have been among the justices but for McConnell, along with Kavanaugh's other former colleagues on the D.C. Circuit Court, former Bush administration colleagues and law clerks, parents, wife, and daughters. For all the scripted pomp, there was an awkward, Trumpian moment. The court clerk read aloud Kavanaugh's presidential commission, and the name of the attorney general who'd authorized it—Jeff Sessions, fired by Trump just the day before. At 10:08, Chief Justice John G. Roberts Jr. administered the judicial oath to Kavanaugh. The junior justice ascended to the bench, to a seat on the end. In just nine minutes, at 10:10, the rites were over. The court adjourned.[1]

•   •   •

For a court with a majority of five of the most conservative men in memory, a natural question was how the four liberal justices viewed life there—the three women especially, given that two of the men had been credibly accused of sexual misconduct. The Supreme Court is, after all, a small club whose members serve together for years, deciding the most consequential and divisive issues of their times. Across the street, members of Congress increasingly had formed partisan tribes since the 1990s; many Republicans refused even to work with Democrats. Justices didn't have that luxury.

Soon after Kavanaugh's investiture, former Obama adviser David Axelrod put the question to Sonia Sotomayor on his podcast. When the two met in the court's stately conference room, beneath portraits of chief justices, he quickly alluded to Kavanaugh's "acrimonious" confirmation and asked, "How does the court and family, community, adjust to those moments?" Sotomayor was clearly ready for the query. She said she would "steal" a story Clarence Thomas had told her: When he arrived on the court—she didn't mention the confirmation battle he'd survived—a justice approached him and said, "I judge you by what you do here. Welcome." Sotomayor added, "And I repeated that story to Justice Kavanaugh when I first greeted him here." She went on, "When you're charged with working together for most of the remainder of your life, you have to create a relationship. The nine of us are now a family, and we're a family with each of us our own burdens and our own obligations to others, our own families. But this is our work family, and it's just as important as our personal family."

Sotomayor acknowledged that many Americans saw the court as no less partisan than Congress or the president. Yet she bristled when Axelrod suggested that its legitimacy was at stake. "We have our share of five-to-four decisions," she said, "but is it partisan or is it because, as I believe, we approach judicial decision making in different ways?" Axelrod, skeptical, countered that she had to know she would likely spend her life in the minority on a conservative court. "I don't know what that word means," she shot back. "Conservative? Liberal? Those are political terms. Do I suspect that I might be dissenting a bit more? Possibly." She referred to her new colleagues, Kavanaugh and Neil Gorsuch: "We've agreed in quite a few cases. We've disagreed in a bunch."[2]

Months later, Ginsburg—by then the star of a documentary and a movie, an icon to the left and feminists everywhere—disappointed many fans by praising Kavanaugh and Gorsuch. In June 2019, she said Anthony M. Kennedy's departure would have negative consequences "for many terms ahead," yet she also lauded Kavanaugh for choosing women for all four of his clerks. That was a first for a justice, she noted, and helped the court achieve a milestone: Women outnumbered men as clerks for the first time.[3] "It's thanks to our new justice, Justice Kavanaugh," she said again in July at Georgetown Law School.[4] On NPR that month, Ginsburg allowed that the court was more conservative—the word Sotomayor shunned—than she would like. But she opposed proposals from the left to weaken conservatives' grip by expanding the court or limiting justices' terms.[5] Ginsburg told another forum that the court was "the most collegial place I have ever worked," and added, "I can say that my two newest colleagues are very decent and very smart individuals." In polarized times, that simple statement made news.[6]

*　　*　　*

The right certainly saw the Supreme Court in partisan terms: With Kavanaugh's confirmation, conservatives celebrated the realization of their decades-long dream of a like-minded court. The secretive Center for National Policy, an elite group mostly of rich evangelical conservatives, happened to be meeting at a hotel in Charlotte, North Carolina, on the weekend the Senate voted. Its gathering turned jubilant. Among attendees were Thomas's wife, Ginni, whose fiery partisan activism, including on matters before the court, was unprecedented for a justice's spouse; Jim DeMint, formerly a South Carolina senator and now president of the Heritage Foundation; U.N. ambassador Nikki Haley, who would soon resign and, many believed, run for president in 2024; Representative Jim Jordan of Ohio, Trump's most outspoken ally in Congress; Herman Cain, the entrepreneur and former presidential candidate whose 2012 campaign collapsed after disclosures of sexual harassment (and who would die in 2020 of COVID-19 soon after attending a Trump rally); and Tony Perkins, leader of the far-right Family Research Council.

The media as usual was barred, but a reporter interviewed participants in the lobby. Cain damned the allegations against Kavanaugh as the work of "a liberal media mob" bankrolled by George Soros. Founding member T. Cullen Davis, a flamboyant Texas tycoon who twice escaped conviction for murder and murder-for-hire amid a bitter divorce, said Kavanaugh would protect Christians' religious liberty. "They're teaching the Muslim religion in school now, but they can't say the name Jesus," Davis said. An attendee who declined to be named said Kavanaugh's confirmation "was God's will."[7]

A far bigger, public celebration came a month later. The Federalist Society's annual convention in mid-November, at the historic Mayflower Hotel near the White House, became an early Thanksgiving for conservatives. Amid the party, however, some dissident skunks warned that the society wasn't living up to its principles. It had made a Faustian bargain, ignoring Trump's heresies and abuses of power in return for picking his judicial nominees. Evidence: Among the convention's discussion panels that year, not one dealt with Trump's violations of norms and the rule of law, including his attacks on judges who didn't rule as he wanted.

The dissidents announced a new group, "Checks & Balances," to spur conservative lawyers to speak out.[8] One founder was George T. Conway III, husband of Trump adviser Kellyanne Conway. Others included Tom Ridge, the former Republican congressman, Pennsylvania governor, and first secretary of homeland security; Peter Keisler, a former Justice Department official; Marisa Maleck, once a Thomas clerk; Stuart Gerson, a past adviser to both Presidents Bush; Paul Rosenzweig, a veteran of the Starr team and George W. Bush's Homeland Security Department; and conservative law professors Jonathan H. Adler and Orin S. Kerr. Leo seethed, taking the group's formation as an affront to the Federalist Society and to him, though the founders insisted that wasn't their intent.

"I want to say to the Federalist Society: We can like the judges, but not Trump's behavior," Conway told me. Rosenzweig said "the most heart-warming feedback" came from the Federalist Society's law school chapters, where students welcomed "a return to principles, in part because they were having trouble selling Trumpism—or selling the Trumpist turn of the Federalist Society—to young conservative lawyers." Whether the Federalist Society would indeed return to its principles was "an open question," Rosenzweig said to me—"just as it's an open question whether the Republican Party will become the Trumpian Party or revert to its traditional conservative norms."[9]

•   •   •

As Leo opened the 2018 conference, he exulted at his group's success, and not just at packing the courts. "I remember not all that long ago when we used to space out the chairs in this room to make the crowd seem bigger," he said. "Now we squeeze seats together as tightly as possible." He introduced the opening speaker—Senator Mike Lee of Utah, one of those on Trump's Supreme Court list. Lee began with a lengthy ice-breaker more baffling than funny, involving a stolen suitcase holding a dead dog. "There's definitely a close corollary to what the Democrats tried to do to Brett Kavanaugh," he concluded, to tepid chuckles. "Character assassination," he called it. He urged conservatives "to chart a new course," and added, "The good news is that, thanks to President Donald Trump and the Republican Senate majority, we have a Supreme Court that should be ready to do its part on this project." It was a stunning statement from a self-professed "constitutional conservative," the sort who claims to support an independent, nonideological judiciary. "Of course," he closed, "no one deserves more credit or more thanks than the men and women of the Federalist Society."[10]

In past years, justices and federal judges generally skipped the society's convention, to maintain an appearance of judicial independence. No longer. Four justices attended the black-tie "Antonin Scalia Memorial Dinner" in Union Station's cavernous Main Hall: Thomas, Samuel Alito, Gorsuch, and Kavanaugh. The newest justice got a standing ovation of nearly a minute from the more than two thousand people there. Of the court's conservatives, only Roberts—whose concern about its perceived partisanship was well known—stayed away. (In 2007, however, he'd sent a video tribute for the society's twenty-fifth anniversary gala.) Also there were about ten federal judges who were on Trump's list of Supreme Court candidates, including Amy Coney Barrett from the Seventh Circuit Court; during one panel discussion at the convention, a participant said to her, to applause, "Welcome back to Washington—and I hope you'll come back for good sometime soon."

In 2017, the gala headliner had been the newly confirmed Gorsuch, who thanked the Federalist Society "from the bottom of my heart." Members figured Kavanaugh might be the 2018 speaker. Yet the controversy surrounding his confirmation remained too fresh and finally, on the day of the gala, it was announced that the entertainment would be the duo of McConnell and McGahn.

Onstage, the two men reveled in their success remaking the judiciary. McConnell noted that Democrats used to try to block the "crazy right-wingers," then paused for his punch line: "Some of them are in the audience."[11] McGahn recalled how he, Leo, and Trump conceived the idea of a list of Supreme Court candidates to reassure wary conservatives about the thrice-married Manhattanite. (Speaking earlier, Orrin Hatch had quipped, "Some have accused President Trump of outsourcing his judicial selection process to the Federalist Society. I say, 'Damn right!'" That story line vexed McGahn, who'd say Trump "in-sourced" the process, given McGahn's own ties on the right.)[12] McConnell was nothing if not candid before his friendly audience. He acknowledged that his quick decision to block any Obama nominee to replace Scalia was based on "political instinct." Contrary to his remarks at the time, he called Obama's choice—he never said Garland's name—"obviously a well-qualified nominee."

Senate Republicans voted to end filibusters of high court nominees, he said, to clear the way for the most far-right justices possible: "No Republican president could get the kind of nominee we'd want with sixty votes!"[13]

(Think Amy Coney Barrett.) The goal? "To do everything we can, for as long as we can, to transform the federal judiciary, because everything else we do is transitory." He added, with self-satisfaction, "I hope you are proud of what we've done."[14]

Before its convention closed, the Federalist Society announced that Kavanaugh would be the headline speaker in 2019. A year later, more than twenty-seven hundred conservatives were on hand to hear him—the largest crowd ever, said society president Eugene Meyer.[15] McGahn, appropriately, introduced Kavanaugh and candidly captured the sense in the room that the justice represented "Mission accomplished"—conservatives' capture of the court. "In the last twenty-five years, we have seen our views go from the fringe—views that in years past would inhibit someone's chances to be considered for the federal bench—to being the center of the conversation. Now we are the mainstream," McGahn said, to applause and whoops. "How far we have come!" Turning to Kavanaugh, McGahn said, "He has stood for principles and paid the price."

Kavanaugh took the stage to a nearly ninety-second standing ovation, which competed with the screeching whistles of a few protestors; they persisted as he spoke until security officials ejected them all. Like Gorsuch before him, Kavanaugh began by thanking the Federalist Society: "I'm forever grateful to all of you." He singled out "my longtime friends, Gene Meyer and Leonard Leo," adding, "I have always been a proud member of the Federalist Society." A half hour later he would end with the refrain he'd lifted from Bush—about being an optimist on the sunrise side of the mountain, "to see the day that's coming." Yet in between he mostly looked backward, bitterly, at his confirmation ordeal more than a year before. Most justices presumably would have avoided the topic, especially before a partisan audience. That Kavanaugh did not was a disturbing decision, recalling his intemperate anger at his Senate hearing. "Last year," he said, "a lot of my friends put themselves on the line for me, and risked great personal and reputational harm. People risked their jobs, their livelihoods. Some of them lost business. They were yelled at, insulted, threatened. Many of my friends lost other friends merely because they supported me. My friends paid a heavy price—way too heavy a price. I'm well aware of that, and it pains me daily." When he retold how his daughter Liza prayed during his confirmation process, he lost composure, then recovered with humor: "Matt Damon would have made it through this."

Meyer had the last word: "Let me say on behalf of everyone here, we thank you for staying in the fight and being willing to serve. Thank you. May the Lord bless you and keep you in the new day of the Supreme Court."

* * *

Months later, Kavanaugh was the honoree at an informal reception at the court hosted by its press corps, a tradition for new justices dating to the 1981 arrival of Sandra Day O'Connor. He brought along his female clerks. Wine was served—the reporters decided against beer—but Kavanaugh clutched a water bottle as he mingled genially. In brief remarks, he thanked them for their coverage. "He thanks everybody for everything," a court official privately told a reporter. Kavanaugh then left for the "highest court in the land"—the basketball court above the Supreme Court chamber.[16]

For all such signs of normality, fallout from Kavanaugh's confirmation kept the controversy alive—in the courts, Congress, the 2020 election campaign, and the national conversation.

Days after Kavanaugh's swearing-in, Roberts sent fifteen complaints against him—from lawyers, doctors, professors, and self-described concerned citizens—to the Judicial Council of the Denver-based Tenth Circuit Court. The complaints had first gone to the D.C. Circuit Court, but Kavanaugh's former colleagues there asked Roberts to assign another circuit to consider them. Dozens more came, eighty-three in all. Many alleged that Kavanaugh had lied under oath in his hearings in 2004, 2006, and 2018, and others cited his intemperance and partisanship at the hearing on the assault allegations.[17] Two months later, on December 18, 2018, the Judicial Council dismissed the complaints, noting that ethics rules apply to lower court judges, not to Supreme Court justices. "The allegations contained in the complaints are serious," the eight-member council said, yet "an intervening event—Justice Kavanaugh's seating on the Supreme Court—has made the complaints no longer appropriate for consideration."[18] Twenty complainants appealed, but the council reaffirmed its decision in March

2019. One judge objected, saying that fairness demanded that a different body handle the appeal; a second judge endorsed that dissent.[19]

In late 2020, Democrats and watchdog groups were still sifting through documents from Kavanaugh's career that Republicans had kept under wraps. The records slowly trickled in, in response to the requests that several senators had filed under the Freedom of Information Act, before Kavanaugh's confirmation, to the National Archives and several federal agencies. No smoking gun turned up in initial deliveries, which were projected to take years to complete. Doing most of the review work was American Oversight, a watchdog nonprofit formed in early 2019 to hold the Trump administration accountable, chiefly with FOIA lawsuits to get access to its records. Democrats in Congress became preoccupied with new Trump administration controversies—not least the president's two impeachments and Senate trials.

The hope was to find evidence strong enough to impeach Kavanaugh for lying under oath. But only once in history had the House impeached a justice, in 1805, and he was acquitted by the Senate.[20] Yet Senate veterans argued that even if nothing damning turned up, Democrats must press for all of Kavanaugh's records on principle: to challenge the precedents Republicans set during his confirmation process. "We cannot have a nomination system in which they can say, 'We're going to set a timetable that's too quick. Then we're going to use the timetable as an excuse to not get the full record. Then if you get the record after the guy's confirmed, it's sour grapes for you to even talk about it,'" said Sam Simon, a counsel to Richard Blumenthal, the senator who led the push for documents. By pursuing records even after confirmation, Simon told me, Democrats could create a disincentive to withholding them in the first place: "If you essentially try to ram somebody through and engage in a cover-up, you will at some point in the future, to use a technical legal term, look like a schmuck."[21]

*   *   *

When Kavanaugh took his seat on Tuesday, October 9, 2018, for his first court session, he did not hang back—he quickly joined in the justices' questioning of the lawyers in the case before them.[22] He still had public relations help from the conservative firm CRC Strategies, which had long worked for Republicans, including Gorsuch after his nomination. At the end of Justice Kavanaugh's first day, CRC flacks sent reporters accounts of his questions from the bench, an article lauding him for having an all-female staff, and a Fox pundit's column favorably predicting that he would support conservatives' priorities.

By the time his first term ended the following June, neither Kavanaugh nor the conservative majority had fulfilled the hyperbolic predictions on the left and right that he'd usher in a right-wing sweep. Instead it was a court in transition. Following Roberts's strategic lead, the justices avoided taking on divisive cases so soon after Kavanaugh's contentious confirmation. In the prior term, conservatives had been on the winning side in most 5–4 rulings. Over 2018–19, the conservative and liberal factions split the close wins, according to Adam Feldman, creator of the *Empirical SCOTUS* blog. That is, in half the decisions, a majority of all five conservatives or four conservatives and one liberal prevailed; in the rest, the majority included the four liberals and a conservative, usually Roberts. Only this much was clear, Feldman said: "The Supreme Court with Kavanaugh is distinctly different from the court with Kennedy. There is no longer a clear swing vote."[23] Roberts emerged as the new center, reflecting the court's rightward shift in trading Kennedy for Kavanaugh. Kavanaugh's early record put him in the middle, too, yet court watchers presciently hesitated to draw conclusions. New justices historically had been cautious, voting often with the majority and only later gravitating right or left.

To the surprise of many court watchers, the two Trump justices disagreed as often as not in the close rulings over their first term together. Gorsuch was the more conservative; he had quickly aligned with Thomas and Alito on the far right. Yet as a westerner, Gorsuch had a libertarian bent that sometimes had him allying with liberals, especially to limit government power in cases of criminal justice and tribal rights. Kavanaugh, a more traditional big-government conservative, supported strong police powers. He and Gorsuch were on the same side in just over half of cases decided by close votes, according to an analysis by scholars at Washington University in St. Louis and the University of Michigan. Kavanaugh agreed nearly as often with Stephen Breyer and Elena Kagan. In contrast, he voted with Roberts 86 percent of the time.[24]

In Kavanaugh's first week, he took a notably harder line than Gorsuch in questioning immigrants' lawyers in a significant case. The issue was whether authorities could indefinitely detain any immigrants who'd committed crimes, even if their offenses were nonviolent, minor, and years old. Kavanaugh said yes. He cited a 1996 law Congress passed after Gingrich-era Republicans took control: "What was really going through Congress' mind in 1996 was harshness on this topic." In contrast, Gorsuch asked, "Is there any limit on the government's power?" The plaintiffs included a grandfather who came to the country as an infant; in 2013 he was arrested to be deported, based on two convictions in the 1990s for drug possession and one in 2002 for having an unloaded pistol in his shed.[25] Kavanaugh and Gorsuch ultimately did end up on the same side, with the other three conservatives, when the court ruled 5–4 for the government in March 2019. Kavanaugh, however, wrote a separate concurrence to insist that the ruling was a narrow one. Breyer, in the four liberals' dissent, rebuked him: "In terms of potential consequences and basic American legal traditions, the question before us is not a 'narrow' one."[26]

The court heard several abortion-related cases in Kavanaugh's first months, but none was a test of his stance on *Roe*—yet. One was more interesting for what it signaled about his possible alliance with Roberts at the center. In December 2018, they joined the liberal justices in declining a case about whether states could ban Medicaid reimbursements to Planned Parenthood clinics; in effect, they sided with Planned Parenthood. (The Medicaid funds did not cover abortions—federal law prohibited that—but instead repaid clinics for other services to low-income patients. Still, Republicans for years had nonetheless sought to "defund" Planned Parenthood because of its abortion services.) Thomas, angry that the court wouldn't hear the case, suggested that Roberts and Kavanaugh were politically cowed: "What explains the court's refusal to do its job here? I suspect it has something to do with the fact that some respondents in these cases are named 'Planned Parenthood.'"[27]

On a later abortion case, however, Roberts and Kavanaugh took opposite sides. Roberts allied with the liberals to block a Louisiana antiabortion law from taking effect while challenges worked through the courts. (It would reach the high court the next year, posing Kavanaugh's first real test on the issue; again the two men would differ.) The law, which required a doctor performing abortions to have admitting privileges in a nearby hospital in case of emergencies, was nearly identical to a Texas law the court struck down in 2016 for obstructing women's access to abortion. Just as half of Texas's forty clinics had closed because of the mandate—hospitals resisted granting admitting privileges to abortion providers—Louisiana would be left with at most one of its three clinics, according to evidence in the lower court trial. Kavanaugh and the other conservatives supported letting the law take effect pending appeals. But he alone wrote to say that opponents could challenge the law later if they could show it had indeed reduced women's access to abortions.[28] As in the deportation case, where he'd described the harsh outcome as "limited," Kavanaugh seemed to be trying to put a softer veneer on a hard-line stand.

In state capitals, meanwhile, conservatives were bringing new anti-abortion cases into the judicial pipeline, expressly because Kavanaugh was on the court. In 2019, a number of red states enacted restrictions that blatantly violated Supreme Court precedents. "What I'm trying to do here is get this case in front of the Supreme Court so *Roe v. Wade* can be overturned," said Alabama state representative Terri Collins, sponsor of a law to criminalize all abortions, without exceptions for rape, incest, or a mother's life, and to mandate stiff prison sentences for doctors.[29]

It was a Supreme Court ruling unrelated to abortion that first showed the flimsiness of Kavanaugh's assurance to Susan Collins of his respect for precedents like *Roe*. He joined the other conservatives in reversing a long-standing ruling on states' liability in private lawsuits. Breyer wrote in the liberals' dissent, "Today's decision can only cause one to wonder which cases the Court will overrule next"—a line widely read as referring to the abortion precedents.[30] When the conservatives struck down another precedent the following month, Kagan echoed Breyer's comment and wrote, "Now one may wonder yet again."[31] Three times in his first term, Kavanaugh would vote to overturn precedents.

In two death penalty cases that raised issues of religious freedom, he baffled court-watchers. In one, he was in the conservative majority that allowed Alabama to execute a Black Muslim inmate without providing an imam at the man's side; the state employed only a Christian chaplain. Kavanaugh said the inmate's challenge came too late. Yet in the second case, which differed little on timing, he joined the majority to block Texas's execution of a white Buddhist prisoner because the man wasn't allowed a spiritual adviser of his faith. He was the only justice to explain his reasoning, writing, "In my view, the Constitution prohibits such denominational discrimination." He didn't address why that view didn't also apply in the Black Muslim's case.[32]

The court announced two of the term's biggest decisions on its last day, and Kavanaugh voted with conservatives—and for the Republican Party's position—in both. He was on the winning side as the court blessed even extremely partisan gerrymandering, deciding 5–4 that federal courts were powerless to second-guess such political decision making.[33] It was a monumental victory for Republicans, who had aggressively harnessed technology in states where they held power to draw lines for local, state, and congressional districts with a precision all but guaranteeing their party an edge for years.

In the second decision, also 5–4, Kavanaugh was in the conservative minority as Roberts joined the liberals to block the Trump administration's plan to add a citizenship question to the 2020 census.[34] Three lower court judges had ruled against the administration, after proceedings that exposed the Republican plan as a power grab to depress Latinos' responses to the census. The evidence included the papers of a deceased party strategist, provided by his estranged daughter: They confirmed that Republicans hoped to discourage Latinos from filling out census forms, for fear that they or their relatives would become targets of Trump's anti-immigrant crackdown. If the census undercounted a group that favored Democrats, Republicans would gain in the next round of redistricting. Roberts, judiciously, essentially called the administration's front man for the ploy, Commerce Secretary Wilbur Ross, a liar. Ross, under oath, had claimed that the Justice Department sought the citizenship question to better enforce the Voting Rights Act. As Roberts wrote, "Altogether, the evidence tells a story that does not match the explanation the secretary gave for his decision."[35] Yet Kavanaugh and the other conservatives bought it.

* * *

Kavanaugh's second year, for the 2019–20 term, proved more revealing. As the court confronted issues it had largely dodged in his freshman term, the decisions confirmed both his conservatism and his willingness to overturn precedent. But Roberts was the defining figure—both chief justice and the court's swing vote, the only justice who was in the majority on every significant decision. Building coalitions when he could, otherwise siding with the four liberals on some of the most politically charged cases, Roberts exerted rare control and steered the court's rulings mostly in line with public opinion. And he ensured, by its rulings on several cases involving Trump, that the court illustrated independence from a president who continued to suggest it was in his pocket. (In early 2019, Trump correctly predicted he'd be sued for diverting federal funds to build his border wall over Congress's opposition; he'd get a "bad ruling" in the lower courts, he told reporters, but "then we will end up in the Supreme Court, and we'll win.")[36]

Conservatives, still resentful that Roberts had saved the Affordable Care Act in 2012, were enraged at the surprise wins for progressives— on abortion limits, immigrant protections, and the rights of gay and transgender people. Yet the right didn't lose: The headline-grabbing decisions were written, mostly by Roberts, in such a way that conservatives could ultimately win in future cases on those divisive social issues. For example, he joined with the liberals to strike down Louisiana's law requiring that doctors at abortion clinics have hospital privileges. Yet he wrote that he did so only because the court had previously declared the similar Texas law unconstitutional; he still believed—like the other conservatives—that the court had erred in the Texas decision, and expressed openness to future abortion challenges.[37] On immigration, Roberts and the liberals blocked an administration order to kill an Obama-era program protecting from deportation so-called Dreamers, hundreds of thousands of young adults brought to the United States as children. Yet his opinion said Trump still could end the policy, *if* he complied with the procedures set out in federal law to justify such regulatory actions—as his administration so far had not.[38] Both Roberts and Gorsuch allied with liberals in the landmark decision to extend to LGBTQ individuals the protections of the 1964 Civil Rights Act against job discrimination on the basis of sex. But the opinion, by Gorsuch, all but invited employers with religious objections to seek exemptions under another federal law, the Religious Freedom Restoration Act.[39]

Even so, many conservatives felt betrayed. Mike Huckabee, the former Arkansas governor and Republican presidential candidate turned conservative commentator, tweeted in late June that Roberts should "Resign Now," because he'd "stabbed the American people in the back more than Norman Bates and 'swings' more than Hugh Hefner in his heyday." Trump cheerleader Matt Schlapp, chairman of the American Conservative Union, told Fox News that Roberts should be impeached. And Senator Josh Hawley of Missouri called for changing the "Republican vetting process" for judges, to give the religious right even more influence.[40] Then there was Trump, who tweeted after the immigration and LGBTQ rulings, "These horrible and politically charged decisions coming out of the Supreme Court are shotgun blasts into the face of people that are proud to call themselves Republicans or Conservatives." He followed up with another tweet: "Do you get the impression that the Supreme Court doesn't like me?"[41]

•   •   •

Kavanaugh did not disappoint conservatives, however: He came down on the "right" side on the abortion, Dreamers, and gay rights decisions, and signaled eagerness to expand gun rights. Even so, he took pains to distance himself from the hard-core rhetoric of Thomas, Alito, and Gorsuch. Occasionally he wrote separate opinions, as if to have it both ways, and cast himself as the "compassionate conservative," in the phrase of his mentor, George W. Bush. Rather than join the right-wing trio's dissent to the Dreamers ruling, Kavanaugh wrote his own, beginning sympathetically, "They live, go to school, and work here with uncertainty about their futures."[42] Similarly, he wrote separately from Alito and Thomas's dissent to the LGBTQ decision, in one passage praising gay people for having "exhibited extraordinary vision, tenacity, and grit" in seeking equal rights.[43]

But for them as well as Dreamers, he wrote that it was up to Congress, not the court, to provide legal protections.

The anticipated alliance of Kavanaugh with Roberts proved episodic at best. For all their similarities—conservative Catholics, country club pals, veterans of Republican administrations and of the Bush-versus-Gore recount fight—the two men were very different. Kavanaugh was the more politically inclined of the two, and less socially awkward. While Kavanaugh had collected mentors from high school on—from priests and professors to judges and a president—Roberts owed no one, including in the Federalist Society and the rest of the conservative legal movement; he had advanced through sheer brilliance and hard work. And more than anyone on the court, the chief justice was protective of its image, determined that it not be seen as partisan. To him, if not Kavanaugh, the institution took precedence over most conservative causes. Activists on the right were wary of Kavanaugh aligning with Roberts, fearing the novice justice couldn't hold his own, that he'd get snookered into compromises.

Behind the scenes, Kavanaugh—a veteran of the horse trading between a White House and Congress—tried his own hand at court politics. Without success, he sought to corral his colleagues into avoiding two of the most dicey matters before them: the Louisiana antiabortion law, and two cases involving House Democrats' subpoenas of Trump's financial records. That insight from the justices' private deliberations came from extraordinary leaks to longtime Supreme Court reporter Joan Biskupic.

In the Louisiana case, Kavanaugh wrote a series of private memos to colleagues in mid-March 2020 to propose that they send it back to the district judge for reconsideration, Biskupic reported on CNN. The justices wouldn't have to take a stand, yet. And *he* wouldn't have to, less than two years after he'd persuaded Senator Collins of his respect for precedents like the one at issue here—the 2016 ruling striking down Texas's antiabortion law. But the justices had already heard oral arguments in the Louisiana case on March 4, and afterward took an initial, private vote: 5–4 against the state law. Roberts sided with the liberals, just as he would in the ultimate ruling, and he had assigned Breyer to write the majority opinion. Now Kavanaugh was suggesting that they set the case aside and tell the district judge to start over. He argued that the judge had ruled against the law without enough evidence to prove that it would force clinics to close. The other justices wouldn't buy it. They were ready to rule.[44] When the court did so in late June, Kavanaugh dissented for much the same reason, that the law's challengers hadn't shown that clinics would inevitably have to shut down. And yet he fully accepted Louisiana's disputed claim that its law would protect women's lives.

In the two cases involving Trump's standoff with House Democrats over his financial records, Kavanaugh proposed a way out in an internal memo and during one of the justices' private teleconferences (the COVID-19 pandemic had put an end to their in-person meetings by early March). He asked: Might the "political question" doctrine apply? That tenet holds that the court should stay out of disputes better left to the political branches to hash out. The justices agreed to put the question to the parties in the Trump cases before oral arguments in April.[45] The parties were puzzled by the court's request for the new filings. Was the court wary of antagonizing the president should it rule against him? If the court wouldn't settle whether the House could subpoena Trump's records, the precedent could weaken Congress's power of government oversight. That might be fine with conservative justices, including Kavanaugh, who favored a strong executive. But inaction also could allow Trump's accountants and his banks to simply hand over his records. All parties in the House case argued that the Supreme Court should—must—decide the issue. In any event, the court still faced a separate dispute between Trump and the Manhattan district attorney, Cy Vance Jr., who wanted the president's tax returns for a criminal investigation of his family business, the Trump Organization.

The Trump cases were a major test for a court that millions of Americans already viewed as partisan. Given the political and constitutional stakes, involving questions of a president's vulnerability to criminal investigation or congressional scrutiny, the chief justice assigned the opinions to himself. But he consulted with each justice, working to produce drafts that would get decisive approval transcending ideology. After all, two landmark rulings of the past half century on executive power were unanimous: the 1974 decision forcing Richard M. Nixon to turn over the Watergate tapes, and the 1997 one holding that Bill Clinton wasn't immune to a civil lawsuit for alleged sexual harassment before he became president.[46]

Roberts didn't get unanimity, but he came close. On July 9, 2020, the court ruled 7–2 in both the House and Vance cases that the president's personal records could be subpoenaed for criminal investigations or congressional oversight.[47] Trump's two appointees, Kavanaugh and Gorsuch, were in the majority, though in a separate concurring opinion they said that prosecutors should have to meet a tougher standard to demand a president's private papers. The dissenters were Thomas and Alito, who opposed the subpoenas but agreed with the others that presidents are not absolutely immune from criminal investigations: "On that point," Roberts wrote, "the Court is unanimous."[48] Roberts had avoided a partisan split on the court, while also balancing the interests of Congress, prosecutors, and the presidency. And the court had protected Trump's immediate political interests: His records wouldn't become public before the 2020 election—the House first had to justify that its subpoenas served a legitimate legislative purpose to receive any papers, and Trump's lawyers had additional tactics available to them to stymie New York prosecutors.

Pro-firearms groups, which had spent millions toward Kavanaugh's confirmation, were disappointed that his first terms didn't bring the gun rights victories they'd banked on. But they didn't blame him. The court in June 2020 declined ten challenges to local gun controls; Roberts, it was widely believed, had privately signaled to colleagues that he wouldn't necessarily provide the necessary fifth conservative vote against the regulations. The court earlier had accepted an appeal by a New York gun group, but declared it moot in April after the city and state killed the regulation at issue. The city and state had successfully defended the regulation in the lower courts, but killed it after the Supreme Court agreed to consider the gun groups' appeal. Their action reflected the general trepidation among gun control advocates about their chances at the high court now that Kavanaugh was there. Kavanaugh joined Roberts and the liberals in holding that the New York case was moot. But he wrote a statement urging the court to consider one of the other pending gun cases—thus giving hope to the pro-gun conservatives who'd backed his confirmation.[49] Roberts's court decided otherwise two months later.

With Kavanaugh's support, Christian conservatives won several victories. The Roberts Court continued to chip at the wall between church and state, and to favor those who don't want to comply with federal laws that conflict with their beliefs. In this term, that included businesses opposed to providing employees insurance coverage for contraceptives, as mandated, and private religious schools seeking to hire and fire lay teachers regardless of antidiscrimination statutes. In one notable case, however, a split court decided against a church—a result that was also interesting for the tension it suggested between Roberts and Kavanaugh.

In that decision, in June 2020, Roberts sided with liberals as the court voted 5–4 not to block California's limit on the size of church congregations during the coronavirus pandemic; an evangelical church had sought the justices' intervention against the cap. For such an emergency petition, the court typically would issue an order without explanation. Yet Kavanaugh wrote a three-page dissent so extravagant in its objections on behalf of the Pentecostal plaintiffs' First Amendment religious rights that Roberts was moved to rebut him, to correct the record, said a person familiar with the court's deliberations.[50]

Kavanaugh wrote that California's cap on the number of worshippers gathered for a service "indisputably discriminates against religion." He complained that many secular businesses weren't subject to the same limit—including, he specified for effect, "cannabis dispensaries."[51] Roberts countered by first describing the dire public health threats from the virus that California officials justifiably sought to mitigate. Contrary to churches being singled out, he wrote, "Similar or more severe restrictions apply to comparable secular gatherings, including lectures, concerts, movie showings, spectator sports, and theatrical performances, where large groups of people gather in close proximity for extended periods of time." An "unelected federal judiciary" shouldn't second-guess local officials' decisions about such public safety measures, Roberts said. He ended with a slap at Kavanaugh's language: "The notice that it is 'indisputably clear' that the Government's limitations are unconstitutional seems quite improbable."[52]

On voting rights questions, including a number that arose because of other steps local and state officials took to allay the pandemic's dangers in an election year, the court conservatives generally stuck together in taking the Republican Party's side—Roberts's worries about public perceptions notwithstanding. That was true in a case whose title said it all: *Republican*

National Committee, et al. v. Democratic National Committee, et al. It was a case, moreover, that raised questions about whether Kavanaugh had shaded the truth—bringing doubts that had dogged him periodically throughout his life all the way onto the nation's highest court.

On April 6, the eve of Wisconsin's party primary elections, all five conservatives sided with the state and national Republican Party to block a district judge's order extending the deadline for receiving mail ballots to six days after the election. The district judge, in ruling for the Democratic plaintiffs, had cited the huge backlog of requests for mail-in ballots from voters fearful of going to the polls amid a spike in coronavirus infections, a backlog that could cause ballots to arrive too late. The Seventh Circuit Court of Appeals upheld his decision. Republicans appealed to the Supreme Court.

Though the high court's opinion was unsigned, like most emergency orders, Kavanaugh is widely believed to have written it for the five conservatives. (All four liberals signed a dissent.) The Republican National Committee had addressed its appeal to him, as the justice responsible for overseeing the Seventh Circuit. In reversing the district and appeals courts' rulings, the Supreme Court's opinion included a factual error about Wisconsin election law and, more crucially, a seriously misleading statement. Five times it said the Wisconsin judge had ordered relief that Democrats hadn't even asked for in their legal filings—the deadline extension for ballots mailed and postmarked after election day. That was "the critical point," the order said. Yet the Democrats' lawyer, John Devaney, had expressly sought such relief during the court hearing, as Ginsburg noted in the liberals' dissent.

"I could not have been clearer," Devaney told me. "It was really jarring to read that decision and to see its reliance on the fact that we supposedly hadn't made that request, when—as Ginsburg pointed out—I very clearly did." Also disappointing, he said, was the order's failure to "acknowledge the significance and relevance of the pandemic to what was before them."[53] Instead, the court—Kavanaugh presumably—explicitly said it was not addressing "the broader question" of the pandemic's impact on the election. For the court to suggest that this election was an ordinary one, Ginsburg responded, "boggles the mind."

Ironically, in reversing the judge's order for a deadline extension, the Supreme Court cited its 2006 precedent against changing voting rules too close to an election. Yet it was acting just hours before election day, when Wisconsin voters had been told for nearly a week that their ballot would be counted if returned by April 13. As Ginsburg wrote, "The Court's order requires absentee voters to postmark their ballots by election day, April 7— *i.e.*, tomorrow—even if they did not receive their ballots by that date." She added, "If a voter already in line by the poll's closing time can still vote, why should Wisconsin's absentee voters, already in line to receive ballots, be denied the franchise?" In the end, tens of thousands of voters were disenfranchised, the state estimated; many others who'd requested mail-in ballots risked infection by going to the polls.[54]

Ginsburg chastised the majority for calling the Wisconsin case a "narrow, technical question" when votes were at stake, much as Breyer had reproached Kavanaugh for calling the deportation case a narrow one. Pinched readings of the law and the Constitution were a recurring trait in Kavanaugh's opinions—like the one supporting the Black Muslim's execution because his appeal was late. His record suggested other aspects after a couple terms on the court: The rhetorical distancing from the hard-right trio of Alito, Thomas, and Gorsuch. His tendency to try to soften a hard-line position, as with his tributes to gay individuals and young immigrants even as he joined rulings against them. His support for the Republican Party position in political cases, like those on gerrymandering, the census, and voting rights. The on-and-off alliance with Roberts at the court's center. And perhaps most of all, his willingness to override precedents. Yet Kavanaugh was still evolving—and so was the court, as would soon become clear.

•   •   •

As Kavanaugh quietly went about his work, Trump kept memories of the justice's confirmation battle alive as a political issue straight through the 2020 election season. On June 18, 2019, the president officially kicked off his reelection campaign with a rally in must-win Florida. Just fifteen minutes into a hundred-minute tirade against Democrats, he turned to the court and Kavanaugh: "They want to pack the court with far-left ideologues and they want to radicalize our judiciary. Look at what they did to a great gentleman, Justice Kavanaugh, highly respected. They didn't just try to win. They tried to destroy him with false and malicious accusations." Trump pointed to Lindsey Graham, who was there, telling the crowd that the senator was doing great in his reelection race, thanks to his red-hot defense of Kavanaugh.[55]

The president name-checked Kavanaugh again days later, when advice columnist E. Jean Carroll became the latest woman to accuse Trump of sexual assault, a rape in 1996. He denied her allegation as he had the others, depicting himself as just another aggrieved man: "When you look at what happened to Justice Kavanaugh, and you look at what's happening to others, you can't do that for the sake of publicity," he told reporters. In an official White House statement, Trump said, "Shame on those who make up false stories of assault to try to get publicity for themselves, or sell a book, or carry out a political agenda—like Julie Swetnick who falsely accused Justice Brett Kavanaugh." No mention of Ford or Ramirez; again, they were conflated with Kavanaugh's less credible accuser.

Trump's response to all such allegations against him or other men—defiant denial and claims of victimhood—underlined why Kavanaugh was never in real danger of losing the president's support. It also helped explain why Kavanaugh himself took the partisan offensive in the Senate—to cement Trump's backing, and in turn that of the compliant Senate Republicans.

Among the Senate Republicans facing elections in 2020, the Kavanaugh vote cut both ways. Graham, the political maverick turned Trump sycophant, vastly improved his party support in pro-Trump South Carolina. His advocacy for Kavanaugh was a main theme of his own campaign kickoff, which Vice President Mike Pence attended to convey Trump's endorsement.[56] In Maine, however, the long-popular Susan Collins confronted a backlash; by mid-2019, handicappers saw her race for a fifth term as a toss-up. Out-of-state money flowed in to oust her. McConnell rallied donors for Collins, but a fund-raiser hosted by the Federalist Society's Leo at his new summer home in Maine drew criticism as well as cash. "Have I lost some votes because of my decision to support Justice Kavanaugh? Yes,

I have," Collins said. "And I'm sad about that because I explained in great depth my decision-making."[57]

For himself, Trump saw Kavanaugh's confirmation—and his court appointments more broadly—only as a political plus. Just ahead of the Federalist Society convention in November 2019, he held an East Room fete with Republican senators for a plainly political purpose: showcasing his record-setting pace of seating judges at all levels. Past presidents had avoided such overt partisanship at the White House, but Trump had no such qualms. (Nine months later he'd accept his party's nomination from the South Lawn.) Graham told Trump that his stand for Kavanaugh was "the defining moment of your presidency," and thanked him "for not pulling the plug." Trump accepted the praise, and said, "You know this and Mitch knows this—there were plenty of other people that were saying, 'Let's go to maybe another choice.'" But both he and Kavanaugh wanted to fight, Trump said. Then, from the White House and before numerous cameras, he got in yet another lick at Kavanaugh's accusers: "Some of those people that came forward—to my way of thinking, all of those people that came forward—it was disgraceful."[58]

* * *

For Ramirez and especially Ford, adjusting to life after the confirmation clash was hard, particularly when some reminder—say, a nasty remark from Trump—would incite online trolls again. In a tweet ahead of the Academy Awards broadcast in February 2019, Trump's son Donald Jr. nominated Ford for a new category: "Best performance in a politically motivated hate crime hoax."[59] Hate messages started up again and, with them, Ford's security fears. Friends urged her to avoid looking at social media—so did her senator, Kamala Harris—to no avail.

Keith Koegler said that when she returned to California after testifying, "a very specific, credible threat" required the family to relocate again. They went to a hotel for a week, their third move since mid-September. Then a Palo Alto couple—strangers—offered their home while they were staying in Europe. Security guards drove the boys to school. Meanwhile, the Fords had work done on their empty house to make it more secure. They were back in by Christmas.[60] One mailing said, "I want you dead." Friend Deepa Lalla said the blowback against Ford was "so much worse" than expected. "I didn't think people would be sending her death threats all the time," Lalla said. "The online trolling, I thought it would go away."[61]

Her first public appearance was at an event in mid–December 2018, two months after Kavanaugh's confirmation; Ford had declined many invitations, but this one she was determined to accept, if only virtually. She recorded a video for a *Sports Illustrated* tribute to former gymnast Rachael Denhollander, the first of many women to allege sexual abuse by Larry Nassar, the doctor for USA Gymnastics. "In stepping forward, you took a huge risk," Ford said to Denhollander, speaking from experience, "and you galvanized future generations to come forward, even when the odds are seemingly stacked against them." She was returning a kind gesture: Denhollander, a conservative, had written after the Kavanaugh vote, "In our rush to get a conservative nominee, we have forgotten that there are hundreds of other survivors out there who are now the teenage survivor I once was, who have heard, 'It doesn't matter what someone did years ago,' who have seen a woman vilified, attacked, and even subjected to death threats after making an allegation of abuse." That message, she said, was "more devastating than we will ever know."[62]

Ford shut down the GoFundMe page started by supporters after she saw claims online that she was enriching herself. The fund closed with $647,610, more than four times its $150,000 goal. On the eve of Thanksgiving 2018, Ford gave thanks on the site to the nearly fourteen thousand contributors, writing, "Your donations have allowed us to take reasonable steps to protect ourselves against frightening threats." Unneeded funds, she said, would go to organizations serving trauma survivors.[63] She later told me that she had donated to local Boys and Girls Clubs, to counseling for low-income students and families in Silicon Valley, and to her alma mater, the University of North Carolina at Chapel Hill, for its counseling center.[64]

The Palo Alto City Council delayed plans to present Ford with a public proclamation, because of security concerns. When she was named months later among California's "Women of the Year," chosen by state legislators, she declined to go to Sacramento; she got her award privately.

Initially she did not return to teaching, but she resumed her biostatistics research and counseled doctoral students individually. In May 2019, she accepted the annual distinguished alumnus award for Pepperdine University's Graduate School of Education and Psychology; the citation noted only Ford's contributions to biostatistics, nothing about her role in the Kavanaugh confirmation.[65] She hired a security detail to accompany her to Pepperdine's Malibu campus for the commencement ceremonies. A friend suggested that she not sit on the stage or, if she did, that she wear a bullet-proof vest. Ford took the stage and spoke unprotected.[66] A month before, *Time* had named her to its annual list of one hundred influential people; Harris wrote the tribute to her. Ford posed for a photo and planned to attend the magazine's gala celebrating the issue in New York—until she saw that Kavanaugh also was included on the list, with a testimonial by McConnell.

Long after Kavanaugh's confirmation, Ford continued to lament that the whole matter was so partisan. She resented Republicans for their treatment of her—especially Grassley's staff, though not him—and Democrats for not rebutting the Senate Republicans' memorandum. She remained grateful to Feinstein for keeping her secret. Most of all, she was shocked that Republicans, led by Trump, continued to slander her. She longed to forget the whole affair, she said, and never see another reminder.[67]

*   *   *

While Ford grappled with her unwanted fame, Ramirez dealt with disillusionment that the Senate and FBI had all but ignored her. She was pained by the rupture with Karen Yarasavage, yet had reconnected with others from Yale. Two months after Kavanaugh's confirmation, about a dozen of the friends gathered on the Massachusetts coast, at the home of Tracy Harmon Joyce. "We all wanted to just get together," said Klaus Jensen, the only man in the group—"reconciling what had happened," and telling old college stories.[68]

Initially hesitant, Ramirez agreed to speak with authors writing books, hoping that by completing and correcting the record about herself, "other people who come forward and speak to power don't have to go through what Dr. Ford did or Anita Hill did, or I did." Her goal: "That some type of process is put in place where people want to actually hear what we want to share." More than two years later, and nearly thirty years after Anita Hill's experience, that goal was no closer in Congress.

Like Ford, Ramirez said she had no regrets. "I never expected that I'd change the outcome, to be completely honest. But what I would do is stand with another survivor and say, 'This happened to me, too.'" As she spoke in her living room, she gestured toward a thick blue binder and a decorative cardboard box beside a sofa; each was full of correspondence from friends and strangers around the world. She reread a few whenever she felt discouraged. People confided stories of sexual trauma, some for the first time. In one message, students at the University of Pittsburgh Medical Center wrote that her account had caused them to alter their approach to victims. "So, yes," she said, "I'd do it again."

"I'm not the same person I was as a teenager, or the same person I was in college," Ramirez told me. Had Kavanaugh acknowledged the same thing in his responses, she said, "that would have fixed it. For me, that would have done it."[69]

EPILOGUE

MINORITY RULE

When President Trump announced on September 9, 2020, that he was again expanding his list of Supreme Court candidates, it got little attention except as a preelection play to his base. There was no opening on the court, and he might lose reelection in eight weeks. Ruth Bader Ginsburg was being treated again for cancer, but say she died—would Republicans be so brazen as to defy history and ram a nominee to confirmation on the eve of a presidential election, after they'd refused to act on an Obama nominee for eight months before the previous one? The question seems laughably naïve now. Of course they would. Yet on September 18, just nine days after Trump released his list, a plugged-in Democratic neighbor confidently insisted the answer was no, they wouldn't. This after she'd just read aloud a text, from a Ginsburg associate, that interrupted the small backyard dinner to celebrate my birthday: The justice had died.

Though Ginsburg's dying wish, dictated to her granddaughter, was "that I will not be replaced until a new president is installed," three days later Trump offered her seat to a very different female jurist.[1] Amy Coney Barrett, only forty-eight, was as conservative as Ginsburg was progressive, especially on reproductive rights. Trump had passed over Barrett in 2018 because Republicans had just fifty-one Senate seats and couldn't afford to lose the votes of Susan Collins and Lisa Murkowski. Now they had fifty-three seats—wiggle room. Barrett's background showed how brazen Trump and Republicans had become about naming someone openly hostile to *Roe*. In 2006, then teaching at Notre Dame's law school, she was among the signers on a full-page ad in the local paper saying, "It's time to put an end to the barbaric legacy of *Roe v. Wade* and restore laws that protect the lives of unborn children."[2] Of course, the formerly pro-choice Trump had promised as much: *Roe* would be overturned automatically if he were president, he said in 2016, "because I am putting pro-life justices on the court."

But Senate Democrats didn't focus on abortion rights in opposing Barrett. Mindful of Catholic voters so close to the election, they were cowed by fear that Republicans would claim Democrats were attacking Barrett's faith—just as Republicans had done in 2017 when Dianne Feinstein, at the hearing on Barrett's nomination to the Seventh Circuit, complained that "the dogma lives loudly within you." The line, memorialized on mugs, T-shirts, and baby onesies that conservatives snapped up, instantly made Barrett a celebrity on the right; within a month, in November of 2017, the novice judge was among the five candidates Trump added to his Supreme Court list (along with Brett Kavanaugh). Now that she was indeed a high-court nominee, Democrats mostly criticized Barrett for her opposition to the Affordable Care Act. With the court about to hear a third Republican challenge to the law, Democrats contended Barrett could decide the matter against it.

They declined to meet with her and boycotted the committee vote on her nomination, refusing to lend it legitimacy. But Democrats rejected calls from allies on the left to somehow force the Senate to a halt in protest. That would simply delay the inevitable in an institution run by Mitch McConnell. The shamelessness with which the Republican leader conspired with Trump to rush Barrett onto the court—after blocking Merrick Garland's confirmation on the "principle" that the voters should have a say—stunned even the most hardened politicos. Trump openly suggested Barrett was needed on the court to decide the election for him.[3] On October 26, eight days before the election finale, with millions of early votes already cast, the Senate confirmed Barrett 52–48. All Democrats were opposed (along with one Republican, Collins), making Barrett the first justice in 150 years to receive not a single vote from the minority party. No justice had ever been confirmed so close to a presidential election; the previous record was a July vote in 1916. Yet this election would give Democrats control of both the presidency and Congress—so much for McConnell's months-long mantra against Garland in 2016: "Give the people a voice in the filling of this vacancy."[4]

With the court's very legitimacy at stake, McConnell's talk of heeding the people was even more cynical than it seemed: Barrett was the fifth justice—along with Roberts, Alito, Gorsuch, and Kavanaugh—to be appointed by a Republican president first elected despite losing the popular vote.[5] She also was the fifth justice—along with Thomas, Alito, Gorsuch, and Kavanaugh—to be confirmed by a narrow majority of senators who, collectively, were elected with many millions fewer votes than the senators who opposed them. Days after her confirmation, the president who nominated her would lose reelection by more than seven million votes, more than twice his popular-vote shortfall in 2016.

The circumstances of Barrett's ascension meant that all three Trump justices came to the court with partisan asterisks: Neil Gorsuch filled the seat stolen from a Democratic president who, unlike Trump, was twice elected by more than a majority of voters. Then there was Kavanaugh, speedily confirmed without a full review of his record, amid complaints he'd lied under oath at his Senate hearings and after a disqualifying show of partisan rage and a sham investigation of assault allegations. His confirmation had sealed conservatives' capture of the Supreme Court. Barrett, even further to the right, cemented it.

•   •   •

Her impact was immediate. Chief Justice John G. Roberts Jr. lost the whip hand on the court. After Kavanaugh arrived, the swing-vote chief had been able to control the five-man conservative faction both by his vote and his power to decide which justices wrote opinions. He'd masterfully shown in the term just ended that he could—by writing the most sensitive opinions himself and occasionally aligning with the liberals—put a thumb on the scale to prevent outcomes that might be seen as political and undermine the court's legitimacy. With Barrett providing a sixth conservative vote and likely to side often with the hard-line justices—she'd chosen Clarence Thomas to administer her oath of office—the right wing was in control. Advocates for reproductive rights, affirmative action, voting rights, gun limits, environmental rules, and labor rights feared the worst.

The first proof of the new dynamic came a month after Barrett's arrival: a 5–4 ruling issued just before midnight on November 25, 2020. It struck down New York's pandemic-related limits on religious services, reversing the court's 5–4 rulings that upheld restrictions in California and Nevada months before. In those rulings, the court had deferred to local and state officials' public-health decisions; the four liberals and Roberts were the majority. Now Ginsburg was gone, and Barrett joined the other four conservatives to form a new majority. More broadly, the outcome seemed to confirm that she would reinforce the conservative court's expansive view of the First Amendment protection of the free exercise of religion, favoring it above other state interests and individual rights even when those laws treated churches no differently from secular places. The Supreme Court's opinion in the New York case was unsigned, but in separate concurrences and dissents several justices exchanged potshots that exposed tensions both personal and ideological.

Kavanaugh said the minority, which included Roberts, favored "wholesale judicial abdication" on the religious liberty question by opposing churches' petitions to be exempted from pandemic restrictions. Gorsuch chastised Roberts, mocking his opinion in the California ruling for having "reached back one-hundred years" to cite a 1905 ruling that "hardly supports cutting the Constitution loose during a pandemic." The chief justice, with uncharacteristic snark, replied that no one was "cutting the Constitution loose" and marveled that Gorsuch took three pages to skewer Roberts's one sentence mentioning the old precedent. Dissenters Sonia Sotomayor and Elena Kagan warned the majority, "Justices of this Court play a deadly game in second guessing the expert judgment of health officials." At the time, the coronavirus was infecting a million Americans weekly.[6]

In another such case six weeks later, on February 5, 2021, Barrett wrote her first opinion when the conservatives partially struck down new restrictions California imposed as illnesses spiked. She agreed with other conservatives, including Roberts this time, that the state's ban on indoor services in areas where infections were highest was unconstitutional. But, parting with the hard-right trio of Thomas, Gorsuch, and Samuel Alito, who opposed all limits on churches, Barrett joined the three liberals, Roberts, and Kavanaugh in allowing California's other restrictions—capping attendance and banning songs and chants—to stand. What was most interesting about the splintered order, however, was the biting dissent from Kagan, typically the liberal faction's most conciliatory justice. She seemed to throw up her hands at dealing with the conservative majority, at least insofar as its favoritism toward conservative religious plaintiffs. "In the worst public health crisis in a century, this foray into armchair epidemiology cannot end well," she wrote. Kagan described actual epidemiologists' support for California's ban on indoor assemblies, and closed with a sting to the court: "If this decision causes suffering, we will not pay. Our marble halls are now closed to the public, and our life tenure forever insulates us from responsibility for our errors. That would seem good reason to avoid disrupting a state's pandemic response. But the court forges ahead regardless, insisting that science-based policy yield to judicial edict."[7]

This debate played out as the justices themselves had been working remotely since closing the court in March 2020. First they'd canceled oral arguments and then, facing a likelihood of a prolonged shutdown, began holding audio conferences by phone—an arrangement that continued into 2021.

Despite the court's shift further right, Alito wasn't satisfied. Two weeks after Barrett joined the court, he was the keynote speaker at the Federalist Society's annual Washington convention—the fourth conservative justice in five years to do the honors. Rather than celebrate the right's 6–3 hold on the nation's highest court, Alito delivered the sort of grievance-filled rant more common to Republican politicians. The evidence at the court to the contrary, he lamented that the free exercise of religion had become "a disfavored right," along with gun rights and free speech. "You can't say that marriage is a union between one man and one woman" without possible reprisals, Alito claimed. "Until very recently that's what the vast majority of Americans thought. Now it's considered bigotry."[8] He got no ovations like Kavanaugh received the year before; this speech was video-streamed because of the pandemic. While Alito didn't say anything he hadn't written on the court, nonpartisan legal scholars joined critics on the left in panning his acrid speech as damaging to the institution.[9] His address, and to that audience, signaled that Roberts was likely waging a losing battle to keep the conservative court from being seen as ideological and out of step with public opinion.

The election-related lawsuits that proliferated through 2020 likewise gave evidence of the court's political bent, and that of Trump-appointed judges in lower courts as well. The conservative justices mostly sided with Republicans in blocking actions by state and federal courts that loosened rules to accommodate voters worried about the coronavirus and postal delays. Overall, nearly three out of four opinions by Trump appointees to federal courts were against relaxing voting rules, compared to 17 percent of decisions from Obama appointees, the *Washington Post* found.[10] Republicans' lawsuits reflected their general calculation that anything that increased voter turnout was bad for their party; as Trump candidly said of pandemic proposals to encourage absentee and mail-in ballots, if his party "ever agreed to it, you'd never have a Republican elected in this country again." The conservative justices, in upholding restrictions, gave short shrift to the once-in-a-century health emergency that prompted local and state officials to seek to relax them. Kavanaugh, in particular, drew rebukes from liberals, law professors, and Kagan for his opinion in late October opposing an extension of Wisconsin's deadline for receiving mailed ballots. He cited the widely disparaged *Bush v. Gore* ruling, as no subsequent opinion ever had, made a factual error, and echoed Trump's criticism of mail-in ballots received after election day.[11]

By luck and circumstance—the presidential election result wasn't close—the court avoided the constitutional crisis many Americans had feared: a repeat of *Bush v. Gore*, but worse, with the losing side rejecting the justices' ruling. Trump's presumption, that he had the 6–3 court in his pocket, vastly raised the stakes for a contested election. "I'm counting on them to look at the ballots, definitely," he'd said of the justices during a debate with Joe Biden September 29. "I hope we don't need them, in terms of the election itself, but for the ballots, I think so."[12] Post-election, the absurdity of the Trump challenges to Biden's victory made it easy for the justices to dismiss them. More than sixty state and federal courts rejected lawsuits based on the Trump camp's conspiracy theories about fraud in states he lost. Among the suitably scathing opinions, one by a Trump judge on the Third Circuit began with a line that summed up the consensus: "Calling an election unfair does not make it so. Charges require specific allegations and then proof. We have neither here."[13]

To make good on his threats to have "his" justices decide the election, Trump joined a suit from Texas's grandstanding Republican attorney general, Ken Paxton, asking the Supreme Court to throw out the votes in four swing states that Biden won. As outrageous as their proposal was, it wouldn't have changed the result: The four states had a combined sixty-two electoral votes; Biden won by seventy-four, 306–232. Yet seventeen Republican state attorneys general and most House Republicans endorsed the preposterous suit, underscoring their party's rot in placing fealty to one man over democratic norms. When the Supreme Court dismissed the suit without comment December 11, Trump tweeted to his millions of followers, "The Supreme Court really let us down. No Wisdom! No Courage!" Twice more, in January and February, the court tossed other suits from Trump and his allies, again without comment.

As usual, the president scorned the rule of law. In rallying supporters to march on Congress on January 6, 2021, he also delivered a less-noted rhetorical attack on the citadel of the other branch of government—the Supreme Court. He singled out Kavanaugh especially, reviving the justice's confirmation controversy. "Look, I'm not happy with the Supreme Court," he said. "They love to rule against me. I picked three people. I fought like hell for them—one in particular. I fought. They all said, 'Sir, cut him loose. He's killing us.'" Trump said he wouldn't do that to Kavanaugh: "He didn't do anything wrong. They're made-up stories." And yet, he whined, the justices "couldn't give a damn...It almost seems that they're all going out of their way to hurt all of us, and to hurt our country." All three of his ungrateful justices were ruling against him, Trump suggested, because the media had called them his "puppets": "They hate that. It's not good on the social circuit."[14]

That the high court, like lower courts, ruled against Trump's election suits was cited by some commentators as cause for celebration: The institutions of government and rule of law had prevailed against his attempted coup. At bottom, however, it simply reflected just how baseless the vanquished president's cases were. A closer election, as in 2000, might have tested the guardrails.

●   ●   ●

Trump's 226 appointments to the trial, appellate, and Supreme courts will stand as one of his foremost legacies, and all but certainly his most enduring: Some appointees, mostly young and with life tenure, will be on the bench late into the twenty-first century. Were Barrett to serve until her late eighties as Ginsburg did, she would be on the court until about 2060; Kavanaugh and Gorsuch could be there past 2050. Trump's three justices in a single term are one more than Obama, George W. Bush, and Bill Clinton each named over two terms. He appointed fifty-four judges to the circuit courts—which are the final word on the overwhelming share of appeals, since the high court accepts few—just one less than Obama over eight years. When Trump left office, his picks comprised one-third of the Supreme Court, 30 percent of the thirteen circuit courts, and more than one-quarter of the judges at the nation's ninety-four district courts. Like Trump's administration and the Republican Party, his appointees are not a diverse group. Seventy-six percent are male (compared to 58 percent for Obama) and 84 percent white (64 percent for Obama).[15]

In McConnell's Senate, confirming Trump judges took precedence over everything else. The right-wing RedState.com wrote—approvingly, of course—of "the bloody-mindedness of Mitch McConnell and Chuck Grassley in ramming those nominees through the system."[16] Six months before the 2020 election, Grassley's successor as Senate Judiciary Committee chairman, Lindsey Graham, urged federal judges in their sixties to retire so Republicans, rightly fearful of losing the Senate majority and the presidency, could fill the seats.[17] McConnell, breaking yet another norm, had the Senate continue to confirm judges after Trump's defeat, vowing he'd "leave no vacancy behind."[18] Since 1897, the Senate had confirmed just one judicial nomination of those pending after the presidents who made them lost election. It confirmed fourteen of Trump's.[19] Even as Republicans complained that Democrats would pack the courts once Biden took office to offset Trump's judges, they actually were continuing to do so.

More than any president before him, Trump picked young lawyers for the lifetime jobs. Many lacked the experience expected of federal judges. Democrat Dick Durbin of Illinois, who in 2021 became chairman of the Senate Judiciary Committee, told me that more than once he'd said to Trump officials at confirmation hearings, "So, let me get this straight: You couldn't find one conservative Republican attorney in the state...who has had any courtroom experience or experience as a state judge?"[20] More often than in past administrations, the American Bar Association rated some nominees "not qualified," which didn't deter Republicans from confirming them. However, forty-four-year-old Jonathan Kobes, an aide to Republican senator Mike Rounds of South Dakota, needed Mike Pence to break a tie for his confirmation to the St. Louis–based Eighth Circuit in 2018. Kobes was the first federal judge in history confirmed by a vice president's vote.[21] Lawrence J. C. VanDyke, nearly forty-seven, was confirmed in late 2019 to the Ninth Circuit, although the ABA found him "not qualified" based on "strong evidence" from sixty lawyers and judges. Its harsh evaluation, which conservatives denounced, said those consulted about him called VanDyke "arrogant, lazy, an ideologue, and lacking in knowledge," and said he "has an 'entitlement' temperament, does not have an open mind, and does not always have a commitment to being candid and truthful."[22]

Some nominees had troubling records regarding their attitudes toward racial minorities, women, and LGBTQ people. Tim Scott of South Carolina, the only Black Republican in the Senate, took to the *Wall Street Journal* to object, "We should stop bringing candidates with questionable track records on race before the full Senate for a vote."[23] Scott was able to block several, given Republicans' slim Senate margin.

All of Trump's choices had one thing in common: serious conservative bona fides. As McConnell had half joked to the Federalist Society, ending the filibuster opened the door to "crazy right-wingers" who never would have been confirmed in the past. Three times Trump nominated forty-year-old Matthew Kacsmaryk, who'd opposed legal protections for LGBTQ people and said they had mental disorders, before Republicans finally approved him for a Texas trial court in 2019. Confirmed to another Texas court that year was Michael J. Truncale, sixty-one, who'd called Obama an "un-American imposter"; the only Republican to oppose him was Obama's 2012 rival, Mitt Romney.

Another example: Neomi Rao, Trump's forty-five-year-old czar against federal regulations, who replaced Kavanaugh on the D.C. Circuit Court that handles most challenges to such rules. Rao seemed a singularly odd choice, given the allegations Kavanaugh had faced during his confirmation: At Yale, she'd written that women who were sexually assaulted bore blame if they'd been drinking. Facing bipartisan opposition initially, she wrote to Judiciary Committee leaders, "If I were to address these issues now, I would have more empathy and perspective."[24] That assuaged Republican Joni Ernst of Iowa, an assault survivor who'd called Rao's writings "abhorrent." Separately, Rao privately reassured Republican Josh Hawley of Missouri, who'd worried that she was soft on abortion. Once on the D.C. court, Rao reliably took the administration's side in cases important to Trump. She opposed Congress's subpoenas of his financial records, for example, and upheld the Justice Department's dismissal of the conviction of his former national security adviser Michael Flynn—a ruling that the full appeals court overturned decisively.

Perhaps the quintessential Republican judge of the Trump-McConnell era, however, was Justin Walker, a baby-faced political networker to rival Kavanaugh in his time. In less than a year between 2019 and 2020, Walker went from being a thirty-eight-year-old associate law professor in Louisville, Kentucky, to a federal district judge there and then a member of the powerful D.C. appeals court. The ABA had advised that Walker, with no trial experience, was unqualified to preside over a district court. That didn't matter to Republican senators: He was a protégé of the majority leader. On March 13, 2020, McConnell and Kavanaugh flew to Louisville to participate in Walker's formal investiture as a federal judge, an event that was remarkable for the openly political banter.

There, McConnell recalled that they'd met when Walker was eighteen; as a favor to Walker's grandfather, the senator talked to the teenager for a school paper on the 1994 "Republican Revolution." The party's takeover of Congress that year was "the most exciting thing that had ever happened in my life," the boy said, in McConnell's recounting. "Clearly he had excellent political taste from quite a young age," McConnell quipped.[25] Walker interned in McConnell's office, worked on Bush's 2004 campaign, and clerked first at the D.C. court for Kavanaugh—who was only too happy to hire a protégé of the Senate Republican leader—and then for Justice Anthony M. Kennedy on Kavanaugh's recommendation. Kavanaugh, in his judicial robe, told the audience that he recalled just where Walker sat when Kavanaugh taught him at Harvard Law School.[26]

Walker, also in a black robe, recognized each mentor. "It has been extremely important to me that Kentucky's senior senator is Mitch McConnell," he said, and then led the audience in applause. As for Kennedy, Walker told a weak joke that would become an issue in his next Senate confirmation hearing; in the telling, he said "the worst words" he'd ever heard was Kennedy's disclosure that Chief Justice Roberts would uphold Obamacare. Of Kavanaugh, Walker joked, "What can I say that I haven't already said"—he paused for effect—"on Fox News?" That nod to his ubiquitous support for Kavanaugh during the confirmation fight was a bit awkward. But what followed—an ideological call to arms—was simply inappropriate from a judge. Walker compared Kavanaugh to St. Paul: "Hard-pressed on every side but not crushed, perplexed but not in despair, persecuted but not abandoned, struck down but not destroyed. Because in Brett Kavanaugh's America, we will not surrender while you wage war on our work or our cause or our hope or our dream." He stopped for applause, then closed by thanking Trump and "the Senate majority," adding snarkily, "And to the Senate minority—no hard feelings."[27]

On the district court, Walker soon sparked a controversy that resonated beyond Louisville. With coronavirus infections peaking, the Democratic mayor had issued a directive against drive-in Easter services. Walker blocked it and lashed out: "On Holy Thursday, an American mayor criminalized the communal celebration of Easter." Twenty pages later he ended with musings on the meaning of Jesus's resurrection to those eager to attend services: "The reason they will be there for each other and their Lord is the reason they believe He was and is there for us."[28] Even a conservative analyst wrote that Walker's rhetoric was "over the top," and that he could have settled the matter with a fifteen-minute phone call among the parties.[29] A liberal commentator, describing Walker's order as more like "a screed against Democrats" on far-right Breitbart.com, said it exemplified what scornful judges called "auditioning" by Trump appointees—as in, primping for a higher court seat by showing off their conservatism. That's what some associates had previously said of Gorsuch and Kavanaugh before their promotions. But Walker didn't need to audition. Eight days earlier Trump had nominated him for the D.C. appeals court. Walker had followed the political path Kavanaugh helped pave for conservative judges years before. Already some on the right had tagged Walker as a future justice. That prospect would have to wait: In 2021, Democrats took over the White House and Senate.

•   •   •

Initially, Democrats' elation at Biden's victory was offset by dismay at their apparent failure to capture a Senate majority. Few expected Democrats could win both runoff elections in Georgia, which would give them control of a 50–50 Senate with Kamala Harris's tiebreaker vote. If McConnell remained in charge, they knew, many Biden judicial nominees would hit a wall. As courts scholar Russell Wheeler at the Brookings Institution had written, "We are reaching the point that confirmations stop unless the same party controls the White House and Senate."[30] Yet the Democratic candidates in Georgia—a Black man and a Jew—amazingly did win their elections January 5, 2021.

Given Democrats' precarious margins in the Senate and House, most liberal activists dropped their unrealistic demand that Congress expand the Supreme Court so Biden could add progressive justices. Even so, after years of Republicans thwarting Obama's nominees and then railroading Trump's, Democrats were primed to act more aggressively than in the past to shape the judiciary. The pressure to do so was bottom-up, from the party's base, donors, and progressive groups. In a break from past elections, more Democratic voters than Republicans had said that an important factor in their choice for president was concern about Supreme Court appointments. That reflected in part a backlash to the Kavanaugh and Barrett confirmations.[31] Emboldened progressives forced eighty-seven-year-old

Feinstein, disdained as too conciliatory toward Republicans, to relinquish her role as party leader on the Senate Judiciary Committee. Durbin became chairman once Democrats took the majority.[32]

Copying a page from Trump and the right, progressive groups were ready with lists of potential judges for Biden. One group was the American Constitution Society, the left's weak imitation of the Federalist Society, now led by former senator Russ Feingold. Activists had canvassed lawyers, law professors, and local officials nationwide during the Trump years to vet prospects for judgeships should a Democrat become president.[33] They emphasized diversity of race and gender, for a judiciary that "looks like America," as Biden put it, but also professional and educational variety: fewer corporate lawyers and prosecutors, more public defenders, labor and legal-aid lawyers, and civil rights advocates. Fewer Ivy Leaguers, more state school alumni. As usual, Democrats didn't focus on judicial philosophy and ideology like Republicans did, though certainly their criteria would yield generally progressive candidates. Activists also urged Senate Democrats to follow Republicans' lead and end the blue slip tradition that gave opposition senators a veto over nominees from their states. Chris Kang, the former Obama adviser, said Senate Republicans mostly from southern states had blocked nearly twenty Obama nominees, all of them women or minorities, by withholding their blue slips.

No question, Democrats would be more partisan going forward. The question was whether they could beat Republicans at the game. Brian Fallon, the former Senate and Hillary Clinton adviser who was Kang's cofounder of the liberal group Demand Justice, was skeptical even as he pressured Democratic leaders. "Mitch McConnell will obliterate norms without batting an eye," he said. "Democrats constitutionally—no pun intended—don't have that gene. They like the system to work. They like the government to function by norms."[34]

That certainly included Biden, long suspect on the left for his record as a moderate institutionalist on the Judiciary Committee, back to the Thomas hearings thirty years before. But the new president was receptive to the partisans' push for a harder line, despite his promise to work with Republicans. He endorsed the call for diverse judicial candidates outside the corporate and prosecutorial mold. He promised a commission to examine potential changes to the judiciary, including term limits and additional judgeships. To expedite nominations, Biden agreed not to wait for ABA evaluations. "People are approaching this with a different sense of urgency," said Paige Herwig, a White House counsel. "And they understand: They saw what the Trump administration did for four years."

Biden didn't inherit nearly as many vacancies as Trump had, though McConnell didn't quite fulfill his vow to leave none behind. Circuit courts had five openings and federal trial courts more than sixty. When Garland finally won Senate confirmation—as Biden's attorney general—his seat on the D.C. appeals court opened. Other vacancies loomed: Some judges had put off retirement rather than let Trump fill their seats, and about sixty were eligible by their age and years of service to take "senior status," a limited role that allows presidents to name a full-time replacement. Those included more than a third of appellate judges.[35]

Rebalancing the Supreme Court, however, was a lost cause. Breyer, eighty-two when Biden took office, was widely expected to retire before long, now that a Democrat would nominate a successor. Biden had promised to make history by naming the first Black woman to the high court. Ideologically, however, that would be an even swap, leaving the court's balance unchanged. From the Supreme Court through lower courts, Republican appointees stood as potential roadblocks to the agenda of Biden and congressional Democrats—what liberal writer and lawyer Dahlia Lithwick called the "dead hand of the Trump administration that strikes down every single thing that Biden does in the coming years."[36]

That specter was evident in the new president's first week: A Trump trial judge in Texas, in a case brought by the state's Republican attorney general, blocked Biden's one-hundred-day moratorium on deportations— his first step in reviewing Trump's inhumane, xenophobic immigration policies. Days later, a three-judge panel of the D.C. Circuit Court—all Trump appointees—gave a green light to a Trump directive to turn away children seeking asylum as health risks, a policy Biden opposed. The Biden administration would face a quandary in deciding whether to appeal such cases all the way to the Supreme Court. More than a year before the election, Wheeler, the judiciary expert, wrote of the potential that the conservative court would stymie laws and regulations from a Democratic president and Congress. That, he wrote, in turn could trigger progressives' attacks on the court's legitimacy, much like in the New Deal era, reviving and intensifying the pressure for court-packing.[37]

•   •   •

It was judicial appointments more than anything, even more than tax cuts, that kept the Republican establishment in thrall to Trump. That was the Faustian bargain party leaders made for five years with the self-dealing charlatan who provoked an existential crisis for their party, and for democracy. "One of the many revealing aspects of the problem is that, while there are exceptions, you will generally not find people saying, 'Yes, I think the president is corrupt. It's deeply wrong when he calls upon the Justice Department to investigate his opponents. People in Charlottesville were not very fine people. POWs and reporters with disabilities should never be mocked. Oh, and we're separating children at the border. But I really like the judges, and that's more important,'" said Peter Keisler, one of the foremost conservative lawyers of his generation, and a Never Trumper. "If you ask somebody to explain the tradeoffs they're making, they will instead almost always minimize or dismissively toss away the deep aberrations that—if it were a president from the other party—they would readily denounce. That kind of moral compromise becomes corrosive." Even so, he told me, "One thing I've learned is that it's not a hostile takeover anymore, if it ever was. Trump has broad support within the Republican Party."[38]

Trump was able first to take ownership of the Republican base, and then to keep it despite defeat and disgrace, because party leaders had done the spadework: For more than two decades, they had played to voters on the right with antigovernment, antimedia, and anti-immigrant rhetoric, false promises, and tolerance of bigots, nationalists, and conspiracists. Party leaders' refrain that government doesn't work became a self-fulfilling prophecy when Republicans, valuing politicking over governing competence, took power—from the Gingrich shutdowns; through Bush's mismanagement of the Iraq war, Hurricane Katrina, and the economy; to Trump's sabotages of Obamacare, the postal service, and more, culminating in his deadly bungling of the pandemic. Unlike his Republican predecessors, the policy-phobic

Trump made little pretense of governing and was unconstrained by either respect for norms and truth or any sense of shame.

From his announcement of his campaign in 2015, he'd given demagogic voice to the grievances of white Americans resentful of economic and demographic changes in a country where they'd be a minority by mid-century. Once he was president, Republican leaders believed they could rein him in and, surrounded by able hands, he'd grow in the office. They couldn't, and Trump didn't. They tolerated his outrages and constant chaos, consoling themselves with tax cuts and conservative judges. Even three years in, after Senate Republicans acquitted Trump after his first impeachment trial—for extorting a foreign leader to provide dirt on Trump's likely election rival—Susan Collins justified the outcome by saying he'd learned his lesson. (Proved wrong, she voted to convict him a year later in his unprecedented second trial.) Republicans like Collins enabled Trump's worst impulses, until he'd cost them control of the House, Senate, and White House and ultimately sent a mob against them on January 6, 2021.

In the final days of his reelection race, Trump revived a staple of his 2016 campaign rallies: He recited the lyrics of an old soul song, "The Snake," perversely reinterpreting it as a xenophobic allegory for "vicious" immigrants biting the naïve Americans who take them in. By 2020, however, it was an apt fable about Republicans: Trump was the snake, and they were the dupes who thought they could tame him. As the reptile hisses to the "tender-hearted woman" as she dies of his venom, "You knew damn well I was a snake before you took me in."[39]

Many Republicans had hoped that voters would save them from Trump in 2020. Some openly wished for a "burn it all down" wipeout of the party's candidates, a comeuppance so complete that there would have to be an anti-Trump reckoning. Raze the forest and allow new growth—a renewed party—the thinking went.[40] The results fell far short of the full repudiation these Republicans desired. Even in decisive defeat, Trump brought out millions of new voters. Unfortunately for him, many more came out for Biden, for a record turnout overall. But other Republicans—including Collins, a target since her Kavanaugh vote—defied the predictions of doom. The party won enough House and Senate races to threaten Democrats' majorities in 2022. Republicans' strength in state legislatures was reinforced—just in time to dominate the postcensus redrawing of state and congressional districts, to favor party candidates for yet another decade even as Democrats got a significantly larger share of the overall vote.

Then Trump seemed to do what the voters hadn't: He fully discredited himself—by his unprecedented refusal to concede, lying about fraud, inciting a riot to stop Congress's constitutional act of certifying Biden's victory, and then failing to defend the Capitol and his vice president. In 2016, a conservative journalist famously criticized the media for obsessing over candidate Trump's rhetorical outrages, writing in the *Atlantic* that "the press takes him literally, but not seriously; his supporters take him seriously, but not literally."[41] Sadly, she turned out to be wrong—Trump's MAGA army took his incitements seriously *and* literally. "Fight for Trump!" the mob chanted as it bloodied cops to breach the Capitol.

Clearer violations of a president's oath to "preserve, protect and defend the Constitution" would be hard to conjure. Yet Trump continued to dominate a party that had become a cult of personality. That much was plain when Congress reconvened in the just-ransacked Capitol on January 6 to finish the election count, and nearly 60 percent of Republicans still voted to block Pennsylvania's and Arizona's electoral votes for Biden, potentially disenfranchising millions of citizens. It was clear a week later, when just ten House Republicans voted to impeach Trump for inciting the insurrection, and yet again on February 13, when just seven of the fifty Senate Republicans voted to convict him. The Senate's 57–43 majority to convict was ten votes short of the necessary two-thirds margin. With reason, Republicans were fearful of Trump's voters—politically and literally, given the violence they'd witnessed and the death threats some were receiving. Trump vowed revenge against those who voted against him, and nearly all were condemned by their state parties, which were controlled by Trump loyalists.

Of the seven senators who supported conviction, just one—Ben Sasse of Nebraska—was considered a possible candidate for Republicans' presidential nomination in 2024. Sasse seemed to be betting, as few other Republicans were, that Trump's grip on the party might ease by then and voters would be open to a young candidate promising a return to conservative ideas over personality politics and grievances. It was a losing gamble. Even before his vote, the Nebraska Republican Central Committee had moved to censure Sasse because he'd simply criticized Trump for his lies and encouragement of the riot. Sasse was defiant. In a video posted on Facebook and YouTube, he told the state party leaders, "Let's be clear about why this is happening. It's because I still believe, as you used to, that politics isn't about the weird worship of one dude." He challenged them: "We're going to have to choose—between conservatism and madness."[42]

The party has chosen madness—the continued "weird worship of one dude." Trumpism had reflected the marriage of the man and the moment: Trump was a charismatic demagogue at a time when the Republican Party, despite its shrinking base of mostly white, older, and rural voters, could still win the White House, majorities in Congress, and, by extension, control of the Supreme Court—thanks to gerrymandering and to the disproportionate edge that less populated states have in both the Senate and the Electoral College under the Constitution. Defying political fundamentals, Trump never tried to expand his base by appealing to voters across racial, gender, generational, and geographic lines. Yet he was elected once, and might have been reelected but for his botched response to the pandemic. Soon Republicans' reliance on white voters would be a losing game, given demographic trends. But politicians' focus extends only to the next election. As most Republicans looked toward the 2022 midterms and the 2024 presidential race, they still saw Trump as the Godfather, whose wrath could mean political death. As Donald Trump Jr. said January 6 in warming the crowd for his dad, "This isn't their Republican Party anymore. This is Donald Trump's Republican Party."

With or without Trump, the party would go on in his image: Its voters were Trumpian before they'd embraced his brand, and they'd soldier on, forcing party officials to fall in line. Long before he'd descended the Trump Tower escalator to run for president, the base was dominated by culture warriors who'd been riled for decades by Rush Limbaugh, his thousands of local imitators, Fox News pundits, and ever more right-wing websites and networks; by 2020 most Republicans got their "news" solely from such sources, willfully closed off from balanced, factual coverage and unpersuadable.[43] They'd followed Newt Gingrich for a time. Disillusioned by George W. Bush, they'd coalesced as the leaderless Tea Party. Finally, they jumped on the Trump Train. He simply harnessed these voters and radicalized them further, giving them license by his own shameless behavior. Once-fringe characters became the faces of the party: white nationalists, bigots, far-right conspiracists, Christian zealots, gun fetishists, and even self-styled paramilitaries.

"The party isn't doomed; it's dead," conservative columnist Kathleen Parker wrote in late January 2021. "The chance to move away from Trumpism, toward a more respectful, civilized approach to governance that acknowledges the realities of a diverse nation and that doesn't surrender to the clenched fist, has slipped away. What comes next is anybody's guess."[44] Yet Lindsey Graham declared two weeks later on Fox News, "Donald Trump is the most vibrant member of the Republican Party. The Trump movement is alive and well." He encouraged Trump's daughter-in-law Lara Trump to run for the Senate, saying, "She represents the future of the Republican Party."

For all the post-election talk of a party at war with itself—embrace Trump or exorcise him—it's not much of a fight. Pick a side? Republican voters were on Trump's. Even party foes agreed he'd win the party nomination if he ran again in 2024 (but not the election). The caveat, of course, was Trump's very real legal liabilities amid ongoing criminal investigations. McConnell, who'd savaged Trump for a "disgraceful dereliction of duty" after January 6, later said he "absolutely" would support Trump as the nominee. In late February, Trump emerged from Mar-a-Lago to claim victory in the presidential straw poll at the annual Conservative Political Action Conference, the once-fringe, now-mainstream Republican winter assembly. A gold idol of the man graced the CPAC convention site.

Republicans eager to run for president, if Trump didn't, competed for his favor. Among these would-be Trump heirs were Senators Josh Hawley of Missouri and Ted Cruz of Texas, who recklessly led his fight to trash the votes of pro-Biden states, and Tom Cotton of Arkansas, who'd proposed sending Army divisions against protestors for racial justice in 2020. Former secretary of state Mike Pompeo sought to pick up Trump's nationalist banner. Pence tried to revive his prospects as the heir apparent, planning a political operation to promote the Trump-Pence record. But, after four years of sycophancy, he'd likely forfeited his claim when he refused to use his ceremonial role presiding at Congress's election certification to try to overturn the result. Whipped up by Trump, the rioters bellowed "Hang Mike Pence!" in the shadow of a gallows. Trump himself declared that a "future Republican Star" was Marjorie Taylor Greene. The new Georgia congresswoman was a QAnon cultist who believed, among other loathsome sentiments, that the school massacres in Newtown, Connecticut, and Parkland, Florida, were hoaxes staged to spur antigun backlashes, and that Nancy Pelosi deserved a bullet to her head.[45]

Polls did suggest some slippage in Trump's stranglehold on the party. The final *Wall Street Journal* and NBC News poll before the election showed that 54 percent of Republicans identified more as supporters of Trump than of the party. In a poll after January 6, the result was a 46–46 split.[46] Surveys by the conservative American Enterprise Institute found a sharper shift—from a majority before the election who said they were more loyal to Trump than party, to 63 percent choosing party over Trump in January. Yet in that same month, eight of ten Republicans held positive views of Trump, three-quarters said he didn't encourage the Capitol riot, and, most disturbing, two-thirds said Biden did not win legitimately.[47]

The antidemocratic drift of the Republican Party was evident before the insurrection. In a paper months before the election, Vanderbilt University political scientist Larry M. Bartels began: "Most Republicans in a January 2020 survey agreed that 'the traditional American way of life is disappearing so fast that we may have to use force to save it.'" Based on their other responses in the survey, Bartels attributed Republicans' attitude chiefly to "ethnic antagonism"—"especially concerns about the political power and claims on government resources of immigrants, African Americans, and Latinos." With a prescience he likely couldn't have imagined, Bartels wrote a half year before the Capitol insurrection: "How concerned should we be that a president who assails 'essential institutions and traditions' of democracy has found millions of followers willing to endorse significant violations of democratic norms, including resort to force in pursuit of political ends, lawlessness by 'patriotic Americans,' and casting doubt on the legitimacy of elections? The simple answer is that no one knows."[48]

Now we do. And the answer is we should be very concerned. The American Enterprise Institute's survey in January 2021 reaffirmed Bartels's finding. A majority of Republicans agreed, "The traditional American way of life is disappearing so fast that we may have to use force to save it." They were simply echoing Trump. Less than forty-eight hours before his mob stormed the Capitol, he was in Georgia campaigning for the state's two doomed Republican senators and continuing to falsely claim victory for himself. "There's no way we lost," he told the crowd, adding, "But we're still fighting it and you'll see what's going to happen." If he failed, he said, "America as you know it will be over. And it will never, I believe, be able to come back again."[49]

The upshot: When one major party comes to believe the other is the threat to that mythic way of life—because that other party, the Democrats, includes minorities, immigrants, feminists, non-Christians—then democracy is too big a gamble, in adherents' view. So Republicans gerrymander political districts. They pass restrictive voting laws to limit turnout of the other party's supporters. And if Republicans still lose, they reject the result or, worse, turn to force or countenance those who do. With Biden in the White House, Trump told his so-called "Save America" rally on January 6, "We're going to have somebody in there that should not be in there and our country will be destroyed. And we're not going to stand for that . . . If you don't fight like hell, you're not going to have a country anymore."[50]

For all the focus on Trump, another Republican leader merits indictment for the damage done, predating Trump: McConnell. After Kavanaugh's confirmation, historian Christopher R. Browning wrote, "If the U.S. has someone whom historians will look back on as the gravedigger of American democracy, it is Mitch McConnell. He stoked the hyperpolarization of American politics to make the Obama presidency as dysfunctional and paralyzed as he possibly could . . . Congressional gridlock in the U.S. has diminished respect for democratic norms, allowing McConnell to trample them even more. Nowhere is this vicious circle clearer than in the obliteration of traditional precedents concerning judicial appointments."[51]

Just as he'd done in early 2009, amid the worst economic crisis since the Depression, in 2021 McConnell opposed a new Democratic president confronting a dual economic and health calamity. In each case, with Republicans stung by election losses, McConnell shamelessly prescribed knee-jerk opposition as a sure way to unite the party. Still majority leader when the House voted January 13 to impeach Trump, the ever-cynical McConnell refused to convene the Senate before Biden's inauguration and then said the Senate trial was unconstitutional because Trump was no longer president. Yet for four years he'd ignored the Constitution as Trump defied the Senate's prerogatives, diverting billions to his border wall over Congress's objections, and dodging the Senate confirmation process by naming "acting" Cabinet secretaries. Far from protecting the Senate as a separate branch of government, McConnell boasted to Sean Hannity of working in "total coordination" with the White House counsel during Trump's first impeachment—as he had during Kavanaugh's confirmation.

For all McConnell's later fulminations against Trump, he was complicit in the lies that provoked an insurrection, not wanting to alienate Trump voters before Georgia's Senate runoffs. He declared after the presidential election that Trump was "100 percent within his rights to look into allegations of irregularities," implicitly giving credence to the bizarre fraud claims. He didn't congratulate Biden until December 15, after the Electoral College voted. Only as the Senate met on January 6, after the Georgia results were in, did McConnell chastise Trump. "Over and over the courts rejected these claims, including all-star judges whom the president himself has nominated," he said. It was too late. We can't know whether McConnell and other Republican leaders might have averted what happened next had they stood up to Trump much earlier—years earlier. The insurrectionists were on their way to defile the chamber as he spoke.[52] Even then, McConnell's cynical enabling of Trumpism continued with his engineering of Trump's acquittal, followed by his Senate speech indicting Trump as vehemently as any Democratic accuser. "There's no question, none," McConnell thundered, "that President Trump is practically and morally responsible for provoking the events of the day...a foreseeable consequence of the growing crescendo of false statements, conspiracy theories, and reckless hyperbole, which the defeated president kept shouting into the largest megaphone on planet Earth." If the insurrection was foreseeable, and it was, why had McConnell been silent until now? "Party over country," as the late senator John McCain used to say disdainfully of colleagues like McConnell.[53]

Reelected in 2020 to a seventh six-year term, at seventy-eight, Mc-Connell will be around for his party's next chapter. Republicans could well retake control of the Senate and House in 2022, given the close margins and the midterm jinx for the president's party. Whether leader of a minority or majority, McConnell is likely to do what he can to obstruct Biden's agenda and especially his judicial nominees. But however the elections for Congress and the White House play out, he can be satisfied that he, more than any single person, ensured that the Supreme Court will almost certainly remain in the conservatives' corner well beyond his lifetime.

ACKNOWLEDGMENTS

Acknowledging the people to whom I feel some debt in completing this project is perhaps the hardest writing job of all. I fear slighting someone, or leaving out another person. Purposely missing are the folks across the political spectrum who shared their insights with me only if they could do so without being identified. As unsatisfying as anonymous sources often are for the reader, they are essential to fully getting the story of what goes on in Washington when candidly confiding information to a journalist can be a career risk. I have tried here, as always, to balance such sourcing with on-the-record interviews and documents.

Special thanks must go to the sources and friends who doubled as grief counselors in the final lonely year of my work, much of it amid the pandemic, when I suffered two blows: first, my beloved mother unexpectedly died of a heart attack just after celebrating her eighty-sixth birthday, and within months my youngest sister was diagnosed with brain cancer and died eight weeks later. To Mom and Connie, I dedicate this book. I cannot imagine enduring these losses without the mutual support of my sisters (and best friends) Pat Cotton and Cathy Calmes and my daughters Sarah and Carrie Hutcheson. In Connie's final days, Carrie kept me company while she competently finished the endnotes for this book. My editor, Sean Desmond, gave me needed space through the bad times even as he encouraged me; from the start he was smart, patient, and unflappable. He drew out my best work. I thank my generous friend and former colleague at the *New York Times*, Maureen Dowd, for bringing us together.

Separated by distance for much of the time from my actual family, I had my Washington family to fill the void. Thank you especially to Beth and Luke Donovan, my friends through three decades of our respective ups and downs; to my "sister" Marcia Hale; to Al Hunt, my former boss (at the *Wall Street Journal*) and forever mentor; to Karen Tumulty, my pal since our career beginnings in Texas; and to Janet Hook, a colleague first at *Congressional Quarterly* in the 1980s and then again at the *Los Angeles Times* Washington bureau, and always a confidant. Besides Janet and Beth, I want to acknowledge my other *CQ* sisters: Pam Fessler, who recently finished her own book, *Carville's Cure: Leprosy, Stigma, and the Fight for Justice*, a compelling account of infectious disease, misinformation, and discrimination; Joan Biskupic, one of the best Supreme Court reporters and biographers ever, whose feedback has been invaluable, and Dale Tate, who's remained a friend across time and miles but now is a neighbor again.

I couldn't have done the reporting and research necessary for this book without the support—and book leave—provided to me by David Lauter, until recently the Washington bureau chief of the *LA Times* and one of the smartest and most insightful journalists in town. Thanks must go, too, to my fellow editors and friends Bob Drogin and Eddie Sanders, as well as to the reporters with whom I've worked closest: Janet, Evan Halper, Noah Bierman, Eli Stokols, Chris Megerian, David Cloud (another repeat colleague, at *CQ* and the *Journal*), Tracy Wilkinson, Don Lee, Noam Levey, Del Wilber, and, not least, David Savage, another authority on the Supreme Court whose brain I picked repeatedly.

Throughout my education in American government and politics, which I've tried to reflect in these pages, I am indebted to the newspaper colleagues who were my teachers, collaborators, and confidants. At the *Journal*, where Al Hunt hired me when I was eight months pregnant, I subsequently shared both professional and parenting experiences with Jerry Seib, David Wessel, Laurie McGinley, David Shribman, John Harwood, Jill Abramson, Alan Murray, Marylu Carnevale, and June Kronholz. Later came Phil Kuntz (rejoining me from *CQ*), Neil King, and Shailagh

Murray, Glenn Simpson, and Mary Jacoby, Sue Davis, Jeanne Cummings, and John McKinnon and Beth Crowley. For years it was my great fortune to work cheek-by-jowl in the Senate press gallery with one of the best congressional reporters ever, David Rogers.

At the *Times*, where I next landed thanks to Jill Abramson and Dean Baquet, I was also blessed to work alongside some of the smartest and nicest people you could know: desk mates Eric Schmitt, Eric Lipton, Charlie Savage, and David Sanger; beat partners Mark Landler, Peter Baker, and Mike Shear; occasional collaborator Carl Hulse; and Jeff Zeleny, Mark Mazzetti, Scott Shane, Binyamin Appelbaum, Adam Liptak, and of course Robert Pear, whose death in 2019 was a loss both to the bureau and to journalism.

Francis O'Brien and Frances Cox provided office space and good company. Tom Spulak and Richard Bates, once hard-to-crack sources and then friends, were more help than either knew; I wish I'd told Richard before his sudden death on New Year's Eve, 2020. Over the years, I'd kid Ruth Marcus of the *Washington Post* that we must have been separated at birth, I felt such a mind-meld reading her columns. We both ended up with book contracts focused on Brett Kavanaugh's confirmation—friendly competitors, as she put it. Her fabulous book, *Supreme Ambition*, came out first, and inevitably contained reporting I've included and footnoted in my own.

I must recognize two political scientists I've long known, Norm Ornstein and Tom Mann. Courageously for two guys who worked in this town, they were perhaps the first to document early on that the Republican Party increasingly bore more of the blame for dysfunction in Washington (and many state capitals), and to attack the "false equivalence" in journalism that defined balanced reporting as seeing equal fault in Democrats and Republicans. Covering Congress, six presidents, and political campaigns, I learned from politicians and operatives of both parties. To name just a few: Bob Dole, Pete Domenici, Tom Daschle, Tom Foley, Leon Panetta, Vin Weber, and Mickey Edwards. *Journal* pollsters from both parties—Peter Hart, Bill McInturff, and the late Bob Teeter—were invaluable instructors over many years.

I'll close with thanks, again, to Sean Desmond—for his editing, his guidance, and ultimately his friendship—and to my agent Gail Ross, who, for all the authors she represents, made me feel when it counted like I was the only one. She never said it would be easy.

NOTES

AUTHOR'S NOTE

1   Geoffrey Kabaservice, *Rule and Ruin: The Downfall of Moderation and the Destruction of the Republican Party, from Eisenhower to the Tea Party* (New York: Oxford University Press, 2012), xvi, xix.

2   Peter Wehner, "The Comprehensive Case Against Donald Trump," RealClearPolitics, September 11, 2016, www.realclearpolitics.com/articles/1016/09/11/the_comprehensive_case_against_donald_trump_131748.html.

PROLOGUE

1   Hugh Hewitt, "The Supreme Court's 30 Years War Is Finally Over," *Washington Post*, October 22, 2018, www.washingtonpost.com/opinions/the-supreme-courts-30-years-war-is-finally-over/2018/10/22/c443d566-d62d-11e8-aeb7-ddcad4a0a54e_story.html?utm_term=.f647be8d5e3c.

2   Much of this prologue is drawn from White House pool reports and transcripts, and the author's contemporaneous viewing and reporting.

3   Justice John Paul Stevens, *Five Chiefs: A Supreme Court Memoir* (New York: Little, Brown, 2011), 207–8.

4   Kevin J. McMahon, "Will the Supreme Court Still 'Seldom Stray Very Far'?: Regime Politics in a Polarized America," *Chicago-Kent Law Review* 93, no. 2 (2018), https://scholarship.kentlaw.iit.edu/cklawreview/vol93/iss2/4.

5   Dana Blanton, "Fox News Poll: Record Number of Voters Oppose Kavanaugh Nomination," Fox News, September 23, 2018, www.foxnews.com/politics/fox-news-poll-record-number-of-voters-oppose-kavanaugh-nomination.

6   "Kavanaugh's Supreme Court Hearing," *At This Hour*, CNN, September 4, 2018, http://transcripts.cnn.com/TRANSCRIPTS/1809/04/ath.02.html.

1: THE EARLY YEARS

1   White House pool reports and transcripts, July 9, 2019.
2   Samantha Semerad Guerry, interview with the author, May 31, 2019.
3   Evgenia Peretz, "'Men for Others, My Ass': After Kavanaugh, Inside Georgetown Prep's Culture of Omertà," *Vanity Fair*, December 17, 2018, www.vanityfair.com /news/2018/12/inside-georgetown-prep-culture-of-omerta-scandal.
4   Catholic Law in Washington, DC, "Commencement Address: The Honorable Brett M. Kavanaugh," YouTube, June 6, 2018, www.youtube.com/watch?v=sggWPCe -Ugk.
5   "Montgomery County Circuit Court: Former Judges," Maryland Manual On-line, Maryland State Archives, August 16, 2016, https://msa.maryland.gov/msa/mdmanual /31cc/former/html/msa12367.html.
6   Douglas C. McGill, "Cosmetics Companies Quietly Ending Animal Tests," *New York Times*, August 2, 1989, www.nytimes.com/1989/08/02/business/cosmetics-companies -quietly-ending-animal-tests.html.
7   Phil Gailey, "Tax-Law Originators Soaked Taxpayers with Barbados Fling," *St. Petersburg Times*, October 30, 1990, 4.
8   Tom Brune, "Roberts Omits Stint with Cosmetics Group," *Newsday*, August 3, 2005, 20.
9   Scott Shane et al., "Influential Judge, Loyal Friend, Conservative Warrior—and D.C. Insider," *New York Times*, July 14, 2018, www.nytimes.com/2018/07/14/us/politics /judge-brett-kavanaugh.html.
10   Brett Kavanaugh, "Judge Brett Kavanaugh Speaks Out," interview by Martha Mac-Callum, *The Story*, Fox News, September 24, 2018, audio, at 9:27, www.foxnews .com/politics/kavanaugh-denies-sexual-misconduct-in-fox-news-exclusive-i-know -im-telling-the-truth.
11   Wesley Morris, "In '80s Comedies, Boys Had It Made. Girls Were the Joke," *New York Times*, October 4, 2018, www.nytimes.com/2018/10/04/movies/brett -kavanaugh-80s-teen-comedies.html.
12   Kavanaugh, "Judge Brett Kavanaugh Speaks Out," at 9:41.
13   Rebecca Nelson, "A Writer Mined His '80s Adolescence in the D.C. Suburbs. Then Came the Kavanaugh Hearings," *Washington Post*, October 22, 2018, www .washingtonpost.com/lifestyle / magazine / a - writer - mined-his-80s-adolescence-in -the-dc-suburbs-then-came-the-kavanaugh-hearings / 2018 / 10 / 19 / 3170fb70-c8ad -11e8-b1ed-1d2d65b86d0c_story.html.
14   Catholic Law in Washington, DC, "The Judge as Umpire Delivered by the Honorable Brett M. Kavanaugh," YouTube, April 1, 2015, www.youtube.com /watch?v=SXKX_whwVzs.
15   Marc Fisher and Perry Stein, "'100 Kegs or Bust': Kavanaugh Friend, Mark Judge, Has Spent Years Writing About High School Debauchery," *Washington Post*, September 21, 2018, www.washingtonpost.com/local/100-kegs-or-bust-kavanaugh-friend -has-spent-years-writing-about-high-school-debauchery / 2018 / 09 / 21/a8e0fe22 -bb55-11e8-a8aa-860695e7f3fc_story.html?utm_term=.ab69f51822cf; Dwight Gar-

ner, "What a Book Critic Finds in Mark Judge's 'Wasted' 21 Years Later," *New York Times*, October 2, 2018, www.nytimes.com/2018/10/02/books/wasted-mark-judge-memoir.html.

16   Elizabeth Rasor, interview with the author, July 14, 2019.

17   Memorandum to Senate Republicans from the Office of the Chairman, Senator Chuck Grassley, "Senate Judiciary Committee Investigation of Numerous Allegations Against Justice Brett Kavanaugh During the Senate Confirmation Proceedings," November 2, 2018, Declaration of Paul Rendon, Exhibit 20, 99–102, www.judiciary.senate.gov/imo/media/doc/2018-11-02%20Kavanaugh%20Report.pdf.

18   Kate Kelly and David Enrich, "Kavanaugh's Yearbook Page Is 'Horrible, Hurtful' to a Woman It Named," *New York Times*, September, 24, 2018, www.nytimes.com/2018/09/24/business/brett-kavanaugh-yearbook-renate.html.

19   "That's a Hoya," *The Little Hoya*, February 1983.

2: FROM WATERGATE'S RUINS TO REAGAN'S REVOLUTION

1   David Grann, "Robespierre of the Right," *New Republic*, October 27, 1997, https://newrepublic.com/article/61338/robespierre-the-right.

2   Geoffrey Kabaservice, *Rule and Ruin: The Downfall of Moderation and the Destruction of the Republican Party, from Eisenhower to the Tea Party* (New York: Oxford University Press, 2012), 346, 349.

3   Ronald Reagan, "1980 Neshoba County Fair Speech," August 3, 1980, transcript published by *Neshoba Democrat*, November 15, 2007, http://neshobademocrat.com/Content/NEWS/News/Article/Transcript-of-Ronald-Reagan-s-1980-Neshoba-County-Fair-speech/2/297/15599.

4   John T. Woolley and Gerhard Peters, "1980," American Presidency Project, UC Santa Barbara, www.presidency.ucsb.edu/statistics/elections/1980.

5   Ronald Reagan, "Inaugural Address," January 20, 1981, American Presidency Project, UC Santa Barbara, www.presidency.ucsb.edu/node/246336.

6   Author interview with a Republican senator who asked to remain anonymous, 1987.

7   Andrew Blasko, "Reagan and Heritage: A Unique Partnership," Heritage Foundation, June 7, 2004, www.heritage.org/conservatism/commentary/reagan-and-heritage-unique-partnership.

8   David Brock, interview with the author, May 22, 2019.

9   Author interview with attendee who asked to speak on background, June 21, 2019.

10   Jill Abramson, "Right Place at the Right Time," *American Lawyer*, June 1986, 100.

11   David Montgomery, "Conquerors of the Courts," *Washington Post Magazine*, January 2, 2019, www.washingtonpost.com/news/magazine/wp/2019/01/02/feature/conquerors-of-the-courts/.

12   Steven M. Teles, *The Rise of the Conservative Legal Movement: The Battle for Control of the Law* (Princeton, NJ: Princeton University Press, 2008), 135–41.

13   Author interviews, November 5, 2018, March 21, 2019.

14   Abramson, "Right Place at the Right Time," 104.

15   Teles, *The Rise of the Conservative Legal Movement*, 147–51.

16   Teles, *The Rise of the Conservative Legal Movement*, 26, 39.

17   George T. Conway III, interview with the author, June 7, 2019.

18   Steven M. Teles, interview with the author, February 26, 2019.

19   Teles, *The Rise of the Conservative Legal Movement*, 1.

20   Interviews with former officials of the Reagan, George H. W. Bush, and George W. Bush administrations.

21   Todd J. Zywicki, "A Great Mind?: Miers Might Vote Right, but What the Court Truly Needs Is Intellectual Leadership," *Legal Times* 28, no. 41 (October 10, 2005): 2, https://mason.gmu.edu/~tzywick2/Legal%20Times%20Mier%20Op%20Ed.pdf.

22   Teles, *The Rise of the Conservative Legal Movement*, 157–61.

23   Annie Grayer, "Brett Kavanaugh Was Concerned with His Federalist Society Membership in 2001, Emails Show," CNN, August 20, 2018, https://edition.cnn.com /2018/08/19/politics/brett-kavanaugh-federalist-society-emails/index.html.

24   The author attended the Federalist Society's 2019 National Lawyers Convention, November 14, 2019.

25   Jason Deparle, "Debating the Subtle Sway of the Federalist Society," *New York Times*, August 1, 2005, www.nytimes.com/2005/08/01/politics/politicsspecial1/debating -the-subtle-sway-of-the-federalist.html.

26   Teles, *The Rise of the Conservative Legal Movement*, 142.

3: THE YALE YEARS AND ONWARD

1   Lisa Miller, "Brett Kavanaugh's Former Roommate Describes Their Debauched Dorm at Yale," *The Cut*, September 26, 2018, www.thecut.com/2018/09 /kavanaugh-roommate-yale-dorm-room.html; Jamie Roche, interview with the author, June 1, 2019.

2   Jamie Roche, interview with the author, June 1, 2019.

3   Memorandum to Senate Republicans from the Office of the Chairman, Senator Chuck Grassley, "Senate Judiciary Committee Investigation of Numerous Allegations Against Justice Brett Kavanaugh During the Senate Confirmation Proceedings," November 2, 2018, Statement of Jamie Roche, Exhibit 28, 133, www.judiciary.senate.gov/imo/medi a/doc/2018-11-02%20Kavanaugh%20Report.pdf.

4   Senate Judiciary Committee, staff interview with Brett Kavanaugh, September 25, 2018, www.judiciary.senate.gov/imo/media/doc/09.25.18%20BMK%20Interview %20Transcript%20(Redacted)..pdf.

5   Todd Kaplan, interview with the author, July 19, 2019.

6   Richard Oh, interview with the author, July 19, 2019; Dan Steinberg, "John Riggins and 'Loosen Up, Sandy,'" *Washington Post*, October 29, 2012, www.washingtonpo st.com/news/dc-sports-bog/wp/2012/10/29/john-riggins-and-loosen-up-sandy/?ar c404=true.

7   Interviews with the author.

8   Daniel Lavan letter to senators, October 4, 2018; Daniel Lavan, interview with the author, September 13, 2019.

9   "Lindsey Graham Erupts During Kavanaugh Hearing," CNN, September 27, 2018, www.cnn.com/videos/politics/2018/09/27/graham-kavanaugh-hearing-a-sham-vpx .cnn/video/playlists/kavanaugh-ford-senate-hearing/; Lynne Brookes, interview with the author, September 7, 2019.

10   Jennifer Langa Klaus, interview with the author, July 3, 2019; Kerry Berchem, inter-view with the author, May 15, 2019.

11   Hailey Fuchs and Britton O'Daly, "A Flag of Underwear: Photo from Kavanaugh's

Time Shows DKE Hijinks," *Yale Daily News*, September 20, 2018, https://yaledailynews
.com/blog/2018/09/20/a-flag-of-underwear-photo-from-kavanaughs-time-shows
-dke-hijinks/.

12   Serena Cho and Alice Park, "DKE Brothers Recall Kegs of Beer, Toga Parties During Kavanaugh's Years," *Yale Daily News*, October 3, 2018, https://yaledailynews
.com/blog/2018/10/03/dke-brothers-recall-kegs-of-beer-toga-parties-during-kav
anaughs-years/.

13   Klaus Jensen, interview with the author, June 26, 2019.

14   Rebecca Dana, "Tang Returns with Drunken Vengeance," *Yale Daily News*, April
26, 2002, https://yaledailynews.com/blog/2002/04/26/tang-returns-with-drunke
n-vengeance/.

15   Fuchs and O'Daly, "A Flag of Underwear."

16   "Decades Before Nomination Brett Kavanaugh Wrote About College Sports," *Yale
Daily News*, July 10, 2018, http://features.yaledailynews.com/blog/2018/07/10
/decades-before-nomination-brett-kavanaugh-wrote-about-college-sports/.

17   Chad Ludington, interview with the author, September 6, 2019; Emily Bazelon
and Ben Protess, "Kavanaugh Was Questioned by Police After Bar Fight in 1985,"
New York Times, October 1, 2018, www.nytimes.com/2018/10/01/us/politics
/kavanaugh-bar-fight.html?searchResultPosition=1; Alice Park and Serena Cho,
"Kavanaugh Involved in Bar Fight During Yale College Years," *Yale Daily News*,
October 2, 2018, https://yaledailynews.com/blog/2018/10/02/kavanaugh
-involved-in-bar-fight-during-yale-college-years/.

18   "Interview with Sen. Chris Coons; Discussion of Ford & Kavanaugh Testimony,"
Cuomo Prime Time, CNN, September 27, 2018, http://transcripts.cnn.com/TRAN
SCRIPTS/1809/27/CPT.01.html.

19   Lynne Brookes, interview with the author, September 7, 2019.

20   Marc Schindler, interview with the author, August 26, 2019.

21   Michael Barr, interview with the author, October 14, 2019.

22   Hailey Fuchs and Adelaide Feibel, "A Sports Junkie Who Ate Pasta with Ketchup:
Law School Friends Reflect on Kavanaugh's Time at YLS," *Yale Daily News*, July 12,
2018, https://yaledailynews.com/blog/2018/07/12/a-sports-junkie-who-ate-pasta
-with-ketchup-law-school-friends-reflect-on-kavanaughs-time-at-yls/.

23   Catholic Law in Washington, DC, "Commencement Address: The Honorable Brett
M. Kavanaugh," YouTube, June, 6, 2018, www.youtube.com/watch?v=sggWPCe
-Ugk.

24   Interview with the author; source asked to remain unidentified.

25   Peter Keisler, interview with the author, June 21, 2019.

26   "From the Bench: Judge Brett Kavanaugh on the Constitutional Statesmanship of
Chief Justice William Rehnquist," American Enterprise Institute, September 18,
2017, www.aei.org/wp-content/uploads/2017/08/from-the-bench.pdf.

27   Felicia Sonmez, Twitter post, September 16, 2018, 8:26 p.m., https://twitter.com
/feliciasonmez/status/1041483381257715712.

28   Interview with the author; source asked to remain unidentified.

29   Interview with the author; source asked to remain unidentified.

30   Sonmez, Twitter post, September 16, 2018; Pema Levy, "Brett Kavanaugh Gave
a Speech About Binge Drinking in Law School," *Mother Jones*, September 17,
2018, www.motherjones.com/politics/2018/09/brett-kavanaugh-gave-a-speech
-about-binge-drinking-in-law-school/.

31   Scott Shane et al., "Influential Judge, Loyal Friend, Conservative Warrior—and D.C. Insider," *New York Times*, July 14, 2018, www.nytimes.com/2018/07/14/us/politics /judge-brett-kavanaugh.html.

32   Interview with the author, June 22, 2019; source asked to remain unidentified.

33   David Kendall, interview with the author, May 10, 2019.

34   U.S. Congress, Senate, Committee on the Judiciary, "Confirmation Hearing on the Nomination of Brett Kavanaugh to Be Circuit Judge for the District of Columbia Circuit," 109th Congress, 2nd Session, May 9, 2006, www.congress.gov/109/chrg /shrg27916/CHRG-109shrg27916.pdf.

35   Scott Glover, "9th Circuit's Chief Judge Posted Sexually Explicit Matter on His Website," *Los Angeles Times*, June 11, 2008, www.latimes.com/local/la-me-kozinski 12-2008jun12-story.html.

36   Scott Glover, "Judge E-mailed Jokes to 'Gag List,'" *Los Angeles Times*, December 8, 2008, www.latimes.com/archives/la-xpm-2008-dec-08-me-gaglist8-story.html.

37   Matt Zapotosky, "Federal Appeals Judge Announces Immediate Retirement Amid Probe of Sexual Misconduct Allegations," *Washington Post*, December 18, 2017, www.washingtonpost.com/world/national-security/federal-appeals-judge -announces-immediate-retirement-amid-investigation-prompted-by-accusations -of-sexual-misconduct/2017/12/18/6e38ada4-e3fd-11e7-a65d-1ac0fd7f097e _story.html.

38   Interview with the author; source asked to remain unidentified.

39   Gary S. Feinerman, interview with the author, October 7, 2019.

40   Interview with the author; source asked to remain unidentified.

4: SUPREME BATTLES: BORK AND THOMAS

1   Orrin Hatch, *Square Peg: Confessions of a Citizen Senator* (New York: Basic Books, 2002), 121.

2   "Bork," Merriam-Webster.com Dictionary, www.merriam-webster.com/dictionary /bork.

3   Jackie Calmes, "'They Don't Give a Damn About Governing': Conservative Media's Influence on the Republican Party," Shorenstein Center on Media, Politics and Public Policy, Harvard Kennedy School, July 27, 2015, https://shorensteincenter.org /conservative-media-influence-on-republican-party-jackie-calmes/.

4   Hatch, *Square Peg*, 134.

5   Mark Gitenstein, *Matters of Principle: An Insider's Account of America's Rejection of Robert Bork's Nomination to the Supreme Court* (New York: Simon & Shuster, 1992), 53.

6   Mark Sherman, "Bork: Nixon Offered Next High Court Vacancy in '73," Associated Press, February 25, 2013, https://news.yahoo.com/bork-nixon-offered-next-high -court-vacancy-73-215733645--politics.html.

7   Tom Shales, "The Bork Turnoff," *Washington Post*, October 9, 1987, www.washingtonpost .com/archive/lifestyle/1987/10/09/the-bork-turnoff/5342ccb1-404c-4540-92af-7f5a4b 6b9b82/.

8   PFAWdotorg, "1987 Robert Bork TV Ad, Narrated by Gregory Peck," YouTube, July 16, 2008, www.youtube.com/watch?v=NpFe10lkF3Y.

9   Gitenstein, *Matters of Principle*, 11.

10   "Senate Vote on the Nomination of Robert H. Bork to the Supreme Court of the United States: Roll Vote No. 348," *Congressional Record* 133:21 (October 23, 1987), 29121, www.senate.gov/reference/resources/pdf/348_1987.pdf.

11   Hatch, *Square Peg*, 133–35.

12   Alexander Burns, "Biden Wants to Work with 'the Other Side.' This Supreme Court Battle Explains Why," *New York Times*, September 7, 2019, www.nytimes.com /2019/09/07/us/politics/joe-biden-bork-supreme-court.html.

13   Linda Greenhouse, "Bork's Nomination Is Rejected, 58–42; Reagan Saddened," *New York Times*, October 24, 1987, www.nytimes.com/1987/10/24/politics/borks -nomination-is-rejected-5842-reagan-saddened.html.

14   Gitenstein, *Matters of Principle*, 15, 17.

15   Linda Greenhouse, "Playing the Long Game for the Supreme Court," *New York Times*, October 25, 2018, www.nytimes.com/2018/10/25/opinion/supreme-court -conservatives-progressives.html.

16   Steven M. Teles, *The Rise of the Conservative Legal Movement: The Battle for Control of the Law* (Princeton, NJ: Princeton University Press, 2008), 167–70.

17   David Brock, *Blinded by the Right: The Conscience of an Ex-Conservative* (New York: Three Rivers Press, 2002), 51.

18   Jane Mayer and Jill Abramson, *Strange Justice: The Selling of Clarence Thomas* (Boston: Houghton Mifflin Harcourt, 1994), 11–14.

19   Hatch, *Square Peg*, 144.

20   Mayer and Abramson, *Strange Justice*, 221, 232.

21   Mayer and Abramson, *Strange Justice*, 221–51.

22   Hatch, *Square Peg*, 150.

23   "Thomas Second Hearing Day 1, Part 1," C-SPAN video, October 11, 1991, www.c-span.org/video/?21974-1/thomas-hearing-day-1-part-1.

24   Janet Napolitano, interview with the author, April 23, 2019.

25   Napolitano, interview, April 23, 2019.

26   Hatch, *Square Peg*, 153–54.

27   Napolitano, interview, April 23, 2019.

28   Hatch, *Square Peg*, 155.

29   U.S. Senate, "U.S. Senate: Roll Call Vote 102nd Congress—1st Session," October 15, 1991, www.senate.gov/legislative/LIS/roll_call_lists/roll_call_vote_cfm.cfm?congress =102&session=1&vote=00220.

30   Brock, *Blinded by the Right*, 107–10.

31   Brock, *Blinded by the Right*, xx, 122.

32   Mayer and Abramson, *Strange Justice*, 8.

33   Mayer and Abramson, *Strange Justice*, 356–57.

34   Jackie Calmes, "Activism of Thomas's Wife Could Raise Judicial Issues," *New York Times*, October 8, 2010, www.nytimes.com/2010/10/09/us/politics/09thomas .html?searchResultPosition=2; Jackie Calmes, "Who's Sorry Now?," *New York Times*, The Caucus, October 20, 2010, https://thecaucus.blogs.nytimes.com/2010/10/20 /whos-sorry-now/?searchResultPosition=1.

35   Jill Abramson, "Do You Believe Her Now?," *New York*, February 19, 2018, http: //nymag.com/intelligencer/2018/02/the-case-for-impeaching-clarence-thomas.html.

36   Brittney McNamara, "Joe Biden to Anita Hill: 'I Owe Her an Apology,'" *Teen Vogue*, December 13, 2017, www.teenvogue.com/story/joe-biden-anita-hill.

37   Janet Hook, "Joe Biden's Handling of Anita Hill's Harassment Allegations Clouds His

Presidential Prospects," *Los Angeles Times*, April 15, 2019, www.latimes.com/politics /la-na-pol-anita-hill-joe-biden-presidential-campaign-20190415-story.html.

38 Angela Wright-Shannon, "Joe Biden Doesn't Owe Me an Apology. Clarence Thomas Does," *Washington Post*, May 1, 2019, www.washingtonpost.com/opinions /joe-biden-doesnt-owe-me-an-apology-clarence-thomas-does/2019/05/01/fb7577 d6-6c2f-11e9-be3a-33217240a539_story.html.

39 Anita Hill, *Speaking Truth to Power* (New York: Doubleday, 1997), 345–54.

5: GINGRICH, STARR, AND A PARTISAN BAPTISM

1 Jackie Calmes and Phil Kuntz, "Newt's House: Republicans' Wins Put Their Attack Tactician in a Position to Lead," *Wall Street Journal*, November 9, 1994, 1.

2 Jackie Calmes, "As Michel Leaves Top House GOP Post, Younger Generation Flexes for Fights," *Wall Street Journal*, October 5, 1993.

3 Calmes and Kuntz, "Newt's House," 1.

4 David Brock, interview with the author, May 22, 2019.

5 Bruce Udolf, interview with the author, April 5, 2019.

6 Paul Rosenzweig, interview with the author, July 3, 2019.

7 Brett Kavanaugh memorandum to Starr and OIC attorneys, "RE: Foster Investigations," March 4, 1995, URTS 16305, Document ID 70105100, 393, Brett Kavanaugh Attorney Work Files, Records of Independent Counsel Kenneth W. Starr, National Archives, www.archives.gov/files/research/kavanaugh/releases /docid-70105100.pdf.

8 Robert B. Fiske Jr., "Report of the Independent Counsel: In Re Vincent W. Foster, Jr.," June 30, 1994, 58.

9 David Johnston, "Appointment in Whitewater Turns into a Partisan Battle," *New York Times*, August 13, 1994, www.nytimes.com/1994/08/13/us/appointment-in -whitewater-turns-into-a-partisan-battle.html.

10 Robert O'Harrow Jr. and Michael Kranish, "After Investigating Clinton White House and Vincent Foster's Death, Brett Kavanaugh Had a Change of Heart," *Washington Post*, August 2, 2018, www.washingtonpost.com/investigations/after -investigating-clinton-white-house-and-vincent-fosters-death-brett-kavanaugh-had -change-of-heart/2018/08/02/66ee2b2c-91f5-11e8-9b0d-749fb254bc3d_story .html?utm_term=.83e40f3c5b6d.

11 Sean Wilentz, "Why Was Kavanaugh Obsessed with Vince Foster?," *New York Times*, September 5, 2018, www.nytimes.com/2018/09/05/opinion/why-was-kavanaugh -obsessed-with-vince-foster.html; Brett Kavanaugh memorandum to Judge Starr, Mark Tuohey, Hickman Ewing, John Bates, "RE: Foster Issues," June 6, 1995, Document ID 70105100, 388–89, Brett Kavanaugh Attorney Work Files, Records of Independent Counsel Kenneth W. Starr, National Archives, www.archives.gov/files /research/kavanaugh/releases/docid-70105100.pdf.

12 Brett Kavanaugh memorandum to Judge Starr, Mark Tuohey, Hickman Ewing, John Bates, Ed Lueckenhoff, Chuck Regini, "Summary of Foster Meeting on 6-15-95," June 16, 1995, URTS 16305, Document ID 70105100, 394–95, Brett Kavanaugh Attorney Work Files, Records of Independent Counsel Kenneth W. Starr, National Archives, www.archives.gov/files/research/kavanaugh/releases/docid-70105100.pdf.

13 Interview with the author; source asked to remain unidentified.

14   Kavanaugh memorandum to Jim Clemente, "RE: Vince Foster," July 15, 1995, Doc-
       ument ID 70105100, 384–87, Brett Kavanaugh Attorney Work Files, Records of
       Independent Counsel Kenneth W. Starr, National Archives, www.archives.gov/files
       /research/kavanaugh/releases/docid-70105100.pdf.

15   Special Agent C. L. Regini memorandum to Brett Kavanaugh, "Death Investigation
       Status," July 18, 1995, URTS 16305, Document ID 70105100, 16, Brett Kavanaugh
       Attorney Work Files, Records of Independent Counsel Kenneth W. Starr, National
       Archives, www.archives.gov/files/research/kavanaugh/releases/docid-70105100.pdf.

16   Fax from Debbie Gershman, June 8, 1995, Document ID 70105100, 421–25, Brett
       Kavanaugh Attorney Work Files, Records of Independent Counsel Kenneth W.
       Starr, National Archives, www.archives.gov/files/research/kavanaugh/releases/docid
       -70105100.pdf.

17   Brett Kavanaugh to File, Memorandum "RE: Meeting with Hamilton," October 21,
       1995, URTS 16304, Document ID 70105002, 173, 421–25, Brett Kavanaugh At-
       torney Work Files, Records of Independent Counsel Kenneth W. Starr, National
       Archives, www.archives.gov/files/research/kavanaugh/releases/docid-70105002.pdf.

18   Brett Kavanaugh to File, Memorandum "RE: Meeting with Hamilton," 131–33,
       167–70.

19   David E. Kendall, interview with the author, May 10, 2019.

20   O'Harrow and Kranish, "After Investigating Clinton White House and Vincent Fos-
       ter's Death, Brett Kavanaugh Had a Change of Heart."

21   Ken Starr, *Contempt: A Memoir of the Clinton Investigation* (New York: Sentinel, 2018),
       144.

22   David Mark, "Bill Clinton Says Kavanaugh Fight Was Payback for Vince Foster,"
       Washington Examiner, May 6, 2019, www.washingtonexaminer.com/news/bill
       -clinton-says-kavanaugh-fight-was-payback-vince-foster.

23   Brian McGrory, "Starr Aide Asks Court to Limit Legal Privilege," *Boston Globe*, June
       9, 1998, 1; David G. Savage, "Justices Skeptical of Effort by Starr to Waive Privilege,"
       Los Angeles Times, June 9, 1998, 1.

24   James Hamilton, interview with the author, June 25, 2019; FDCH Political Tran-
       scripts, Hamilton press conference, June 25, 1998.

25   Kendall, interview, May 10, 2019.

26   Author interviews and contemporary news sources, including *The Clinton Affair* (TV
       series), A&E, 2018, www.amazon.com/dp/B07KMM57W8/ref=pe_385040_11
       8058080_TE_M1DP; Don van Natta Jr. and Jill Abramson, "The President's Trial:
       The Lawsuit; Quietly, a Team of Lawyers Kept Paula Jones's Case Alive," *New York
       Times*, January 24, 1999, www.nytimes.com/1999/01/24/us/president-s-trial
       -lawsuit-quietly-team-lawyers-kept-paula-jones-s-case-alive.html; Susan Schmidt,
       Peter Baker, and Tony Locy, "Clinton Accused of Urging Aide to Lie," *Washington
       Post*, January 21, 1998, www.washingtonpost.com/wp-srv/politics/special/clinton
       /stories/clinton012198.htm; Ben Terris, "George Conway Is the Man at the Center
       of Everything," *Washington Post*, May 14, 2017, www.washingtonpost.com/lifestyle
       /style/george-conway-is-the-man-at-the-center-of-everything/2017/05/13/e0720
       ad6-366b-11e7-b412-62beef8121f7_story.html.

27   George T. Conway III, interview with the author, June 7, 2019.

28   "Independent Counsel Statute Future," C-SPAN video, February 19, 1998, www.c
       -span.org/video/?101056-1/independent-counsel-statute-future; Ruth Marcus,
       "Probe Bogs Down in Tangle of Privilege," *Washington Post*, February 26, 1998, 11.

29   Michael D. Shear and Adam Liptak, "The Partisan Battle Brett Kavanaugh Now Regrets," *New York Times*, August 4, 2018, www.nytimes.com/2018/08/04/us/politics/brett-kavanaugh-clinton-impeachment.html.

30   "Kenneth Starr Appreciation Dinner," C-SPAN video, November 30, 1999, www.c-span.org/video/?153930-1/kenneth-starr-appreciation-dinner.

31   "Declaration of Dan E. Moldea," Declaration to the Senate Judiciary Committee, September 3, 2018, 2–3, www.moldea.com/Affidavit-OIC-09032018.pdf.

32   Dan E. Moldea, "Brett Kavanaugh Exposed as Ken Starr's Designated Leaker," *National Memo*, September 11, 2018, www.nationalmemo.com/brett-kavanaugh-exposed-ken-starr-designated-leaker/; "Affidavit of Dan E. Moldea," United States District Court for the District of Columbia, August 24, 1998, www.moldea.com/DEM-OIC-AFF-08241998.pdf; Adam Liptak, "Secret Report on Starr Inquiry Leaks Is Released, but Doesn't Name Kavanaugh," *New York Times*, August 23, 2018, www.nytimes.com/2018/08/23/us/politics/starr-leaks-report-brett-kavanaugh.html.

33   David Brock, "I Knew Brett Kavanaugh During His Years as a Republican Operative. Don't Let Him Sit on the Supreme Court," NBC News, September 7, 2018, www.nbcnews.com/think/opinion/i-knew-brett-kavanaugh-during-his-years-republican-operative-don-ncna907391.

34   "The Reliable Source," *Washington Post*, December 8, 1998, C3.

35   David Brock, *Blinded by the Right: The Conscience of an Ex-Conservative* (New York: Three Rivers Press, 2002), 306; Brock, interview, May 22, 2019.

36   Michael Kranish, "Brett Kavanaugh Memo Proposed Explicit Questions for President Bill Clinton," *Washington Post*, August 20, 2018, www.washingtonpost.com/politics/brett-kavanaugh-memo-detailed-explicit-questions-for-clinton/2018/08/20/c0854616-a488-11e8-8fac-12e98c13528d_story.html.

37   Ken Gormley, *The Death of American Virtue: Clinton vs. Starr* (New York: Broadway Books, 2010), 552.

38   Susan Schmidt and Michael Weisskopf, *Truth at Any Cost: Ken Starr and the Unmaking of Bill Clinton* (New York: HarperCollins, 2000), 253.

39   Gormley, *The Death of American Virtue*, 571.

40   Bob Woodward, "A Prosecutor Bound by Duty," *Washington Post*, June 15, 1999, 1.

41   Starr, *Contempt*, 249.

42   "The Starr Report: One Year Later," *Burden of Proof* (transcript), CNN, September 9, 1999.

43   Judi Nardella Hershman, interview with the author, June 26, 2019; interview with author, source asked to remain unidentified.

44   "Kenneth Starr Appreciation Dinner."

45   Jackie Calmes and John Harwood, "Gingrich Gone, GOP Is Still Left Struggling to Craft Its Message," *Wall Street Journal*, November 10, 1998, 1.

46   Jackie Calmes, "Why Congress Hews to the Party Lines on Impeachment," *Wall Street Journal*, December 16, 1998, 1.

47   Schmidt and Weisskopf, *Truth at Any Cost*, 2–3.

48   Judi Hershman, Copy of "Statement to Senators," October 2, 2018; Judi Hershman, multiple interviews with the author, 2019.

49   Judi Hershman, "I'll Never Forget Brett Kavanaugh's Anger," *Slate*, November 5, 2018, https://slate.com/news-and-politics/2018/11/brett-kavanaugh-ken-starr-heidi-heitkamp-republican-campaign-democrat.html.

50   *The Clinton Affair*, A&E; Shear and Liptak, "The Partisan Battle Brett Kavanaugh Now Regrets."

51 Alison Mitchell, "The President's Acquittal: The Overview; Clinton Acquitted Decisively: No Majority for Either Charge," *New York Times*, February 13, 1999, www.nytimes.com/1999/02/13/us/president-s-acquittal-overview-clinton-acquitted-decisively-no-majority-for.html.

52 Orrin Hatch, *Square Peg: Confessions of a Citizen Senator* (New York: Basic Books, 2002), 198, 201.

53 Starr, *Contempt*, 307.

6: BECOMING A "BUSHIE"

1 Monique O. Madan, "New Supreme Court Nominee Kavanaugh Has Ties to Big Florida Moments," *Miami Herald*, July 9, 2018, www.miamiherald.com/news/nation-world/national/article214604235.html.

2 "Responses of Brett M. Kavanaugh to the Written Questions of Senator Durbin," Question 16, November 19, 2004, https://archive.org/stream/gov.gpo.fdsys.CHRG-108shrg24853/CHRG-108shrg24853_djvu.txt.

3 Jackie Calmes, "Deja Vu, as Bush Makes a Pledge: No New Taxes," *Wall Street Journal*, January 7, 2000.

4 Jackie Calmes and John Harwood, "Gingrich Gone, GOP Is Still Left Struggling to Craft Its Message," *Wall Street Journal*, November 10, 1998, 1.

5 David Rogers, Jeanne Cummings, and Jackie Calmes, "Jeffords Considers Defecting from GOP, Threatening Party's Majority in Senate," *Wall Street Journal*, May 23, 2001.

6 Jackie Calmes, "Republican Advantage on Issue of National Security Erodes," *Wall Street Journal*, September 1, 2006, 1.

7 Neil Lewis, "President Moves Quickly on Judgeships," *New York Times*, March 11, 2001, 34.

8 Dana Milbank, "White House Counsel Office Now Full of Clinton Legal Foes," *Washington Post*, January 30, 2001, A08.

9 Dana Milbank, "Whitewater Lawyer Turned Proponent of Presidential Power," *Washington Post*, October 15, 2002, 17.

10 Scott Shane et al., "Influential Judge, Loyal Friend, Conservative Warrior—and D.C. Insider," *New York Times*, July 14, 2018, www.nytimes.com/2018/07/14/us/politics/judge-brett-kavanaugh.html; Joan Biskupic, "A Presumption of Perfection Derails Trump's Sure Bet," CNN, September 24, 2018, www.cnn.com/2018/09/24/politics/kavanaugh-presumption-of-perfection-trump/index.html.

11 Amanda Hollis-Brusky, *Ideas with Consequences: The Federalist Society and the Conservative Counterrevolution* (New York: Oxford University Press, 2015), 154–55.

12 Caroline Fredrickson, interview with the author, June 14, 2019.

13 Catholic Law in Washington, DC, "Commencement Address: The Honorable Brett M. Kavanaugh," YouTube, June 6, 2018, www.youtube.com/watch?v=sggWPCe-Ugk.

14 Elisabeth Bumiller, "White House Letter; A Trusted Aide Relishes Trailer-Park Life in Texas," *New York Times*, December 1, 2003, www.nytimes.com/2003/12/01/us/white-house-letter-a-trusted-aide-relishes-trailer-park-life-in-texas.html.

15 Stephanie Kirchgaessner, "Dining Club Emails Reveal Kavanaugh's Close Ties to Trump's Solicitor General," *Guardian*, October 25, 2018, www.theguardian.com/us-news/2018/oct/25/brett-kavanaugh-eureka-club-noel-francisco-emails.

16   Brett Kavanaugh, Email Correspondence with peers, September 10, 2001, www
     .judiciary.senate.gov/imo/media/doc/09-06-18%20GWB%20Document%20Produ
     ction%20%20-%20Booker%203.pdf.

17   Nomination of Judge Brett Kavanaugh, of Maryland, to be an Associate Justice of the
     United States Supreme Court Questions for the Record, Questions for Judge Kav-
     anaugh, Submitted September 10, 2018, Questions from Senator Sheldon
     Whitehouse,   129–30,   www.judiciary.senate.gov/imo/media/doc/Kavanaugh%
     20Responses%20to%20Questions%20for%20the%20Record.pdf; author interviews
     with senators and aides.

18   Greg Jaklewicz and Timothy Chipp, "Abilenians Fondly Regard Ashley Estes, wife
     of Trump Supreme Court nominee Brett Kavanaugh," *Abilene Reporter News*, July 13,
     2018, www.reporternews.com/story/news/local/2018/07/13/abilene-tx-love-wife
     -trump-supreme-court-nominee-ashley-estes-kavanaugh/778674002/.

19   Mary Clare Glover, "Weddings of the Rich & Famous," *Washingtonian*, February 19,
     2008, www.washingtonian.com/2008/02/19/weddings-of-the-rich-famous/.

20   David Kendall, interview with the author, May 10, 2019.

21   Jeremy Paris, interview with the author, May 9, 2019.

22   "Manny Miranda," SourceWatch, last edited October 11, 2017, www.sourcewatch.org
     /index.php/Manny_Miranda; Michael Crowley, "Miranda Rights," *New Republic*, July
     25, 2005, https://newrepublic.com/article/63407/miranda-rights.

23   Unredacted copy of the report of the investigation of Senate sergeant-at-arms Wil-
     liam Pickle for the Senate Judiciary Committee into computer breaches, Pickle
     Report, March 4, 2004, https://cryptome.org/judiciary-sys.htm.

24   Lisa Graves, interview with the author, February 6, 2019.

25   "Executive Session," *Congressional Record* 149:164 (November 12, 2003), S14722,
     www.congress.gov/crec/2003/11/12/CREC-2003-11-12-pt3-PgS14683.pdf.

26   Pickle Report, https://cryptome.org/judiciary-sys.htm.

27   Neil A. Lewis, "Report Finds Republican Aides Spied on Democrats," *New York
     Times*, March 5, 2004, www.nytimes.com/2004/03/05/us/report-finds-republican
     -aides-spied-on-democrats.html.

28   Charlie Savage, "US to Probe Taking of Computer Files," *Boston Globe*, April 27,
     2004, A2.

29   Beryl A. Howell, "Real World Problems of Virtual Crime," *Yale Journal of Law and
     Technology* 7, Iss. 1 (2005): 104–22, https://digitalcommons.law.yale.edu/yjolt/vol7
     /iss1/5/.

30   Graves, interview; Paris, interview.

31   Crowley, "Miranda Rights," https://newrepublic.com/article/63407/miranda-rights.

32   "Conservatives Honor Two Stars: Susette Kelo, Manuel Miranda," *Human Events*,
     February   16,   2006,   https://humanevents.com/2006/02/16/conservatives-honor
     -two-stars-susette-kelo-manuel-miranda/.

33   U.S. Congress, Senate, Committee on the Judiciary, "Confirmation Hearing on the
     Nomination of Brett Kavanaugh to be Circuit Judge for the District of Columbia
     Circuit," 108th Congress, 2nd Session, April 27, 2004, www.govinfo.gov/content
     /pkg/CHRG-108shrg24853/pdf/CHRG-108shrg24853.pdf; U.S. Congress, Sen-
     ate, Committee on the Judiciary, "Confirmation Hearing on the Nomination of
     Brett Kavanaugh to be Circuit Judge for the District of Columbia Circuit," 109th
     Congress, 2nd Session, May 9, 2006, www.congress.gov/109/chrg/shrg27916
     /CHRG-109shrg27916.pdf.

34 "Standing Committee on the Federal Judiciary," Federal Judiciary, American Bar Association, www.americanbar.org/groups/committees/federal_judiciary/.

35 Edward Whelan, "Lowering the Bar: The Corrupt ABA Judicial Evaluation Process," *Weekly Standard*, June 12, 2006.

36 United States Senate, "Statement of Stephen. L. Tober on behalf of the Standing Committee on Federal Judiciary of the American Bar Association concerning the Nomination of Brett Michael Kavanaugh to be Judge of the United States Court of Appeals for the District of Columbia Circuit before the Committee on the Judiciary," May 8, 2006, https://images1.americanprogress.org/il80web20037/ThinkProgress /2006/aba_kavanaugh.pdf.

37 "EPIC v. NARA: Seeking Public Release White House Records Concerning Kavanaugh's Work on Warrantless Wiretapping, Patriot Act, and Other Surveillance Programs," Epic.org, Electronic Privacy Information Center, https://epic.org /foia/nara/kavanaugh/; "Records on Brett M. Kavanaugh," Digital Library, George W. Bush Presidential Library and Museum, www.georgewbushlibrary.smu.edu/en /Digital-Library---2/BrettMKavanaughRecords; James Risen and Eric Lichtblau, "Bush Lets U.S. Spy on Callers Without Courts," *New York Times*, December 16, 2005, www.nytimes.com/2005/12/16/politics/bush-lets-us-spy-on-callers-without -courts.html?searchResultPosition=9.

38 Eric Lichtblau, *Bush's Law: The Remaking of American Justice* (New York: Random House, 2008), 225.

39 Barton Gellman and Jo Becker, "Pushing the Envelope on Presidential Power," *Washington Post*, June 25, 2007, http://voices.washingtonpost.com/cheney/chapters /pushing_the_envelope_on_presi/; Ari Shapiro, "Federal Judge Downplayed Role in Detainee Cases," *All Things Considered*, NPR, June 26, 2007, www.npr.org/templates /story/story.php?storyId=11433231.

40 Thomas Ferraro, "Democratic Senator Seeks Probe of a Bush Judge," Reuters, June 28, 2007, www.reuters.com/article/us-usa-detainees-judge-idUSN27324079 20070628.

41 David Espo, "Evolution of a Deal on Senate Fight over Judicial Nominees," Associated Press, May 28, 2005; author's contemporary reporting and interviews with current and former Senate Judiciary Committee lawyers, 2019; Ronald Weich, interview with the author, April 3, 2020.

42 U.S. Congress, Senate, Committee on the Judiciary, "Confirmation Hearing on the Nomination of Brett Kavanaugh to be Circuit Judge for the District of Columbia Circuit," 109th Congress, 2nd Session, May 9, 2006, 42, www.congress.gov/109 /chrg/shrg27916/CHRG-109shrg27916.pdf.

43 "Senator Schumer on Brett Kavanaugh Nomination," C-SPAN video, May 25, 2006, www.c-span.org/video/?c4739027/senator-schumer-brett-kavanaugh-nomin ation&playlist=97888b340e3bdebbe3d178fe371e0885.

44 "On the Nomination PN1179: Brett M. Kavanaugh, of Maryland, to be United States Circuit Judge for the District of Columbia Circuit," Senate Vote 159, 109th Congress (May 26, 2006), available from: www.govtrack.us/congress/votes /109-2006/s159.

45 "Judge Kavanaugh Swearing-In Ceremony," C-SPAN video, June 1, 2006, www.c -span.org/video/?192795-1/judge-kavanaugh-swearing-ceremony.

46 Paul Bedard, "Washington Whispers," *U.S. News & World Report*, November 6, 2006.

47 President George W. Bush, Letter to Brett M. Kavanaugh, May 31, 2006,

www.whitehouse.gov/wp-content/uploads/2018/09/BMK-Departure-Letter-from
-GWB-1920x2764.jpg.

7: THE JUDGE AVOIDS A TEA PARTY

1   Jackie Calmes, "Republican Rebels of '94 Now Face Their Own Revolt," *Wall Street Journal*, November 3, 2006, 1.

2   Thomas E. Mann and Norman J. Ornstein, *The Broken Branch: How Congress Is Failing America and How to Get It Back on Track* (New York: Oxford University Press, 2006), 7.

3   Calmes, "Republican Rebels," 1.

4   Orrin Hatch, *Square Peg: Confessions of a Citizen Senator* (New York: Basic Books, 2002), viii–xiii.

5   Dennis Romboy, "Former Utah Sen. Bob Bennett Now Dealing with Stroke," *Deseret News*, April 21, 2016, www.deseret.com/2016/4/21/20587180/former-utah -sen-bob-bennett-now-dealing-with-stroke#utah-sen-bob-bennett-celebrates-his -victory-with-republican-supporters-tuesday-nov-3-1998-at-the-double-tree-hotel; Frank Thorp V, "GOP Senator Bob Bennett Apologized to Muslims for Trump While on Deathbed," NBC News, May 19, 2016, www.nbcnews.com/politics /2016-election/gop-senator-bob-bennett-apologized-muslims-trump-while-deathb ed-n576566.

6   Jackie Calmes, "'They Don't Give a Damn About Governing': Conservative Media's Influence on the Republican Party," Shorenstein Center on Media, Politics and Public Policy, Harvard Kennedy School, July 27, 2015, https://shorensteincenter.org /conservative-media-influence-on-republican-party-jackie-calmes/.

7   Robert Draper, *Do Not Ask What Good We Do: Inside the U.S. House of Representatives* (New York: Free Press, 2012), xv–xix.

8   Calmes, "'They Don't Give a Damn About Governing.'"

9   Author interviews with Kavanaugh acquaintances who asked to remain unidentified; Nan Aron, interview with the author, October 31, 2018.

10   Scott Shane et al., "Influential Judge, Loyal Friend, Conservative Warrior—and D.C. Insider," *New York Times*, July 14, 2018, www.nytimes.com/2018/07/14/us/politics /judge-brett-kavanaugh.html.

11   Emily Peck, "Brett Kavanaugh Liked Female Clerks Who Looked a 'Certain Way,' Yale Student Was Told," *Huffington Post*, September 19, 2018, www.huffpost .com/entry/yale-student-brett-kavanaugh-clerkship-look_n_5ba2f051e4b0181540 d9e2bb.

12   Interview with the author; source asked to remain unidentified.

13   Stephanie Kirchgaessner and Jessica Glenza, "'No Accident' Brett Kavanaugh's Female Law Clerks 'Looked Like Models,' Yale Professor Told Students,'" *Guardian*, September 20, 2018, www.theguardian.com/us-news/2018/sep/20/brett-kavanaug h-supreme-court-yale-amy-chua.

14   Interview with the author; source asked to remain unidentified.

15   Amy Chua, "Kavanaugh Is a Mentor to Women," *Wall Street Journal*, July 12, 2018, www.wsj.com/articles/kavanaugh-is-a-mentor-to-women-1531435729; "Daughter of 'Tiger Mom' Chua Picked as Kavanaugh Law Clerk," Associated Press, June 10, 2019, https://apnews.com/6d04c4f10b7e4071b4e3223fb39a510c.

16   Dahlia Lithwick, interview with the author, July 18, 2019.

17   Linda Greenhouse, "Women Suddenly Scarce Among Justices' Clerks," *New York Times*, August 30, 2006, www.nytimes.com/2006/08/30/washington/30scotu s.html.

18   Seven-Sky v. Holder, 661 F.3d 1 (D.C. Cir. 2011), https://scholar.google.com /scholar_case?case=12283140068462647556&q=661+F.3d+1&hl=en&as_sdt=4.

19   Michael Cooper, "Conservatives Sowed Idea of Health Care Mandate Only to Spurn It Later," *New York Times*, February 14, 2012, www.nytimes.com/2012/02/15 /health/policy/health-care-mandate-was-first-backed-by-conservatives.html.

20   Heller v. District of Columbia, 670 F.3d 1244 (D.C. Cir. 2011), https://scholar.google.com /scholar_case?case=8354949939576611637&hl=en&as_sdt=6&as_vis=1&oi=scholarr.

21   EPA v. EME Homer City Generation, L.P., 572 U.S. 489 (2014), www.supremecourt .gov/opinions/13pdf/12-1182_553a.pdf.

22   Steven Pearlstein, "The Judicial Jihad Against the Regulatory State," *Washington Post*, October 13, 2012, www.washingtonpost.com/business/the-judicial-jihad-against-the -regulatory-state/2012/10/12/d9eb080c-13ca-11e2-bf18-a8a596df4bee_story.html.

23   SeaWorld of Florida LLC v. Perez, 748 F.3d 1202 (D.C. Cir. 2014), www.govinfo.gov /content/pkg/USCOURTS-caDC-12-01375/pdf/USCOURTS-caDC-12-01375 -0.pdf.

24   Steven H. Aden, J.D., "Priests for Life v. U.S. HHS: Judge Kavanaugh's Dissent," Americans United for Life, July 11, 2018, https://aul.org/2018/07/11/priests-for -life-v-u-s-hhs-judge-kavanaughs-dissent/.

25   Brett M. Kavanaugh, "From the Bench: The Constitutional Statesmanship of Chief Justice William Rehnquist," 2017 Walter Berns Constitution Day Lecture, American Enterprise Institute, Washington, D.C., September 18, 2017, http://lc.org/PDFs /Attachments2PRsLAs/2018/071018KavanaughSpeech2017.pdf.

26   Garza v. Hargan, 874 F.3d 735 (D.C. Cir. 2017), www.cadc.uscourts.gov/internet /opinions.nsf/C81A5EDEADAE82F2852581C30068AF6E/$file/17-5236-1701167 .pdf.

27   Steven H. Aden, J.D., "Garza v. Hargan: Why Didn't Judge Kavanaugh Join Judge Henderson's Dissent?," Americans United for Life, July 16, 2018, https://aul.org /2018/07/16/garza-v-hargan-why-didnt-judge-kavanaugh-join-judge-hendersons -dissent/.

8: NUCLEAR WAR AND A SUPREME STEAL

1   Manu Raju, "Republicans Warn Obama on Judges," *Politico*, March 2, 2009, www.politico.com/story/2009/03/republicans-warn-obama-on-judges-019526.

2   Chris Kang, interview with the author, December 17, 2018.

3   Kristine Lucius, interview with the author, January 22, 2019.

4   Interviews with senators and their counsels, 2018–2019; author's contemporaneous reporting for the *Wall Street Journal*.

5   Mike McCurry, interview with the author, October 17, 2018; Orrin Hatch, *Square Peg: Confessions of a Citizen Senator* (New York: Basic Books, 2002), 179–81.

6   Hatch, *Square Peg*, 180.

7   Paul Richter, "Clinton Picks Moderate Judge Ruth Ginsburg for High Court: Judiciary: President Calls the Former Women's Rights Activist a Healer and Consensus

Builder. Her Nomination Is Expected to Win Easy Senate Approval," *Los Angeles Times*, June 15, 1993, www.latimes.com/archives/la-xpm-1993-06-15-mn-3237-story.html.

8   Neil A. Lewis, "G.O.P., Its Eyes on High Court, Blocks a Judge," *New York Times*, June 13, 1998, www.nytimes.com/1998/06/13/nyregion/gop-its-eyes-on-high-court-blocks-a-judge.html.

9   Neil A. Lewis, "President Moves Quickly on Judgeships," *New York Times*, March 11, 2001, 34.

10   Carl Hulse, *Confirmation Bias: Inside Washington's War over the Supreme Court, from Scalia's Death to Justice Kavanaugh* (New York: HarperCollins, 2019), 65–67.

11   U.S. Congress, Senate, Committee on the Judiciary, "Confirmation Hearing on the Nomination of Brett Kavanaugh to be Circuit Judge for the District of Columbia Circuit," 108th Congress, 2nd Session, April 27, 2004, www.govinfo.gov/content/pkg/CHRG-108shrg24853/pdf/CHRG-108shrg24853.pdf.

12   Author interviews with current and former Senate aides, contemporaneously and in 2018–2019.

13   Jeffrey Toobin, "Advice and Dissent," *New Yorker*, May 26, 2003, 42.

14   Carl M. Cannon, "The Uncompromising Mr. Bush," *Washington Post*, May 29, 2005, B01.

15   Robert Bork, interview by Tucker Carlson, *The Situation with Tucker Carlson*, NBC News, October 14, 2005, www.nbcnews.com/id/9623345#.XdSJWpNKg_U.

16   Lucius, interview.

17   Robert Barnes, "Conservative Judges' Gun Ruling in Agreement with Sotomayor," *Washington Post*, June 3, 2009, www.washingtonpost.com/wp-dyn/content/article/2009/06/02/AR2009060203379.html.

18   David Axelrod, "A Surprising Request from Justice Scalia," CNN, March 9, 2016, www.cnn.com/2016/02/14/opinions/david-axelrod-surprise-request-from-justice-scalia/index.html.

19   Nina Totenberg, "Solicitor General Holds Views Close to Her Chest," NPR, December 22, 2009, www.npr.org/templates/story/story.php?storyId=121712227.

20   Carl Hulse, "Senate Confirms Kagan in Partisan Vote," *New York Times*, August 5, 2010, www.nytimes.com/2010/08/06/us/politics/06kagan.html.

21   Peter Baker and Jeff Zeleny, "Obama Picks Kagan as Justice Nominee," *New York Times*, May 9, 2010, www.nytimes.com/2010/05/10/us/politics/10court.html.

22   Jennifer Duck, interview with the author, February 8, 2019.

23   Kang, interview; Hulse, *Confirmation Bias*, 198–201; Kevin Freking, "In Rare Move, GOP Ignores Tammy Baldwin on Federal Judge Selection," Associated Press, May 11, 2018, https://madison.com/wsj/news/local/govt-and-politics/in-rare-move-gop-ignores-tammy-baldwin-on-federal-judge/article_d72df696-bc5c-5944-b6fd-88fc0c1a444f.html.

24   Ed Beeson, "Trump's Turn: How Far Right Can the President Pull the Courts?," *Law360*, March 12, 2018, www.law360.com/articles/1020197.

25   Jason Zengerle, "How the Trump Administration Is Remaking the Courts," *New York Times Magazine*, August 22, 2018, www.nytimes.com/2018/08/22/magazine/trump-remaking-courts-judiciary.html; Barry J. McMillion, "U.S. Circuit and District Court Nominations During President Trump's First Year in Office: Comparative Analysis with Recent Presidents," R45189, U.S. Congressional Research Service, May 2, 2018, https://fas.org/sgp/crs/misc/R45189.pdf.

26   Hulse, *Confirmation Bias*, 10–15.

27   Hulse, *Confirmation Bias*, 12.

28   Dick Durbin, interview with the author, June 4, 2019.

29   Jeff Flake, interview with the author, June 6, 2019.

30   Valerie Jarrett, interview with the author, June 5, 2019.

31   Author's contemporary reporting, and interviews with Obama administration aides.

32   Jarrett, interview; Hulse, *Confirmation Bias*, 34, 45–46, 120–21.

33   Statement from the office of Senate majority leader Bill Frist, distributed by States News Service, April 27, 2006.

34   Statement from Bill Frist, April 27, 2006.

35   United States Senate, "Statement of Karol Corbin Walker on Behalf of the Standing Committee on the Federal Judiciary American Bar Association, Concerning the Nomination of the Honorable Merrick B. Garland to Be an Associate Justice of the Supreme Court of the United States to the Committee on the Judiciary," June 21, 2016, https://obamawhitehouse.archives.gov/sites/whitehouse.gov/files/document s/ABA%2BStatement%2BRating%2Bfor%2BChief%2BJudge%2BGarland.pdf.

36   Jarrett, interview.

37   Jesse Byrnes, "Trump: Republicans 'Have No Choice' but to Vote for Me," *The Hill*, July 28, 2016, https://thehill.com/blogs/blog-briefing-room/news/289716-trump -republicans-have-to-vote-for-me-because-of-supreme-court.

38   Nan Aron, interview with the author, October 31, 2018.

39   Nan Aron, interview.

40   Flake, interview.

41   Kang, interview.

42   Philip Bump, "A Quarter of Republicans Voted for Trump to Get Supreme Court Picks—and It Paid Off," *Washington Post*, June 26, 2018, www.washingtonpost.com /news/politics/wp/2018/06/26/a-quarter-of-republicans-voted-for-trump-to-get -supreme-court-picks-and-it-paid-off/.

9: THE LURE OF A LIST

1   CBSN, "Full CBS News South Carolina Republican Debate," YouTube, February 15, 2016, www.youtube.com/watch?v=Un3OhYs-tCE; author's contemporary reporting.

2   Matt Flegenheimer, "Ted Cruz Calls Donald Trump's Sister, a Judge, an 'Extremist,'" *New York Times*, February 15, 2016, www.nytimes.com/politics/first-draft/2016 /02/15/ted-cruz-calls-donald-trumps-sister-a-judge-an-extremist/.

3   Carl Hulse, *Confirmation Bias: Inside Washington's War over the Supreme Court, from Scalia's Death to Justice Kavanaugh* (New York: HarperCollins, 2019), 50–55.

4   David Lat, "A Look Inside the Conservative Judge-Making Machine," *Above the Law*, November 16, 2018, https://abovethelaw.com/2018/11/a-look-inside-the -conservative-judge-making-machine/.

5   Jenna Johnson, "Donald Trump to Release List of Top Picks for the Supreme Court," *Washington Post*, March 21, 2016, www.washingtonpost.com/news/post-politics/wp /2016/03/21/donald-trump-to-release-list-of-his-top-picks-for-the-supreme-court/.

6   Steven M. Teles, interview with the author, February 26, 2019; Eugene Meyer, "The Federalist Society Doesn't Participate in Judicial Selection and Confirmation," *Washington Post*, July 12, 2019, www.washingtonpost.com/opinions/the-federalist

-society-doesnt-participate-in-judicial-selection-and-confirmation/2019/07/12/8e
b28222-a345-11e9-a767-d7ab84aef3e9_story.html.

7   Republican National Lawyers Association, "Donald Trump gave some insight into
    his judicial selection process . . . ," Facebook post, June 16, 2016, https://facebook
    .com/TheRepLawyer/posts/10156921809790618.

8   Author interview with a member of the Federalist Society who asked to remain un-
    identified; Peter Keisler, interview with the author, June 21, 2019.

9   Alan Rappeport and Charlie Savage, "Donald Trump Releases List of Possible Su-
    preme Court Picks," *New York Times*, May 18, 2016, www.nytimes.com/2016/05
    /19/us/politics/donald-trump-supreme-court-nominees.html; Sheryl Gay Stolberg,
    "A Different Timpanist," *New York Times*, June 10, 2005, www.nytimes.com/2005
    /06/10/politics/a-different-timpanist.html.

10 Jill Colvin and Mark Sherman, "Trump Unveils List of Potential Picks for Supreme
    Court Seat," Associated Press, May 18, 2016, https://apnews.com/c68d11041efe47c
    c918fe3d7d2da4edb.

11 John Malcolm, "The Trump List of Possible Justices Is Great but Two Names Are Miss-
    ing," Heritage Foundation, December 13, 2016, www.heritage.org/election-integrity
    /commentary/the-trump-list-possible-justices-great-two-names-are-missing.

12 Joan Biskupic, "A Presumption of Perfection Derails Trump's Sure Bet," CNN, Sep-
    tember 24, 2018, www.cnn.com/2018/09/24/politics/kavanaugh-presumption-of
    -perfection-trump/index.html.

13 Hulse, *Confirmation Bias*, 142–43.

14 Sarah McCammon, "Inside Trump's Closed-Door Meeting, Held to Reassure 'The
    Evangelicals,'" NPR, June 21, 2016, https://www.npr.org/2016/06/21/483018976
    /inside-trumps-closed-door-meeting-held-to-reassures-the-evangelicals.

15 Leigh Ann Caldwell, "Supreme Court a Rare GOP Rallying Point on Trump,"
    NBC News, June 23, 2016, www.nbcnews.com/politics/2016-election/some
    -conservatives-use-supreme-court-sole-reason-back-trump-n597841.

16 Hugh Hewitt, "It's the Supreme Court, Stupid," *Washington Examiner*, July 31, 2016,
    www.washingtonexaminer.com/its-the-supreme-court-stupid.

17 Philip Bump, "A Quarter of Republicans Voted for Trump to Get Supreme Court
    Picks—and It Paid Off," *Washington Post*, June 26, 2018, www.washingtonpost.com
    /news/politics/wp/2018/06/26/a-quarter-of-republicans-voted-for-trump-to-get
    -supreme-court-picks-and-it-paid-off/.

18 Author interview; source asked to remain unidentified.

19 Adam Liptak, "How Trump Chose His Supreme Court Nominee," *New York Times*,
    February 6, 2017, www.nytimes.com/2017/02/06/us/politics/neil-gorsuch-trump
    -supreme-court-nominee.html.

20 Jessica Taylor, "Yes, All This Happened. Trump's First 2 Weeks as President," NPR,
    February 4, 2017, www.npr.org/2017/02/04/513473827/yes-all-this-happened
    -trumps-first-2-weeks-as-president.

21 Sen. Chuck Grassley, "Working to Secure Iowa's Judicial Legacy," *Des Moines Register*,
    April 14, 2015, www.desmoinesregister.com/story/opinion/columnists/iowa-view
    /2015/04/15/working-secure-iowas-judicial-legacy/25801515/.

22 Robert Farley, "Trump's Hollow Complaint," FactCheck.org, May 18, 2018,
    www.factcheck.org/2018/05/trumps-hollow-complaint/.

23 Barry J. McMillion, "U.S. Circuit and District Court Nominations During President
    Trump's First Year in Office: Comparative Analysis with Recent Presidents,"

R45189, U.S. Congressional Research Service, May 2, 2018, https://fas.org/sgp/crs/misc/R45189.pdf.

24 Adam Liptak and Maggie Haberman, "Inside the White House's Quiet Campaign to Create a Supreme Court Opening," *New York Times*, June 28, 2018, www.nytimes.com/2018/06/28/us/politics/trump-anthony-kennedy-retirement.html.

25 Ruth Marcus, *Supreme Ambition: Brett Kavanaugh and the Conservative Takeover* (New York: Simon & Schuster, 2019), 3.

26 Nan Aron, interview with the author, October 31, 2018.

27 Hulse, *Confirmation Bias*, 1–4; author interviews with Republicans who asked to remain unidentified.

28 "Supreme Court Nominee Brett Kavanaugh Confirmation Hearing, Day 2, Part 2," C-SPAN video, September 5, 2018, www.c-span.org/video/?449705-10/supreme-court-nominee-brett-kavanaugh-confirmation-hearing-day-2-part-2.

29 Hulse, *Confirmation Bias*, 206–7; Mollie Hemingway and Carrie Severino, *Justice on Trial: The Kavanaugh Confirmation and the Future of the Supreme Court* (Washington, DC: Regnery, 2019), 1–3; author contemporary interviews.

30 "Supreme Court Nominee Brett Kavanaugh Confirmation Hearing, Day 2, Part 2."

31 Benny Johnson, "Movement Conservatives Fume at Trump SCOTUS Favorite: 'This Is the Low-Energy Jeb Bush Pick,'" *Daily Caller*, July 3, 2018, https://dailycaller.com/2018/07/03/conservatives-trump-supreme-court-brett-kavanaugh/.

32 Kevin Daley and Saagar Enjeti, "These Are Trump's Two Top Picks for the Supreme Court," *Daily Caller*, July 2, 2018, https://dailycaller.com/2018/07/02/top-picks-trump-supreme-court/.

33 Written responses from Senator Susan Collins to author questions, December 3, 2019.

34 Hemingway and Severino, *Justice on Trial*, 14–20.

35 Maggie Haberman and Jonathan Martin, "McConnell Tries to Nudge Trump Toward Two Supreme Court Options," *New York Times*, July 7, 2018, www.nytimes.com/2018/07/07/us/politics/trump-mcconnell-supreme-court.html.

36 Interviews with the author; sources asked to remain unidentified.

10: THE MODEL NOMINEE

1 White House pool reports and transcripts, July 9, 2018.

2 Mollie Hemingway and Carrie Severino, *Justice on Trial: The Kavanaugh Confirmation and the Future of the Supreme Court* (Washington, DC: Regnery, 2019), 71, 74.

3 Author interviews with Republicans; sources asked to remain unidentified.

4 Author interview with adviser to Senator Chuck Schumer, February 8, 2019; "Senator Schumer on Brett Kavanaugh Nomination," C-SPAN video, May 25, 2006, www.c-span.org/video/?c4739027/senator-schumer-brett-kavanaugh-nomination&playlist=97888b340e3bdebbe3d178fe371e0885.

5 Author interviews with Democratic senators and counsels on the Senate Judiciary Committee; Senator Dick Durbin, interview with the author, June 4, 2019.

6 United States Senator for Maine Susan Collins, "Senator Collins Meets with Judge Brett Kavanaugh," press release, August 21, 2018, www.collins.senate.gov/newsroom/senator-collins-meets-judge-brett-kavanaugh.

7 Elise Viebeck and Gabriel Pogrund, "Sen. Susan Collins Says Kavanaugh Sees Roe v.

Wade as 'Settled Law,'" *Washington Post*, August 21, 2018, https://beta.washingtonpost .com/powerpost/sen-susan-collins-said-kavanaugh-sees-roe-v-wade-as-settled-law /2018/08/21/214ae5dc-a54c-11e8-8fac-12e98c13528d_story.html.

8   Mike Davis, interview with the author, June 27, 2019; author interviews with Republican and Democratic Senate aides; Tony Mauro, "From Private Practice to Gorsuch Clerk to Senate Staff: A Denver Lawyer's Career Whirlwind," Law.com, August 16, 2017, www.law.com/supremecourtbrief/almID/1202795662879/?mcod e=1202617652897&curindex=21&slreturn=20200714171312.

9   Jake Sherman and Anna Palmer, *The Hill to Die On: The Battle for Congress and the Future of Trump's America* (New York: Broadway Books, 2019), 303.

10 Author interview, June 6, 2019.

11 Jeremy Paris, interview with the author, May 9, 2019.

12 Laurie Rubiner, interview with the author, February 6, 2019; author interviews with other meeting participants.

13 Alan J. Borsuk, "Judge Brett Kavanaugh Calls for 'Rules of the Road' for Separation of Powers Issues," *Marquette University Law School Faculty Blog*, March 5, 2015, https://law.marquette.edu/facultyblog/2015/03/judge-brett-kavanaugh-calls-for-rul es-of-the-road-for-separation-of-powers-issues/.

14 Author interview with Democratic Senate leadership aide.

15 Rubiner, interview.

16 William A. Burck, Brigham Q. Cannon, and Evan A. Young, Letter to Chairman Charles Grassley, August 31, 2018, www.judiciary.senate.gov/imo/media/doc /2018-08-31%20Burck%20to%20Grassley%20-%20Accounting%20of%20Kavanaug h%20WHCO%20Records.pdf.

17 Helaine Greenfeld, interview with the author, February 8, 2019.

18 Author interview with Republican party strategist who asked to remain unidentified, October 26, 2019.

19 Author interviews with Republicans, including Mike Davis, June 27, 2019.

20 Klaus Jensen, interview with the author, June 26, 2019; Jennifer Langa Klaus, interview with the author, July 3, 2019; Klaus Jensen, text messages to the author, June– September 2019.

21 Kerry Berchem, interviews and text messages with the author, May–December 2019.

22 Fatima Goss Graves, interview with the author, November 15, 2018.

23 Molly Langmuir, "What's Next for *New Yorker* Reporter Jane Mayer?," *Elle*, February 27, 2019, www.elle.com/culture/a26537529/jane-mayer-new-yorker-interview -kavanaugh/.

11: ONE WOMAN'S CIVIC DUTY

1   This chapter reflects interviews with Ford, her friends and associates; their emails and texts; "Supreme Court Nominee Brett Kavanaugh Sexual Assault Hearing, Professor Blasey Ford Testimony," C-SPAN video, September 27, 2018, www.c-span.org /video/?451895-1/professor-blasey-ford-testifies-sexual-assault-allegations-part-1; Memorandum to Senate Republicans from the Office of the Chairman, Senator Chuck Grassley, "Senate Judiciary Committee Investigation of Numerous Allegations Against Justice Brett Kavanaugh During the Senate Confirmation Proceedings,"

November 2, 2018, www.judiciary.senate.gov/imo/media/doc/2018-11-02%20 Kavanaugh%20Report.pdf.

2   "History of Holton-Arms," Holton-Arms School, www.holton-arms.edu/about /history-of-holton-arms.

3   "History of Holton-Arms"; Samantha Guerry, interviews with the author, May 31, 2019–2020; *The Scribe*, Holton-Arms School Yearbook, 1982.

4   Christine Ford, interviews with the author, 2019–2020.

5   Memorandum to Senate Republicans from the Office of the Chairman, Senator Chuck Grassley, "Senate Judiciary Committee Investigation of Numerous Allegations Against Justice Brett Kavanaugh During the Senate Confirmation Proceedings," November 2, 2018, Declaration of Russell Ford, Exhibit 6, 54–56, www.judiciary.senate.gov/imo /media/doc/2018-11-02%20Kavanaugh%20Report.pdf.

6   Keith Koegler, interviews with the author, February 26, 2019, and April 12, 2019.

7   Anna Eshoo, interview with the author, April 10, 2019.

8   Michael Bromwich, interview with the author, November 14, 2018; John Clune, interview with the author, May 17, 2019.

9   Michele Dauber, interview with the author, April 11, 2019, and subsequent emails exchanged through October 2019; Jennifer Duck, interviews with the author, December 7, 2018–2020; Debra Katz, interviews with the author, April 18 and 29, 2019, and subsequent emails; Katherine Spillar, interviews with the author, October and December 2019.

10   Eshoo, interview.

11   Katz, interviews; Lisa Banks, interview with the author, April 29, 2019.

12   Memorandum to Senate Republicans from the Office of the Chairman, Senator Chuck Grassley, "Senate Judiciary Committee Investigation of Numerous Allegations Against Justice Brett Kavanaugh During the Senate Confirmation Proceedings," November 2, 2018, Polygraph Examination Report, Exhibits 10 and 11, 65–71, www.judiciary.senat e.gov/imo/media/doc/2018-11-02%20Kavanaugh%20Report.pdf.

13   Katz, interviews; Banks, interview; Koegler, interviews; Ford, interviews; Ricki Seidman, interviews with the author, October 30, 2018–2020.

14   Author interview with a member of the Burning Tree Country Club, April 2019; source asked to remain unidentified.

12: QUESTIONS OF CREDIBILITY

1   Author interview with Senate Democratic leadership aide, February 8, 2019.

2   Author interviews with several members of the Senate Judiciary Committee and their counsels.

3   Author interview with Republican strategist who asked to remain unidentified.

4   "Supreme Court Nominee Brett Kavanaugh Confirmation Hearing, Day 1, Part 2," C-SPAN video, September 4, 2018, www.c-span.org/video/?449704-2/senators -judge-brett-kavanaugh-make-opening-statements-confirmation-hearing.

5   C-SPAN video coverage, September 5–6, 2018: "Supreme Court Nominee Brett Kavanaugh Confirmation Hearing, Day 2, Part 1," September 5, 2018, www.c-span.org /video/?449705-1/supreme-court-nominee-brett-kavanaugh-confirmation-hearing -day-2-part-1; "Supreme Court Nominee Brett Kavanaugh Confirmation Hearing, Day 2, Part 2," September 5, 2018, www.c-span.org/video/?449705-10/supreme

-court-nominee-brett-kavanaugh-confirmation-hearing-day-2-part-2; "Supreme Court Nominee Brett Kavanaugh Confirmation Hearing, Day 2, Part 3, " September 5, 2018, www.c-span.org/video/?449705-11/supreme-court-nominee -brett-kavanaugh-confirmation-hearing-day-2-part-3; "Supreme Court Nominee Brett Kavanaugh Confirmation Hearing, Day 2, Part 4," September 5, 2018, www.c-span.org/video/?449705-14/supreme-court-nominee -brett-kavanaugh-confirmation-hearing-day-2-part-4; "Supreme Court Nominee Brett Kavanaugh Confirmation Hearing, Day 3, Part 1," September 6, 2018, www.c-span.org/video/?449706-1/supreme-court-nominee-brett -kavanaugh-confirmation-hearing-day-3-part-1; "Supreme Court Nominee Brett Kavanaugh Confirmation Hearing, Day 3, Part 2," September 6, 2018, www.c-span.org/video/?449706-101/supreme-court-nominee-brett-kavanaugh -confirmation-hearing-day-3-part-2; "Supreme Court Nominee Brett Kavanaugh Confirmation Hearing, Day 3, Part 3," September 6, 2018, www.c-span.org/video/?449706-2/supreme-court-nominee-brett-kavanaugh -confirmation-hearing-day-3-part-3; "Supreme Court Nominee Brett Kavanaugh Confirmation Hearing, Day 3, Part 4," September 6, 2018, www.c-span.org/video/?449706-102/supreme-court-nominee-brett-kavanaugh -confirmation-hearing-day-3-part-4; "Supreme Court Nominee Brett Kavanaugh Confirmation Hearing, Day 3, Part 5," September 6, 2018, www.c-span.org/video/?449706-3/supreme-court-nominee-brett-kavanaugh -confirmation-hearing-day-3-part-5; "Supreme Court Nominee Brett Kavanaugh Confirmation Hearing, Day 3, Part 6," September 6, 2018, www.c-span.org/video/?449706-4/supreme-court-nominee-brett-kavanaugh -confirmation-hearing-day-3-part-6; "Supreme Court Nominee Brett Kavanaugh Confirmation Hearing, Day 3, Part 7," September 6, 2018, www.c-span.org/video/?449706 -103/supreme-court-nominee-brett-kavanaugh-confirmation-hearing-day-3-part-7.

6   Email exchange between James Ho and Brett M. Kavanaugh, "RE: Pro-choice op-eds in support of Justice Owen?," March 24, 2003, https://int.nyt.com/data /documenthelper/269-kavanaugh-email-re-whether-roe/e6dbbda94dd204fe02af /optimized/full.pdf.

7   U.S. Congress, Senate, Committee on the Judiciary, "Confirmation Hearing on the Nomination of Brett Kavanaugh to Be Circuit Judge for the District of Columbia Circuit," 108th Congress, 2nd Session, April 27, 2004, www.govinfo.gov/content /pkg/CHRG-108shrg24853/pdf/CHRG-108shrg24853.pdf; U.S. Congress, Senate, Committee on the Judiciary, "Confirmation Hearing on the Nomination of Brett Kavanaugh to Be Circuit Judge for the District of Columbia Circuit," 109th Congress, 2nd Session, May 9, 2006, www.congress.gov/109/chrg/shrg27916 /CHRG-109shrg27916.pdf.

8   Sen. Patrick Leahy, Twitter thread on Miranda emails, October 3, 2018, 6:13 p.m., https://twitter.com/SenatorLeahy/status/1047610549100580869.

9   Lisa Graves, interview with the author, February 6, 2019; Lisa Graves, "I Wrote Some of the Stolen Memos That Brett Kavanaugh Lied to the Senate About," *Slate*, September 7, 2018, https://slate.com/news-and-politics/2018/09/judge-brett-kavanaugh-should -be-impeached-for-lying-during-his-confirmation-hearings.html.

10   Michael Kranish, "Leahy Says Kavanaugh Was 'Not Truthful' About Democratic Documents," *Washington Post*, September 7, 2018, www.washingtonpost.com/politics/leahy -says-kavanaugh-was-not-truthful-about-democratic-documents/2018/09/07/babfb

4aa-b2d9-11e8-a20b-5f4f84429666_story.html?utm_term=.6b0ec511583b.

11 Salvador Rizzo, "Brett Kavanaugh's Unlikely Story About Democrats' Stolen Documents," *Washington Post*, September 20, 2018, www.washingtonpost.com/politics /2018/09/20/brett-kavanaughs-unlikely-story-about-democrats-stolen-documents/.

12 Neil A. Lewis, "A Judge, a Renomination and the Cross-Burning Case That Won't End," *New York Times*, May 28, 2003, www.nytimes.com/2003/05/28/us/a-judge -a-renomination-and-the-cross-burning-case-that-won-t-end.html?module=inline.

13 Email exchanges between Brett M. Kavanaugh et. al., May 10, 2003–June 2, 2003, www.dropbox.com/sh/cc4u94lgyncygn6/AABPGJkIiq5ND7KJuX7kXUX9a?dl=0 &preview=08-Booker-Confidential+-+Kavanaugh+Hearing.pdf; Charlie Savage, "Democrats Question Kavanaugh's Testimony About Bush Nominee," *New York Times*, August 16, 2018, www.nytimes.com/2018/08/16/us/politics/brett-kavanau gh-pickering-nomination.html.

14 Brett M. Kavanaugh, email to John C. Yoo, "Re: 4A Issue," September 17, 2001, https://int.nyt.com/data/documenthelper/264-purported-kavanaugh-e-mail-to/70 2e332fddd3bf0416f3/optimized/full.pdf#page=1.

15 Washington v. Glucksberg, 521 U.S. 702 (1997), https://scholar.google.com/scholar _case?case=17920279791882194984&hl=en&as_sdt=6&as_vis=1&oi=scholar.

16 Brett M. Kavanaugh, "From the Bench: The Constitutional Statesmanship of Chief Justice William Rehnquist," 2017 Walter Berns Constitution Day Lecture, American Enterprise Institute, Washington, D.C., September 18, 2017, www.aei.org/wp -content/uploads/2017/12/From-the-Bench.pdf.

17 Eliana Johnson, "Trump's Supreme Court Search Unleashes Fierce Politicking," *Politico*, July 4, 2018, www.politico.com/story/2018/07/04/trump-supreme-court -pick-brett-kavanaugh-694787; Ruth Marcus, *Supreme Ambition: Brett Kavanaugh and the Conservative Takeover* (New York: Simon & Schuster, 2019), 83.

18 Heidi Bond, "I Received Some of Kozinski's Infamous Gag List Emails. I'm Baffled by Kavanaugh's Responses to Questions About Them," *Slate*, September 14, 2018, https://slate.com/news-and-politics/2018/09/kavanaugh-kozinski-gag-list -emails-senate-hearings.html.

19 Interview with the author, June 7, 2019; source asked to remain unidentified.

20 United States Senate Committee on the Judiciary, "Nomination of the Honorable Brett M. Kavanaugh to be an Associate Justice of the Supreme Court of the United States (Day 5)," video, September 27, 2018, www.judiciary.senate.gov/meetings /nomination-of-the-honorable-brett-m-kavanaugh-to-be-an-associate-justice-of -the-supreme-court-of-the-united-states-day-5.

13: A LEAK, AND A LEAP

1 This chapter initially draws from the author's interviews with Christine Ford, her friends and lawyers, senators, their aides, advocacy group leaders, and reporters.

2 Lily Adams, interview with the author, October 17, 2019.

3 Ryan Grim, "Dianne Feinstein Withholding Brett Kavanaugh Document from Fellow Judiciary Committee Democrats," *The Intercept*, September 12, 2018, https://theintercept .com/2018/09/12/brett-kavanaugh-confirmation-dianne-feinstein/.

4 Author interviews with witnesses.

5 Helaine Greenfeld, interview with the author, February 8, 2019.

6   Laurie Rubiner, interview with the author, February 6, 2019.

7   Ronan Farrow and Jane Mayer, "A Sexual-Misconduct Allegation Against the Supreme Court Nominee Brett Kavanaugh Stirs Tension Among Democrats in Congress," *New Yorker*, September 14, 2018, www.newyorker.com/news/news-desk/a-sexual-misconduct-allegation-against-the-supreme-court-nominee-brett-kavanaugh-stirs-tension-among-democrats-in-congress.

8   Nicholas Fandos and Michael S. Schmidt, "Letter Claims Attempted Assault by a Teenage Brett Kavanaugh," *New York Times*, September 14, 2018, www.nytimes.com/2018/09/14/us/politics/kavanaugh-assault-allegation-letter.html.

9   Emma Brown, "California Professor, Writer of Confidential Brett Kavanaugh Letter, Speaks Out About Her Allegation of Sexual Assault," *Washington Post*, September 16, 2018, www.washingtonpost.com/investigations/california-professor-writer-of-confidential-brett-kavanaugh-letter-speaks-out-about-her-allegation-of-sexual-assault/2018/09/16/46982194-b846-11e8-94eb-3bd52dfe917b_story.html?utm_term=.5208111a2d73.

10   Samantha Guerry, interview with the author, May 31, 2019.

11   Author interviews with Republicans who asked not to be identified.

12   Michael Bromwich, interviews with the author, November 14, 2018, and January 31, 2019.

13   Anita Hill, "How to Get the Kavanaugh Hearings Right," *New York Times*, September 18, 2018, www.nytimes.com/2018/09/18/opinion/anita-hill-brett-kavanaugh-clarence-thomas.html?action=click&module=Opinion&pgtype=Homepage.

14   Gabriel Pogrund and David Weigel, "'Don't Get Rattled': Social Conservatives Rally Behind Embattled Supreme Court Pick," *Washington Post*, September 21, 2018, www.washingtonpost.com/politics/dont-get-rattled-social-conservatives-rally-behind-embattled-court-pick/2018/09/21/3b9057b6-bc4d-11e8-8792-78719177250f_story.html.

15   Ben Sales, "There Are Now 500,000 Negative Tweets About George Soros Every Day. Many Claim He's Funding George Floyd Protests," Jewish Telegraphic Agency, June 3, 2020, www.jta.org/2020/06/03/united-states/there-are-now-500000-negative-tweets-about-george-soros-every-day.

16   Donald J. Trump, Twitter post, October 5, 2018, 9:03 a.m., https://twitter.com/realDonaldTrump/status/1048196883464818688?s=20.

17   Carl Hulse, *Confirmation Bias: Inside Washington's War over the Supreme Court, from Scalia's Death to Justice Kavanaugh* (New York: HarperCollins, 2019), 247.

18   Christine Ford, text messages exchanged with Leland Keyser, September 17, 2018–June 13, 2019.

19   Laura Collins, "'Christine Ford Threw Her Under the Bus.' Strained 'Sex Assault' Witness Leland Keyser Is Seen for the First Time as Close Family Member Confirms She Did NOT Corroborate School Friend Ford's Story to FBI," *Daily Mail*, October 3, 2018, www.dailymail.co.uk/news/article-6235463/Christine-Fords-high-school-friend-blindsided-named-corroborating-witness.html; Amy Lamare, "Who Is Leland Keyser? New Details on Christine Blasey Ford's High School Best Friend," *Your Tango*, October 3, 2018, www.yourtango.com/2018317652/who-is-leland-keyser-new-details-on-christine-blasey-ford-highschool-best-friend.

14: A CLASSMATE'S SECRET, REVEALED

1   This chapter draws from the author's multiple interviews with Debbie Ramirez, her mother, friends, lawyers, and Yale classmates.

2   Dana James, interview with the author, May 31, 2019.

3   Cherríe Moraga and Gloria E. Anzaldúa, eds., *This Bridge Called My Back: Writings by Radical Women of Color*, (New York: Kitchen Table/Women of Color Press, 1983), www.goodreads.com/book/show/313110.This_Bridge_Called_My_Back.

4   James, interview.

5   Lynne Brookes, interview with the author, September 20, 2019, and emails exchanged with the author.

6   Kathy Charlton, interviews and text messages with the author, May 17, 2019–August 2020; David Todd declined to speak for the record.

7   Debbie Ramirez, interviews with the author, May 16 and 18, 2019; Jamie Roche, interview with the author, June 1, 2019; subsequent emails and texts with each.

8   Kerry Berchem, interviews and text messages with the author, May–December 2019.

9   Richard Oh, interview with the author, July 19, 2019; Kenneth Appold, emails exchanged with the author, March 12 and September 15, 2019; Ronan Farrow and Jane Mayer, "Senate Democrats Investigate a New Allegation of Sexual Misconduct, from Brett Kavanaugh's College Years," *New Yorker*, September 23, 2018, www.newyorker.com / news/news-desk/senate-democrats-investigate-a-new -allegation-of-sexual-misconduct-from-the-supreme-court-nominee-brett-kavana ughs-college-years-deborah-ramirez.

10 Lisa Ryan, "What 'Credible Information' Does Michael Avenatti Have on Kavanaugh?," *The Cut*, September 24, 2018, www.thecut.com/2018/09/michael -avenatti-kavanaugh-judge-client-tweets.html.

11 Stan Garnett, interview with the author, May 20, 2019, and subsequent emails.

12 John Clune, interview with the author, May 17, 2019, and subsequent emails and calls.

13 Emails among John Clune, William Pittard, Stan Garnett, Mike Davis, Heather Sawyer, and Jennifer Duck, September 23–25, 2018.

14 William Pittard, letter to Chuck Grassley and Dianne Feinstein, September 26, 2018.

15 Mitch McConnell, "Judge Kavanaugh Is a Man of Strong Character and Tremendous Integrity," remarks made on the Senate floor, September 24, 2018, www.republicanleader.senate.gov/newsroom / remarks/judge-kavanaugh-is-a-man -of-strong-character-and-tremendous-integrity-.

16 Gabriel Sherman, "'Cut Bait': As the Kavanaugh Nightmare Escalates, Trump Is Gripped with Uncertainty as Ivanka Suggests Cutting the Judge Loose," *Vanity Fair*, September 18, 2018, www.vanityfair.com/news/2018/09/kavanaugh-allegations -trump-ivanka.

17 President Donald J. Trump, "Remarks by President Trump on Federal Judicial Confirmation Milestones," East Room of the White House, Washington, DC, November 6, 2019, www.whitehouse.gov/briefings-statements/remarks-president -trump-federal-judicial-confirmation-milestones.

18 Author interview with a Republican strategist who asked to remain unidentified.

19 Donald J. Trump, Twitter post, September 24, 2018, 5:33 p.m., https://twitter.com /realDonaldTrump/status/1044339078257356801?s=20.

20 Samuel Chamberlain, "Kavanaugh Denies Sexual Misconduct in Fox News Ex-

clusive: 'I Know I'm Telling the Truth,'" Fox News, September 24, 2018, www.foxnews.com/politics/kavanaugh-denies-sexual-misconduct-in-fox -news-exclusive-i-know-im-telling-the-truth.

21   Michael Bromwich, interviews with the author, November 14, 2018, and January 31, 2019; Debra Katz, interview with the author, April 29, 2019.

22   Stephanie Saul, Robin Pogrebin, Mike McIntire, and Ben Protess, "In a Culture of Privilege and Alcohol at Yale, Her World Converged with Kavanaugh's," *New York Times*, September 25, 2018, www.nytimes.com/2018/09/25/us/politics/deborah -ramirez-brett-kavanaugh-allegations.html.

23   Karen Yarasavage and Kevin Genda declined interviews.

24   Men of Yale, "An Open Letter from Men of Yale in Support of Deborah Ramirez, Christine Blasey Ford and others," *Medium*, September 25, 2018, https://medium.com /@yalemen80s/an-open-letter-from-men-of-yale-in-support-of-deborah-ramirez -christine-blasey-ford-and-others-ffc878fd600a.

25   John McCormack, "The Lasting Damage of the Kavanaugh Confirmation Battle," *Weekly Standard*, October 12, 2018, www.washingtonexaminer.com/weekly-standard/how-the -kavanaugh-battle-damaged-the-court-congress-the-media-and-the-country.

26   Author interview with a Democratic counsel who asked to remain unidentified; Mike Davis, interview with the author, June 27, 2019.

27   Kaitlan Collins, "Aides Quietly Stunned by Trump's Respectful Handling of Ka-vanaugh Accuser," CNN, September 20, 2018, www.cnn.com/2018/09/20 /politics/donald-trump-kavanaugh-accuser/index.html.

28   Donald J. Trump, Twitter post, September 21, 2018, 9:14 a.m., https://twitter.com /realDonaldTrump/status/1043126336473055235.

29   Donald J. Trump, Twitter post, September 21, 2018, 9:29 a.m., https://twitter.com /realDonaldTrump/status/1043130170612244481.

30   Aaron Blake and Transcript courtesy of Bloomberg Government, "President Trump's U.N. Press Conference, Annotated," *Washington Post*, September 26, 2018, www .washingtonpost.com/politics/2018/09/26/president-trumps-un-press-conference -annotated/.

31   Author interviews with Ford, friends, and lawyers.

32   Ashley Schapitl, interview with the author, February 8, 2019.

15: SHE SAID . . .

1   Much of this chapter is based on interviews with Christine Ford, her lawyers and friends, and senators and committee aides of both parties; "Supreme Court Nominee Brett Kavanaugh Sexual Assault Hearing, Professor Blasey Ford Testimony," C-SPAN video, September 27, 2018, www.c-span.org/video/?451895-1/professor-blasey -ford-testifies-sexual-assault-allegations-part-1.

2   David Bauder, "More Than 20 Million People Watched Kavanaugh Hearing," Asso-ciated Press, September 28, 2018, https://apnews.com/caa510f21dcd4c569a4c8ea91 f587a44/More-than-20-million-people-watched-Kavanaugh-hearing.

3   Author interviews with Republicans who asked to remain unidentified.

4   "FBI Expanding Probe into Kavanaugh," *The Beat with Ari Melber*, MSNBC, Octo-ber 1, 2018, www.msnbc.com/transcripts/msnbc-live-with-ari-melber/2018-10-01.

5   Janet Napolitano, interview with the author, April 23, 2019.

6   Chris Coons, interview with the author, September 17, 2019.

7   Debbie Ramirez, interview with the author, May 18, 2019.

8   Ed Whelan, Twitter post, September 21, 2018, 8:38 a.m., https://twitter.com /edwhelaneppc/status/1043117304152817664?lang=en.

9   Jeff Flake, interview with the author, June 6, 2019; Alex Isenstadt and Kevin Robillard, "Flake Announces Retirement as He Denounces Trump," *Politico*, October 24, 2017, www.politico.com/story/2017/10/24/flake-retiring-after-2018-244114.

10   Jessica Contrera and Ian Shapira, "Christine Blasey Ford's Family Has Been Nearly Silent Amid Outpouring of Support," *Washington Post*, September 27, 2018, www.washingtonpost.com/local/christine-blasey-fords-own-family-has-been-nearly -silent-amid-outpouring-of-support/2018/09/26/49a3f4a6-c0d6-11e8-be77-51633 6a26305_story.html.

11   Author interviews with a Burning Tree Country Club member, several Republicans, and Christine Ford.

12   Christine Ford, interview with the author, April 11, 2019.

13   Mitch McConnell, *The Long Game: A Memoir*, paperback ed. (New York: Sentinel, 2019), 273.

14   Interviews with the author; sources asked to remain unidentified.

15   John McCormack, "The Lasting Damage of the Kavanaugh Confirmation Battle," *Weekly Standard*, October 12, 2018, www.washingtonexaminer.com/weekly -standard/how-the-kavanaugh-battle-damaged-the-court-congress-the-media-and -the-country.

16   Author's recording of Kavanaugh remarks to Federalist Society National Lawyers Convention, Washington, D.C., November 14, 2019.

17   Carl Hulse, *Confirmation Bias: Inside Washington's War over the Supreme Court, from Scalia's Death to Justice Kavanaugh* (New York: HarperCollins, 2019), 253; Peter Baker and Nicholas Fandos, "Show How You Feel, Kavanaugh Was Told, and a Nomination Was Saved," *New York Times*, October 6, 2018, www.nytimes.com/2018/10 /06/us/politics/kavanaugh-vote-confirmation-process.html.

16: . . . HE SAID

1   This chapter draws from the hearing video and transcript, supplemented by author interviews; CNBC Television, "Brett Kavanaugh, Christine Blasey Ford Testify Before U.S. Senate—Thursday, Sept. 27 2018," YouTube, September 27, 2018, www.youtube.com/watch?v=MvaFzCrYcXI.

2   Sheldon Whitehouse, interview with the author, July 18, 2019.

3   "Kavanaugh Hearing Cold Open—SNL," *Saturday Night Live*, YouTube, September 29, 2018, www.youtube.com/watch?v=VRJecfRxbr8.

4   Whitehouse, interview.

5   Dick Durbin, interview with the author, June 4, 2019, and interviews with Senate aides.

6   Chris Coons, interview with the author, September 17, 2019.

7   Peter Baker and Nicholas Fandos, "Show How You Feel, Kavanaugh Was Told, and a Nomination Was Saved," *New York Times*, October 6, 2018, www.nytimes.com /2018/10/06/us/politics/kavanaugh-vote-confirmation-process.html; Philip Rucker, Ashley Parker, Sean Sullivan, and Seung Min Kim, " 'Willing to Go to the

Mat': How Trump and Republicans Carried Kavanaugh to the Cusp of Confirmation," *Washington Post*, October 5, 2018, www.washingtonpost.com/politics/willing
-to-go-to-the-mat-how-trump-and-republicans-carried-kavanaugh-to-the-cusp-of
-confirmation/2018/10/05/7cdf0d0e-c81c-11e8-b1ed-1d2d65b86d0c_story.html?
utm_term=.3a42faeb2e0d.

8   Fox News, Twitter post, September 27, 2018, 10:50 p.m., https://twitter.com/Fox
     News/status/1045505877384613888.

9   Keith Koegler, interview with the author, April 12, 2019.

10   William Pittard, interview with the author, March 27, 2019.

11   Jeff Flake, interview with the author, June 6, 2019.

12   Janet Napolitano, interview with the author, April 23, 2019.

13   Letter from Robert M. Carlson, President of the American Bar Association, to
     Chairman Charles E. Grassley and Ranking Member Dianne Feinstein of the Senate
     Judiciary Committee, September 27, 2018, www.americanbar.org/content/dam
     /aba/administrative/federal_judiciary/senator-grassley-from-aba-9-27-18.pdf.

14   Aidan McLaughlin, "Brett Kavanaugh Classmate Tears into His 'Blatant Lying': I've
     Witnessed Him Stumbling Drunk," *Mediaite*, September 27, 2018, www.mediaite
     .com/tv/kavanaugh-classmate-tears-into-him-over-drinking-denial-ive-witnessed
     -him-stumbling-drunk/.

15   Mike McIntire, Linda Qiu, Steve Eder, and Kate Kelly, "At Times, Kavanaugh's Defense
     Misleads or Veers Off Point," *New York Times*, September 28, 2018, www.nytimes.com
     /2018/09/28/us/politics/brett-kavanaugh-fact-check.html?action=click & module
     =Ribbon&pgtype=Article.

16   "Chad Ludington's Statement on Kavanaugh's Drinking and Senate Testimony," *New
     York Times*, September 30, 2018, www.nytimes.com/2018/09/30/us/politics/chad
     -ludington-statement-brett-kavanaugh.html.

17   Debbie Ramirez and Vikram Shah, interviews with the author, May 18, 2019.

18   Erica Songer, interview with the author, June 24, 2019.

19   Mike Davis, interview with the author, June 27, 2019.

20   "Flake to Vote for Kavanaugh; Flake Confronted by Rape Victims; Judiciary Com-
     mittee Hearing," CNN News Room, transcript, September 28, 2018,
     http://transcripts.cnn.com/TRANSCRIPTS/1809/28/cnr.02.html.

21   Coons, interview.

22   "Senate Judiciary Meeting on Brett Kavanaugh Nomination," C-SPAN video, Sep-
     tember 28, 2018, www.c-span.org/video/?452084-1/senator-flake-calls-delaying
     -kavanaugh-vote-fbi-background-check-reopen.

23   Chris Coons and Erica Songer, interview with the author, September 17, 2019.

24   Flake, interview.

25   Flake, interview; Coons, interview.

26   Author interviews with multiple people in the room; Flake, interview.

27   Whitehouse, interview.

17: THE "INVESTIGATION" THAT WASN'T

1   Jeff Flake, interview with the author, June 6, 2019.

2   Author interviews with Democrats and Republicans.

3   Flake, interview.

4   William Pittard, interview with the author, March 27, 2019; Debbie Ramirez, interview with the author, May 18, 2019.

5   Michael Bromwich, interviews with the author, November 14, 2018, and January 31, 2019; author emails with Justice officials.

6   Michael D. Shear, Sheryl Gay Stolberg, Maggie Haberman, and Michael S. Schmidt, "Details of F.B.I.'s Kavanaugh Inquiry Show Its Restricted Range," *New York Times*, September 29, 2018, www.nytimes.com/2018/09/29/us/politics/kavanaugh-fbi -inquiry.html.

7   John Clune, interview with the author, May 17, 2019.

8   "President Trump Campaign Rally in Wheeling, West Virginia," C-SPAN video, September 29, 2018, www.c-span.org/video/?451998-1/president-trump-campaign s-west-virginia-republican-senate-candidate-patrick-morrissey.

9   Chris Coons, interview with the author, September 17, 2019; Coons, letter to Donald McGahn, October 2, 2018.

10 Stan Garnett, interview with the author, May 20, 2019; Ramirez, interview; Clune, interview; Pittard, interview; and subsequent author emails with all four individuals.

11 Devlin Barrett, Josh Dawsey, Seung Min Kim, and Matt Zapotosky, "White House Agrees to Expand Kavanaugh Probe Slightly as McConnell Signals Vote Is Imminent," *Washington Post*, October 1, 2018, www.washingtonpost.com/politics/trump -adds-to-confusion-over-scope-of-fbi-investigation-of-kavanaugh-accusations/2018 /10/01/1aa5e922-c561-11e8-b1ed-1d2d65b86d0c_story.html.

12 Senate Judiciary Committee, "Supplemental FBI Investigation Executive Summary," October 4, 2018, www.judiciary.senate.gov/press/rep/releases/supplemental-fbi -investigation-executive-summary; Author interviews.

13 Memorandum to Senate Republicans from the Office of the Chairman, Senator Chuck Grassley, "Senate Judiciary Committee Investigation of Numerous Allegations Against Justice Brett Kavanaugh During the Senate Confirmation Proceedings," November 2, 2018, Affidavit of Elizabeth Rasor, 82–83, www.judiciary.senate.gov /imo/media/doc/2018-11-02%20Kavanaugh%20Report.pdf.

14 Kate Snow, "Kavanaugh Accuser Julie Swetnick Speaks Out on Sexual Abuse Allegations," NBC News, October 1, 2018, www.nbcnews.com/politics/supreme-court /kavanaugh-accuser-julie-swetnick-speaks-out-sexual-abuse-allegations-n915641.

15 Emails and phone calls with Mary Davison, Montgomery County custodian of records, September 20–26, 2019; Julie Swetnick, interview with the author, October 6, 2019.

16 "President Trump Rally in Mississippi," C-SPAN video, October 2, 2018, www .c-span.org/video/?452371-1/president-trump-holds-rally-mississippi.

17 Bromwich, interview, November 14, 2018.

18 Interview with FBI official who declined to be identified, October 9, 2019; Jane Mayer and Ronan Farrow, "The Confusion Surrounding the F.B.I.'s Renewed Investigation of Brett Kavanaugh," *New Yorker*, October 1, 2018, www.newyorker.com /news/news-desk/the-confusion-surrounding-the-fbis-renewed-investigation-of -brett-kavanaugh.

19 Sarah Baker, interview with the author, October 16, 2018.

20 David M. Hardy, chief of the Record/Information Dissemination Section, U.S. Department of Justice, Federal Bureau of Investigation, letter to House Speaker Nancy Pelosi, August 7, 2019.

21 The following two sections are based on the individuals' interviews with the author and correspondence from lawyers for Christine Ford and Debbie Ramirez; memorandum to Senate Republicans from the Office of the Chairman, Senator Chuck Grassley, "Senate Judiciary Committee Investigation of Numerous Allegations Against Justice Brett Kavanaugh During the Senate Confirmation Proceedings," November 2, 2018, www.judiciary.senate.gov/imo/media/doc/2018-11-02%20Kavanaugh%20Report.pdf.

22 Kirsten Leimroth, interview with the author, April 30, 2019; Jim Gensheimer, interview with the author, April 28, 2019.

23 Elizabeth Rasor, interview with the author, July 14, 2019.

24 Vikram Shah, interview with the author, May 18, 2019; Mary Ann LeBlanc, interview with the author, May 21, 2018, and subsequent emails exchanged with the author.

25 James Roche, "I Was Brett Kavanaugh's College Roommate," *Slate*, October 3, 2018, https://slate.com/news-and-politics/2018/10/brett-kavanaugh-college-roommate-jamie-roche.html.

26 Jamie Roche, interview with the author, June 1, 2019.

27 "Interview with Sen. Chris Coons; Discussion of Ford & Kavanaugh Testimony," transcript, *Cuomo Prime Time*, CNN, September 27, 2018, http://transcripts.cnn.com/TRANSCRIPTS/1809/27/CPT.01.html; Lynne Brookes, "Kavanaugh 'Lied' in Interview, Drank to Excess, Classmate from Yale Says," interview from appearance on *Good Morning America*, ABC News, September 28, 2018, https://abcnews.go.com/GMA/News/video/kavanaugh-lied-interview-drank-excess-classmate-yale-58146577; Lynne Brookes, interview with the author, September 7, 2019.

28 "Classmate: Kavanaugh Drank Heavily," video, *Cuomo Prime Time*, www.cnn.com/videos/politics/2018/09/29/liz-swisher-yale-classmate-sloppy-drunk-bts-cuomo-vpx.cnn.

29 Jane Mayer and Ronan Farrow, "The F.B.I. Probe Ignored Testimonies from Former Classmates of Kavanaugh," *New Yorker*, October 4, 2018, www.newyorker.com/news/news-desk/will-the-fbi-ignore-testimonies-from-kavanaughs-former-classmates.

30 Jane Mayer, interview with the author, September 12, 2019.

31 Kenneth Appold, emails exchanged with the author, March 12–13, 2019, and September 13-16, 2019.

32 Richard Oh, interview with the author, July 19, 2019.

33 Mark Krasberg, interview with the author, September 16, 2019; Sheryl Gay Stolberg and Michael D. Shear, "F.B.I. to End Kavanaugh Inquiry as Soon as Wednesday, with Vote Coming This Week," *New York Times*, October 2, 2018, www.nytimes.com/2018/10/02/us/politics/kavanaugh-fbi-background-check.html.

34 Daniel Lavan, interviews with the author, September 13 and 16, 2019.

35 Mayer and Farrow, "The F.B.I. Probe Ignored Testimonies," *New Yorker*, www.newyorker.com/news/news-desk/will-the-fbi-ignore-testimonies-from-kavanaughs-former-classmates.

36 "Chad Ludington's Statement on Kavanaugh's Drinking and Senate Testimony," *New York Times*, September 30, 2018, www.nytimes.com/2018/09/30/us/politics/chad-ludington-statement-brett-kavanaugh.html?module=inline.

37 Chad Ludington, interview with the author, September 6, 2019.

38 Jennifer Langa Klaus, interview with the author, July 3, 2019.

39 Lisa Miller, "Brett Kavanaugh's Former Roommate Describes Their Debauched

Dorm at Yale," *The Cut*, September 26, 2018, www.thecut.com/2018/09/kavanaugh-roommate-yale-dorm-room.html; John Clune, letter via email to FBI supervisory agent Todd E. Stanstedt, "Re: Follow up to Deborah Ramirez Interview," September 30, 2018.

40   Marc Schindler, interview with the author, August 26, 2019.

41   Kathy Charlton, interview with the author, May 18, 2019, and subsequent emails.

42   Affidavit of Ramirez's friend, sworn on October 4, 2018 (she asked that her name be redacted except for the FBI); William Pittard, letter to FBI director Christopher A. Wray, October 4, 2018 (affidavit attached without redactions); Ramirez, interview.

43   Kerry Berchem, interviews and text messages with the author, May–December 2019.

44   Michael R. Bromwich and Debra S. Katz, letter to FBI director Christopher A. Wray, "Re: Supplemental Background Investigation of Judge Brett Kavanaugh," September 29, 2018.

45   Author interviews from late October 2018 into 2020 with individuals who had first- or secondhand knowledge of the Stier account alleging that he saw Kavanaugh assault a woman other than Debbie Ramirez.

46   United States Senate, memorandum from Rachel Mitchell to All Republican Senators, "Re: Analysis of Dr. Christine Blasey Ford's Allegations," September 30, 2018, https://assets.documentcloud.org/documents/4952137/Rachel-Mitchell-s-analysis.pdf.

47   Emma Brown and Seung Min Kim, "Experts Question GOP Prosecutor's Memo on Christine Blasey Ford," *Washington Post*, October 1, 2018, www.washingtonpost.com/investigations/experts-question-gop-prosecutors-memo-on-christine-blasey-ford/2018/10/01/85a454c0-c5a2-11e8-b1ed-1d2d65b86d0c_story.html?utm_term=.6563cf55467a.

48   Senators Richard J. Durbin, Dianne Feinstein, Patrick J. Leahy, Sheldon Whitehouse, Richard Blumenthal, Mazie K. Hirono, Cory A. Booker, and Kamala D. Harris, letter to Chairman Charles E. Grassley, October 3, 2018.

49   Author interview with a former FBI agent who served at the time of the Senate's Kavanaugh investigation; the agent asked to remain unidentified.

50   Coons, interview.

51   Rebecca Shabad and Frank Thorp V, "Some Undecided GOP Senators on Kavanaugh Call FBI Report 'Reassuring' and 'Thorough,'" NBC News, October 4, 2018, www.nbcnews.com/politics/congress/grassley-says-new-fbi-report-kavanaugh-includes-no-new-info-n916601.

52   Dick Durbin, interview with the author, June 4, 2019.

53   "Senate Judiciary Committee Hearing on FBI Oversight," C-SPAN video, July 23, 2019, www.c-span.org/video/?462772-1/senate-judiciary-committee-hearing-fbi-oversight.

54   Senators Sheldon Whitehouse and Chris Coons, letter to FBI director Christopher A. Wray, August 1, 2019, www.whitehouse.senate.gov/imo/media/doc/2019-08-01%20Ltr%20to%20FBI%20Wray%20re%20supplemental%20Kavanaugh%20investigation.pdf; author correspondence with Whitehouse and Coons Senate offices.

55   Garnett, interview.

56   Ramirez, interview.

57 "'This Is How Victims Are Isolated and Silenced': Deborah Ramirez Releases Statement Prior to Kavanaugh Confirmation Vote," *Denver Post*, October 6, 2018, www.denverpost.com/2018/10/06/deborah-ramirez-statement-kavanaugh-confirmation/.

18: CONFIRMATION

1 "Senator Murkowski Voted Against Kavanaugh. Read Her Remarks Declaring Why," *New York Times*, October 5, 2018, www.nytimes.com/2018/10/05/us/politics/lisa-murkowski-brett-kavanaugh-vote.html.

2 Author interviews with Republicans who declined to be identified.

3 Philip Rucker, Ashley Parker, Sean Sullivan, and Seung Min Kim, "'Willing to Go to the Mat': How Trump and Republicans Carried Kavanaugh to the Cusp of Confirmation," *Washington Post*, October 5, 2018, www.washingtonpost.com/politics/willing-to-go-to-the-mat-how-trump-and-republicans-carried-kavanaugh-to-the-cusp-of-confirmation/2018/10/05/7cdf0d0e-c81c-11e8-b1ed-1d2d65b86d0c_story.html?utm_term=.3a42faeb2e0d.

4 Author interview, May 16, 2019; source asked to remain unidentified.

5 Author interview, June 6, 2019; source asked to remain unidentified.

6 Author interviews; sources asked to remain unidentified.

7 "Open Letter to the United States Senate from Law Professors Around the Country," October 4, 2018, 1, available at: www.scribd.com/document/390196814/Open-Letter-to-the-U-S-Senate?secret_password=IoF5vZqqJ5zO5QjtuuTk.

8 Adam Liptak, "Retired Justice John Paul Stevens Says Kavanaugh Is Not Fit for Supreme Court," *New York Times*, October 4, 2018, www.nytimes.com/2018/10/04/us/politics/john-paul-stevens-brett-kavanaugh.html.

9 "ABA Standing Committee on the Federal Judiciary Reopens Evaluation of Kavanaugh," American Bar Association, press release, October 5, 2018, www.americanbar.org/news/abanews/aba-news-archives/2018/10/aba-standing-committee-on-the-federal-judiciary-reopens-evaluati/.

10 Brett M. Kavanaugh, "I Am an Independent, Impartial Judge," *Wall Street Journal*, October 4, 2018, www.wsj.com/articles/i-am-an-independent-impartial-judge-1538695822.

11 Judi Hershman, interviews with the author, 2019.

12 Mitch McConnell, *The Long Game: A Memoir*, paperback ed. (New York: Sentinel, 2019), 275.

13 *PBS NewsHour*, "Collins: 'I Will Vote to Confirm Judge Kavanaugh,'" YouTube, October 5, 2018, www.youtube.com/watch?v=ZUEPFO6zgGM.

14 Author witnessed event; Mike DeBonis, "In Fierce Speech for Kavanaugh, Collins Sheds Her Swing-Vote Image," *Washington Post*, October 5, 2018, www.washingtonpost.com/powerpost/in-fierce-speech-for-kavanaugh-collins-sheds-her-swing-vote-image/2018/10/05/3ab05984-c8de-11e8-9b1c-a90f1daae309_story.html.

15 *PBS NewsHour*, "WATCH: Sen. Manchin Drowned Out by Protestors as He Explains Kavanaugh 'Yes' Vote," YouTube, October 5, 2018, www.youtube.com/watch?time_continue=1&v=sYvRM1Hk8Iw&feature=emb_title.

16 Liz Ruskin, "Murkowski: Kavanaugh Debate Now About 'Victims and Their Ability to Tell Their Story,'" Alaska Public Media, September 26, 2018, www.alaskapublic

.org/2018/09/26/murkowski-kavanaugh-debate-now-about-victims-and-their
-ability-to-tell-their-story/.

17 "Sen. Lisa Murkowski's Senate Speech on Why She Opposed Kavanaugh," *Anchorage Daily News*, October 8, 2018, www.adn.com/politics/2018/10/05/sen-lisa-murkowskis -full-senate-speech-on-why-shes-not-supporting-kavanaugh/.

18 *PBS NewsHour*, "Watch: Senate Votes on Confirmation of Brett Kavanaugh," YouTube, October 6, 2018, www.youtube.com/watch?v=O7XtthDPaV8.

19 Paulina Dedaj, "Pence Faces Kavanaugh Protestors, Tells Security Detail 'Let's Do It' as He Walks down Senate Steps," Fox News, October 6, 2018, www.foxnews.com /politics/pence-faces-kavanaugh-protesters-tells-security-detail-lets-do-it-as-he -walks-down-senate-steps.

20 Author interviews.

21 Sarah Palin, Twitter post, October 5, 2018, 3:06 p.m., https://twitter.com /SarahPalinUSA/status/1048288254422728704?s=20.

22 President Donald J. Trump, "Remarks by President Trump upon Arrival of Air Force One," Topeka Regional Airport, Topeka, Kansas, October 6, 2018, www .whitehouse.gov/briefings-statements/remarks-president-trump-upon-arrival-air -force-one-topeka-kansas/.

23 CNN, "Anti-Kavanaugh Protestors Bang on the Doors of the Supreme Court," YouTube, October 6, 2018, www.youtube.com/watch?v=IRnmnxVtDqg.

24 Laurie Rubiner, interview with the author, February 6, 2019.

25 Sarah Baker, interview with the author, October 16, 2018; author interview with a former FBI agent who asked to remain unidentified, October 9, 2019.

26 Jonathan Martin, "Court Battle Shifts Political Terrain for Senators in Heartland," *New York Times*, October 7, 2018, www.nytimes.com/2018/10/07/us/politics /supreme-court-kavanaugh-senators-midterms-heartland.html.

27 Donald J. Trump, Twitter post, November 3, 2018, 9:38 a.m., https://twitter.com /realDonaldTrump/status/1058715144442781696.

28 "Lady Gaga: Dr. Ford Spoke Up to Protect Us," video, *The Late Show with Stephen Colbert*, October 4, 2018, www.cbs.com/shows/the-late-show-with-stephen-colbert/video/F1fBll CZgv_vaBVaX3TbQcgwu3RCWEIx/lady-gaga-dr-ford-spoke-up-to-protect-us/.

29 Ana Navarro, interview by David Axelrod, *The Axe Files with David Axelrod*, podcast audio, October 11, 2018, https://podtail.com/en/podcast/the-axe-files-with-david -axelrod/ep-276-ana-navarro/.

30 Jeffrey M. Jones, "Americans Still Closely Divided on Kavanaugh Confirmation," Gallup, October 3, 2018, https://news.gallup.com/poll/243377/americans-closely -divided-kavanaugh-confirmation.aspx.

31 Dana Bash, "Heidi Heitkamp Was Ready to Vote 'Yes' on Kavanaugh. Then She Watched Him with the Sound Off," CNN, October 8, 2018, www.cnn.com/2018 /10/08/politics/heidi-heitkamp-kavanaugh-cnn-interview/index.html.

32 Jonathan Martin, "#MeToo Is a 'Movement Toward Victimization,' G.O.P. Senate Candidate Says," *New York Times*, October 8, 2018, www.nytimes.com/2018/10 /08/us/politics/heidi-heitkamp-kevin-cramer-metoo.html.

33 "McSally Campaign Seeks to Explain Defeat in Post-election Memo," *Washington Post*, November 2018, http://apps.washingtonpost.com/g/documents/politics /mcsally-campaign-seeks-to-explain-defeat-in-post-election-memo/3325/.

34 Memorandum to Senate Republicans from the Office of the Chairman, Senator Chuck Grassley, "Senate Judiciary Committee Investigation of Numerous Allegations

Against Justice Brett Kavanaugh During the Senate Confirmation Proceedings," November 2, 2018, www.judiciary.senate.gov/imo/media/doc/2018-11-02%20Kav anaugh%20Report.pdf.

35 Memorandum, "Senate Judiciary Committee Investigation of Numerous Allegations Against Justice Brett Kavanaugh," 5–6, 8, and Exhibit 15, 85; author interviews with Republican senators and several with Christine Ford.

36 Debbie Ramirez, interview with the author, May 18, 2019; Christine Ford, interview with the author, April 11, 2019.

37 Memorandum to Senate Republicans, 5, 6, 79.

38 Mark Gauvreau Judge, *Wasted: Tales of a Gen X Drunk* (Minnesota: Hazelden, 1997).

39 Memorandum to Senate Republicans, 3.

40 Author interview with a senior Republican aide, June 27, 2019.

41 Memorandum to Senate Republicans, 3.

42 Memorandum to Senate Republicans, 7-10.

43 Memorandum to Senate Republicans, 8.

44 Memorandum to Senate Republicans, 6.

45 Memorandum to Senate Republicans, 7.

46 Memorandum to Senate Republicans, 10.

47 Memorandum to Senate Republicans, 9.

48 Memorandum to Senate Republicans, 11, and Exhibits 6–9, 54–64.

49 Memorandum to Senate Republicans, 12, and Exhibit 14, 80–83.

50 Memorandum to Senate Republicans, 13, and Exhibit 20, 99–102.

51 Memorandum to Senate Republicans, 13, and Exhibit 22, 106–7.

52 Ramirez, interview.

53 In interviews with the author, several of Kavanaugh's Yale classmates and other individuals familiar with the committee Republicans' investigation identified Smith and others whose names are redacted in the memorandum.

54 Memorandum to Senate Republicans, Exhibit 32, 211.

55 Memorandum to Senate Republicans, 17, and Exhibit 30, 137.

56 Memorandum to Senate Republicans, Exhibit 31, 138–209.

57 Kathy Charlton, interviews with the author, May 17–18, 2019.

58 Memorandum to Senate Republicans, 17–23, and Exhibits 41 and 42, 277–85.

59 Memorandum to Senate Republicans, 27–28; Chairman Charles E. Grassley, letter to Attorney General Jeff Sessions and FBI director Christopher A. Wray, November 2, 2018, www.judiciary.senate.gov/imo/media/doc/2018-11-02%20CEG%20to% 20DOJ%20FBI%20(Munro-Leighton%20Referral)%20with%20redacted%20enclosu res.pdf.

60 Goss Graves, interview with the author, November 5, 2018.

61 Kerry Berchem, interview with the author, May 16, 2019.

62 Stan Garnett, interview with the author, May 20, 2019.

63 United States Senator for California Dianne Feinstein, "Feinstein Statement on Republican Kavanaugh Memo," press release, November 5, 2018, www.feinstein.senate.gov /public/index.cfm/press-releases?ID=1B7B44A7-78E1-454A-9FC9-302D5093F834.

64 Helaine Greenfeld, interview with the author, February 8, 2019.

19: JUSTICE KAVANAUGH

1   White House pool reports for November 8, 2018; interviews with attendees.

2   Sonia Sotomayor, interview by David Axelrod, *The Axe Files with David Axelrod*, podcast audio, minutes 1:45 to 7:20, November 17, 2018, https://omny.fm/shows /the-axe-files-with-david-axelrod/ep-287-sonia-sotomayor.

3   Adam Liptak, "Ginsburg Hints at Sharp Divisions Ahead as Supreme Court Term Nears End," *New York Times*, June 10, 2019, www.nytimes.com/2019/06/10/us /politics/ruth-bader-ginsburg-supreme-court-decisions.html.

4   "Justice Ruth Bader Ginsburg Discusses Gender Equality, in Life and in Law," *George-town Law*, July 5, 2019, www.law.georgetown.edu/news/justice-ginsburg-discusses -her-pursuit-of-gender-equality-in-life-and-law/.

5   Nina Totenberg, "Justice Ginsburg: 'I Am Very Much Alive,'" NPR, July 24, 2019, www.npr.org/2019/07/24/744633713/justice-ginsburg-i-am-very-much-alive.

6   Duke University School of Law, "Justice Ruth Bader Ginsburg Discusses the 2018– 19 Supreme Court Term," YouTube, July 30, 2019, www.youtube.com /watch?v=FRjGoX-ZrQo&feature=youtu.be.

7   Lee Fang, "At Secretive Retreat, Evangelicals Celebrate Brett Kavanaugh's Confir-mation," *The Intercept*, October 7, 2018, https://theintercept.com/2018/10/07 /brett-kavanaugh-evangelicals-council-for-national-policy/.

8   Adam Liptak, "Conservative Lawyers Say Trump Has Undermined the Rule of Law," *New York Times*, November 14, 2018, www.nytimes.com/2018/11/14/us /politics/conservative-lawyers-trump.html.

9   George T. Conway III, interview with the author, June 7, 2019; Paul Rosenzweig, interview with the author, June 21, 2019.

10   Senator Mike Lee, Opening Address to the 2018 National Lawyers Convention of the Federalist Society, Mayflower Hotel, Washington D.C., November 15, 2018, https://feds oc.org/conferences/2018-national-lawyers-convention?#agenda-item-opening.

11   Josh Gerstein, "Gorsuch Takes Victory Lap at Federalist Dinner," *Politico*, No-vember 16, 2017, www.politico.com/story/2017/11/16/neil-gorsuch-federalist -society-speech-scotus-246538.

12   David Lat, "A Look Inside the Conservative Judge-Making Machine," *Above the Law*, November 16, 2018, https://abovethelaw.com/2018/11/a-look-inside-the-conservative -judge-making-machine/?rf=1.

13   Lat, "A Look Inside the Conservative Judge-Making Machine."

14   David Montgomery, "Conquerors of the Courts," *Washington Post Magazine*, Janu-ary 2, 2019, www.washingtonpost.com/news/magazine/wp/2019/01/02/feature /conquerors-of-the-courts/.

15   This section is based on the author's attendance and recording at the Antonin Scalia Memorial Dinner of the Federalist Society's National Lawyers Convention, Novem-ber 14, 2019.

16   Author interviews with reporters in attendance.

17   "Tenth Circuit Judicial Council Issues Order on Complaints Against Justice Brett M. Kavanaugh," United States Court of Appeals for the Tenth Circuit, last modified March 15, 2019, www.ca10.uscourts.gov/ce/misconduct/kavanaugh-complaints.

18   Timothy M. Tymkovich, Chief Circuit Judge, et al., "In Re: Complaints Under the Judicial Conduct and Disability Act," Judicial Council of the Tenth Circuit, Decem-ber 18, 2018, www.uscourts.gov/courts/ca10/10-18-90038-et-al.O.pdf.

19   David Tighe, Circuit Executive and Secretary to the Judicial Council of the Tenth Circuit, "In: Re: Complaints Under the Judicial Conduct and Disability Act," Judicial Council of the Tenth Circuit, March 15, 2019, Briscoe, dissenting, Lucero, disqualified, www.uscourts.gov/courts/ca10/10-18-90038-et-al.J.pdf.

20   "Has a Justice ever been impeached?," FAQs–General Information, Supreme Court of the United States, www.supremecourt.gov/about/faq_general.aspx.

21   Sam Simon, interviews with the author, March 25 and June 6, 2019.

22   David G. Savage, "Newly Seated Justice Kavanaugh Joins Questioning During First Oral Argument," *Los Angeles Times*, October 9, 2018, www.latimes.com/politics/la-na-pol-kavanaugh-immigrant-20181009-story.html.

23   Adam Feldman, "Empirical SCOTUS: Changes Are Afoot—5–4 Decisions During October Term 2018," *SCOTUSblog*, July 8, 2019, 12:24 p.m., www.scotusblog.com/2019/07/empirical-scotus-changes-are-afoot-5-4-decisions-during-october-term-2018/.

24   Adam Liptak and Alicia Parlapiano, "A Supreme Court Term Marked by Shifting Alliances and Surprise Votes," *New York Times*, June 29, 2019, www.nytimes.com/2019/06/29/us/supreme-court-decisions.html?searchResultPosition=13.

25   Adam Liptak, "At Immigration Argument, Justice Kavanaugh Takes Hard Line," *New York Times*, October 10, 2018, www.nytimes.com/2018/10/10/us/politics/kavanaugh-immigration-supreme-court-case.html; David G. Savage, "Kavanaugh Backs Trump Administration on Jailing and Deporting Immigrants for Crimes Committed Years Earlier," *Los Angeles Times*, October 10, 2018, www.latimes.com/politics/la-na-pol-court-jail-immigrants-20181010-story.html.

26   Nielsen v. Preap, 586 U.S. ___ (2019), March 19, 2019, Breyer, J., dissenting, p. 4, www.supremecourt.gov/opinions/18pdf/16-1363_a86c.pdf.

27   Gee v. Planned Parenthood of Gulf Coast, 585 U.S. ___ (2018), Thomas, J., dissenting, www.supremecourt.gov/opinions/18pdf/17-1492_g3bi.pdf.

28   June Medical Services L.L.C. v. Gee, 586 U.S. ___ (2019), Kavanaugh, J., dissenting from grant of application for stay, www.supremecourt.gov/opinions/18pdf/18a774_3ebh.pdf.

29   Emily Wax-Thibodeaux, "Restrictive Abortion Bill Weighs on Alabama Republicans, Who Struggle with Lack of Exceptions for Rape, Incest," *Washington Post*, May 13, 2019, www.washingtonpost.com/national/restrictive-abortion-law-weighs-on-alabama-republicans-who-struggle-with-lack-of-exceptions-for-rape-incest/2019/05/13/bec7b736-759e-11e9-b3f5-5673edf2d127_story.html.

30   Franchise Board of California v. Gilbert P. Hyatt, 587 U.S. ___ (2019), May 13, 2019, Breyer, J., dissenting, p. 13, www.supremecourt.gov/opinions/18pdf/17-1299_8njq.pdf.

31   Knick v. Township of Scott, Pennsylvania, 588 U.S. ___ (2019), June 21, 2019, Kagan, J. dissenting, p. 19, www.supremecourt.gov/opinions/18pdf/17-647_m648.pdf.

32   Robert Barnes, "Brett Kavanaugh Pivots as Supreme Court Allows One Execution, Stops Another," *Washington Post*, March 30, 2019, www.washingtonpost.com/politics/courts_law/brett-kavanaugh-pivots-as-supreme-court-allows-one-execution-stops-another/2019/03/29/26b28b32-5245-11e9-88a1-ed346f0ec94f_story.html.

33   Rucho v. Common Cause, 588 U.S. ___ (2019), June 27, 2019, Kavanaugh, J., concurring in judgment, p. 5, www.supremecourt.gov/opinions/18pdf/18-422_9ol1.pdf.

34   Department of Commerce v. New York, 588 U.S. ___ (2019), June 27, 2019, Thomas, J., concurring in part and dissenting in part, p. 1, www.supremecourt.gov/opinions/18pdf/18-966_bq7c.pdf.

35   Adam Liptak, "Supreme Court Green-Lights Gerrymandering and Blocks Census

Citizenship Question," *New York Times*, June 27, 2019, www.nytimes.com/2019 /06/27/us/politics/supreme-court-gerrymandering-census.html?module=inline.

36   *PBS NewsHour*, "WATCH: 'We'll End Up in the Supreme Court,' Trump Predicts for Emergency Declaration," YouTube, February 15, 2019, www.youtube.com /watch?v=lYqkzWGWkiE.

37   June Medical Services L.L.C. v. Russo, 591 U.S. ___ (2020), June 29, 2020, Roberts, C.J., concurring in judgment, www.supremecourt.gov/opinions/19pdf/18-1323 _c07d.pdf.

38   Department of Homeland Security v. Regents of the University of California, 591 U.S. ___ (2020), June 18, 2020, www.supremecourt.gov/opinions/19pdf/18-587 _5ifl.pdf.

39   Bostock v. Clayton County, 590 U.S. ___ (2020), June 15, 2020, www.supremecourt .gov/opinions/19pdf/17-1618_hfci.pdf.

40   Robert Costa, "Trump Supporters Hope to Use Conservative Anger at Chief Justice Roberts to Energize Troubled Campaign," *Washington Post*, July 1, 2020, www .washingtonpost.com/politics/trump-john-roberts-abortion-supreme-court/2020 /06/30/34513f92-bae8-11ea-80b9-40ece9a701dc_story.html.

41   Donald J. Trump, Twitter post, June 18, 2020, 11:08 a.m., https://twitter.com/real DonaldTrump/status/1273633632742191106; Donald J. Trump, Twitter post, June 18, 2020, 11:10 a.m., https://twitter.com/realDonaldTrump/status/1273634152433 188865?s=20.

42   Department of Homeland Security v. Regents of the University of California, 591 U.S. ___ (2020), June 18, 2020, Kavanaugh, J., concurring in part and dissenting in part, p. 2, www.supremecourt.gov/opinions/19pdf/18-587_5ifl.pdf.

43   Bostock v. Clayton County, 590 U.S. ___ (2020), June 15, 2020, Kavanaugh, J., dissenting, p. 27, www.supremecourt.gov/opinions/19pdf/17-1618_hfci.pdf.

44   Joan Biskupic, "How Brett Kavanaugh Tried to Sidestep Abortion and Trump Financial Doc Cases," CNN, July 29, 2020, www.cnn.com/2020/07/29/politics/brett -kavanaugh-supreme-court-abortion-trump-documents/index.html.

45   Biskupic, "How Brett Kavanaugh Tried to Sidestep Abortion and Trump Financial Doc Cases."

46   Joan Biskupic, "Inside the Supreme Court's Internal Deliberations over Trump's Taxes," CNN, July 30, 2020, www.cnn.com/2020/07/30/politics/supreme-court -trump-taxes-financial-documents/index.html.

47   Trump v. Mazars USA, LLP, 591 U.S. ___ (2020), July 9, 2020, www.supremecourt .gov/opinions/19pdf/19-715_febh.pdf.

48   Trump v. Vance, 591 U.S. ___ (2020), July 9, 2020, Roberts, C.J., p. 17, www .supremecourt.gov/opinions/19pdf/19-635_o7jq.pdf.

49   New York State Rifle & Pistol Assn., Inc. v. City of New York, 590 U.S. ___ (2020), April 27, 2020, www.supremecourt.gov/opinions/19pdf/18-280_ba7d.pdf.

50   Author interview with a source close to the court who asked to remain unidentified.

51   South Bay United Pentecostal Church v. Gavin Newsom, Governor of California, 590 U.S. ___ (2020), May 29, 2020, Kavanaugh, J., dissenting, pp. 1–3, www .supremecourt.gov/opinions/19pdf/19a1044_pok0.pdf#page=4.

52   South Bay United Pentecostal Church v. Gavin Newsom, Governor of California, 590 U.S. ___ (2020), May 29, 2020, Roberts, C.J., concurring, pp. 1–3, www .supremecourt.gov/opinions/19pdf/19a1044_pok0.pdf.

53   John Devaney, interview with the author, September 4, 2020.

54 Republican National Committee v. Democratic National Committee, 589 U.S. ___ (2020), April 6, 2020, Ginsburg, J., dissenting, pp. 3–5, www.supremecourt.gov /opinions/19pdf/19a1016_o759.pdf; Jim Rutenberg and Nick Corasaniti, "How a Supreme Court Decision Curtailed the Right to Vote in Wisconsin," *New York Times*, April 13, 2020, www.nytimes.com/2020/04/13/us/wisconsin-election -voting-rights.html.

55 Donald J. Trump, "Speech: Donald Trump Announces His 2020 Candidacy at a Political Rally in Orlando—June 18, 2019," https://factba.se/transcript/donald -trump-speech-maga-rally-reelection-orlando-june-18-2019.

56 White House pool report, March 30, 2019.

57 Colin Woodard, "Why Did Trump's 'Judge Whisperer' Buy a House on the Maine Coast," *Central Maine*, August 18, 2019, www.centralmaine.com/2019/08/18/why -did-trumps-judge-whisperer-buy-a-house-on-the-maine-coast/.

58 President Donald J. Trump, "Remarks by President Trump on Federal Judicial Con- firmation Milestones," East Room of the White House, Washington, D.C., November 6, 2019, www.whitehouse.gov/briefings-statements/remarks-president -trump-federal-judicial-confirmation-milestones.

59 Donald Trump Jr., Twitter post, February 24, 2019, 7:46 p.m., https://twitter.com /DonaldJTrumpJr/status/1099832970997833730?s=20.

60 Keith Koegler, interview with the author, February 26, 2019.

61 Deepa Lalla, interview with the author, May 8, 2019.

62 Emily Stewart, "'In Stepping Forward, You Took a Huge Risk': Christine Blasey Ford Honors Rachael Denhollander, Who Spoke Up About Larry Nassar," *Vox*, December 12, 2018, www.vox.com/identities/2018/12/12/18137535/christine -blasey-ford-sports-illustrated-rachael-denhollander.

63 "Help Christine Blasey Ford," GoFundMe, last updated November 21, 2018, www.gofundme.com/help-christine-blasey-ford.

64 Christine Ford, interviews with the author, September 2019.

65 Anastassia Kostin, "Christine Blasey Ford Presented with Distinguished Alumnus Award," *Pepperdine University Graphic*, June 3, 2019, http://pepperdine-graphic.com /christine-blasey-ford-presented-with-distinguished-alumnus-award/.

66 Author interviews with Ford and the friend.

67 Author interviews with Ford and the friend.

68 Klaus Jensen, interview with the author, June 26, 2019.

69 Debbie Ramirez, interview with the author, May 18, 2019.

EPILOGUE

1 Nina Totenberg, "Justice Ruth Bader Ginsburg, Champion of Gender Equality, Dies at 87," Weekend Edition Saturday, NPR, September 18, 2020, https://www.npr.org /2020/09/18/100306972/justice-ruth-bader-ginsburg-champion-of-gender-equality -dies-at-87.

2 Adam Liptak, "Amy Coney Barrett, Trump's Supreme Court Pick, Signed Anti- Abortion Ad," *New York Times*, October 1, 2020, https://www.nytimes.com/2020 /10/01/us/amy-coney-barrett-abortion.html.

3 Peter Baker, "Trump Says He Wants a Conservative Majority on the Supreme Court in Case of an Election Day Dispute," *New York Times*, September 23, 2020,

https://www.nytimes.com/2020/09/23/us/elections/trump-supreme-court-election
-day.html.

4   Mitch McConnell, "McConnell On Supreme Court Nomination," Remarks made on the Senate floor, March 16, 2020, https://www.republicanleader.senate.gov /newsroom/remarks/mcconnell-on-supreme-court-nomination.

5   Russell Wheeler, "McConnell's Fabricated History to Justify a 2020 Supreme Court Vote," *Brookings*, September 24, 2020, https://www.brookings.edu/blog/fixgov /2020/09/24/mcconnells-fabricated-history-to-justify-a-2020-supreme-court-vote/.

6   *Roman Catholic Diocese of Brooklyn v. Cuomo*, 592 U. S. ____ (2020), November 25, 2020, https://www.supremecourt.gov/opinions/20pdf/20a87_4g15.pdf.

7   *South Bay United Pentecostal Church v. Newsom*, 592 U. S. ____ (2021), February 5, 2021, Kagan, J., dissenting in judgment, pp. 10–15, https://www.supremecourt.gov /opinions/20pdf/20a136_bq7c.pdf#page=10.

8   "Supreme Court Justice Samuel Alito Speech Transcript to Federalist Society," November 12, 2020, https://www.rev.com/blog/transcripts/supreme-court-justice -samuel-alito-speech-transcript-to-federalist-society.

9   Kimberly Wehle, Twitter post, November 12, 2020, 9:07 p.m., https://twitter.com /kimwehle/status/1327085636558467079; Michael McGough, "Opinion: Alito's Federalist Society Speech Was Bad for the Supreme Court," *Los Angeles Times*, November 13, 2020, https://www.latimes.com/opinion/story/2020-11-13/opinion -alitos-federalist-society-speech-was-bad-for-the-supreme-court; "Justice Alito's Brazen Political Speech to FedSoc Underscores Need for Ethics Code," *Fix the Court*, November 13, 2020, https://fixthecourt.com/2020/11/ftc-justice-alitos-speech -fedsoc-scotus-needs-ethics-code/.

10   Ann E. Marimow and Matt Kiefer, "Judges Nominated by President Trump Play Key Role in Upholding Voting Limits Ahead of Election Day," *Washington Post*, October 31, 2020, https://www.washingtonpost.com/politics/2020/10/31/trump -judges-voting-rights/?arc404=true&itid=lk_inline_manual_20.

11   Robert Barnes, "Kavanaugh's Bush v. Gore Citation Draws Scrutiny Ahead of Another Divisive Election," *Washington Post*, October 27, 2020, https://www.washington-post.com/politics/courts_law/brett-kavanaugh-bush-gore-wisconsin-election/2020/10 /27/799fe8aa-1876-11eb-befb-8864259bd2d8_story.html; *Democratic National Committee v. Wisconsin State Legislature*, 592 U. S. ____ (2020), October 26, 2020, Kavanaugh, J., concurring in judgment, pp. 6–23, https://www.supremecourt.gov/opinions/20pdf/20 a66_new_m6io.pdf#page=6.

12   "Trump Says He'd Ask Court to 'Look at the Ballots,'" *New York Times*, Video, 1:19, September 29, 2020, https://www.nytimes.com/video/us/elections/100000007368 957/trump-ballots-debate-video-clip.html.

13   *Donald J. Trump v. Secretary Commonwealth of Pennsylvania*, D.C. No. 4:20–cv–02078, November 27, 2020, https://www2.ca3.uscourts.gov/opinarch/203371np.pdf.

14   "Donald Trump Speech 'Save America' Rally Transcript" (speech, Washington, D.C., January 6, 2021), 31:50, https://www.rev.com/blog/transcripts/donald -trump-speech-save-america-rally-transcript-january-6.

15   John Gramlich, "How Trump Compares with Other Recent Presidents in Appointing Federal Judges," Pew Research Center, January 13, 2021, https://www.pewresearch.org /fact-tank/2021/01/13/how-trump-compares-with-other-recent-presidents-in-appoin ting-federal-judges/; "Biographical Directory of Article III Federal Judges, 1789–Present," Federal Judicial Center, https://www.fjc.gov/history/judges/search/advanced-search.

16   Streiff, "WARNING. Trump Administration May Be Surrendering to Dianne Fein-
        stein on Ninth Circuit Nominations," *Red State*, January 30, 2019, https://redstate
        .com/streiff/2019/01/30/warning-trump-administration-may-surrendering-dianne-f
        einstein-ninth-circuit-nominations-n100472.

17   John Wagner, "Senate Confirms 200th Judicial Nominee from Trump, a Legacy That
        Will Last Well Beyond November," *Washington Post*, June 24, 2020, https:
        //www.washingtonpost.com/politics/senate-confirms-200th-judicial-nominee-from
        -trump-a-legacy-that-will-last-well-beyond-november/2020/06/24/8e8d7048-b61a
        -11ea-a510-55bf26485c93_story.html.

18   "Mitch McConnell Leaves No Vacancy Behind," Team Mitch, https://www.team
        mitch.com/mitch-mcconnell-leaves-no-vacancy-behind/.

19   Russell Wheeler, "Trump's Last-Minute Judicial Appointments: Impact on Norms
        and on Biden's Appointment Opportunities," *Brookings*, January 22, 2021,
        https://www.brookings.edu/blog/fixgov/2021/01/22/trumps-last-minute-judicial
        -appointments-impact-on-norms-and-on-bidens-appointment-opportunities/.

20   Dick Durbin, interview with the author, June 4, 2019.

21   Debra Cassens Weiss, "Pence Breaks Tie to Confirm 8th Circuit Nominee with 'Not
        Qualified' Rating from ABA Committee," *ABA Journal*, December 12, 2018,
        https://www.abajournal.com/news/article/pence_breaks_tie_to_confirm_8th_circuit
        _nominee_with_not_qualified_rating.

22   William C. Hubbard, Letter to Chairman Lindsey Graham and Ranking Member Di-
        anne Feinstein, October 29, 2019, http://cdn.cnn.com/cnn/2019/images/10/30/2019
        .10.29_chair_rating_letter_to_graham_and_feinstein_re_nomination_of_lawrence_j.c.
        _vandyke.pdf.

23   Sen. Tim Scott, "Only the Best Candidates for Federal Courts," *Wall Street Journal*,
        December   6,   2018,   https://www.wsj.com/articles/only-the-best-candidates-for
        -federal-courts-1544127307.

24   Neomi Rao, Letter to Chairman Lindsey Graham and Ranking Member Dianne
        Feinstein, February 11, 2019, https://www.judiciary.senate.gov/imo/media/doc
        /Letter%20from%20N.%20Rao%20to%20SJC.pdf.

25   Walker Investiture, "Judge Justin Walker Investiture Part Two," YouTube video, 6:53,
        March 13, 2020, https://www.youtube.com/watch?v=vEi3H1tArBY.

26   Walker Investiture, "Judge Justin Walker Investiture Part Three," YouTube video,
        9:41, March 13, 2020, https://www.youtube.com/watch?v=r6HnWd1F-q0.

27   Walker Investiture, "Judge Justin Walker Investiture Part Four—Judge Walker
        Speech," YouTube video, 12:57, March 13, 2020, https://www.youtube.com
        /watch?v=k5iUfudxuM8.

28   *On Fire Christian Center, Inc. v. Greg Fischer, et al.*, United States District Court, West-
        ern District of Kentucky, 62 (2020), https://www.courtlistener.com/recap
        /gov.uscourts.kywd.116558/gov.uscourts.kywd.116558.6.0.pdf.

29   Josh Blackman, "Courts Should Not Decide Issues That Are Not There," *Reason*,
        April 12, 2020, https://reason.com/volokh/2020/04/12/courts-should-not-decide
        -issues-that-are-not-there/.

30   Russell Wheeler, "Senate Obstructionism Handed a Raft of Judicial Vacancies to
        Trump—What Has He Done With Them?," *Brookings*, June 4, 2018, https://www
        .brookings.edu/blog/fixgov/2018/06/04/senate-obstructionism-handed-judicial-vac
        ancies-to-trump/.

31   "4. Important Issues in the 2020 Election," Pew Research Center, August 13, 2020,

https://www.pewresearch.org/politics/2020/08/13/important-issues-in-the-2020-ele
ction/; "Exit Polls," CNN, https://www.cnn.com/election/2020/exit-polls/presi
dent/national-results.

32   Jennifer Haberkorn, "Dianne Feinstein Won't Seek Top Senate Judiciary Committee
Spot," *Los Angeles Times*, November 23, 2020, https://www.latimes.com/politics
/story/2020-11-23/feinstein-judiciary-committee.

33   Carl Hulse, "Progressive Groups Urge Biden to Move Quickly on Diverse Slate of
Judges," *The New York Times*, December 11, 2020, https://www.nytimes.com/2020
/12/11/us/progressive-groups-biden-judges.html.

34   Brian Fallon, interview with the author, October 12, 2018.

35   Ann E. Marimow and Matt Viser, "Biden Moves Quickly to Make His Mark on
Federal Courts After Trump's Record Judicial Nominations," *Washington Post*, February 3, 2021, https://www.washingtonpost.com/local/legal-issues/biden-judge
-nominations/2021/02/02/e9932f3a-6189-11eb-9430-e7c77b5b0297_story.html.

36   "Biden's Vision for Federal Court Reform," NPR, February 14, 2021,
https://news.wbfo.org/post/bidens-vision-federal-court-reform.

37   Russell Wheeler, "Pack the Court? Putting a Popular Imprint on the Federal Judiciary," *Brookings*, April 3, 2019, https://www.brookings.edu/blog/fixgov/2019/04
/03/pack-the-court-putting-a-popular-imprint-on-the-federal-judiciary/.

38   Peter Keisler, interview with the author, June 21, 2019; subsequent emails exchanged
with the author, February 23, 2021.

39   Bailey Aldridge, "Trump Recites 'The Snake' at NC rally—Reviving His Controversial Readings of the Song," *Charlotte Observer*, November 2, 2020, https://www
.charlotteobserver.com/news/state/north-carolina/article246891632.html.

40   Charles Sykes, "Burn It All Down?," *Bulwark*, July 27, 2020, https://thebul
wark.com/burn-it-all-down/.

41   Salena Zito, "Taking Trump Seriously, Not Literally," *Atlantic*, September 23, 2016,
https://www.theatlantic.com/politics/archive/2016/09/trump-makes-his-case-in-pi
ttsburgh/501335/.

42   The Hill, "Ben Sasse EVISCERATES Donald Trump and the Nebraska GOP State
Central Committee," YouTube video, 5:07, February 4, 2021, https://www.youtube
.com/watch?v=BKsBVSa653E.

43   Mark Jurkowitz, Amy Mitchell, Elisa Shearer, and Mason Walker, "U.S. Media Polarization and the 2020 Election: A Nation Divided," Pew Research Center, January
24, 2020, https://www.journalism.org/2020/01/24/u-s-media-polarization-and
-the-2020-election-a-nation-divided/.

44   Kathleen Parker, "Opinion: The GOP Isn't Doomed. It's Dead," *Washington Post*,
January 29, 2021, https://www.washingtonpost.com/opinions/the-gop-isnt-doom
ed-its-dead/2021/01/29/07d08c3a-6271-11eb-afbe-9a11a127d146_story.html.

45   Reis Thebault, "Rep. Marjorie Taylor Greene's Endorsement of Conspiracy Theories, Violence Sparks Calls for Her Resignation—Again," *Washington Post*, January
27, 2021, https://www.washingtonpost.com/politics/2021/01/26/marjorie-taylor
-greene-facebook-violence/.

46   Hart Research Associates/Public Opinion Strategies, Study #210016: NBC News
Survey, January 10–13, 2021, https://assets.documentcloud.org/documents
/20457943/210016-nbc-news-january-poll-1-17-21-release.pdf.

47   Daniel A. Cox, "After the Ballots Are Counted: Conspiracies, Political Violence, and
American Exceptionalism," Survey Center on American Life, February 11, 2021,

https://www.americansurveycenter.org/research/after-the-ballots-are-counted-con spiracies-political-violence-and-american-exceptionalism/.

48   Larry M. Bartels, "Ethnic Antagonism Erodes Republicans' Commitment to De-
      mocracy," *Proceedings of the National Academy of Sciences of the United States of America*
      117, no. 37 (September 15, 2020): 22752–22759, first published August 31, 2020,
      https://www.pnas.org/content/117/37/22752.

49   "Donald Trump Rally Speech Transcript Dalton, Georgia: Senate Runoff Election,"
      January 4, 2021, https://www.rev.com/blog/transcripts/donald-trump-rally-speech
      -transcript-dalton-georgia-senate-runoff-election.

50   "Donald Trump Speech 'Save America' Rally Transcript January 6," January 6, 2021,
      https://www.rev.com/blog/transcripts/donald-trump-speech-save-america-rally-tran
      script-january-6.

51   Christopher R. Browning, "The Suffocation of Democracy," *New York Review*, Oc-
      tober 25, 2018, https://www.nybooks.com/articles/2018/10/25/suffocation-of
      -democracy/.

52   "Mitch McConnell Senate Speech Transcript January 6: Rejects Efforts to Overturn Presi-
      dential Election Results," January 6, 2021, https://www.rev.com/blog/transcripts/mitch
      -mcconnell-senate-speech-on-election-confirmation-transcript-january-6.

53   "Mitch McConnell Speech Transcript After Vote to Acquit Trump in 2nd Impeachment
      Trial," February 13, 2021, https://www.rev.com/blog/transcripts/mitch-mcconnell
      -speech-transcript-after-vote-to-acquit-trump-in-2nd-impeachment-trial.

INDEX

ABOUT THE AUTHOR

Jackie Calmes has been a journalist in Washington for nearly four decades, most recently as the White House editor in the *Los Angeles Times* bureau. She was a White House correspondent for the *New York Times* during the Obama administration, as well as a national politics reporter and chief economic correspondent. During eighteen years at the *Wall Street Journal*, she covered Congress and the White House and ultimately became the chief political correspondent. She first worked in Washington as a reporter for *Congressional Quarterly*. A native of Ohio, she began her career in Texas, where she covered state government and politics from Austin for the *Dallas Morning News* and, before that, for the Harte-Hanks newspaper chain.